THE AFGHANISTAN PAPERS

A Selection of Leaked US Military Field Reports from the Afghan War

Edited by Lenny Flank

Red and Black Publishers, St Petersburg, Florida

Library of Congress Cataloging-in-Publication Data

The Afghanistan papers : a selection of leaked US military field reports from the Afghan War / edited by Lenny Flank.
    p. cm.
  ISBN 978-1-61001-000-9
1. Afghan War, 2001---Sources. 2. United States--Armed Forces--Afghanistan--Sources. 3. Afghan War, 2001---Stability operations--Sources. 4. Afghan War, 2001---Civil action--Sources. 5. Afghan War, 2001---Casualties--Sources. 6. Counterinsurgency--Afghanistan--Sources. I. Flank, Lenny.
   DS371.412.A364 2010
   958.104'74--dc22

2010039197

Red and Black Publishers, PO Box 7542, St Petersburg, Florida, 33734
Contact us at: info@RedandBlackPublishers.com
    Printed and manufactured in the United States of America

Contents

Preface   5

Glossary   7

    The Documents

Assassinations   19

Blue on Blue   46

Blue on White   54

Weapons Caches   66

Detainees   114

Demonstrations   145

Enemy Actions   191

IEDs   274

Preface

In October 2001, in the wake of the 9-11 terror attacks on the World Trade Center and the Pentagon, the US launched a military invasion known as "Operation Enduring Freedom" to destroy the Al Qaeda bases and training camps in Afghanistan and to remove the ruling Islamic-extremist Taliban from power. Although the Taliban government quickly fell, the surviving members of Al Qaeda and the Taliban formed a guerrilla insurgency to drive the occupying US forces out of Afghanistan and overthrow the US-backed government. American troops, later joined by international forces from NATO allies, have been waging a counter-insurgency campaign to eliminate the Taliban/Al Qaeda forces. The war has dragged on for nine years.

The classified documents in this volume were leaked to the public in the summer of 2010. They represent a series of snapshots, from the point of view of the troops on the ground, of the Afghan War from 2004 to 2010. The documents consist of after-action reports filed by the actual units on the field. These reports are used by US intelligence and military authorities to develop a broader picture of what is really happening on the ground. Most of the 91,000 reports are monotonous and repetitive, because the war itself is monotonous and repetitive. For most troops, the war consists of endlessly repeating routine boring tasks—until the unexpected instant when a roadside bomb suddenly detonates or a hidden ambush opens fire, and you or your nearby companion falls dead or wounded.

From the leaked documents, this volume selects around 800 which are the most illustrative of the reality of the Afghan War on the ground, and which contain interesting insights into how the war is being fought on both sides. The reports are written in the terse matter-of-fact style preferred by the military, and are filled with military jargon, acronyms and abbreviations. To help the reader make sense of these, a glossary is given of the most common terms.

The only alteration that has been made to the files is to remove all the sourcing and filing information. Otherwise, the reports, complete with hurried typos and misspellings, are exactly as the soldiers in the field wrote them. The documents are, unfortunately, not an easy read. The profusion of acronyms and jargon can be daunting. However, the documents contain a tremendous wealth of very detailed and illuminating information about the Afghanistan War, and it comes from the very best of all possible sources—the troops who are there. It is therefore well worth making the effort needed to read and understand them.

The documents are grouped according to broad categories. "Assassination" refers to insurgent attacks on Afghan government officials, militia leaders, or other targeted individuals, and to American attacks on targeted individuals on the "kill or capture list". "Blue on Blue" refers to friendly-fire incidents where American forces have inadvertently fired on other American or allied troops. "Blue on White" refers to incidents in which death or injury to civilians occurs as a result of US actions. "Weapons Caches" refers to police actions to uncover hidden weapons and explosives. "Detainees" refers to the arrest and confinement of suspected Taliban/Al Qaeda sympathizers or supporters. "Demonstrations" refers to political rallies or protests against Afghan government officials or US occupation forces. "Enemy Actions" refers to actual combat resulting from insurgent ambushes. "IEDs" refers to incidents involving the use of Improvised Explosive Devices, the favorite weapon of the Afghan insurgency.

Taken as a whole, the documents provide an overview, written by the troops themselves, of the war in Afghanistan. The picture that emerges is that of a beleaguered government that lacks popular support (there is one report of civilians throwing rocks at Afghan army troops, who then responded with lethal gunfire, another report of an Afghan security officer "beating an old man in an alley", and yet another report of an organized protest by local Afghans against an Afghan Army officer who was "harassing and beating" civilians), propped up by an American military that also lacks popular support and is viewed as a foreign occupying army. One report perceptively concludes, after describing three separate incidents in which civilians were killed, that these reactions "underscore the challenge of addressing the serious security problems facing Afghanistan while minimizing civilian casualties and disruption to the lives of local residents".

The Taliban and Al Qaeda insurgents, meanwhile, operate by ambushing American and Kabul forces with gunfire and improvised explosives, and by assassinating government officials or those who cooperate with the Americans.

American efforts to win "hearts and minds" seem to have, the documents show, largely failed, and there seems to be widespread resentment against the American presence. Not only is the US viewed as an invader (and despite the presence of troops from several NATO nations, the war remains essentially an American undertaking, under American command), but Americans are seen as hostile to the Muslim religion that is so central to Afghan life. Whether we like the Taliban or not (and they are decidedly not nice people), it is clear that they hold the hearts and minds of most Afghans, and that no political solution is possible in Afghanistan without the cooperation of the Taliban.

As in all guerrilla wars, it is often impossible to tell who is the enemy and who is a civilian, since the insurgents make every effort to blend in among the people. American troops, therefore, inevitably resort to treating *all* civilians as potential enemies—which is a certain way to lose popular support. In one case, US troops fired at Afghans they thought were burying a roadside IED and killed one, only to learn that they were just innocent civilians digging an irrigation ditch. In another report, an American, referring to a detained Afghan, makes the telling comment, "He is just like all the others, just a terrorist."

The Afghans themselves are experienced guerrilla fighters, having forced the Soviet Union to withdraw after their ill-fated 1979 invasion. But at the same time, Afghans are torn by faction fighting between the warlords who lead the various independent tribes. Their loyalty to the Kabul government (or any other) is tenuous at best. A number of reports refer to clashes and disputes between neighboring tribes over land ownership; in one reported incident, a riot broke out amongst Afghan Army troops when officers of one tribe began harassing soldiers from another tribe— 22 soldiers were wounded in the ensuing fight.

Such ethnic clashes are symptoms of a much deeper problem in Afghanistan. For most Afghans, particularly those from rural regions, tribal loyalty comes above national identity, and the real source of political authority is the tribal warlord and the traditional elders, who owe little or no loyalty to the Kabul government. In essence, the Afghan national government's authority barely extends outside of the capitol city (President Karzai has been referred to in the press, only half-jokingly, as "the Mayor of Kabul"). In a very real sense, Afghanistan is not a single nation, but a loose amalgamation of many different tribes, many of whom are traditional enemies of each other. These tribal tensions not only make the American task of defending "the Afghan government" much harder, but they are exploited by the Taliban to win local support from one tribal leader or another, thereby strengthening the insurgency.

What these documents clearly show, in the end, is that the United States has made very little if any progress in the past nine years towards winning this war. Ambushes and roadside bombs can occur everywhere and are increasing in frequency, and American troops are not safe anywhere unless they move in large heavily-armed groups or convoys. The number of insurgent weapons caches that are uncovered has not declined in either number or area, and for every cache found, there are probably a dozen more that are not. In the early stages of the insurgency, the guerrillas were heavily dependent on their safe havens across the Pakistan border, and Taliban operations were limited largely to the area of east Afghanistan near Pakistan. Recently, however, incidents of attacks, ambushes and insurgent caches and camps have expanded into nearly every area of the country, indicating that the insurgency itself is expanding.

In short, there are no signs of a military victory.

Glossary of Military Jargon and Acronyms

A/C—"Aircraft", usually referring to fixed-wing airplanes

AAF—"Anti-Afghan Forces". The insurgency, consisting of the Taliban, Al Qaeda, and several small splinter groups.

ABP—"Afghan Border Police". An Afghan Government police force.

ACK—"Acknowledged"

ACM—"Anti-Coalition Militia". The locally-organized insurgency units.

AFG—"Afghan".

AIHRC—"Afghan Independent Human Rights Commission".

AMF – "Afghan Military Forces"

ANA – "Afghan National Army". The armed forces of the Kabul Government.

ANAP – "Afghan National Auxiliary Police". A police force of the Kabul Government.

ANBP – "Afghan National Border Police". An Afghan Government police force.

Angel – A Marine KIA.

ANP – "Afghan National Police".

ANSF – "Afghan National Security Forces". The security and police units of the Kabul Government.

AO – "Area of Operations"

AQ – "Al Qaeda". One of the two major anti-government insurgency groups.

ASG – "Area Support Group".

ASV – "Armored Security Vehicle".

ATT – "At this time"

ATTK – "Attack"

AUP – "Afghan Uniformed Police"

BAF – "Bagram Air Field". The primary American base in Afghanistan.

BBIED – "Bike-borne Improvised Explosive Device". The low-tech version of a car-bomb, in which explosives are strapped to a bicycle or motorcycle.

BCT – "Brigade Combat Team". An American military unit.

BDA – "Battle Damage Assessment". An evaluation of the actual damage done to the enemy by an attack or action.

BDE – "Brigade". A military unit.

Beaten Zone – the area of fire in which bullets or other ordnance actually impact.

BFT – "Blue Force Tracking". Efforts made to identify friendly forces in the area so they are not accidentally hit.

BG – "Brigadier General".

Blue Force – An American or other friendly military unit.

Blue on Blue – Friendly fire, in which a unit inadvertently fires on another allied unit.

BN – "Battalion". A military unit.

BPT – "Be prepared to"

BRF – "Brigade Reconnaissance Force". A scouting unit.

BSN – Camp Bastion. An important American military base.

BTIF – Bagram Theater Internment Facility. The primary American military detention center for suspected insurgents. Also known as "Bagram Prison".

BTL — "Battalion". A military unit.

Buzz Saw — A method of signaling at night, in which a light stick is waved over the head in a circle.

C//NF — "Confidential, No Foreigners". A security code indicating that this report is not to be shared with non-Americans.

C/S — "Call Sign". The code name used to identify oneself on the radio.

CAS — "Close Air Support". An air strike against nearby targets that are engaging American troops.

CAT C — "Category C". A medical designation for a severely-wounded priority patient.

CCIR — "Command's Critical Information Requirements". The intelligence needed by a military commander for a mission.

CD — "Commander"

CND — "Canadian"

CDR — "Commander"

CF — "Coalition Forces". The NATO and other allied forces that joined the US in Afghanistan.

CHOPS — "Chief of Operations".

CIV — "Civilian"

CIVCAS — "Civilian Casualties"

CJ2 -- Designation for the American intelligence and security command in Afghanistan.

CJ3 — Designation for joint special operations in Afghanistan.

CJTF — "Combined Joint Task Force". A military unit.

CJSOTF — "Combined Joint Special Operations Task Force". A Special Forces unit.

CO — "Commanding Officer"

COL — "Colonel"

COP — "Chief of Police". The local Afghan police supervisor.

COP — "Combat Outpost". A small military camp.

COY — "Company". A small American military unit.

CP — "Check Point". A roadblock or other security post.

Cpt — "Captain"

CSH — "Combat Support Hospital". A field hospital for treating casualties.

CWIED — "Command Wired Improvised Explosive Device". A homemade bomb which is rigged with an electrical wire and detonated by a nearby person with a switch.

Daisy Chain—A number of explosives that are wired together to blow up at the same time.

DC—"District Center". A local command center.

DF—"Direct Fire". Weapons fire directed against a visible target.

DOI—"Date of Incident"

DOS—"Department of State". The US State Department.

DSHKA—A Soviet-made heavy machine gun, usually left over from the 1979 war.

DETREP—"Detailed report"

DOW—"Died of Wounds"

DTMF—"Dual-Tone Multi-Frequency". An electronic chip used to generate the keypad signals in cellphones. It can be used to construct radio-detonated bombs.

ECM—"Electronic-Countermeasures". A device that sends out radio signals ahead of a convoy to detonate radio-controlled IED's before the vehicle reaches them.

ECP—"Entry Control Point". A security gate or checkpoint.

EKIA—"Enemy Killed In Action"

ENG BDE—"Engineer Brigade". Engineers are specially trained to handle mines and improvised explosive devices.

EOD—"Explosive Ordnance Disposal". An engineer trained to defuse unexploded mines or IEDs.

EOF: "Escalation of Force". An exchange of fire with an enemy.

ETT—"Embedded Training Team". An American group that trains Afghan units.

EVAC—"Evacuation"

FB—"Forward Base". An advance American military post.

FF—"Friendly Forces"

FIR—"First Impressions Report". A preliminary initial report.

FO—"Forward Observer"

FOB—"Forward Operations Base"

FP—"Firing Point". A place where machine guns or other weapons are located.

FRA—"French"

FSB—"Forward Support Base". A supply dump.

GBU—"Glide Bomb Unit". An aerial bomb.

GCTF—"Global Counter Terrorism Forces"—The US forces engaged in the "War on Terror".

GHZ—"Ghazni". Ghazni Province is an active area of operations.

GIROA—"Government of the Islamic Republic of Afghanistan". The Kabul government being defended by the US.

GMRLS — An American multiple-rocket launcher.

GSW — "Gun Shot Wound"

HEAT — "High Explosive Anti-Tank". A rocket with a shaped-charge warhead designed to penetrate armor

HELO — "Helicopter"

HHB — "Headquarters, Headquarters Battalion"

HIIDE — "Handheld Interagency Identity Detection Equipment". A scanner that identifies people through biometric measurements.

HIMARS — An American multiple rocket launcher

HLZ — "Helicopter Landing Zone"

HME — "Homemade Explosives"

HMLA — "Helicopter, Marines, Light Attack". A Marine helicopter unit.

HRT — "Hostage Rescue Team"

HET — "Human Exploitation Team". Interrogators.

HVI — "High Value Individual". A captured Al Qaeda or Taliban insurgency leader.

HWY — "Highway"

IAW — "In accordance with"

IAW EOF SOP — "In accordance with escalation of force standard operating procedures". American forces are provided with "rules of engagement" that cover what they can and cannot do in any operation.

ICOM — Radio communications

IDF — "Indirect Fire". Weapons fire against a target that lies out of sight.

IED — "Improvised Explosive Device". A homemade bomb, usually fashioned from an unexploded artillery shell or aerial bomb. IEDs are the favorite weapon of the Afghan insurgency.

ILLUM — "Illumination". A mortar or artillery shell that gives off a bright light, used to illuminate the battlefield at night.

INFIL — "Infiltrate"

INS — "Insurgents"

INTSUM — "Intelligence Summary"

IO — "Information Operations". American and Afghan propaganda. Often used for Psyops.

IOT — "In order to"

IR — "Incident Report". An after-action report describing the facts of an event.

IR — "Infrared". A heat-sensing device used for night vision or to guide heat-seeking weapons.

IROA—"Islamic Republic of Afghanistan". The Kabul government being defended by the US.

ISAF—"International Security Assistance Force". The American allies in Afghanistan. Also known as "Coalition Forces".

ISN—"Internment Serial Number". The identifying number assigned to prisoners at American camps.

ISO—"In Support Of"

ISR—"Intelligence, Surveillance, and Reconnaissance"

IVO—"In the vicinity of"

JAF—"Jalalabad Air Field". An important US base.

JBAD—"Jalalabad". A city near the Afghan-Pakistani border. An active area for insurgents and an important American base of operations.

JDAM—"Joint Direct Attack Munition". An American device that converts an ordinary "dumb bomb" into a guided "smart bomb".

JDCC—"Joint District Coordination Center"

JDOC—"Joint Defense Operations Center"

Jingle trucks—common Afghan civilian vehicles that are decorated with numerous bells and bright colors

JOC—"Joint Operations Center"

JPEL—"Joint Prioritized Effects List". The "hit list" of priority individuals to be arrested or killed.

JTAC—"Joint Terminal Air Controller". An observer who directs air strikes.

JUGROOM—Fort Garmsir, an American base in Afghanistan.

KAF—"Kandahar Air Field". An important US base.

KAIA—"Kabul International Airport". The airport in the Afghan capital, used for both civilian and military flights.

KDZ—"Kunduz". An area of operations in Afghanistan.

KIA—"Killed In Action".

KJI—"Kajaki". An area of operations in Afghanistan.

KMTC—"Kabul Military Training Center". Where Afghan forces are trained by American personnel.

KPRT—"Kabul Province Reconstruction Team". A group in charge of rebuilding damaged civilian infrastructure.

L:—"Location"

LEP—"Law Enforcement Professionals"

LKG—"Lashkar Gar". An area of operations.

LN—"Local National". An Afghan.

LNO—"Liason Officer". An American who coordinates US operations with the Kabul government.

LTC—"Lieutenant Colonel".

Luna—A German-made unmanned aerial drone

LZ—"Landing Zone".

M240b—A machine gun

M249—A machine gun

M4—An American rifle. A version of the Vietnam-era M16, it is the standard US infantry battlefield weapon.

MAM—"Military Age Male"

MAR—"Marines". US Marine Corps.

MED OPS—"Medical Operations"

MED TM—"Medical Team"

MEDEVAC—"Medical Evacuation"

MEY PRT—"Meymanah Province Reconstruction Team"

MG—"Machine Gun"

MHL—"Mehtar Lam". An area of operations.

MM—"Military Message"

MOD—"Ministry of Defense". The Kabul government's department of defense.

MOI—"Ministry of Interior". The Kabul government's security service.

MP—"Military Police"

MS—"Military Support"

MSN—A military nurse

MSR—"Main Supply Route"

MTF—"More to follow"

MTT—"Military Training Team"

N/I C—"NATO/ISAF Confidential" A security code indicating that this report is not to be shared outside of NATO.

NAI—"Named Area of Interest". A targeted area.

NC—"Non-Combatant". A civilian.

NCO—"Non-Commissioned Officer". The lowest levels of American military officers.

NDS—"National Directorate of Security". The Kabul government's intelligence service.

NFI—"Not further identified"

NFTR—"Nothing further to report"

NMC – "Non-Mission Capable"

NOFORN – "No foreigners". A security classification limiting distribution to American forces.

NSTR – "Nothing significant to report"

OBJ – "Objective". Persons on the kill/capture list are given OBJ codenames.

OC – "Outcome"

OCC-P – "Operations Command Center-Provincial"

OCCD – "Operations Coordination Center District"

ODA – "Operational Detachment Alpha". US Special Forces.

OGA – "Other Government Agency". Refers to non Defense Department parts of the US government. Usually indicates the CIA or other intelligence organization.

OIC – "Officer in Charge"

OMF – "Opposing Military Forces"

OP – "Operation". An action by military or security forces.

OP – "Observation Post". A site, usually temporary, used to watch enemy areas.

OP GRID – "Operation Grid". The map coordinates used for an operation.

OP SUM – "Operation Summary".

ORSA – "Operations Research and Systems Analysis". The process of integrating all the various individual incident reports into a coherent over-all picture.

PA – "Physician Assistant". A medic.

PAK – "Pakistan"

PAKMIL – "Pakistan Military"

PAO – "Public Affairs Officer". US military official who deals with the press.

PAX – People or persons.

PB – "Patrol Base".

PBIED – "Pedestrian-Borne Improvised Explosive Device". A suicide bomber with an explosive vest.

PEF – "Poppy Eradication Force". The Afghan police who have responsibility for controlling the opium/heroin trade. The drug trade is a major source of funding, for the insurgency as well as the local Afghan tribal warlords.

PEN – Penich. A base of operations.

PHQ – "Police Headquarters"

PID – "Positive identification"

PKM – A machine gun

PL or PLT – "Platoon". A small military unit.

PLT SJT – "Platoon Sargeant"

PMT—"Police Mentor Team"

POA—"President of Afghanistan"

POC—"Point of Contact"

POI—"Point of Impact"

POO—"Point of Origin"

PPIED—"Pressure-plate Improvised Explosive Device. A buried bomb that is detonated when a vehicle drives over it or a person steps on it.

PRED—An American-made Predator unmanned aerial drone

PRO COY—"Protection Company". An armed escort.

PRT—"Provincial Reconstruction Team"

PSO—"Post Security Officer"

PT—"Patient". A medical casualty.

PTS—"Peace Through Strength". An amnesty program run by the Kabul government to encourage and support defectors from the Taliban and Al Qaeda forces.

Qalat--A walled Afghan compound.

QRF—"Quick Response Force"

RB—"Roadblock"

RC(N)--"Regional Command, North"

RC CENTRAL—"Regional Command, Central"

RC(E)--"Regional Command, East"

RC(S) -- "Regional Command, South"

RC(W)--"Regional Command, West"

RCAG—"Regional Corps Assistance Group"

RC(C.)--"Regional Command, Capitol". The commander in the Kabul area.

RCIED—"Radio-Controlled Improvised Explosive Device". A homemade bomb that is set off at a distance by an operator with a radio or cell phone.

RCP—"Route Clearance Patrol". An armed convoy to sweep a road clear of insurgents and IEDs.

RDS—"Rounds". Bullets or ammunition.

RFS—"Resident Field Squadron"

ROE—"Rules of Engagement". A set of guidelines that specify what actions can or cannot be taken by American troops during an operation.

ROLE 3--An American military surgical hospital

RPG—"Rocket-propelled grenade". Used to attack buildings and armored vehicles.

RPK — A machine gun

RPT — "Report"

RTB — "Return to Base"

RTE — "Route"

S-2 -- Military intelligence officer

S-5 -- Officer who coordinates a military unit's actions with the local civilian authority.

SALT — "Size, Activity, Location, Time"

SALTUR — "Size, Activity, Location, Time, Unit, Result"

SALUTE — "Size, Activity, Location, Unit, Time, Effect"

S: -- Size

S//REL — "Selective Release". A security code indicating that a report is to be released only to specified agencies.

SA7 -- Russian-made shoulder-launched antiaircraft missile

SAF or SAFIRE — "Small Arms Fire". Rifle fire.

SAF or SAFIRE — "Surface to Air Fire". Antiaircraft or antihelicopter fire.

SAW — A machine gun

SFG — "Special Forces Group"

Shura — A meeting of Afghan tribal leaders

SIED — "Suicide Improvised Explosive Device". A bomb detonated by a suicide bomber.

SIGACT — "Significant Activity"

SIR — "Serious Incident Report"

SOF — "Special Operations Force"

SOG — "Special Operations Group"

Solatia — A payment made to civilians for damage or deaths caused by American actions.

SOP — "Standard Operating Procedures"

SOTF — "Special Operations Task Force"

SOTG — "Special Operations Task Group"

SPC — "Specialist". An Army rank.

Spider — An electronic device that receives radio signals, used in remote-detonated bombs

SQD or SQN — "Squadron".

Squirter — A person seen running away, or someone who attempts to get away from US forces

SSE—"Sensitive Site Exploitation". The process of gathering intelligence from a captured enemy location.

SVBIED—"Suicide Vehicle-Borne Improvised Explosive Device". A homemade bomb delivered by truck or car. A suicide car bomb.

SWO—"Surface Warfare Officer"

SWT—"Scout Weapons Team".

T: -- "Time"

TB—"Taliban". One of the two primary insurgent groups.

TBC—"To be confirmed"

TBD—"To be decided"

TCP—"Traffic Control Point". A checkpoint.

TERP—An interpreter.

TF—"Task Force".

TFK—"Task Force Kandahar"

TG—"Tactical Group"

TIC—"Troops in contact" with enemy forces

TOC—"Tactical Operations Center"

TTPs—"Tactics, Techniques and Procedures"

TQ—"Tactical Questioning"

UAH—"Up-Armored Humvee". A reinforced Humvee vehicle used for convoy duty.

UAV—"Unmanned Aerial Vehicle". A drone flown by remote control, used for reconnaissance and attack.

UH1--An American helicopter

UH60--An American helicopter

UI—"Unidentified"

UNAMA—"United Nations Assistance Mission in Afghanistan".

UNK—"Unknown"

USFOR-A—"United States Forces in Afghanistan"

UXO—"Unexploded Ordnance"

VBIED—"Vehicle-Borne Improvised Explosive Device". A car bomb.

VCP—"Vehicle Check Point"

VIC—"Vicinity"

VOIED—"Vehicle-Operated Improvised Explosive Device". A homemade mine that is buried in the road. Driving over the mine's pressure plate sets it off.

VP—"Vulnerable Point"

VPB—"Vehicle Patrol Base"

VSA—"Vital Signs Absent". Dead—a fatal casualty.

WIA—"Wounded in Action"

X-SPRAY--Field test used to indicate whether someone has been in contact with explosives

The Documents

Assassination

Like all insurgencies, Afghanistan is a dirty war. The Taliban/Al Qaeda insurgency is not strong enough militarily to stand in direct combat with US military forces. As a result, the Afghan insurgents have adopted classic guerrilla strategy, avoiding large-scale battlefield combat and instead focusing on small-scale hit-and-run raids and ambushes, which constantly nibble at the Americans without giving them any suitable targets for their superior firepower. Since guerrilla warfare is a political fight, not a military one, the purpose of the insurgent attacks is simply to wear down the occupier's will, to drag him into an ever-deepening quagmire, and to convince him in the end that the fight is no longer worth continuing. That strategy worked well for the Afghans against the Soviet Union—and it is working equally well against the United States.

The insurgent fighter therefore has two basic methods; assassinations and ambushes. In assassinations, the insurgent's goal is to demoralize, terrorize and break the will of his opponent by systematically attacking the government's officials and its supporters. We label them as "terrorists", but the Afghan insurgency's attacks are not simply directed at random civilians—they are carefully targeted, meticulously planned, and aimed towards definite political ends.

The US forces also practice their own form of assassination, which they refer to as "kinetic strikes on command nodes". These consist of targeted raids or remote missile or air attacks on those Taliban and Al Qaeda leaders who have been precisely located, particularly those on the JPEL—Joint Prioritized Effects List—also known as the "capture or kill list". By October 2009, the JPEL had over 2,000 names on it. A secretive unit called Task Force 373, presumably American Special Forces, has apparently been given the task of hunting down the people named in the JPEL. In 2009, TF 373 killed insurgent leader Shah Agha in a targeted raid. A few weeks later, they launched a "capture/kill operation" against Taliban subcommander Amir Jan Mutaki. One of the raids, to kill or capture a Taliban leader named Qarl Ur-Rahman, led to a mistaken firefight with Afghan police instead. In another attack, on Al Qaeda leader Abu Layth Libi, TF 373 used a multiple-rocket launcher to blow up his compound, killing 7 civilians. The documents reveal that steps were taken to hide the involvement of the US unit: "The knowledge that TF 373 conducted a HIMARS strike must be protected."

The goal of the American assassination program is the same as the insurgent's—to weaken and terrorize the enemy's leadership. The American program is, however, inherently more difficult and less effective, since the insurgents, unlike the Afghan government, do not have a single unified political and military structure—instead, the insurgency is a loose-knit coalition of ever-changing forces, including Taliban, Al Qaeda, and various local tribal warlords, which operate more or less independently of each other. Removing a particular insurgent commander, therefore, does not have as much operational or political impact as removing an Afghan government official—while American assassinations of insurgent leaders, when they become known, have far more negative impact both on Afghan popular support and on the political sensibilities of the American public.

Reference ID: AFG20040214n7
Latitude: 32.51665878
Date: 2004-02-14 00:12
Category: Assassination
Detained: 0

Region: RC SOUTH
Longitude: 67.41665649
Type: Enemy Action
Affiliation: ENEMY

	Enemy	Friend	Civilian	Host Nation
Killed in Action	0	0	0	1
Wounded in Action	0	0	0	0

(S//REL GCTF) TB ATTACK HOME AND ASSASINATE AN AMF COMMANDER IN SHAJOY

Reference ID: AFG20050122n62
Latitude: 32.82471848
Date: 2005-01-22 00:12
Category: IED Explosion
Detained: 0

Region: RC SOUTH
Longitude: 65.42888641
Type: Explosive Hazard
Affiliation: ENEMY

	Enemy	Friend	Civilian	Host nation
Killed in action	0	0	1	0
Wounded in action	0	0	0	0

(DEH RAWOOD/ RCIED ATTACK ON LN OFFICIAL) IN A DELAYED REPORT, ON 22 JAN HAJI WAZIR (THE YARDAK SECURITY CHIEF) AND HIS FAMILY WERE KILLED IN AN RCIED ATTACK 21KM N OF DEH RAWOOD. THE HAJI WAZIR HAD MANY ENEMIES, GOVERNOR JAN MOHAMMED IS CONDUCTING AND INVESTIGATION AND ASSERTS THAT MULLAH GHAFOR, A MID-LEVEL TB CDR AND IED TRAINER CONDUCTED THE ATTACK.

Reference ID: AFG20050719n114
Latitude:
Date: 2005-07-19 00:12
Category: IED Explosion
Detained: 0
Region: RC WEST
Longitude:
Type: Explosive Hazard
Affiliation: ENEMY

	Enemy	Friend	Civilian	Host nation
Killed in action	1	0	0	0
Wounded in action	0	0	0	0

On 19 July, at about 0730 hrs, a BBIED went off on an alleged suicide bomber targeting Enjeel district Chief of Police. As a result, the attacker was instantly killed, but no injures to anyone else was reported. Police investigation is ongoing.

Reference ID: AFG20050814n125
Latitude:
Date: 2005-08-14 00:12
Category: IED Explosion
Detained: 0
Region: RC EAST
Longitude:
Type: Explosive Hazard
Affiliation: ENEMY

	Enemy	Friend	Civilian	Host nation
Killed in action	0	0	0	0
Wounded in action	0	0	0	0

At 0900 hrs an n IED detonated under a culvert in Shobi Kalay village of Tere Zayi district as WJ Candidate Mohammed Quyum was passing in his vehicle. Quyum was unhurt and there was no significant damage to his vehicle.

Reference ID: AFG20051202n191
Latitude: 31.96858978
Date: 2005-12-02 12:12
Category: IED Explosion
Detained: 0
Region: RC SOUTH
Longitude: 65.96700287
Type: Explosive Hazard
Affiliation: ENEMY

	Enemy	Friend	Civilian	Host nation
Killed in action	0	0	5	1
Wounded in action	0	0	2	0

(Delayed Report) ANP reported an RCIED strike against a local GOA official 11km S of FOB Tiger II to TF Bayonet. At 0107Z, TF Gundevil reported while traveling down the roadway the Shah Wali Kot district leader vehicle was struck by an RCIED. Vehicle had eight personnel inside. As a result of the detonation ANP reported five passengers killed including the district leader, and three passengers injured. The vehicle was destroyed by the blast. Injured were ground EVACD to KAF. TF Gun Devil sent a patrol to investigate the site. Upon arrival and further investigation TF Gun Devil determined the IED was remote detonated. ANP detained five personnel for questioning in connection with the strike. No CF were present during the incident. No further injuries or damages were reported

Reference ID: AFG20060901n377
Latitude: 33.31718445
Date: 2006-09-01 07:07
Region: RC EAST
Longitude: 67.80709839
Type: Enemy Action

Category: Assassination   Affiliation: ENEMY
Detained: 0

	Enemy	Friend	Civilian	Host Nation
Killed in Action	0	0	1	4
Wounded in Action	0	0	0	0

(Delayed Report) In the Shahbaz Shopping Area, the district commissioner of Muqur was ambushed and killed. He was enroute to Muqur District. At the same time his police escorts were also killed.

Reference ID: AFG20060910n384   Region: RC EAST
Latitude: 33.31718445   Longitude: 67.80709839
Date: 2006-09-10 14:02   Type: Enemy Action
Category: Assassination   Affiliation: ENEMY
Detained: 0

	Enemy	Friend	Civilian	Host Nation
Killed in Action	0	0	1	0
Wounded in Action	0	0	0	0

(Delayed Report) The remains of the Education Director who was abducted on 5 Sep 06 were found on 10 Sep 06.

Reference ID: AFG20061010n408   Region: RC EAST
Latitude: 33.36402893   Longitude: 69.84312439
Date: 2006-10-10 00:12   Type: Enemy Action
Category: Assassination   Affiliation: ENEMY
Detained: 0

	Enemy	Friend	Civilian	Host Nation
Killed in Action	0	0	1	0
Wounded in Action	0	0	0	0

(Delayed Report) Bak Mullah, Mullawi Khalil Ahmad, was allegedly targeted and killed late this afternoon. Sub-Governor reports he believes Mullah Ahmad was killed by insurgents in the area for outwardly supporting the Government. ANP investigation in progress. Note. Mullah Ahmad replaced Mullah Zinul Abidin after his death in mid-Jul. Abidin was killed in a raid by US Coalition Forces for supporting insurgency operations. (DBC 19 Jul / 368-71 refers).

Reference ID: AFG20061122n476   Region: RC SOUTH
Latitude: 31.03955841   Longitude: 65.7148819
Date: 2006-11-22 00:12   Type: Enemy Action
Category: Assassination   Affiliation: ENEMY
Detained: 0

	Enemy	Friend	Civilian	Host Nation
Killed in Action	0	0	1	0
Wounded in Action	0	0	0	0

(Delayed Report) District 4- in the afternoon a woman member of the Kandahar Provincial Council escaped death when two assassins attempted to kill her when she was shopping. Her husband was killed in the incident.

Reference ID: AFG20061125n415
Latitude: 31.03955841
Date: 2006-11-25 00:12
Category: Assassination
Detained: 0

Region: RC SOUTH
Longitude: 65.7148819
Type: Enemy Action
Affiliation: ENEMY

	Enemy	Friend	Civilian	Host Nation
Killed in Action	0	0	1	0
Wounded in Action	0	0	0	0

(Delayed Report) a municipal official was returning home in the early evening when he was shot and killed by gunmen.

Reference ID: AFG20061202n451
Latitude: 34.96220779
Date: 2006-12-02 00:12
Category: Assassination
Detained: 0

Region: RC EAST
Longitude: 71.09215546
Type: Enemy Action
Affiliation: ENEMY

	Enemy	Friend	Civilian	Host Nation
Killed in Action	0	0	3	0
Wounded in Action	0	0	0	0

Korangal Area, the murdered bodies of three men were found in the Sawatalo Sar Area. The three men were laborers who were abuducted by TB from the Pech District. All three were shot execution style. A forth person is still missing.

Reference ID: AFG20061224n401
Latitude: 33.51749039
Date: 2006-12-24 10:10
Category: Assassination
Detained: 0

Region: RC EAST
Longitude: 68.83654022
Type: Enemy Action
Affiliation: ENEMY

	Enemy	Friend	Civilian	Host Nation
Killed in Action	0	0	1	0
Wounded in Action	0	0	0	0

At 241015ZDEC06 TF VANGUARD reported the Zormat Chief of Interior Affairs (Abdul Rahman) was kidnapped and murdered 39km East of FB Ghazni. Unit reported he was kidnapped from Tatanak and his body was discovered in Payendakhel. Chief of Interior Affairs was in charge of issuing Taskaras(Afghan National Photo IDs) for Zormat District. It is believed that he was denying groups in Sahak Taskaras for change of identity. This is also believed to be the same group that stole an ANA truck in Ghazni. ANP/ANA are investigating. Event closed at 1315Z. ISAF Tracking # 12-302

Reference ID: AFG20070106n621
Latitude: 33.33086014
Date: 2007-01-06 03:03
Category: Assassination
Detained: 0

Region: RC EAST
Longitude: 69.8638916
Type: Enemy Action
Affiliation: ENEMY

	Enemy	Friend	Civilian	Host Nation
Killed in Action	0	0	0	0
Wounded in Action	0	0	0	0

At 060330ZJAN07, TF WOLFPACK reported PCC reported NDS COL was ambushed and killed vic Khost City. PCC reported COL was traveling to work on his motorcycle when he was attacked. Assailants escaped on motorcycles. It is unknown if this is criminal or enemy related. NDS investigating. ISAF Tracking# 01-074.

Reference ID: AFG20070112n526
Latitude: 34.19045639
Date: 2007-01-12 00:12
Category: Assassination
Detained: 0

Region: RC WEST
Longitude: 62.13847733
Type: Enemy Action
Affiliation: ENEMY

	Enemy	Friend	Civilian	Host Nation
Killed in Action	0	0	1	0
Wounded in Action	0	0	2	0

3 armed men broke into a residence and killed a former district governor and wounded 2 other civilians.

Reference ID: AFG20070126n464
Latitude: 33.62928391
Date: 2007-01-26 00:12
Category: Assassination
Detained: 0

Region: RC EAST
Longitude: 69.39308167
Type: Enemy Action
Affiliation: ENEMY

	Enemy	Friend	Civilian	Host Nation
Killed in Action	0	0	1	0
Wounded in Action	0	0	0	0

Gardea (Jan 26). The Taliban militants have killed a man in Paktia on charges of spying for the US and Afghan forces. The body of the slain man was found hanging in a tree on Friday. A spokesman for the Taliban in that area reported man was killed three days prior. "He was involved in spying for the Afghan and foreign forces"; said the spokesman. However, residents said the slain was innocent and had nothing to do with the government or the foreign forces. An elder of the Balakht village said the deceased was running a shop in Kabul and he had come home to meet his family. "He was on the way from the market to his house when he was kidnapped by armed men."; The Paktia police chief confirmed the incident.

Reference ID: AFG20070126n477
Latitude: 34.55408859
Date: 2007-01-26 08:08
Category: Assassination
Detained: 0

Region: RC CAPITAL
Longitude: 69.32198334
Type: Enemy Action
Affiliation: ENEMY

	Enemy	Friend	Civilian	Host Nation
Killed in Action	0	0	1	0
Wounded in Action	0	0	0	0

(Delayed Report) At 260830ZJAN07 the NPCC received a report that a member of Parliament, Mohammad Islam, was shot by an unknown suspect near his residence in the Karteh Parwan area in Kabul city. Mohammad Islam is a member of Parliament from Samangan Province. Information relayed to RC-East from CSTC-A. Event closed at 0830Z.

Reference ID: AFG20070313n658
Latitude: 33.14292908
Date: 2007-03-13 00:12
Category: Assassination
Detained: 0
Region: RC EAST
Longitude: 68.09076691
Type: Enemy Action
Affiliation: ENEMY

	Enemy	Friend	Civilian	Host Nation
Killed in Action	0	0	1	0
Wounded in Action	0	0	0	0

The provincial Chief of Police informed the PRT that a senior mullah was killed last night in Qarabagh District. Mullah Jamal Adin, who lived in the village of Nawroz Kel (grid 42S VB 152675), was shot twice in the head and then decapitated because of his support of the IRoA and coalition forces. The Chief of Police is sending men from Ghazni to investigate and did not have any further details.

Reference ID: AFG20070405n671
Latitude: 33.34667969
Date: 2007-04-05 11:11
Category: Assassination
Detained: 0
Region: RC EAST
Longitude: 69.92101288
Type: Enemy Action
Affiliation: ENEMY

	Enemy	Friend	Civilian	Host Nation
Killed in Action	0	0	0	1
Wounded in Action	0	0	1	0

At approx. 1600L (1130Z), Khowst PCC reported that the NDS LTC Sadet Khan was assassinated by 2xUI men riding motorcycles. This occurred in the Mandu Khel Village, Matun District about 1KM East of the PCC. They utilized Mekarap pistol (believed to be a russian model). The LTC was riding in a taxi when attacked. The driver, Toor s/o Ajeb Khan was also injured and is currently at Khowst Hospital.

Reference ID: AFG20070407n747
Latitude: 33.3685112
Date: 2007-04-07 12:12
Category: Assassination
Detained: 9
Region: RC EAST
Longitude: 70.0136795
Type: Enemy Action
Affiliation: ENEMY

	Enemy	Friend	Civilian	Host Nation
Killed in Action	0	0	1	0
Wounded in Action	0	0	1	0

At 1210Z NDS reports that Mohammad Anwar, the Chief Mullah of the Pro Government Mullah Council, and his son were traveling through Mahdi Khel Village (WB 943 926), Matun District (approx 4km east of FOB Salerno.) As they were traveling home a group of fighters who were waiting exited a white corolla and fired on the Mullah and his son. The attackers then returned to their vehicle and fled towards Khowst City. The Mullah was dead within 10 minutes of the attack. Local nations brought the Mullah and his son into a local residence until ANP arrived on the scene. ANP brought the Mullah and the son to Khowst Hospital, the Mullah was dead on arrival and the son was later released and sent home without any security. The Taliban released to the Ariana TV at 1900 that they were the ones responsible for the Mullahs death.

Analyst Comments: This attack is part of a continuing trend of targeted assassinations and attacks within the province. These attacks have likely been planned for some time, and it is probable that we will continue to see these targeted assassinations as insurgents become emboldened by their successes. These successful assassinations send a very powerful IO message and will undoubtedly have a significant impact on the perception of security in the province. NDS has indicated through the PCC that they believe the Mullahs funeral, to be held tomorrow, is likely to be a target for a suicide bomber, and has coordinated for an increased ANP presence at the event.

Reference ID: AFG20070416n639
Latitude: 33.36462021
Date: 2007-04-16 16:04
Category: Assassination
Detained: 0

Region: RC EAST
Longitude: 69.99127197
Type: Enemy Action
Affiliation: ENEMY

	Enemy	Friend	Civilian	Host Nation
Killed in Action	0	0	0	0
Wounded in Action	0	0	0	0

On 16 April at approx. 2100 local Mullah Ghulam Haidar was assassinated by small caliber wounds to the head and chest. NDS reported the pro-IRoA/CF supporter was killed in Kundi village, aka Mongal village, adjacent to FOB Salerno. He was found dead in his home, there were no witnesses.

Reference ID: AFG20070422n668
Latitude: 33.48308182
Date: 2007-04-22 00:12
Category: Assassination
Detained: 0

Region: RC EAST
Longitude: 68.42723846
Type: Enemy Action
Affiliation: ENEMY

	Enemy	Friend	Civilian	Host Nation
Killed in Action	0	0	0	1
Wounded in Action	0	0	0	0

The Associated Press: Afghan Intelligence Officer Beheaded
 Assailants abducted and beheaded an Afghan intelligence service employee In Ghazni province. According to reports an intelligence service employee was invited to a home, then kidnapped and beheaded Sunday by the Taliban, deputy governor Mohammad kazim Allayar said Monday. He said the owner of the house is under investigation.

Reference ID: AFG20070427n639
Latitude: 33.30628967
Date: 2007-04-27 02:02
Category: Assassination
Detained: 0

Region: RC EAST
Longitude: 69.89372253
Type: Enemy Action
Affiliation: ENEMY

	Enemy	Friend	Civilian	Host Nation
Killed in Action	0	0	1	1
Wounded in Action	0	0	1	0

270245Z Apr 07 Khowst PCC reports the Chief Detective of Tani Police killed by unkown number of gunmen, his brother was also killed, and a relative was wounded in the attack. Location VIC ANP checkpoint at WB 832 856. Attackers used white station wagon car and headed toward Mando Zayi. Tani ANP is currently conducting an investigation at the scene.

Reference ID: AFG20070427n667
Latitude: 34.93901062
Date: 2007-04-27 17:05
Category: Other (Hostile Action)
Detained: 0

Region: RC EAST
Longitude: 70.96878052
Type: Enemy Action
Affiliation: ENEMY

	Enemy	Friend	Civilian	Host Nation
Killed in Action	0	0	1	1
Wounded in Action	0	0	1	0

INSURGENT COMMANDER HABIB ((JAN)), CURRENTLY LOCATED IN KAKI BANDEH, PECH DISTRICT, KUNAR PROVINCE, AFGHANISTAN, PLANS TO MOVE TO AN UNIDENTIFIED LOCATION IN THE SHURYAK VALLEY WITHIN 24 TO 48 HOURS FROM 27 APR 2007. JAN WILL CONDUCT MOVEMENT FROM KAKI BANDEH WITH AN UNIDENTIFIED NUMBER OF FIGHTERS. JAN PLANS TO CROSS THE PECH RIVER USING ONE OF THREE POSSIBLE BRIDGES, TO INCLUDE BARKANDAY BRIDGE //MGRS: 42SXD79806805//, SEYAMATA BRIDGE (CNA), OR KHARAMOR BRIDGE (CNA). AFTER CROSSING ONE OF THESE THREE BRIDGES, JAN WILL PROCEED TO AN UNKNOWN LOCATION IN THE SHURYAK VALLEY. JAN WILL USE THE LOW LIGHT OF EITHER THE BREAK OF DAWN OR DUSK TO CROSS THE RIVER UNOBSERVED. JAN WILL BE EQUIPPED WITH AN ICOM RADIO, WHICH HE WILL USE TO COMMUNICATE WITH SPOTTERS ON THE SOUTH SIDE OF THE RIVER. SPOTTERS ARE TASKED TO WATCH FOR COALITION FORCES AND WILL WARN JAN IF SUCH FORCES ARE IN THE AREA. JAN IS LEAVING KAKI BANDEH BECAUSE OF CURRENT COALITION OPERATIONS AND HIS FEAR OF BEING CAPTURED.

Reference ID: AFG20070430n534
Latitude: 35.41905975
Date: 2007-04-30 04:04
Category: Assassination
Detained: 0

Region: RC EAST
Longitude: 71.37133789
Type: Enemy Action
Affiliation: ENEMY

	Enemy	Friend	Civilian	Host Nation
Killed in Action	0	0	1	0
Wounded in Action	0	0	0	0

300556Z TF Titan reports the leader of the Kamdesh Security Shura (Fazal Ahad) was assassinated by an enemy element of UNK size while traveling along the MSR VIC Kamdesh with 3x other shura members. Fazal Ahad's vehicle was stopped by an unknown number of personnel, and he was fatally wounded. The 3x other shura members fled east to Mirdesh where it is believed they are currently located. The remains of Fazal Ahad are currently located at the ANP station adjacent to Camp Keating. Elements of CJSOTF are moving to the area where Fazal Ahad was assassinated to investigate further, and were told the following: At 0330Z, Fazal Ahad, Aziz Khan, and Abdul Aziz of Barge Matal and Mohamadullah of Saret left Mandigal in a Taxi. They were traveling to Gaziabad IOT bring unidentified Kushtuzi elders to Kamdesh IOT resolve the Kamdesh/Kushtuz conflict. At 0430z, the previously mentioned individuals were stopped by 6x armed individuals in the road. The fighters secured Fazal Ahad and told the others they could leave now and live or follow them and die. After Aziz Khan, Abdul Aziz, and Mohamadullah fled towards Mirdesh LNs report hearing a gunshot and discovering Fazal Ahads body. ANP are continuing to search for the assassins. NFTR. ISAF Tracking# 04-563.

Reference ID: AFG20070502n629
Latitude: 34.58201981
Date: 2007-05-02 15:03
Category: Assassination
Detained: 0

Region: RC CAPITAL
Longitude: 69.1253891
Type: Enemy Action
Affiliation: ENEMY

	Enemy	Friend	Civilian	Host Nation
Killed in Action	0	0	1	0
Wounded in Action	0	0	0	0

At 1535z KCP reported to RC(C) that a member of the Afghan Parliment representing KAPISA province was assassinated as he exited his house.
ISAF Tracking # 05-052

Reference ID: AFG20070507n782
Latitude: 33.30057907
Date: 2007-05-07 02:02
Category: Assassination
Detained: 2

Region: RC EAST
Longitude: 69.93447876
Type: Enemy Action
Affiliation: ENEMY

	Enemy	Friend	Civilian	Host Nation
Killed in Action	0	0	2	0
Wounded in Action	0	0	0	0

PCC reports that two individuals were assassinated in Gurbuz just before 0230Z/0700L this morning at WB 87 85. One of the individuals was identified as Habib Shah who was KPF. The other was his cousin Kasi Shah. Two men were arrested and confessed to killing the KPF soldier. The two men were named Omar and Wazir, they were arrested with two AK-47s and are currently being held at the ANP HQ in Khowst City.

The following debrief is from the FOB Chapman Daily Security Meeting held on 07 May 2008, ANP was not present during the meeting:
KPF
KPF reported that this morning at approximately 07:25 a KPF solider was shot dead on the way to work. The soldier was identified as Habib ((SHAH)) s/o Mohamed ((HASAN)). The solider and his cousin were killed when a white station wagon drove up to them near the Shamal Bridge and began shooting. Eye witnesses (small boys in the area) advised the ANP of their description and they were subsequently able to locate the suspects and apprehend them. They are currently in custody at the Gurbaz District Center.
KPF then reported that yesterday that a KPF patrol was ambushed while on the way to BCP 10, near Mirsapir, Spera District. Unfortunately, a KPF solider was killed in the exchange. The solider was identified as Kamil ((KHAN)) s/o Jahan ((SHAH)); the body was turned over to family members this morning.
ANP
ANP representative was not present this morning, probably due to the shooting this morning at the Shamal Bridge.
ABP
NSTR
NDS
NDS learned that approximately 70 ACM, commanded by Toor ((KHAN)), from Surkah Village in Spera District are being housed at the Atah Khel Madrassa in Rezu Village, Speara. NDS stated this group is armed with both heavy and light weapons. This group is apparently being trained by two Mullahs who are identified as ((AZIZULLAH)) and Torin ((GUHL)). NDS wasnt able to provide a specific time or method of any intended attack.
Another group of 20-30 ACM was reported to be located at the Asar Khel Madrassa which is located in the Spera District. The commander is identified as Talib ((NOOR ZAMAN)). The HQN commander in this area is assessed to be Zangin ((ZADRAN)).
NDS also advised that 40 more ACM fighters are located at Shinkai Mountain, in the Shamal District. Source stated he observed these fighters while cutting fire wood in the area. An unidentified individual approached source and advised him to stop what he was doing and move on, and asked that he not reveal what he saw here. NDS opined that these three groups could be planning a coordinated attack against the Spera District Center.
Lastly, NDS reported that 105 ACM fighters, commanded by ((SAKHIJAN)) who is from Almrah Village, Nadir Shah Kot District, are located at their HQ in Alrazmak, Miram Shah in the Barbari Compound near the Razmak Bus Station in Miram Shah City. They apparently have one black Hilux and one white station wagon. Their weapons inventory consists of 5 PKs, 2 RPGs and other small arms. This group is supposedly funded by Siraj ((HIQANNI)). Their intentions are to carry out ground assaults on various border checkpoints located in the southern parts of Khost Province. Most of the fighters are reported to be from the Wazri Tribe in Pakistan.
End of report.
Headquarters
International Security Assistance Force Afghanistan

NEWS RELEASE [2007-XXX: Draft]
Afghan Security Guard, cousin killed in Khowst

FORWARD OPERATING BASE SALERNO, Afghanistan Insurgents shot and killed an Afghan security guard and his cousin May 7 at 7:25 a.m. in Gurbaz District, Khowst. (For the rest of the release, see attachment)

Reference ID: AFG20070517n775
Latitude: 35.02999878
Date: 2007-05-17 14:02
Category: Assassination
Detained: 0

Region: RC EAST
Longitude: 71.35236359
Type: Enemy Action
Affiliation: ENEMY

	Enemy	Friend	Civilian	Host Nation
Killed in Action	0	0	0	0
Wounded in Action	0	0	0	1

At 171403z, TF Titan reports one enemy bomb targeting the Dangam Police Chief and requests MEDEVAC for 1 ANP (Dangam Police Chief) with sharpnel injuries to upper torso and head at HLZ Duke IVO YD 146 789. ANP was drinking tea in a local national's home when a prepositioned bomb exploded and the local national brought the Dangam Police Chief to Camp Monti for medical assistance. MM(E) 05-17F approved to ABAD. W/U HLZ DUKE at 1453, W/D ABAD at 1503z. At 1818, ABAD requests patient transfer of the Dangam Police Chief to BAF along with an exchange of 1 vent, 1 propac, and 1 suction. MM(E) 05-17G approved from BAF to ABAD to BAF. W/D ABAD at 1944z, W/U ABAD at 2025z, W/D BAF at 2116z. M/C. NFTR.

Reference ID: AFG20070606n851
Latitude: 35.12229156
Date: 2007-06-06 03:03
Category: Assassination
Detained: 0

Region: RC EAST
Longitude: 69.23267365
Type: Enemy Action
Affiliation: ENEMY

	Enemy	Friend	Civilian	Host Nation
Killed in Action	0	0	1	0
Wounded in Action	0	0	0	0

Parwan Governor Taqwa called this morning to inform the PRT that the owner/director of Radio Solh (Peace Radio) in Parwan, Zakiya Zaki was murdered last night in Jabal Saraj. Zakiya Zaki was known for her pro-IROA stance and had been highly supportive of CF reconstruction efforts. She was also a former member of the National Assemby Loya Jirga. Her radio was established in October 2001 after an agreement with Ahmed Shah Masood. She was one of the most prominent women in Parwan Province. MTF as situation develops.
PRT S-2 Comment: This is the second incident involving the assassination/attempted assassination of a prominent female in Parwan Province. The first was what the ANP described as an attempted assassination of the Parwan Minister of Education Azizi Sedat on 30 May 07. Information on this specific incident is still vague, as reporting indicates the IED was likely a small-calibur mortar or fireworks.

Reference ID: AFG20070610n771
Latitude: 31.59741974

Region: RC SOUTH
Longitude: 65.70863342

Date: 2007-06-10 05:05　　　　　　Type: Enemy Action
Category: Assassination　　　　　　Affiliation: ENEMY
Detained: 0

	Enemy	Friend	Civilian	Host Nation
Killed in Action	0	0	1	0
Wounded in Action	0	0	0	0

At 0548Z TF Kandahar reported unknown enemy shot and killed Kandahar Afghan National Police director of Admin GEN. Mohammad Dawood. After getting his hair cut in district 3, Director. Adm was returning home and was shot and killed. Ministry of Information indicated that they felt that he was specifacilly targeted. ISAF Event # 06-252.

Reference ID: AFG20070611n787　　　Region: RC EAST
Latitude: 34.27045822　　　　　　　　Longitude: 70.06186676
Date: 2007-06-11 19:07　　　　　　　　Type: Friendly Fire
Category: BLUE-BLUE　　　　　　　　Affiliation: FRIEND
Detained: 0

	Enemy	Friend	Civilian	Host Nation
Killed in Action	4	0	0	7
Wounded in Action	0	0	0	4

Initial Report (12 0430Z June)
- TF 373 was conducting an operation 43 Km south-west of Jalalabad (OBJ Carbon)
- Mission was a kill / capture of the senior TB commander (Qari Ur-Rahman) for attacks and planning in Nangarhar, and a cousin of Anwar al-Haqs
- This was a combination of Helicopter and Ground Assault forces
- Approximately one hour into the operation, the unit suffered a hard compromise and a firefight ensued
- AC-130 was on station and engaged personnel who were engaging TF 373 forces with SAF and RPGs
- ICOM chatter was intercepted stating enemy maneuver intentions on the TF 373 force
- AC-130 engaged and reported positive effects on 3 x vehicles moving to reinforce the element engaged with TF 373
- The original mission was aborted and TF-373 broke contact and returned to FOB Fenty
- BDA No TF-373 casualties, 4 x EKIA, 1 x Detainee, 3 x vehicles, 5-6 x personnel down IVO of the vehicle strikes, unknown number of small arms / heavy weapons and RPGs, and 1 x radio
Followup Report
- 7 x ANP KIA, 4 x WIA (evacuated to the JBAD Hospital)
- 4 x EKIA
Executive Summary from Meeting with Gov Sherzai, (12 0730Z Jun 07):
The following personnel attended the meeting with Gov Sherzai: Lt Col Phillips (PRT CDR), LTC Milhorn (TF RAPTOR), Danny Hall (DoS), LTC Muhamadullah (Deputy CDR, Unit 03), and Najib (PRT TERP).
Governor Sherzai began the meeting by describing the event as an unfortunate incident that occurred between friends and he further emphasized that he does not

want to see this happen again. Though not completely opposed to night operations, he strongly encourages better coordination.

Lt Col Phillips inquired of any press coverage and the governor indicated that he had pre-taped the following comments:

Afghan security forces conducted a joint operation with Coalition Forces (CF) to fight the enemy.The governor cited recent attacks by TB against police checkpoints, adding that many police were still cautious of any activity in the surrounding areas

The governor described that the joint patrol was misdirected resulting in close contact made with police from Unit 03. He indicated that Unit 03 reacted by engaging CF first. CF then responded when attacked, resulting in numerous casualties.

The governor emphasized this incident as a complete misunderstanding, again citing recent TB activities within the area and the immediate response to a perceived threat by both forces.

Lt Col Phillips acknowledged the Governors concern and reiterated our support to prevent these types of events from occurring again.

The governor indicated that he had received $2000 from OGA and he, himself, donated an additional $10,000 to Families/Elders for initial funeral expenses.

The governor reported that his Deputy Governor, Afghan National Police Chief, and several line directors were already working to prevent any demonstrations. The governor also reported that MOI and President Karzais office had also been notified. Governor Sherzai advised that CF in Kabul should host a press conference to prevent negative messages from being used by the insurgents.

When Lt Col Phillips emphasized the need for continued night operations, Governor Sherzai did not retaliate. The governor acknowledged that many of the tribal elders and mullahs were opposed to night ops. He only re-emphasized the need for improved coordination and intelligence sharing. If not done, bad things will continue to happen, he said.

The governor outlined future events to address many of the new concerns:

On Sunday, 17 Jun 07, he will host a Shura at the governors compound inviting 10 tribal elders and leaders from each of the 22 districts across Nangarhar Province. The governor requested that a general officer be present from Kabul (originally citing GEN McNeil). Media will also be invited with no press conference to follow.

Within the next few days, he will host the Families and Soldiers of Unit 03 at the compound for a funeral service and solatia event in an effort to show how much he cares for his children (the police).

Lt Col Phillips further expressed his concern about the inability of ANSF to conduct night ops on their own and further concurred with the governors proposal that all operations should be conducted jointly. The governor responded with agreement and stressed that ANSF should be in the lead with CF in trail.

After the governor concluded with his comments, I expressed my condolences to LTC Muhamadullah and the governor and reiterated our emphasis to conduct joint patrols routinely. Additionally, I expressed my concern for the derogatory remarks made by LTC Safi, the Unit 03 Commander in Khogyani, and suggested that we meet in the near future. LTC Muhamadullah suggested that we meet with LTC Safi within the next few days and follow-up with a meeting in Khogyani.

In closing, Governor Sherzai requested that the three trucks destroyed by CF be replaced. He added that MOI had committed to sending three additional trucks to Unit 03, and at least 30 to the governor for distribution amongst his 22 sub-governors and special staff. He indicated that he had given four of his personal vehicles to sub-governors, of which all had been destroyed by IEDs.

13 June 07 Meeting with BG Gul Nabi (Director of Education and Training for MOI) who was doing the official MOI investigation of the Force 03 incident. Key points from the meeting:

Our sequence of events as discussed last night are the same as he received from Force 03, the ANP, and the Governor

He stressed that they clearly understand this was an accident, and trust between all involved is still strong

Appreciated our recommended coordination adjustments to ensure this type of incident does not occur again

Recommended three events in conjunction with this event: Shura with elders, shura with security personnel, and solitia payment in small group

=SUN, 17 JUN, Elder shura at Nangarhar Governors Compound followed by lunch, BG Votel and B6 attend (PAO, LNO, IO, PSO, and RTO), Time is TBD, Purpose: apology and stress changes to prevent this in the future

= MON, 18 JUN, Security Shura with ANSF personalities followed by lunch, B6 is senior guy (PAO, LNO, IO, PSO, RTO, and JAG), B6 would like to do even on FOB Fenty, Time is TBD, Purpose: Quick remarks on what happened and apologies, questions from the group, encourage attendees to express feelings

=TUE, 19 JUN, Solatia payment to families, B6 can do it or have the PRT CDR do it, location will be Governors Compound, Purpose: express condolences, Time is TBD

Reference ID: AFG20070617n853
Latitude: 33.0050087
Date: 2007-06-17 21:09
Category: Other
Detained: 7

Region: RC EAST
Longitude: 68.70246124
Type: Friendly Action
Affiliation: FRIEND

	Enemy	Friend	Civilian	Host nation
Killed in action	6	0	7	0
Wounded in action	0	0	0	0

NOTE: The following information (TF-373 and HIMARS) is Classified Secret / NOFORN. The knowledge that TF-373 conducted a HIMARS strike must be kept protected. All other information below is classified Secret / REL ISAF.

(S) Mission: O/O SOTF conducts kinetic strike followed with HAF raid to kill/capture ABU LAYTH AL LIBI on NAI 2.

(S)Target: Abu Layth Al Libi is a senior al-Qaida military commander, Libyan Islamic Fighting Group (LIFG) leader. He is based in Mir Ali, Pakistan and runs training camps throughout North Waziristan. Collection over the past week indicates a concentration of Arabs IVO objective area.

Result: 6 x EKIA; 7 x NC KIA, 7 x detainees

(S) Summary: HAF departed for Orgun-E to conduct link-up and posture to the objective immediately after pre-assault fires. On order, 5 rockets were launched and destroyed structures on the objective (NAI 2). The HAF quickly inserted the assault force into the HLZ. ISR reported multiple UIMs leaving the objective area. The assault force quickly conducted dismounted movement to the target area and established containment on the south side of the objective. During the initial assault, dedicated air assets engaged multiple MAMs squirting off the objective area. GFC

assessed 3 x EKIA squirters north and 3 x EKIA squirters south of the compound were neutralized from air asset fires. The assault force quickly maneuvered with a SQD element on the remaining squirters. The squirter element detained 12 x MAMs and returned to the objective area. GFC passed initial assessment of 7 x NC KIA (children). During initial questioning, it was assessed that the children were not allowed out of the building, due to UIMs presence within the compound. The assault force was able to uncover 1 x NC child from the rubble. The MED TM immediately cleared debris form the mouth and performed CPR to revive the child for 20 minutes. Due to time restrictions, TF CDR launched QRF element to action a follow-on target (NAI 5). They quickly contained the objective and initiated the assault. The objective was secured and the assault force initially detained 6 x MAMs. The GFC recommended that 7 MAMs be detained for additional questioning. The TF CDR assessed that the assault force will continue SSE. The local governor was notified of the current situation and requests for assistance were made to cordon the AO with support from ANP and local coalition forces in search of HVI. A PRT is enroute to AO.
1) Target was an AQ Senior Leader
2) Patterns of life were conducted on 18 June from 0800z 1815z (strike time) with no indications of women or children on the objective
3) The Mosque was not targeted nor was it struck initial reports state there is no damage to the Mosque
4) An elder who was at the Mosque stated that the children were held against their will and were intentionally kept inside
UPDATE: 18 0850Z June 07
- Governor Khapalwak has had no success yet in reaching President Karzai (due to the Presidents busy schedule today) but expects to reach him within the hour (PoA reached later in the afternoon ~ 1400Z)
- The Governor conducted a Shura this morning, in attendance were locals from both the Yahya Yosof Khail & Khail Districts
- He pressed the Talking Points given to him and added a few of his own that followed in line with our current story
- The atmospherics of the local populous is that they are in shock, but understand it was caused ultimately by the presence of hoodlums
    - the people think it is good that bad men were killed
    - the people regret the loss of life among the children
- The Governor echoed the tragedy of children being killed, but stressed this couldve been prevented had the people exposed the presence of insurgents in the area
- The Governor promised another Shura in a few days and that the families would be compensated for their loss
- Tthe Governor was asked what the mood of the people was and he stated that "the operation was a good thing, and the people believe what we have told them"
- Additionally, the people accused the Yahya Khail Chief of Police and his officers of corruption and collusion with TB in the area
- The Governor and the Provincial NDS Chief relieved the CofP and his officers, disarmed them, and they are currently detained and enroute to Sharana at this time unknown as to total numbers detained (MTF on this incident)

Reference ID: AFG20070623n705 Region: RC SOUTH
Latitude: 32.05575943 Longitude: 64.84205627

	Date: 2007-06-23 00:12 Category: Assassination Detained: 0			Type: Enemy Action Affiliation: ENEMY	

	Enemy	Friend	Civilian	Host Nation
Killed in Action	0	0	5	0
Wounded in Action	0	0	0	0

AV24a Headline: Decapitated bodies of Afghan truck drivers discovered
Media: BBC Monitoring (Pajhwok Afghan News, Kabul)
Date: 23 June 2007
Security officials today said that they have discovered the decapitated bodies of six truck drivers who supplied food items to the Afghan and foreign forces stationed in Sangin District of southern Helmand province.
The drivers were returning to Kandahar from Sangin in three trucks after delivering foodstuffs to the troops, the district police chief, Gholam Rasul, informed Pajhwok Afghan News. The Taleban captured them in the Haiderabad area of Greshk District and torched their trailers.
Qari Yusof Ahmadi [the Taleban spokesman] confirmed the killing of five drivers, saying that they had repeatedly warned drivers to stop supplying foodstuffs and fuel to the foreign forces.

Reference ID: AFG20070702n741   Region: RC EAST
Latitude: 33.43104935   Longitude: 69.99848938
Date: 2007-07-02 03:03   Type: Enemy Action
Category: Assassination   Affiliation: ENEMY
Detained: 0

	Enemy	Friend	Civilian	Host Nation
Killed in Action	0	0	1	0
Wounded in Action	0	0	1	0

THE DEPUTY CHIEF OF EDUCATION WAS ASSASINATED APPROX ONE HOUR AGO IN THE SABARI DISTRICT AT VIC GRID WB 9282 9952 NEAR THE VILLAGE OF KHONI KANDOW. THE DEPUTY CHIEF NAME WAS SAID OSMAN SON OF QASIM. THERE WAS A DOCTOR TRAVELING WITH HIM AT THE TIME AND HIS NAME IS MAMOOR SON OF WAZIR. HE WAS FOUND ALIVE AND WAS TRANSPORTED TO KWOST HOSPITAL. THEY WERE ATTACKED BY SMALL ARMS FIRE AS THEY WERE MOVING SOUTH FROM THE ROADSIDE. NFTR ATT. ANP AND NDS ARE ON SITE AND INVESTIGATING.
Excerpt from TF Professional INTUM 02 JUL 07 (S//REL USA, ISAF, NATO) At approx 02 0230Z JUL 07 Said Osman s/o Qasim, the Deputy Chief of Education, was assassinated near the village Khoni Kandow (WB 9282 9952), Sabari District. Mamoor s/o Wazir, a local doctor, was traveling with him at the time. Mamoor was wounded and transported to Khowst Hospital and is reportedly stable. ANP questioned Mamoor however he does not remember much, only that an unknown number of ACM attacked them from the right side of the road. He also said that he believes that they were attacked from the mountains vic WB 9282 9952. The two personnel were traveling in a car south, towards Khowst City, when they received small arms fire from the roadside.
Headquarters
International Security Assistance Force Afghanistan

NEWS RELEASE [2007-XXX: Draft]
Prominent educator murdered
FORWARD OPERATING BASE SALERNO, Afghanistan (2 July) The deputy chief of education for Khowst province was shot and killed by a gunman near the village of Khoni Kandow in the Sabari District, Khowst Province, around 7 a.m., today.
SEE ATTACHMENTS FOR COMPLETE RELEASE
EXCERPT FROM INTSUM DATED 05 JUL 07: FIVE AL QAEDA OPERATIVES IN A WHITE TOYOTA COROLLA ASSASSINATED SARAN ((WAL)), DIRECTOR OF SABARI HIGH SCHOOL//MGRS: 42SWC9272602807//, SABARI DISTRICT, KHOST PROVINCE, AFGHANISTAN (AF) ON 02 JULY 2007. ANOTHER MAN WAS KILLED IN THE SAME ATTACK. (SOURCE COMMENT-I THINK THE SECOND MAN WAS SARAN WALS BODYGUARD.) THE AL QAEDA MEMBERS STAY IN THE MOUNTAINS OF THE SABARI DISTRICT, AND USE RADIOS TO COMMUNICATE WITH ONE ANOTHER. (SOURCE COMMENT-I DONT KNOW IN WHICH MOUNTAINS THE AL QAEDA MEMBERS HIDE.) THE AL QAEDA MEMBERS RECEIVED 30,000 PAKISTANI RUPPEES (500 USD) FOR THE ASSASSINATION FROM THE PAKISTANI GOVERNMENT. (SOURCE COMMENT-THE PAKISTAN GOVERNMENT WANTS THE CHILDREN OF AF TO BE UNEDUCATED SO THAT THEY ARE MORE SUSCEPTIBLE TO AL QAEDA INFLUENCE.)
(FIELD COMMENT-ASSASSINATION CONFIRMED IN TF PROFESSIONAL INTSUM, DATED 03 JULY 2007.) (DOI: 20070702)

Reference ID: AFG20070714n937
Latitude: 33.43341064
Date: 2007-07-14 13:01
Category: Assassination
Detained: 0
Region: RC EAST
Longitude: 69.37651825
Type: Enemy Action
Affiliation: ENEMY

	Enemy	Friend	Civilian	Host Nation
Killed in Action	0	0	2	0
Wounded in Action	0	0	2	0

At 141300ZJUL07 Sub-Governor of Schwack was assaulted. His 2 bodyguards were KIA IVO 42S WB 35000 99400. Governor was evacuated to FOB Lightning for treatment. Attack was initiated by RPG and small arms unknown number of ACM. (Shwak sub-governor) is reported in stable condition at an ANA hospital on FOB Lightening and may be transported to either an ANA or American hospital in the morning for additional treatment. NFTR. Event closed out at 1848Z. NTFR ATT. ISAF Tracking#07-337.
HEADQUARTERS
INTERNATIONAL SECURITY ASSISTANCE FORCE
AFGHANISTAN
NEWS RELEASE [2007 - : DRAFT]
District governor survives apparent assassination attempt
FORWARD OPERATING BASE SALERNO, Khowst, Afghanistan (14 July)   An unknown number of assailants killed two civilians and injured two others, including the district governor, as a result of an attack in Schwack District, Paktya Province, today.
FOR THE COMPLETE PRESS RELEASE, SEE ATTACHMENT

Reference ID: AFG20070720n811
Latitude: 36.70116043
Date: 2007-07-20 06:06
Category: Assassination
Detained: 2
Region: RC NORTH
Longitude: 67.10249329
Type: Enemy Action
Affiliation: ENEMY

	Enemy	Friend	Civilian	Host Nation
Killed in Action	0	0	1	0
Wounded in Action	0	0	0	0

At 0630Z RC NORTH reported 2 assassins killed a high ranking muslim cleric. ANP arrested the assassins. Event closed. ISAF Tracking # 07-482

Reference ID: AFG20070805n920
Latitude: 34.53594971
Date: 2007-08-05 12:12
Category: Assassination
Detained: 0
Region: RC CAPITAL
Longitude: 69.19069672
Type: Enemy Action
Affiliation: ENEMY

	Enemy	Friend	Civilian	Host Nation
Killed in Action	0	0	0	0
Wounded in Action	0	0	1	0

AT 051230ZAUG07, ASSASSINATION ATTEMPT WAS MADE ON AIT HOST NATION TRUCKING COMPANY REPRESENTATIVE IN THE EASTERN PORTION OF KABUL AT (42S WD 17500 21600) IN EAST SIDE KABUL. HE IS AIT TRUCKING COMPANY'S REPRESENTATIVE TO THE 450TH MCB. REPRESENTATIVE'S CAR WAS HIT BY OTHER CARS AND THEN ATTK WITH SAF. ASSASSINATION ATTEMPT WAS NOT SUCCESSFUL. REPRESENTATIVE'S BODYGUARD WAS WIA. 1 LN INJ

Reference ID: AFG20070919n971
Latitude: 35.58345032
Date: 2007-09-19 11:11
Category: Assassination
Detained: 0
Region: RC WEST
Longitude: 63.32891846
Type: Enemy Action
Affiliation: ENEMY

	Enemy	Friend	Civilian	Host Nation
Killed in Action	0	0	0	0
Wounded in Action	0	0	0	0

At 1140Z RC WEST reported at 1250Z COL Amanulah ANP CMDR in BALA MURGHAB informed via phone to the PRT IOT about an insurgenst attack at 41S NV 298 378, 90.7km northeast of PRT QUAL-E-NOW, BALA MORGHAB in BADGHIS province. CMDR stated, that the ANP member was at the bazaar, insurgents in police uniform shoot him in his back. These information were confirmed by HUMINT team in the area. Due to the seriousness of the injury the CMDR requested a MEDEVAC. It is not confirmed, that the assailants were insurgents. At 160415Z The ANP died of his wounds. Event closed at 0527Z. ISAF tracking # 09-519.

Reference ID: AFG20071001n950
Latitude: 36.76227951
Region: RC NORTH
Longitude: 67.20741272

Date: 2007-10-01 13:01   Type: Enemy Action
Category: Assassination   Affiliation: ENEMY
Detained: 0

	Enemy	Friend	Civilian	Host Nation
Killed in Action	0	0	1	0
Wounded in Action	0	0	0	0

At 1330Z TF Phoenix reported 1x Jamit party leader was assasinated IVO Mazar E Sharif. The leader was pro-coalition and a friend of the Balkh governor. ISAF Tracking # 10-029

Reference ID: AFG20071003n1014   Region: RC EAST
Latitude: 33.3825798   Longitude: 69.9439621
Date: 2007-10-03 11:11   Type: Enemy Action
Category: Assassination   Affiliation: ENEMY
Detained: 0

	Enemy	Friend	Civilian	Host Nation
Killed in Action	0	0	0	2
Wounded in Action	0	0	0	0

At approximately 031143ZOCT 07, NDS COL Wali Badsha was assassinated northeast of Khowst city near grid WB 878 914. The assassination occurred when his vehicle was ambushed by personnel on motorcycles armed with AK 47s; COL Wali Badshah and his driver, Sobat Khan were both killed in the attack; the brother of Wali Badshah, Sultan Sha was also wounded in the attack. The attack occurred as COL Badsha was en route home from Khowst NDS HQ. NDS is currently investigating. Event closed at 1953Z. ISAF Tracking #10-093.
Update:
On 06 OCT 07, NDS reported the assassination of Wali Badshah was accomplished from a motorcycle with two assailants riding the bike. The motorcycle was described as old and in poor condition. The motorcycle had to be jumpstarted after the attack in the area of Patora Village (unlocated), home to many government officials. Because of this, people in the area feel the government is not effective. COL Wali Badsha was an intell officer working in the Khost area.
Report closed out, nothing more to follow.

Reference ID: AFG20071113n1026   Region: RC EAST
Latitude: 33.37055969   Longitude: 68.45713043
Date: 2007-11-13 07:07   Type: Enemy Action
Category: Assassination   Affiliation: ENEMY
Detained: 0

	Enemy	Friend	Civilian	Host Nation
Killed in Action	0	0	1	0
Wounded in Action	0	0	0	0

At about 0730z TF 2Fury received a report from the Ghazni PCC that a judicial official had been killed in Andar District, vic VB 495 925. The judicial official was working as a liaison for the possible PTS of OBJ SEASIDE. The OBJ arranged a meeting with judicial official to discuss the matter in the village of Chahar Divari (VB 495 925). The official arrived at the agreed meeting point. It is believed that OBJ SEASIDE then killed the official. The officials brother recovered the remains around 0900z and moved to FB 4 Corners (VB 5478 8814) to meet with CFs. The brother states that the judicial official was shot in the back, most likely while trying to running away, and he had talked to his brother just prior to the meeting. TF 2Fury will continue to gather information on this event and pass the IO themes.

Reference ID: AFG20071218n1150
Latitude: 31.62198067
Date: 2007-12-18 05:05
Category: Assassination
Detained: 0

Region: RC SOUTH
Longitude: 65.68052673
Type: Enemy Action
Affiliation: ENEMY

	Enemy	Friend	Civilian	Host Nation
Killed in Action	0	0	0	0
Wounded in Action	0	0	0	0

At 1330Z, TF Kandahar reported the secretary of the Governor of Kandahar was assonated, he was shot in the back in front of his house, by an unknown number of insurgents at 41R QR 54265 01658, Kandahar district, Kandahar Province. He was brought to the hospital of Mirwais where he was pronounced dead. The funeral will be held at 19 0530Z at the Eidgah Moaque and he will be buried before sunset.
Event closed at 19 0527Z.
ISAF Tracking# 12-501

Reference ID: AFG20080122n1167
Latitude: 32.62015915
Date: 2008-01-22 12:12
Category: Assassination
Detained: 0

Region: RC WEST
Longitude: 62.47409058
Type: Enemy Action
Affiliation: ENEMY

	Enemy	Friend	Civilian	Host Nation
Killed in Action	0	0	0	0
Wounded in Action	0	0	0	0

Contractor Killed IVO Shewan 22JAN08: According to the 207TH CORPS G2, The contractor that provided Class1 supplies to the ANA in Shewan was killed, he was believed to be killed by the TB. The incident accord IVO Spin Mosque (41S MS 50662 09301) (Source: Silverback in Farah Rud) NFI. EVENT CLOSED.

Reference ID: AFG20080210n1210
Latitude: 34.37376022
Date: 2008-02-10 04:04
Category: Assassination
Detained: 0

Region: RC WEST
Longitude: 62.21168137
Type: Enemy Action
Affiliation: ENEMY

	Enemy	Friend	Civilian	Host Nation
Killed in Action	0	0	0	0
Wounded in Action	0	0	0	0

GOZARA DISTRICT GOVERNOR AND HIS SON WERE ATTACKED IN HERAT 100400Z FEB 08, SUNDAY, CRITICALLY WOUNDING THE GOVERNOR AND KILLING HIS 18-YEAR-OLD SON; THE ATTACK OCCURRED AS THE

GOVERNOR STEPPED OUT OF HIS CAR. THERE IS CONFLICTING INFORMATION REGARDING THE SITE OF THE ATTACK; TWO LOCATIONS SITED ARE: THE FIVE STAR HOTEL AND THE GOVERNOR⊦S RESIDENCE.. THE ATTACK WAS EXECUTED BY 3 - 4 UNKNOWN ASSAILANTS IN A TOYOTA COROLLA WHO DEPARTED THE SCENE IMMEDIATELY. LACK OF ADDITIONAL INFORMATION OPENS SPECULATION AS TO THE ORIGINS OF THE ATTACKERS, WHETHER THESE ARE TALIBAN MILITANTS, WHO ARE WAGING AN INSURGENCY AGAINST THE GOVERNMENT, OR IS ATTRIBUTABLE TO COMMON CRIME.

ARSIC-WEST S2 COMMENTS: COLONEL GULAM AHMAD, GUZARA DISTRICT COMMANDER, BELIEVES GULAM YAHYA IS RESPONSIBLE, EVEN THOUGH HE HAS NOT YET CLAIMED RESPONSIBILITY. NFI. EVENT CLOSED.

Reference ID: AFG20080210n1211
Latitude: 34.12449265
Date: 2008-02-10 04:04
Category: Assassination
Detained: 0

Region: RC WEST
Longitude: 62.27017593
Type: Enemy Action
Affiliation: ENEMY

	Enemy	Friend	Civilian	Host Nation
Killed in Action	0	0	1	0
Wounded in Action	0	0	2	0

At 0400Z, RC West reported that an unknown number of insurgents engaged the Governor of Gozara's (sub-governor of Herat) vehicle with small arms fire at 41S MT 327 762, Gozara district of Herat. The shooting occurred in the 8th District of Herat City. The Governor, Gholam Nazrat, and one of his party members were wounded and his son was killed. The governor and his party member were taken to the closest hospital for treatment.

Update: Both Governor Nazart and the wounded party member are in critical condition at the local hospital.
(1 x Afghan Civilian KIA - Governor's son, 2 x Afghan Civlian WIA (Governor and party member)
ISAF tracking # 02-140

Reference ID: AFG20080311n1218
Latitude: 34.23490143
Date: 2008-03-11 01:01
Category: Raid
Detained: 30

Region: RC WEST
Longitude: 62.18777084
Type: Friendly Action
Affiliation: FRIEND

	Enemy	Friend	Civilian	Host nation
Killed in action	3	0	0	0
Wounded in action	0	0	0	0

At 0130Z, RC-West reported that several insurgents, Gulam Yahya, Mullah Sanging and Haffizullah, were suspected of meeting at house located at 41S MT 252 885, Ghaslambaf village, Guzara District, Herat. ABP reported that there were 2 x separate weapons caches of Iranian mines and assorted small arms and ammunition at the site. BDA: 3 x ACM KIA. 30 x INS arrested, 3 of them unnamed High Value Targets. ABP and PMT returned to garrison. ISAF Tracking # 03-256

Reference ID: AFG20080319n1198
Latitude: 32.37125015
Date: 2008-03-19 05:05
Category: Assassination
Detained: 0

Region: RC WEST
Longitude: 62.15705109
Type: Enemy Action
Affiliation: ENEMY

	Enemy	Friend	Civilian	Host Nation
Killed in Action	0	0	0	0
Wounded in Action	0	0	0	0

(S//REL TO USA, NATO, AND ISAF) FORMER DELARAM DISTRICT ANP CHIEF GUNNED DOWN IN FARAH CITY ANP AND NDS REPORTING RECEIVED TODAY STATES THAT QADER QAHRMAN WAS KILLED TODAY IN FRONT OF AZIZ BANK AS HE WAS SHOPPING AT THE BAZAAR IN FARAH CITY THIS MORNING. THE GUNMAN USED SMALL ARMS AND WAS ON A MOTORCYCLE AT THE TIME OF THE ATTACK. FARAH CITY ANP ARE INVESTIGATING THE MURDER AND HAVE THREE MEN IN CUSTODY INCLUDING ADAM YAHYA, WHO IS THE BROTHER OF THE LATE MULLAH YAHYA, FORMER DISTRICT MANAGER OF DELARAM. (PRT FARAH S2; DOI: 19 MAR 08)
NFI. EVENT CLOSED

Reference ID: AFG20090601n1857
Latitude: 34.31847382
Date: 2009-06-01 21:09
Category: Raid
Detained: 0

Region: RC EAST
Longitude: 68.7286377
Type: Friendly Action
Affiliation: FRIEND

	Enemy	Friend	Civilian	Host nation
Killed in action	4	0	0	0
Wounded in action	1	0	0	0

"Operation CDO Jump Nerkh Reinforcement : The initial post op roll up for 373's op. In the target building there were 4 EKIA's, in an adjacent building there was 1 EKIA JACKPOT which was reported to be Shah Agha. The enemy TTP was that Agha and OBJ Piedmont would switch handsets and it looks like that is what happened. They had TOUCHDOWN also. There was an unknown number of AK-47's, chest racks with ammo, grenades, and IED making material. Also 5 woman and 11 children were protected.
The Commando's inserted to the HLZ ISO Operation Commando Nerkh without issue.
2-87 has recovered the vehicle (an ASV and not an MRP as previously reported) from Site 2 to COP Blackhawk. 2-87 was waiting until exfil of 373 and insertion of the Commando's before moving to recover at Site 1.
TF 373 will send a complete final roll up as soon as exfil is complete.

Reference ID: AFG20090613n1827
Latitude: 33.66980743
Date: 2009-06-13 07:07
Category: Detain
Detained: 2

Region: RC EAST
Longitude: 69.45780182
Type: Friendly Action
Affiliation: FRIEND

	Enemy	Friend	Civilian	Host Nation
Killed in Action	0	0	0	0
Wounded in Action	0	0	0	0

Event Title:D16 0708Z
Zone:null
Placename:ISAF#06-971
Outcome:Effective
UNIT: TF DENALI 1/B W/ANP
TYPE: DETAINEE
TIMELINE:
INDIVIDUAL WALKED UP TO 1/B CONVOY WHEN THEY DECIDED TO HIIDE HIM. WHEN HIS NAME WAS INPUTED INTO THE HIIDE HIS NAME CAME UP WITH INSTRUCTIONS TO EITHER KILL HIM OR ARREST HIM. WHICH MAKES HIM A PRIMARY TARGET. INDIVIDUALS NAMES ARE:
MULLAH JULANI AND GHAGHA IS HIS BODY GUARD.
WE ARE STILL WAITING FOR THE NAME OF THE BODY GUARD.
ANP SAYS THAT THEY WILL NOT DETAIN INDIVIDUAL DUE TO THE FACT THAT HE HAS CONNECTION IN THE GOV.
ALSO 1/B FOUND A CACHE IN AREA OF DETAINEES. SEE CHILD.
UPDATE 1029Z: 1/B CURRENTLY HAVE CONTROL OF DETAINEES AND WILL BE BRINGING THEM BACK TO FOB GARDEZ FOR FURTHER QUESTIONING. AND THE ANP HAVE CONTROL OF CACHE.
SUMMARY:
2 X DETAINEES
MULLAH JULANI
GHAGHA-HIS BODY GUARD
0 X DMG
0 X INJ
EVENT: 1100Z CLOSED

Reference ID: AFG20090622n1922   Region: RC EAST
Latitude: 33.81812286   Longitude: 68.95992279
Date: 2009-06-22 12:12   Type: Friendly Action
Category: Raid   Affiliation: FRIEND
Detained: 0

	Enemy	Friend	Civilian	Host nation
Killed in action	0	0	0	0
Wounded in action	0	0	0	0

"Who: OP RAFALKAT ((QASIM))
What: Level II Capture/Kill
Where: Charkh District, Wardack Province
When: 21 0900-1845L JUN 09
Why: Qasim is the head Taliban of Charkh District. He is a murderer or innocent women and children and is known to also attack ANSF and CF. A hard line criminal. Initial Results: The assaulters were flexible and conducted two combined/joint air assault/clearing operations. No Jackpot, Qasim coward in the face of ANSF and Coalition Forces for over 9 hours and hid among women and children.

His fighters also coward and hid in wells and culverts. The ANSF detained 3 x POIs with various documentation and in possession of over 40 mortar rounds, other explosives and 4 rockets (destroyed), 1 x RPG system, 17 various weapon systems recovered. More SSE to come from TQ and other devices recovered from the various objectives.
The POIs will be processed through the ANP.

Reference ID: AFG20090624n1819
Latitude: 33.80693817
Date: 2009-06-24 21:09
Category: Raid
Detained: 2
Region: RC EAST
Longitude: 68.50307465
Type: Friendly Action
Affiliation: FRIEND

	Enemy	Friend	Civilian	Host nation
Killed in action	8	0	0	0
Wounded in action	0	0	1	0

"TF-373 actioned objective Millersville, a capture / kill operation against Amir Jan Mutaki (Sayed Abad and Tangi Valley Taliban sub-commander who has taken part in ambushes against ISAF convoys on highway 1.) They do not yet know whether they captured or killed the target. Outside the objective building, six enemy were killed by fire from spectre gunships and SAF. One of the dead was wearing a suicide vest that failed to detonate. Two of the dead had handsets. Inside the compound, there were two military-aged men, three women, and six children. One of the children was bitten by the assaulting element's military working dog, which the PJ with the team assessed as minor and treated on site. They also found IED making materials, RPG's, multiple AK-47s, 1xRPK, grenades, chest rigs, and pistols.
Amir Jan Mutaki (Targeted Individual) confirmed as one of the EKIAs.
2 x Detainees: BDA: 8 EKIA

Reference ID: AFG20090701n1948
Latitude: 33.91292191
Date: 2009-07-01 21:09
Category: Raid
Detained: 15
Region: RC EAST
Longitude: 68.62930298
Type: Friendly Action
Affiliation: FRIEND

	Enemy	Friend	Civilian	Host nation
Killed in action	0	0	0	0
Wounded in action	0	0	0	0

02 0130L TF-10 Operation Kabori Mahee in order to capture/kill Sar Gul in Bahadurkhel, Sayad Abad resulted in 15xPAX detained. In the past 30 days there was 1xComplex attack involving an IED strike and IDF.

Reference ID: AFG20090703n1965
Latitude: 33.91322327
Date: 2009-07-03 19:07
Category: Raid
Detained: 1
Region: RC EAST
Longitude: 68.93710327
Type: Friendly Action
Affiliation: FRIEND

	Enemy	Friend	Civilian	Host nation
Killed in action	0	0	0	0
Wounded in action	0	0	0	0

TF 373 conducted a kill/capture mission tagreting Mirwais in a village just north of Ebad. 373 conduct a tactical callout and was able to exploit the site with no shot fired. On the objective, there were 4x MAM, 2x Females, 6x Children, 7x Communication devices. One of the MAMs indentified himself as the target. Conducting TSE ATT.

Reference ID: AFG20090728n2155
Latitude: 33.90333557
Date: 2009-07-28 18:06
Category: Raid
Detained: 2

Region: RC EAST
Longitude: 68.93439484
Type: Friendly Action
Affiliation: FRIEND

	Enemy	Friend	Civilian	Host nation
Killed in action	0	0	0	0
Wounded in action	0	0	0	0

TF 373 actioned OBJ Haida, Mohammad Aziz Mutmain. 373 conducted a soft breach of the target. ATT OBJ Haida has been detained. On the OBJ there were 13xMAMs, 8xFemales, 4xChildren. Of the 13xMAMs, two were detained to include the TGT. No weapons were found, however a fake ID making kit and fake election cards were found.

Reference ID: AFG20090731n1143
Latitude: 33.41489792
Date: 2009-07-31 03:03
Category: Raid
Detained: 3

Region: RC EAST
Longitude: 70.13709259
Type: Friendly Action
Affiliation: FRIEND

	Enemy	Friend	Civilian	Host nation
Killed in action	0	0	0	0
Wounded in action	0	0	0	0

Mission:
Romeo 01 conducted deliberate kill/capture operation of OBJ Granite Peak
Units/ Attendees4-25 BCT 2-377 FTF
Summary of Events
SI led CF and ANSF to location. FMV was over target location via CAS. While CAS was reported no individuals left the area. Isolation team reached objective and isolation was established within 2 minutes. There was no SI Lock on the objective, there were three MAMs present. Through TQ Romeo 01 was given the name, RHAMATULLAH; which correlates with the name currently being tracked for OBJ Granite Peak. The call was made that all three would be detained and brought back to FOB Salerno for HUMINT exploitation.
HCT 08 conducted the TQ and ascertained all three were being deceptive, with one possibly being a hard-line Taliban follower. SSE on the objective was cold.
Based off of TQ a the three MAMs have been placed in the custody of the BTIF for further exploitation.
Timeline

0120L ROMEO 01 REPORTS THAT HE HAS A POSSIBLE JP FROM THE 3 X MAMS. ROMEO WAS INSTRUCTED TO DETAIN ALL 3 X MAMS
0225L ROMEO 01 EXFIL to SAL

Reference ID: AFG20090803n2084
Latitude: 32.19192123
Date: 2009-08-03 19:07
Category: Raid
Detained: 0
Region: RC SOUTH
Longitude: 64.96577454
Type: Friendly Action
Affiliation: FRIEND

	Enemy	Friend	Civilian	Host nation
Killed in action	4	0	0	0
Wounded in action	0	0	0	0

TF42 conducted kinetic operations ISO Op Bers Simi in order to disrupt EF IED facilitation and supply lines. Area was secured and searched leading to the discovery of weapons and IED components. IED manufacturing facility was discovered, searched, exploited and destroyed.

Reference ID: AFG20090817n2166
Latitude: 36.98802185
Date: 2009-08-17 06:06
Category: Assassination
Detained: 0
Region: RC NORTH
Longitude: 66.28087616
Type: Enemy Action
Affiliation: ENEMY

	Enemy	Friend	Civilian	Host Nation
Killed in Action	0	0	1	0
Wounded in Action	0	0	0	0

ABDUL RAHIM, A CANDIDATE FOR THE JAWZJAN PROVINCIAL COUNCIL WAS ASSASSINATED BY INS.

Reference ID: AFG20090905n2245
Latitude: 36.31137848
Date: 2009-09-05 19:07
Category: Raid
Detained: 0
Region: RC NORTH
Longitude: 68.82511139
Type: Friendly Action
Affiliation: FRIEND

	Enemy	Friend	Civilian	Host nation
Killed in action	2	0	0	0
Wounded in action	2	0	0	0

OCC-P BAGHLAN INFORMED PRT PEK OPS THAT THE ANP, LED BY THE COP PREPARED AN AMBUSH AGAINST INS A CAHAR SAMBA TEPA. THEY CONFISCATED 3 X AK47(NO SERIAL NUM), 1 X RPG7 LAUNCHER, 12 X RPG7 ROUNDS, 12 X AK MAGAZINES, 2 X MINES 1 X TOYOTA VEHICLE.

Reference ID: AFG20090919n2226
Latitude: 34.33778
Date: 2009-09-19 09:09
Region: RC WEST
Longitude: 62.19875336
Type: Enemy Action

Category: Assassination Affiliation: ENEMY
Detained: 0

	Enemy	Friend	Civilian	Host Nation
Killed in Action	0	0	1	1
Wounded in Action	0	0	3	3

report received that on 191330LSEP09 Provincial Reconstruction Team Herat reported that there was an explosion caused by a RCIED in HERAT downtown (41SMT2630099900). According to unofficial source, the explosion was very close to HAJI SULTANs house. The source reported also that Ghulam Yahya Akbari has taken the responsibility of a bombing at the home of Haji Sultan. A female, with her two children, was leaving a bath house and was walking by the home of Haji Sultan when an IED detonated. The female's 6 years old daughter was killed in the blast, second child (a boy) along with female/ mother seriously injured. Haji Sultan was also injured and is currently being secured at a local hospital. Haji Sultan is a civilian and not any sort of government official.
UPDATE: HAJI SULTAN AND THE MOTHER DIED OF THEIR WOUNDS. IN THE ATTACK A MAN AND ANOTHER CHILD WERE ALSO INJURED

Reference ID: AFG20091230n2353 Region: RC SOUTH
Latitude: 31.66861153 Longitude: 65.61972809
Date: 2009-12-30 07:07 Type: Enemy Action
Category: Assassination Affiliation: ENEMY
Detained: 0

	Enemy	Friend	Civilian	Host Nation
Killed in Action	0	0	1	0
Wounded in Action	0	0	0	0

OCCP-K reported via Email:
The village elder (ABDUL QAUM) of MANARA village was assassinated at approx 0700D* while he was praying in the mosque.
No further details known ATT.
BDA: 1 x LN Killed.

Blue on Blue

"Friendly fire" incidents, in which an army mistakenly fires upon units of its own side, have always been a problem in modern warfare. Modern military weapons are effective at ranges far beyond visual, and in the confusion of battle it is not hard to lose track of where one's own troops are. Modern military equipment often has elaborate precautions built in to allow identification of friend from foe, but "blue on blue" attacks, though not as common as before, still happen. They are demoralizing for troops, particularly in guerrilla fights where one hardly ever gets a glimpse of the enemy anyway, but still falls victim to ambushes and surprise attacks. It's bad enough to be killed by an unseen enemy who seems to be everywhere. Getting killed by one's own side only adds to the frustration. Many of the friendly-fire incidents involve non-American troops, indicating that command coordination is poor among the coalition forces. And, the reports indicate, everyone is a little jumpy and trigger-happy when surrounded by insurgents who appear suddenly from the civilian population and attack—making cases of mistaken identity potentially lethal.

Friendly fire incidents are also demoralizing to the people back home. In a democratic society like the United States, where the people ultimately decide how long a war goes on and when it stops, friendly fire casualties can have a particularly deep effect, since it makes the war seem even more hopeless and futile, and can hasten the political decision to stop the fighting.

Reference ID: AFG20060304n208
Latitude: 31.55846024
Date: 2006-03-04 19:07
Category: BLUE-BLUE
Detained: 0

Region: RC SOUTH
Longitude: 65.84230042
Type: Friendly Fire
Affiliation: FRIEND

	Enemy	Friend	Civilian	Host Nation
Killed in Action	0	0	0	0
Wounded in Action	0	0	0	0

TF Aegis reported Blue on Blue fire 6K North of KAF. At 2045z TF Aegis reported 6x warning shots were fired at a unknown vehicle. A coalition SOTF patrol then notified TF Aegis that they were moving through their AO. TF Aegis will investigate further. No damage or injuries reported.

Reference ID: AFG20060903n347
Latitude: 31.54976082
Date: 2006-09-03 04:04
Category: BLUE-BLUE
Detained: 0

Region: RC SOUTH
Longitude: 65.43344879
Type: Friendly Fire
Affiliation: FRIEND

	Enemy	Friend	Civilian	Host Nation
Killed in Action	0	4	0	0
Wounded in Action	0	7	1	0

At 030414Z Sept 06 received SAF & RPGS from sawtooth building. returned fire 1x GBU dropped on it. Sawtooth building is heavily damaged. only 4x sections remain standing. no activity observed. Casualties 4x CDN KIA 4X CDN WIA.
At 030419Z Sep received SAF and RPG fire on op, a total of WIA in these hour 7x CDN, and 4x CDN KIA and 1x WIA interpreter.

Reference ID: AFG20070415n732
Latitude: 34.75141907
Date: 2007-04-15 18:06
Category: BLUE-BLUE
Detained: 0

Region: RC EAST
Longitude: 70.86927795
Type: Friendly Fire
Affiliation: FRIEND

	Enemy	Friend	Civilian	Host Nation
Killed in Action	0	0	0	0
Wounded in Action	0	0	0	2

151845Z D5 was conducting scheduled fires and the 81 went short;said it was a bad round and landed in the OP grid: XD71100 47070 wounding two ASG Soldiers. MM(E)04-15F
Line 1 XD71100 47070
Line 2

Line 3 1a laceration to chest and abdomen
Line 1d left foot
Line 4 hoist required
Line 5 1 litter and 1ambulatory
Line 6 n
Line 7 ir buzz saw
Line 8 Delta ASG
Line 9 hilltop
vitals are bp is 138/96 chest wounds 4" to 6" long and 2 cm wide shrapnel in left bicep has both bracal and radial pulse
19:19Z the medic says they can stablize til am but cannot ground evac due to the terrian
19:24Z Medic on ground, consulted with Chosin PA and confirms they can keep patients stable until the morning when better illum.
19:34Z If anything changes with patients, we will advise, but for now ask that medevac be conducted in morning.

Reference ID: AFG20070712n849
Latitude: 33.15853882
Date: 2007-07-12 17:05
Category: BLUE-BLUE
Detained: 0

Region: RC EAST
Longitude: 68.05754852
Type: Friendly Fire
Affiliation: FRIEND

	Enemy	Friend	Civilian	Host Nation
Killed in Action	0	0	0	0
Wounded in Action	0	0	0	2

12 1755ZJUL07 2Fury element located at the Qarabagh DC, VB 1656 7295, got a report that an ANP check point located at VB 024 651 was attacked by an unknown number of TB w/ 2 ANP WIA. At the time of the report not in contact. The 2Fury element, a squad from Apache Thunder, with 3v, 9US, 1 terp, 9 ANP and ANP Police Chief left the DC at 1802z to recover casualties and help with security. ISR assets were pushed to the grid given but could not locate any type of activity. ISR then found the convoy and followed them to the location. The ANP led the 2Fury element to the location of the CP, actual location was VB 12116 69258. Upon arrival they discovered there was 1 ANP wounded with a single GSW to the upper right thigh caused by friendly fire. There was no TB contact. The wounded ANP was ground evac'd to the Qarabagh DC to receive treatment at the Qarabagh Clinic, next to the district center. NFTR, Event closed at 1802Z
ISAF Tracking# 07-292.

Reference ID: AFG20070805n934
Latitude: 34.54388046
Date: 2007-08-05 19:07
Category: BLUE-BLUE
Detained: 0

Region: RC CAPITAL
Longitude: 69.28227234
Type: Friendly Fire
Affiliation: FRIEND

	Enemy	Friend	Civilian	Host Nation
Killed in Action	0	0	0	0
Wounded in Action	0	0	0	0

At 1940Z TF Phoenix reported on route to Camp Dogan where coalition forces are stationed a US patrol from Camp Phoenix fired at a civilian vehicle carrying coalition personel. NO injuries but damage to civilian vehicle. Dismounted US patrol was not in cooridination with CF's.Event Closed. ISAF Tracking #08-099

Reference ID: AFG20070823n859　　　Region: RC SOUTH
Latitude: 32.34920883　　　　　　　　Longitude: 65.08226013
Date: 2007-08-23 13:01　　　　　　　 Type: Friendly Fire
Category: BLUE-BLUE　　　　　　　　Affiliation: FRIEND
Detained: 0

	Enemy	Friend	Civilian	Host Nation
Killed in Action	0	3	0	0
Wounded in Action	0	2	0	0

At 1354Z TF Helmand reported that 2-3 insurgents attacked a compound in the Kajaki district, Helmand province, with small arms fire and RPGs. Friendly forces returned fire with mortars and crew serve weapons. Close air support was on station (2xF-15s). At 1429Z TF Helmand requested a medevac for 4 UK, 3 WIA with various status on injuries and 1 UK KIA. At 1751Z, TF Helmand is searching grid 41S PR 9635 8085, which the POI of the 1xGBU-12 (500 lbs JDAM). At 2009Z, friendly forces has arrived in Kajaki and are at COP getting briefed before deploying. Friendly forces are at ground level but still a large amount of rubble to sort through about to happen with other friendly forces handling over another friendly forces. At 2016Z consttant attcks on helos with RPGs were reported. At 2124Z an update was reported, that the search continues for missing individual. At 2159Z body is reported as found in compound 549. Extraction to HLS LANCASTER is planed by first light. Update reported at 2239Z search of site denied by level 1 CD. Minimal damage assesed at this time UK asset will complete task. Event update at 0042Z all C/S are back in COP ZBG and PAZ are extracting from KJI. A/C is now servicable. TIC closed at 0138Z. UPDATE: 3x UK KIA, 2x UK WIA. ISAF Tracking # 08-640.

Reference ID: AFG20070920n893　　　Region: RC SOUTH
Latitude: 31.87821007　　　　　　　　Longitude: 64.76875305
Date: 2007-09-20 03:03　　　　　　　 Type: Friendly Fire
Category: BLUE-BLUE　　　　　　　　Affiliation: FRIEND
Detained: 0

	Enemy	Friend	Civilian	Host Nation
Killed in Action	0	0	0	0
Wounded in Action	0	0	0	1

At 0322Z TF Helmand reported in the vicinity of FOB Arnhem, Nahri Sarraj district in Helmand province; during a resupply ANA observed and engaged a friendly forces resupply with small arms fire. Friendly forces returned fire with small arms fire resulting in 1 ANA casualty. ANA casualty was medevac'd MM(S) 09-20B, which was mission complete at 0614Z. TIC closed at 0616Z. ISAF tracking # 09-655.

Reference ID: AFG20080114n1240　　 Region: RC SOUTH
Latitude: 32.07688141　　　　　　　　Longitude: 64.84715271

Date: 2008-01-14 18:06 Type: Friendly Fire
Category: BLUE-BLUE Affiliation: FRIEND
Detained: 0

	Enemy	Friend	Civilian	Host Nation
Killed in Action	0	0	0	1
Wounded in Action	0	0	0	0

At 1830Z, TF Helmand reported 3-4x insurgents were positively identified laying IEDs at 41S PR 7434 5045 IVO checkpoint Norfolk, 0.6km southwest of Paygharakay in the Sangin district Helmand province. Friendly forces engaged with Javelin due to low visibility and PB Inkerman with 81mm mortars being out of range.

Update: TF Helmand element that provided force protection to Sangin DC PID 3/4 PAX conducting suspicious activities in the area of the old governors compound. FF fired a warning shout with 338mm and 50mm illumination. THE INS took no action in response to these challenges. FF engaged with Javelin. The Javelin operator locked on to the single heat source and engaged target. FF confirmed 1 x INS killed. Immediately following the Javelin engagement ANA reported an attack in PB Tufan 3. It was discovered that the heat source selected was not that of the possible INS, but that of the roof sentry position on PB Tufan 3. BDA: 1 x ANA KIA. Incident is under investigation.

Event closed at 1935Z.
ISAF tracking # 01-270.

Reference ID: AFG20080219n1161 Region: RC SOUTH
Latitude: 31.9883709 Longitude: 66.71814728
Date: 2008-02-19 05:05 Type: Friendly Fire
Category: BLUE-BLUE Affiliation: FRIEND
Detained: 0

	Enemy	Friend	Civilian	Host Nation
Killed in Action	0	0	0	0
Wounded in Action	0	0	0	0

At 0503Z, TF Zabul reported that 3x insurgents engaged an observation point with small arms at 42R TA 84414 41422 in teh Jeldak district, Zabul province. Friendly forces developed the situation.

At 0529Z, TF Zabul reported that the individuals that fired against them were identified as Afghan National Army individuals. They were informed of there mistake and ceased fire.

Event closed at 0602Z.
ISAF Tracking # 02-340

Reference ID: AFG20080521n1255 Region: RC EAST
Latitude: 33.17214584 Longitude: 68.79621124
Date: 2008-05-21 12:12 Type: Friendly Fire
Category: BLUE-BLUE Affiliation: FRIEND
Detained: 0

	Enemy	Friend	Civilian	Host Nation
Killed in Action	0	0	0	1
Wounded in Action	0	0	0	0

ON 21 MAY 08 AT APPROXIMATELY 1700L AN ANP SOLDIER AT A BAZAAR GOT INTO A FIGHT WITH TWO NATIONAL DEFENSE SOLDIERS (NDS). THE ANP RETURNED TO THE ANP HQ COMPOUND TO RETRIEVE HIS AK-47. THE ANP SOLDIER EXITED THE COMPOUND AND GUNFIRE WAS EXCHANGED WITH THE NDS SOLDIERS. THE NDS SOLDIERS HAD A DSHKA MOUNTED ON A VEHICLE AND THE NDS SOLDIERS KILLED THE ANP. ANA, PMT, AND ETT WERE INVOLVED AFTER THE FACT. PRIMARY FOCUS WAS SEPARATING THE TWO AND CREATING A TRUCE BETWEEN ANP AND NDS LEADERSHIP.
BDA: 1 X ANP KILLED

Reference ID: AFG20080628n1371
Latitude: 34.10028076
Date: 2008-06-28 08:08
Category: BLUE-BLUE
Detained: 0
Region: RC EAST
Longitude: 68.76365662
Type: Friendly Fire
Affiliation: FRIEND

	Enemy	Friend	Civilian	Host Nation
Killed in Action	0	0	0	0
Wounded in Action	0	0	0	1

REFERENCE PAKTIKA PMT SIR A002:
PAKTIKA PMT-TEAM 2 REPORTS THAT AT APPROXIMATELY 0600L, THE PAKTIKA AND THE GHANZI PMTS WERE RETURNING FROM THE JALABAD REGIONAL TRAINING FACILITY, AND WERE TRAVELING SOUTH BOUND ON MSR OHIO. APPROXIMATELY 1 MILE FROM ROUTE GEORGIA, A TRACTOR TRAILER OPERATED BY A LOCAL NATIONAL LOST CONTROL OF THE VEHICLE, AND THE VEHICLE OVERTURNED. AN INVESTIGATION WAS INITIATED BY THE REPORTING OFFICER WITH THE ASSISTANCE OF THE GHAZNI PMT PERSONNEL AND ANP. DURING THE INVESTIGATION IT WAS DISCOVERED THAT AN ANP POLICE OFFICER (IDENTIFIED AS ABDUEL JABAR ASSIGNED TO THE SARHHAWZA POLICE DISTRICT) WAS SHOT ONCE IN THE UPPER THIGH. WHILE THE ANP OFFICER WAS BEING TREATED BY SPC WARD (PAKTIKA PMT MEDIC), THE REPORTING OFFICER NOTIFIED THE 2 BCT TOC AND REQUESTED A MEDEVAC VIA BFT (REQUEST SENT IN 0615 HOURS). AT 0700 HOURS, THE MEDEVAC ARRIVED ON SCENE AND TRANSPORTED THE PATIENT TO THE NEAREST CSH. THE REPORTING OFFICER CONDUCTED A PRELIMINARY INVESTIGATION TO DETERMINE AS HOW THE ANP OFFICER RECEIVED THE GUNSHOT WOUND. WITH THE ASSISTANCE OF ASSIGNED PAKITKA PMT INTERPRETERS, THE UNDERSIGNED DETERMINED THAT THE ANP OFFICER MAY HAVE BEEN A VICTIM OF FRIENDLY FIRE FROM HIS OWN ANP. ACCORDING TO WITNESSES (ANP OFFICERS), THE TRUCK ACCELERATED AND SWERVED INTO THEIR CONVOY. THE ANP OFFICERS FEARING THAT THE TRUCK MIGHT BE A POSSIBLE VBIED DISCHARGED SEVERAL ROUNDS AT THE TRUCK. NO US FORCES FIRED ROUNDS. AT APPROXIMATELY 0600, THE PAKTIKA AND THE GHANZI PMTS WERE RETURNING FROM THE JALABAD REGIONAL TRAINING FACILITY, AND WERE TRAVELING SOUTH BOUND ON MSR OHIO. APPROXIMATELY 1 MILE FROM ROUTE GEORGIA, A TRACTOR TRAILER OPERATED BY A LOCAL NATIONAL LOST CONTROL OF THE VEHICLE, AND

THE VEHICLE OVERTURNED. AN INVESTIGATION WAS INITIATED BY THE REPORTING OFFICER WITH THE ASSISTANCE OF THE GHAZNI PMT PERSONNEL AND ANP. DURING THE INVESTIGATION IT WAS DISCOVERED THAT AN ANP POLICE OFFICER (IDENTIFIED AS ABDUEL JABAR ASSIGNED TO THE SARHHAWZA POLICE DISTRICT) WAS SHOT ONCE IN THE UPPER THIGH. WHILE THE ANP OFFICER WAS BEING TREATED BY SPC WARD (PAKTIKA PMT MEDIC), THE REPORTING OFFICER NOTIFIED THE 2 BCT TOC AND REQUESTED A MEDEVAC VIA BFT (REQUEST SENT IN 0615 HOURS). AT 0700 HOURS, THE MEDEVAC ARRIVED ON SCENE AND TRANSPORTED THE PATIENT TO THE NEAREST CSH. THE REPORTING OFFICER CONDUCTED A PRELIMINARY INVESTIGATION TO DETERMINE AS HOW THE ANP OFFICER RECEIVED THE GUNSHOT WOUND. WITH THE ASSISTANCE OF ASSIGNED PAKITKA PMT INTERPRETERS, THE UNDERSIGNED DETERMINED THAT THE ANP OFFICER MAY HAVE BEEN A VICTIM OF FRIENDLY FIRE FROM HIS OWN ANP. ACCORDING TO WITNESSES (ANP OFFICERS), THE TRUCK ACCELERATED AND SWERVED INTO THEIR CONVOY. THE ANP OFFICERS FEARING THAT THE TRUCK MIGHT BE A POSSIBLE VBIED DISCHARGED SEVERAL ROUNDS AT THE TRUCK. NO US FORCES FIRED ROUNDS. AS A NOTE, FOB GHAZNI TOC WAS NOTIFIED BY CPT CURTISS (GHAZNI PMT CHIEF) AND BY THE FOB RUSHMORE TOC OF THE ACCIDENT AND THE NEED FOR ENGINEER ASSETS AND LOCAL ANP TO SECURE THE SCENE.
BDA: 1 X ANP WOUNDED

Reference ID: AFG20081122n1557
Latitude: 31.4878006
Date: 2008-11-22 19:07
Category: BLUE-BLUE
Detained: 0

Region: RC SOUTH
Longitude: 65.86040497
Type: Friendly Fire
Affiliation: FRIEND

	Enemy	Friend	Civilian	Host Nation
Killed in Action	0	0	0	0
Wounded in Action	0	0	0	0

TFK/ JDOC
S: VEHICLE DROVE ERRATICALLY AT PATROL AND FAILED TO STOP AFTER BEING SIGNALLED
A: PATROL CARRIED OUT EOF FIRST WITH MINIFLARES, VEHICLE STILL FAILED TO STOP, PATROL THEN FIRED 3X RDS 7.62MM TOWARDS THE REAR OF VEHICLE RESULTING IN 1X REAR TIRE DAMAGED. NO CASUALTIES, MINOR DAMAGE TO 1X REAR TIRE
L: 41RQQ7172387209
T: 222340D NOV 2008
A: AFTER CONDUCTING FOLLOW UP ACTION, THE PATROL DISCOVERED THAT THE VEHICLE WAS TF71, ALL DETAILS WERE EXCHANGED FOR FOLLOW UP ACTION IF REQUIRED.
RESIDENT FIELD SQN(BRITTISH SECURITY PATROL) RETURNING FROM SECURITY PATROLS VIC KAF REPORTED THAT VEHICLE APPROACHED CONVOY FROM THE REAR, DRIVING ERRATICALLY. VEHICLE WAS SIGNALLED TO STOP BY RFS WITH PENFLARES. VEHICLE DID NOT OBEY SIGNALS TO STOP. RFS THEN ENGAGED VEHICLE WITH 3X 7.62MM,

DAMAGING 1X REAR TIRE OF THE VEHICLE. OCCUPANT OF VEHICLE WAS NOT INJURED. UPON FOLLOW ON ACTION, ALL DETAILS AND POC'S WERE DOCUMENTED FOR REPORTING PURPOSES AND LATER ACTIONS IF REQUIRED.
KAF JDOC STATED THAT RC-S WILL BE SUBMITTING AN ISAF CRITICAL INCIDENT REPORT THROUGH ISAF ON THIS INCIDENT
SOLDIER IS DETERMINED TO BE US SPECIAL FORCES (7 SFG, TF71). NFTR.
EVENT CLOSED 230115D

Reference ID: AFG20090703n1902
Latitude: 34.53951645
Date: 2009-07-03 06:06
Category: BLUE-BLUE
Detained: 0
Region: RC CAPITAL
Longitude: 69.21523285
Type: Friendly Fire
Affiliation: FRIEND

	Enemy	Friend	Civilian	Host Nation
Killed in Action	0	0	0	0
Wounded in Action	0	0	0	0

RC(C) reported a blue on blue incident. C/S 203 (2 x Toyota Stingray GBR from UK FP & Tpt Coy) were pulling out from Route Purple onto Highway 7 to turn right. They pulled out behind a US Military Cargo Truck and another US Military Armoured vehicle. The US Military Cargo Truck moved over to the right hand lane and the driver waved C/S 203 to go past him. C/S 203 had driven past the US Military Armoured vehicle, it pulled out onto the road and continued in the same direction as C/S 203. The US Military Armoured vehicle then started to indicate that he wanted C/S 203 to move over. C/S 203 obliged and moved over to the right hand side of the carriageway allowing both the US vehicles to drive past C/S 203. C/S 203 then started to drop back and create distance between themselves and the 2 x US vehicles. C/S 203 were approximately 50 70m behind the 2 x US vehicles when the front vehicle of C/S 203 saw a muzzle flash from the top cover of the US Military Armoured vehicle, and heard a loud impact on the bonnet of their vehicle. C/S 203 pulled over immediately to check for any damage or casualties. They made a quick assessment and then continued on their return journey to HQ ISAF.

Reference ID: AFG20090831n1231
Latitude: 31.76895905
Date: 2009-08-31 01:01
Category: BLUE-BLUE
Detained: 0
Region: RC SOUTH
Longitude: 64.49530792
Type: Friendly Fire
Affiliation: FRIEND

	Enemy	Friend	Civilian	Host Nation
Killed in Action	0	0	0	0
Wounded in Action	0	0	0	0

LD BG reported AH-1 (COBRA) gunship engaged NW sanger of FF locn in BABAJI AO (BLUE on BLUE) without reason while Black Hawks were collecting ISAF Mil pax from the same location. No FF casualties were sustained. COBRA than conducted a strafing run from the south into the NW part of the FF location, and missed the NW sangar by 15 metres. COBRA then strafed Rte KRONOS up to a compound at GR 41R PR 414 160. The strafing run went into an area where locals are known to move

frequently IOT go to pray. No civ cas reported ATT. ISAF Mil troops had liased on Sun 30 Aug specifying intent to extract from FF location. No casualties were sustained.
ISAF Mil have spoken to TFH Air desk. ISAF Mil JTAC has confirmed no request for hot airspace, and not authorised to engage. ISAF Mil are going to get guntapes from the COBRA and the Blackhawks. FF are now observing.
UPDATE 311105D*
Full investigation is being carried out. BG & TFH hold no further info.
***Event closed at 311118DD*

Reference ID: AFG20091130n2287 Region: RC WEST
Latitude: 35.61453247 Longitude: 63.31005478
Date: 2009-11-30 08:08 Type: Friendly Fire
Category: BLUE-BLUE Affiliation: FRIEND
Detained: 0

	Enemy	Friend	Civilian	Host Nation
Killed in Action	0	0	0	0
Wounded in Action	0	1	0	0

S: 1 x US shot in lower extremity
A: Barbarian 26 reported that 1 x US WIA from a ND in the lower extremity (Left Heel)
L: vic. Akazia School 41S NV 25835 43563
T: 300800LNov09
R: Awaiting 9-line
Correction the origin of the ND is US. Blue on Blue
0858L: Evaluation From DOC determined GW does not warrant a MEDEVAC.

Blue on White

Civilian casualties have always presented difficulties in guerrilla and counter-insurgency warfare. Unlike in conventional warfare, where the opposing population can be considered an enemy and treated accordingly, guerrilla insurgencies are, above all, political struggles, not military ones—and the hearts and minds of the population is precisely what both sides are struggling for. Every civilian who is killed or injured, even unintentionally, produces new sympathy for the insurgents and new resentments against the government and its defenders.

Several incidents have caused particular outrage amongst Afghans. In one incident, a guided bomb malfunctioned and hit a village. In another, a Polish unit that had hit an IED mortared a village where they thought the insurgents were hiding, hitting a wedding party. A French unit opened fire on a schoolbus that came too close to a convoy, and an American unit killed a number of civilians when it opened fire on a local bus. In another incident, British forces fired on some interpreters, and the US noted that it was "not able to get the complete story" from them.

The United States, whose military power is designed to be unleashed to the fullest extent, finds itself at a tremendous disadvantage in a counter-insurgency fight. It cannot use the full force of its military firepower, since an unacceptably high level of civilian "collateral damage" will destroy any sympathy the US may have from the local population—as well as produce political discontent back home.

The United States, therefore, has been forced to keep its military power on a very short leash in Afghanistan, and has tightly constrained itself, with a web of "rules of engagement", to avoid actions which produce civilian casualties or which offend the feelings of the local population, such as shooting into mosques. Some of the more hawkish critics may view this as "fighting with one hand tied behind our backs", but this criticism ignores the realities of guerrilla war and counter-insurgency. It cannot be overemphasized that insurgent war is *political* war, not military—it is not about winning battles or killing as many of the enemy as possible. That is simply not what wins a guerrilla war. Counter-insurgency is a battle for hearts and minds, not a battle for territory and attrition. And that is why a counter-insurgent force like the US in Afghanistan simply *must* limit its firepower, in the interests of reducing civilian casualties as low as possible. To do any less would be to repeat the mistakes of Vietnam—to win every military battle, but ultimately to lose the war in the only arena that really counts in an insurgency, the arena of popular support.

Reference ID: AFG20070328n674
Latitude: 34.75244904
Date: 2007-03-28 12:12
Category: Attack
Detained: 0

Region: RC CAPITAL
Longitude: 69.13437653
Type: Enemy Action
Affiliation: ENEMY

	Enemy	Friend	Civilian	Host nation
Killed in action	0	0	0	0
Wounded in action	0	0	0	0

Classification: SECRET / NOFORN
CSTC-A DCG for Pol-Mil Affairs
Daily Cable Summaries
28 March 2007
(S/NF) PRT TARIN KOWT: DUTCH ACCIDENTLY KILL CIVILIANS DEFENDING VILLAGE FROM INSURGENTS: (Source: AMEMBASSY KABUL 01019, 28 Mar 07) Dutch direct fire on an apparent enemy target in support of a village under Taliban attack ended tragically. Four villagers engaged in the fight to defend Chenartu were killed and another seven wounded. The Dutch have launched an official investigation and have engaged in a proactive public relations campaign to prevent political fallout here and in the Netherlands. Although the decision to fire was justified, the danger is that, having had this action go awry, they will hesitate in the future with negative consequences for security in the province.

Reference ID: AFG20070622n814
Latitude: 33.19190979
Date: 2007-06-22 19:07
Category: GREEN-WHITE
Detained: 0

Region: RC EAST
Longitude: 68.1048584
Type: Friendly Fire
Affiliation: FRIEND

	Enemy	Friend	Civilian	Host Nation
Killed in Action	0	0	0	0
Wounded in Action	0	0	0	0

A 2Fury unit stationed at the Qarabagh District Center reported taking small arms fire at 22 1910ZJUN07. Upon investigation they discovered a NDS agent stationed at the DC guarding the NW perimeter fired at 2 pax walking with flashlights IVO the DC. The 2 pax ran off. The DC was not recieving small arms fire. NFTR

Reference ID: AFG20070816n891
Latitude: 32.43878937
Date: 2007-08-16 10:10
Category: BLUE-GREEN
Detained: 0

Region: RC EAST
Longitude: 68.35555267
Type: Friendly Fire
Affiliation: FRIEND

	Enemy	Friend	Civilian	Host nation
Killed in action	0	0	6	0
Wounded in action	0	0	3	0

These are the facts as I know them. All of this is subject to change.

The morning of the incident, around 1030L, the RCP hit an IED near the village. A patrol from C Coy responded and hit asecond IED. They identified 4x ACM responsible for the IEDs andcaptured two and thetwo others escaped.Theycollected a lot of SIGINTindicating that the individuals were still around. They were searching for the remaining individuals when around 1600L, 4x ACM were seen moving vicinity of the village. It is not clear if they were hiding in the village or just passing through. There was only one section of two vehicles involved in the TIC. They fired their 12.7mm MG at the individuals, but the weapon jammed. The ACM then returned fire. They then emplaced their mortars. They fired a total of 26 rounds according to one report. They fired over and then short and then three rounds impacted within a compound. One impacted on the roof of the house, one impacted in the court yard, and the last went through the roof and detonated within the house. There was a wedding celebration going on in the house, which explains the high number of casualties. As soon as the PBG soldiers saw where the rounds impacted, they moved immediately to the compound to provide assistance. The 4x ACM escaped.

This information is still to sketchy to assess a cause for the inaccurate rounds.

Current Casualty list:6x KIA (1x male, 4 female, one baby)

3x WIA (all female, one of which was 9 months pregnant)

All of the casualties were from the Jalal Zaid Tribe, but not all were from the village, because some were from out of town for the wedding. This will spread the negative effect to a larger area then itwould of otherwise. Today, there were 120 locals rioting at the gate ofFOB Waza Khwa protesting the deaths.

I am not able to talk to the individual soldiersdirectly, because the formal investigation has to be conducted by their Prosecutor. His name is LTC Dariusz Raczkiewicz. He is currently in Ghazni and will be here ina day or two. The individuals conducting their informal investigation are a MP investigator, WO Humeniuk Karol and aCounter Intelligence guy named LTC Radoslaw Jagiello. They are also not allowed to question the soldiers that were involved. Their inability to question the soldiers is causing much of the faulty reporting.

Tomorrow at 0830L, there will be a Shura at the Waza Khwa DC. I will attend it with the C Coy Commander, the Charlie 2/508 Commander,and the two guys conducting the informal investigation. At 1100L a flight will take a contingent from the families of the injured females to OE.

Reference ID: AFG20071021n961
Latitude: 34.55213165
Date: 2007-10-21 00:12
Category: BLUE-WHITE
Detained: 0
Region: RC CAPITAL
Longitude: 69.36927795
Type: Friendly Fire
Affiliation: FRIEND

	Enemy	Friend	Civilian	Host Nation
Killed in Action	0	0	0	0
Wounded in Action	0	0	3	0

At 0045Z, TF Phoenix reported that a civilian vehicle with three MPRI interpreters and a driver were fired upon in downtown Kabul by a military-type vehicle that was brown with a gunner on top. Three of the occupants were wounded, two critically and one non-critically. The injured were taken to the hospital in downtown Kabul, condition unknown. It has been confirmed that there were no US forces located in the vicinity of the event that may have been involved. More to follow!

Initial reports indicated 3 interpreters were wounded from friendly fire from a military-type vehicle in downtown Kabul. It has been confirmed that the interpreters vehicle was fired upon by an UK vehicle near Camp Blackhorse, wounding 2 of the interpreters.

(UPDATE 2) BDA: 2 X LN TERPS WOUNDED, NO DEATHS ASSOCIATED WITH THIS INCIDENT

INVESTIGATION IS CONTROLLED BY THE BRITISH. WE NOT ABLE TO GET THE COMPLETE STORY. THIS EVENT BELONGS TO THE BRITISH ISAF FORCES.
ISAF Tracking # 10-521

Reference ID: AFG20080210n1209
Latitude: 32.8044281
Date: 2008-02-10 02:02
Category: BLUE-WHITE
Detained: 0
Region: RC WEST
Longitude: 62.54199982
Type: Friendly Fire
Affiliation: FRIEND

	Enemy	Friend	Civilian	Host Nation
Killed in Action	0	0	0	0
Wounded in Action	0	0	0	0

24 YEAR OLD MALE LN KILLED BY SPANISH CONVOY AS THEY WERE TRAVELING IN A WHITE SURACHE NORTH ALONG ROUTE 1 (41S MS 5712 2970) IVO BALA BELUK, FARAH PROVINCE, AT APPROX 101330L FEB08. THE LN↑S VEHICLE PULLED INTO THE ANCOP HEADQUARTERS AND NAVY CORPSMAN FABROS PRONOUNCED HIM DEAD ON ARRIVAL. THE DECEASED WAS STRUCK IN THE RIGHT EYE, KILLING HIM. THE DRIVER WAS STRUCK IN THE RIGHT EAR; HMS FABROS TREATED THE DRIVER FOR A CLIPPED RIGHT EAR AND GLASS FRAGMENTATION ON THE NECK. THERE ARE TWO VERSIONS REGARDING THE CIRCUMSTANCES SEQUENCE OF EVENTS IN THE SHOOTING INCIDENT.
LN VERSION: COUSIN OF THE DECEASED RIDING IN THE VEHICLE (GULBUDIN) INDICATED THAT THE SPANISH CONVOY APPROACHED FROM THEIR REAR, MOVING NORTH. THE WHITE SURACHE PULLED OVER SLOWLY, WAS PASSED BY THE CONVOY, AND THE LAST VEHICLE IN THE SPANISH CONVOY SHOT THROUGH THEIR WINDSHIELD.

SPANISH VERSION: CONVOY COMMANDER INDICATED THE SHOOTING WAS AN ACCIDENT, BUT THAT THE SURACHE MAY HAVE BEEN SHOT DUE TO NOT FOLLOWING DIRECTIONS. THE CONVOY COMMANDER SAYS THE VEHICLE PULLED OVER, BUT ATTEMPTED TO PULL BACK INTO THE SPANISH CONVOY. HIS REAR VEHICLE DID INDEED SHOOT IN AN ATTEMPT TO PUSH THE VEHICLE OVER. HE CANNOT SAY CLEARLY IF HIS GUNNER FIRED TO DISABLE OR TO KILL. IN THE RIGHT EYE AND CHEST. NFI. Event Closed.

Reference ID: AFG20080505n1329
Latitude: 33.16999817
Date: 2008-05-05 13:01
Category: BLUE-WHITE
Detained: 0
Region: RC EAST
Longitude: 68.78999329
Type: Friendly Fire
Affiliation: FRIEND

	Enemy	Friend	Civilian	Host Nation
Killed in Action	0	0	1	0
Wounded in Action	0	0	0	0

[20:14] <PBG_LNO_OPS> S: PCC REPORTS THAT A LOCAL NATIONAL WAS SHOT BY A US CONVOY
[20:14] <PBG_LNO_OPS> A: AFTER TALKING TO SHARANA PRT INITIAL INVESTIGATION HAS DETERMINED THAT A PRT CONVOY RETURNING TO FOB SHARANA FIRED A WARNING SHOT THAT RICOCHET OFF THE GROUND AND MAY HAVE HIT THE LN
[20:14] <PBG_LNO_OPS> L: UNKNOWN
[20:14] <PBG_LNO_OPS> T: 1515Z
[20:14] <PBG_LNO_OPS> R: NONE, LN IS CURRENTLY AT SHARANA HOSPITAL, PRT IS CONDUCTING INVESTIGATION AND WILL UPDATE THE SITUATION.
[20:19] <PBG_LNO_OPS> UPDATE TO LN SHOOTING: ETT HAS CONFIRMED THAT THE LN HAS DIED OF WOUNDS

Reference ID: AFG20080615n1272
Latitude: 32.87607574
Date: 2008-06-15 03:03
Category: BLUE-WHITE
Detained: 0
Region: RC EAST
Longitude: 68.95061493
Type: Friendly Fire
Affiliation: FRIEND

	Enemy	Friend	Civilian	Host Nation
Killed in Action	0	0	1	0
Wounded in Action	0	0	1	0

TYPE: POSSIBLE IED IMPLACERS
TIMELINE:
AT 0336Z, C/2-506 ENGAGED 2 X POSSIBLE IED IMPLACERS VIC CHARBARAN, D.C. THE SUSPECTED AAF WERE LN'S DIGGING AN IRRIGATION DITCH 30 METERS OFF RTE CHARGERS. THE SUSPECTED AAF (LN), WAS KIA, AND THE OTHER LN RAN OFF AND COULD NOT BE LOCATED. THE LOCAL ANP DELIVERED THE LN BODY TO THE FAMILY. A HHA DROP WILL OCCUR LATER TODAY AND A SHURA WILL BE HELD WEDNESDAY WITH THE

LOCALS. AN IO MESSAGE IS CURRENTLY BEING DEVELOPED ABOUT DIGGING NEAR ROADS.
SUMMARY:
POSSIBLE IED IMPLACERS
42SVB 95380 37550
D1 0336Z
BDA:
LN KIA: 1
LN WIA: 1
EVENT CLOSED 0703Z
ISAF # 06-0654
Update
OFFENSIVE engagement w/ Alleged CIVCAS
UPDATE
First Impression report complete
Update
Second Impression report complete
UPDATE
Investigation report complete
Based on latest update changes in title and category

Reference ID: AFG20080909n1379 Region: RC EAST
Latitude: 33.58015823 Longitude: 69.82315826
Date: 2008-09-09 06:06 Type: Friendly Fire
Category: BLUE-WHITE Affiliation: FRIEND
Detained: 0

	Enemy	Friend	Civilian	Host Nation
Killed in Action	0	0	2	0
Wounded in Action	0	0	17	0

ISAF #09-383
UNIT: TF GLORY
TYPE: GBU MALFUNCTION
AT 0608Z IN RESPONSE TO A KNOWN UXO POINTED AT ZAMBAR (107MM ROCKET FROM THE D2 SIGACT) TF GLORY REQUESTED BONE 1-1 DROP A GBU 31 IOT RENDER IT NMC. DURING THE DROP THE TAILKIT OF THE GBU 31 MALFUNCTIONED CAUSING THE GBU TO DROP UNGUIDED INTO A BALLISTIC TRAJECTORY. THE GBU DROPPED INTO A QUALAT AT GRID 42SWC 76390 15910 2788 METERS AT A 270 DEGREE HEADING FROM THE INTENDED TARGET. STILL WORKING CASUALTIES AND QRF FROM FOB SALERNO
UPDATE: AS OF 0709Z MEDEVAC BIRDS AND DMR (3xUH 60's) WILL BE USED FOR QRF INSERTION FROM SAL INTO A NSHLZ. 0H 58 QRF ARE ALSO OVER THE SITE IOT SECURE THE NSHLZ. STILL PENDING APPROVAL
UPDATE: AT 0716 OH 58'S OBSERVED APROX 25 PAX GOING THROUGH THE POI SITE. PAX ARE NOT SHOWING ANY HOSTILE INTENT AT THIS TIME
UPDATE: 0730z PCC REPORTED TO TF GLORY THAT ANP ARE TAKING 7x LN WIA TO KHOST HOSPITAL. STILL NO CONFIRMED NUMBER OF TOTAL CASUALTIES, AND BREAKDOWN.

UPDATE: AT 0734 AP40 (308) AP36(291) & AP41(314) WENT W/U SAL WITH THE QRF PACKAGE
UPDATE: AT 0745 AP40 (308) AP36(291) & AP41(314) WENT W/D NSHLZ WITH THE QRF PACKAGE. ALSO WARRIOR ALPHA CHECKED ON STATION
UPDATE: 19xANA ALONG WITH 2xETT; 1 TERP WILL BE INSERTED TO THE SITE AS WELL IOT PROVIDE ANSF PRESENCE TO THE SITUATION.
UPDATE: AT 0820z AP36(291) & AP41(314) ARRIVED AT CLARK TO PICK UP THE ANA AND ETT GOING W/U AT 0832z.
UPDATE: AT 0847z ANA AND ETT'S INSERTED UPDATE: GLORY 5 RECIEVED A REPORT FROM GLORY 6 THAT THERE ARE CONFIRMED 2x LN KIA, 2x LN WIA; AND 8 OTHER LNS ARE BEING LOOKED AT BY MEDICS
UPDATE: 1000z GLORY 6 FOUND THE TAILKIT OF THE GBU 31 AT WC 76481 15802
UPDATE: 1005z DUDE 03 OFF STATION
UPDATE: 1010z HAWG 55 ON STATION
UPDATE: AT 1046 MEDEVAC (MM(E) 09-09E) WAS INITIATED TO MEDEVAC 14xLN WIA (1xESCORT) EOD PRELOADED ON THE CHASE BIRD TO EXPLOIT THE SITE FOR THE TAILFIN. (MEDEVAC INFORMATION CAN BE FOUND IN THE MEDEVAC ICON INSIDE THE ASSOCIATIONS BOX)
UPDATE: 1128Z MEDEVAC WILL TAKE ANOTHER TURN IOT PICK UP AN ADDITIONAL 3 PATIENTS
UPDATE: AT 1144 DO26(883) AP40 (308) [MED BIRDS] AP42(429) WENT W/U SAL IN ORDER TO EXFIL
UPDATE 1150z MEDEVAC WHEELS DOWN HLZ
UPDATE: 1154z MEDEVAC WHEELS UP HLZ ENROUTE TO SAL
UPDATE: 1200z HAWG 57 CONDUCTING BATTLE HANDOFF WITH HAWG 55
UPDATE: UH-60s WHEELS UP SAL ENROUTE TO HLZ FOR EXFIL

Reference ID: AFG20081002n1400
Latitude: 34.57512665
Date: 2008-10-02 04:04
Category: Escalation of Force
Detained: 0
Region: RC CAPITAL
Longitude: 69.39794922
Type: Friendly Action
Affiliation: FRIEND

	Enemy	Friend	Civilian	Host nation
Killed in action	0	0	0	0
Wounded in action	0	0	8	0

ISAF #10-049
INFO;DTG of Report: 020845SEP08 (as reported by villagers from Tangi Kalay) 201ST
S: 4xLN WIA
A: FRA BG vehicles opened fire on a bus that came too close to convoy
L: IVO Tangi Kalay village, 42SWD 365 260(12 NE OF CAMP PHOENIX)
T: 02 0820L OCT 08
R: TAG received reports from villagers via phone and others who arrived at front gate. TAG confirmed incident with Camp Warehouse TOC LNO 1LT Logan. KMTC ANA personnel are BPT respond with QRF and medical care. Camp Warehouse is preparing medical units to respond. According to LN reports as of 0853, most of the children have been put into taxis by LNs IOT evacuate them to CF medical facilities.

At 0900: ISAF is reporting that at least 5 wounded children have arrived at Camp Warehouse,
8x LN CHILDREN WIA

Reference ID: AFG20081212n1518
Latitude: 33.86717987
Date: 2008-12-12 06:06
Category: Escalation of Force
Detained: 0

Region: RC EAST
Longitude: 68.63316345
Type: Friendly Action
Affiliation: FRIEND

	Enemy	Friend	Civilian	Host nation
Killed in action	0	0	4	0
Wounded in action	0	0	11	0

ISAF # 12-0471
S-UNK
A-SAF/RPG
L-VC 66071 47490
T-0622z
U-ABLE 2-6
R-RETURN FIRE, REQUESTING CAS.
TF RED CURRAHEE (ABLE 2-6)
SAF/RPG
TIMELINE: 0600z ABLE 2-6 WAS CONDUCTING A DISMOUNTED PATROL IVO OF COP HAFT ASIAB ON THE WEST SIDE OF MSR OHIO. ABLE 2-6 ATTEMPTING TO CROSS MSR OHIO TO RETURN TO COP HAFT ASIAB. SOUTHERN SECURITY ELEMENT NOTICED A BUS MOVING FROM SOUTH TO NORTH ALONG MSR OHIO. SOLDIER WENT INTO MIDDLE OF THE ROAD AND PUT BOTH HANDS IN THE AIR, ATTEMPTING TO MAKE THE VEHICLE STOP. VEHICLE DID NOT SLOW DOWN OR MAKE ATTEMPT TO STOP. SOLDIER TOLD SQUAD LEADER THAT THE VEHICAL DID NOT STOP. tHE SQUAD LEADER FIRED A WARNIN SHOT OVER THE BUS. SOLDIER TOLD THE SQUAD LEADER THAT THE VEHICLE DID NOT STOP AND THE SQUAD LEADER PLACED 1x5.56mm TRACER RD INTO THE VEHICLE'S ENGINE BLOCK. VEHICLE AGAIN DID NOT STOP OR SLOW DOWN. SQUAD LEADER AUTHORIZED SAW GUNNER (IAW EOF SOP) TO FIRE ON THE VEHICLE WITH M-249. VEHICLE STOPPED WITH 4xLN KIA, 11xLN WIA. ATT CASUALTIES HAVE BEEN CASEVACED.
UPDATE: 0622z ABLE 2-6 RECEIVES SAF/RPG FROM THE SOUTH WHILE CASEVAC OF LN'S TO HAFT ASAIB. ABLE 3-6 WAS LAUNCHED TO RE-ENFORCE ABLE 2-6.
UPDATE: 0627z ABLE 2-6 FLT VC 66071 47490 RECEIVING FIRE FROM 150 DEGREES AT 300m.
UPDATE: 0633Z, 7 X LN WIA WERE MEDEVAC TO BAF, 4 X LN WIA WERE MEDEVAC TO SALERNO.
UPDATE: 0636z HAWG 53 CHECKS ONSTATION ATT.
UPDATE: 0650z ABLE 2-6 IS NO LONGER IN CONTACT ATT.
UPDATE: 0733z SHADOW IS ONSITE OVER THE TIC SITE ATT.
UPDATE: 0820z ABLE 2-6 IS CURRENTLY COLLECTING STATEMENTS FROM LN'S ANA INVESTIGATING INCIDENT.

FRIENDLY FOLLOW UP: HAWG 53 (A-10'S), ABLE 3-6, SHADOW
SUMMARY:
4xLN KIA
11xLN WIA (7 X BAF, 4 X SAL)
EVENT CLOSED 1555Z

Reference ID: AFG20090526n1719   Region: UNKNOWN
Latitude: 32.5011673   Longitude: 69.26773071
Date: 2009-05-26 15:03   Type: Friendly Fire
Category: GREEN-WHITE   Affiliation: FRIEND
Detained: 0

	Enemy	Friend	Civilian	Host Nation
Killed in Action	0	0	2	0
Wounded in Action	0	0	3	0

Event Title:INFO 0839Z
Zone:null
Placename:null
Outcome:Effective

TF East Paktika SOUTH OP, ANA ROUNDS: 82MM HE NUMBER OF ROUNDS: UNKNOWN *THERE ARE NO US FORCES AT SOUTH OP* TIMELINE: 0839Z: SOUTH OP REPORTS 5 X PAX DIGGING IN A KNOWN BAD AREA, JLENS CONFIRMS 0848Z: LILLEY REPORTS THAT SOUTH OP FIRED MORTARS 0916Z: LILLEY REPORTS THEY DID NOT DO ANY DAMAGE BY SHOOTING MORTARS UPDATE: 2220Z THE PAKISTAN LNO RECEIVED A REPORT FROM THE 11TH CORP THAT A FAMILY WAS STRUCK WITH IDF IN A PASS IVO OF OP SOUTH, FOB LILLEY (42SWA 24638 96099) THE FAMILY WAS REPORTEDLY MOVING SHEEP FROM AFGHANISTAN TO PAKISTAN WHEN THEY WERE HIT. THE FAMILY MOVED ACROSS THE BORDER AND INFORMED THE PAK BORDER CHECK STATION OF THE INCIDENT BDA: 3X LN WIA (2 WOMEN, 1 CHILD) 2X LN KIA (MALES) **NO COALITION FORCES ROUNDS WERE FIRED IN THIS EVENT** ///CLOSED AT 1720Z///

Reference ID: AFG20090616n1906   Region: RC EAST
Latitude: 34.98443222   Longitude: 70.85583496
Date: 2009-06-16 10:10   Type: Friendly Fire
Category: BLUE-WHITE   Affiliation: FRIEND
Detained: 0

	Enemy	Friend	Civilian	Host Nation
Killed in Action	0	0	0	0
Wounded in Action	0	0	0	0

Event Title:D11 1055Z
Zone:null
Placename:ISAF #06-1189
Outcome:null

0430z C/1-26 was conducting a planned observer training on KE 2370. all rounds were reported to have been observed landing in VIC KE 2370. Approx 1 hour after the last rnd landed, the Distric Governor called C/1-26 CDR and stated that the mortar rounds might have injured someone in the village of Wodi Gerum. C/1-26CDR informed the Governer that they had watched all of the rounds and that none of them had landed near any villages. The governor told C/1-26CDR he would look into it and call back. 3/C/1-26 was dispatched to investigate. when 3/C/1-26 arrived he noticed a large group of people carrying a body down to the villiage of Wodi Gerum from the north. 3/C/1-26 l/u with the head Shuraelder, Haji Raouf Khan, of Wodi Gerum, who told him that one shepard had been injured and one child and 10 sheep were killed while they were up in the mountains. According to #/C/1-26 the elders were not angry or particularly upset as they know we frequently use KE2370 to fire on. They were wanted to arrange a time to come to the district center or FOB Blessing to discuss compensation for the family of the child and for the sheep that were injured and killed. CLOSED

Reference ID: AFG20090711n1960
Latitude: 34.75622559
Date: 2009-07-11 04:04
Category: BLUE-WHITE
Detained: 0
Region: RC EAST
Longitude: 71.01533508
Type: Friendly Fire
Affiliation: FRIEND

	Enemy	Friend	Civilian	Host Nation
Killed in Action	0	0	0	0
Wounded in Action	0	0	5	0

S- 2 AAF
A-DISKHA FIRE
L (F)42SXD 8446 4786
L (E)42SXD 83098 47850
T-0437
U-3/D/1-32ND
R-SAF,105MM
0437 COP BADEL REPORTS THAT ITS A 2 MAN FIGHTING POSITION WITH A DISHKA.
0439 FIRE MISSION POSTED KE 3012 AT GRID 42SXD 83098 47850 105MM FROM COP FORTRESS
0447 3/D/1-32ND HAS SUPPRESSED THE ENEMY
0450 END OF FIRE MISSION THE ENEMY HAVE BEEN SUPPRESSED
0456 3/D/1-32ND IS GREEN ON M/W/E
0504 PALEHORSE 45 AND 47 REPORTS SEEING 5-7 PEOPLE GETTING LOADED INTO A WHITE PICK UP TRUCK HEADING TOWARDS ABAD. THE CIVILIANS WERE BEING HELPED BY LOCAL NATIONALS. PALEHORSE HAS FOLLOWED THE VEHICLE TO ASADABAD HOSPITAL. 2/D/1-32ND WENT TO THE HOSPITAL AND WAS INSTRUCTED TO GO TO FOB WRIGHT UNTILL FURTHER NOTICE.
UPDATE: 1 X 105 ROUND SHOT OVER TARGET. LANDED IN A FIELD AND LEFT 5 LN WOUNDED.
0546 PALEHORSE HAS OBSERVED 50 PEOPLE AT THE HOSPITAL IN ASADABAD. GATHERING OUTSIDE.
0606 OCEAN 7 (PMT out of Fob Fiaz) REPORTED THAT THE LOCALS HAVE BLOCKED THE ROAD AT GRID 42SXD 86649 48093 WITH ROCKS

0749 ABAD OCCP REPORTED THAT 3 FEMALES 4 MALES WERE INJURED CURRENTLY 6 ARE AT THE ABAD HOSPITAL 1 FEMALE HAD TO BE EVAC TO JALALABAD CIVILIAN HOSPITAL THE DISPOSITION OF THE CASUALTIES WERE GIVEN TO 2/D/1-32 BY THE HOSPITAL DIRECTOR. ONE FEMALE SUFFERED TRAUMA TO THE FACE, BROKEN CHEEK BONE ,NASAL CAVITY DAMAGE AND WAS UNCONSCIOUS AT THE TIME OF EVAC URGENT SURGICAL AND IN CRITICAL CONDITION THEY ARE FROM THE VILLAGE OF QUALAH WONAH
ROUNDS FIRED:
105MM X4 HE/VT
TOW MISSLE X1
.50 CAL 250 ROUNDS
5.56 LINKED 150 ROUNDS

Reference ID: AFG20090924n2070
Latitude: 34.39581299
Date: 2009-09-24 06:06
Category: GREEN-WHITE
Detained: 0

Region: RC EAST
Longitude: 68.87979126
Type: Friendly Fire
Affiliation: FRIEND

	Enemy	Friend	Civilian	Host Nation
Killed in Action	0	0	0	0
Wounded in Action	0	0	0	0

Event Title:D5 0500Z
Zone:1xLN KIA
Placename:ISAF #09-2256
Outcome:null
OMLT LNO 5w's
WHO:20x OMLT with 4 vics, 1xTeam of Catamount with 1x Humvee, 10x Hungary SF with 2x Humvee and 9x ANA with 1x Ranger truck.
WHERE: FOB Airborne shooting range.
WHEN: 240930LSEPT2009 TIME OF FIRST REPORT.
HOW: unk
WHAT: CPT Boton reports they were at the range from 0600 to 0900 having a competition. They were shooting at 100 Meter targets and behind the targets they were hills to stop the rounds from going anywhere. Only aimpoint scope was use and small arms weapons were all 5.56mm.
 WHY: LOCAL NATIONAL KIA GUN SHOT WOUND TO ABDOMEN
0700Z: ANA COMANDER REPORTS TO FRENCH OMLT THE ANA SOLDIERS WHEN TO THE RANGE AFTER THE COMPETITION AND SHOT THE KUSHI.
0716Z UPDATE: ANA REPORTED TO THE OMLT THAT THEY HAVE SPOKE WITH THE KUCHI FAMILY AND ARE TAKING FULL REPOSIBILITY FOR THE ANA SOLDIERS ACTIONS.
1036Z SUMMARY: 1 LN KIA ON FOB AIRBORNE RANGE, INVESTIGATION LAUNCHED AND ANA REPORTED SHOOTING THE KUCHI. THEY HAVE TAKEN FULL RESPONSIBILITY AND HAVE TALKED WITH THE FAMILY OF THE DECEASED LN.
EVENT OPENED: 0500Z
EVENT CLOSED: 1036Z

Reference ID: AFG20091020n2526
Latitude: 32.7272377
Date: 2009-10-20 12:12
Category: GREEN-WHITE
Detained: 0

Region: RC EAST
Longitude: 69.28509521
Type: Friendly Fire
Affiliation: FRIEND

	Enemy	Friend	Civilian	Host Nation
Killed in Action	0	0	0	0
Wounded in Action	0	0	0	0

At 1230D* TF 3 Geronimo reported that ABP were moving from Margah COP to FOB Shkin when they were engaged by a LN. The LN thought the ABP were taliban. ABP returned fire and shot the LN Male in the HIP.
At 1303D* ABP CASAVACD the LN Male to FOB Boris. The patient was later MEDEVACD to FOB Orgun-E on MM(E)10-20C as WIA (CAT A). There were no further damages or injuries reported. NFTR
This event closed at 1506D*

Reference ID: AFG20091130n2300
Latitude: 32.63220596
Date: 2009-11-30 11:11
Category: GREEN-WHITE
Detained: 0

Region: RC SOUTH
Longitude: 65.88856506
Type: Friendly Fire
Affiliation: FRIEND

	Enemy	Friend	Civilian	Host Nation
Killed in Action	0	0	1	0
Wounded in Action	0	0	2	0

ANA was conducting an independent patrol. ANA was moving via CP GHARMAB when LN's threw rocks at them.
ANA engaged LN's resulting in 3 x LN wounded. The casualties were brought to TK hospital where 1 x LN DOW (nephew of ABDUL BAQI KHAN, PTC teacher). ANP went to the GOVERNORS COMPOUND to disarm and arrest ANA assuming they were the perpetrators. ANP arrested 3 x ANA from GOVERNORS COMPOUND but later released them.
UPD1-020422D*
There was no ISAF involvement, FF have NFTR on the incident.
BDA: 1 x LN DOW, 2 x LN wounded.
This Incident closed by RC (S) at: 021602D*NOV2009

Reference ID: AFG20091220n2717
Latitude: 33.39113617
Date: 2009-12-20 14:02
Category: BLUE-WHITE
Detained: 0

Region: RC WEST
Longitude: 62.25163269
Type: Friendly Fire
Affiliation: FRIEND

	Enemy	Friend	Civilian	Host Nation
Killed in Action	0	0	0	0
Wounded in Action	0	0	1	0

S: 1x Civilain
A: Gunshot wound to Chest (sucking chest wound)
L: Shindand (41S MS 304 949)

T: 201015LDec09
R: The patient was sent to Herat. When asked what happened he stated that he was driving toward one of the gates and was told to stop by a guard. He did not stop so the guard fired. Patient stated that he was a civilian not ANA.

Weapons Caches

In a guerrilla fight, the occupying counter-insurgent army is no longer a military force using firepower against an opposing army in the field—in many ways, the counter-insurgent soldier becomes not much more than a policeman. And like any policeman in a violent gang-ridden neighborhood, he has two basic goals—remove the weapons from the streets, and remove as many of the fighters as possible. One of the aims of the American counter-insurgency in Afghanistan, therefore, has been to find and remove weapons from the insurgent's hands, to weaken them and lessen their ability to attack. This is done by patrols (called "meet and greets") which encourage civilian informants to give information leading to enemy stockpiles, and by "cordon and clear" actions, which seal off suspicious areas and then actively search for insurgent suspects and hidden weapon caches.

In the first years of the Afghan insurgency, most of the weapons being used were leftovers from the war against the Soviets (one report in fact mentions the discovery by American forces of an old but still serviceable Soviet Army supply dump). Indeed, some of the weapons that have been discovered in the hands of the insurgents are old bolt-action rifles and submachine guns, like the British Lee-Enfield and the Soviet PPSh, that date all the way back to the Second World War. The favorite weapon of the insurgency—the improvised explosive device, or roadside bomb—was made from old Soviet mortar and artillery munitions, or from crude homemade explosives.

These still make up a large part of the insurgency's arsenal today, and American troops still uncover large caches of homemade explosives and Soviet-era guns. Increasingly, however, the insurgents are obtaining newer Russian and Chinese-manufactured munitions, and even a small amount of Italian, Iranian, and Pakistani weapons. The most reliable sources for the insurgency, however, are unexploded American ordnance. These can litter a battlefield after a fight; one of the reports describes a farmer who gathered a number of unexploded shells in his fields. The Taliban/Al Qaeda insurgency has demonstrated that they are perfectly capable of resisting US troops effectively using nothing more than cell phones and American dud bombs, and leftover AK-47s from 1979.

It is not unusual for US troops to find large amounts of opium or hashish in insurgent weapons caches, and the illegal drug trade plays a central role in the war. Afghanistan is one of the poorest countries on earth, and for many rural farmers, growing marijuana or opium poppies is their only source of income. This drug trade is controlled by the local tribal leaders, and the insurgency receives a large portion of its funding through drug trafficking with sympathetic tribal figures. In addition, the illegal drug trade produces political conflict. The US military funds a Poppy Eradication Program, which aims to cut off the flow of drug money to the guerrillas. Every time US troops destroy a poppy field, however, they are destroying an Afghan family's sole livelihood, and are creating local enemies; by actively defending the poppy fields, on the other hand, the insurgents win local friends. The result is a situation where the US tries to weaken the guerrillas by destroying the illegal drug trade, but in doing so only increases local resentment for the occupation and increases sympathy for the Taliban.

Reference ID: AFG20040101n2
Latitude: 2004-01-01 00:12
Date: 2004-01-01 00:12
Category: Cache Found/Cleared
Detained: 0
Region: RC EAST
Longitude: 70.92027283
Type: Friendly Action
Affiliation: FRIEND

	Enemy	Friend	Civilian	Host Nation
Killed in Action	0	0	0	0
Wounded in Action	0	0	0	0

USSF FINDS CACHE IN VILLAGE OF WALU TANGAY: USSF CONDUCTED A MEET AND GREET IN THE VILLAGE OF WALU TANGAY. USSF MEMBERS WERE APPROACHED BY A LOCAL BOY WHO SPOKE OF A CACHE IN A CAVE ON A NEARBY HILL. USSF MEMBERS INVESTIGATED AND FOUND A CACHE CONSISTING OF THIRTEEN 82MM MORTAR ROUNDS, SIXTY RPG ROUNDS, FIFTEEN BOXES 12.7X108MM AMMO (85 ROUNDS PER BOX), FIVE BOXES NON-DISINTEGRATING 12.7X108MM LINK, AND ONE DSHK BARREL LOCATED IN A CAVE AT 350107.26N 0705513.00E. USSF CONFISCATED THE AMMO. THE REST WAS BLOWN IN PLACE.

Reference ID: AFG20040103n1
Latitude: 31.62694931
Date: 2004-01-03 06:06
Category: Cache Found/Cleared
Detained: 0
Region: RC SOUTH
Longitude: 65.7416687
Type: Friendly Action
Affiliation: FRIEND

	Enemy	Friend	Civilian	Host Nation
Killed in Action	0	0	0	0
Wounded in Action	0	0	0	0

(M) KAF PRT REPORTS FINDING ROCKET IVO KAF PRT SITE. MARSHALL 16 SALUTE REPORT AS FOLLOWS: S- 1 X RKT (TYPE UNKNOWN), A- UNK, L- VIC 41RQR 599 023, U- UNK, T- 0630Z, E- UNK, ELEMENT ON SITE SECURING SCENE. 0654Z UPDATE TO KAF PRT RKT: ROCKET IS 107 MM VIC (41 RQR 60060 02337) IS 400 METERS FROM PRT AND IS AIMED AT KAF PRT SITE. EOD IS RESPONDING AT THIS TIME. MARSHALL IS SECURING SITE. PRT HAS BEEN NOTIFIED. UPDATE THE ROCKET WAS TAKEN TO KAF BY EOD.

Reference ID: AFG20040104n2
Latitude: 32.89999008
Date: 2004-01-04 00:12
Category: Cache Found/Cleared
Detained: 0
Region: RC EAST
Longitude: 69.26526642
Type: Friendly Action
Affiliation: FRIEND

	Enemy	Friend	Civilian	Host Nation
Killed in Action	0	0	0	0
Wounded in Action	0	0	0	0

TF 1-87 REPORTS FINDING THREE CACHES SOUTH OF ORGUN-E. S- CACHE, A- CURRENTLY SEARCHING COMPOUND AT 42SWB 2471 3928, L- 42SWB 24815 40239, U- UNK, T- 040933JAN04, E- 19X RPG'S, 2X AT MINES, 6X CASES 82MM MORTAR BOOSTERS, 3X CASES HEAT TABS, 15X RPG BOOSTERS, 3X CLAYMORES, AND 1 107 ROCKET. CACHE AT 42SWB 24815 40239 WAS DESTROYED. AT 1046Z CTF WARRIOR REPORTS TF 1-87 FINDS SECOND CACHE. S- WEAPON CACHE FOUND, A- UNK, L- 42SWB 247 392, U-UNK, T- 040955JAN04, E-FOUND: 30 MINES, 20 RPG ROUNDS, PENCIL TIMERS, DYNAMITE, AND MORTAR ROUNDS (NUMBER UNKNOWN). 1347Z UPDATE FOR THIRD CACHE SOUTH OF ORGUNE. S: 574 X RPG-9 ROUNDS, 700 X RPG-9 BOOSTERS, 1X 40 MM FRONT-LINE ARTILLERY ROUNDS, 18X 82MM MTRS, 1X 82MM MTR RND (US MADE), 10X ROLLS OF DET CORD, 70X LAND-MINE BOOSTERS, 100X BLASTING CAPS, 10X M5

Reference ID: AFG20040106n1
Latitude: 32.79249954
Date: 2004-01-06 00:12
Category: Cache Found/Cleared
Detained: 0

Region: RC EAST
Longitude: 69.08860779
Type: Friendly Action
Affiliation: FRIEND

	Enemy	Friend	Civilian	Host Nation
Killed in Action	0	0	0	0
Wounded in Action	0	0	0	0

CACHE FOUND INSIDE OF THE SAROBI GOVERNMENT COMPOUND: A CACHE WAS DISCOVERED IN A BACK ROOM OF A GOVERNMENT COMPOUND IVO 3247.557N 06905.319E IN SAROBI. THE GOVERNOR COMPOUND MISSION WAS TO PROVIDE MEDICAL, VETERINARY AND HUMANITARIAN AID ASSISTANCE. THE CACHE CONSISTED OF THE FOLLOWING: 574 X RPG-9 ROUNDS; 700 X RPG-9 BOOSTERS; 1 X 40MM FRONT LINE ARTILLERY ROUNDS; 18 X 82MM MORTAR ROUNDS; 1 X 82MM MORTAR ROUND (US MFG); 10 X ROLLS OF TRIP WIRE; 10 X ROLLS OF DET CORD; 70 X TNT TYPE LAND MINE BOOSTER; 100 X BLASTING CAPS; 10 X M-5 MOUSE TRAPS 5 BOXES WITH 2 PER BOX; 35 X U/I TYPE LAND MINE BOOSTERS; 30 X TIME PENCILS (7 GREEN, 7 YELLOW, 7 WHITE, 9 RED); 50 X SQUIBS; 68 X OZ STRIKER FUSES; 12 X MK-7 AT MINE WITH FUSES; 6 X ITALIAN 2.4 AT MINE; 7 X ITALIAN TC-6 AT MINE; 1 X PAKISTANI TM-46 AT MINE.
(S//REL ISAF) THE MAYOR, MOHAMMAD GUL, AND THE CHIEF OF POLICE, ABDUL BAQI, WERE ABSENT, WITH THE MAYOR REPORTEDLY IN SHARONA AND THE POLICE CHIEF IN GOWMAL. HABIB ULLAH, A POLICE OFFICER, AND NEMAT ULLAH, THE SECOND IN COMMAND FOR THE POLICE DEPARTMENT BOTH SAID THAT FOUR PEOPLE KNEW OF THE CACHE: ABDUL BAQI, SAGEEN FROM NAKA, DAWLAT KHAN (PAKTIKA PROVINCE POLICE CHIEF) FROM KHUORJANA, AND GOVERNOR MOHAMMAD ALI JALALI. THEY WERE BOTH SCARED THAT THE CACHE WOULD BE GONE WHEN THE MAYOR AND POLICE CHIEF RETURNED. HABIB ASKED FOR A LETTER DECLARING THAT US FORCES TOOK THE CACHE AND THAT THE TWO INDIVIDUALS DID NOT VOLUNTARILY HAND OVER THE CACHE. THEY SAID THAT THE ITEMS WERE THERE FROM THE PREVIOUS LEADERSHIP AT

LEAST THREE MONTHS AGO. THEY CLAIMED THAT THEY DID NOT KNOW THE EXACT SOURCE OF THE CACHE.

Reference ID: AFG20040108n4
Latitude: 34.21749878
Date: 2004-01-08 00:12
Category: Cache Found/Cleared
Detained: 0

Region: RC EAST
Longitude: 70.33305359
Type: Friendly Action
Affiliation: FRIEND

	Enemy	Friend	Civilian	Host Nation
Killed in Action	0	0	0	0
Wounded in Action	0	0	0	0

(M) USSF LOCATE AND DESTROY TWO ROCKETS IN NANGARHAR PROVINCE: USSF RECEIVED INTELLIGENCE INFORMING THEM OF TWO ROCKETS EMPLACED WITH FUSES AIMED TOWARDS THE JALALABAD AIRFIELD. WHEN USSF LINKED UP WITH THEIR MOBILE REACTION FORCE ESCORT, THE MRF COMMANDER INFORMED USSF THAT A ROCKET HAD IMPACTED NEAR THE JALALABAD AIRFIELD IVO 342408.90N 0702953.31E THE NIGHT BEFORE (04 JAN 04).
(S//REL GCTF) ON 05 JAN 04, USSF AND MRF ARRIVED IVO 341302.82N 0701958.83E AND COULD NOT DRIVE ANY FURTHER. TWO ROCKETS AND TWO FUSES COVERED BY ROCKS WERE FOUND. USSF BLEW THE ROCKETS IN PLACE. (NFI)

Reference ID: AFG20040110n4
Latitude: 33.39167023
Date: 2004-01-10 00:12
Category: Cache Found/Cleared
Detained: 0

Region: RC EAST
Longitude: 69.95276642
Type: Friendly Action
Affiliation: FRIEND

	Enemy	Friend	Civilian	Host Nation
Killed in Action	0	0	0	0
Wounded in Action	0	0	0	0

TF 1-501 REPORTS CACHE FOUND BEHIND HOUSES NORTH OF FB SALERNO. S-20X-30X DSHKA BARRELS, A- FOUND IN A HOLE 20-30FT DEEP BEHIND THE HOUSES, L- 42SWB 886 951, T- 1137Z.

Reference ID: AFG20040110n8
Latitude: 33.54693985
Date: 2004-01-10 00:12
Category: Cache Found/Cleared
Detained: 0

Region: RC EAST
Longitude: 69.08389282
Type: Friendly Action
Affiliation: FRIEND

	Enemy	Friend	Civilian	Host Nation
Killed in Action	0	0	0	0
Wounded in Action	0	0	0	0

USSF RECOVERS CACHE IVO SAHAK (GARDEZ) ON 07 JAN 04 USSF SEARCHED 2 COMPOUNDS FOR A SUSPECTED AMMUNITION CACHE SITE IVO THE

VILLAGE OF SAHAK. COMPOUND 1 IS LOCATED AT 333248.61N 0690502.43E AND COMPOUND 2 IS LOCATED AT N 333218.58N 0690445.31E.

(S//REL TO USA AND GCTF) IN COMPOUND #1 THE FOLLOWING ITEMS WERE RECOVERED: 1 X RCIED (TRANSMITTER, RECEIVER W/ BLASTING CAP, EXPLOSIVE DEVICE), POMZ STICK MINE BODY, 1 X .303 ENFIELD RIFLE, 1 X AK47, 4 X AK47 MAGAZINES, 1 X BOX; 1 X BAG OF 7.62 AMMUNITION, 1 X BOX OF .303 AMMUNITION AND MISCELLANEOUS PAPERS, DOCUMENTS AND PICTURES. INITIAL REVIEW OF DOCUMENT EVIDENCE SEIZED FROM THE ROOM OF NAZAR KHAN AND SAID MOHAMMAD SHOWS LETTER TO/FROM SAMOOT AND NAZAR KHAN AS WELL AS TB RECEIPTS FOR WEAPONS. (A FULL REPORT IS EXPECTED).

(S//REL TO USA AND GCTF) THE RCIED WAS FOUND BURIED APPROXIMATELY; UNDERGROUND, WRAPPED IN A PLASTIC BAG. COMPONENTS WERE A WIRELESS DOORBELL TRANSMITTER AND RECEIVER. THE ACTUAL EXPLOSIVE WAS CONTAINED INSIDE A METAL PIPE. BOTH THE TRANSMITTER AND RECEIVER HAD BEEN MODIFIED (TRANSISTORS AND CAPACITORS SOLDERED TO CIRCUIT BOARDS) TO INCREASE THE RANGE OF THE DEVICE. THE BUZZER/SPEAKER HAD BEEN REMOVED FROM THE RECEIVER AND REPLACED WITH A NON-ELECTRIC DETONATOR (MODIFIED WITH AN ELECTRIC SQUIB AND WIRE LEADS). THE PUSH BUTTON ON THE TRANSMITTER CASE WAS REMOVED TO EXPOSE A RECESSED MICRO-SWITCH TO PREVENT ACCIDENTAL INITIATION OF DEVICE. THERE IS NO BRAND NAME ON THE UNIT, BUT IT STATES CHANNEL 301 ON BOTH PIECES. A 9-VOLT BATTERY POWERED THE TRANSMITTER AND 2 AA BATTERIES POWERED THE RECEIVER. THE PIPE BOMB IS 200MM IN LENGTH AND 50MM IN DIAMETER. EOD ASSESSMENT IS THAT THIS IED WAS FULLY FUNCTIONAL AND THE PIPE WAS POSSIBLY DESIGNED AS A BOOSTER TO BE USED IN THE FUSE WELL OF A LARGE MUNITION. SMALL PIECES OF CLOTH WERE TIED INTO THE BRANCHES OF A TREE ABOVE THE BURIED IED. THIS IS BELIEVED TO BE A FLAG/LOAD SIGNAL FOR HELP IN LOCATING THE DEVICE.

(S//REL TO USA AND GCTF) I

Reference ID: AFG20040111n1
Latitude: 33.75999832
Date: 2004-01-11 00:12
Category: Cache Found/Cleared
Detained: 0

Region: RC EAST
Longitude: 69.48665619
Type: Friendly Action
Affiliation: FRIEND

	Enemy	Friend	Civilian	Host Nation
Killed in Action	0	0	0	0
Wounded in Action	0	0	0	0

USSF RECOVERS CACHE IVO KHALILAN VILLAGE: USSF RECOVERED A CACHE DURING A PATROL NORTH OF GARDEZ. THE CACHE, IVO KHALILAN (334536N 692912E), CONSISTED OF VARIOUS ITEMS TO INCLUDE: ONE RCIED (PIPE BOMB), ONE CASE DETONATION CORD (APPROX. 100 FT.), NINETY-ONE 82MM MORTAR ROUNDS (RUSSIAN), NINETY-EIGHT 82MM MORTAR ROUNDS (CHINESE), NINE POM-Z STICK MINES, FORTY M-6 FUSES, ELEVEN 82MM MORTAR PROPELLANT CHARGES, TWENTY-FIVE BOXES DHSK

ROUNDS, NINETEEN 107MM ARTILLERY ROUNDS (CHINESE). EOD X-RAYED THEN SHOT THE END CAP OFF OF THE PIPE. THE DEVICE CONTAINED AN ELECTRIC SQUIB IN BAG OF SMOKELESS POWDER. NO MAIN CHARGE WAS PRESENT, BUT DUE TO SMELL AND MOISTURE PRESENT INSIDE PIPE, EOD SUSPECTS THAT LIQUID FUEL WAS PRESENT. EOD STATES THAT A WELL-TRAINED INDIVIDUAL MANUFACTURED THE RCIED. THE WIRES WERE SHUNTED AND THEN COVERED BY ALUMINUM TAPE.

Reference ID: AFG20040111n5
Latitude: 32.37778091
Date: 2004-01-11 00:12
Category: Cache Found/Cleared
Detained: 0
Region: RC WEST
Longitude: 62.11943817
Type: Friendly Action
Affiliation: FRIEND

	Enemy	Friend	Civilian	Host Nation
Killed in Action	0	0	0	0
Wounded in Action	0	0	0	0

(S//REL TO USA, GCTF AND /ISAF) WEAPONS CACHE FOUND: EOD TEAM DISPOSED OF 13,000 POUNDS OF EXPLOSIVE WEIGHT REMOVED FROM THREE MUNITIONS CACHES ADJACENT TO THE AIRFIELD. (MINISTRY OF TRANSPORTATION) MOT-1 ENCOUNTERED A WEAPONS CACHE AT 324514.73N 0623528.09E. THE CACHE SITE IS DIRECTLY OFF OF HIGHWAY 1, A FEW KM NORTH OF JUNCTION WITH HIGHWAY 517 TO FARAH CITY (322239.59N 0620710.33E). THIS CACHE IS LOCATED IN THE AREA WHERE ATTACKS AGAINST AFGHAN NGO EMPLOYEES AND BANDITRY ALONG HIGHWAY 1 HAVE BEEN REPORTED.

Reference ID: AFG20040117n3
Latitude: 32.90528107
Date: 2004-01-17 00:12
Category: Cache Found/Cleared
Detained: 0
Region: RC EAST
Longitude: 69.26721954
Type: Friendly Action
Affiliation: FRIEND

	Enemy	Friend	Civilian	Host Nation
Killed in Action	0	0	0	0
Wounded in Action	0	0	0	0

(S//REL GCTF) CACHE RECOVERY IVO SHEY KHAN: ON THE NIGHT OF 14 JAN 04, A WALK-IN CONTACT FROM SHEY KHAN REPORTED THE PRESENCE OF A CACHE IN THE PIR KOWTI VALLEY, NORTH OF SHEY KHAN (IVO 3253.874N 06916.039E). THE CONTACT STATED THAT THERE WAS A SMALL CACHE OF AMMUNITION BURIED IN THE SIDE OF THE MOUNTAIN AND OFFERED TO LEAD US TO THE CACHE. HE STATED THAT HE DID NOT WANT TO BE SEEN LEADING US TO THE CACHE AND WE ASSURED HIM THAT HE COULD REMAIN IN OUR VEHICLE DISGUISED. THE CONTACT AGREED, BUT MADE INTIMATION THAT HE EXPECTED TO BE PAID FOR HIS TROUBLE. THE CACHE CONSISTED OF THE FOLLOWING: FIFTEEN HUNDRED 7.62 X 39MM ROUNDS, TWENTY-FOUR 82MM MORTAR ROUNDS, SEVENTEEN HUNDRED 12.7MM API ROUNDS, TWENTY FIVE HUNDRED 12.7MM BALL ROUNDS, TWENTY CANS OF 14.5MM BALL AMMUNITION, TWELVE DSHK METAL LINK

BELTS, SIX ANTI-PERSONNEL MINES. THE CACHE WAS LOCATED AT 3254.318N 06916.040E.

Reference ID: AFG20040119n5
Latitude: 30.99555969
Date: 2004-01-19 00:12
Category: Cache Found/Cleared
Detained: 0

Region: RC SOUTH
Longitude: 66.28943634
Type: Friendly Action
Affiliation: FRIEND

	Enemy	Friend	Civilian	Host Nation
Killed in Action	0	0	0	0
Wounded in Action	0	0	0	0

(S//REL GCTF) CACHE FOUND TO THE WEST OF SPIN BOLDAK: DURING A PATROL IN THE VICINITY OF SPIN BOLDAK FB ON DECEMBER 11TH, A VILLAGER TOLD A TF WARRIOR PATROL THERE WERE SEVERAL ROCKETS HIDDEN NEAR HIS VILLAGE. THIS VILLAGER BELONGS TO THE LOCAL SOURCES NETWORK THAT A US FORCES ELEMENT HAS BEEN BUILDING FOR THE PAST FEW MONTHS. THE CACHE IS LOCATED SIX KILOMETERS WEST OF THE FB IVO 305943.75N 0661721.73E. THE CACHE WAS DUG IN THE SAND AND LOCATED ONE HUNDRED METERS AWAY FROM A VILLAGE. IT WAS 2 METERS LARGE, 4 METERS LONG AND 1.50 METERS DEEP. THE CACHE CONTAINED THE FOLLOWING: TWELVE 122MM ROCKETS, SEVENTY-FOUR 107MM ROCKETS, NINETEEN 100MM SHELLS, TWENTY 122 MM FUSES, ONE HUNDRED - 107MM FUSES, ONE HUNDRED AND TWENTY BOXES OF 14.5MM CARTRIDGES AND AROUND ONE THOUSAND 14.5 MM AND 12.7 MM MIXED CARTRIDGES. THE MUNITIONS HAVE SOVIET AND CHINESE ORIGIN.

Reference ID: AFG20040221n4
Latitude: 31.62055016
Date: 2004-02-21 00:12
Category: Cache Found/Cleared
Detained: 0

Region: RC SOUTH
Longitude: 65.89943695
Type: Friendly Action
Affiliation: FRIEND

	Enemy	Friend	Civilian	Host Nation
Killed in Action	0	0	0	0
Wounded in Action	0	0	0	0

3-6 FA REPORTS FINDING CACHE NE OF KANDAHAR. S- 12X 107MM ROCKETS, A- FOUND DURING PATROL, L- 41R QR 75030204, T- 0730Z. ROCKETS FOUND DURING MP PATROL EAST OF KANDAHAR CITY. EOD MOVING TO THE SCENE AND WILL MAKE ASSESSMENT TO MOVE ROCKETS OR DESTROY IN PLACE. NFI.

Reference ID: AFG20040228n8
Latitude: 34.32276917
Date: 2004-02-28 00:12
Category: Cache Found/Cleared
Detained: 0

Region: RC CAPITAL
Longitude: 69.38054657
Type: Friendly Action
Affiliation: FRIEND

	Enemy	Friend	Civilian	Host Nation
Killed in Action	0	0	0	0
Wounded in Action	0	0	0	0

CJSOTF-A REPORTS RECOVERING 2X CACHES IVO ZORMAT AND SHARONA. S- 14X AK-47 TYPE RIFLES, PKM MACHINE GUN, NUMEROUS RDS OF MIXED AMMUNITION, RPG-7 LAUNCHER, 10X RPG ROCKETS, MISC. DOCUMENTS, A- CJSOTF-A ELEMENT WITH ANA DISCOVERED CACHE DURING CONOP, L- IVO SWAK AREA (42S WC 350 980), T- 28900ZFEB04. SALT REPORT FOR 2ND CACHE TO FOLLOW. S- 1X ANTI-TANK MINE, 3X RPG RDS, A- LN LED ODA 2075 TO CACHE, L- IVO SHARONA (42SUB 812687), T- 28900ZFEB04. REMARKS: EOD DESTROYED MINE IN PLACE. NFI

Reference ID: AFG20040301n10
Latitude: 34.19971848
Date: 2004-03-01 00:12
Category: Cache Found/Cleared
Detained: 0
Region: RC EAST
Longitude: 70.15721893
Type: Friendly Action
Affiliation: FRIEND

	Enemy	Friend	Civilian	Host Nation
Killed in Action	0	0	0	0
Wounded in Action	0	0	0	0

CJSOTF-A REPORTS CACHE FOUND DURING PATROL IVO TORA BORA. SALT REPORT TO FOLLOW. S- APPROX 1000+ ASSORTED MORTAR AND ARTILERY ROUNDS, A- DISCOVERED CACHE DURING PATROL, L- VICINTY WAZIR VALLEY, TORA BORA (42S XC 0661 8492), T- 010500ZMAR04. REMARKS: ALL SERVICABLE ROUNDS WILL BE TRANSPORTED TO THE MRF COMPOUND, ODA WILL SUPERVISE THE MRF IN THE DESTRUCTION OF ALL UNSERVACABLE ROUNDS, ACCURATE ROUND COUNT WILL BE SENT LATER. NFI.

Reference ID: AFG20040302n7
Latitude: 33.32387924
Date: 2004-03-02 00:12
Category: Cache Found/Cleared
Detained: 0
Region: RC EAST
Longitude: 69.93250275
Type: Friendly Action
Affiliation: FRIEND

	Enemy	Friend	Civilian	Host Nation
Killed in Action	0	0	0	0
Wounded in Action	0	0	0	0

SMALL CACHE RECOVERED IVO KHOWST: ON 02 MAR 04, A USSF PATROL WAS IVO 331926N 0695557E WHEN THEY WERE APPROACHED BY LOCAL CLAIMING KNOWLEDGE OF NEIGHBOR WHO WAS AN EX- TALIBAN (TB) MEMBER. THE LOCAL CLAIMED HE HAD SEEN HIS NEIGHBOR RECENTLY HIDING WEAPONS IN HIS HOME. THE LOCAL ALSO SAID HE WITNESSED APPROXIMATELY TEN VEHICLES GOING IN AND OUT OF THE NEIGHBOR'S COMPOUND ON A DAILY BASIS. WHEN SURROGATE FORCES LOOKED AT THE NEIGHBOR'S HOME FROM OVER A WALL, AN ANTENNAE SYSTEM (MULTI-PRONGED HOUR GLASS SHAPED DIPOLE) WAS SPOTTED ON THE ROOF. THE AMF THEN CONDUCTED A CORDON AND SEARCH OF THE

NEIGHBOR'S COMPOUND. THE FOLLOWING ITEMS WERE FOUND: ONE FN-FAL PAKISTANI MADE ASSAULT RIFLE, ONE DI-POLE ANTENNAE, 2 X MICRO-CASSETTE RECORDERS WITH TAPES (BEING INTERPRETED), 2 X CHEST RIGS, SEVERAL LOADED MAGAZINES AND LOOSE FN-FAL AMMO, AND ONE HOME-MADE RADIO SYSTEM.

Reference ID: AFG20040312n12
Latitude: 32.19194031
Date: 2004-03-12 00:12
Category: Cache Found/Cleared
Detained: 0
Region: RC EAST
Longitude: 68.36472321
Type: Friendly Action
Affiliation: FRIEND

	Enemy	Friend	Civilian	Host Nation
Killed in Action	0	0	0	0
Wounded in Action	0	0	0	0

(S//REL GCTF) CJSOTF-A REPORTS FINDING CACHE DURING CORDON AND SEARCH SW OF SHKIN. S- (4)X RPG RDS WITH BOOSTERS AND WEAPONS CLEANING MATERIALS. A- ODA 2074 DISCOVERED CACHE DURING COMPOUND SEARCH, L- 42SVA4013161899, T- 121320ZMAR04. NFI.

Reference ID: AFG20040325n11
Latitude: 33.29917145
Date: 2004-03-25 00:12
Category: Cache Found/Cleared
Detained: 0
Region: RC EAST
Longitude: 69.91443634
Type: Friendly Action
Affiliation: FRIEND

	Enemy	Friend	Civilian	Host Nation
Killed in Action	0	0	0	0
Wounded in Action	0	0	0	0

TF 1-501 CONDUCTED SENSITIVE SITE EXPLOTATION SOUTH OF KHOWST. S- CACHE, A- SSEL WB8514 8484, T- 1245Z, E- 2 AK-47, 1 ENFIELD RIFLE, 1 ICOM RADIO, 2 CELL PHONES, PAKISTANI PASSPORTS, AND LARGE AMOUNT OF AMMUNITION.

Reference ID: AFG20040328n12
Latitude: 31.61667061
Date: 2004-03-28 00:12
Category: Cache Found/Cleared
Detained: 0
Region: RC SOUTH
Longitude: 65.71665955
Type: Friendly Action
Affiliation: FRIEND

	Enemy	Friend	Civilian	Host Nation
Killed in Action	0	0	0	0
Wounded in Action	0	0	0	0

(S//REL GCTF) AT 281217ZMAR04, TF 3-6 FA FOUND A CACHE WHILE CLEARING A TEXTILE FACTORY IN AO EISENHOWER IVO KANDAHAR CITY. THE CACHE CONTAINED 2000 X ENFIELD RIFLES, 50-70 X 82MM & 120MM MORTAR ROUNDS, 1 X DSHK, 50 X AP ROUNDS, 1 X RPK (9MM), RPGS ROUNDS, 50 X CASES OF 23MM AMMO, 20-30 RPGS LAUNCHERS (OLD), 2 X

82MM RECOILLESS RIFLE, NUMEROUS AP MINES, DET CORD, AND 7 X 107MM FUSES. NFI.

Reference ID: AFG20040402n9
Latitude: 33.99528122
Date: 2004-04-02 00:12
Category: Cache Found/Cleared
Detained: 0

Region: RC EAST
Longitude: 68.64916992
Type: Friendly Action
Affiliation: FRIEND

	Enemy	Friend	Civilian	Host Nation
Killed in Action	0	0	0	0
Wounded in Action	0	0	0	0

TF 2-87 RECOVERS CACHE AND DETAINS L/N NE OF GHAZNI. SALUTE REPORT FOLLOWS: S-(1) DETAINEE (NAME: NAMIJULLAH) A-AFTER DETAINING THE INDIVIDUAL, THE WOMAN OF THE COMPOUND REMOVED THEIR BURKAS AND SHOWED US FORCES CONTRABAND ENCASED WITHIN THE COMPOUND WALLS THAT CONTAINED 100 X GRENADES AND 100 BLOCKS OF PLASTIC EXPLOSIVE (4" X 2"). SEARCH OF COMPOUND CONTINUES. L-VC 676617 (NEAREST COMPOUND TO OBJ ANCHOR) U-UNK T-0836 E-100 X GRENADES/100 X BLOCKS OF PLASTIC EXPLOSIVES. TF STONEWALL IS CURRENTLY CONTACTING THE HARC FOR ANY INFORMATION ON NAMIJULLAH. UPDATE: 100X82MM RDS, DETERMINED UNSTABLE BY EOD (FUSE, CORRODED), WILL DESTORY. UNDETERMINED AMOUNT AND CALIBER OF SMALL ARMS AMMO, WILL BE DESTROYED. ADDITION TO EARLIER REPORT OF 85 X 82MM MORTAR RDS- 1XSM BOX OF BLASTING CAPS

Reference ID: AFG20040408n16
Latitude: 32.78887939
Date: 2004-04-08 00:12
Category: Cache Found/Cleared
Detained: 0

Region: RC EAST
Longitude: 69.0938797
Type: Friendly Action
Affiliation: FRIEND

	Enemy	Friend	Civilian	Host Nation
Killed in Action	0	0	0	0
Wounded in Action	0	0	0	0

CTF WARRIOR REPORTS 3X DETAINED FROM CORDON AND SEARCH IVO SAROBI, SALT REPORT FOLLOWS: S-3X DETAINEES, A-FOUND A BOX OF DEMOLITIONS AT A BAKERY DETAINED 3XPAXS, DETONATORS AND FUSES TO 107MM ROCKETS, U.S. ELEMENTS HAVE CONTROL OVER EXPLOSIVES, L-42SWB 088 279 IVO SAROBI, T- 0031Z 08 APR 04.

Reference ID: AFG20040505n12
Latitude: 34.52471924
Date: 2004-05-05 00:12
Category: Cache Found/Cleared
Detained: 0

Region: RC EAST
Longitude: 68.78250122
Type: Friendly Action
Affiliation: FRIEND

	Enemy	Friend	Civilian	Host Nation
Killed in Action	0	0	0	0
Wounded in Action	0	0	0	0

(S//REL GCTF) 5 MAY: AN ISAF SPOKESMAN REPORTED THE SEIZURE OF A LARGE WEAPONS CACHE 34 KM WEST OF KABUL CITY. THE CACHE INCLUDED 650 ARTILLERY AND MORTAR ROUNDS AND COULD HAVE BEEN USED FOR AN EXTREMIST ATTACK ON THE AFGHAN CAPITAL. AFGHAN SECURITY OFFICERS WERE REPORTED TO HAVE ARRESTED 7 SUSPECTS AND SEIZED A HOME MADE BOMB IN A SEPARATE OPERATION IN THE CITY. (RSO)

Reference ID: AFG20040521n12
Latitude: 33.94610977
Date: 2004-05-21 09:09
Category: Cache Found/Cleared
Detained: 0
Region: RC EAST
Longitude: 69.69471741
Type: Friendly Action
Affiliation: FRIEND

	Enemy	Friend	Civilian	Host Nation
Killed in Action	0	0	0	0
Wounded in Action	0	0	0	0

(S//REL GCTF) CJSOTF REPORTS A LARGE CACHE OF HEAVY WEAPONS AND ORDINANCE 90K SW OF JALALABAD. ESTIMATED 200X 82MM MORTARS, 2X OR MORE DSHKS, MULTIPLE MORTAR TUBES, 1X US MORTAR SIGHT, 1X TRAILER/DSHK MOUNT, ALL KINDS OF AMMO FOR IT, AP MINES.

Reference ID: AFG20040523n23
Latitude: 33.5625
Date: 2004-05-23 01:01
Category: Cache Found/Cleared
Detained: 0
Region: RC EAST
Longitude: 69.8861084
Type: Friendly Action
Affiliation: FRIEND

	Enemy	Friend	Civilian	Host Nation
Killed in Action	0	0	0	0
Wounded in Action	0	0	0	0

(S//REL GCTF) USSF REPORTS CACHE FOUND IVO SALERNO: ON 23 MAY 04 AT 0120Z, THERE WAS A CACHE FOUND IN AN UNDERGROUND COMPOUND FILLED WITH GRAIN (333345.96N 695310.83E). THE CACHE CONSISTED OF SIX RECOILLESS HEAT ROUNDS, FIFTY 82MM HEAT FUSES, ONE 107MM FUSES, ONE HUNDRED AND TWENTY 20MM ROUNDS, EIGHT HUNDRED AND TWENTY FIVE API DSHKA ROUNDS, ONE RPK, ONE THOUSAND TWO HUNDRED AND TWENTY AP DSHKA ROUNDS. (23 MAY 04, SIGACT #6363)

Reference ID: AFG20040706n33
Latitude: 34.00582886
Date: 2004-07-06 14:02
Category: Cache Found/Cleared
Detained: 0
Region: RC EAST
Longitude: 69.26055145
Type: Friendly Action
Affiliation: FRIEND

	Enemy	Friend	Civilian	Host Nation
Killed in Action	0	0	0	0
Wounded in Action	0	0	0	0

(S//REL GCTF) PMO REPORTS 551ST RECOVERED A LARGE CACHE 2000 METERS NW OF BAF. SALT REPORT AS FOLLOWS: S- 75X ROUNDS OF RECOILLESS RIFLE 88MM, 62X HEAT ROUNDS, 13X FRAG HIGH EXPLOSIVE ANTI TANK ROUNDS AND 40LBS OF BULK TNT. ALL CLOSE TO THE SAME AREA, THERE WAS A STASH OF 3,000X AIRCRAFT FLARES. A- N/A. L- GRID AS FOLLOWS: 42S WD 234 696 (2000M NW OF BAF). T- 1430Z. AFOSI REPORTED THAT CACHE WAS IN A VERY GOOD CONDITION, ORIGINAL PACKAGING, ESTIMATING THAT IT HAD BEEN THERE LESS THAN A MONTH. OSI, 551 MP AND AF EOD CONDUCTED A CONTROLLED DETONATION AND DESTROYED ITEMS.

Reference ID: AFG20041206n77
Latitude: 35.04027939
Date: 2004-12-06 07:07
Category: Cache Found/Cleared
Detained: 0

Region: RC EAST
Longitude: 69.27749634
Type: Friendly Action
Affiliation: FRIEND

	Enemy	Friend	Civilian	Host Nation
Killed in Action	0	0	0	0
Wounded in Action	0	0	0	0

TF EAGLE REPORTS CACHE 8K N BAF. AT 0707Z THE FOLLOWING SALT REPORT WAS SENT: S- 6X 107MM ROCKETS, A- ROCKETS AIMED AT 180 DEGREES W/ ELEVATION OF 40 DEGREES TOWARDS BAF. L- 42S WD 2531 7756. T- 0700Z. REMARKS: OSI INTERVIEWED L/N WHO FOUND DEVICE. OSI AND AF EOD CONFISCATED ROCKETS AND AIMING DEVICES. UPDATE 0726Z: ALL ROCKETS WERE WIRED TO ELECTONIC DEVICES. DEVICES WERE ALSO CONFISCATED BY OSI.

Reference ID: AFG20050201n67
Latitude: 31.64999962
Date: 2005-02-01 12:12
Category: Cache Found/Cleared
Detained: 0

Region: RC SOUTH
Longitude: 64.94999695
Type: Friendly Action
Affiliation: FRIEND

	Enemy	Friend	Civilian	Host Nation
Killed in Action	0	0	0	0
Wounded in Action	0	0	0	0

TF STEEL REPORTS CACHE 40K SE GERESHK. SALT FOLLOWS: S- 9X AK-47, 2X RPGS, 31X MAGAZINES, 26X RPG ROUNDS, 3X PKM, 2X BELTS (DRUM), 9X AMMO VESTS, 2X PINEAPPLE HAND GRENADES, A- CACHE CONFISCATED FROM UNAUTHORIZED PERSONNEL MANNING AN ILLEGAL CHECKPOINT, L- 41R PR 84880 04494, T- 1200Z. REMARKS: ALL ITEMS APPEAR SERVICEABLE. WEAPONS ARE IN TF STEEL POSSESSION FOR DDR PROCESSING. RPG ROUNDS HAVE BEEN TURNED OVER TO EOD.

Reference ID: AFG20050206n94
Latitude: 31.62388039
Date: 2005-02-06 11:11
Category: Cache Found/Cleared
Detained: 0

Region: RC SOUTH
Longitude: 65.52610016
Type: Friendly Action
Affiliation: FRIEND

	Enemy	Friend	Civilian	Host Nation
Killed in Action	0	0	0	0
Wounded in Action	0	0	0	0

TF BRONCO 3-7 FA REPORTS CACHE 13K W KANDAHAR. AT 1114Z THE FOLLOWING SALT REPORT WAS SENT: S- UNK NUMBER OF AP MINES, 1000X RECOILLESS RIFLE ROUNDS, UNK AMOUNT OF DSHK AMMUNITION, 1X SA-7 W/ BATTERY PACK, AND VARIOUS SMALL ARMS, A- CACHE, L- 41R QR 39627 01526, T- 1110Z. REMARKS: CACHE WAS FOUND AT 530TH AMF HQ. CACHE IS SERVICEABLE AND WILL BE TURNED IN TO ASP. SEE IIR 7 398 9730 05 FOR FURTHER DETAILS ON SA-7 CONDITION.

Reference ID: AFG20050211n89
Latitude: 33.36500931
Date: 2005-02-11 13:01
Category: Cache Found/Cleared
Detained: 0

Region: RC WEST
Longitude: 62.29916
Type: Friendly Action
Affiliation: FRIEND

	Enemy	Friend	Civilian	Host Nation
Killed in Action	0	0	0	0
Wounded in Action	0	0	0	0

TF LONGHORN REPORTS ROCKET DISCOVERY 6K SE SHINDAND. AT 1458Z THE FOLLOWING SALT REPORT WAS SENT: S- 2X ROCKETS, A- WIRED TOGETHER ON A TIMING DEVICE, L- 41S MS 3482 9200, T- 1358Z. REMARKS: L/N REPORTED LOCATION OF ROCKETS TO UNIT. EOD ATTEMPTING TO DISARM THE ROCKETS AND BLOW IN PLACE.

Reference ID: AFG20050303n68
Latitude: 34.69556046
Date: 2005-03-03 13:01
Category: Cache Found/Cleared
Detained: 0

Region: RC EAST
Longitude: 70.14305115
Type: Friendly Action
Affiliation: FRIEND

	Enemy	Friend	Civilian	Host Nation
Killed in Action	0	0	0	0
Wounded in Action	0	0	0	0

TF THUNDER REPORTS ROCKETS POINTED TOWARD METHER LAM FOB. AT 1346Z THE FOLLOWING SALT REPORT WAS SENT S: 3X 122MM ROCKETS WITH 6X POINT DETONATING FUSES, 1X REMOTE FIRING SYSTEM A: LIMA 3 RECEIVED HUMIT THAT THERE WERE ROCKETS POINTED TOWARD THE METHER LAM FOB. L: METHER LAM 42S XD 047 399 T: 1320Z REMARKS: LIMA 3 SENT OUT A PATROL TO THE AREA AND DISCOVERED THE ROCKETS AS WELL AS DETAINED 4X INDIVIDUALS IN THE DIRECT VICINITY OF THE ROCKETS FOR QUESTIONING. LIMA 3 IS CURRENTLY SEARCHING THE

VILLAGE IVO THE ROCKETS. UPDATE 1456Z LIMA 3 IS STILL SEARCHING THE VILLAGE WHERE THEY FOUND THE ROCKETS. THE ROCKETS WERE LOCATED IN A BUILDING BUT NO WIRES WERE ATTACHED. EOD AND LIMA QRF IS CURRENTLY IN ROUTE FROM JBAD TO THE VILLIAGE.

Reference ID: AFG20050306n101
Latitude: 33.34276962
Date: 2005-03-06 11:11
Category: Cache Found/Cleared
Detained: 0

Region: RC WEST
Longitude: 62.32915878
Type: Friendly Action
Affiliation: FRIEND

	Enemy	Friend	Civilian	Host Nation
Killed in Action	0	0	0	0
Wounded in Action	0	0	0	0

TF PEACEKEEPER REPORTS CACHE IVO SHINDAND.
(S//REL TO USA, ISAF AND NATO) AT 1139Z, 06 MARCH 2005, TF PEACEKEEPER RECOVERED A CACHE IVO SHINDAND WHILE CONDUCTING AN ANTI-ROCKET PATROL. THE PATROL WAS ALERTED TO A HOUSE THAT WAS UNDER CONSTRUCTION BY A LOCAL NATIONAL. IN THE HOUSE, 41S MS 376 895, TF PEACEKEEPER RECOVERED 4 X RPG ROUNDS, 4 X RPG LAUNCHERS, AND 2 X AK-47S. EOD ASSESSED THE SITUATION AND TOOK POSSESSION OF THE EQUIPMENT. NFI

Reference ID: AFG20050306n104
Latitude: 33.19916916
Date: 2005-03-06 13:01
Category: Cache Found/Cleared
Detained: 0

Region: RC EAST
Longitude: 69.26277161
Type: Friendly Action
Affiliation: FRIEND

	Enemy	Friend	Civilian	Host Nation
Killed in Action	0	0	0	0
Wounded in Action	0	0	0	0

REPORT FROM 2-27/1-508TH FOLLOWS:
S: 20 X RECOILESS RIFLE RDS
A: CACHE RECOVERED
L: 42S WB 245734 (IVO ZEROK)
T: 06 MAR 1343Z
R: THIS IS THE SECOND LOCATION SEARCHED REVEALED BY NDS INFORMANT. LOCAL POLICE RECOVERED THE ABOVE SERVICEABLE MUNITIONS AND BRINGING THEM TO A/2-27. THE 3RD CACHE WILL BE EXPLORED AT FIRST LIGHT ON 07 MAR.

Reference ID: AFG20050311n91
Latitude: 34.89611053
Date: 2005-03-11 08:08
Category: Cache Found/Cleared
Detained: 0

Region: RC EAST
Longitude: 70.30110931
Type: Friendly Action
Affiliation: FRIEND

	Enemy	Friend	Civilian	Host Nation
Killed in Action	0	0	0	0
Wounded in Action	0	0	0	0

TF THUNDER REPORTS CACHE 25K NE OF METHAR LAM. AT 1157Z THE FOLLOWING SALT REPORT WAS SENT: S: 2X RUSSIAN BOLT ACTION RIFLES, 1X SAWED-OFF SHOTGUN, 3X RPG RDS, 3X FRAG GRENADES, 2X ANTENNAS, 1X ICOM RADIO, 1X DETONATOR, A: CACHE, L: 42S XD 189 623 T: 0800Z. REMARKS: CACHE IS SERVICEABLE. CACHE WILL BE BROUGHT BACK TO FOB METHAR LAM FOR DESTRUCTION. DESCRIPTION OF DETONATOR FOUND AT CACHE IS BLACK BOX, "TALL"; WIDE, LONG RED COVER ON TOP WITH WIRES AND ELECTRIC CONNECTORS ON TOP POWERED BY 9 VOLT BATTERIES.

Reference ID: AFG20050319n72
Latitude: 33.16389084
Date: 2005-03-19 05:05
Category: Cache Found/Cleared
Detained: 0

Region: RC SOUTH
Longitude: 66.1727829
Type: Friendly Action
Affiliation: FRIEND

	Enemy	Friend	Civilian	Host Nation
Killed in Action	0	0	0	0
Wounded in Action	0	0	0	0

S: 75X LBS OPIUM, 8X LBS HASHISH, 1X LBS UNK WHITE POWDER, 2X BOXES RANDOM LOOSE SMALL ARMS AMMUNITION, A: CACHE, L: 42S TB 3634 7304 T: 0545Z. REMARKS: ITEMS DISCOVERED IN COMPOUND STATED TO BE THE HOME OF LOCAL ELDER. THIS ELDER IS NOT CURRENTLY PRESENT BUT SAID TO BE VISITING TARIN KOWT.

Reference ID: AFG20050710n131
Latitude: 33.45682907
Date: 2005-07-10 12:12
Category: Cache Found/Cleared
Detained: 3

Region: RC EAST
Longitude: 70.02223206
Type: Friendly Action
Affiliation: FRIEND

	Enemy	Friend	Civilian	Host Nation
Killed in Action	0	0	0	0
Wounded in Action	0	0	0	0

TF Devil reported a cache 11km NE of Salerno at 0805Z. The cache consisted of 3X AKs, 2X Springfields, 1X K98, 1X PSBL, 1X RPK, 1X double barrel shotgun, 1X RPG launcher, 10X RPG rounds, 12X grenades, 14X mags, 12X dishka rounds, 3000X AK rounds. A TF Devil element went to the town of Yaqubi, Sabari Dist, when ANP asked for help to secure some suspicious individuals causing trouble in the area. TF Devil secured the outer compound and ANP went into the compound. 4X individuals were detained from the compound. 1X PAX was released and 3 PAX were brought back to the RIF. EOD secured the cache and transported it back to SAL for destruction at a later date.

Reference ID: AFG20050821n104
Latitude: 31.00175095
Date: 2005-08-21 05:05
Category: Cache Found/Cleared
Detained: 0

Region: RC SOUTH
Longitude: 66.37818909
Type: Friendly Action
Affiliation: FRIEND

	Enemy	Friend	Civilian	Host Nation
Killed in Action	0	0	0	0
Wounded in Action	0	0	0	0

CJSOTF reports a rocket launch site 2 km W of Spin Buldak at 0551Z. 2x 107mm rockets on improvised launch pads were found. The area was booby trapped with a third rocket. EOD is onsite. 2300Z Update: EOD blew the rockets in place.

Reference ID: AFG20050823n141
Latitude: 34.5273819
Date: 2005-08-23 16:04
Category: Cache Found/Cleared
Detained: 0

Region: RC WEST
Longitude: 65.25213623
Type: Friendly Action
Affiliation: FRIEND

	Enemy	Friend	Civilian	Host Nation
Killed in Action	0	0	0	0
Wounded in Action	0	0	0	0

TF Phoenix reports cache recovery IVO Chagcharan. TF Phoenix reports recovering the following items hidden inside walls and buried up to 4ft deep: 800x 82mm mortars, numerous RPGs, 30x mortar fuses, 2000x armor piercing12.7mm and 14.5mm rounds.

Reference ID: AFG20050916n168
Latitude: 33.47200012
Date: 2005-09-16 13:01
Category: Cache Found/Cleared
Detained: 0

Region: RC EAST
Longitude: 68.89463043
Type: Friendly Action
Affiliation: FRIEND

	Enemy	Friend	Civilian	Host Nation
Killed in Action	0	0	0	0
Wounded in Action	0	0	0	0

TF Devil reports a building with possible explosives in it 13km W of Zormat at 1340Z. A Devil element has setup the outer ring of Cordon and ANA is searching the area under ANP supervision. The information leading to the search came from a reliable source. Nothing siginificant was found in the building.

Reference ID: AFG20051222n180
Latitude: 31.6404705
Date: 2005-12-22 12:12
Category: Cache Found/Cleared
Detained: 0

Region: RC SOUTH
Longitude: 65.72042847
Type: Friendly Action
Affiliation: FRIEND

	Enemy	Friend	Civilian	Host Nation
Killed in Action	0	0	0	0
Wounded in Action	0	0	0	0

(Delayed report) On 22 December, TF Bayonet reported a cache in Kandahar City. ANP searched a cemetery based on source reporting and found 20 x AP mines. The type of mines was unknown. ANP secured the mines and transported them to Kandahar City ANP HQ. Comment: This is the 5th cache uncovered in a cemetery since AUG 05.41R QR 580 038 The cache was transported to KAF and destroyed.

Reference ID: AFG20060113n202
Latitude: 34.54756165
Date: 2006-01-13 13:01
Category: Cache Found/Cleared
Detained: 1

Region: RC CAPITAL
Longitude: 69.25415039
Type: Friendly Action
Affiliation: FRIEND

	Enemy	Friend	Civilian	Host Nation
Killed in Action	0	0	0	0
Wounded in Action	0	0	0	0

TF Phoenix reported cache discovered IVO Kabul. At 1323Z TF Phoenix reported two 107mm mortar discovered in the back of a LN truck. EOD cleared the truck and KCP detained the LN.

Reference ID: AFG20060117n224
Latitude: 31.61455917
Date: 2006-01-17 12:12
Category: Cache Found/Cleared
Detained: 0

Region: RC SOUTH
Longitude: 65.75128174
Type: Friendly Action
Affiliation: FRIEND

	Enemy	Friend	Civilian	Host Nation
Killed in Action	0	0	0	0
Wounded in Action	0	0	0	0

(Delayed report) On 17 January, TF Bayonet reported 2 x artillery shells found in Kandahar City. The artillery shell were being transported on a donkey. The person associated with the donkey evaded AHP forces.

Reference ID: AFG20060216n226
Latitude: 34.92354202
Date: 2006-02-16 09:09
Category: Cache Found/Cleared
Detained: 0

Region: RC EAST
Longitude: 69.28028107
Type: Friendly Action
Affiliation: FRIEND

	Enemy	Friend	Civilian	Host Nation
Killed in Action	0	0	0	0
Wounded in Action	0	0	0	0

A LN reported to TF Eagle that he knew the location of a cache site 3km S of BAF. At 1349Z, TF Eagle reported they received a report of a possible cache site. A patrol was sent to the site to verify and a cache was discovered. Cache consisted of: 18x claymores, 15x PMN-2 mines, eight YM-1 mines, four PMN mines, three Type 69 mines, three TM-57 mines, one HOSAM grenade, 12x M6 fuses, and two MJ1 fuses. Cache was recovered and taken to BAF to be destroyed. No damages or injuries were reported.

Reference ID: AFG20060506n313
Latitude: 34.88034058
Date: 2006-05-06 05:05
Category: Cache Found/Cleared
Detained: 0

Region: RC EAST
Longitude: 71.03334808
Type: Friendly Action
Affiliation: FRIEND

	Enemy	Friend	Civilian	Host Nation
Killed in Action	0	0	0	0
Wounded in Action	0	0	0	0

TF Chosin reported 3x cache discovered 5KM E of ABAD. At 0518Z, TF Chosin reported 3x cache discovered containing a spool of wire (possible time fuse or det cord, gas powered jackhammer, 5x AK-47s, 5x bolt action rifles, and 1x PKM, 2x Enfield rifles, 2x RPG rounds, 100+ 7.62mm rds, 12x grenades, 8x grenade fuses, HIG paperwork, and a Afghan icom hand mic. Three males were detained at site and are being questioned. Unit plans on bringing the detainees to ABAD tomorrow.

Reference ID: AFG20060518n331
Latitude: 33.38246155
Date: 2006-05-18 11:11
Category: Cache Found/Cleared
Detained: 0

Region: RC EAST
Longitude: 70.07082367
Type: Friendly Action
Affiliation: FRIEND

	Enemy	Friend	Civilian	Host Nation
Killed in Action	0	0	0	0
Wounded in Action	0	0	0	0

TF Wolfpack reported a LN turned in a cache to QRF and EOD 14 KM N of Khowst PRT. TF Wolfpack reported that a LN (Kimat Gul) turned in 25x AP mines to QRF and EOD team in Ayub Khel. LN was paid according to SRP. NFTR. [UPDATED ON 05/18/2006 2155]:

Reference ID: AFG20060608n307
Latitude: 34.22121048
Date: 2006-06-08 05:05
Category: Cache Found/Cleared
Detained: 0

Region: RC EAST
Longitude: 70.17642212
Type: Friendly Action
Affiliation: FRIEND

	Enemy	Friend	Civilian	Host Nation
Killed in Action	0	0	0	0
Wounded in Action	0	0	0	0

At 0520Z,TF Chosin reported a small cache discovered while conducting a cordon and search of a suspected area linked to a previous IED attacks 35 km SW of JBAD. Patrol discovered 6 tupperware containers (8-10" diameter and 3" deep) containing black powder, a car battery, and wires. TF Paladin recovered the items for exploitation. No individuals have been detained ATT.

Reference ID: AFG20060725n316
Latitude: 34.96210861
Date: 2006-07-25 09:09

Region: RC EAST
Longitude: 71.05496979
Type: Friendly Action

The Afghanistan Papers 83

Category: Cache Found/Cleared   Affiliation: FRIEND
Detained: 0

	Enemy	Friend	Civilian	Host Nation
Killed in Action	0	0	0	0
Wounded in Action	0	0	0	0

At 0932Z, TF Chosin reports a cache found approx 14km E of Camp Blessing. TF Chosin reports US and ANA soldiers found two caches in close proximity of each other in a rock cut out consisting of food (bread, onions), 2 AK-47s with folding stock, 5 AK47 magazines, 200 expended 7.62 casings, bloody bandages, a notebook in URDU described as an IED instruction manual, a black assault vest containing grenades, ammunition belt, brown mens clothing, and a cooking pot. All items will be brought back to Asadabad for further exploitation.

Reference ID: AFG20060911n342   Region: RC SOUTH
Latitude: 31.56671906   Longitude: 65.43357086
Date: 2006-09-11 07:07   Type: Friendly Action
Category: Cache Found/Cleared   Affiliation: FRIEND
Detained: 0

	Enemy	Friend	Civilian	Host Nation
Killed in Action	0	0	0	0
Wounded in Action	0	0	0	0

(DELAYED REPORT) At 0719Z ISAF reported discovering a building filled with garage door openers. A second building which appeared to be a bomb making factory was also discovered 250 meters from the first building. The second building contained 2-3X 500lb bombs. EOD and TF Paladin will exploit and clear both sites.

Reference ID: AFG20061022n460   Region: RC EAST
Latitude: 34.95759201   Longitude: 70.38803101
Date: 2006-10-22 21:09   Type: Friendly Action
Category: Cache Found/Cleared   Affiliation: FRIEND
Detained: 0

	Enemy	Friend	Civilian	Host Nation
Killed in Action	0	0	0	0
Wounded in Action	0	0	0	0

(DELAYED REPORT)At 2200Z Kalagush PRT reports NDS discovered 1x jingle truck and 1x Hilux truck carrying explosives approximately 35km northeast of FOB Mehtar Lam. TF Paladin moved to the site to exploit the findings, and discovered the following: 153x bags of Ammonium Nitrate (finely processed for explosive purposes), and 159x cans of suspected magnesium paste (which multiplies explosive strength 2-3 times). TF Paladin states that only liquid fuel would be needed to create a slurry, and a trigger charge to complete a large explosive device. The material is being confiscated by the Kalagush PRT, and will be disposed of through TF Paladin. NDS is continuing the investigation, and will deliver further details when they are obtained.Update: The bags of ammonium nitrate were farm size, approximately 75 lbs. plastic bags, different lables to include some "sugar" and some in russian. The cans with the metallic substance were about the size of a can of paste wax, and similar in construction, silver in color, no lables. They were inside boxes labled tetracyclene. Event closed at 2228Z. ISAF Tracking number 10-519.

Reference ID: AFG20061112n470
Latitude: 31.60940933
Date: 2006-11-12 07:07
Category: Cache Found/Cleared
Detained: 0

Region: RC SOUTH
Longitude: 66.0820694
Type: Friendly Action
Affiliation: FRIEND

	Enemy	Friend	Civilian	Host Nation
Killed in Action	0	0	0	0
Wounded in Action	0	0	0	0

(Delayed Report) At 120725Z Nov 06, FF reported several fighting men who fled from the patrol when they entered a village 25 km E of KAF (DAMAN District, KANDAHAR Province). A weapons cache was discovered. FF observed males fleeing from location. FF BIPd 200x 20mm and 5x 82 mm. Afterwards they found a tunnel with 300x DISHKA rounds. Rounds were recovered to bring back to KAF. Tunnel was blown. Humanitarian assistance was done with locals, and gained some Intel. Incident closed at 1116Z.

Reference ID: AFG20061126n422
Latitude: 35.04240036
Date: 2006-11-26 10:10
Category: Cache Found/Cleared
Detained: 0

Region: RC EAST
Longitude: 71.23948669
Type: Friendly Action
Affiliation: FRIEND

	Enemy	Friend	Civilian	Host Nation
Killed in Action	0	0	0	0
Wounded in Action	0	0	0	0

(DELAYED REPORT) At 261010ZNOV06 TF Chosin reports discovering 10x RPGs (full system) hidden is haystacks. TF met with village elders and if owner is not turned in, unit will search every house in the village.

Reference ID: AFG20061205n495
Latitude: 32.63666916
Date: 2006-12-05 14:02
Category: Cache Found/Cleared
Detained: 4

Region: RC SOUTH
Longitude: 65.50475311
Type: Friendly Action
Affiliation: FRIEND

	Enemy	Friend	Civilian	Host Nation
Killed in Action	0	0	0	0
Wounded in Action	0	0	0	0

At 051437ZDEC06 CJSOTF elements conducted a combat recon patrol IVO Deh Rawod in order to search for a possible IED cache. The ANA searched several compounds and located 2X Italian AT mines (TC-6) and IED materials including a battery box, batteries, and wire. The mines were destroyed in place and the four brothers that lived in one of the compounds were taken into custody by the patrol.The patrol returned to the FB without incident.

Reference ID: AFG20061212n512
Latitude: 33.43907928
Date: 2006-12-12 12:12
Category: Cache Found/Cleared
Detained: 0

Region: RC EAST
Longitude: 69.27971649
Type: Friendly Action
Affiliation: FRIEND

	Enemy	Friend	Civilian	Host Nation
Killed in Action	0	0	0	0
Wounded in Action	0	0	0	0

(DELAYED REPORT)At 121633ZDEC06 TF Vanguard reports ANA discovered a cache during a cordon and search 2x days ago approximately 14km southeast of FOB Gardez containing the following items: 100x DSHK rounds, 2700x PKM rounds, 1000x AK rds, 23x AK mags, 20x fuses, 200m det cord, 30x bomb fuses, 100m white electrical wire, 100m black electrical wire, 49KG plastic explosives, 2x military tarps, 10x ANA canteens, 10x ammo vests, 4x RPG rds, 1x grenade, 20x rocket/arty fuses, and 20x recoilless rifle rds. ANA forces detained 1x individual in the search (the name of the individual detained was not passed to CF). NFTR.

Reference ID: AFG20061217n496
Latitude: 34.95934296
Date: 2006-12-17 00:12
Category: Cache Found/Cleared
Detained: 0

Region: RC EAST
Longitude: 69.61868286
Type: Friendly Action
Affiliation: FRIEND

	Enemy	Friend	Civilian	Host Nation
Killed in Action	0	0	0	0
Wounded in Action	0	0	0	0

Asad Abad Village, police recovered a cache with 2 AK47s, 1 kg opium, ten rockets, and PK machine gun ammo.

Reference ID: AFG20061225n460
Latitude: 34.1199913
Date: 2006-12-25 13:01
Category: Cache Found/Cleared
Detained: 0

Region: RC EAST
Longitude: 70.25467682
Type: Friendly Action
Affiliation: FRIEND

	Enemy	Friend	Civilian	Host Nation
Killed in Action	0	0	0	0
Wounded in Action	0	0	0	0

(DELAYED REPORT) At 251330ZDEC06, CJSOTF reported a reliable source identified the location of a significant cache. CJSOTF personnel were able to negotiate the removal of the cache from ACM control. Cache consisted of 7 X thermobaric rocket launchers which are in good condition and appeared to be from the same lot number or have similar numbers. NFTR.

Reference ID: AFG20070114n612
Latitude: 32.34777832
Date: 2007-01-14 11:11

Region: RC EAST
Longitude: 68.53988647
Type: Friendly Action

Category: Cache Found/Cleared   Affiliation: FRIEND
Detained: 0

	Enemy	Friend	Civilian	Host Nation
Killed in Action	0	0	0	0
Wounded in Action	0	0	0	0

At 141410ZJAN07 TF Catamount reports ANA/ETTs from Waza Khawa, discovered an IED affiliated cache consisting of the following: approximately 4x detenators (the same type of detonators that were used in an IED against the ANA when ANA RIPd in northern Waza Khawa in October); several burlap bags full of the insides of anti-personnel mines; chest-high cases of armor piercing DSKA rounds; several burlap bags full of MTR charges; several wood crates containing plastic explosives; and artillery Rounds (type and number unknown). ANA were drawn to this location following an ANA soldier receiving a threatening night letter. The trail ended in a small village where the cache was found. ANA/ETTs have the site secured. 0526Z Unit reported discovering a second hidden cache in the same village with AT Mines, DSHKA ammo, mortar rounds and a possible rocket launcher. 0721Z Unit reported Paladin requested additional EOD team and 15 cases of C4 to destroy cache. 0759Z Unit reported cache consisted of: 5k of propellant, approx 150 possibly more grenades, 60x 107 mm rockets, 150 mortar rounds, 122 launcher w/ sight, 22 AT mines w/ 3x boxes fuzes, 2k pkm rds, several hundred Dshka rds, 60 or 70 mm recoilless rifle, 2 pkm barrels and 25 pkm drum magazines. 160600 JAN Unit reported discovering a 3rd and 4th cache site vic the Caches discovered on 14 and 15 JAN. Third Cache consisted of Western 82mm mortar rounds (western, dated 1983), several drums of PKM ammo, several crates of AK47 ammo and magazines and several cases of plastic explosives. Only data on the 4th Cache is that it contains a case of AK47s. 1025Z Unit reported Paladin detained 8 PAX and are moving them to Salerno FDS.At 161250Z EOD completed exploitation and detonation of all Cache items and are RTB. EOD will forward completed report. Event Closed at 161251ZJAN07. ISAF Tracking # 01-236.

Reference ID: AFG20070218n610   Region: RC SOUTH
Latitude: 32.91596985   Longitude: 66.56617737
Date: 2007-02-18 08:08   Type: Friendly Action
Category: Cache Found/Cleared   Affiliation: FRIEND
Detained: 0

	Enemy	Friend	Civilian	Host Nation
Killed in Action	0	0	0	0
Wounded in Action	0	0	0	0

At 0208Z 18 February, C/S F22 reported an IED cache containing blasting caps, wire, partially built IED, insurgent propaganda, battery and battery box. ANA conducted a search of the compound and questioned suspicious individuals. NFI.

Reference ID: AFG20070224n470   Region: RC EAST
Latitude: 34.88063812   Longitude: 70.90950775
Date: 2007-02-24 00:12   Type: Friendly Action
Category: Cache Found/Cleared   Affiliation: FRIEND
Detained: 0

	Enemy	Friend	Civilian	Host Nation
Killed in Action	0	0	0	0
Wounded in Action	0	0	0	0

240045Z A/1-32 IN discovered a small cache and detained one individual while conducting Operation Grab Hatchet. As Attack 6, Attack 40, Attack 21 and ANA approached the village of Marsta Naw while conducting Operation Grab Hatchet, the prophet team picked up iCOM traffic indicating that the CF patrol was being observed. 3 enemy pax were observed by the LRAS team as moving down the draw away from Attack position. Attack 21 engaged 1 enemy pax as he was attempting to flee the area. Attack 21 is currently conducting BDA ATT. In the house, Attack 6 reports that they have 3 RPG rounds, 1 RPG launcher, 5 loaded AK magazines, 2 bolt action rifles. They currently have 3 x pax in custody, plus 1 x returned with them on his own accord. All elements are RTB. NFTR. ISAF Tracking# 02-349.

Reference ID: AFG20070326n545
Latitude: 31.91155052
Date: 2007-03-26 08:08
Category: Cache Found/Cleared
Detained: 0
Region: RC SOUTH
Longitude: 67.58911133
Type: Friendly Action
Affiliation: FRIEND

	Enemy	Friend	Civilian	Host Nation
Killed in Action	0	0	0	0
Wounded in Action	0	0	0	0

At 0820Z TF Zabul reported finding a weapons cache which included detonation cord (time device), IED making materials and US mortars.ISAF#03-536

Reference ID: AFG20070411n631
Latitude: 34.83581924
Date: 2007-04-11 08:08
Category: Cache Found/Cleared
Detained: 1
Region: RC EAST
Longitude: 70.97083282
Type: Friendly Action
Affiliation: FRIEND

	Enemy	Friend	Civilian	Host Nation
Killed in Action	0	0	0	0
Wounded in Action	0	0	0	0

110853Z TF Chosin reports a patrol in Gatigal Bandeh discovered a cache consisting of the following: animals, flour, grain, corn, medical supplies, 1x US litter, clothing, paperwork, photos, 1x TC6 mine, 8x blasting caps, 1x SONY wireless receiver, and ANA have detained 1x adult male (Izat Gul), who had an AK in his possession and whose name was heard frequently in intel reports. The Bandeh was unoccupied, but the items looked recently used. The items will be confiscated by the patrol for further exploitation. NFTR.

Reference ID: AFG20070422n686
Latitude: 33.4100914
Date: 2007-04-22 05:05
Category: Cache Found/Cleared
Detained: 0
Region: RC EAST
Longitude: 68.16536713
Type: Friendly Action
Affiliation: FRIEND

	Enemy	Friend	Civilian	Host Nation
Killed in Action	0	0	0	0
Wounded in Action	0	0	0	0

At approx 24 0550Z APR 2007, C25 finds a cache VIC 42S VA 22394 97062 of 5 grenades, 3 AK-47 magazines1x Pressure plate (the plate not the IED), assorted IED making materials, tubes and wires, 2x lb blocks of SYMTEX explosives, 1x Enfield style rifle (old bolt action rifle), 100x RPK rnds, 2x Taliban training manuals, 1x Paper with Taliban commander names and numbers, // 4/73 has the papers and taking them to Sharona, 1x Launcher style weapon with a bipod, C25 cannot determine type. The compound as owned by Mohammad. C25 is securing the AO and 4-73 EOD is going to exploited the site. This the first know cache site to be found in this area. It is quite possible that there are more cache sites in the area. CF will continue to conduct patrols in the area and question local nationals on more caches in the area.

Reference ID: AFG20070518n718
Latitude: 34.51667023
Date: 2007-05-18 07:07
Category: Cache Found/Cleared
Detained: 2

Region: RC CAPITAL
Longitude: 69.18332672
Type: Friendly Action
Affiliation: FRIEND

	Enemy	Friend	Civilian	Host Nation
Killed in Action	0	0	0	0
Wounded in Action	0	0	0	0

On 18 May 2007, the National Directorate of Security (NDS) 90 apprehended two (2) individuals in a residence in Kabul City in possession of four (4) SIED vest as well as AK-47 rifles and fragmentation grenades. CEXC Kabul was notified by another U.S. Government agency and gained access on 22 May to observe the devices. CEXC Kabul did not view the AK-47s or the grenades. The investigation is ongoing and being conducted by NDS 90. Items Recovered: a. Four (4) SIED vest; consisting of black cloth material containing bulk explosives, fragmentation and woven with detonating cord within. b. Bulk explosive unmeasured quantity. NDS 90 retains custody of the evidence.c. Fragmentation ball bearings and dry wall screws. NDS 90 retains custody of the evidence. d. Eight (8) rocker type switches. NDS 90 retains custody of the evidence. e. Three (3) power source 9V Duracell batteries. NDS 90 retains custody of the evidence. f. Electric detonators unknown number. g. Residue Tape various amount was turned over to CEXC Kabul. CEXC Report: CEXC_AFG_347_07.

Reference ID: AFG20070604n714
Latitude: 34.35111618
Date: 2007-06-04 00:12
Category: Cache Found/Cleared
Detained: 0

Region: RC EAST
Longitude: 70.56681061
Type: Friendly Action
Affiliation: FRIEND

	Enemy	Friend	Civilian	Host Nation
Killed in Action	0	0	0	0
Wounded in Action	0	0	0	0

FF discovered IED making material located in mud hut, AT/AP mines covered by bags with wires running out. ANP secured the site.

Reference ID: AFG20070618n771
Latitude: ------------
Date: 2007-06-18 12:12
Category: Cache Found/Cleared
Detained: 0

Region: RC EAST
Longitude: ---------
Type: Friendly Action
Affiliation: FRIEND

	Enemy	Friend	Civilian	Host Nation
Killed in Action	0	0	0	0
Wounded in Action	0	0	0	0

On 18 Jun, Afghan Military Forces located a cache IVO MGRS 42S YD 02800 67600 which consisted of 42 individual M142 Multi-Purpose Firing Devices. These devices can be used as booby-trap devices set for pressure, pressure-release, tension and tension release. The firing devices were unopened and contained inside three ammo cans (14 in each can). All M142 Firing Devices were turned over to U.S. Forces in ABAD.

Reference ID: AFG20070805n877
Latitude: 32.64050293
Date: 2007-08-05 00:12
Category: Cache Found/Cleared
Detained: 0

Region: RC EAST
Longitude: 69.06289673
Type: Friendly Action
Affiliation: FRIEND

	Enemy	Friend	Civilian	Host Nation
Killed in Action	0	0	0	0
Wounded in Action	0	0	0	0

A CF air strike was conducted on Objective Volunteer, following which TF Eagle sent out a team to carry out a battle damage assessment (BDA) and site exploitation. They recovered the items listed below and found one dead enemy combatant.
ITEMS RECOVERED:
a.Seven Mod 5 devices:
(1) Mod 5 #1: This Mod 5 device is housed in a gray plastic container.
(2) Mod 5 #2: This Mod 5 device is in a black and purple card board box labeled Battery Charger DC 12V 9V Toshiba Electronics. The device itself is housed in a gray plastic container.
(3) Mod 5 #3: This Mod 5 device is in a black and purple card board box labeled Battery Charger DC 12V 9V Toshiba Electronics. The device itself is housed in a gray plastic container.
(4)Mod 5 #4: This Mod 5 device is in a white, yellow, and blue card board box labeled Maxwell ELECTRONIC CHARGER 12V 3.5A. The device itself is housed in a gray plastic container.
(5) Mod 5 #5: This Mod 5 device is in a white, yellow, and blue card board box labeled Maxwell ELECTRONIC CHARGER 12V 3.5A. The device itself is housed in a gray plastic container.
(6) Mod 5 #6: This Mod 5 device is in a white, yellow, and blue card board box labeled Maxwell ELECTRONIC CHARGER 12V 3.5A. The device itself is housed in a gray plastic container
(7) Mod 5 #7: This Mod 5 device is in a white, yellow, and blue card board box labeled Maxwell ELECTRONIC CHARGER 12V 3.5A. The device itself is housed in a gray plastic container

b. One Remote FOB Trigger (RFT) housed in a black plastic box with a SONY CAR DOOR LOCK sticker on the front of it. The box 1111 handwritten on one side in white marker.
c. Six (6x) electric blasting caps.
d. Seven (7x) non-electric blasting caps.
e. Three (3x) MUV pressure/pull firing devices.
f. Four (4x) MUV2 pressure/pull firing devices.
g. Six (6x) boosters for the grenade fuze or MUV firing devices.
h. One (1x) roll of orange detonating cord.
i. Two (2x) Pakistani P5 MK1 claymore mines.
j. One (1x) Pakistani P4 MK2 anti personnel landmine.
k. One (1x) P3 MK1 anti tank landmine.
l. One (1x) F1 hand grenade with the top part of a Bulgarian striker/release grenade fuze.
m. Two (2x) rolled lengths of multi strand silver colored wire with tan insulation.
n. One (1x) ICOM IC-V8 radio set to 161.00 MHz.

Reference ID: AFG20070809n907 Region: RC EAST
Latitude: 33.34160233 Longitude: 69.95465088
Date: 2007-08-09 09:09 Type: Friendly Action
Category: Cache Found/Cleared Affiliation: FRIEND
Detained: 0

	Enemy	Friend	Civilian	Host Nation
Killed in Action	0	0	0	0
Wounded in Action	0	0	0	0

CEXC traveled to Lahore, Punjab to review IED components seized by local authorities. After reviewing the evidence CEXC determined that the seized IED components consisted of a cache of partially constructed MOD 5 Radio Controlled IED (RCIED) and related electronic components used to build the MOD 5, lap top computer, chemicals for making improvised explosives and aluminum containers used to deploy the explosive charges. The seizure was part of a larger operation and investigation, highlighted in open source reporting below.

From the SAP20070702005002 Daily Times (Internet Version-WWW) in English 0000 2 July 2007 - 0000 2 July 2007 [Description of Source: Lahore Daily Times (Internet Version-WWW) in English -- Internet version of the independent, moderate daily, run by veteran journalist Najam Sethi and published by the Friday Times group. Strong critic of radical and jihadi elements. Provides extensive coverage of activities of jihadi/militant groups. Caters to the educated middle class, with an estimated hardcopy circulation of 20,000; root URL as of filing date: http://www.dailytimes.com.pk]

The police have arrested eight terrorist suspects here with links to banned militant outfit Jaish-e-Muhammad and the Taliban, police said. The eight men are believed to have been behind an attack on a missionary school near Murree on August 5, 2002, killing six Pakistanis; and a grenade attack on a church in Taxila four days later in which four nurses were killed, Lahore police chief Malik Muhammad Iqbal told a press conference on Sunday.

The suspects include Safeer Ahmed, alias Muhammad Azeem, alias Umair, who was wanted by the Punjab government, which had a Rs 1 million bounty on his head.

Safeer, Mufti Sagher Ahmed, Ghulam Qadir and Muhammad Yasir Wifaq were arrested from a bus stand on Saturday night, while Muhammad Siddique, Abdul Moeed, Ubaidullah Asghar and Syed Muhammad Masood were arrested from a house in Iqbal Park, Ittefaq Town in a predawn operation on Sunday.

Capital City Police Officer (CCPO) Iqbal said that Safeer was planning terrorist plots in Lahore. He said they had been trained in use of firearms and making remote-controlled bombs "in a neighbouring country". Police also seized a large quantity of arms, ammunition and bomb-making material from the suspect hideout in Ittefaq Town.

He said the suspects had confessed they were part of the Jamiatul Furqan, a splinter group of the Jaish-e-Muhammad, which was banned in 2002. They had also confessed to the attacks in Murree and Taxila, he said.

AFP adds: A senior police official told AFP that the suspects supplied suicide bombers and explosive devices to Taliban fighters in Afghanistan. He said the eight-member group was based in Quetta, and used to collect materials and volunteers from Punjab. "During the interrogation they confessed to having carried out a series of suicide bombings and bomb blasts against foreign forces in Afghanistan over the past several years," he said.

"The suspects were preparing remote-controlled devices for the Taliban in Afghanistan," the official said, adding that they had "links" with former mujahedin leader Jalaluddin Haqqani and his pro-Taliban son Siraj Haqqani.

ITEMS RECOVERED:

a. One representative MOD 5 DTMF decoder circuit board measuring approximately 65 mm L x 42 mm W. This circuit board is partially populated with electronic components

b. One representative MOD 5 RF circuit board measuring approximately 70 mm L x 37 mm W. This circuit board was not populated with any electronic components but is marked and labeled for assembly.

c. One 20 pin MT 8870 DTMF Decoder chip. This chip is not programmable and is stock to be installed on the DTMF Decoder board of the MOD 5 circuit card mentioned above.

d. 9 aluminum containers were seized as well but noit turned over. The container lids had a rubber gasket attached and closed on to the container by screwing the lid down. The lids, once closed, could be sealed by placing a lock through one of the 4 holes drilled through the lip of the lid and the body of the container. These holes lined up when the container was closed properly. Also identified was one small hole drilled through the side of the lid. It is speculated that these containers were being used to place bulk explosive in and primed through the hole in the lid.

e. The chemicals found were bundled in 16 bags each weighing 25 kilograms each. A test was conducted on a sample of the chemicals using the HAZMAT ID (IR) field machine with a match to Potassium Chlorate with a 97% accuracy.

Reference ID: AFG20070825n807
Latitude: 34.08327103
Date: 2007-08-25 02:02
Category: Cache Found/Cleared
Detained: 0

Region: RC EAST
Longitude: 70.23618317
Type: Friendly Action
Affiliation: FRIEND

	Enemy	Friend	Civilian	Host Nation
Killed in Action	0	0	0	0
Wounded in Action	0	0	0	0

At 1930Z, TF 1 Fury reports discovering a signifcan weapons Cache in the Suleimankheyl Pass. The cache was found in a hidden room of a house. Cache included the following:

2 x DISKA barrels
2 x DISKA
14 x Cans DISKA rds
14 x 80mm rds
3 x RPG rds(Russian)
34 x mortar rds (Chinese)
2 x rds (heat Chinese)
1 x mortar tube,
5 x 107rds
1 x Recoiless rifle
2 x 8ft tube launchers
1 x initiator device
1 x tripod
3 x new barreled rocket launchers
14 x Barrel rocket launchers

Unit is continuing to assess the serviceability of the systems/munitions and is working ICW EOD to furthur exploit the cache. On the 29th all ordnance was loaded and transported to the disposal site. All LN in the area were evacuated and the cache was destroyed. The following items were not destroyed, but turned over to C Co. 1/508 for dispersal to ANA/ANP: 29 Chinese Projo.s type 65 in excellent condition and still in the originally shipping containers, still sealed tight, 107 cases of 12.7mm and 14.5mm small arms mixed.

The following hardware was transported back to FOB Fenty via C Co. 1/508: 2 x 14.5 Anti-aircraft receivers and barrels, 2 x 12.7mm Dishka Barrels, 1 x 30 Cal. Machine gun with tri-pod, 4 x twin launches of unknown type, 1 x Quad launcher of unknown type, 2 x 8 tubes of unknown type, 1 x mechanism of unknown type, and 1 x control device of unknown type.

Nothing to follow.

Reference ID: AFG20070924n834
Latitude: 34.87162018
Date: 2007-09-24 07:07
Category: Cache Found/Cleared
Detained: 0

Region: RC EAST
Longitude: 71.15258789
Type: Friendly Action
Affiliation: FRIEND

	Enemy	Friend	Civilian	Host Nation
Killed in Action	0	0	0	0
Wounded in Action	0	0	0	0

The team and security responded to an ANP station to recover 2 ea RPO-Z 92mm Russian Incendiary Rockets, 9 ea PMN, AP, Russian Landmine, 10 ea P4MK2, Pakistani, Anti-Personnel Landmines, 1 ea Italian, TC6, AT Landmine, 1 ea PG-18 and 2 ea DTMF receivers. The team transported recovered ordnance and contents from their SHA to a disposal site and disposed of all ordnance by detonation. The following items were retained for intelligence and biometric data; both RPO-'s and DTMF receivers.

Ordnance Recovered
2 ea USSR RPO-Z Missiles
2 ea DTMF Receiver
Ordnance Destroyed
10 ea Pakistani P4MK2 Landmine
9 ea USSR PMN Landmine
1 ea Italian TC-6 Landmine
1 ea USSR RPG-18 Rocket
10 ea US M549 Projectile
500 ea US .50 cal API

Reference ID: AFG20071003n984
Latitude: 32.68138885
Date: 2007-10-03 04:04
Category: Cache Found/Cleared
Detained: 0

Region: RC EAST
Longitude: 67.7155838
Type: Friendly Action
Affiliation: FRIEND

	Enemy	Friend	Civilian	Host Nation
Killed in Action	0	0	0	0
Wounded in Action	0	0	0	0

At 0450Z TF 2Fury reported an IED discovery in Gelan District at UB 79582 16696. The IED was not placed, but buried in a garden for suspected future use. The IED was described as a 3ft long tube, 6in in diameter with a blasting cap and wire taped to the IED. A battery box, batteries, and belt of ammo were also discovered. While continuing to search and secure the area, the element reported discovering a 105mm round, EFP. QRF and EOD from FOB Warrior moved to investigate at 0710z. At 0803z the QRF struck an IED (see associated report) and a secondary QRF moved with recovery assets. At 0922z the element securing the cache and IED received 1x107mm. LN kids in the area report the round was fired from vic UB 80899 16625 and POI was 300 West of the friendly location. No injuries or damage was reported. At 0928z ISR came on station and began to search for any suspicious activity IVO of the reported POO. At 1221z the element reports finding an additional cache at UB 79577 16681 that included a bookbag of 7.62mm ammo, 2 x chest racks, AT and AP Mines, bolt action rifle, 107mm rockets, and other IED making materials. The element will remain on site over night and return with all items recovered. At 0530z the element returned to FOB Warrior with NFTR. Event closed at 0530Z.

Reference ID: AFG20071121n1044
Latitude: 33.89471817
Date: 2007-11-21 10:10
Category: Cache Found/Cleared
Detained: 0

Region: RC WEST
Longitude: 62.23822021
Type: Friendly Action
Affiliation: FRIEND

	Enemy	Friend	Civilian	Host Nation
Killed in Action	0	0	0	0
Wounded in Action	0	0	0	0

At 211430L1107 at //MGRS: 41S MT 29564 50744// 30 KM south FSB HERAT, IVO RING ROAD 1, Guzara District, Herat Province, AF, ODA reported to RC-W that they found an ammunition cache containing about 250 artillery shells of various calibres and 50 81mm mortar rounds.

Reference ID: AFG20071130n996
Latitude: 33.80738068
Date: 2007-11-30 07:07
Category: Cache Found/Cleared
Detained: 0

Region: RC EAST
Longitude: 69.81787872
Type: Friendly Action
Affiliation: FRIEND

	Enemy	Friend	Civilian	Host Nation
Killed in Action	0	0	0	0
Wounded in Action	0	0	0	0

ODA 3321 DEVELOPS AND MAINTAINS A ROBUST MSO NETWORK THROUGHOUT THE CHAMKANI AREA. THE TEAM DOES NOT MEASURE SUCCESS BY THE AMOUNT OF MUNITIONS TURNED IN, BUT BY THE AMOUNT OF NEW ATMOSPHERICS WE GAIN FOR FUTURE OPERATIONS. IN ADDITION, WE BEAT THE INS (INSURGENTS) TO THE IO PUNCH. INS PURCHASE MUNITIONS FROM LOCALS, NOT JUST TO USE, BUT AS A WAY OF GAINING THE LOCALS TRUST AND RESPECT. FOLLOWING AN EXTENDED CRP IN THE MOQBIL TRIBAL AREA, LOCAL MEN TURNED IN 200, NEW IN BOX, AT MINE PRESSURE FUSES (AS SEEN BELOW). THE MEN STATED THAT DUE TO THE INCREASED IROA SECURITY PRESENCE IN THE AREA, THEY FELT THAT THEY SHOULD TURN IN THE FUSES TO THE FIREBASE. END RESULT IS GREATER COOPERATION FROM LOCAL ELDERS, REDUCED IED THREAT, POSITIVE IO EFFECTS, BETTER SECURITY AND THE CONTINUED TREND OF SEPARATING THE INSURGENT FROM THE POPULATION.
16 CACHES TURNED IN.
119 X RPG Rounds
85 X Hand Grenades
24 X Anti Personal Mines
11 X 82MM Recoilless Rounds
14 X 82MM Mortar Rounds
6   x Anti Tank Mines
200 X Anti Tank Mine Fuses
3   X RCIED
4   X PKM
2   X RPD
1   X RPG Launcher

Reference ID: AFG20080110n1197
Latitude: 34.25687027
Date: 2008-01-10 16:04
Category: Cache Found/Cleared
Detained: 3

Region: RC EAST
Longitude: 70.19146729
Type: Friendly Action
Affiliation: FRIEND

	Enemy	Friend	Civilian	Host Nation
Killed in Action	0	0	0	0
Wounded in Action	0	0	0	0

At 1518z the PTDS spotted 3 men digging in the road (42S XC 0970 9128) the ANA and ANP were dispacted to location at 1605z. The ANA and ANP arrive 2 men ran from the target location at 1631. The ANA and ANP setup cordon and requsted EOD. QRF and EOD was send from FOB Khogyani. The ANSF began a search area and detained 3 men and recover 2- PG-7 rockets, 1- PG-22 rockets, 3-Rocket propellant, 31- 75mm propelling charge for artillery charges for artillery rounds, 1- Block bulk HE 5 lbs and a 2- D cell battery. After SSE of the cache in Nawe Kaza the three individuals were BATS and turned over to ANP. ANP will maintain presence the house tonight. In the morning the ANP and ANA will go back to the site and finish SSE with LN press for IO.

Timeline of events below:
1518z The PTDS observed 3 men digging in the road
1605z ANA SP from FOB Khogyani to linkup with ANP to investigate the site
1613z ANA and ANP completed linkup and begin movement to suspected cache site
1625z ANA and ANP reach objective site XC 0970 9128 begin cordon and search
1631z two paxs were seen running away from location ANP was in pursue
1640 ANA & ANP secure building and await EOD support
ETT, EOD, & RECCE sp Khogyani to ANP and ANA location
1716z ETT and EOD link-up with ANA and ANP. RECCE provides outer cordon
1804z ANP/ANA detain one PAX
1818z EOD conducting SSE
1837z ANA detained 2nd PAX
2016z Operation complete Wolverine submits a roll up 3 Detained and cache found

Reference ID: AFG20080124n1040
Latitude: 33.5973587
Date: 2008-01-24 04:04
Category: Cache Found/Cleared
Detained: 0

Region: RC EAST
Longitude: 69.22760773
Type: Friendly Action
Affiliation: FRIEND

	Enemy	Friend	Civilian	Host Nation
Killed in Action	0	0	0	0
Wounded in Action	0	0	0	0

On 24 JAN, the Gardez District ANP seized four tons of marijuana seed. They also seized 1960 kilograms of powder and 2310 liters of the chemicals required to convert opium into heroin (NFI). The marijuana is currently being stored in a container at the Provincial ANP HQ, and the drug making supplies are in a separate storage facility at the governors compound because of the lack of evidence storage at the Provincial ANP HQ.

Reference ID: AFG20080125n1118
Latitude: 31.50555801
Date: 2008-01-25 10:10
Category: Cache Found/Cleared
Detained: 0

Region: RC SOUTH
Longitude: 65.43044281
Type: Friendly Action
Affiliation: FRIEND

	Enemy	Friend	Civilian	Host Nation
Killed in Action	0	0	0	0
Wounded in Action	0	0	0	0

At 1030Z, TF Kandahar detained 6 x insurgents who had 1 x AK-47, 4 x grenades and IED making materials in their possession at 41R QQ 30823 88193 IVO Musa Kata, 1.4km northeast of PB Sperwan Ghar in the Panjwayi district, Kandahar province. Friendly forces on patrol received a tip from a local national of an IED factory. They discovered the cache and detained the personnel after searching the compound. All PAX failed the GSR test. Two detainees, one of them is believed to be a high value target, were transferred to Kandahar AF. The remaining four detainees were turned over to the ANSF.
At 1538Z, an airlift from PB Sperwan Ghar to KAF was pending movement. No BDA was reported. Event closed at 1536Z.
ISAF tracking # 01-459

Reference ID: AFG20080207n1268 Region: RC NORTH
Latitude: 36.22111893 Longitude: 68.77189636
Date: 2008-02-07 00:12 Type: Friendly Action
Category: Cache Found/Cleared Affiliation: FRIEND
Detained: 0

	Enemy	Friend	Civilian	Host Nation
Killed in Action	0	0	0	0
Wounded in Action	0	0	0	0

07 FEB - OLD BAGHLAN (42SVF 795 085) village, BAGHLAN-I JADID district - ANA/ANP common OP, arrested (01) TB sympathizer (Mullah MAHMADULLAH). (6) RPG grenades, (1) BM-1 rocket launcher, approximately two hundred (200) ammunition for different rifles, (2) bad-condition AKs, (01) old carbine

Reference ID: AFG20080212n1159 Region: RC WEST
Latitude: 32.75249863 Longitude: 62.60363007
Date: 2008-02-12 12:12 Type: Friendly Action
Category: Cache Found/Cleared Affiliation: FRIEND
Detained: 0

	Enemy	Friend	Civilian	Host Nation
Killed in Action	0	0	0	0
Wounded in Action	0	0	0	0

At an unspecified time on 12 FEB 2008, ANP and CF conducted a clear and search operation IVO Sozanak Village (CNA), Bala Baluk District, Farah Province, AF. As a result of the seizure ANP confiscated 1 x PKM and 2 x AK-47. The weapons were turned over to CF. NFI. EVENT CLOSED.

Reference ID: AFG20080427n1278 Region: RC CAPITAL
Latitude: 34.49808121 Longitude: 69.18408203
Date: 2008-04-27 08:08 Type: Friendly Action
Category: Cache Found/Cleared Affiliation: FRIEND
Detained: 0

	Enemy	Friend	Civilian	Host Nation
Killed in Action	0	0	0	0
Wounded in Action	0	0	0	0

RC CAPITAL REPORTED FF DISCOVERED A 40mm MORTAR SETUP WITH A BATTERY AND TIMER AIMED AT KABUL 6KM S OF CAMP PHOENIX. NFTR.

Reference ID: AFG20080503n1322
Latitude: 32.15047455
Date: 2008-05-03 19:07
Category: Cache Found/Cleared
Detained: 0
Region: RC SOUTH
Longitude: 63.44113922
Type: Friendly Action
Affiliation: FRIEND

	Enemy	Friend	Civilian	Host Nation
Killed in Action	0	0	0	0
Wounded in Action	0	0	0	0

ARSIC WEST UNIT ETT REPORTED THAT DURING AN OPERATION JOIN ANA, ON A SIDE OF KHASROD RIVER, CLOSE TO DELARAM PB THEY SEIZED ABOUT 150 LBS OF OPIUM AND SOME WEAPONS, ACTUALLY UNKNOWN TYPE AND THE AMOUNT. THE DRUG IS UNDER CUSTODY ON US ARSIC COMPOUND IN DELARAM. NFI. ATT.

Reference ID: AFG20080514n1346
Latitude: 34.50912094
Date: 2008-05-14 03:03
Category: Cache Found/Cleared
Detained: 0
Region: RC CAPITAL
Longitude: 69.64927673
Type: Friendly Action
Affiliation: FRIEND

	Enemy	Friend	Civilian	Host Nation
Killed in Action	0	0	0	0
Wounded in Action	0	0	0	0

A TF SUROBI UNIT REPORTED THE DISCOVERY OF 8X 76MM ROCKETS AND 2KG OF HASHISH 14KM SW OF FOB SUROBI. NFTR.

Reference ID: AFG20080519n1272
Latitude: 34.3865509
Date: 2008-05-19 18:06
Category: Cache Found/Cleared
Detained: 0
Region: RC EAST
Longitude: 70.66402435
Type: Friendly Action
Affiliation: FRIEND

	Enemy	Friend	Civilian	Host Nation
Killed in Action	0	0	0	0
Wounded in Action	0	0	0	0

SUMMARY OF EVENTS
(S//REL) On 26JUN08, an EOD technical advisor (civilian contractor) for the State Departments Weapons Removal and Abatement (WRA) Program, accompanied by two personnel from the United Nations Development Program (UNDP) group, Disarmament of Illegal Armed Groups (DIAG), turned into CEXC-JAF six (6x) mobile phones which appeared to be modified to serve as RCIED receivers. The DIAG personnel turned over a copy of a written report from ANP/ABP which related some

of the circumstances of the recovery. According to the report as translated by the CIED Team JAF interpreter, fifteen (15x) police men and one (1x) border police officer came across a Taliban element in the Soori Village, Nazyan District, Nangarhar Province at approximately 191850ZMAY08. The patrol engaged the Taliban element in a firefight for approximately 20 minutes, at the conclusion of which the Taliban escaped but left behind what the report describes as six (6x) fuses, six (6x) electric remote controls, and 264 fuses and other explosive materials. The CEXC investigator was unable to determine the exact location of the recovery. Along with the IED materials, the ANP and ABP forces recovered a Taliban note, addressed from Nandar Commander (translation) to Khoona Commander (translation). Of the items reported recovered by ANP/ABP in the report, CEXC-JAF only received the six (6x) mobile phones.

ITEMS RECOVERED

(C//REL) Six (6x) mobile phones. The battery for each phone was removed prior to receipt at CEXC-JAF. Each of the phones was modified with the addition of one or two wires protruding from the interior of the phone. CEXC-JAF did not receive any additional sources of power with the mobile phones, nor did the ANP/ABP reports refer to recovering any additional power sources. To the knowledge of the investigator, these cell phones have not previously been exploited for forensic communication data such as sent/received calls, etc. CEXC-JAF received the following mobile phones which the investigator is sending to Level II/III for additional exploitation:

1. Nokia Model 6100, Type NPL-2, IMEI: 35252 (remainder of IMEI is illegible)
2. Nokia Model 1100, Type: RH-18, IMEI: 35939900/871432/4
3. Nokia Model 1100, Type: RH-18, IMEI: 35667100/4882849/9
4. Nokia Model 1100, Type: RH-18, IMEI: 35226301/208770/4
5. Nokia Model 3310, Type: NHM-5NX, IMEI: 350845/10/122019/6
6. Samsung Model Unknown, Type: SGH-N620, IMEI: 352179/00/448929/ (remainder of IMEI is illegible)

(C//REL) One (1x) copy of Taliban note recovered at the scene by ANP and ABP. CEXC JAF interpreter translated the note as from Nandar Commander to Khoona Commander.

Reference ID: AFG20080530n1210
Latitude: 31.07545471
Date: 2008-05-30 12:12
Category: Cache Found/Cleared
Detained: 0
Region: RC SOUTH
Longitude: 64.17337799
Type: Friendly Action
Affiliation: FRIEND

	Enemy	Friend	Civilian	Host Nation
Killed in Action	0	0	0	0
Wounded in Action	0	0	0	0

EOD was notified that 1BN 6th Charlie Co. had found a weapons cache inside of a house on the outside of Jugrom Fort.

Reference ID: AFG20080602n1297
Latitude: 31.05698395
Region: RC SOUTH
Longitude: 64.20506287

Date: 2008-06-02 23:11 Type: Friendly Action
Category: Cache Found/Cleared Affiliation: FRIEND
Detained: 0

	Enemy	Friend	Civilian	Host Nation
Killed in Action	0	0	0	0
Wounded in Action	0	0	0	0

At approximately 020700LJUN08 EOD Team 1 arrived on scene for weapons cache response. Items that were found are as follows:
9 x British SAPI plates 2 x Canteens
1 x British optics 2 x PIR
1 x Morphine pen 6 x Lithium Batteries
1 x Pair goggles 2 x Radios
3 x British pop up flares 3 x Bayonets
5 x Backpacks 1 x 203 Launcher
2 x Vests 1 x Rifle
4 x CamelBaks 31 x Rifle magazines
1 x Helmet 1 x Ammo can 7.62mm
2 x Ammo can 5.56mm 1 x Mortar tube
Items were taken by EOD Team 3 for further inspection and exploitation.

Reference ID: AFG20080704n1333 Region: RC CAPITAL
Latitude: 34.50705338 Longitude: 69.69719696
Date: 2008-07-04 11:11 Type: Friendly Action
Category: Cache Found/Cleared Affiliation: FRIEND
Detained: 0

	Enemy	Friend	Civilian	Host Nation
Killed in Action	0	0	0	0
Wounded in Action	0	0	0	0

A TF SUROBI UNIT REPORTED THE DISCOVERY OF A CACHE 13KM S OF FOB SUROBI: TYPE 65 82MM RDS, 2 MINES A/P PMN, 70KG HASHISH.

Reference ID: AFG20080714n1398 Region: RC EAST
Latitude: 34.71207428 Longitude: 70.95301056
Date: 2008-07-14 05:05 Type: Friendly Action
Category: Cache Found/Cleared Affiliation: FRIEND
Detained: 0

	Enemy	Friend	Civilian	Host Nation
Killed in Action	0	0	0	0
Wounded in Action	0	0	0	0

ANP conducted a random vehicle stop of a taxi on 14JUL08. Habi Bullah, the driver and another man were in the vehicle. ANP discovered a pistol, 2 fragmentation grenades, 2 circuit boards, 1 ICOM radio, 1 cell phone in the possession of Bullah. Bullah remained in the custody of ANP and was transported by ANP to an Afghan facility in Kabul on 15JUL08. ANP provided one circuit board to Cpt.Demer on 15JUL08. Cpt. Demer provided the circuit board to ABAD CIED at FOB Fortress.

Reference ID: AFG20080731n781
Latitude: 33.28752136
Date: 2008-07-31 12:12
Category: Cache Found/Cleared
Detained: 0
Region: RC EAST
Longitude: 69.35934448
Type: Friendly Action
Affiliation: FRIEND

	Enemy	Friend	Civilian	Host Nation
Killed in Action	0	0	0	0
Wounded in Action	0	0	0	0

UNIT: TF PANTHER (1/C)
TYPE: Cache Found
TIMELINE: 1218Z 1/C reported finding items at target 6.
 11 x Abandoned huts
Hut # 1 cache:
 - 5 x Sleeping bags
 - 8 x AA batteries
 - 1 x Flashlight
 - 1 x Field expedient antenna attached to regular antenna
 - 1 x Stove
 - Clothes for approximately 5 PAX
Hut # 2 cache:
 - 8 x Sleeping bags
 - 120 x AA batteries
 - 25 x D batteries
 - 3 x Empty ammo crates (AK-47)
 - 1 x Stove with unknown type of food
HUT #3 (APPEARS TO BE AID STATION)
 - 2 x books with over 100 phone numbers
 - 25 x sleeping bags
 - 9 x bags of food (various types)
 - 2 x cans of cooking oil
 - 1 x grenade fuse
 - unk # of Gauze and IV Bags
 - 2 x pressure cookers
 - multiple notebooks with name of known Taliban CDR. Phone numbers and addresses in PAKISTAN.
SUMMARY:
BDA:
EVENT: CLOSED 1150Z

Reference ID: AFG20080818n1455
Latitude: 34.26202011
Date: 2008-08-18 13:01
Category: Cache Found/Cleared
Detained: 0
Region: RC EAST
Longitude: 70.31991577
Type: Friendly Action
Affiliation: FRIEND

	Enemy	Friend	Civilian	Host Nation
Killed in Action	0	0	0	0
Wounded in Action	0	0	0	0

Between 172215ZAUG08 and 181300ZAUG08, SFODA 7321 and 3rd CO, 1st (3/1) CDOs conducted an operation IVO Chaparhar District, Nangarhar Province, IOT kill/capture OBJ RALEIGH (NASRATULLAH S/O ABDUL HAQ, Taliban Commander/IED facilitator) and disrupt AAF safe havens and IED cells operating in Chaparhar. As part of that operation, SFODA 7321 and 3/1 CDOs searched NASRATULLAHs residence, designated as building 1, IVO 42S XC 21520 91997. SFODA 7320 EOD and CIED Team JAF TET collected explosives, a PMN landmine, detonating cord with a blasting cap, documents, photographs, computer, monitor and keyboard. In addition CIED Team JAF TET photographed, entered into HIIDEs and obtained rolled fingerprints from eleven (11) military age males (including NASRATULLAH, capture tag #4926053) who were present on the objective.

Reference ID: AFG20080828n1428
Latitude: 34.68578339
Date: 2008-08-28 10:10
Category: Cache Found/Cleared
Detained: 0

Region: RC CAPITAL
Longitude: 69.05567932
Type: Friendly Action
Affiliation: FRIEND

	Enemy	Friend	Civilian	Host Nation
Killed in Action	0	0	0	0
Wounded in Action	0	0	0	0

TUR EOD team discovered a cache consisting of 4x 107mm Type 63 rockets, 1x 122 mm rocket, 15x 82 mm mortars, 1x 82mm mortar, 11x OG-7 rockets, 24x fuze, Chinese PD MP1a/1b, 1x AP mine, 4x Chinese Type 69 AP mine, 4x AK-47, 5x AK-46 magazines, 1x grenade fuze

Reference ID: AFG20080901n1380
Latitude: 34.14515686
Date: 2008-09-01 06:06
Category: Cache Found/Cleared
Detained: 0

Region: RC EAST
Longitude: 71.06383514
Type: Friendly Action
Affiliation: FRIEND

	Enemy	Friend	Civilian	Host Nation
Killed in Action	0	0	0	0
Wounded in Action	0	0	0	0

0634z: IN DITCH, POSSIBLY UNEARTHED FROM A WASHOUT DUE TO RECENT RAIN. WRA UNCOVERED 1 60mm ROUND, 3 82mm CHINESE MORTARS, 1 81mm IRANIAN, 1 .50 CAL ROUND, 1 40mm ROCKET, AND FRAGMENTS.

Reference ID: AFG20080923n1386
Latitude: 34.61365128
Date: 2008-09-23 09:09
Category: Cache Found/Cleared
Detained: 0

Region: RC CAPITAL
Longitude: 68.98363495
Type: Friendly Action
Affiliation: FRIEND

	Enemy	Friend	Civilian	Host Nation
Killed in Action	0	0	0	0
Wounded in Action	0	0	0	0

RC-C reported the discovery of a cache in Paghman district, consisting of: 10x fuses, 2Kg of TNT, 50 grams of plastic explosives, 2x artillery fuses,1x Russian hand grenade, 2x 82mm mortar shells, 2x RPG-7's, 20Kg of explosives/additional charges, 1x anti-aircraft weapon barrel, and 1x Russian PPSh-41 sub-machine gun . The items were removed by NDS, and were sent to the NDS HQ in Paghman for storage.

Reference ID: AFG20081005n1472
Latitude: 34.6830864
Date: 2008-10-05 04:04
Category: Cache Found/Cleared
Detained: 0
Region: RC CAPITAL
Longitude: 69.037117
Type: Friendly Action
Affiliation: FRIEND

	Enemy	Friend	Civilian	Host Nation
Killed in Action	0	0	0	0
Wounded in Action	0	0	0	0

RC-C reported the discovery of a cache in Shakar Dara district that consisted of: 13x 107 mm Chinese HE Rockets, 118x 82 mm Chinese HE Mortars, 114x Russian MP-1B Fuses, 250x Chinese M6 Fuses, 16x Russian PDV-429 Fuses, and 10x Russian MRVU Fuses. FRA EOD removed the items and stored them at the Pol-e Charki Ammunition Storage site (CNA).

Reference ID: AFG20081102n1425
Latitude: 34.63597107
Date: 2008-11-02 16:04
Category: Cache Found/Cleared
Detained: 0
Region: RC CAPITAL
Longitude: 69.70372772
Type: Friendly Action
Affiliation: FRIEND

	Enemy	Friend	Civilian	Host Nation
Killed in Action	0	0	0	0
Wounded in Action	0	0	0	0

DELAYED REPORT
FRA BG reported during a NFO patrol in Surobi lake area, French unit discovered a cache consisting of :
- 20 x 82mm mortar bombs
- 3 x 122 mm shells.
Removal planned on 03 Nov.
UPDATE-1057D*
Cache removal is postponed to 04 Nov.

Reference ID: AFG20081030n1416
Latitude: 31.5723362
Date: 2008-10-30 17:05
Category: Cache Found/Cleared
Detained: 0
Region: RC SOUTH
Longitude: 64.32136536
Type: Friendly Action
Affiliation: FRIEND

	Enemy	Friend	Civilian	Host Nation
Killed in Action	0	0	0	0
Wounded in Action	0	0	0	0

ANP with PMT while manning CP BOLAN found IED components (3 x containers containing approx 20KG of HME, numerous initiation devices, pressure plates and batteries). ANP have cordoned the cache area and EOD is informed.
UPDATE 2210D*
EOD will exploit as a routine task and the final report will be submitted through C-IED chain.No casualties or damage reported.
***Event closed at 2210D*.

Reference ID: AFG20081031n892 Region: RC EAST
Latitude: 34.29849243 Longitude: 70.40947723
Date: 2008-10-31 16:04 Type: Friendly Action
Category: Cache Found/Cleared Affiliation: FRIEND
Detained: 0

	Enemy	Friend	Civilian	Host Nation
Killed in Action	0	0	0	0
Wounded in Action	0	0	0	0

ISAF #11-006;
TF VALIANT CACHE
1630z ODA found a cache in w/ COMPOSITION OF CACHE: -
21 CHINESE CARTRIDGE, 82MM, HEAT, TYPE 65 -
6 CHINESE CARTRIDGE, 75-MM, RR,HEAT - 7 U.S.S.R. GRENADE, HAND, DEFENSIVE, F-1 - 1 U.S.S.R. LANDMINE, APERS, FRAG, MON-90 - 1 CHINESE CARTRIDGE, 75-MM, HE, TYPE 52 COMMENTS: -All munitions appeared to be in good conditions, most of them still in their containers. EFFECTS: - Cache in hands of CF and is unable to be used for attacks. - AOB personnel were able to negotiate the removal of the munitions from the cache site. NFI---- EVENT CLOSED

Reference ID: AFG20081110n1529 Region: RC SOUTH
Latitude: 31.85551643 Longitude: 65.70030975
Date: 2008-11-10 11:11 Type: Friendly Action
Category: Cache Found/Cleared Affiliation: FRIEND
Detained: 0

	Enemy	Friend	Civilian	Host Nation
Killed in Action	0	0	0	0
Wounded in Action	0	0	0	0

At 1214Z, TF Kandahar reported a Weapons Cache Find:
FF were conducting a Recon Patrol in ARD when they discovered a Weapons CACHE with small IEDs, Det Cord, Electronic Components, SA ammo, Rockets, Medical Supplies, and buried crates that still await exploitation. ANA detained 8x INS for questioning. No injuries or damages reported. BDA: 8x INS Detained.
At 1457Z, TF Kandahar reported:
FF reported spotting 2x Potential IED sites on route Murphy at grid: 41R QR 55000 26400 and 41R QR 55000 26200. INS with an AK-47 is observing FF. FF are escorting integral Engineers to the location to exploit. All 8x detained INS have been released by the ANA as FF moved to establish a cordon and await the arrival of the Engineers. After EOD exploited the site the Cache items reported were: 1x chest rig with ammo, 9x IED Pressure Plate, Medical supplies to include 10x IV bags, a car battery and

other kind of battery power sources, 9x 82mm rounds, 21feet of Det. Cord, 2.5 -3 lbs of HME, 1x Led Enfield Rifle with ammo, 4x AK-47 rifles with mag and ammo and 45 rounds of PKM link ammo. NFTR. Event closed at 1345Z.
ISAF # 11-0532

Reference ID: AFG20081116n1568
Latitude: 31.48744965
Date: 2008-11-16 11:11
Category: Cache Found/Cleared
Detained: 0

Region: RC SOUTH
Longitude: 65.31811523
Type: Friendly Action
Affiliation: FRIEND

	Enemy	Friend	Civilian	Host Nation
Killed in Action	0	0	0	0
Wounded in Action	0	0	0	0

At 170510ZNOV08, RC South reported a Cache Find. While conducting compound searches ISO OP JANUBI TAPU, FF found an extensive cache of weapons and IED components, (various mortars, rockets, shells, mines and grenades), various explosives (HME, cordite and C4), assorted IED components include, pressure plates, detonators, switches, fuses and rolls of command wires.
TF Paladin is on site and are cataloguing. Forensic evidence will be recovered for further investigation and a full list will be passed up the normal C-IED chain.
The ammo and explosives will be BIP.
NFTR. Event closed at 0548Z.
ISAF # 11-0876

Reference ID: AFG20081118n1593
Region: RC SOUTH
Latitude: 31.50680733
Longitude: 65.2833786
Date: 2008-11-18 11:11
Type: Friendly Action
Category: Cache Found/Cleared
Affiliation: FRIEND
Detained: 0

	Enemy	Friend	Civilian	Host Nation
Killed in Action	0	0	0	0
Wounded in Action	0	0	0	0

At 1945Z, TF Kandahar reported a Weapons Cache Find:
FF were conducting a Clearance Patrol ISO OP Janubi Tapu, when they carried out a Routine Search of a compound and discovered approx. 35kg of heroin split down into 4.5 kg bags. FF also found 2x hand grenades and a quantity of IED Components. No injuries or damages reported. NFI att.
At 2100Z, TF Kandahar reported:
At 2058Z, all IED Components, Heroin and Hand Grenades have been recovered by FF. NFTR. Event closed at 2058Z.
ISAF # 11-0970

Reference ID: AFG20081119n1496
Region: RC SOUTH
Latitude: 31.1287632
Longitude: 64.19833374
Date: 2008-11-19 06:06
Type: Friendly Action
Category: Cache Found/Cleared
Affiliation: FRIEND
Detained: 0

	Enemy	Friend	Civilian	Host Nation
Killed in Action	0	0	0	0
Wounded in Action	0	0	0	0

At 0655Z, TF Helmand reported a UXO Cache Find. While conducting a security patrol, FF reported a LN farmer found and collected a UXO Cache of 25x 81mm ILLUM mortar rounds and 1x 51mm HE mortar from his field. FF marked the site and EOD TM will exploit the site as a routine task. NFTR. Event closed at 0627Z. ISAF # 11-0981

Reference ID: AFG20081215n1558
Latitude: 34.63393402
Date: 2008-12-15 15:03
Category: Cache Found/Cleared
Detained: 0

Region: RC CAPITAL
Longitude: 69.57601929
Type: Friendly Action
Affiliation: FRIEND

	Enemy	Friend	Civilian	Host Nation
Killed in Action	0	0	0	0
Wounded in Action	0	0	0	0

A RC-E unit (NFI) reported finding a cache, which consisted of: 9 kilograms (20 lbs) of home made explosives, a cell phone, an alarm clock, fifty meters of wire, and a soldering set.
BDA: None reported. All materials were taken to Bagram AF for further exploitation.

Reference ID: AFG20081219n1543
Latitude: 31.62343025
Date: 2008-12-19 10:10
Category: Cache Found/Cleared
Detained: 0

Region: RC SOUTH
Longitude: 64.17879486
Type: Friendly Action
Affiliation: FRIEND

	Enemy	Friend	Civilian	Host Nation
Killed in Action	0	0	0	0
Wounded in Action	0	0	0	0

K Coy 42 CDO conducting OP SOND CHARA, reported FF were investigating INS FP's when they found 210 kg of (wet) opium, 1x pump action shotgun, 3x white Toyota Corolla's, 1x chest webbing and belts of ammo. TFH BPO has been informed and FF are seeking for ANP assistance to hand over the find.
NFTR.
***Event closed at 1530D*

Reference ID: AFG20081218n1625
Latitude: 34.07027817
Date: 2008-12-18 06:06
Category: Cache Found/Cleared
Detained: 0

Region: RC EAST
Longitude: 70.66564178
Type: Friendly Action
Affiliation: FRIEND

	Enemy	Friend	Civilian	Host Nation
Killed in Action	0	0	0	0
Wounded in Action	0	0	0	0

At 0705Z, RC East reported a CACHE find. FF reported a CACHE (2x hand grenades and 5x mines without fuses) and drug (35kg of Poppy and 2kg of Hash) find. The drugs were turned into the Counter Narcotics Team and the munitions were turned into Afghan EOD. No casualties or damage was reported. NFTR. Event closed at 0645Z.
ISAF # 12-755

Reference ID: AFG20081224n1494
Latitude: 34.54764175
Date: 2008-12-24 10:10
Category: Cache Found/Cleared
Detained: 0

Region: RC CAPITAL
Longitude: 69.03891754
Type: Friendly Action
Affiliation: FRIEND

	Enemy	Friend	Civilian	Host Nation
Killed in Action	0	0	0	0
Wounded in Action	0	0	0	0

***DELAYED REPORT*
ITA BG with KCP on a joint patrol in Rural District of Paghman, found an ex-ammo depot, probably used by the Russian Army. The bunkers were completely filled with earth and a military excavator was transported to the site and under the control and direction of EOD Team Leader was recovered a considerable amount of ordnance, during two days of work. List A are the ordnances stored in KCP Paghman HQ, List B, the ordnances removed by ITA BG soldiers.
LIST A; RECOVERED MATERIAL ON THE 24 TH DECEMBER 2008 KCP PAGHMAN
4x RUSSIAN ROCKETS 122mm HE 9M28F
1x RUSSIAN ROCKETS 122mm HE 9M22F
13x CHINESE ROCKETS 107mm HE, Type63-2
2x CHINESE ROCKETS 107mm Incendiary, Type63-1
2x RUSSIAN PROJECTILE 100mm HE OF32
5x CHINESE PROJECTILE 82MM, HEAT, Type65
19x RUSSIAN MORTAR BOMB 82MM, HE, O832DU
4x AUSTRIAN MORTAR BOMB 82MM, HE, 83LD
2x RUSSIAN PROJECTILE 57mm HEI O271
50x RUSSIAN ANTIAIRCRAFT AMMUNITION 14,5 mm
14x RUSSIAN ROCKET FUZES PD V25
5x RUSSIAN ROCKET FUZES PD V14
2x RUSSIAN ROCKET FUZES PDSD V5
1x PAKISTAN A/T MINE P3MK1
LIST B; RECOVERED MATERIAL ON THE 25TH DECEMBER 2008 ITA BG3
84x RUSSIAN PROJECTILE 57mm HE O271

2x CHINES PROJECTILE 82MM, HEAT, Type65
1x RUSSIAN PROJECTILE 23mm HEI OFZ
2x RUSSIAN ANTIAIRCRAFT AMMUNITION 14,5 mm
1x CHINESE ROCKET FUZES for 107mm
7x RUSSIAN PROJECTILE FUZES for 57mm.
***Event closed at 272310D*

Reference ID: AFG20081229n1538   Region: RC SOUTH
Latitude: 31.60942459   Longitude: 65.52394104
Date: 2008-12-29 09:09   Type: Friendly Action
Category: Cache Found/Cleared   Affiliation: FRIEND
Detained: 0

	Enemy	Friend	Civilian	Host Nation
Killed in Action	0	0	0	0
Wounded in Action	0	0	0	0

At 1216Z, RC South reported a CACHE find. While conducting a clearance patrol ISO OP ATAL 47, FF reported a CACHE (medical supplies, 1000x rounds of DISHK ammo, AUP/ANP uniforms, various IED making material and yellow smoke grenades) find. EOD is on site and is exploiting. FF believe this to be a INS C2 center. No casualties or damage reported. NFI att.
At 1719Z, RC South reported:
At 1655Z, EOD BIP the device and RTB. NFTR. Event closed at 1655Z.
ISAF # 12-1265

Reference ID: AFG20090114n1694   Region: RC SOUTH
Latitude: 32.83581161   Longitude: 65.97214508
Date: 2009-01-14 07:07   Type: Friendly Action
Category: Cache Found/Cleared   Affiliation: FRIEND
Detained: 0

	Enemy	Friend	Civilian	Host Nation
Killed in Action	0	0	0	0
Wounded in Action	0	0	0	0

At 1235Z, RC South reported a Weapons Cache Find. While conducting OP TURA GHAR, FF reported they found a weapons cache of 3x Lee Enfield, 3x AK-47, 1500 9mm, 5x 56mm rounds, 7x 62mm rounds, chest rig, and 9x full magazines. FF recovered the findings and continued on with their missions. No casualties or damage reported. NFTR. Event closed at 1228Z.
ISAF # 01-589

Reference ID: AFG20090203n1635   Region: RC NORTH
Latitude: 35.93821716   Longitude: 68.65786743
Date: 2009-02-03 10:10   Type: Friendly Action
Category: Cache Found/Cleared   Affiliation: FRIEND
Detained: 0

	Enemy	Friend	Civilian	Host Nation
Killed in Action	0	0	0	0
Wounded in Action	0	0	0	0

At 1223Z, RC North reported a Weapons Cache Find. FF reported they found a Weapons Cache of illegal arsenal by ANA consisting of 64x PG7V Rocket, 170x BM1 type of Inflammatory, 50x VOG-17 Rifle Grenade, 4x Crates of 14.5mm Ammo, 7x Crates of PMC Ammo, 30x Battery Ignition, and 2x 57mm Anti-Aircraft Missile. The confiscated materials were transported to the ANP station for later disposal. No reports of casualties or damage. NFI att.
At 1219Z, RC North reported:
NFTR. Event closed at 1219Z.
ISAF # 02-120

Reference ID: AFG20090227n1676
Latitude: 36.66685486
Date: 2009-02-27 07:07
Category: Cache Found/Cleared
Detained: 0

Region: RC NORTH
Longitude: 68.91539764
Type: Friendly Action
Affiliation: FRIEND

	Enemy	Friend	Civilian	Host Nation
Killed in Action	0	0	0	0
Wounded in Action	0	0	0	0

At 1257Z, RC North reported a Weapons Cache Find:
FF were conducting a Sweep Mission in the area between PRT Camp and PRT Airfield when they discovered a Weapons Cache consisting of 38x UXOs and secured them for later disposal. PRT KDZ EOD has reported back to PRT KDZ Camp. The cache consisted of the following: 22x 76mm HE Grenades, 1x 100, HR Grenade, 1x Spall AP Mine POMSZ, 1x 82mm Mortar Grenade, 2x Rifle Grenades VOG 25, 6x Rifle Grenades VOG 17, 1x Propelling Charge RG-15, 3x Fuses and 1x Bomb AO 2.5.
At 1421Z, RC North reported:
NFTR. Event closed at 1415Z.
ISAF # 02-1172

Reference ID: AFG20090304n1583
Latitude: 33.98513794
Date: 2009-03-04 05:05
Category: Cache Found/Cleared
Detained: 0

Region: RC EAST
Longitude: 69.25765228
Type: Friendly Action
Affiliation: FRIEND

	Enemy	Friend	Civilian	Host Nation
Killed in Action	0	0	0	0
Wounded in Action	0	0	0	0

At 0649Z, RC East reported a Weapons Cache Find. FF reported that they discovered 2x Jingle Trucks containing 1x IED (ready for emplacement), 3x bags of hash, 3x 82mm Mortar Rounds, 1x Rocket, 1x Box of Unk Ammo, 12x Unk Mortar Rounds. The ANP are transporting the contraband to NDS(National Defense Security) compound. EOD has been notified. No casualties or damage reported. NFI att.
At 1539Z, RC East reported:

At 0900Z, ANP contacted FF and reported they originally discovered the UXOs and loaded them into the 2x Jingle Trucks to move them to a safe site for a Controlled Detonation. NFI att.
At 1600Z, RC East reported:
NFTR. Event closed at 1200Z.
ISAF # 02-149

Reference ID: AFG20090304n1599
Latitude: 45.54703522
Date: 2009-03-04 11:11
Category: Cache Found/Cleared
Detained: 0

Region: UNKNOWN
Longitude: 60.91264343
Type: Friendly Action
Affiliation: FRIEND

	Enemy	Friend	Civilian	Host Nation
Killed in Action	0	0	0	0
Wounded in Action	0	0	0	0

At 1148Z, RC South reported a Weapons Cache Find. FF reported that while conducting clearance patrol South of PB YUBRAJ, FF found 4x AP Mines, black in color, flat bottom and possible Italian made. FF secured and cordoned the area. AP Mines will be marked and avoided until IEDDT can exploit at a later time. NFI att.
At 1310Z, RC South reported:
NFTR. Event closed at 1310Z.
ISAF # 03-0173

Reference ID: AFG20090305n1762
Latitude: 36.65288162
Date: 2009-03-05 11:11
Category: Cache Found/Cleared
Detained: 0

Region: RC NORTH
Longitude: 68.90170288
Type: Friendly Action
Affiliation: FRIEND

	Enemy	Friend	Civilian	Host Nation
Killed in Action	0	0	0	0
Wounded in Action	0	0	0	0

At 1205Z, RC North reported a Weapons Cache Find. FF reported ANSF turned in 35x UXOs and 1x CWIED to NDF HQ KUNDUZ for disposal. EOD destroyed all ordnance at SR WADI. No casualties or damage reported.
At 1315Z, RC North reported:
NFTR. Event closed at 1310Z.
ISAF # 03-0243

Reference ID: AFG20090408n1819
Latitude: 31.59502602
Date: 2009-04-08 12:12
Category: Cache Found/Cleared
Detained: 0

Region: RC SOUTH
Longitude: 64.37588501
Type: Friendly Action
Affiliation: FRIEND

	Enemy	Friend	Civilian	Host Nation
Killed in Action	0	0	0	0
Wounded in Action	0	0	0	0

At 1640Z, RC South reported IED (Component) find:
FF reported finding probable TNT blocks and numerous commercial batteries. All items have been recovered to Lashkar Gah PRT. At 1848Z, IED components were handed over to EOD team at LKG. NFTR. Event closed at 1858Z.
ISAF #04-0339

Reference ID: AFG20090411n1746
Latitude: 31.49712563
Date: 2009-04-11 05:05
Category: Cache Found/Cleared
Detained: 0

Region: RC SOUTH
Longitude: 65.41278076
Type: Friendly Action
Affiliation: FRIEND

	Enemy	Friend	Civilian	Host Nation
Killed in Action	0	0	0	0
Wounded in Action	0	0	0	0

At 1538Z, RC South reported a Cache Find:
FF reported while conducting an offensive patrol, they found a cache consisting of 2x ANA uniforms, 10x PKMs and ammunition at grid 41R QQ 29166 87220. FF also detained 2x LNs. Cache was brought to PB Sperwan Ghar. FF found a second cache at grid 41R QQ 29222 87166. Cache was detected by metal detector and K9 unit. Cache consisted of 120x RPG rounds, 20x 82mm recoilless rounds, 1x mortar round, 1x AT mine and 3x boxes of grenades (60). UXOs were destroyed in 5x controlled detonations. NFI att.
At 1806Z, FF RTB. Event closed at 1821Z.
ISAF #04-0492

Reference ID: AFG20090417n1839
Latitude: 31.62592316
Date: 2009-04-17 08:08
Category: Cache Found/Cleared
Detained: 0

Region: RC SOUTH
Longitude: 64.88934326
Type: Friendly Action
Affiliation: FRIEND

	Enemy	Friend	Civilian	Host Nation
Killed in Action	0	0	0	0
Wounded in Action	0	0	0	0

At 0925Z, RC South reported a IED Components find:
FF reported while conducting an offensive patrol, they found 5x pressure plates, wires, tubing (for waterproofing) and blasting caps. There were no intact IEDs or explosives found. At 1335Z, materials were taken to FOB Ramrod. NFTR. Event closed at 1343Z.
ISAF #04-0735

Reference ID: AFG20090514n1870
Latitude: 34.64000702
Date: 2009-05-14 04:04
Category: Cache Found/Cleared
Detained: 0

Region: RC CAPITAL
Longitude: 69.07341766
Type: Friendly Action
Affiliation: FRIEND

	Enemy	Friend	Civilian	Host Nation
Killed in Action	0	0	0	0
Wounded in Action	0	0	0	0

At 1214Z, RC Capital reported a Weapons Cache Find. FRA BG reported that while conducting a patrol they found a Weapons Cache consisting of 54x Chinese 82mm projectiles. The projectiles have been recovered by FRA EOD. No casualties or damage reported. NFI att.
ISAF # 05-0784

Reference ID: AFG20090515n1796
Latitude: 32.72071838
Date: 2009-05-15 10:10
Category: Cache Found/Cleared
Detained: 0

Region: RC SOUTH
Longitude 65.90911865
Type: Friendly Action
Affiliation: FRIEND

	Enemy	Friend	Civilian	Host Nation
Killed in Action	0	0	0	0
Wounded in Action	0	0	0	0

11 BG conducting an offensive patrol ISO OP MANI GHAR 2, FF found a weapons cache consisting of 2 x Lee Enfield, 1 x Garant, 2 x PMK barrel and 3 x mortar sights(82mm). FF have collected the finds, which will be dealt with at the end of the operation. No casualties or damage reported.
***Event closed at 0010D*

Reference ID: AFG20090529n1741
Latitude: 31.63488007
Date: 2009-05-29 08:08
Category: Cache Found/Cleared
Detained: 0

Region: RC SOUTH
Longitude: 65.7286911
Type: Friendly Action
Affiliation: FRIEND

	Enemy	Friend	Civilian	Host Nation
Killed in Action	0	0	0	0
Wounded in Action	0	0	0	0

While Un-mentored ANP conducted a NFO patrol, they found an AP mine of UNK type with a watch attached to it. ANP cordoned the site. PRT QRF and EOD deployed to cordon and collect.
UPDATE 2001D*
EOD conducted a BiP and PRT have returned to base. Nothing further to report. No casualties or damage reported.
***Event closed 2056D*

Reference ID: AFG20090702n1886
Latitude: 31.77322769
Date: 2009-07-02 06:06
Category: Cache Found/Cleared
Detained: 0

Region: RC SOUTH
Longitude: 64.4797287
Type: Friendly Action
Affiliation: FRIEND

	Enemy	Friend	Civilian	Host Nation
Killed in Action	0	0	0	0
Wounded in Action	0	0	0	0

** DELAYED REPORTING - REPORT DERIVED FROM CEXC REPORT 09/CEXC-A/2019 **
The IED factory found was a facility utilized to manufacture "Graphite Pressure Plates". The adjacent room consisted of abandoned pieces of metal pressure plates in which future construction seemed to be abandoned. JFEOD blew everything in place. Items recovered:
6 x Graphite Pressure Plates, batteries (AA), Documents, RDX, Potassium Nitrate, Ammonium Nitrate, explosive samples, Multiple pieces of metal pressure plate material. See associated CEXC report and Cache Report for additional details.

Reference ID: AFG20090718n1940
Latitude: 31.01061249
Date: 2009-07-18 02:02
Category: Cache Found/Cleared
Detained: 0
Region: RC SOUTH
Longitude: 66.39596558
Type: Friendly Action
Affiliation: FRIEND

	Enemy	Friend	Civilian	Host Nation
Killed in Action	0	0	0	0
Wounded in Action	0	0	0	0

FF reported that while conducting NFO patrol they found a Explosives Cache consisting of 350kg of Gunpowder and 3100kg Aluminum Phosphate. FF collected all material and turned it over to ANP for destruction. No ISAF action required. No casualties or damage reported. NFTR. Event closed.

Reference ID: AFG20090718n1980
Latitude: 31.51202011
Date: 2009-07-18 06:06
Category: Cache Found/Cleared
Detained: 0
Region: RC SOUTH
Longitude: 65.56233978
Type: Friendly Action
Affiliation: FRIEND

	Enemy	Friend	Civilian	Host Nation
Killed in Action	0	0	0	0
Wounded in Action	0	0	0	0

1-12 INF reported that while conducting a patrol, FF found a cache consisting of suicide vests, 3x AK-47, 1x RPG, 10x RPG rounds, 12x 81mm mortars, 10x ANSF uniforms and sleeping bags. FF confiscated all items. NFI att.
FF also found 1x suicide vest, 1x DsHK (with tripod and ammo), 1x PKM, yellow jugs, batteries, wires, det cord, ball bearings, medical supplies, IV bags and kitchen equipment. All items found were destroyed or turned over to ANSF as appropriate. No casualties or damage reported. Event closed at 1801Z.
Update: See attached Task Force Kandahar Counter-IED Tactical Exploitation Report.

Reference ID: AFG20090922n2151
Latitude: 30.54704857
Region: RC SOUTH
Longitude: 63.81791306

Date: 2009-09-22 04:04 Type: Friendly Action
Category: Cache Found/Cleared Affiliation: FRIEND
Detained: 0

	Enemy	Friend	Civilian	Host Nation
Killed in Action	0	0	0	0
Wounded in Action	0	0	0	0

WHEN: 22 0922D SEP 09
WHO: 2D LAR
WHERE: 41R NP 78451 79690, 3.3KM E OF COP KHAN NESHIN CASTLE
WHAT: IED CACHE
EVENT: WHILE CLEARING A COMPOUND FROM WHICH 2DLAR HAD RECENTLY TAKEN DETAINEES, 2D LAR DISCOVERED (18) HOMEMADE BLASTING CAPS, MADE FROM PENS AND HME. ADDITIONALLY THEY FOUND BATTERIES, AND TIRE TUBES. 2D LAR UP THE MATERIALS AND BROUGHT THEM TO KHAN NESHIN CASTLE FOR FUTURE DISPOSAL.
BDA: NO CASUALTIES OR DAMAGE REPORTED.
ISAF # 09-2133 (CLOSED)

Detainees

The second task of the counter-insurgent policeman, along with removing weapons, is to place as many of the armed gang members in jail as possible to get them off the streets, and to obtain as much useful intelligence information as he can in order to track down more members and capture them, until he has broken the organization. US occupation troops use a variety of standard police measures, including fingerprinting, DNA testing, biometric devices, and a network of informants, to identify and track down suspected insurgents. American forces in Afghanistan have been vigilant in rounding up suspected insurgent supporters, incarcerating them in various prison camps, and extracting information from them. Reports indicate that children as young as 11 and 14 have been arrested, and then questioned or detained. The total number of Afghans who have been detained at one time or another must be massive. The US also maintains a list of specific individuals who are targeted for detention.

In situations where the counter-insurgent does not have the support of the population, however, this is an extremely difficult task. Without the active cooperation of the public, among whom the guerrillas must swim, it is an impossible task, particularly for an outside power, to track down and penetrate the insurgent resistance network.

Although the documents here do not go into the treatment of these prisoners or the legality of their captivity, it is in precisely that area where the US has done the most to cripple its own counter-insurgency efforts — not just in Afghanistan, but also in its simultaneous guerrilla fight in Iraq. By resorting to torture in its interrogations and by declaring that it doesn't have to follow international laws and treaties regarding the treatment of prisoners, the United States has lost the once-universal sympathy of the rest of the world, has destroyed much of the political support of the American people towards the war, and has handed Al Qaeda and the Taliban the opportunity to organize a global army of supporters and defenders who are willing to take up weapons against the United States.

Reference ID: AFG20061013n419
Latitude: 33.31472015
Date: 2006-10-13 03:03
Category: Detain
Detained: 0

Region: RC EAST
Longitude: 69.70474243
Type: Friendly Action
Affiliation: FRIEND

	Enemy	Friend	Civilian	Host Nation
Killed in Action	0	0	0	0
Wounded in Action	0	0	0	0

At 130330ZOCT06 TF WOLFPACK reported NDS capture 3x individuals 20km West of Khowst in Kadhi village. The 3 individuals were directly involved in a VBIED (Black Toyota Sedan) expected to target CF/GOA vic Khowst. NDS was unable to secure the vehicle. NFTR.

Reference ID: AFG20070201n561
Latitude: 34.42556
Date: 2007-02-01 06:06
Category: Detain
Detained: --

Region: RC EAST
Longitude: 70.45285034
Type: Friendly Action
Affiliation: FRIEND

	Enemy	Friend	Civilian	Host Nation
Killed in Action	--	--	--	--
Wounded in Action	--	--	--	--

(DELAYED REPORT) On 22JAN07 CJSOTF received information from a source that an individual would be delivering IED components and explosives from Pakistan to Jalalabad. The source advices that the delivery would be made to a hat shop located in downtown JBAD. ABP provided physical surveillance of the shop intended. ABP detained 2xINS on 28JAN07. Items recovered on the scene were 2.5pds Orange RDX explosives , 3pds white RDX explosives (removed from PG-7), 2pds of propellant, 1x200gram Block of TNT with black time fuse and non-electric blasting cap, and 1xChemical pencil. NFTR. CEXC Report: CEXC_AFG_092_07.

Reference ID: AFG20070201n563
Latitude: 35.01166916
Date: 2007-02-01 08:08
Category: Detain
Detained: 1

Region: RC EAST
Longitude: 69.31667328
Type: Friendly Action
Affiliation: FRIEND

	Enemy	Friend	Civilian	Host Nation
Killed in Action	0	0	0	0
Wounded in Action	0	0	0	0

(DELAYED REPORT) At 010830ZFEB07 OSI received a DTMF MOD 4 device from ANP. OSI reported that the device was taken from a LN that ANP arrested following a 25JAN07 raid on a house in Jamchi Village where they found a cache consisting of military ordnance mortar rounds, artillery shells, AP mines, 55mm rockets and a mosque clock. OSI turned in the device to BAF CEXC. CEXC Report: CEXC_AFG_067_07. NFTR.

Reference ID: AFG20070826n804
Latitude: 33.47941971
Date: 2007-08-26 05:05
Category: Detain
Detained: 0

Region: RC EAST
Longitude: 69.37133789
Type: Friendly Action
Affiliation: FRIEND

	Enemy	Friend	Civilian	Host Nation
Killed in Action	0	0	0	0
Wounded in Action	0	0	0	0

On 26 August 2007, ANA/ANP with CF as observers conducted a tactical screening of three detainees associated with a suspected VBIED along the K-G Pass. Comment: The suspected was due to be exploited by TF Paladin assets on 26 August 2007, as of this report the team had not began that exploitation. End Comment. The detainees are two Afghans and one Russian. The below is a summary of the tactical questioning of the detainees by ANA/ANP with CF as observers:
Name: Jawed (Detainee 1)
Fathers Name: Momin
Age: 26
Profession: Teacher at the Ibrahim bin Adam Madrassa in Kabul (located in the Chaharasai District)
District: Chaharasai
Province: KabulJawed
Name: Khwani (Detainee 2)
Fathers Name: Abdul Ghafor
Age: 22
Profession:
Village: Ilyas Khel
District: Chaharasai
Province: KabulKhwani
Name: Andre Batoloff Vladimirovich (Detainee 3)
Islamic Name: Abdul Ahmad
Age: 28
POB: RussiaAndre Batoloff Vladimirovich
Abdul Ahmad (Islamic Name)
Detainee 1, did not want to identify himself to ANA/ANP after a couple of times he identified himself as Jawed. The detainee from this point answered most questions that the ANA/ANP asked. The detainee stated that he and his friend went to Khowst Province to the Yaqubi Village to meet with Gul Khan who the detainee had loaned some money to. Detainee 1 called Detainee 2 and asked him to travel with him to Khowst, to which Detainee 2 agreed too. The pair arrived at Gul Khans in the Yaqubi Village and Gul tells Jawed that he does not have Jaweds money. Instead of paying Jawed his money Gul gives Jawed a truck and tells him to take a woman to Logar and she knows where to go from there. Jawed stated they all got in the vehicle and started their move to Pul-e-Alam. Jawed stated that he did not ask who the woman was or exactly where she was going in Logar. Jawed stated he did not ask the woman any questions and was not concerned with it, he was just doing what Gul Khan asked him to do. ANA/ANP Comment: This guy is a liar and is hiding information, he is crooked. End Comment.
Detainee 2 stated he was called by Detainee 1 and asked to go to Khowst with him to see a friend. Detainee 2 stated when they arrived in Khowst they met with Gul Khan

and he said he did not have the money so he was would give them a vehicle instead and told them to take an unidentified woman to the Logar Province. ANA/ANP Comment: This man is not honest and he is trying to protect himself. He is just like all the others just a terrorist and not a good Afghan. End Comment.

Detainee 3: Is a Russian national who is trying to get through Afghanistan to make it to Tajikistan to get back into Russia. Background: Detainee 3 converted to Islam about three years ago. The detainee is a gas mine engineer back at his home in Nizhnevartovsk, Russia. The detainee traveled from Moscow, Russia to Teheran, Iran to Quetta, PK. Once the detainee arrived in Quetta, PK he moved by bus to Mir Ali and onward to Miram Shah. Once in Miram Shah the detainee was moved and stayed with other in villages between Miram Shah and Degan, PK. The detainee stated he come to PK with the intent of studying Islam. While in the Miram Shah area the detainee stated he studied under an Abdullah. When asked where he got his money from or if he had any money. The detainee responded that he had dollars from his job back in Russia and once he got to Pakistan he exchanged the money he had into Rupee. The detainee identified that the villages and madrassas that he stayed had many foreign fighters there. He stated that all the men in the areas that he stayed in and around were armed with AK-47s and RPGs. The groups in the areas that he stayed were Tajiks, some Arabs, Uzbeks, Turkish and Pashtu. When asked how long he had been in PK, the detainee stated he had been in PK for about ten and half months. When asked why he came to Pakistan? The detainee stated again that he was there to learn more about Islam and study. While the detainee was in Miram Shah and Mir Ali he stated that he was taken out to the mountains to train and shoot weapons. The detainee stated he only fired a Kalashnikov rifle firing about 30 rounds. When asked was he a jihadi? The detainee responded no and stated he was only there to study Islam not to fight anyone. The detainee stated he only spent one and half months in Mir Ali and the remainder of his time in was spent between Miram Shah and Degan in small villages. The detainee said that he was not allowed to go to the bazaar or into the villages, he did not know why. The detainee stated he was trying to get through Afghanistan to make it back to Russia. The detainee stated since he no official papers he was told in PK by Abdullah, NFI, that it was be easy to cross the border into Afghanistan and then go to Tajikistan and onward to Russia. The detainee stated he came into Afghanistan yesterday, 25 August 2007, on the road from Degan, PK. The detainee stated he was given a burkha and a small bag to put his clothes in and told to get into a white Toyota Corolla. The vehicle had a driver and it drove him into Afghanistan across the border into the Khowst area where he was dropped off and basically instructed to wait and someone would pick him up and that is what happened. Detainee 3 was picked up and driven by Detainees 1 and 2, detainee 3 was not told where he was going or being taken. The detainee stated he kept the burkha on until they were stopped and detained by ANP. When asked about the explosives in the vehicle the detainee stated that he knew nothing about them and all he was just riding to get to Tajikistan to make it back to his home in Russia. Detainee 3 provided his residence address in Nizhnevartovsk, Russia, Tyumenskaya, Nizhnzevartovsk Mira 60/4 APT 88 Floor 7, 44-26-58.

TF Fury Comment/Observation: Detainee 3 seemed to be forthcoming with his information and did not evade or try to mislead. The tactical questioning was conducted in Russian and translated into Pashtu/Dari. Detainee became emotional when it was suggested that he was to be used as a suicide bomber or as part of a VBIED attack. The ANA/ANP both assess detainee 3 was actually trying to return to his home in Russia. Detainee 3 seemed nave as he did not speak much Urdu or Pashtu limiting interaction with the other detainees who only spoke Pashtu. Detainee told the ANA/ANP screener that all he was trying to do is learn how to be a good Muslim and learn the Holy Koran and this was not what a good Muslim does. Concur with ANA/ANP assessment that detainee was unknowingly going to be used a suicide bomber or part of a VBIED attack. End Comment.

CEXC conducted SSE of the VBIED and control detonated the vehicle on FB Lightning.

Reference ID: AFG20080906n1552
Latitude: 34.53055573
Date: 2008-09-06 07:07
Category: Detain
Detained: 0
Region: RC CAPITAL
Longitude: 69.17979431
Type: Friendly Action
Affiliation: FRIEND

	Enemy	Friend	Civilian	Host Nation
Killed in Action	0	0	0	0
Wounded in Action	0	0	0	0

An FBI source advised that Mullah Burham, an IED facilitator from Kapisa Province, Tagab Valley, may be in NDS custody. In an attempt to determine if these individuals were one in the same person, biometrics and photographs were collected from Burham on 9/6/08. It was later determined by photograph ID that they are the same individual. It is requested that the collected biometrics be compared to previous IED incidents in the Tagab Valley.

Reference ID: AFG20080924n1330
Latitude: 34.75190735
Date: 2008-09-24 06:06
Category: Detain
Detained: 3
Region: RC EAST
Longitude: 69.38052368
Type: Friendly Action
Affiliation: FRIEND

	Enemy	Friend	Civilian	Host Nation
Killed in Action	2	0	0	0
Wounded in Action	1	0	0	0

t 0420Z - SLAYER 26 SENDS SITREP THAT THE ANA HAVE SURGUL SURROUNDED IN PACHA HAK AND AFGHAN CID REQUEST CF ASSISTANCE. At 0600Z - SLAYER 26 REPORTS: ANA HAVE CAPTURED SURGUL AND 2x OTHER LNs. ONE OTHER LN WAS KIA. ANA ARE NOW CONDUCTING A SEARCH OF THE AREA. SLAYER 26 REPORTS: THERE ARE NOW 2x INS KIA. 1x WIA HAS BEEN CAPTURED. THEY ARE NOT IN CONTACT ATT. THE GRID THAT THE ANA CAPTURED SURGUL IS IVO 42SWD 34828 45597
At 0631Z - SURGUL WAS TAKEN BY THE ANA AND HAVE LEFT THE SCENE ATT. SLAYER 26 IS GOING BACK TO UPPER PACHA HAK NOW
At 0756Z - SLAYER 26 CONDUCTED AN ADDITIONAL SEARCH OF THE AREA AND IS EN ROUTE BACK TO THE DANDAR VPB
At 0757Z - EVENT CLOSED
SIGACT 24 0605Z SEP 08: ANA contacted SLAYER Base and informed them that they had Surgul surrounded in the village of Pacha Hak. They requested Coalition Forces reinforcements. SLAYER 26 moved from the Dandar VPB to the area, vic 42S WD

34828 45597. Upon arrival, SLAYER 26 reported that the ANA had captured Surgul alive. 2x other INS were KIA and 1x WIA INS is also in ANA custody. SLAYER and ANA elements are clearing the area ATT. 24 0750Z SEP 08: SLAYER 26 reports that the ANA have left Pacha Hak, taking Surgul and other INS detainees to a secure location. SLAYER 26 conducted an additional search of the area and is en route back to the Dandar VPB. MC.

Reference ID: AFG20081022n1480
Latitude: 34.6088028
Date: 2008-10-22 15:03
Category: Detain
Detained: 1

Region: RC CAPITAL
Longitude: 69.72312927
Type: Friendly Action
Affiliation: FRIEND

	Enemy	Friend	Civilian	Host Nation
Killed in Action	0	0	0	0
Wounded in Action	0	0	0	0

A FRA platoon on NFO patrol has captured 1 x suspect who should be Mollha GAI (Supposed insurgent probably involved in the 18th AUG08 ambush against French Troops). Currently this man is on FOB TORA and will be soon transport to WAREHOUSE by helicopter.
UPDATE 1800D*
Captured person has been brought to CW and investigation is ongoing for the moment.
***Event closed at 241645D*1 Detained None(None) Insurgent

Reference ID: AFG20081024n1388
Latitude: 34.51864243
Date: 2008-10-24 11:11
Category: Detain
Detained: 1

Region: RC CAPITAL
Longitude: 69.11254883
Type: Friendly Action
Affiliation: FRIEND

	Enemy	Friend	Civilian	Host Nation
Killed in Action	0	0	0	0
Wounded in Action	0	0	0	0

From 232200D* FF conducted technical and covert physical surveillance against Mullah ASAMUDDIN. ASAMUDDIN was eventually fixed at the above location at 241105D* and FF conducted a hard stop on ASAMUDDIN. ASAMUDDIN was detained and handed over to the NDS. No casualties or damage reported.
***Event closed at 252250D*1 Detained None(None) Insurgent

Reference ID: AFG20081025n1417
Latitude: 31.4275341
Date: 2008-10-25 13:01
Category: Detain
Detained: 5

Region: RC SOUTH
Longitude: 64.28575897
Type: Friendly Action
Affiliation: FRIEND

	Enemy	Friend	Civilian	Host Nation
Killed in Action	0	0	0	0
Wounded in Action	0	0	0	0

TF 42 while conducting detention operation enter the compound and detained 5x MAMs.
It was confirmed that the JPEL taget was detained. No casualties or damage reported. Detainees are in NDS custody.
***Event closed at 271758D*5 Detained None(None) Insurgent

Reference ID: AFG20081026n1333
Latitude: 34.52324295
Date: 2008-10-26 01:01
Category: Detain
Detained: 9

Region: RC CAPITAL
Longitude: 69.22777557
Type: Friendly Action
Affiliation: FRIEND

	Enemy	Friend	Civilian	Host Nation
Killed in Action	0	0	0	0
Wounded in Action	0	0	0	0

TF 36, TF 52 and the CRU (Crisis Response Unit - Afghan Spec. Police) during OP DEGALE II prosecuted a strike against WAHIDULLAH at his compound. Entry to the compound was gained at 0120D* and the compound was secured at 0132D*. WAHIDULLAH and 8 x LN (unknown males) were detained and are now in NDS custody.
***Event closed at 0120D*1 Detained None(None) Insurgent
8 Detained None(None) Local Civilian

Reference ID: AFG20081028n1531
Latitude: 32.04904938
Date: 2008-10-28 12:12
Category: Detain
Detained: 0

Region: RC SOUTH
Longitude: 66.73404694
Type: Friendly Action
Affiliation: FRIEND

	Enemy	Friend	Civilian	Host Nation
Killed in Action	0	0	0	0
Wounded in Action	0	0	0	0

This report is based on scant information, provided verbally by a member of the unit. Task Force 77 (TF 77) conducted a site exploitation of an area between three villages in Tarnak va Jaldak on 28 October 2008. TF 77 took six individuals were taken into custody and the detainees are currently in the custody of the ANA. TF 77 located a detonator, eight AA batteries, one nine volt battery, tape and wiring in a dry river bed.
Please see attached reports for further information.
This SIGACT is associated with CEXC # 08-2161.

Reference ID: AFG20081028n1542
Latitude: 32.17634201
Date: 2008-10-28 19:07
Category: Detain
Detained: 0

Region: RC SOUTH
Longitude: 66.5141449
Type: Friendly Action
Affiliation: FRIEND

	Enemy	Friend	Civilian	Host Nation
Killed in Action	0	0	0	0
Wounded in Action	0	0	0	0

TFZ BTL NCO reported that ANA (2/2/205) whilst conducting a follow up action to previous IED event 10-1315, detained 10 x poss INS IVO IED strike. At the same time ANP detained a further 12 x pax with Humvee parts in MIZAN DC. All pax were taken to FOB MIZAN and FF will send a full report, once the investigation is completed. RC(S) considers this event closed until the results of pending investigation have been compiled, completed and released. No casualties or damage reported.
***Event closed at 2208D*.10 Arrested Insurgent
12 Arrested Local Civilian

Reference ID: AFG20081030n1399   Region: RC EAST
Latitude: 34.2468338   Longitude: 70.84938812
Date: 2008-10-30 10:10   Type: Friendly Action
Category: Detain   Affiliation: FRIEND
Detained: 0

	Enemy	Friend	Civilian	Host Nation
Killed in Action	0	0	0	0
Wounded in Action	0	0	0	0

On 301030ZOCT08, Noorullah s/o Ghulam Habib, Technical Assistant, Nangarhar ANP Counterterrorism Department (ANP/CT), contacted SABT Francisco and advised ABP had detained one (1) individual at Torkham Gate (42S XC 9310 7766) while traveling from Pakistan to his home in the vicinity of Khogyani (42S XC 106 922) Afghanistan, with possible IED materials. Noorullah advised the individual had three (3) notebooks with handwritten notes of detailed instructions on the construction of IEDs and the use of other military ordnance, and three (3) DVDs appearing to be insurgent propaganda videos in his possession at the time of arrest. SABT Francisco inquired about ANPs intentions and Noorullah advised ANP intended to prosecute the individual. On 301045ZOCT08, CIED Team JAF, responded to the Nangarhar ANP HQ in Jalalabad to conduct an interview, biometrics, photographs, and fingerprinting.
Please see attached reports for further information.
This SIGACT is associated with CEXC # 2293.

Reference ID: AFG20090105n1663   Region: RC SOUTH
Latitude: 31.73921585   Longitude: 65.72024536
Date: 2009-01-05 09:09   Type: Friendly Action
Category: Detain   Affiliation: FRIEND
Detained: 0

	Enemy	Friend	Civilian	Host Nation
Killed in Action	0	0	0	0
Wounded in Action	0	0	0	0

3 RCR BG Recce SQN conducting a NFO patrol found a crater and CW leading from crater to a LN compound. No IED was found from the area. FF administered a GSR (Gun Shot Resident) test to a LN living in the compound, which he failed. FF

detained the LN as a POSS trigger man and IED emplacer and extracted him to KAF. FF continued on task.
***event closed at 1045D*1 Detained None(None) Local Civilian

Reference ID: AFG20090123n1613   Region: RC SOUTH
Latitude: 32.37514496   Longitude: 64.77241516
Date: 2009-01-23 11:11   Type: Friendly Action
Category: Detain   Affiliation: FRIEND
Detained: 0

	Enemy	Friend	Civilian	Host Nation
Killed in Action	0	0	0	0
Wounded in Action	0	0	0	0

B Coy 2 RGR providing FP to PB WOQAB saw an INS spotter at Gr 41S PR 6639 8296 observing FF patrol as it was returning from patrol. QRF with embedded ANP arrested him and an investigation is being conducted.
UPDATE 1720D*
FF have returned to PB WOQAB.
***Event closed at 1720D*.1 Arrested None(None) Insurgent

Reference ID: AFG20090210n1684   Region: RC NORTH
Latitude: 36.75761414   Longitude: 68.81513977
Date: 2009-02-10 17:05   Type: Friendly Action
Category: Detain   Affiliation: FRIEND
Detained: 2

	Enemy	Friend	Civilian	Host Nation
Killed in Action	0	0	0	0
Wounded in Action	0	0	0	0

At 11 1000D*, EUPOL reported about an operation by ANP and ANA between 10 2130D* and 11 0400D* in BAGHI SHERKAT, where INS meeting took place. Result of operation was 2 x INS captured, 1 x AK 47 and 1 x TOYOTA TOWN ACE confiscated. The INS's and confiscated materials are in the hand of NDS. NFTR.
***Event closed at 11 1037D*2 Detained None(None) Insurgent

Reference ID: AFG20090218n1677   Region: RC SOUTH
Latitude: 31.51355743   Longitude: 65.76551819
Date: 2009-02-18 06:06   Type: Friendly Action
Category: Detain   Affiliation: FRIEND
Detained: 0

	Enemy	Friend	Civilian	Host Nation
Killed in Action	0	0	0	0
Wounded in Action	0	0	0	0

Joint RFS (Regiment Field Squadron) at KAF reported that in a deliberate detaiment operation, FF detained ABSAL KHAN. The detainee was highlighted by OSI elements at KAF as having possible links to IED facilitation. The detainee is being moved to THF at KAF.1 Detained None(None) Insurgent

Reference ID: AFG20090220n1606
Latitude: 31.49478149
Date: 2009-02-20 02:02
Category: Detain
Detained: 0

Region: RC SOUTH
Longitude: 65.22205353
Type: Friendly Action
Affiliation: FRIEND

	Enemy	Friend	Civilian	Host Nation
Killed in Action	0	0	0	0
Wounded in Action	0	0	0	0

A Coy 2-2 INF reported that while conducting a dismounted NFO patrol, LN guided FF to a compound housing a suspected INS. FF detained 1 x PAX and moved him to HUTAL DC and later to NDS. There were no casualties or damage reported. BDA: see personnel details.
***Event closed at 21 0824D*1 Detained None(None) Local Civilian

Reference ID: AFG20090225n1608
Latitude: 32.836586
Date: 2009-02-25 12:12
Category: Detain
Detained: 2

Region: RC SOUTH
Longitude: 65.99256134
Type: Friendly Action
Affiliation: FRIEND

	Enemy	Friend	Civilian	Host Nation
Killed in Action	0	0	0	0
Wounded in Action	0	0	0	0

1 platoon MRTF conducting a NFO patrol detained 2 x persons who tested positive on TNT type explosives.
FF took both detainees to PB MARSHAL. There were no casualties or damage reported.
UPDATE 2133D*
Detainees will be taken to FOB RIPLEY in the morning.
***Event closed at 2146D*2 Detained None(None) Local Civilian

Reference ID: AFG20090321n1685
Latitude: 31.66373634
Date: 2009-03-21 07:07
Category: Detain
Detained: 6

Region: RC SOUTH
Longitude: 65.64308167
Type: Friendly Action
Affiliation: FRIEND

	Enemy	Friend	Civilian	Host Nation
Killed in Action	0	0	0	0
Wounded in Action	0	0	0	0

Un-mentored ANA reported that while conducting a NFO, FF detained 3 x PAX in ARGHANDAB DC believed to be related to IED activities. 2x detainees confessed to being triggerman for an IED strike at GR 41RQR506062 which resulted in 1 x LN killed and 3x LN injured. Details unconfirmed. (TFK have no details of this IED explosion or that the wounded LNs were transported to a local hospital). FF transported all the detainees to SP ARGHANDAB. All detainees tested positive for explosives. During the questioning of the detainees, a cellphone rang. When answered, the person on the other end asked have you done the job and how many have you killed.

FF intend to move all detainees to CAMP HERO for further processing. There were no casualties or damage reported.
UPDATE 1538D*
3x FAM arrived at SP Arghandab to collect their friends, and they were subsequently questioned. During questioning they also tested positive for explosives and have been detained.
UPDATE 2002D*
ANA intends to hand over the detainees to AUP. No word of timings yet. OMLT is working on getting as much data as possible prior to transfer.
BDA:6 Detained None(None) Insurgent

Reference ID: AFG20090416n1748
Region: RC EAST
Latitude: 33.33957291
Longitude: 69.90695953
Date: 2009-04-16 06:06
Type: Friendly Action
Category: Detain
Affiliation: FRIEND
Detained: 5

	Enemy	Friend	Civilian	Host Nation
Killed in Action	0	0	0	0
Wounded in Action	0	0	0	0

UNIT: TF STEEL
TYPE: SUICIDE BOMBER
WHO: LN; SAPPER IS ASSUMING RESPONSIBILITY FOR THE DETAINEES.
WHERE: KHOWST PROVINCE
INITIAL REPORT: @ 0630 TF STEEL RECIEVED A REPORT ON TWO MEN THE REPORT FOLLOWS: ANP DETAINED A MAN NAME NOT KNOWN WHO WAS LATER SHIPPED TO kHOWS T ANP HQ IN KHOWST CITY. THE MAN SAID HE WAS FROM PAKTIKA, VISITING HIS ILL FATHER IN MIRAAM SHAH, NWA, PAK. HE WAS CAPTURED BY THE TALIBAN AND FORCED TO BE A SUICIDE BOMBER. HE WAS BROUGHT TO A BED-DOWN LOCATION NORTH OF MASHI KALAY, AND INSTRUCTED TO WALK INTO THE GORBUZ DC AND IDENTIFY THE CF COMPOUND AND ENTRANCE AND THE ANP CHIEF AND HIS OFFICE LOCATION. THE MAN WAS DETAINED DURING HIS RECON. AFTER PROMISE OF IMMUNITY (WHICH IS AN EMPTY PROMISE) FROM THE ANP INVESTIGATORS, THE MAN SAID THAT HE WOULD BRING ANP TO THE BED-DOWN LOCATION. HE SAID THERE WAS ANOTHER MAN, NAMED AHMED. HE WAS A YOUNG MAN 18-22 YEARS OF AGE BLUE EYES, AND RED IN COLOR, POSSIBLY BEARD POSSIBLY DYED OR REDDISH TINTED SKIN. ANP MAY CONDUCT OPERATION TO AREA NEAR MASHI KALAY IOT IDENTIFY AND SEARCH BED-DOWN LOCATION. MAN ALSO INFORMED THE ANP INVESTIGATORS THAT HTE BOMBER VESTS WERE ACTUALLY GARMENTS WORN NEAR GROIN AREA DUE TO CULTURAL BOUNDARIES OFTEN HAVING ANSF NOT SEARCH THAT AREA.
ANP INVESTIGATORS BELIEVE THIS MAN WOULD ATTACK IN CONCERT WITH OTHERS, CONDUCTING A COORDINATED STRIKE SIMILAR TO THE ATTACKS ON SALERNO UTILIZING VBIEDS. FIRST BOMBER WOULD TARGET GUARDS IN WADDI, NEXT WOULD TARGET ANP/ASG, FOLLOW ON 2 OR 3 WOULD TARGET HARDENED STRUCTURES AND AREAS IN CF COMPOUND AND ANP. ALSO ANP EXPRESSED CONCERN OF A MAN IN A BURKHA BEING

ABLE TO INFILTRATE THE CLINIC AT GORBUZ DC AND ENTER THE ANP COMPOUND VIA THIS ROUTE UNDETECTED. AT LEAST ONE OF THE ABOVE MEN HAD A FAKE I.D.
UPDATE: 1106Z THERE ARE NOW 5 DETAINEES AND A TC-6 MINE FOUND
SUMMARY:
2 X SUICIDE BOMBERS
5 X DETAINEES
5 TOTAL DETAINEES
EVENT: CLOSED 0900Z

Reference ID: AFG20090419n1730
Latitude: 32.06111526
Date: 2009-04-19 10:10
Category: Detain
Detained: 2

Region: RC SOUTH
Longitude: 64.85190582
Type: Friendly Action
Affiliation: FRIEND

	Enemy	Friend	Civilian	Host Nation
Killed in Action	0	0	0	0
Wounded in Action	0	0	0	0

A Coy 2 RIFLES reported that while providing FP to PB WISHTAN, FF observed 2 x PAX on a motorcycle who failed to follow instructions. FF fired 1 x (5.56mm) warning shot causing the PAX to stop. The PAX were then questioned. The interpeter was not happy with the story and one of the LN had an old GSW and star and crescent tattoo on the web of his hand. FF detained both LN. FF will transport 2 x detainees to FOB JACKSON.
UPDATE 2003D*
FF questioned the detainees and released them afterwards. No significant Information has been gathered from the questioning.
***Event closed 2006D*

Reference ID: AFG20090428n1802
Latitude: 31.47031593
Date: 2009-04-28 06:06
Category: Detain
Detained: 1

Region: RC SOUTH
Longitude: 65.28638458
Type: Friendly Action
Affiliation: FRIEND

	Enemy	Friend	Civilian	Host Nation
Killed in Action	0	0	0	0
Wounded in Action	0	0	0	0

C Coy R22R reported that FF detained 1 x PAX which is tested positive for explosive powder. FF preparing all documents for DETREP.

Reference ID: AFG20090502n1750
Latitude: 31.84223175
Date: 2009-05-02 14:02
Category: Detain
Detained: 2

Region: RC SOUTH
Longitude: 64.22278595
Type: Friendly Action
Affiliation: FRIEND

	Enemy	Friend	Civilian	Host Nation
Killed in Action	0	0	0	0
Wounded in Action	0	0	0	0

4 Mercian BSN FP reported that while conducting a NFO patrol, FF observed 4 x PAX with 2 x motorcycle possibly cutting the perimeter wire of BSN. FF QRF deployed to investigate and identified a hole in the fence. FF stopped 2x PAX and confiscated 1 x motorcycle until further notice. 2 x PAX are juveniles between 16-19 years of age.
2 x PAX are under age and have been released with motorcycle. No casualties or damage reported.
***Event closed at 2320D*

Reference ID: AFG20090507n1837 Region: RC SOUTH
Latitude: 31.53120422 Longitude: 65.79338074
Date: 2009-05-07 07:07 Type: Friendly Action
Category: Detain Affiliation: FRIEND
Detained: 1

	Enemy	Friend	Civilian	Host Nation
Killed in Action	0	0	0	0
Wounded in Action	0	0	0	0

DELAYED REPORT
NMCC reported that one suspected man with 1 Ak-47 was arrested, 2 Kg IED, 55 auto parts of RCIED, 50 time delay fuse and 370 gram hashish were discovered in a clean up operation conducted by ANP, ANA and NDS in relative areas of Kandahar City.
***Event closed at 082135D*MAY1 Arrested None(None) Local Civilian

Reference ID: AFG20090509n1755 Region: RC SOUTH
Latitude: 31.53120422 Longitude: 65.79338074
Date: 2009-05-09 07:07 Type: Friendly Action
Category: Detain Affiliation: FRIEND
Detained: 3

	Enemy	Friend	Civilian	Host Nation
Killed in Action	0	0	0	0
Wounded in Action	0	0	0	0

NMCC LNO reported that in a joint mop-up operation of ANA, ANP and NDS in Loy Weyala Area, 3 x suicide bombers were arrested and 21kg explosives, 1 pistol, 2 AT IEDs and 2 hand grenades were seized. No casualties or damage reported.
***Event closed at 101200D*3 Arrested None(None) Insurgent

Reference ID: AFG20090516n1789 Region: RC SOUTH
Latitude: 31.61775589 Longitude: 65.53453827
Date: 2009-05-16 03:03 Type: Friendly Action
Category: Detain Affiliation: FRIEND
Detained: 0

	Enemy	Friend	Civilian	Host Nation
Killed in Action	0	0	0	0
Wounded in Action	0	0	0	0

A Coy 2R22R BG conducting an Offensive patrol ISO OP SHIN MENGARAY arrested 3 x INS after tested positive for X-Spray and items of interest. FF has detainees and will transfer them to imbedded MP's for processing and transfer to KAF. No casualties or damage reported.
UPDATE 2342D*
Detainees are in control of MPs.They will be moved to KAF with 12 detainees from event 05-0930. TFK will inform if any problems with detainee transfer.
***Event closed 2344D*3 Detained None(None) Insurgent

Reference ID: AFG20090516n1792
Latitude: 31.51263428
Date: 2009-05-16 04:04
Category: Detain
Detained: 1

Region: RC SOUTH
Longitude: 65.48828125
Type: Friendly Action
Affiliation: FRIEND

	Enemy	Friend	Civilian	Host Nation
Killed in Action	0	0	0	0
Wounded in Action	0	0	0	0

B Coy TF 2-2 conducting an Offensive patrol ISO OP SHIN MENGARAY observed 1 x INS attempting to leave Senjaray area. INS had a fake ID and a laundry list of ammunition to purchase. FF arrested the INS. No casualties or damage reported.
UPDATE 2347D*
ANA with TF 2-2/B searched and detained the INS. INS is in ANA custody.
***Event closed 2349D*1 Detained None(None) Insurgent

Reference ID: AFG20090516n1834
Latitude: 31.60813332
Date: 2009-05-16 13:01
Category: Detain
Detained: 13

Region: RC SOUTH
Longitude: 65.54360962
Type: Friendly Action
Affiliation: FRIEND

	Enemy	Friend	Civilian	Host Nation
Killed in Action	0	0	0	0
Wounded in Action	0	0	0	0

C Coy 2R22R reported that FF conducted an Offensive patrol ISO Op SHIN MENGARAY detained 1 x FAM. FAM was posessing an electrical wire, a remote control, a grenade fuse and he tested positive for X-Spray. Detainee will be taken to FOB WILSON at first light (17 May).
UPDATE 2327D*
11 Detainees were arrested in addition to detainee above. Detainees were in proximity to materials used in IED fabrication. Compound is known to be used by INS. Detainees will be moved with detainees from event 0917 to KAF on 17 May. TFK will inform if any problems with detainee movement. BDA: 13 Detainees, ED materials.
***Event closed 2358D*13 Detained None(None) Local Civilian

Reference ID: AFG20090524n1742
Latitude: 31.62321472

Region: RC SOUTH
Longitude: 65.52442169

Date: 2009-05-24 09:09 Type: Friendly Action
Category: Detain Affiliation: FRIEND
Detained: 0

	Enemy	Friend	Civilian	Host Nation
Killed in Action	0	0	0	0
Wounded in Action	0	0	0	0

While B Coy 2R22R BG with PsyOps team conducted a NFO patrol. Suspicious FAM talking on a cell phone, giving details of FF movements. FF approached the FAM and tested for X-Spray. The FAM tested positive, was detained and will be transported to FW for processing. No casualties or damage reported.
UPDATE 2028D*
After processing at FOB WILSON, FAM was detained. FAM is due to be transferred to KAF (251530May09) for further questioning. Nothing further to report.

Reference ID: AFG20090526n1674 Region: RC SOUTH
Latitude: 31.53788757 Longitude: 65.6235199
Date: 2009-05-26 04:04 Type: Friendly Action
Category: Detain Affiliation: FRIEND
Detained: 0

	Enemy	Friend	Civilian	Host Nation
Killed in Action	0	0	0	0
Wounded in Action	0	0	0	0

While B Coy R22R conducted an offensive patrol ISO Op KALAY they observed 1 x PAX run from the site of a freshly dug hole. 1 x PAX was apprehended and tested positive for x-spray. The 1 x PAX was taken as CDN detainee and transported to DAND DC for processing. No casualties or damage reported.
UPDATE 1523D*
1 x detainee will be transported to KAF (27 May 09) for TQ. No casualties or damage reported.
***Event closed at 1548D*1 Detained None(None) Insurgent

Reference ID: AFG20090605n1906 Region: RC SOUTH
Latitude: 30.71499634 Longitude: 65.54824066
Date: 2009-06-05 04:04 Type: Friendly Action
Category: Detain Affiliation: FRIEND
Detained: 0

	Enemy	Friend	Civilian	Host Nation
Killed in Action	0	0	0	0
Wounded in Action	0	0	0	0

Weapons Coy un-mentored ANA (1/1/205) reported that while conducting a NFO patrol, FF detained 1 x INS who was held 2 x detonators in his possession. INS is currently in ANA custody at FW.
UPDATE 1009D*
No CF involvement requested. ANA processed the detainee.
***Event closed at 1010D*1 Detained None(None) Insurgent

Reference ID: AFG20090610n1918
Latitude: 31.87118149
Date: 2009-06-10 21:09
Category: Detain
Detained: 0

Region: RC SOUTH
Longitude: 64.21438599
Type: Friendly Action
Affiliation: FRIEND

	Enemy	Friend	Civilian	Host Nation
Killed in Action	0	0	0	0
Wounded in Action	0	0	0	0

DELAYED REPORT
MEB BHG reported that FF observed 1 x un-escorted PAX moving around the forward ammunition supply point at night. LN has been detained by SOG. The detainee was taken for further questioning to BSN detainee holding facility. 1 x PAX detained. No casualties or damage reported ATT. NFTR.
***Event closed at 1544D*1 Detained not otherwise specified(NOS) Local Civilian

Reference ID: AFG20090617n1975
Latitude: 32.51650238
Date: 2009-06-17 06:06
Category: Detain
Detained: 1

Region: RC SOUTH
Longitude: 67.21034241
Type: Friendly Action
Affiliation: FRIEND

	Enemy	Friend	Civilian	Host Nation
Killed in Action	0	0	0	0
Wounded in Action	0	0	0	0

ANA (3/2/205) with US ETT reported that while conducting a NFO patrol, FF PID 3-5 INS who were fleeing from area. FF detained 1 x INS (unconfirmed) and continued pursuing the remaining ones. No casualties or damage reported.
***Event closed at 1656D*1 Detained None(None) Insurgent

Reference ID: AFG20090623n1816
Latitude: 32.22838974
Date: 2009-06-23 04:04
Category: Detain
Detained: 1

Region: RC SOUTH
Longitude: 63.13903427
Type: Friendly Action
Affiliation: FRIEND

	Enemy	Friend	Civilian	Host Nation
Killed in Action	0	0	0	0
Wounded in Action	0	0	0	0

OPS BOX TRIPOLI
F COY 2/3 USMC reported while conducting a NFO patrol, FF detained 1 x 11 year old INS who was acting as an observer for the INS emplacing IEDs this morning. The boy has admitted that he was acting as an spotter. FF also detained the boys father who is suspected to have connections to INS.
UPDATE 2143D*
The detainees are processed. NFTR. BDA: 2 x detainee.
***Event closed 2207D*2 Detained None(None) Insurgent

Reference ID: AFG20090626n1775
Latitude: 36.20517731
Date: 2009-06-26 10:10
Category: Detain
Detained: 0

Region: RC NORTH
Longitude: 64.67079163
Type: Friendly Action
Affiliation: FRIEND

	Enemy	Friend	Civilian	Host Nation
Killed in Action	0	0	0	0
Wounded in Action	0	0	0	0

DELAYED REPORT
During a joint cordon and search operation in ATEH KHAN KWAJA 41SPA502080 and ORTEPAH 41SPA503068 conducted by ANP, ANA and PRT MEY TU, 30x persons were arrested by ANP, and have been transported to MEY for further interogation. ANA and ANP found 3x UNK type of anti-personnel mines which were disposed by ANA EOD. During the operation ANA fired 1 x RPG rocket which did not detonate. This UXO also was treated and neutralised by ANA on the scene. No casualties or damage reported.30 Arrested None(None) Local Civilian

Reference ID: AFG20090627n1947
Latitude: 33.0727005
Date: 2009-06-27 19:07
Category: Detain
Detained: 0

Region: RC EAST
Longitude: 69.22905731
Type: Friendly Action
Affiliation: FRIEND

	Enemy	Friend	Civilian	Host Nation
Killed in Action	0	0	0	0
Wounded in Action	0	0	0	0

Event Title:INFO 1157Z
Zone:null
Placename:Wurzana Kalay, E Paktika
Outcome:null
At 1157Z, TF 3 Geronimo reported that HHC (Jackal-6), while conducting patrolling and COIN operations in Wurzana Kalay Village, captured and detained a HVT (Obj Noah) and 3 other INS at 42S WB 2138 5937, 17km NE of FOB Orgun-E, Zirok District, Paktika. HHC, with an attached CF SIGINT enabler team were assessing polling sites for future operations when a HVI SIGINT hit was acquired. HHC conducted a cordon of the area in question partnered with ANA and ANP. After losing signal once and then reacquiring it, HHC assembled a force of CF and ANA to close in on the HVT signal. FF then confronted the target on the street (with another MAM) for TQ and that questioning led to the additional TQ and detainment of two more MAMs, after they had all admitted association with the target. A fifth detainee was determined to be a 14 year old male and was turned over to the Orgun NDS.

Reference ID: AFG20090628n2001
Latitude: 31.51528549
Date: 2009-06-28 11:11
Category: Detain
Detained: 1

Region: RC SOUTH
Longitude: 65.39675903
Type: Friendly Action
Affiliation: FRIEND

	Enemy	Friend	Civilian	Host Nation
Killed in Action	0	0	0	0
Wounded in Action	0	0	0	0

DELAYED REPORT
B Coy 2R22R BG reported that while conducting an offensive patrol ISO OP TORA ARWA 2, FF took a detainee after he was observing FF and was tested positive for X-spray. The detainee was taken by CAN troops and he has a cell phone and phonebook with known ICOM persons on it. BDA: 1 x AC detained. No casualties or damage reported.
UPDATE 0737D*
NFTR.
***Event closed at 0737D*1 Detained None(None) Local Civilian

Reference ID: AFG20090702n1889
Latitude: 31.61679077
Date: 2009-07-02 07:07
Category: Detain
Detained: 0

Region: RC SOUTH
Longitude: 65.57504272
Type: Friendly Action
Affiliation: FRIEND

	Enemy	Friend	Civilian	Host Nation
Killed in Action	0	0	0	0
Wounded in Action	0	0	0	0

TFK DO reported that FF detained 1 x LN who could not PID himself, but claims to be a civsec from USPI. Currently held at Camp Nathan Smith for questioning. BDA: 1 x LN detained. NFTR
***Event closed at 2159D*1 Detained None(None) Local Civilian

Reference ID: AFG20090705n1996
Latitude: 31.3902092
Date: 2009-07-05 07:07
Category: Detain
Detained: 22

Region: RC SOUTH
Longitude: 64.31890106
Type: Friendly Action
Affiliation: FRIEND

	Enemy	Friend	Civilian	Host Nation
Killed in Action	0	0	0	0
Wounded in Action	0	0	0	0

TFL 1/5 USMC reported while manning PB JAKER, FF detained 22 x FAM, who are suspected to have some information about IED network. In addition FF found 1 x weapon, IED materials and a instruction letter for a known HVT. No casualties or damage reported.22 Detained None(None) Local Civilian

Reference ID: AFG20090705n2031
Latitude: 31.79708481
Date: 2009-07-05 14:02
Category: Detain
Detained: 4

Region: RC SOUTH
Longitude: 64.61360168
Type: Friendly Action
Affiliation: FRIEND

	Enemy	Friend	Civilian	Host Nation
Killed in Action	0	0	0	0
Wounded in Action	0	0	0	0

TF THOR 3-1 reported while conducting a NFO, FF observed 4 x FAM carrying 1 x RPK, 1 x RPG and 9 x RPG rounds and are in possession of ANA paperwork. FF detained the 4 x FAM and turned them over to ANA to verify their ID. No casualties or damage reported.
UPDATE 2202D*
The detained LN were brought to ANA, because the claimed that they were ANA. They had no ID or paperwork that showed conection to ANA. ANA claimed the LN were not ANA. They are now considered to be INS and had been handed over to ANA. Nothing further to report.
***Event closed at 2209D*4 Detained None(None) Local Civilian

Reference ID: AFG20090713n1891 Region: RC SOUTH
Latitude: 31.64667892 Longitude: 65.63943481
Date: 2009-07-13 04:04 Type: Friendly Action
Category: Detain Affiliation: FRIEND
Detained: 1

	Enemy	Friend	Civilian	Host Nation
Killed in Action	0	0	0	0
Wounded in Action	0	0	0	0

B Coy 2 R22R BG reported that while conducting a NFO patrol, FF found 1 x FAM in a compound with a big quantity of food. FF conducted a tactical questioning and tested the FAM for explosive residue. He tested positive and was detained. BDA: 1 x AC detained.
UPDATE 1603D*
Detainee was moved to KAF. NFTR.
***Event closed at 1653D*1 Detained None(None) Local Civilian

Reference ID: AFG20090718n1979 Region: RC SOUTH
Latitude: 32.83643341 Longitude: 65.9838028
Date: 2009-07-18 06:06 Type: Friendly Action
Category: Detain Affiliation: FRIEND
Detained: 3

	Enemy	Friend	Civilian	Host Nation
Killed in Action	0	0	0	0
Wounded in Action	0	0	0	0

While AUS MRTF conducted an offensive patrol ISO OP TUFANI BABAR, FF cordoned off and searching an area, FF detained 3 x INS. INS were quistioned by the MRTF and brought to FOB RIPLEY IAW EAMR 0809.
UPDATE 1528D*
The 3 x detainees have now arrived at FOB. No casualties or damage reported.
***Event closed at 1532D*3 Detained afghan(AFG) Insurgent

Reference ID: AFG20090721n1893
Latitude: 31.44408417
Date: 2009-07-21 01:01
Category: Detain
Detained: 1

Region: RC SOUTH
Longitude: 64.33286285
Type: Friendly Action
Affiliation: FRIEND

	Enemy	Friend	Civilian	Host Nation
Killed in Action	0	0	0	0
Wounded in Action	0	0	0	0

MEB 1/5 USMC reported while conducting a NFO patrol, FF detained 1 x FAM with documentation on hand which indicates suggested involvement with INS leadership. FF will bring the 1 x FAM to COP NAWA and intent to hand him over to ANCOP.
UPDATE 0731D*
Legal units are working on with the detainee. Additional information will be delivered through their channels. NFTR. BDA: 1 x FAM detained.
***Event closed at 0732D*1 Detained None(None) Insurgent

Reference ID: AFG20090723n1929
Latitude: 32.79458618
Date: 2009-07-23 11:11
Category: Detain
Detained: 0

Region: RC SOUTH
Longitude: 65.93874359
Type: Friendly Action
Affiliation: FRIEND

	Enemy	Friend	Civilian	Host Nation
Killed in Action	0	0	0	0
Wounded in Action	0	0	0	0

ANA (2/4/205) with AUS OMLT reported while providing FP to PB QUDUS, FF detained 1 x LN which conducted supsicious activity and brought the detainee back to PB QUDUS. No casualties or damage reported.
***Event closed at 232311D*1 Detained None(None) Local Civilian

Reference ID: AFG20090730n1936
Latitude: 30.98060036
Date: 2009-07-30 14:02
Category: Detain
Detained: 2

Region: RC SOUTH
Longitude: 64.17071533
Type: Friendly Action
Affiliation: FRIEND

	Enemy	Friend	Civilian	Host Nation
Killed in Action	0	0	0	0
Wounded in Action	0	0	0	0

HEN: 30 1910D JULY 09
WHO: 2/8 GOLF
WHERE: 41R PQ 1179 2804, PB KOSTAY
WHAT: DETAINEEE
EVENT: UNIT DETAINED (1) IND WHO WAS CONNECTED TO THE ATTACK WHICH OCCURRED 30 1737D JUL09 RESULTING IN (2) US KIA. THE IND WAS DETAINED .5 MI SOUTH OF THE ATTACK ALONG ECP COWBOYS. THE DETAINEE WAS TRANSPORTED TO PB KOSTAY. AT 0056D 2/8 REPORTED TAKING ANOTHER DETAINEE. ICOMM CHATTER HAD AN INDIVIDUAL SAY THEY PASSED A CHECKPOINT THAT WAS IN REFERENCE TO REDSKINS 1.

WHEN ABP SEARCHED THE VEHICLE AND THE FOUR INDIVIDUALS IN IT, THEY SAID THREE OF THEM WERE LOCALS AND THE FOURTH UNKNOWN AND SUSPICIOUS LOOKING. THE DETAINEE WAS TRANSPORTED TO PB KOSTAY. BOTH DETAINEES WILL BE TRANSFERRED TO FOB DEHLI TO UNDERGO TQ BY HET TEAM.
ISAF REF # 07-2699(CLOSED), 07-2716 (CLOSED)

Reference ID: AFG20090730n1937
Latitude: 30.98060036
Date: 2009-07-30 14:02
Category: Detain
Detained: 1
Region: RC SOUTH
Longitude: 64.17071533
Type: Friendly Action
Affiliation: FRIEND

	Enemy	Friend	Civilian	Host Nation
Killed in Action	0	0	0	0
Wounded in Action	0	0	0	0

2/8 USMC reported while conducting a NFO patrol, FF detained 1 x INS who tested positive for X-spray.
UPDATE 0551D*
At 302330D* FF searched an vehicle and detained 1 x suspected INS on GR 41R PQ 1230 2742. It is suspected that he was involved in the INS ATTACK from ev #07-2699.
***Event closed at 310802D*2 Detained None(None) Insurgent

Reference ID: AFG20090803n2028
Latitude: 32.29258728
Date: 2009-08-03 10:10
Category: Detain
Detained: 1
Region: RC WEST
Longitude: 62.72810745
Type: Friendly Action
Affiliation: FRIEND

	Enemy	Friend	Civilian	Host Nation
Killed in Action	0	0	0	0
Wounded in Action	0	0	0	0

****EVENT CLOSED BUT WAITING FOR SJA FOLLOW-UP****
WHEN: 03 1430D AUG 09
WHO: FOX 2/3
WHERE: 41S MR 744 729 12KM NW OF FOB BAKWA
WHAT: JPEL TARGET DETAINEE
EVENT: RDBN REPORTED THAT A JPEL TGRT, ABDUL BARI, WOULD BE AT GRID 41S MR 744 729 FOR A WHILE. FOX 2/3 LAUNCHED A PATROL TO INTERCEPT. ONCE THERE, HE WAS DETAINED AND TRANSPORTED BACK TO FOB BAKWA. ANOTHER PATROL WITH ANP WAS DISPATCHED FROM BAKWA TO CONTINUE SEARCHING THE COMPOUND. FULL DETAINEE REPORT WILL BE COMPLETED ONCE MORE INFO IS ACQUIRED.
INITIAL DETAINEE REPORT SUBMITTED.
CONFISCATED AS EVIDENCE: (1) AK-47, (1) EMPTY MAGAZINE, (1) FULL MAGAZINE, EXPENDED CASINGS, BLOODY SHOES AND SHIRT.
NOTE: DETAINEE HAD SCRATCHES ON HIS BODY.
BDA: NO CASUALTIES OR DAMAGE REPORTED.
ISAF REF # 08-0235 (CLOSED)

Reference ID: AFG20090808n2113
Latitude: 30.57980347
Date: 2009-08-08 11:11
Category: Detain
Detained: 6

Region: RC SOUTH
Longitude: 63.84614944
Type: Friendly Action
Affiliation: FRIEND

	Enemy	Friend	Civilian	Host Nation
Killed in Action	0	0	0	0
Wounded in Action	0	0	0	0

WHEN: 08 1622D AUG 09
WHO: 2D LAR
WHERE: 41R NP 81132 83340 6.7KM NE OF KHAN NESHIN CASTLE
WHAT: DETAINEE
EVENT: 2D LAR DETAINED (6) INDIVIDUALS AT SNAP VCP WHILE PERFORMING A SCREEN LINE TO THE NORTH TO GUARD SCOUT OPS ALONG RTE UNIFORM.
BDA: (6) DETAINEES, NO CASUALTIES OR DAMAGE REPORTED.
ISAF REF # 08-0696 (CLOSED)

Reference ID: AFG20090811n2082
Latitude: 30.97009468
Date: 2009-08-11 10:10
Category: Detain
Detained: 1

Region: RC SOUTH
Longitude: 64.19477844
Type: Friendly Action
Affiliation: FRIEND

	Enemy	Friend	Civilian	Host Nation
Killed in Action	0	0	0	0
Wounded in Action	0	0	0	0

WHEN: 11 1500D AUG 09
WHO: GOLF 2/8
WHERE:41R PQ 1410 2690
WHAT: DETAINEE
EVENT: WHILE ON PATROL, GOLF 2/8 DETAINED A MAN WHO WAS OBSERVING THE PATROL. ABDULLAH ALI, THE DETAINEE, GAVE INCONSISTENT ANSWERS TO TACTICAL QUESTIONING AND HAS (1) 7.62MM ROUND IN HIS POSESSION. ADDITIONALLY, HE REFUSED TO GIVE THE PATROL HIS GRANDFATHERS NAME WHICH CAUSED THE PATROL LEADER TO SUSPECT HE WAS LYING ABOUT HIS OWN IDENTITY.
DETAINEE REPORT IS PENDING AND WILL BE FORWARDED THROUGH NORMAL CHAIN.
BDA: NO CASUALTIES OR DAMAGE REPORTED.
ISAF REF # 08-0987 (CLOSED)

Reference ID: AFG20090814n2200
Latitude: 32.50624466
Date: 2009-08-14 14:02
Category: Detain
Detained: 1

Region: RC WEST
Longitude: 63.56061172
Type: Friendly Action
Affiliation: FRIEND

	Enemy	Friend	Civilian	Host Nation
Killed in Action	0	0	0	0
Wounded in Action	0	0	0	0

WHEN: 14 1900D AUGUST 09
WHO: FOX 2/3
WHERE: 41S NR 5266 9669 10 MI SW OF GOLESTAN
WHAT: DETAINEE
EVENT: WHILE CONDUCTING MOUNTED SECURITY OPERATIONS IN THE BUJI BAST PASS, FOX 2/3 DETAINED (1) INDIVIDUAL ALLAH DAD 14KM SOUTH WEST OF FOB GOLESTAN. ALLAH DAD WAS DETAINED DUE TO HIGH EVIDENCE LINKING HIM AS AN IED EMPLACER.
BDA: NO CASUALTIES OR DAMAGES REPORTED.
ISAF REF # 08-1278 (CLOSED)

Reference ID: AFG20090815n2088
Latitude: 31.73052025
Date: 2009-08-15 14:02
Category: Detain
Detained: 3

Region: RC SOUTH
Longitude: 65.71657562
Type: Friendly Action
Affiliation: FRIEND

	Enemy	Friend	Civilian	Host Nation
Killed in Action	0	0	0	0
Wounded in Action	0	0	0	0

At 151905AUG2009 TF Hellraiser reported TF Buffalo reports while conducting a patrol 2nd PLT B Co 1-17 IN observed 1x FAM digging in the road VIC 41RQR5738613777. When the individual noticed the US forces he fled. US forces dismounted and pursued the individual approximately 50 M into the treeline where they found him with two other FAM with wires in their possession. All 3x FAM were detained and brought to FOB Frontenac for Tactical Questioning. All three individuals were X-Sprayed and one tested positive for TNT. The names of the three individuals are Agha Mahmad, Ghalam Nabi Talimesher, and Neaz Mohammed. Detainess were turned over to ANP. Detainee reports are attached. No casualties or injuries reported. NFI ATT
 DELETED DUPLICATE SIGACT 41RQR57386137772009-08#1412.01 ***
Summary from deleted SIGACT: B COY 1-17 INF reported while conducting a NFO patrol, FF spotted 1 x FAM digging on the road. FF dismounted from STRYKERS and pursued individual. UPDATE 0407D* FF found the INS 50m in treeline with 2 x other FAM's. All 3 FAM's were detained at aprox 2100D* and were taken back to FOB FRONTEMAC for tactical questioning. Ins were found with wire in their possession. NFI at this time. BDA: 3 x FAM DETAINED.3 Detained Local Civilian.

Reference ID: AFG20090817n2148
Latitude: 32.6579895
Date: 2009-08-17 04:04
Category: Detain
Detained: 1

Region: RC SOUTH
Longitude: 65.98104858
Type: Friendly Action
Affiliation: FRIEND

	Enemy	Friend	Civilian	Host Nation
Killed in Action	0	0	0	0
Wounded in Action	0	0	0	0

While TFU MRTF conducted a cordon and search operation, FF detained 1 x LN named Abdul Malik, during this operation. FF intended to complete operation and returned to PB ATIQ to complete the Person Under Control investigation. No casualties or damage reported.
UPDATE 2238D*
FF reported PUC is released after questioning, no further reason to detain, NFTR.
***Event closed at 172244D*1 Detained None(None) Local Civilian

Reference ID: AFG20090818n2057   Region: RC SOUTH
Latitude: 30.99440956   Longitude: 64.17116547
Date: 2009-08-18 03:03   Type: Friendly Action
Category: Detain   Affiliation: FRIEND
Detained: 3

	Enemy	Friend	Civilian	Host Nation
Killed in Action	0	0	0	0
Wounded in Action	0	0	0	0

While 3-11 USMC conducted a NFO patrol, FF received INTEL from LN about POSS INS using an abandoned compound for their operations. At 172200D* FF set up an OP to observe that location. At 180800D* 3 x INS were detained at that house and questioned on site. Detainee reports to follow.
UPDATE 1221D*
Detailed detainee report to follow. NFTR. No casualties or damage reported.
***Event closed at 1243D*
UPDATE 181449D*
FF discovered 10 bags of 46%ammonium nitrate in the same compound where detainee were taken. A terrain model was located behind the house. FF also reported jugs, chemical and scales. EOD is enroute to investigate, NFTR.3 Detained None(None) Insurgent

Reference ID: AFG20090818n2082   Region: RC SOUTH
Latitude: 31.32467842   Longitude: 64.20383453
Date: 2009-08-18 05:05   Type: Friendly Action
Category: Detain   Affiliation: FRIEND
Detained: 3

	Enemy	Friend	Civilian	Host Nation
Killed in Action	0	0	0	0
Wounded in Action	0	0	0	0

WHEN: 18 0940D AUG 09
WHO: 3/11
WHERE: 41R PQ 14538 66211 1.4KM SOUTH OF FIDDLERS GREEN
WHAT: DETAINEES
EVENT: 3/11 DISPATCHED A PATROL TO ASSIST WITH THE ARSIC IED STRIKE, AND DETAINED (3) INDIVIDUALS FROM A KNOWN COMPOUND OF INTEREST. THESE DETAINEES ARE BELIEVED TO BE INVOLVED IN IED

ACTIVITIES ALONG THE 605. ONE OF THE DETAINEES IS MISSING FINGERS AND IS WEARING "SKETCHER" SANDALS. SKETCHER FOOTPRINTS HAVE BEEN FOUND AROUND MULTIPLE IED SITES ON THE 605.
THE COMPOUND THAT THE DETAINEES WERE TAKEN FROM WAS SEARCHED, AND IED PRECURSOR CHEMICALS, AND A TERRAIN MODEL WERE FOUND. EOD ARRIVED AND COMPLETED THE SITE EXPLOITATION. UNIT ASSESS THE COMPOUND AS AN IED STORAGE/ EN SUPPLY BUILDING.
BDA: (3) DETAINEES
ISAF REF # 08-1687 (CLOSED)

Reference ID: AFG20090824n1956
Latitude: 31.65504265
Date: 2009-08-24 11:11
Category: Detain
Detained: 1
Region: RC SOUTH
Longitude: 65.64926147
Type: Friendly Action
Affiliation: FRIEND

	Enemy	Friend	Civilian	Host Nation
Killed in Action	0	0	0	0
Wounded in Action	0	0	0	0

While 1 PLT A COY 1-17 INF conducted a NFO patrol, 2 x PAX came up positive on X-SPRAY for TNT. FF are investigating ATT. At 1618D* FF took an HCT team to location of TCP to do tactical Questioning. FF released 1 x PAX and 1 x PAX was handed over to ANP, NFTR
***Event closed at 2257D*1 Detained None(None) Not known

Reference ID: AFG20090824n2022
Latitude: 31.07015991
Date: 2009-08-24 14:02
Category: Detain
Detained: 1
Region: RC SOUTH
Longitude: 64.19403076
Type: Friendly Action
Affiliation: FRIEND

	Enemy	Friend	Civilian	Host Nation
Killed in Action	0	0	0	0
Wounded in Action	0	0	0	0

WHEN: 24 1900D AUGUST 09
WHO: FOX 2/8
WHERE: 41R PQ 13910 37990 1 MI NE OF PB HASSAN ABAD
WHAT: DETAINEES
EVENT: FOX 2/8 DETAINED (1) INDIVIDUAL WHO REPORTEDLY PLACED IED'S AND FIRED ROCKETS DURING THE ELECTION.
BDA: (1) DETAINEES
ISAF # 08-2874 (CLOSED)
*** DELETED DUPLICATE REPORT 41RPQ13910379902009-08#2874.01 ***
Summary from deleted report: ***DELAYED REPORT***
F COY 2/8 USMC reported while conducting a NFO patrol, FF found 1 x INS placing IED's and detained him. Nothing further to report.
***Event closed at 250604D*1 Detained None(None) Insurgent

Reference ID: AFG20090825n2004
Latitude: 31.13296318
Date: 2009-08-25 14:02
Category: Detain
Detained: 4

Region: RC SOUTH
Longitude: 65.90490723
Type: Friendly Action
Affiliation: FRIEND

	Enemy	Friend	Civilian	Host Nation
Killed in Action	0	0	0	0
Wounded in Action	0	0	0	0

DELAYED REPORT
While 1/5 USMC conducted a NFO patrol, LNs were stopped by FF after the vehicle they were riding in was declared as a BOLO by FF (Be ON Look Out) . FF found a ID making card machine and a digital camera. Tactical questioning proves the LNs were lying. No casualties or damage reported.
***Event closed at 0647D*4 Detained None(None) Local Civilian

Reference ID: AFG20090829n2077
Latitude: 31.06011963
Date: 2009-08-29 13:01
Category: Detain
Detained: 4

Region: RC SOUTH
Longitude: 64.18698883
Type: Friendly Action
Affiliation: FRIEND

	Enemy	Friend	Civilian	Host Nation
Killed in Action	0	0	0	0
Wounded in Action	0	0	0	0

WHEN: 29 1800D AUGUST 09
WHO: FOX 2/8
WHERE:41R PQ 1325 3687 PB HASSAN ABAD
WHAT: DETAINEES
EVENT: AFTER A C2 NODE ENGAGEMENT, HEAVY VEH TRAFFIC BEGAN TO HEAD NORTH ON RTE COWBOYS. FOX 2/8 CONDUCTED A SNAP VCP AT THE FRONT ECP OF PB HASSAN ABAD. (4) DETAINEES WERE TAKEN INTO CUSTODY; (1) IS POSSIBLY A HIGH LEVEL COMMANDER AND A KNOWN IED FACILITATOR, (1) POSSESSED DOG TAGS OF A MARINE AND TESTED POSITIVE FOR NITRATE, (1) RESISTED WHEN SEARCHED, (1) POSSESSED A PPIED TESTER AND TESTED POSITIVE FOR NITRATE.
BDA: NO CASUALTIES OR DAMAGES REPORTED.
ISAF # 08-3304 (CLOSED)

Reference ID: AFG20090830n1985
Latitude: 31.70777893
Date: 2009-08-30 05:05
Category: Detain
Detained: 0

Region: RC SOUTH
Longitude: 65.60635376
Type: Friendly Action
Affiliation: FRIEND

	Enemy	Friend	Civilian	Host Nation
Killed in Action	0	0	0	0
Wounded in Action	0	0	0	0

AT 053030AUG09 (Z) TF Stryker reports TF Buffalo (1-17 IN) detained 4 individual MAMs VIC 41RQR470110 in the Arghandab district of Kandahar Province during operation Oportunity Hold. They were detained after exhibiting suspicious behavior at OBJ Gold TCP on 29 Aug 2009. TSE PLT processed detainee evidence on 30 Aug 2009. Sami Mohammad had silver Fuji Fine digital camera with pics of Speedy Moisture Tester with ball bearings and unknown powder placed inside and a dial indicator on the other end. The Afghan Water and Duck Company later vouched for them and petitioned for their release. The 4 MAMs were released into the custody of the AWDC. NFATT

Reference ID: AFG20090905n2177
Latitude: 31.01706696
Date: 2009-09-05 05:05
Category: Detain
Detained: 5

Region: RC SOUTH
Longitude: 64.23684692
Type: Friendly Action
Affiliation: FRIEND

	Enemy	Friend	Civilian	Host Nation
Killed in Action	0	0	0	0
Wounded in Action	0	0	0	0

WHEN: 05 0947D SEP 09
WHO: 2/8 CAAT BLACK
WHERE: 41R PQ 1806 3215, 7.3KM NE OF COP KOSHTAY
WHAT: DETAINEES
EVENT: 2/8 CAAT BLACK DETAINED (5) INDIVIDUALS. (4) WERE SPOTTED ON FOOT HASTILY TRYING TO LEAVE THER AREA AS THE PATROL APPROACHED. THE INDIVIDUALS REFUSED TO STOP UPON REQEUST. THE 5TH WAS FLEEING IN THE OPPOSITE DIRECTION, CARRYING A SHOVEL. (1) OF THE DETAINEES HAD AN AK-47 UNDER HIS CLOTHES. THE DETAINEES WERE TRANSPORTED TO FOB DEHLI FOR QUESTIONING.
BDA: (5) DETAINEES
ISAF # 09-0449 (CLOSED)

Reference ID: AFG20090907n2159
Latitude: 30.93466568
Date: 2009-09-07 05:05
Category: Detain
Detained: 2

Region: RC SOUTH
Longitude: 64.15184021
Type: Friendly Action
Affiliation: FRIEND

	Enemy	Friend	Civilian	Host Nation
Killed in Action	0	0	0	0
Wounded in Action	0	0	0	0

Reported by RC(S) at 070535D*
E COY 2/8 USMC conducted a framework patrol. FF detained 2 x INS who are believed to have shot at ISAF forces. The detainees tested positive for X-spray and desciption matches that of INS fleeing from eastern desert. After questioning by ANA their stories remain inconsistent. INS remain under questioning to rule out all suspicion. Both detainees are now held at COP SHER.
UPDATE 0643D*
NFTR. BDA: 2 x detained LN
***Event closed at 070643D*2 Detained afghan(AFG) Local Civilian

Reference ID: AFG20090908n2259
Latitude: 30.97876549
Date: 2009-09-08 14:02
Category: Detain
Detained: 4

Region: RC SOUTH
Longitude: 64.17425537
Type: Friendly Action
Affiliation: FRIEND

	Enemy	Friend	Civilian	Host Nation
Killed in Action	0	0	0	0
Wounded in Action	0	0	0	0

WHEN: 08 1850D SEP 09
WHO: GOLF 2/8
WHERE: 41R PQ 1213 2784 (COP KOSHTAY)   41R PQ 12895 27985 (C1T CMPD2)
WHAT: (4) DETAINEE'S
EVENT: UNIT DETAINED (4) INDIVIDUALS. (2) IND WERE THE DRIVERS AND OWNERS OF THE VEH THAT G CO DROPPED ARTY RNDS ON (09-0763). THE OTHER (2) IND WERE IN A COMPOUND WITH IED MANUFACTURING MATERIALS. THE UNIT ALSO DISCOVERED A COMMAND WIRE RUNNING TO THE COMPOUND. INDIVIDUALS ARE CURRENTLY BEING DETAINED AT COP KOSHTAY.
BDA: NO CASUALTIES OR DAMAGE REPORTED.
ISAF # 09-0937 (CLOSED)

Reference ID: AFG20090910n2088
Latitude: 31.57139969
Date: 2009-09-10 01:01
Category: Detain
Detained: 1

Region: RC SOUTH
Longitude: 65.43401337
Type: Friendly Action
Affiliation: FRIEND

	Enemy	Friend	Civilian	Host Nation
Killed in Action	0	0	0	0
Wounded in Action	0	0	0	0

TF1-12 A16 conducted a framework patrol. FF detained 1 x FAM who was on a known IED hotspot kneeling in a wadi in closed proximity to CF and ran when spotted. FF detained FAM fo questioning. BDA: 1 x FAM detained.
***Event closed by RC(S) at 101633D*1 Detained None(None) Insurgent

Reference ID: AFG20090912n2169
Latitude: 31.06020927
Date: 2009-09-12 13:01
Category: Detain
Detained: 0

Region: RC SOUTH
Longitude: 64.18698883
Type: Friendly Action
Affiliation: FRIEND

	Enemy	Friend	Civilian	Host Nation
Killed in Action	0	0	0	0
Wounded in Action	0	0	0	0

WHEN: 12 1820D SEP 09
WHO: F 2/8
WHERE: 41R PQ 1325 3688 IVO PB HASSAN ABAD
WHAT: DETAINEE'S

EVENT: F 2/8 DETAINED AN INDIVIDUAL WHO WAS SEEN NEAR THE FRONT ECP. THE INDIVIDUAL TESTED POSITIVE FOR X-SPRAY AND WAS BROUGHT IN FOR TQ.
BDA:
ISAF # 09-1284 (CLOSED)

Reference ID: AFG20090927n2188
Latitude: 31.6203022
Date: 2009-09-27 05:05
Category: Detain
Detained: 1

Region: RC SOUTH
Longitude: 65.06427002
Type: Friendly Action
Affiliation: FRIEND

	Enemy	Friend	Civilian	Host Nation
Killed in Action	0	0	0	0
Wounded in Action	0	0	0	0

At 270930SEP09 (L) TF Stryker reported TF Legion (2/B/2-1 IN) detained an individual VIC 41RPR958002, Maywand district, Kandahar province. TF Legion conducted a dismounted patrol through the northern portion of Pir Zadeh when they noticed a suspicious individual. ANP attempted to get the individual to stop but he took off running. ANP fired 1x Warning shot in the air and the individual still did not stop. ANP pursued and detained the individual. Villagers indicated he had mental illness, but TF Legion was unable to confirm that with the line of questioning. Individual was detained and brought to COP Rath. NFTR ATT.

Reference ID: AFG20090929n2107
Latitude: 31.51394081
Date: 2009-09-29 02:02
Category: Detain
Detained: 0

Region: RC SOUTH
Longitude: 65.42977905
Type: Friendly Action
Affiliation: FRIEND

	Enemy	Friend	Civilian	Host Nation
Killed in Action	0	0	0	0
Wounded in Action	0	0	0	0

ANA 2KDK with C COY 2R22R BG reported while conducting a NFO patrol that FF spotted 1 x FAM acting suspicious.
The FAM was alleged to have killed LN for ISAF collaboration. During a patrol of a village FF were advised of a FAM locals claimed to be INS. This report corroborated earlier suspicion about the FAM and FF detained the FAM.
The detainee was taken to PBSG and subsequently transported to KAF dtention centre for further questioning.
UPDATE 292149D*
Detainee was transported to KAF and is in MP custody, NFTR.
***Event closed at 292205D*1 Detained afghan(AFG) Insurgent

Reference ID: AFG20091007n2265
Latitude: 32.47423172
Date: 2009-10-07 04:04

Region: RC WEST
Longitude: 63.50965118
Type: Friendly Action

Category: Detain Affiliation: FRIEND
Detained: 2

	Enemy	Friend	Civilian	Host Nation
Killed in Action	0	0	0	0
Wounded in Action	0	0	0	0

OPS BOX TRIPOLI
F COY 2/3 USMC reported while conducting a NFO patrol that ANA found 2 x INS with IED making materials, FF detained both INS. ANA also found 4 AK mag., 100lbs of fertilizer, 1000lbs sugar, 1 russian grenade fuse, 1 BINO, 1 cell phone, 1 moped battery, 1 x 35mm camera, 1 jug of unknown substance, a photo album of possible TB members and 1000ft of wire.
UPDATE 713467D*(M)
Detainees will be processed and properly reported. NFI ATT.
BDA: 2 x DETAINEE
***Event closed at 071411D* OCT20092 Detained afghan(AFG) Insurgent

Reference ID: AFG20091009n2173 Region: RC SOUTH
Latitude: 31.48554802 Longitude: 64.34655762
Date: 2009-10-09 07:07 Type: Friendly Action
Category: Detain Affiliation: FRIEND
Detained: 6

	Enemy	Friend	Civilian	Host Nation
Killed in Action	0	0	0	0
Wounded in Action	0	0	0	0

WHEN: 09 1200D OCT 09
WHO: 1/5 BRAVO CO
WHERE: 41R PQ 27900 84200, 2.7KM NE OF COP SPIN GHAR
WHAT: DETAINEES
EVENT: 1/5 RECEIVED INTELLIGENCE THAT A BAND OF THUGS WERE SETTING UP ILLEGAL CHECKPOINTS AND EXTORTING LOCALS IN THE AREA. ON THE MORNING OF 9 OCTOBER, A SQUAD FROM B CO 1/5 SET UP A CHECK POINT AND WITNESSED 6 INDIVIDUALS CARRYING WEAPONS MOVING FROM SOUTH TO NORTH ON RTE SHINER, SHORTLY AFTER THE INDIVIDUALS RETURNED. THE SQUAD STOPPED THE INDIVIDUALS AND BEGAN QUESTIONING THEM. THE INDIVIDUALS CLAIMED THAT THEY WERE PROVIDING SECURITY TO A NEARBY GRAVEL TRUCK CONVOY THAT WAS HEADING TO FOB GERONIMO. WHILE QUESTIONING THE INDIVIDUALS THE SQUAD BEGAN TAKING SPORADIC SMALL ARMS FIRE FROM MULTIPLE DIRECTIONS. CO B NOTIFIED THE 1/5 MAIN AT GERONIMO WHO SPOKE TO THE SECURITY DETACHMENT FOR THE RECENTLY ARRIVED GRAVEL TRUCKS. THIS LEGITIMATE SECURITY TEAM WAS NOT MISSING ANY PERSONNEL AND COULD NOT VERIFY THE IDENTITY OF THE INDIVIDUALS BEING QUESTIONED. AT THIS POINT, BASED ON THE SMALL ARMS FIRE AND THE LACK OF ANY IDENTIFICATION, THE INDIVIDUALS WERE TAKEN INTO CUSTODY. THE DETAINEES ARE CURRENTLY BEING HELD AT COP SPIN GHAR.
BDA: NO CASUALTIES OR DAMAGE REPORTED.
ISAF # 10-0787 (CLOSED)

Reference ID: AFG20091012n2242
Latitude: 31.57075882
Date: 2009-10-12 09:09
Category: Detain
Detained: 0

Region: RC SOUTH
Longitude: 65.3818512
Type: Friendly Action
Affiliation: FRIEND

	Enemy	Friend	Civilian	Host Nation
Killed in Action	0	0	0	0
Wounded in Action	0	0	0	0

TF 1-12 INF reported while conducting a NFO patrol that FF spotted 3 x FAM with AK47s and RPG in a ditch.
The FAMs entered the VEH and sped off E on HWY 1. RW and SCANEAGLE tracked the VEH, FF arrested the FAMs and searched the VEH. The FAMs claim to be PSC, questioning ongoing.
BDA: 3 x detainee.
UPD1-121418D*
FF found 3 x AK 47 and 15 x mags. 3 x person claimed to be USPI but did not have ID. They were moved to FW where a PSC rep with adequate papers vouched for their identity to the unit's satisfaction. They were released, NFTR.
BDA: 3 x detainees released.

Reference ID: AFG20091023n2187
Latitude: 31.3289566
Date: 2009-10-23 07:07
Category: Detain
Detained: 0

Region: RC SOUTH
Longitude: 65.94764709
Type: Friendly Action
Affiliation: FRIEND

	Enemy	Friend	Civilian	Host Nation
Killed in Action	0	0	0	0
Wounded in Action	0	0	0	0

At 230654OCT09(Z) TF SAINT reports 3/B/8-1 identified suspicious Male VIC 41RQQ8048769813, on HWY 4 in SPIN BOLDAK District, Kandahar Province. While en route from KAF to Spin Boldak, male tried to cover bicycle along side of road and flee on foot from patrol, 3/B/8-1 yelled warning then fired pin flare, male then returned mounted bicycle and tried again to flee area. 3/B/8-1 surrounded individual, dismounted and detained hiim. After detaining individual, 3/B/8-1 tested twice with X-Spray both times male tested positive for TNT. Dismounted teams checked culverts in the vicinity while man was entered into HIIDES. Once complete 3/B/8-1 returned to FOB with detained individual. HIIDES returned Mosin Agha, age 15, as 50% match for "Someone of Interest", all pertinent detainee paperwork was completed, HUMINT team questioned individual gained no INTEL and detainee was turned over to ABP. NFTR ATT.

Reference ID: AFG20091027n2340
Latitude: 32.08057785
Date: 2009-10-27 11:11
Category: Detain
Detained: 0

Region: RC SOUTH
Longitude: 64.84096527
Type: Friendly Action
Affiliation: FRIEND

	Enemy	Friend	Civilian	Host Nation
Killed in Action	0	0	0	0
Wounded in Action	0	0	0	0

B COY 3 RIFLES reported that while conducting an independent patrol, FF oberved an IED EXPLOSION. FF then observed the area and found a 1 x LN hiding in the bushes close to the seat of explosion. The LN has been detained.
The IED EXPLOSION was a possible CWIED.
UPD1-271456D*
At 1438D* were attacked by INS with SAF. FF possition was IVO GR 41S PR 7445 5178. FF observed for INS .
UPD2-271927D*
All C/S back in FOB, NFTR.
UPD3-272150D*
C-IED reported - sus CWIED IVO SGN. Not exploited. NFTR.
BDA: 1 x LN detained.
Event closed 271951D*
This Incident closed at: 272235D*OCT2009

Demonstrations

A large number of protests, demonstrations and sometimes riots have taken place in Afghanistan, directed against either the Kabul government or the US occupation.

The purpose of a demonstration is, of course, to demonstrate—to show the opponent that there are large numbers of people who actively oppose him. Demonstrations and protests also let people who may be in sympathy with the aims of the insurgency, but who cannot or will not carry out armed actions, to express their feelings in a concrete way. It allows both sides the opportunity to carry out propaganda efforts to win the sympathy of the local population; reports mention American "information operations" and "psyops" being organized to "counter" the demonstrations. One report mentions a Pakistani wedding party that was taken for a demonstration, indicating that American forces actively monitor their zones to watch for civilian gatherings. Several reports mention American military assets being dispatched to demonstrations as a "show of force".

Demonstrations can also serve as a recruiting tool for the insurgency; people who are attracted to demonstrations may actively join the insurgency, either as non-combat support or as actual fighters.

Several demonstrations concerned the effect that occupation forces were having on the local population; reports describe protests when the water to a village was cut off by an American construction project, and when local shopkeepers were moved to make room for new military buildings. One protest occurred after American forces killed a young woman during a "cordon and search" operation. Another protest took place when a group of locals confronted American authorities demanding to know the whereabouts of people who had been detained in a recent raid. Several demonstrations were in protest of some perceived insult to Islam; as a Christian culture occupying a Muslim country where religion is central, the Americans are inherently viewed as a hostile outside power.

Other reports describe demonstrations that were made up of local Afghans demanding jobs, and a number of protests were directed against the government's drug-control efforts. One group of auxiliary police staged a protest after they hadn't been paid for six months.

Although demonstrations like these may not be political in nature, they directly impact the "hearts and minds" effort to win civilians over to the government's side, and can cause friction and resentment between civilians and American forces. The saying "All politics is local", is just as true among Afghan farmers as it is among American voters.

Reports also mention demonstrations against Taliban violence, and demonstrations to demand increased security protection from insurgent attacks.

Reference ID: AFG20040503n9
Latitude: 33.55833054
Date: 2004-05-03 00:12
Category: Demonstration
Detained: 0

Region: RC EAST
Longitude: 68.44000244
Type: Non-Combat Event
Affiliation: Neutral

	Enemy	Friend	Civilian	Host Nation
Killed in Action	0	0	0	0
Wounded in Action	0	0	0	0

(S//REL GCTF) AN ESTIMATED 100 OR MORE SUPPORTERS OF A JUDGE FROM KHUGIANI WHO WAS RECENTLY ARRESTED ALONG WITH 5 BY THE PRT TOOK PART IN THE DEMONSTRATION. . THEY MOVED THEIR PROTEST DOWN TOWN AFTER BEING TOLD IT WAS PRT THAT WAS INVOLVED NOT UN. THERE IS NO LIKELIHOOD THAT THIS DEMONSTRATION WILL HAVE A DIRECT EFFECT ON THE ELECTION PROCESS. (RSO)

Reference ID: AFG20040611n30
Latitude: 36.37194824
Date: 2004-06-11 12:12
Category: Demonstration
Detained: 0

Region: RC NORTH
Longitude: 65.85333252
Type: Non-Combat Event
Affiliation: Neutral

	Enemy	Friend	Civilian	Host Nation
Killed in Action	0	0	0	0
Wounded in Action	0	0	0	15

(S//REL GCTF) (DELAYED REPORT) TF VICTORY REPORTS LARGE DEMONSTRATION HAS RESULTED IN 15X INJURIES TO ANP IVO SHEBERGHAN. UK PRT RECEIVED INITIAL REPORTS FROM GEN FAZLI (PRT ATA LIAISON OFFICER). INFORMATION WAS PASSED TO COP BALKH THAT DEMONSTRATORS HAVE STOPPED 100X ANP ON THE WAY TO SAR E POL. THE LOCATION HAS BEEN CONFIRMED AS SAYED ABAD (CENTRED ON 41S QA 5629) LOCATED BETWEEN SAR E POL AND SHEBERGHAN. THIS INCIDENT IS REPORTED TO HAVE EVOLVED AND THE ANP ARE NOW REPORTED TO BE BESIEGED BETWEEN DEMONSTRATORS IN SAR E POL AND JUMBESH MILITIA TO THEIR NORTH. 15X ANP ARE REPORTED TO HAVE BEEN INJURED IN THE DEMONSTRATIONS. 1100Z UPDATE : ANP FORCE HAVE EXTRACTED FROM SAYED ABAD (CENTRED ON 41S QA 5629) AND ARE CURRENTLY ENROUTE

BACK TO MAZAR E SHARIF. THE COMMANDER WILL THEN REPORT TO UK PRT TO REPORT ON EVENTS OF THE DAY. MOT HOTEL IS STILL ENROUTE TO SAR E POL. THEY WILL MEET UP WITH LOCAL POLICE AND CONFIRM GROUND TRUTH AS TO THE EVENTS OF THE DAY. NFITR.

Reference ID: AFG20040815n48
Latitude: 35.99139023
Date: 2004-08-15 10:10
Category: Demonstration
Detained: 0
Region: RC NORTH
Longitude: 68.63916016
Type: Non-Combat Event
Affiliation: Neutral

	Enemy	Friend	Civilian	Host Nation
Killed in Action	0	0	0	0
Wounded in Action	0	0	0	0

(FOUO) AT 1000HRS THERE WAS A DEMONSTRATION, OF ABOUT 100 PEOPLE, AGAINST THE REPLACEMENT OF THE PRESENT GOVERNOR. THE DEMONSTRATION MOVED PAST THE UNOPS COMPOUND AND SHOUTED THAT UNOPS SHOULD PREVENT THE CENTRAL GOVERNMENT FROM REPLACING THE PRESENT GOVERNOR. THERE WAS NO VIOLENCE OR THREAT AGAINST ANYONE AND THE POLICE MOVED WITH THE DEMONSTRATORS THROUGH THE TOWN. THEY ALL DISPERSED AT 1200HRS AND THE SITUATION IS NORMAL IN PUL-I-KUMRI.

Reference ID: AFG20041104n53
Latitude: 32.94583893
Date: 2004-11-04 05:05
Category: Demonstration
Detained: 0
Region: RC EAST
Longitude: 69.49416351
Type: Non-Combat Event
Affiliation: Neutral

	Enemy	Friend	Civilian	Host Nation
Killed in Action	0	0	0	0
Wounded in Action	0	0	0	0

CJSOTF REPORTS PAK CIV PROTEST 4K NE LWARA. AT 0506Z THE FOLLOWING SALT REPORT WAS SENT: S- APPROX. 200X PAKISTANI CIV, A- DEMONSTRATION, L- 42S WB 462 454, T- 0500Z. REMARKS: PAKISTANI CIVILIANS ARE ASSEMBLED INSIDE AFGHAN BORDER. APPEARS TO BE A DEMONSTRATION/PROTEST. UPDATE 0613Z: PAK LNO REPORTS THE ASSEMBLY TO BE FUNERAL PROCESSION, NOT A PROTEST. NFI.

Reference ID: AFG20050514n71
Latitude: 34.39533997
Date: 2005-05-14 06:06
Category: Demonstration
Detained: 0
Region: RC EAST
Longitude: 68.86509705
Type: Non-Combat Event
Affiliation: Neutral

	Enemy	Friend	Civilian	Host Nation
Killed in Action	0	0	0	0
Wounded in Action	0	0	0	0

TF Thunder reports 200X personnel gathering 26K SW of Kabul (42S VD 876 060) at 0600Z. The crowd is gathering in front of the Maydan Shar Gov. Compound. It was a peaceful demonstration and has dispersed.

Reference ID: AFG20050409n102
Latitude: 34.43527985
Date: 2005-04-09 13:01
Category: Demonstration
Detained: 0

Region: RC EAST
Longitude: 70.45610809
Type: Non-Combat Event
Affiliation: Neutral

	Enemy	Friend	Civilian	Host Nation
Killed in Action	0	0	0	0
Wounded in Action	0	0	0	0

CJSOTF REPORTS PROTESTERS AT JBAD. THE FOLLOWING SALT REPORT WAS SENT: S: UNK, A: PROTESTERS HAVE CONGREGATED, L: 42S XD 338 114, T: 1301Z. REMARKS: THE PROTEST BEGAN AT THE UN FACILITY. TO DEFUSE THE SITUATION, 140 REQUESTS PERMISSION FOR A UN HUMAN RIGHTS INDIVIDUAL WITH AN INTERPRETER TO SPEAK TO RAHIM, ASSESS HIS SITUATION, AND INFORM THE PROTESTERS OF HIS CONDITION. 140 CONFIRM THAT THEY HAVE A UN REP. AND INTERPRETER PRESENT TO DO THIS, WILL EXECUTE ATT TO COUNTER THE IO CAMPAIGN BY THE PROTESTERS.

Reference ID: AFG20050412n86
Latitude: 31.65527916
Date: 2005-04-12 08:08
Category: Demonstration
Detained: 0

Region: RC SOUTH
Longitude: 65.07556152
Type: Non-Combat Event
Affiliation: Neutral

	Enemy	Friend	Civilian	Host Nation
Killed in Action	0	0	0	0
Wounded in Action	0	0	0	0

TF BRONCO REPORTS DEMONSTRATION 51K SE OF GERESK. THE FOLLOWING SALT REPORT WAS SENT: S: 100X LNS, A: DEMONSTRATING, L: 41R PR 96802 04105, T: 0830Z. REMARKS: LNS DEMONSTRATING BECAUSE OF CPEF DESTROYING THEIR POPPY FIELDS. CPEF PERSONNEL HAS CURRENTLY PULLED OUT OF THE AREA. ANP IS TRYING TO DEFUSE THE SITUATION ATT. 1154Z UPDATE TO SALT : SHOTS WERE FIRED ONE ANP WAS INJURED WHILE RUNNING FOR COVER (RAN INTO A VEHICLE). GEN AGBHAR (ANP GEN. FROM KABUL) ORDERED GEN. AMERI TO STOP ERADICATION UNTIL SITUATION WAS DEFUSED. GEN. AMERI IS STILL TRYING TO NEGOTIATE WITH THE LOCAL ELDERS. CPEF RETURNED BACK TO THE FOB UNTIL SITUATION IS RESOLVED. NFI.

Reference ID: AFG20050430n68
Latitude: 34.34091187
Date: 2005-04-30 06:06

Region: RC WEST
Longitude: 62.20438004
Type: Non-Combat Event

Category: Demonstration Affiliation: Neutral
Detained: 0

	Enemy	Friend	Civilian	Host Nation
Killed in Action	0	0	0	0
Wounded in Action	0	0	0	0

TF THUNDER REPORTS DEMONSTRATION AT HERAT. THE FOLLOWING SALT REPORT WAS SENT: S: 100-200X LN, A: DEMONSTRATION, L: HERAT CITY (OUTSIDE GOVERNORS COMPOUND (UN COMPOUND), T: 0615Z. REMARKS: DEMONSTRATING AGAINST THE HERAT GOVERNOR AND ANA DUE TO AN INCIDENT THAT HAPPENED LAST NIGHT. THE DEMONSTRATION STARTED OUTSIDE THE UN COMPOUND AND THEN MOVED TO THE GOVERNORS COMPOUND. ATT THE DEMONSTRATION IS CALM AND IN THE PARK SOUTH OF THE GOVERNORS COMPOUND.
GRID FOR HERAT IS 41S MU 26820 00243

Reference ID: AFG20050511n113 Region: RC EAST
Latitude: 34.40942001 Longitude: 70.49043274
Date: 2005-05-11 06:06 Type: Non-Combat Event
Category: Demonstration Affiliation: Neutral
Detained: 0

	Enemy	Friend	Civilian	Host Nation
Killed in Action	0	0	37	0
Wounded in Action	0	0	10	0

3/3 Marines reports demonstration in Jalalabad City. TF THUNDER reported that the size of the demonstration is 250x pax. The crowd is becoming unruly and is throwing rocks, burning tires and vandalizing buildings. Gunshots were also fired. Gov Din Mohammad of Nangarhar is requesting a show of force. At 0606Z ANA reports that streets into city are blocked by fires. At 0609Z 3/3 requests AH-64s for show of force. At 0623Z, the crowd dispersed into two different groups. One group is located IVO 42S XD 3669 0879 the second group is IVO 42S XD 3698 0856. AT 0636Z JBAD PRT reports that DIA and UNAMA are secured ATT. The riot generated the following 9 line. A 13 y/o LN was struck by vehicle. PT is listed as urgent surgical; 1X ventilator is required. PT is suffering a head injury bleeding from ears and mouth, and left femur fracture. No enemy in area, PZ is at JBAD PRT LZ. CJTF76 approves medevac mission 05-11A at 0745Z. Medevac is canceled due to PTS Status. PT is being casvac'd to JBAD hospital. At 0810Z the UN JEMB security operations manager in Kabul requests the immediate evacuation of their JBAD provincial staff at 42S XD 3132 1114. The international staff consists of 3X PAX and 1X US citizen. ANA and private guards are outside the facility ATT, but they claim the situation is critical. Gunfire is reported, but it is not directed at the building. At 0824Z the governors office contacted the 3/3 Marines and reports that the situation is under control in JBAD. At 0828Z the UN officer rescinds his request for evacuation. At 0831Z Sabre 6 reports that local authorities are dealing with fires IVO 42S XD 3202 as the ANA/ANP secure the area. At 0841Z ODB reports that the governors house, PK consulate, and several other GOA buildings are being burned. They also report that this is the first day of a planned 2-day riot. As of 0800z it was reported that all NGOs were accounted for and evacuated from Jalalabad.

Reference ID: AFG20050511n114
Latitude: 33.33776093
Date: 2005-05-11 07:07
Category: Demonstration
Detained: 0

Region: RC EAST
Longitude: 69.9573288
Type: Non-Combat Event
Affiliation: Neutral

	Enemy	Friend	Civilian	Host Nation
Killed in Action	0	0	0	0
Wounded in Action	0	0	0	0

TF THUNDER reports students demonstrating at Khowst University approximately 200X LN are downtown at the University at 0740Z.

Reference ID: AFG20050511n115
Latitude: 38.1336174
Date: 2005-05-11 08:08
Category: Demonstration
Detained: 0

Region: UNKNOWN
Longitude: 71.80373383
Type: Non-Combat Event
Affiliation: Neutral

	Enemy	Friend	Civilian	Host Nation
Killed in Action	0	0	0	0
Wounded in Action	0	0	0	0

3-116th reports a demonstration 51K N OF Ghazni. The crowd has Taliban flags and is shouting anti-coalition and anti-American slogans at 0725Z. A PLT is moving IVO FOB Ghazni to conduct security. Local police have sent patrols to the area of the demonstration. It is believed that the demonstrators have come from the Logar Province. At 0913Z received a report that the demonstration is over.

Reference ID: AFG20050512n95
Latitude: 33.31718445
Date: 2005-05-12 05:05
Category: Demonstration
Detained: 0

Region: RC EAST
Longitude: 67.80709839
Type: Non-Combat Event
Affiliation: Neutral

	Enemy	Friend	Civilian	Host Nation
Killed in Action	0	0	0	0
Wounded in Action	0	0	0	0

TF THUNDER reports a large demonstration in the Jaghatu district. 3-116th submitted the report that the crowd is moving north on ring road and may try to block movement on the RTE 1 between Jaghatu and Kabul. At 0906Z received that MP element went to SAYD ABAD and reported that all is normal. 3 MP gun trucks and ANA will move north to Chaki district and asses the area. Eng, Nor 3 and the rest of the warlord element will continue to Maydan Shahr and assess things in that area. NFI.

Reference ID: AFG20050513n88
Latitude: 33.60113907
Date: 2005-05-13 10:10
Category: Demonstration
Detained: 0

Region: RC EAST
Longitude: 69.22202301
Type: Non-Combat Event
Affiliation: Neutral

	Enemy	Friend	Civilian	Host Nation
Killed in Action	0	0	1	0
Wounded in Action	0	0	4	0

CJSOTF reports demonstration IVO GARDEZ. Initially approximately 60X demonstrators gathered for a protest where 1X demonstrator was shot in leg and transported to Gardez hospital. The ANP is dealing with demonstration. Earlier that morning CJSOTF facilitated the establishment of the Emergency Operation Center (EOC) at the local government compound. The EOC is maintaining communication with Police/Government/CF. The UNAMA compound is secured by elements of TF Thunder. At 1005Z CJSOTF reported a second group of approximately 300 locals has linked-up with first group. Demonstrators appear to be taking some direction from the police. Group is moving north toward Tera Pass (CNA).

CJSOTF recommends all CF units stay off roads between Tera Pass and Gardez. At 1007Z a large group of demonstrators (over 100) began to move toward FB Gardez (42s wc 20598 17955). At 1053Z the crowd was 50M from north check point throwing rocks and a second group is 300M away and moving toward the check point. During the incident, the police shot five people. One died at the hospital and four are in stable condition. The police verified that the individual who died was a spectator and not a demonstrator and that he was shot unintentionally. At least two of the other four were shot for attempting to wrestle weapons away from the police. It was not verified that the demonstrators were armed with anything more than slingshots.

Reference ID: AFG20050513n89
Latitude: 33.31718445
Date: 2005-05-13 11:11
Category: Demonstration
Detained: 0

Region: RC EAST
Longitude: 67.80709839
Type: Non-Combat Event
Affiliation: Neutral

	Enemy	Friend	Civilian	Host Nation
Killed in Action	0	0	0	0
Wounded in Action	0	0	0	1

3-116th reports demonstration in Ghazni City. This is a continuation of the demonstration from the past few days. Approximately 1000X locals were gathered where the old city starts and the demonstrators then proceeded down Ring Road. At 1050Z, the chief of police of Ghazni was shot in the chest and was taken to the FOB for medical assistance. 3-116th is putting together a reaction force to assist the police and ANA, 3-116th has comms with the ETTS. CJTF76 approves MEDEVAC mission 05-13C at 11338Z for the police chief. W/U at 1154Z. W/D at 1513Z. He was taken in to surgery and it is believed that the Police Chief should fully recover.

Reference ID: AFG20050513n90
Latitude: 34.98777008
Date: 2005-05-13 11:11
Category: Demonstration
Detained: 0

Region: RC WEST
Longitude: 63.13254929
Type: Non-Combat Event
Affiliation: Neutral

	Enemy	Friend	Civilian	Host Nation
Killed in Action	0	0	1	0
Wounded in Action	0	0	1	0

TF LONGHORN reports demonstration in the city of QALA-E-NAW (41S NU 1209771695). Gunfire was reported during the demonstration towards the direction of the ANP. ANP returned fire killing 1X LN and wounding another LN. The ANA remained in their compound and the ANP handled the situation. The demonstration has dissipated ATT.

Reference ID: AFG20050514n82
Latitude: 33.32746887
Date: 2005-05-14 05:05
Category: Demonstration
Detained: 0

Region: RC EAST
Longitude: 68.50682068
Type: Non-Combat Event
Affiliation: Neutral

	Enemy	Friend	Civilian	Host Nation
Killed in Action	0	0	0	0
Wounded in Action	0	0	0	0

TF Thunder reports a possible demonstration 21K SE of Ghazni PRT (42S VB 541 877) at 0550Z. The district police chief and the provincial governor have requested a show of force/ assessment of the village. They claim this is a continuation of the demonstrations in Ghazni city from yesterday. 3-116th is moving a patrol to the village to investigate. At 0713Z the patrol didn't find any demonstrators in Andar district.

Reference ID: AFG20050519n91
Latitude: 32.10393143
Date: 2005-05-19 07:07
Category: Demonstration
Detained: 0

Region: RC SOUTH
Longitude: 66.03710175
Type: Non-Combat Event
Affiliation: Neutral

	Enemy	Friend	Civilian	Host Nation
Killed in Action	0	0	0	0
Wounded in Action	0	0	0	0

TF SWORD reports demonstration 7K NE of FOB Tiger 2 at 0400Z. A small crowd of approximately 30X LN were blocking the road between 0400 and 0600z, protesting road construction in Jabey Village IVO 42S TA 204 558. The Eng Bn Cdr has arranged a meeting at FOB Tiger II for 200900z May to resolve the issue with local populace.

Reference ID: AFG20050525n89
Latitude: 34.95383835
Date: 2005-05-25 07:07
Category: Demonstration
Detained: 0

Region: RC EAST
Longitude: 68.88641357
Type: Non-Combat Event
Affiliation: Neutral

	Enemy	Friend	Civilian	Host Nation
Killed in Action	0	0	0	0
Wounded in Action	0	0	0	0

TF Sword reported that 30-40 LN are staging a non-violent gathering 1K NE of BAF. The gathering consists of adults and children protesting the road upgrade construction and expansion by the US. Baseops has coordinated for local police to arrive on scene and all coalition forces have cleared the AO and are RTB.

Reference ID: AFG20050526n95
Latitude: 34.95383835
Date: 2005-05-26 07:07
Category: Demonstration
Detained: 0

Region: RC EAST
Longitude: 68.88641357
Type: Non-Combat Event
Affiliation: Neutral

	Enemy	Friend	Civilian	Host Nation
Killed in Action	0	0	0	0
Wounded in Action	0	0	0	0

TF Sword reports demonstration outside of BAFS gate at 0718Z. Approximately 40 LN protesting on road clearing IVO of tower 10. Sword 6 has reached and agreement with the village elders. Mission will continue. Sword 6 has a follow up meeting with the elders on Saturday. There are 2x ANP on site of incident.

Reference ID: AFG20050726n118
Latitude: 34.95383835
Date: 2005-07-26 04:04
Category: Demonstration
Detained: 0

Region: RC EAST
Longitude: 68.88641357
Type: Non-Combat Event
Affiliation: Neutral

	Enemy	Friend	Civilian	Host Nation
Killed in Action	0	0	0	0
Wounded in Action	0	0	0	0

TF Eagle reported a demonstration 4km W of BAF at 0442Z. MP Bn reported an unruly crowd of 75X LN throwing rocks and yelling. MP Bn reported approx 2000X LN IVO AMF gate, enroute to ECP 1 at 0530Z. Crowd is demonstrating operations of last night. Peacekeeper 6 deployed to demonstration area and TF Guardian notified to take the appropriate action at the PUC facility at 0543Z. TF Eagle reported crowd has pinned themselves against AMF gate and the ANP is attempting to gain control at 0545Z. Eagle 8A reported shots fired outside of ECP 1 by the ANP at 0611Z. No reports of injured or damage to equipment ATT. At 0955Z there are approximately 300X LNs still in the vicinity of the main gate of BAF and another 100 LNs seen moving towards the main gate by way of nearby roads. Unknown object burning 15-20m from the gate and a jingle truck about 200m from the main gate with 20-30 LNs. At 1015Z 50 LNs throwing rocks at the Gunslinger 12 convoy returning to BAF. An unknown number of vehicles were damaged by small arms fire and 4X soldiers were hit by rocks. 3-4 shots fired, none from US soldiers. ANP is attempting to control crowd. There are no injuries or damage to equipment to report. At 1022Z no inbound local national traffic into BAF. At 1115Z the crowd at ECP 1 still about 200-300 demonstrators. TF Peacekeeper has investigated reports of shots fired out side of ECP 1. Determined was only 1X gunman at 1101Z. At 1127Z TF Eagle reported that the crowd had calmed down and no injuries were reported. At 1313Z access to BAF is limited to in and outbound foot traffic for ECP 1and 5. ECP 10 is limited to coalition vehicles for in and outbound traffic. 270733ZJUL05: Yesterday a TF Devil convoy was struck with enemy fire. Vehicles had bullet holes. No injuries were reported.

Reference ID: AFG20050904n119
Latitude: 33.33594131
Date: 2005-09-04 07:07

Region: RC EAST
Longitude: 69.90960693
Type: Non-Combat Event

Category: Demonstration Affiliation: Neutral
Detained: 0

	Enemy	Friend	Civilian	Host Nation
Killed in Action	0	0	0	1
Wounded in Action	0	0	3	0

TF Devil reports a protest 5km W of FB Chapman at 0650Z. 2000-3000 LN are protesting a land dispute over a new ANA compound and moving towards the governors compound. 150x ANP, 80x NDS, and 20x ABP are on scene. The crowd became violent. 3x protestors WIA, 2x of whom were shot by KPF as they climbed over the wall of the governor's compound; 1x off-duty ANP was struck by a rock in the head and KIA. The governor was relocated to a nearby compound. ANA and NDS worked with village elders to resolve the conflict. The crowd has dispersed.

Reference ID: AFG20051130n157 Region: RC EAST
Latitude: 32.66579819 Longitude: 68.45449829
Date: 2005-11-30 06:06 Type: Non-Combat Event
Category: Demonstration Affiliation: Neutral
Detained: 0

	Enemy	Friend	Civilian	Host Nation
Killed in Action	0	0	0	0
Wounded in Action	0	0	0	0

TF Devil reported a demonstration IVO Ghazni. At 0712Z, Task Force Alamo fuel convoy that was enroute to Maydan Shar was forced to return to the FOB due a road closure caused by a demonstration. TF Alamo reported the roadway was blocked by burning tires, and that the Afghan National Police (ANP) were on scene. At 0804Z, the Afghan National Army (ANA) were sent to assist the ANP. Task Force Alamo reported the reason of the demonstration was in response to the ANP attempting to arrest a local Afghan male for criminal activity the day prior. There were no coalition forces present, and the local government did not request coalition forces assistance. There were no injuries or damages reported.

Reference ID: AFG20060206n258 Region: RC EAST
Latitude: 34.25572968 Longitude: 70.8137207
Date: 2006-02-06 06:06 Type: Non-Combat Event
Category: Demonstration Affiliation: Neutral
Detained: 0

	Enemy	Friend	Civilian	Host Nation
Killed in Action	0	0	0	0
Wounded in Action	0	0	0	0

ANP reported to TF Devil a protest in Bari Kowt. At 0634Z, ANP reported that an unknown sized group was protesting the arrest of a local judge by the ANP. Two local shops were burned in the protest, and the LN were throwing rocks. No anti coalition sentiment was reported, and no CF were involved in the incident.

Reference ID: AFG20060206n259 Region: RC EAST
Latitude: 34.7609787 Longitude: 70.14582825

Date: 2006-02-06 06:06
Category: Demonstration
Detained: 0
Type: Non-Combat Event
Affiliation: Neutral

	Enemy	Friend	Civilian	Host Nation
Killed in Action	0	0	1	0
Wounded in Action	0	0	2	1

ANA and ANP reported to TF Devil a lethal protest in Mitharlam. At 0642Z, TF Devil reported that 400X LN were protesting the editorial cartoon, and had begun throwing rocks. The ANSF forces had fired warning shots to attempt to disband the protest. TF Devil reported that one LN was killed, one LN was injured, and one ANP was injured in the incident. At 1100Z TF Devil reported that the protest had dispersed.

Reference ID: AFG20060206n261
Latitude: 34.98035812
Date: 2006-02-06 07:07
Category: Demonstration
Detained: 0
Region: RC EAST
Longitude: 69.27719116
Type: Non-Combat Event
Affiliation: Neutral

	Enemy	Friend	Civilian	Host Nation
Killed in Action	0	0	3	0
Wounded in Action	0	0	0	0

TF Eagle reported a lethal demonstration outside AMF Gate at BAF. TF Eagle reported at 0753Z approximately 1000 to 1500 personnel were demonstrating against the editorial cartoon. Crowd tried to force its way through AMF Gate and ANP forces fired warning shots. 1X US vehicle was stuck outside the gate and windows on the vehicle were broken by the demonstrators. Inbound and outbound traffic was rerouted through T-10 ATT. TF Eagle reported that three LN were killed when the attempted to storm the BAF gate, but at this time it is unknow who killed the LN. At 1406Z, TF Eagle reported that the crowds had dispersed.

Reference ID: AFG20060206n262
Latitude: 34.53684998
Date: 2006-02-06 08:08
Category: Demonstration
Detained: 0
Region: RC CAPITAL
Longitude: 69.19288635
Type: Non-Combat Event
Affiliation: Neutral

	Enemy	Friend	Civilian	Host Nation
Killed in Action	0	0	0	0
Wounded in Action	0	0	0	0

TF Phoenix reported a demonstration in the Kabul AO. TF Phoenix reported at 0833Z 200-300 protesters were reported by Camp Eggers. ISAF and US HQ directed coalition forces to stay away from the area. Protesters were demonstrating against the editorial cartoon and shouting anti-American slogans. At 0857Z TF Phoenix reported that Camp Eggers was locked down, and that protesters were throwing rocks. Update: TF Phoenix reported at 0943Z crowd congregated in front of the Ministry of Foreign Affairs IVO Camp Eggers and was calm and under control. At 1430Z, TF Phoenix reported that the crowd had dispersed. TF Phoenix reported that property was damaged, but there were no casualties.

Reference ID: AFG20060207n260
Latitude: 34.78263855
Date: 2006-02-07 05:05
Category: Demonstration
Detained: 0

Region: RC EAST
Longitude: 70.10935974
Type: Non-Combat Event
Affiliation: Neutral

	Enemy	Friend	Civilian	Host Nation
Killed in Action	0	0	0	0
Wounded in Action	0	0	0	0

TF Devil reported a protest over an editorial cartoon 14km NW of Metharlam. At 0517Z, TF Devil reported that 500X LN were gathered around the ANP station in Alishang. No damage or injuries reported. No violence occurred and the crowd dispersed.

Reference ID: AFG20060207n261
Latitude: 34.97916031
Date: 2006-02-07 05:05
Category: Demonstration
Detained: 0

Region: RC EAST
Longitude: 70.91059113
Type: Non-Combat Event
Affiliation: Neutral

	Enemy	Friend	Civilian	Host Nation
Killed in Action	0	0	0	0
Wounded in Action	0	0	0	0

TF Devil reported a protest 1km SE of Camp Blessing. At 0517Z, TF devil reported that 200X LN were protesting in Nangalam. The reason for the protest was unknown. No damage or injuries were reported. No violence occurred and the crowd dispersed.

Reference ID: AFG20060207n262
Latitude: 34.55408859
Date: 2006-02-07 05:05
Category: Demonstration
Detained: 0

Region: RC CAPITAL
Longitude: 69.32198334
Type: Non-Combat Event
Affiliation: Neutral

	Enemy	Friend	Civilian	Host Nation
Killed in Action	0	0	0	0
Wounded in Action	0	0	0	0

TF Phoenix reported four peaceful protests in Kabul. At 0548Z, TF Phoenix reported that 50X LN were one route Yellow, 50X LN were in front of the KAIA, 400X LN were near CP1 on route Pegasus, and 30x LN were N of CP1 on route Pegasus. ISAF elements were dispatched to all protest sites. Update: At 0859Z TF Phoenix reported all Kabul demonstrations had disbursed.

Reference ID: AFG20060207n264
Latitude: 34.42292023
Date: 2006-02-07 06:06
Category: Demonstration
Detained: 0

Region: RC EAST
Longitude: 70.44735718
Type: Non-Combat Event
Affiliation: Neutral

	Enemy	Friend	Civilian	Host Nation
Killed in Action	0	0	0	0
Wounded in Action	0	0	0	0

TF Devil reported five different protests over a political cartoon in JBAD. At 0610Z, TF Devil reported no damage or injuries had occurred. No violence occurred and the crowd dispersed.

Reference ID: AFG20060207n267
Latitude: 35.92234039
Date: 2006-02-07 08:08
Category: Demonstration
Detained: 0
Region: RC NORTH
Longitude: 64.77687836
Type: Non-Combat Event
Affiliation: Neutral

	Enemy	Friend	Civilian	Host Nation
Killed in Action	0	0	0	0
Wounded in Action	0	0	0	0

TF Phoenix reported rioting in Maimana. At 0813Z TF Phoenix reported that a PRT element in Maimana was receiving SAF and rock throwing into the compound from a group of approximately 200 rioters who had occupied an ANA building outside the PRT compound. PRT requested air assets as a show of force. MOD authorized a company of ANA to calm the riot and stop the violence. A convoy of 18 ETTs and 15 ANA where sent to Maimana to contol the rioting. CF reported the rioting has disburse. NFTR.

Reference ID: AFG20060208n227
Latitude: 18.51077271
Date: 2006-02-08 03:03
Category: Demonstration
Detained: 0
Region: UNKNOWN
Longitude: 68.69004822
Type: Non-Combat Event
Affiliation: Neutral

	Enemy	Friend	Civilian	Host Nation
Killed in Action	0	0	3	0
Wounded in Action	0	0	10	2

TF Bayonet reported demonstration near FOB Lagman. At 0657Z TF Bayonet reported a group of approximately 300 LNs were protesting the hiring of Pakistan workers at an ANA compound. One group of protesters fired shots into the air, and a second group set 2X jingle trucks on fire and 2X fuel trucks on fire. The protesters also set the Qalat boy"s school on fire and engaged ANA forces with small arms fire. TF Rock fired 6X mortar illumination rounds to disperse the crowd. ANA forces dispersed the crowd. 10X LN"s were injured, 3X LN"s were killed, and 2X ANA were WIA.

Reference ID: AFG20060208n229
Latitude: 34.51251984
Date: 2006-02-08 05:05
Category: Demonstration
Detained: 0
Region: RC CAPITAL
Longitude: 69.17430878
Type: Non-Combat Event
Affiliation: Neutral

	Enemy	Friend	Civilian	Host Nation
Killed in Action	0	0	0	0
Wounded in Action	0	0	0	0

TF Phoenix reported a demonstration in Kabul. At 0620Z TF Phoenix reported a group of LNs gathering along RTE Blue. No violence reported, KMNB notified. ANP and ISAF units directed to monitor situation. TF Phoenix reported that the crowd dispersed at 0633Z.

Reference ID: AFG20060208n230
Latitude: 33.99398041
Date: 2006-02-08 10:10
Category: Demonstration
Detained: 0
Region: RC EAST
Longitude: 68.83757782
Type: Non-Combat Event
Affiliation: Neutral

	Enemy	Friend	Civilian	Host Nation
Killed in Action	0	0	0	0
Wounded in Action	0	0	0	0

TF Devil reported peaceful demonstration 56KM S of Gardez. At 1100Z TF Devil reported approximately 350 LNs were protesting the Mohammed political cartoon. Several protesters reported to be armed with sticks. No violence reported. Protest was moving in the direction of a Turkish road construction crew. USPI armed guards have secured the area. USF is monitoring the situation. At 1224Z, TF Devil reported that the demonstration had dispersed.

Reference ID: AFG20060209n236
Latitude: 33.91062927
Date: 2006-02-09 11:11
Category: Demonstration
Detained: 0
Region: RC EAST
Longitude: 68.65493011
Type: Non-Combat Event
Affiliation: Neutral

	Enemy	Friend	Civilian	Host Nation
Killed in Action	0	0	0	1
Wounded in Action	0	0	0	2

NDS reported to TF Devil a violent demonstration over a political cartoon 50km NE of Ghazni. At 1224Z, TF Devil reported that one ANP was killed and two ANP were injured in the demonstration. The ANP have secured the area and have not requested any assistance from CF. No CF were involved.

Reference ID: AFG20060210n219
Latitude: 34.55408859
Date: 2006-02-10 11:11
Category: Demonstration
Detained: 0
Region: RC CAPITAL
Longitude: 69.32198334
Type: Non-Combat Event
Affiliation: Neutral

	Enemy	Friend	Civilian	Host Nation
Killed in Action	0	0	0	0
Wounded in Action	0	0	0	0

TF Phoenix reported a violent demonstration in Kabul. At 1126Z TF Phoenix reported a violent demonstration in Kabul. A group of approximately 1000 LNs were moving

W on Violet from V7 and demonstrators were throwing rocks at US convoys. TF Phoenix reported that the protest disbanded at 1339Z.

Reference ID: AFG20060211n210
Latitude: 33.62928391
Date: 2006-02-11 06:06
Category: Demonstration
Detained: 0

Region: RC EAST
Longitude: 69.39308167
Type: Non-Combat Event
Affiliation: Neutral

	Enemy	Friend	Civilian	Host Nation
Killed in Action	0	0	0	0
Wounded in Action	0	0	0	0

TF Devil reported 2X peaceful protests. The first protest occurred in Gardez at 0330Z and 300 LNs were in attendance. Protest lasted 1.5 hours and ended peacefully at 0500Z. No USF responded to protest. The second protest occurred in Khulbesat and involved an unknown number of LNs. Protest ended peacefully at 0615Z and no USF were involved. A third peaceful protest was reported by CFC-A. At 0710Z CFC-A reported that a group of approximately 2000 LN's were marching from the Presidential Mosque in Kabul to the Minister of Finance building. No damage or injuries were reported. In addition, a fourth protest was also reported by CFC-A. At 0742Z CFC-A reported that approximately 500 LN's were peacefully protesting at the Ministry of Education building in Kabul. No violence was reported. All protests were over the political cartoon depiction of the Prophet Mohammed.

Reference ID: AFG20060329n196
Latitude: 34.95306015
Date: 2006-03-29 02:02
Category: Demonstration
Detained: 0

Region: RC EAST
Longitude: 69.27139282
Type: Non-Combat Event
Affiliation: Neutral

	Enemy	Friend	Civilian	Host Nation
Killed in Action	0	0	0	0
Wounded in Action	0	0	0	0

At 1130Z TF Tiger reported 20 LNs demonstrating outside of BAF gate 3. At 0340Z TF Tiger had an element at gate 3, and the gathering enlarged to 150 pax demonstrating and requesting to talk to military personnel. Demonstrators were preventing freedom of movement for contractors and their workers from Contrak International. The TF Tiger S5, IO, and S3 talked with local leaders in order to understand the complaints. Complaints were as followes: 1. Contractors working on base were hiring people from Kabul and not hiring people from the local villages. S5 informed the leaders that they became aware of this issue recently and were working a solution to this problem. 2. Since Contrak International arrived, they did not have water flowing through their villages. They claimed to know exactly where the stream stopped flowing. S5 took LNs to the stream outside Tower 24 to assess the situation. The stream was dry. S5 told LNs that he would schedule something next week between him, the LNs, and Engineering to seek solutions to this issue or create an alternative to resolve this issue. TF Tiger reported the demonstration ended peacefully at 0430Z.

Reference ID: AFG20060421n242
Latitude: 32.51029968
Date: 2006-04-21 16:04
Category: Demonstration
Detained: 0

Region: RC EAST
Longitude: 68.86234283
Type: Non-Combat Event
Affiliation: Neutral

	Enemy	Friend	Civilian	Host Nation
Killed in Action	0	0	0	0
Wounded in Action	0	0	0	0

At 1706Z, TF Catamount reported that the Orgun-E Police Chief reported approximately 100 personnel were demonstrating on the high ground above the Bandar Afghan Border Check Point in Gomal. TF Catamount informed the Commander of the Afghan Border Patrol. At 1805Z, a B-52 was brought on station to conduct a show of force over the demonstration. 32x flares were dropped and the Police Chief reported vehicles and personnel dispersed. No damage to equipment or personnel.
 [UPDATED ON 22/04/2006 0107]: [UPDATED ON 22/04/2006 0421]: [UPDATED ON 22/04/2006 0628]: [UPDATED ON 22/04/2006 0959]:

Reference ID: AFG20060425n229
Latitude: 34.95306015
Date: 2006-04-25 05:05
Category: Demonstration
Detained: 0

Region: RC EAST
Longitude: 69.27139282
Type: Non-Combat Event
Affiliation: Neutral

	Enemy	Friend	Civilian	Host Nation
Killed in Action	0	0	0	0
Wounded in Action	0	0	0	0

TF Tiger reported a demonstration near ECP3. At 0500Z, TF Tiger reported LNs blocking the entrance to ECP3, and possibly throwing rocks. The Provincial Governor was notified, and Gov stated he will send ANP out to location. At 0518Z, MRF is enroute to ECP, ANP is on site. AT 0626Z, TF Tiger reported Demonstration at ECP 3 has ended and LN's are leaving the area, MRF has been recalled.

Reference ID: AFG20060426n220
Latitude: 34.95306015
Date: 2006-04-26 05:05
Category: Demonstration
Detained: 0

Region: RC EAST
Longitude: 69.27120209
Type: Non-Combat Event
Affiliation: Neutral

	Enemy	Friend	Civilian	Host Nation
Killed in Action	0	0	0	0
Wounded in Action	0	0	0	0

TF Tiger reported a demonstration at ECP3. At 0610Z TF Tiger reported about 30x PAX were demonstrating outside of ECP3 about hiring of labor from Kabul and issues with water outside of BAF. ANP were dispatched to the site, and at 0618Z TF Tiger reported the demonstration was under control. At 0800Z, TF Tiger declared demonstration over.

Reference ID: AFG20060426n221
Latitude: 33.54298019
Date: 2006-04-26 06:06
Category: Demonstration
Detained: 0

Region: RC EAST
Longitude: 68.42326355
Type: Non-Combat Event
Affiliation: Neutral

	Enemy	Friend	Civilian	Host Nation
Killed in Action	0	0	0	0
Wounded in Action	0	0	0	0

TF Iron Gray reported a peaceful demonstration approximately 150x LNs in Ghazni City. At 0606z TF Iron Gray reported approximately 150x LNs demonstrating over the movement of local vendors shops, moving past the Ghazni PCC station in Ghazni City. At 0840Z, TF Iron Gray reported the demonstration had been dispersed by the Ghazni ANP without incident. The shops were moved for Urban renewal. Shop owners were upset because their customer base was in the old area.

Reference ID: AFG20060427n234
Latitude: 34.95306015
Date: 2006-04-27 03:03
Category: Demonstration
Detained: 0

Region: RC EAST
Longitude: 69.27139282
Type: Non-Combat Event
Affiliation: Neutral

	Enemy	Friend	Civilian	Host Nation
Killed in Action	0	0	0	0
Wounded in Action	0	0	0	0

TF Tiger reported 15-20x LNs gathering outside of ECP3. At 0322Z TF Tiger reported LNs had started gathering outside the gate. The local governor was notified and asked to have ANP handle the situation. Because of the recent demonstrations the last few days, the ANP where asked to be at the gate before daylight for the next week. At 0411Z TF Tiger reported 30-40x LNs had gathered at ECP3, and the LNs had built a rock wall about knee high across the road in front of ECP3. At 0623Z TF Tiger reported the demonstration was broken up and traffic had resumed. At 0643Z TF Tiger reported approximately 20x LNs were gathering near Tower 4 along the fence line. The LNs refused to leave and ANP were dispatched to location and were speaking with the LN's. The demonstration concerned LNs wanting jobs, and they dispersed from fence line and ANP left the area.

Reference ID: AFG20060429n212
Latitude: 34.91802979
Date: 2006-04-29 04:04
Category: Demonstration
Detained: 0

Region: RC EAST
Longitude: 69.25647736
Type: Non-Combat Event
Affiliation: Neutral

	Enemy	Friend	Civilian	Host Nation
Killed in Action	0	0	0	0
Wounded in Action	0	0	0	0

TF Tiger reported a demonstration 300m from ECP 3. At 0433Z, TF Tiger reported a gathering of 30X LN's gathering near ECP 3 in addition to a partial rock wall across the road. PMO is contacting ANP to disperse the crowd. At 0553Z, TF Tiger reported gathering has dispersed.

Reference ID: AFG20060924n306
Latitude: 32.60460281
Date: 2006-09-24 00:12
Category: Demonstration
Detained: 0

Region: RC WEST
Longitude: 62.30756378
Type: Non-Combat Event
Affiliation: Neutral

	Enemy	Friend	Civilian	Host Nation
Killed in Action	0	0	0	0
Wounded in Action	0	0	0	0

(DELAYED REPORT) At 0000z, more than 100 elders and LNs gathered in the provincial capital to protest against CF that were currently being conducted and ongoing within Farah Province. In particular, they were protesting the killing of a young LN female following a recent search operation within Farah City on 22 September. The demonstrators warned that they would take the law into their own hands if CF continued with search operations in their areas.

Reference ID: AFG20061017n435
Latitude: 31.54394913
Date: 2006-10-17 05:05
Category: Demonstration
Detained: 0

Region: RC SOUTH
Longitude: 65.45436096
Type: Non-Combat Event
Affiliation: Neutral

	Enemy	Friend	Civilian	Host Nation
Killed in Action	0	0	0	0
Wounded in Action	0	0	0	0

At 170510Z, TF Phoenix reported a large mob in the town of BAZAAR-E-PANJWAI, 80m N of PANJWAYI DC, PANJWAYI District, KANDAHAR Province). A mob of approximately 300 people gathered in the town and started fires, which obscured FF Ops. The mob appeared to attack large trucks, believed to be gravel trucks that are providing ISAF with gravel. TF Phoenix, with ANA, responded to the scene, calmed down the situation, and met local elders. RAVEN 6 reported MOB was very upset over the murder of a local vendor, RAVEN 6 tried to sort out situation. TF Phoenix and ANA moved crowd away from Basar Panjawai District Center peacefully but forcefully. The KANDAK Comd 3/1/201 met with local elders in Basar Panjawai, crowd dispersed. During this time, 1x ANP officer was viewed beating an old man in alley, RAVEN 6 with KANDAK Comd remained in Shura with local leaders. Incident closed at 171134L. (TFK)

Reference ID: AFG20061113n471
Latitude: 34.23389816
Date: 2006-11-13 05:05
Category: Demonstration
Detained: 0

Region: RC EAST
Longitude: 70.97229767
Type: Non-Combat Event
Affiliation: Neutral

	Enemy	Friend	Civilian	Host Nation
Killed in Action	0	0	2	0
Wounded in Action	0	0	4	0

(Delayed Report) At 130500ZNOV06, TF Chosin reported ANP arrived at a civil disturbance, reportedly fired into the crowd, killing two LNs and injuring four LNs 45KM SE from JAF. The Muhmand Dar and the Shinwar tribes were in a dispute when the Shinwar tribe kidnapped four Muhmand Dar LNs. In response, the Muhmand Dara tribe erected illegal checkpoints along MSR Illinois. A crowd of 100 LNs formed and ANP arrived at the scene providing crowd control. A Muhmand Dar tribal leader successfully negotiated the release of the four kidnapped LNs. There was no Coalition Force involvement in the incidents. Event closed at 1632z. ISAF Tracking number 11-216

Reference ID: AFG20061118n482
Latitude: 37.034832
Date: 2006-11-18 00:12
Category: Demonstration
Detained: 0
Region: RC NORTH
Longitude: 71.44797516
Type: Non-Combat Event
Affiliation: Neutral

	Enemy	Friend	Civilian	Host Nation
Killed in Action	0	0	0	0
Wounded in Action	0	0	0	0

(Delayed Report) People in the area have been demonstarting for the past two days against the activities of illegally armed groups. Some 500 people from the north part of the district gathered to demand the disarmament of the illegally armed group.

Reference ID: AFG20061119n467
Latitude: 32.477108
Date: 2006-11-19 00:12
Category: Demonstration
Detained: 0
Region: RC EAST
Longitude: 68.74184418
Type: Non-Combat Event
Affiliation: Neutral

	Enemy	Friend	Civilian	Host Nation
Killed in Action	0	0	0	0
Wounded in Action	0	0	0	0

(Delayed Report) SMALL PEACEFUL PROTEST AT PROVINCIAL GOVERNOR'S COMPOUND. At 190637ZNOV06, The Paktika PCC reported a protest underway at the Governor's Compound, ANP gate in Sharan. The PCC ANP desk reported a crowd of appoximately 100 LNs from Khayer Khot and Yousefkhel districts gathered to protest against an ANA platoon leader who had been harassing and beating LNs in these districts. The protest was apparently peaceful, however, the Sharan ANP at the gate fired warning shots (in the air) at the gate to apparently "gain control" of the crowd. No injuries occured. The protest leaders were escorted into the NDS area on the compound where they met with representatives of the ANP and ANA. Apparently the ANA platoon leader being protested against had already been relieved, a fact the protestors were not aware of. The meeting ended after approx 2 hrs at which point all the protesters departed peacefully.

Reference ID: AFG20061120n404
Latitude: 34.55408859
Date: 2006-11-20 00:12
Category: Demonstration
Detained: 0
Region: RC CAPITAL
Longitude: 69.32198334
Type: Non-Combat Event
Affiliation: Neutral

	Enemy	Friend	Civilian	Host Nation
Killed in Action	0	0	0	0
Wounded in Action	0	0	0	0

(Delayed Report) District 6, Parliament Building, during the course of a morning a small crowd (200 or so) people from Wardak Province staged a peaceful demonstration outside parliament apparently demanding the removal of their provincial governor.

Reference ID: AFG20061214n540
Latitude: 33.36402893
Date: 2006-12-14 00:12
Category: Demonstration
Detained: 0

Region: RC EAST
Longitude: 69.84312439
Type: Non-Combat Event
Affiliation: Neutral

	Enemy	Friend	Civilian	Host Nation
Killed in Action	0	0	0	0
Wounded in Action	0	0	0	0

(Delayed Report) A rally was conducted today in Mando Zayi to protest the Coalition Mission. Following information is provided:
- Rally conducted from 1000-1300 local, with estimated 200-400 people. (Please note that there are conflicting numbers of those in attendance with ranges listed above. More than likely crowd size was closer to the lower limit.)
- No reports of violence
- Majority of those in attendance were from Mando Zayi Tribe (same tribe of those killed). Scant participation from Ismail Khel Tribe (other predominant tribe in District)
- Major theme is anger at the Coalition for the mission and other missions this past summer / early fall (Mullah killed (Jul) and non-combatant woman killed (Sep)). There appears to be no anti-Coalition sentiment beyond these incidents in other words, no all out anti-Coalition theme.
- Populace angry over four specific issues.
  o Those at the compound all say that dialect of the interpreter was from Kandahar. Because of this they believed they were being attacked by Taliban, and thus, were defending themselves
  o Coalition press release states that four suspected terrorists were killed. Many are highly emotional and upset at what they believe is the insensitivity of this report since they all believe those killed were innocent and it is exacerbated because most believe the Coalition knows this to be true
  o District Police Chief has repeatedly stated in interviews that there were no Afghan Security Forces with the Coalition during the mission
  o Alleged beatings of those collected for questioning. Pictures of males with cuts and bruises continue to be shown on the TV
- As of 2115 local, coverage of the rally has already hit the evening TV and radio reports for local / national stations. Initial reports are hitting the internet. Specifically, Pajhwok News
- Possible rally again tomorrow
Will continue to monitor and report.

Reference ID: AFG20070105n510
Latitude: 36.82089996
Date: 2007-01-05 00:12
Category: Demonstration
Detained: 0

Region: RC NORTH
Longitude: 65.84416199
Type: Non-Combat Event
Affiliation: Neutral

	Enemy	Friend	Civilian	Host Nation
Killed in Action	0	0	0	0
Wounded in Action	0	0	0	0

At 1100hr local, about 700 General Dostum supporters took part in a demonstration in the city center protesting against Turktabaran Shora activity while the Chairman of Shora AAkbar Bai was out of Shibirighan visiting Mazar-E Sharif. The demonstration resulted in the Turktabaran Shora Office being completely distroyed, a guest house and two car burnt. Provincial police failed to stop disturbances.

Reference ID: AFG20070106n617
Latitude: 34.96220779
Date: 2007-01-06 00:12
Category: Demonstration
Detained: 0

Region: RC EAST
Longitude: 71.09215546
Type: Non-Combat Event
Affiliation: Neutral

	Enemy	Friend	Civilian	Host Nation
Killed in Action	0	0	0	0
Wounded in Action	0	0	0	0

Hundreds of district residents participated in a protest action to denounce the PAK border fence initiative. They reportedly chanted anti-PAK slogans and burned PAK flags. Demo remained peaceful.

Reference ID: AFG20070106n626
Latitude: 34.9343605
Date: 2007-01-06 06:06
Category: Demonstration
Detained: 0

Region: RC EAST
Longitude: 69.23816681
Type: Non-Combat Event
Affiliation: Neutral

	Enemy	Friend	Civilian	Host Nation
Killed in Action	0	0	0	0
Wounded in Action	0	0	0	0

At 060630ZJAN07 TF Tiger reported there was a gathering of LN personnel at the BAF ANP CP. Bagram Bazaar area outside of BAF is closed and the ANP is trying to secure the area. The Bagram District Leader Kabir has requested further ANP assistance. According to several LNs at the site, the demonstrators are protesting the hanging of Saddam Hussein and are also protesting against the Governor of Parwan, Governor Taqwa. UPDATE 0716Z: Governor Taqwa and General Mawlana report: 30 x ANP at the ANP gate outside of ECP1; 50 x ANP at the intersection of Routes Nevada and Alaska; 200 x ANP QRF available and under the control of Gen Mawlana currently moving towards Bagram from Charikar; Crowd is dispersing and getting smaller. UPDATE 0721Z: Crowd has dispersed from ANP gate. Demonstration has ended with no incident. NFTR. ISAF tracking #01-072.

Reference ID: AFG20070111n509
Latitude: 35.00851059
Date: 2007-01-11 06:06
Category: Demonstration
Detained: 0

Region: RC EAST
Longitude: 69.1654892
Type: Non-Combat Event
Affiliation: Neutral

	Enemy	Friend	Civilian	Host Nation
Killed in Action	0	0	0	0
Wounded in Action	0	0	0	0

At 110600zJAN07 TF Tiger reported a gathering of approx 5000 LN in Charikar. The LNs were protesting GEN Mawlannas announcement of his removal from office. All routes are in the area were closed. The MOI is currently in Charikar. The demonstration was later reported to be only 300-400 LNs who were demonstrating peacefully. Update at 0808z: Crowd has been dispersed. Governor has addressed the crowd and settled concerns.
ISAF Event # 01-169

Reference ID: AFG20070114n595
Latitude: 36.82089996
Date: 2007-01-14 00:12
Category: Demonstration
Detained: 0

Region: RC NORTH
Longitude: 65.84416199
Type: Non-Combat Event
Affiliation: Neutral

	Enemy	Friend	Civilian	Host Nation
Killed in Action	0	0	0	0
Wounded in Action	0	0	0	0

A demonstration turned violent at a government food distribution program. District government buildings were torched and looted.

Reference ID: AFG20070120n536
Latitude: 34.87134933
Date: 2007-01-20 08:08
Category: Demonstration
Detained: 0

Region: RC EAST
Longitude: 70.42236328
Type: Non-Combat Event
Affiliation: Neutral

	Enemy	Friend	Civilian	Host Nation
Killed in Action	0	0	0	0
Wounded in Action	0	0	0	0

At 200809ZJAN07 TF Irongray reported ANP reported there was a riot in the village of Paryana. ANP were on site and ANA were dispatched to assist. 0942Z Unit reported ANP were conducting Poppy eradication when a counter drug agent spotted 20 armed men with AK47 and RPGs. LN villagers became vocal with ANP and ANP requested ANA backup. No CF assistance requested. ISAF TRACKING # 01-316.

Reference ID: AFG20070125n500
Latitude: 34.26401138

Region: RC EAST
Longitude: 70.21764374

Date: 2007-01-25 07:07
Category: Demonstration
Detained: 0
Type: Non-Combat Event
Affiliation: Neutral

	Enemy	Friend	Civilian	Host Nation
Killed in Action	0	0	6	0
Wounded in Action	0	0	8	0

AT 250735ZJAN07 TF CHOSIN land dispute in KHOGYANI district. Land dispute between 3 tribes has resulted in 6 villager KIA, 8 villager WIA, and 12 arrested by ANP. The Provincial ANP QRF from Jalalabad has been sent to site. ISAF Tracking # 01-385

Reference ID: AFG20070130n469
Latitude: 34.95383835
Date: 2007-01-30 00:12
Category: Demonstration
Detained: 0
Region: RC EAST
Longitude: 68.88641357
Type: Non-Combat Event
Affiliation: Neutral

	Enemy	Friend	Civilian	Host Nation
Killed in Action	0	0	0	0
Wounded in Action	0	0	0	0

(Delayed Report) When we arrived at the Govs, there were rickshaws lining the road. We found out that the drivers were not able to get renewed licenses. The ANP were telling them they could not drive on the roads in Parwan. It was a peaceful demonstration.

Reference ID: AFG20070201n550
Latitude: 34.27793121
Date: 2007-02-01 00:12
Category: Demonstration
Detained: 0
Region: RC EAST
Longitude: 70.46929169
Type: Non-Combat Event
Affiliation: Neutral

	Enemy	Friend	Civilian	Host Nation
Killed in Action	0	0	0	0
Wounded in Action	0	0	0	0

(Delayed Report) UNAMA and local officials reported 300-400 protesters at a local mosque who were upset at the arrest of the Director or Canals, Dr Asef. Among the complaints was the involvement of CF even though the Afghans acknowledged that the CF were playing just a supportive role. Some protesters called for Dr Asef to be released on bail until the trial. Another topic of protest was recent radio broadcast attributed to the CF that accused Sherzod elder Zabid Zahir and Provincial Council member Tahlir Omar of corruption and anti-government activity. Peaceful demonstration. Anti-Coalition.

Reference ID: AFG20070207n606
Latitude: 34.27793121
Date: 2007-02-07 00:12
Category: Demonstration
Detained: 0
Region: RC EAST
Longitude: 70.46929169
Type: Non-Combat Event
Affiliation: Neutral

	Enemy	Friend	Civilian	Host Nation
Killed in Action	0	0	1	0
Wounded in Action	0	0	2	4

(Delayed Report) At 0000Z, PRT JALALABAD reported that the Governors poppy eradication efforts received a bit of a set back in the Shinwar district as people reacted negatively to the eradication. Protests led to rock throwing which supposedly led to the crowd shooting at the police. Four ANP were injured and two civilians were injured and one killed. The ANP Chief is investigating. The Governor is still in Kabul and his return and status is unknown.

Reference ID: AFG20070214n650
Latitude: 34.53506851
Date: 2007-02-14 05:05
Category: Demonstration
Detained: 0

Region: RC CAPITAL
Longitude: 69.16364288
Type: Non-Combat Event
Affiliation: Neutral

	Enemy	Friend	Civilian	Host Nation
Killed in Action	0	0	0	0
Wounded in Action	0	0	0	0

At 140510ZFEB07 CFC-A reported 350 LN demonstrating peacefully in Kabul over extortion of bus drivers and shop owners in Kabul. The demonstrators moved from PD10 to KCP HQ. The demonstration dispersed and hour and a half later and 10 representatives went to the Parliament building to discuss their issues and seek a resolution.

Reference ID: AFG20070215n595
Latitude: 32.9346199
Date: 2007-02-15 09:09
Category: Demonstration
Detained: 0

Region: RC EAST
Longitude: 69.45353699
Type: Non-Combat Event
Affiliation: Neutral

	Enemy	Friend	Civilian	Host Nation
Killed in Action	0	0	0	0
Wounded in Action	0	0	0	0

At 0930Z TF Catamount reports 100x LN personnel meeting at the front gate of FB Tillman. The group arrived in peaceful manner, and TF Catamount and OCF personnel met with the group. The group wanted to discuss the whereabouts of personnel detained from their village during a raid a couple days prior. The personnel left peacefully, and there is NFTR.

Reference ID: AFG20070215n635
Latitude: 32.9346199
Date: 2007-02-15 09:09
Category: Demonstration
Detained: 0

Region: RC EAST
Longitude: 69.45353699
Type: Non-Combat Event
Affiliation: Neutral

	Enemy	Friend	Civilian	Host Nation
Killed in Action	0	0	0	0
Wounded in Action	0	0	0	0

At 0930Z TF CATAMOUNT reports receiving 100 LN personnel meeting at the front gate of FOB Tillman. The group arrived in peaceful manner. The group wanted to discuss the CDE issue that occurred on 13 FEB 07 in Gayan.

Reference ID: AFG20070220n584
Latitude: 34.57138824
Date: 2007-02-20 13:01
Category: Demonstration
Detained: 0

Region: RC CAPITAL
Longitude: 69.23932648
Type: Non-Combat Event
Affiliation: Neutral

	Enemy	Friend	Civilian	Host Nation
Killed in Action	0	0	0	0
Wounded in Action	0	0	0	0

At 0600Z outside Kabul a group of 20-30 middle aged men and children were observed holding placards with pictures of IEDs, RPGs, and AT mines.

Reference ID: AFG20070223n524
Latitude: 34.51799011
Date: 2007-02-23 03:03
Category: Demonstration
Detained: 0

Region: RC CAPITAL
Longitude: 69.12747192
Type: Non-Combat Event
Affiliation: Neutral

	Enemy	Friend	Civilian	Host Nation
Killed in Action	0	0	0	0
Wounded in Action	0	0	0	0

At 0350Z, NPCC reported that 600 local nationals had gathered at the Olympic Stadium in Kabul for the demonstration in support of the amnesty bill that recently passed. At 0445Z, the NPCC reported 5000 people and 311 vehicles at the stadium. At 0450Z, the Afghan Air Corps announced that it would launch a helicopter to monitor demonstration activity from the air. Air Corps launched 1 Mi17. Observation mission complete (1.3 hrs). Negative knowledge as to the routing of the execution order. Two Mi35s and 1 Mi17 remain on stand by. Wing directive: Mi35 is NOT armed; show of force only. At 0500Z, the NPCC reported an unconfirmed 20,000 demonstrators at the stadium with PA equipment.
At 0514Z, ISAF reported that they were monitoring the situation, which was still calm with more than 5000 local nationals, including Rashid Dostum, as well as Tajik and Hazara leaders. ISAF reported that Routes Indigo and Crimson were not crowded. At 0525Z, NMCC reported the stadium being approximately half full, with about 8000-10000 demonstrators.
At 0605Z, the NPCC reported 8 vehicles with armed men heading from PD 11 (Northwest Kabul) to the Olympic Stadium. NPCC reports that the armed men in vehicles belong to a member of Parliament
At 0630Z, NMCC reports that it looks like the speeches are over and some of the crowd is starting to disperse and reboard the buses. ISAF confirms this report. It is unclear how many people are leaving and/or staying. At 0715Z, NPCC is reporting that the crowd at the stadium has dispersed into smaller groups. One group is reported to be headed down RTE Violet to CTC, another group to Pol-e-Charki and ISAF is reporting a group heading towards the French Embassy. At 0735Z, NMCC

reports that three large groups left the stadium and went to three separate mosques near the stadium
0632Z: NPCC is recanting its report of 70,000 and now estimating 25,000
ISAF 02-341

Reference ID: AFG20070226n504
Latitude: 34.66827011
Date: 2007-02-26 09:09
Category: Demonstration
Detained: 0

Region: RC EAST
Longitude: 70.59229279
Type: Non-Combat Event
Affiliation: Neutral

	Enemy	Friend	Civilian	Host Nation
Killed in Action	0	0	0	0
Wounded in Action	0	0	0	0

At 0930Z, TF Chosin reported a crowd protesting poppy eradication, the crowd torched two tractors intended to be used for eradication of poppy. The protesters threw stones at, and fired on narcotics police. ANP defended by returning fire at the hostile protesters, resulted in 2LN wounded and 1LN killed. ANP will have extra plice from Jalalabad on site for anticipation of adverse reaction from crowd. ISAF Tracking # 02-394

Reference ID: AFG20070226n510
Latitude: 34.40118027
Date: 2007-02-26 13:01
Category: Demonstration
Detained: 0

Region: RC EAST
Longitude: 70.50007629
Type: Non-Combat Event
Affiliation: Neutral

	Enemy	Friend	Civilian	Host Nation
Killed in Action	0	0	0	0
Wounded in Action	0	0	0	0

AFP: Man Killed as Villagers Block Officials From Destroying Poppies
JPP20070226088007 Hong Kong AFP in English 1110 GMT 26 Feb 07
[OSC Transcribed Text]
JALALABAD, Afghanistan, Feb 26, 2007 (AFP) - A man was killed Monday when police opened fire on around 300 villagers blocking efforts to dig up opium poppies in Afghanistan, an official said.
Demonstrators also fired on and threw stones at counter narcotics police in the eastern province of Nangarhar, said Abdul Akbar, a district governor.
They torched two tractors brought to the district to plough up poppies and blocked a main road, he said.
"About 300 people came out from their houses and started the demonstration against the police forces. The police fired on them and as a result a man has died" he said.
There has been a handful of similar incidents this year as Afghanistan redoubles efforts to slash opium production, which jumped by 50 percent last year and accounts for 90 percent of world supply.
[Description of Source: Hong Kong AFP in English -- Hong Kong service of the independent French press agency Agence France-Presse]

Reference ID: AFG20070228n622
Latitude: 34.12231827
Date: 2007-02-28 08:08
Category: Demonstration
Detained: 0

Region: RC EAST
Longitude: 70.81086731
Type: Non-Combat Event
Affiliation: Neutral

	Enemy	Friend	Civilian	Host Nation
Killed in Action	0	0	0	0
Wounded in Action	0	0	0	0

At 0800Z TF Chosin reported a crowd threw rocks at a poppy eradication team 42km SW of Jalalabad. ANP fired warning shots in response and more ANP are being sent. Provincial and district officials were at the site dealing with the incident.
ISAF Tracking# 02-427.

Reference ID: AFG20070306n688
Latitude: 34.47253036
Date: 2007-03-06 05:05
Category: Demonstration
Detained: 0

Region: RC EAST
Longitude: 70.36765289
Type: Non-Combat Event
Affiliation: Neutral

	Enemy	Friend	Civilian	Host Nation
Killed in Action	0	0	0	0
Wounded in Action	0	0	0	0

At 0515Z TF SPARTAN reported Protest at Nangarhar University . Reports varied as to violence level from peaceful to window breaking. Several sources including ANP and UNAMA reported the protest. Protestors may have blocked Highway 1. Crowd appeared to be either contained in the University Area or moving west out of Jalalabad city. In addition, there were reports of HiG members in the crowd inciting them.
At 0618Z TF CHAMBERLAIN reported that ISR showed only a small group of 15-30 people in the protest area.
ISAF Tracking # 03-119

Reference ID: AFG20070308n684
Latitude: 34.43502045
Date: 2007-03-08 00:12
Category: Demonstration
Detained: 0

Region: RC EAST
Longitude: 70.43663788
Type: Non-Combat Event
Affiliation: Neutral

	Enemy	Friend	Civilian	Host Nation
Killed in Action	0	0	0	0
Wounded in Action	0	0	0	0

The people were outraged by the arrests of three people in Nangarhar. Through the press and through phone calls we were notified that approximately 150 Afghans from Chaparhar district marched to Jalalabad in protest of the operation. Some reports indicated there were thousands of protestors, however these were greatly exaggerated. OCF released talking points about last nights PUCing at 1545L today. IO put together a press release comprised of the talking points and pushed it out ASAP to all local media. Four to five media called this morning and early afternoon asking for details.

Reference ID: AFG20070308n696
Latitude: 34.30899048
Date: 2007-03-08 09:09
Category: Demonstration
Detained: 0

Region: RC EAST
Longitude: 70.39649963
Type: Non-Combat Event
Affiliation: Neutral

	Enemy	Friend	Civilian	Host Nation
Killed in Action	0	0	0	0
Wounded in Action	0	0	0	0

080909Z 1-32 IN reports a non violent protest of approximately 5000-6000 people, occurred between 0600Z-0730Z vic Chaparhar and JBAD. The protesters were demanding the release of 3x individuals detained in a raid last night. The Assistant Nangarhar Governor and ANP QRF arrived on the scene and dispersed the crowd without incident.
ISAF 03-176

Reference ID: AFG20070318n626
Latitude: 34.8503685
Date: 2007-03-18 00:12
Category: Demonstration
Detained: 0

Region: RC EAST
Longitude: 71.13276672
Type: Non-Combat Event
Affiliation: Neutral

	Enemy	Friend	Civilian	Host Nation
Killed in Action	0	0	0	0
Wounded in Action	0	0	0	0

Arriving to visit Gov Deedar at his compound, PRT CMDR and DOS came accross about 100 protesting Aux Police that have not been paid in 6 months. Many of these Aux police in attached photos have been a stabilizing force along the main LOCs and have been diligently working and will be enveloped in the ANAP program. However, many of the group today have been working and have opted not ot become ANAP. All of the group were angry because Gen Jalal, Kunar ANP Chief, had told them that Gov Deedar had their back pay. PRT CMDR explained the process and that Gov Deedar did not in fact have their salaries. Some were happy to be starting training soon for ANAP

Reference ID: AFG20070322n633
Latitude: 34.94884109
Date: 2007-03-22 08:08
Category: Demonstration
Detained: 0

Region: RC EAST
Longitude: 69.25408173
Type: Non-Combat Event
Affiliation: Neutral

	Enemy	Friend	Civilian	Host Nation
Killed in Action	0	0	0	0
Wounded in Action	0	0	0	0

Gladius 6 Category 2 interpreter received a call from General Salim regarding the construction outside tower 19. He stated that the people of Jangadam do not want to give up any of their land. They are currently protesting outside the construction site. Gen Salim fears the people may possibly begin massing and could get up to 100 people to try to fight for their land. TF Cincinatius is currently sending their PAO

and an interpreter to the site to explain to the people it is only a de-mining operation not a construction project.

Reference ID: AFG20070402n596
Latitude: 34.24534988
Date: 2007-04-02 05:05
Category: Demonstration
Detained: 0
Region: RC EAST
Longitude: 70.72810364
Type: Non-Combat Event
Affiliation: Neutral

	Enemy	Friend	Civilian	Host Nation
Killed in Action	0	0	0	0
Wounded in Action	0	0	0	0

At 0509Z TF Vanguard reported LNs were protesting at the Bati Kot District Center. The protest was peaceful at the time, but some demonstrators have AK47s and RPGs. The Nangarhar Governor, and ANP were on the scene, and have arrested approximately 15 protestors. It is believed the protestors were upset about poppy eradication efforts in Bati Kot. The ANP did not requesting CF support, and the protest seemed to be calming down and possibly dispersing. At 0750Z ANP report the protest ended without violence, and there is NFTR.
1358Z reports of 5 x LN wounded, 2 ANP wounded
ISAF Tracking # 04-025

Reference ID: AFG20070402n606
Latitude: 34.15187836
Date: 2007-04-02 05:05
Category: Demonstration
Detained: 0
Region: RC EAST
Longitude: 69.08677673
Type: Non-Combat Event
Affiliation: Neutral

	Enemy	Friend	Civilian	Host Nation
Killed in Action	0	0	1	0
Wounded in Action	0	0	0	0

At 0555Z TF PHOENIX reported a demonstration against the ANP in the vicinity of Pul E Alam. Gunfire broke out between ANP & local nationals, approximately 300 rounds expended, no U.S. involvement, ANP & NDS are remaining in the inner cordon and holding positions at this point. One civilian KIA is confirmed at this point. The crowd would not disperse so the ANP General detained 6 tribe elders that were leading the dispute. As of 0800Z: the scene was under control and the crowd was dispersing. ISAF 04-026.
UPDATE: 3 x Tribes (tribe names undetermined) fighting over land and other issues. RTE Utah was blocked with the crowd, burning tires, and big rocks. The ANP General with ANP from Pul-E-Alam responded to control the crowd. The ANP General began trying to get the crowd to disperse when the ANP fired on the crowd. 1 LN KIA was reported, however, the ANP said they did not shoot into the crowd, they shot above the crowd. The crowd would not disperse so the ANP General detained 6 tribe elders that were leading the dispute. As of 0800Z: the scene was under control and the crowd was dispersing
020555Z TF DIABLO REPORTS DEMONSTARTION THAT LED TO 1 CIV KIA
On 020555ZAPR07, the ANP, NDS, ANA, and CF operated to disarm the villages of Dehenow and Ahmadzai, who have been fighting over disputed land rights. CF had

two TCP/Blocking positions along the east/west MSR, and four security positions to the northeast to support the disarmament. The ANP hired bulldozers to tear down walls built on the disputed land. At 42S WC 085805, the people massed and claimed to be approaching the ANP to ask them questions about the situation. The ANP were frightened and fired onto the crowd. Initially, the shots were disciplined, but the 10m firefight degraded to a SPENDEX. No other forces were involved. One civilian KIA, and 3 civilian WIA- unconfirmed by gov/CF forces. Once shots were fired, the TCP in the bazaar moved to collocate with the western TCP, and the northeastern security positions were recalled to the same site. The citizens of Tangi Wahjan massed in the bazaar and on the bridges and blocked off the roads with several rock and brick piles; they burned piles of tires and then massed on RTE UTAH. The people blocked off RTE UTAH to the north and south of the intersection, and further south approximately 1.5km. Dissipated four hours later.

There is a land dispute between the Ahmadzzi and Dehenow tribes (historical, go figure). The Dehenow tribe began building on what the Ahmadzzi tribe thought was their land.

Things we know:

The ANP XO hired two bulldozers to knock down walls built by Dehenow on the disputed land

The ANP CDR XO (COL Latifi) asked CF to provide security for the bulldozer operation to pay for the bulldozer; the request was denied. We were already in our positions when the bulldozer issue arose and therefore provided security by proxy.

ANP claimed to fire shots over the crowds; however there were casualties (see story board)

Elders from each tribe detained by ANP to attempt to control the situation

Things Hades 6 (CPT Matthews) is confirming time now. She is moving to the Logar Governors compound.

Did he order the ANP to knock down the walls built by Dehenow tribe or was the ANP acting alone Apparently, there was a meeting (sometime yesterday morning) between the NDS/ANA/ANP and they decided together that the walls should be knocked down; the governor gave his approval.

After two Shuras yesterday between the tribes, another Shura was scheduled today, time TBD. The Shura I organized for last night was cancelled by the Governor yesterday. I did not find out until no one showed up; additionally, no one told the Dehenow elders, as they showed up late and I had to explain to them that the governor had canceled the Shura. There were two Shuras conducted today-Dehenow and Ahmadzai. They were kept separate. The Dehenow say that all they want is a decision made and they will abide by it; the Ahmadzai say that they want justice served (the lower courts have already ruled in favor of Dehenow, but the Ahmadzai have appealed and want judgement by the high court) and will abide by a decision if justice is served. I hope to organize a Shura between the two groups soon (within two weeks). If the High Court can reach a ruling, then both groups should be present for the verdict as that lends legitimacy. This facet of the issue is outside of my scope of influence; assistance is requested from Brigade and Division, to push the issue to a speedy, but judicious, resolution.

Governors intent to solve this situation between the tribes; ISAF/ANSF support needed, etc.The governor was not present at the Shura; the sub-governor, who is barely even a figurehead, attended and spoke fewer than three sentences. The governor has made very clear in the past that he has no inclination to resolved this or any land dispute as he feels that is the MOIs job. The MOI has not given its subordinate leaders the authority needed to resolve these issues at the lowest level possible.

Determine the ANPs way ahead for security in the area. There is a checkpoint in the area roughly centered between the two rival groups. The checkpoint is currently manned at approximately 50 personnel. We will continue to push the ANP to patrol the area day and night, but not give the indication of martial law. We will also patrol the area and support ANP-led HA distribution. Additionally, a site survey was done two days ago; we will use this to nominate CERP projects. We are brainstorming to figure out what civil service project the ANP may do to reestablish the relationship.

TF Diablo way ahead:
Continue to show presence in the area
Continue to promote/assist with Shura between the local government, ANP and the two tribes.
Continue KLE with Logar Gov, ANP CDR, and elders from the Ahmadzzi and Dehenow tribes.

Reference ID: AFG20070406n770
Latitude: 34.75244904
Date: 2007-04-06 12:12
Category: Demonstration
Detained: 0

Region: RC CAPITAL
Longitude: 69.13437653
Type: Non-Combat Event
Affiliation: Neutral

	Enemy	Friend	Civilian	Host Nation
Killed in Action	0	0	1	0
Wounded in Action	0	0	0	0

CSTC-A DCG for Pol-Mil Affairs
Daily Cable Summaries
6 April 2007
(U) AEF ERADICATION EFFORTS CONFRONT THOUSANDS OF PROTESTERS IN HELMAND: (Source: AMEMBASSY KABUL 01131, 6 Apr 07)
Thousands of protesters in Helmand province thwarted the Afghan Eradication Forces (AEF) attempts to eradicate poppy in the provinces Nahi Sirraj district on April 6; efforts will resume tomorrow. The AEFs planned activity followed intense negotiations with ISAF, UK Task Force Helmand, and GoA officials to gain consent for eradication in the district. The protesters complained to Helmand Deputy Governor Haji Pir Mohammad, who joined the AEF in its attempt to move to poppy fields, that the AEFs presence was unfair given Governor Wafas earlier promises that there would be no more eradication in the district. GoA officials, for four hours, attempted to reach a compromise with the protesters but were forced to send the AEF back to their base camp. The AEF will attempt to eradicate in Nahi Sirraj again on April 7

Reference ID: AFG20070411n617
Latitude: 34.50984955
Date: 2007-04-11 05:05
Category: Demonstration
Detained: 0

Region: RC CAPITAL
Longitude: 69.1536026
Type: Non-Combat Event
Affiliation: Neutral

	Enemy	Friend	Civilian	Host Nation
Killed in Action	0	0	0	0
Wounded in Action	0	0	0	0

WE HAVE CONFIRMED REPORTS OF A DEMONSTRATION MARCH PROCEEDING SOUTH ROUTE GREEN FROM G-2 IN THE DIRECTION OF G-3. WE HAVE UNCONFIRMED REPORTS STATING THAT THE DEMONSTRATION IS IN RESPONSE TO ANP INTERFERANCE WITH LOCAL VENDORS. THERE IS AN ANP PRESENCE AT THE DEMONSTRATION.

Reference ID: AFG20070415n715
Latitude: 34.5305481
Date: 2007-04-15 08:08
Category: Demonstration
Detained: 0
Region: RC CAPITAL
Longitude: 69.17980194
Type: Non-Combat Event
Affiliation: Neutral

	Enemy	Friend	Civilian	Host Nation
Killed in Action	0	0	0	0
Wounded in Action	0	0	0	0

APPROXIMATELY 20 SHOPKEEPERS FROM BAGRAM CAME TO CAMP EGGERS EXPRESSING THEIR DISPLEASURE AT THE SEISURE OF GOODS FROM THEIR SHOPS BY COALITION FORCES. THE GOODS IN QUESTION ARE MILITARY PROPERTY SEIZED IN THE BAGRAM AREA. THE SHOPKEEPERS WERE TOLD TO CONTACT THE ANP AND LEFT CAMP EGGERS WITHOUT INCIDENT.

Reference ID: AFG20070417n669
Latitude: 34.75381088
Date: 2007-04-17 02:02
Category: Demonstration
Detained: 0
Region: RC EAST
Longitude: 70.10678864
Type: Non-Combat Event
Affiliation: Neutral

	Enemy	Friend	Civilian	Host Nation
Killed in Action	0	0	0	0
Wounded in Action	0	0	0	0

170238Z TF Diamondbacks report that ANP arrested 4-5 personnel approximately 10km northwest of FOB Mehtar Lam, and today, 15-20 personnel are causing civil unrest in the town in order to get the 4-5 arrested individuals released. ANA/ETTs responded, and at 0550Z report there is no significant activity at the village, and the ANA are RTB. NFTR.

Reference ID: AFG20070418n683
Latitude: 34.5305481
Date: 2007-04-18 12:12
Category: Demonstration
Detained: 0
Region: RC CAPITAL
Longitude: 69.17980194
Type: Non-Combat Event
Affiliation: Neutral

	Enemy	Friend	Civilian	Host Nation
Killed in Action	0	0	0	0
Wounded in Action	0	0	0	0

There was a peaceful demonstration near the corner of Route Green. The demonstration was reportedly in reference to disabled local nationals asking for human rights. The demonstration was peaceful and lasted only 15 minutes. (DELAYED REPORT)

Reference ID: AFG20070501n681
Latitude: 34.53055954
Date: 2007-05-01 07:07
Category: Demonstration
Detained: 0

Region: RC CAPITAL
Longitude: 69.17543793
Type: Non-Combat Event
Affiliation: Neutral

	Enemy	Friend	Civilian	Host Nation
Killed in Action	0	0	0	0
Wounded in Action	0	0	0	0

Approximately 200 Afghans are protesting at the Iranian Embassy. This is a registered protest and the ANP/ANA are on the scene. ANP has closed the road between Camp Eggers and the Iranian Embassy. Traffic in the area is extremely heavy due to the road closures.
The Afghans are protesting the deportation of male heads of households from Iranian refugee camps and expected to remain peaceful.
010830Z The protest at the Embassy of Iran has ended and the roads are being reopened.

Reference ID: AFG20070503n708
Latitude: 33.29494095
Date: 2007-05-03 07:07
Category: Demonstration
Detained: 0

Region: RC WEST
Longitude: 62.15901947
Type: Non-Combat Event
Affiliation: Neutral

	Enemy	Friend	Civilian	Host Nation
Killed in Action	0	0	0	0
Wounded in Action	0	0	0	0

At 0730Z TF Phoenix reported the ANA Corps commander, Brigade commander and Deputy Minister of Defense have relayed that there is a large demonstration near the Subgovernor's house in Shindand. ANA QRF is standing by if needed. The demonstration was about the increase in the level of violence over the past week. The citizens are extremely disgruntled over the security situation within the area. At 1023Z ANA reported the crowd had dispersed and left the area. ISAF Tracking# 05-063.

Reference ID: AFG20070503n719
Latitude: 34.75244904
Date: 2007-05-03 12:12
Category: Demonstration
Detained: 0

Region: RC CAPITAL
Longitude: 69.13437653
Type: Non-Combat Event
Affiliation: Neutral

	Enemy	Friend	Civilian	Host Nation
Killed in Action	0	0	0	0
Wounded in Action	0	0	0	0

(C) PRT JALALABAD: FALLOUT FROM MILITARY OPERATION IN NANGARHAR: (Source: AMEMBASSY KABUL 01478, 2 May 07)
On the night of April 28, Coalition and Afghan National Security Forces (ANSF) conducted an operation against a suicide bomb cell in the vicinity of Bati Kot, about 20 miles southeast of Jalalabad. In the course of the operation, four insurgents as well as a woman and teenage girl were killed. Two other girls, a 15 year-old and a three year-old, were injured. The following day between 500-1,000 area residents temporarily blocked the highway linking Jalalabad and the border to protest the deaths as well as the evacuation of the two injured females to the US medical facility at the Bagram Airfield (BAF) without the escort of a male relative. Particularly coming against the backdrop of the March 4 incident in Nangahar in which US Marine Special Forces killed 15 civilians and injured 35 others after coming under attack, Governor Sherzai quickly returned to the province to help quell concerns. With the help of his intervention, along with a visit by two village elders to the BAF medical facility, the situation appeared to be calming as of April 30. This incident, and the public affairs fall-out of a separate clash in Shindand District of Heart Province on April 28-29 in which ANA and US forces were involved and in which civilians were allegedly killed, underscore the challenge of addressing the serious security problems facing Afghanistan while minimizing civilian casualties and disruption to the lives of local residents. President Karzai expressed concern that these incidents could affect popular attitudes toward ISAF and the Coalition in a May 2 meeting with his security advisors, the Ambassadors from US, EU, NATO and UN SRSG, and COMISAF. Karzai said a fourth day of demonstrations was underway in Jalalabad (today's was peaceful) and called for better coordination before and after military (especially SOF) operations. He assigned MOD Wardak to engage with COMISAF on this matter.

Reference ID: AFG20070516n726
Latitude: 34.68817139
Date: 2007-05-16 23:11
Category: Demonstration
Detained: 0

Region: RC EAST
Longitude: 70.59557343
Type: Non-Combat Event
Affiliation: Neutral

	Enemy	Friend	Civilian	Host Nation
Killed in Action	0	0	0	0
Wounded in Action	0	0	0	0

ON A SECOND VISIT TO THIS AREA, VILLAGE ELDER YOSEF DESIRED SOME HUMANITARIAN ASSISTANCE ON A FEW ITEMS, THOSE INCLUDED WERE: BLANKETS, SCHOOL KITS, HYGIENE KITS AND TEACHER KITS. THIS WAS DELIVERED TO THE DISTRICT CENTER OF DARI NUR AND DISTRIBUTED BY THE VILLAGE ELDERS THERE. WHILE THERE CA PERSONNEL CONDUCTED AN ONGOING ASSESSMENT OF HE LOCAL C C CLINIC AND OTHER ONGOING PROJECTS THERE.

Reference ID: AFG20070521n715
Latitude: 34.75244904
Date: 2007-05-21 12:12

Region: RC CAPITAL
Longitude: 69.13437653
Type: Non-Combat Event

Category: Demonstration Affiliation: Neutral
Detained: 0

	Enemy	Friend	Civilian	Host Nation
Killed in Action	0	0	0	0
Wounded in Action	0	0	0	0

(C) RED MOSQUE ISSUE FLARES UP AGAIN: (Source: AMEMBASSY ISLAMABAD 02270, 21 May 07)
In what has become a recurring spectacle in Islamabad, mosque supporters and seminary students-- better known as the Red Mosque brigade-- have again "kidnapped" police to draw attention to their demands. On May 18, the Red Mosque (Lal Masjid) "brigade" captured four plain-clothes police officers outside the mosque and held them as ransom for the release of eleven religious students associated with the Red Mosque. (Note. The eleven students had been arrested earlier on various charges, including raiding video shops. End Note.) Mosque leader Maulana Abdul Rashid Ghazi accused the police of spying on the mosque and threatened violence in response. (Note. Press contacts who meet regularly with Maulana Ghazi have reported that he is likely bluffing on the threat of violence and wants to pursue negotiations. End Note.)

Reference ID: AFG20070609n784 Region: RC CAPITAL
Latitude: 34.52787018 Longitude: 69.16670227
Date: 2007-06-09 05:05 Type: Non-Combat Event
Category: Demonstration Affiliation: Neutral
Detained: 0

	Enemy	Friend	Civilian	Host Nation
Killed in Action	0	0	0	0
Wounded in Action	0	0	0	0

At 0545Z, RC Capital reported approximately 400 people gathering between the finance ministry and justice ministry in order to demonstrate against the attempted murder of the Attorney General yesterday afternoon (08Jun07). The demonstration was peaceful and concluded at 0625Z. ISAF Event # 06-229.

Reference ID: AFG20070630n710 Region: RC EAST
Latitude: 34.71697998 Longitude: 70.95585632
Date: 2007-06-30 13:01 Type: Non-Combat Event
Category: Demonstration Affiliation: Neutral
Detained: 0

	Enemy	Friend	Civilian	Host Nation
Killed in Action	0	0	0	0
Wounded in Action	0	0	0	0

At 1310, TF Rock reported a riot consisting of aprox. 200 local national blocking the ABAD-JBAD road. The cause of the riot appeared to be the recent rocket attack and the locals' feeling that CF were doing too little to protect and secure the district. The locals were burning tires and preventing traffic from passing through. The aproximate center of the riot at time of reporting, as observd by friendly elements, was XD 791 434. Sub-governor Safi and Police Chief Dawood arrived with ANP and

ANA to control the riot and to ensure that it did not get out of hand. The mob disbursed at 1330z without incident.
ISAF Tracking # 06-777.

Reference ID: AFG20070701n798
Latitude: 32.37551117
Date: 2007-07-01 05:05
Category: Demonstration
Detained: 0

Region: RC WEST
Longitude: 62.12192917
Type: Non-Combat Event
Affiliation: Neutral

	Enemy	Friend	Civilian	Host Nation
Killed in Action	0	0	0	0
Wounded in Action	0	0	0	3

At 0500Z RC(W) reported a violent riot in front of the governers compound in Farah city. The crowed fired AK-47s at the compound while the ANP were guarding it. The demonstrators were protesting the death of a doctors son who was kidnapped and beheaded in the desert. Quick responce force was launched to assess. The ANP and ANA had the situation under control. 3 ANP were WIA. The WIA were treated at Farah PRT. ISAF Tracking # 07-009

Reference ID: AFG20070805n901
Latitude: 34.52875137
Date: 2007-08-05 06:06
Category: Demonstration
Detained: 0

Region: RC CAPITAL
Longitude: 69.17870331
Type: Non-Combat Event
Affiliation: Neutral

	Enemy	Friend	Civilian	Host Nation
Killed in Action	0	0	0	0
Wounded in Action	0	0	0	0

At 0640Z RC Capital reported a peaceful demonstration under KCP control in front of UNAMA. 60 people demonstrated IOT collect information about a mass grave discoved two weeks ago in PD17. ISAF tracking number 08-110

Reference ID: AFG20070816n901
Latitude: 34.52965164
Date: 2007-08-16 12:12
Category: Demonstration
Detained: 0

Region: RC CAPITAL
Longitude: 69.18089294
Type: Non-Combat Event
Affiliation: Neutral

	Enemy	Friend	Civilian	Host Nation
Killed in Action	0	0	0	0
Wounded in Action	0	0	0	0

SIGACT: 07-08-005
REPORTING UNIT: CAMP EGGERS BDOC
EVENT TYPE: Peaceful demonstration outside Camp Eggers
DTG: 16 1620L AUG 2007
GRID: IVO 42S WD 165 210

PROVINCE: Kabul
DISTRICT: Kabul
REMARKS: Peaceful demonstration at UNAMA compound just outside Camp Eggers ECP 1. Approx 150 participants in attendance and ANP are on scene. Due to the demonstration, ECP 1 is not accessable from outside the compound. All traffic should be directed through South Gate. The demonstration is in support of the 3 LN that worked a demining company that were killed by the Taliban

Reference ID: AFG20070829n802
Latitude: 34.51881027
Date: 2007-08-29 05:05
Category: Demonstration
Detained: 0

Region: RC CAPITAL
Longitude: 69.1917572
Type: Non-Combat Event
Affiliation: Neutral

	Enemy	Friend	Civilian	Host Nation
Killed in Action	0	0	0	0
Wounded in Action	0	0	0	0

At 0515Z RC Capital reported that in the vicinity Camp Phoenix, Kabul province; an estimated 200-400 ex-officers are claiming for there salaries and rights which were promised by the government. At 0700Z Demonstrators have passed M.O.D. and are moving toward UNAMA. MTF. Event closed at 1100Z. ISAF tracking number 08-829.

Reference ID: AFG20080302n1140
Latitude: 36.70886993
Date: 2008-03-02 00:12
Category: Demonstration
Detained: 0

Region: RC NORTH
Longitude: 67.11092377
Type: Non-Combat Event
Affiliation: Neutral

	Enemy	Friend	Civilian	Host Nation
Killed in Action	0	0	0	0
Wounded in Action	0	0	0	0

On 2 Mar 08, ~1,000 Afghans, incensed by the republication of Prophet Mohammad's caricature in Danish & Dutch papers, marched in the northern city of Mazar-e Sharif near the Blue Mosque on Sunday demanding withdrawal of Danish and Dutch troops from the country. The protesters also condemned plans by a right-wing Dutch politician to broadcast an anti-Koran film. Although the rally remained peaceful, demonstrators set the Danish and Dutch flags ablaze. Afghanistan's religious affairs ministry has called the reprinting of Prophet Mohammad's cartoons as an attack against Islam. The cartoons were first printed in Danish papers in 2005 and sparked violent protests across the Muslim world and reprinted by several other Western publications in 2006 in which dozens of people, some in , were killed. "We demand the...withdrawal of Danish and Dutch soldiers from Afghanistan," said Mawlavi Shoaib, a religious figure and one of the organizers. "Down with and . We urge the Muslim community to voice their concerns" chanted the protesters. The protestors warned they would launch bigger demonstrations, unless their demands over the expulsion of Dutch and Danish forces were met by the Afghan government. NFI

Reference ID: AFG20080311n1223
Latitude: 34.24172974
Date: 2008-03-11 05:05
Category: Demonstration
Detained: 0

Region: RC WEST
Longitude: 62.2221489
Type: Non-Combat Event
Affiliation: Neutral

	Enemy	Friend	Civilian	Host Nation
Killed in Action	0	0	0	0
Wounded in Action	0	0	0	0

LATE REPORTING: PLANNED BUSINESS CLOSURES AND POSSIBLE DEMONSTRATIONS IN HERAT CITY ON 11 MARCH 2008 LOCAL BUSINESS OWNERS PLAN TO CLOSE THEIR SHOPS FOR THE DAY STARTING ON THE MORNING OF 11 MARCH 2008 TO SHOW DISSATISFACTION WITH GOVERNOR ((ANWARI)). IT IS POSSIBLE DEMONSTRATIONS MAY SPAWN FROM THIS SHOW OF PROTEST. NO FURTHER INFORMATION WAS PROVIDED REGARDING SPECIFIC LOCATIONS AND ADDITIONAL DETAILS REGARDING THE PLANNED BUSINESS CLOSURES AND/OR POSSIBLE DEMONSTRATIONS WERE UNKNOWN. THE PLANNED BUSINESS CLOSURES MAY BE A FOLLOW-ON ACTION TO THE RECENT STRIKE BY LOCAL DOCTORS. ACCORDING TO OPEN SOURCE REPORTING OVER 600 DOCTORS AND HEALTH WORKERS IN HERAT PROVINCE WENT ON STRIKE ON 8 MARCH 2008 IN PROTEST AGAINST THE ABDUCTION OF THE SON OF A DOCTOR EARLIER THAT DAY. THE DOCTORS SAY THEY WILL CONTINUE THEIR STRIKE INDEFINITELY UNLESS MEASURES ARE TAKEN TO ENSURE SECURITY IN THAT PROVINCE. ADDITIONALLY, ON 8 MARCH 2008, THE REGIONAL HOSPITAL OF HERAT, ALL HEALTH CLINICS, HEALTH CENTERS, AND DRUG STORES WERE CLOSED IN PROTEST AGAINST THE ABDUCTION OF THE DOCTOR'S SON. NFI. EVENT CLOSED.

Reference ID: AFG20080322n1233
Latitude: 36.06287003
Date: 2008-03-22 09:09
Category: Demonstration
Detained: 0

Region: RC NORTH
Longitude: 68.58914185
Type: Non-Combat Event
Affiliation: Neutral

	Enemy	Friend	Civilian	Host Nation
Killed in Action	0	0	0	0
Wounded in Action	0	0	0	0

PRT PEK received the information about a demonstration in Casma-I-Ser(42SVE 630910) at 221400MAR08 as the result of the GE SF activity in the village which was carried on early in the morning. According to several source, there were approximately 300-600 local civilians who were taking part in the gathering. They were shouting anti ISAF slogans. They were blocking the MSR Uranus. The ANP is on the spot to handle the situation. NFI. Event Closed.

Reference ID: AFG20080328n1258
Latitude: 34.95018005
Date: 2008-03-28 05:05

Region: RC EAST
Longitude: 69.2665863
Type: Non-Combat Event

Category: Demonstration   Affiliation: Neutral
Detained: 0

	Enemy	Friend	Civilian	Host Nation
Killed in Action	0	0	0	0
Wounded in Action	0	0	0	0

(U) Key Leader Engagement (281100ZMarch08/ Bagram, Province, Afghanistan).
Country: (U) Afghanistan (AFG).
Subject: Key Leader Engagement with Local Elders
WARNING: (U) This is an information report, not finally evaluated intelligence. This report is classified S E C R E T RELEASEABLE to USA, GCTF, ISAF and NATO.
(S//REL USA, ISAF, NATO) Summary: During the engagement with Local Elders outside tower 14 the following topic was discussed: Western Land Usage
1.   (S//REL USA, GCTF, ISAF, NATO) Western Land Usage
1A. (S//REL USA, ISAF, NATO) Cincinnatus 6 met with 5 men identified as local village elders, along with known rabble rouser Gold Teeth. These 6 individuals appeared to be the leaders of a peaceful, orderly demonstration of approximately 200-300 Afghans. There were no women observed in the crowd, but approximately a quarter of the protestors were children.
The local elders made the following claims/requests:
There are 14 villages and 10k individuals that will be displaced
Coalition Forces have already plotted a fence line out to the road.
GIRoA must compensate the people because of the 40th article of the Constitution
GIRoA does not speak for the peoplecommunication must flow through the village elders
The villages are not against CF or construction. They were among the first to welcome CF, but that doesn't give CF the right to take their property.
The fliers that CF hand out are making locals angry.
Pressure Governor Taqwa to sit down with the village elders. The Governor has ignored their attempts to date.
Cincinnatus 6 advised the village elders that Governor Taqwa was their governor, and it was their responsibility to contact him. The leaders responded that they had made attempts to contact the governor, and that a group of 50 of their villagers had gone to the governor⊢s compound. Governor Taqwa was not their, they said, but was in India seeking medical treatment. One of the leaders claimed that they only had two options should CF move the fence¶ move to the mountains, or leave Afghanistan. Cincinnatus 6 pointed out that the government had designated land for any displaced individuals, but the village elders claimed that no such land was ever promised them, or shown to them.
Finally, Gold Teeth stated that today was not a good day to negotiate. The elders would prefer that Cincinnatus 6 attend their shura the following day (30 Mar 08). Cincinnatus 6 countered that he would not attend, but he would call Governor Taqwa and ask that he speak with the elders. The elders claimed that such efforts were futile, as the governor never listened to them.
(S//REL USA, ISAF, NATO) Analyst Comments: Cincinnatus 6 explained that a year ago he laid out CF plans for western land usage, and gave the elders 30 days to work out land grants with their government. After those 30 days, Cincinnatus 6 gave them another 30 days. But the time for 30 day reprieves is over. Cincinnatus 6 stated that the conversation was over, that he would contact the governor, and that the elders had 24 hours to settle matters with their government.

At that time the negotiation ended, and the elders were escorted outside the gate. It appeared that the crowd was beginning to disperse, and Cincinnatus 6 left Tower 14.

Reference ID: AFG20080422n1277
Latitude: 34.00947571
Date: 2008-04-22 20:08
Category: Demonstration
Detained: 0

Region: RC EAST
Longitude: 69.02748871
Type: Non-Combat Event
Affiliation: Neutral

	Enemy	Friend	Civilian	Host Nation
Killed in Action	0	0	0	0
Wounded in Action	0	0	0	0

APACHE X-RAY WAS NOTIFIED BY ANP THAT THE TALIBAN HAD SET FIRE TO THE JUYAK BOYS SCHOOL. WARHAWK 1-1 ARRIVED AT LOCATION AND WITH 4 U.S. 10 ANP. WARHAWK 1-1 LINKED UP WITH THE HEADMASTER FOR BOYS (CHIEF NAIK MOHHAMAD) SAID NAMED INFORMED WARHAWK ELEMENT THAT 80 AAF (POSSIBLE 4-6) ENTERED SCHOOL AND STATED THAT "THEY SHOULD'NT ALLOW GIRLS TO ATTEND THIS SCHOOL. THEY COVERED THE GUARDS HEADS AND TOOK THEM TO AN UNKNOWN LOCATION AND BEAT THEM. THE GUARDS WERE RELEASED IOT PASS ON THE INFORMATION. THE OTHER AAF SET FIRE TO THE SCHOOL. THE HEADMASTER CHIEF STATED THAT HE HAD NO PRIOR WARNING. rESUALT: TOTAL DAMAGE TO SCHOOL WAS 1 AND A HALF OF THE TWO ROOM SCHOOL DESTROYED BY FIRE AND SMOKE.
ASSESSMENT: PREVIOUS REPORTING HAS INCLUDED THREATS AGAINST GIRLS SCHOOLS, THIER STAFF AND THE GIRLS THAT ATTEND THE SCHOOL. THESE REPORTS WERE STRICKTLY FOCUSED ON GIRLS SCHOOLS AND MAY HAVE CHANGED DIRECTION OF INFLUENCE TO ALL SCHOOLS. ATTACKS ON SCHOOLS INFLICT FEAR AND PREVENT EDUCATION TO CHILDERN TO WHO ARE EASILY INFLUENCED. THESE ATTACKS WILL CONTINUE AS LONG AS AAF HAS FREEDOM OF MOVEMENT WITHIN AO.
EVENT CLOSED

Reference ID: AFG20080428n1286
Latitude: 35.95051575
Date: 2008-04-28 00:12
Category: Demonstration
Detained: 0

Region: RC NORTH
Longitude: 68.70615387
Type: Non-Combat Event
Affiliation: Neutral

	Enemy	Friend	Civilian	Host Nation
Killed in Action	0	0	0	0
Wounded in Action	0	0	0	0

PRT PEK received an information about a demonstration at the textile factory in Pol-e Khumri town. Employees were taking part in the demonstration. The reason for the demo was some confusion about the service flat (work provided apartment). As a part of the privatisation development in Afghanistan, it is planned to privatise the textile factory. According to the old regulation, after 40 years work at the factory the service flat become their own property. The new owners of the factory want to cancel this rule, and according to the new regulation, the workers have to pay rent for a service flat as long as the live their. If the worker dies, their family is not allowed to stay there longer. This was the reason for the demonstration.

Reference ID: AFG20080522n1294
Latitude: 34.53031158
Date: 2008-05-22 09:09
Category: Demonstration
Detained: 0

Region: RC WEST
Longitude: 65.27068329
Type: Non-Combat Event
Affiliation: Neutral

	Enemy	Friend	Civilian	Host Nation
Killed in Action	0	1	2	0
Wounded in Action	0	1	7	10

REFERNCE ISAF INCIDENT # 05-0881:
RC WEST AND PRT CHG REPORT THAT THERE IS A VIOLENT DEMONSTRATION COMPOSED OF 200 PEOPLE AGAINST ISAF AT THE PRT GATE.
UPDATE REMARKS AS OF 1525L: REPORTS INDICATE THAT THE DEMONSTRATION IS A RESULT OF THE SHOOTING OF THE KORAN BY A AMERICAN SOLDIER IN IRAQ. ROCKS AND FIRE BOMBS HAVE BEEN THROWN OVER THE FENCE. SHOTS HAVE BEEN FIRED INSIDE THE CAMP. QRF ENROUTE. CAS OVERHEAD.
ORIGINAL BDA: 1 KIA NATO/ISAF (LIT), 2 WIA NATO/ ISAF (LIT), 1 KILLED LN, 4 WOUNDED LN.
UPDATE BDA: 1 X NATO/ISAF (LIT) KIA, 1 NATO/ISAF (LIT) WIA, 10 X ANP WIA, 2 X LN KILLED, 7 X LN WOUNDED

Reference ID: AFG20080901n1375
Latitude: 34.54372787
Date: 2008-09-01 01:01
Category: Demonstration
Detained: 0

Region: RC CAPITAL
Longitude: 69.27268219
Type: Non-Combat Event
Affiliation: Neutral

	Enemy	Friend	Civilian	Host Nation
Killed in Action	0	0	0	0
Wounded in Action	0	0	0	0

Approximately 500 LNs marched along Route Violet from V5-V3 in response to an NDS raid in Ud Kheyl (Grid: 42S WD 240 220), which occurred during the previous night and resulted in the death of three LNs and the arrest of four other LNs. NDS had reportedly raided the private residence in Ud Kheyl IOT apprehend a known criminal who had just returned from Pakistan; the suspect was killed along with two infant children, and his wife was seriously wounded. LNs reported that the NDS had used excessive force in clearing the house with automatic rifles and hand grenades. Furthermore, NDS reportedly detained four family members of the victim without due evidence the non-hostile demonstration would not be stopped until they were released. The crowed dispersed at approx. 1000L.

Reference ID: AFG20081016n1477
Latitude: 34.34317017

Region: RC WEST
Longitude: 62.1954422

Date: 2008-10-16 00:12 Type: Non-Combat Event
Category: Demonstration Affiliation: Neutral
Detained: 0

	Enemy	Friend	Civilian	Host Nation
Killed in Action	0	0	0	0
Wounded in Action	0	0	0	0

The event took place yesterday eveing, the demonstration today
EUPOL patrol reported that a crowd (not peaceful) is demonstrating after an attempted kidnapping a famous businessman of HERAT called Hajy Jalil Sarrafj - not previously reported. During this attempt a bodyguard was killed and the kidnappers captured the brother of the businessman.
UPDATE 1608D*
The demonstration is now peaceful and under ANP control.
***Event closed at 71138D*1 Killed None(None) Local Civilian
1 Captured/Detained None(None) Local Civilian

Reference ID: AFG20081031n889 Region: RC CAPITAL
Latitude: 34.55773926 Longitude: 69.0294342
Date: 2008-10-31 15:03 Type: Non-Combat Event
Category: Demonstration Affiliation: Neutral
Detained: 0

	Enemy	Friend	Civilian	Host Nation
Killed in Action	0	0	0	0
Wounded in Action	0	0	0	22

RC-C reported a riot between ANA soldiers within KMTC. The riot reportedly began after Hazara NCOs harassed and beat Pashtun soldiers. Pashtun soldiers from the 1st, 2nd, and 3rd Kandak joined the riot and the protesting soldiers began throwing rocks at KMTC ANA permanent party and ANA MPs. The ANA MPs fired an unknown number of warning shots; the rioters were not responsive to the shots. KMTC TAG QRF was deployed to the scene to assist the ANA MPs. The ANA KMTC commander, General Ali Ahmad, also responded to the scene and was able to calm the rioting soldiers. The riot had dispersed by 2145L.
BDA: 22x ANA NBI

Reference ID: AFG20081202n1529 Region: RC CAPITAL
Latitude: 34.52014542 Longitude: 69.18144226
Date: 2008-12-02 12:12 Type: Non-Combat Event
Category: Demonstration Affiliation: Neutral
Detained: 0

	Enemy	Friend	Civilian	Host Nation
Killed in Action	0	0	0	0
Wounded in Action	0	0	0	3

ANP reported that a demonstration is ongoing at the Afghan Parliament. A group of approx 150-200 refugees from PD 6 and 7 (in the area of the former Russian Embassy) are protesting in support of their request to GIRoA for land. The refugees are a "mixed-bag" of various ethnic groups from across the country and are led by an elder. At one point the protest turned violent. Three ANP were injured by stones thrown by the protesters. It is unknown what the ANP response was. MTF.3 Wounded in Action None(None) ANP

Reference ID: AFG20081225n1509
Latitude: 34.68009949
Date: 2008-12-25 09:09
Category: Demonstration
Detained: 0

Region: RC EAST
Longitude: 69.68391418
Type: Non-Combat Event
Affiliation: Neutral

	Enemy	Friend	Civilian	Host Nation
Killed in Action	0	0	0	0
Wounded in Action	0	0	0	0

Note: RCAC Relaying ANA Reporting
ANA report as of 0900Z, there is a demonstration of approximately 2000 LN. The demonstration is currently non-violent, but closing MSR Vermont.
0900Z: The fourth Kandak CDR is holding a Shura at the locaiton of the Demonstration with the villagers to explain why a compound was raided and individuals were taken away.
Debrief from Shura:
LN Very upset with CF, the capture/kill of the four individuals.
EndState: The ANA will conduct security for funerals on 26DEC; the villagers demand the return of the detainees immediately.

Reference ID: AFG20081226n1481
Latitude: 31.62542534
Date: 2008-12-26 12:12
Category: Demonstration
Detained: 0

Region: RC SOUTH
Longitude: 65.05365753
Type: Non-Combat Event
Affiliation: Neutral

	Enemy	Friend	Civilian	Host Nation
Killed in Action	0	0	0	0
Wounded in Action	0	0	0	0

2008-12#1086
C Coy 2-2 Inf providing FP to FOB HUTAL, reported FF observed a large group of LNs protesting (burning tires and blocking RRS with rocks). The group is moving from 41RPR93550144 to 41RPR95999988. FF are observing from the FOB and launched a UAV (Scan eagle) for overwatch. The protest is believed to be related to the wounding of a LN in event number 12-1073.
UPDATE 1214D*
The group consist of approx 200-300 LN's, TFK info OPS are developing strategy to respond to this protest.
UPDATE 1432D*
Pattern of life returned to normal. ANP cleaned the debris, rocks and tires from the road and RTB. Protest over. No casualties or damage reported.
***Event closed at 1432D*

Reference ID: AFG20081231n950
Latitude: 34.59062576

Region: RC CAPITAL
Longitude: 69.76714325

Date: 2008-12-31 16:04   Type: Non-Combat Event
Category: Demonstration   Affiliation: Neutral
Detained: 0

	Enemy	Friend	Civilian	Host Nation
Killed in Action	0	0	0	0
Wounded in Action	0	0	0	0

FRA BG reported a demonstration close to SUROBI dam to protest against CF strikes in UZBEEN valley. 200 LN gathered and blocked the JALALABAD road. A US convoy from JALALABAD to KABUL with 6 armoured vehicles blocked by the crowd. Convoy turned back to JALALABAD at 1700D*. Some shoots from crossroad VIOLET / CRIMSON were performed. No casualties reported. A UAV is on the site and screening ATT. A FRA GAZELLE RECCE helicopter is planned from 1745D*, a FRA QRF from FOB TORA is ready to move and is currently in direct link with ANA.
UPDATE 1835D*
FRA BG at FOB TORA reported that, ANA may have shot on the demonstrators resulting civilian casualties (TBC). The demonstration is now dislocated. RC(C) air assets are screening the spot ATT.

Reference ID: AFG20090124n1534   Region: RC SOUTH
Latitude: 31.59574699   Longitude: 65.48100281
Date: 2009-01-24 06:06   Type: Non-Combat Event
Category: Demonstration   Affiliation: Neutral
Detained: 0

	Enemy	Friend	Civilian	Host Nation
Killed in Action	0	0	0	0
Wounded in Action	0	0	0	1

ISAF #MM(S)01-24E
N COY 3 RCR reported a large gathering of 300+ LN on RRS are staging a protest at GR 41R QQ 354 983. Some rocks are been seen thrown to the ANP. At 1120D*, N COY 3 RCR has spoken with the Elders that are present; they agreed to try to disperse the crowd. At 1154D*, based on the advice of the Elders the LN were dispersing at that time. The PEF was probably going to push through. At 1338D*, 1 x LN wounded was reported at FOB WILSON. Circumstances state that he was a participant in the protest on RRS. A Private security convoy attempted to transit through remains of protesters. (Small groups of LNs). LN threw rocks at the convoy. Private security probably shot the LN.
UPDATE 1509D*
BDA: 1 x LN Wounded (Cat B) (GSW Right shoulder) MEDEVAC IAW MM(S) 01-24E to ANA CAMP HERO MTF.
***Event closed at 1509D*1 Wounded None(None) Local Civilian

Reference ID: AFG20090201n1590   Region: RC CAPITAL
Latitude: 34.58184052   Longitude: 69.24751282
Date: 2009-02-01 05:05   Type: Non-Combat Event
Category: Demonstration   Affiliation: Neutral
Detained: 0

	Enemy	Friend	Civilian	Host Nation
Killed in Action	0	0	0	0
Wounded in Action	0	0	0	0

KCP LNO reported that, there was a demonstation performed today with 400 demonstrators at the Deh Sabz District. The demonstrators potested unfair GIRoA land policies. The district headquarters is located in the village of Tarakhel. Demonstration started at 01100D* and came to an end at 011230D*.NFI. No casualties or damage reported.

Reference ID: AFG20090329n1626
Latitude: 33.0803833
Date: 2009-03-29 08:08
Category: Demonstration
Detained: 0

Region: RC EAST
Longitude: 68.69399261
Type: Non-Combat Event
Affiliation: Neutral

	Enemy	Friend	Civilian	Host Nation
Killed in Action	0	0	0	0
Wounded in Action	0	0	0	0

ISAF # 03-1580
S:300-400 CIVILIAN LOCAL NATIONALS
A:PROTESTING AGAINST LOCAL GIROA FOR THE KILLING OF LOCAL GIROA DETAINEE MOVING NORTH ON ROUTE AUDI HEADING TOWARD FOB RUSHMORE
L: 42 SVB 7144 6024
T:29 MARCH 0837z
U:1-501 / 203 ANA
R:PUSHING GERONIMO6 AND QRF TO ATTEMPT TO ASSIST IN A PEACEFUL RESOLUTION OF THE SITUATION. REQUESTING AWT IN SUPPORT.
UPDATE: APPROX 0900z CROWD ARRIVES TO THE OUTSKIRTS OF THE TOWN OF SHARANA. THE ANP HALTED THE CROWD BEFORE THEY ENTERED THE TOWN. THE CHEIF OF POLICE CALLED THE ELDERS FORWARD AND ESCORTED THEM TO THE GOVERNOR'S COMPOUND WHERE THEY SAT AND HAD A SHURA WITH THE GOVERNOR. THE GOVERNOR PLEDGED TO INVESTIGATE THE INCIDENT OF THE UNARMED DETAINEE BEING SHOT AND TO AUGMENT THE YAYA KHEL ANP WITH BETTER OFFICERS. THE ELDERS EXPRESSED VARIOUS OTHER CONCERNS AND LEFT THE GOVERNOR'S COMPOUND TO RETURN TO THE CROWD WITH WORD THAT THEY HAD COME TO AN AGREEMENT WITH THE GOVERNOR. THE CROWD SEEMED TO ACCEPT THE SITUATION AND BEGAN TO PEACEFULLY DISPERSE.
UPDATE:0953z SIOUX 6 REPORTS THAT CROUD IS UNDER CONTROL AND IS ENROUTE BACK TO FOB SHARANA WITH GERONIMO6
SUMMARY: 0 X CASUALTIES
0 X DAMAGE
EVENT : CLOSED   1116z

Reference ID: AFG20091002n2208
Latitude: 32.16315079

Region: RC SOUTH
Longitude: 63.42741394

Date: 2009-10-02 07:07　　　　　　　　Type: Non-Combat Event
Category: Demonstration　　　　　　　Affiliation: Neutral
Detained: 0

	Enemy	Friend	Civilian	Host Nation
Killed in Action	0	0	0	0
Wounded in Action	0	2	0	2

ECHO 2/3 COMPANY REPORTED A LARGE GATHERING OF LOCAL NATIONALS PROTESTING AND BURNING TIRES NEAR THE DELARAM ANP STATION. INTEL SOURCES REPORTED THAT PROPAGANDA ABOUT A MARINE BURNING A KORAN, SHOOTING & DRAGGING A DOG CARCASS INTO A MOSQUE, AND SMEARING EXCREMENT INSIDE A MOSQUE WAS BEING DISCUSSED AS THE CAUSE OF THE UNREST. INITIALLY AN UNKNOWN NUMBER OF VEHICLES TRANSPORTED DEMONSTRATORS INTO THE DELARAM AREA VIA RTE. 606. THE MOB ATTACKED FACILITIES AT THE, NDS CONSTRUCTION SITE AND CONTINUED TO MOVE EAST. POLICE CHIEF AND ELDERS WERE AWARE OF THE DEMONSTRATION AND ADVISED COALITION FORCES NOT INTERFERE. THE MOB THEN ATTACKED THE ANP STATION WITH STONES AND BRICKS, INEFFECTIVE SMALL ARMS FIRE. SCAN EAGLE WAS RE TASKED TO SCAN RTE 606 FROM DELARAM DC HEADING SOUTH. 2/3 COC OBSERVED, VIA SCAN EAGLE, A LARGE GATHERING OF MOTORCYCLES, CIVILIAN VEHICLES, AND ESTIMATED 150 LOCAL NATIONALS ON FOOT PROCEEDING NORTH ON RTE 606 TOWARDS RTE 1. THE MOB ARRIVED AT THE NDS CONSTRUCTION COMPANy, OVERRAN THE COMPOUND AND BEGAN SETTING FIRES INSIDE. THE COMPOUND APPEARED TO BE EMPTY AND BURNED QUICKLY. THE MOB LEFT THE NDS CONSTRUCTION COMPANY AND CONTINUED TO PROCEED EAST ON RTE 1 TOWARDS DELARAM DC. 2/3 COC RECEIVED REPORTS OF (1) LN KILLED AND (1) LN WOUNDED FROM THE MOB ON RTE 606. REPORT WAS NEVER CONFIRMED. NO CF ABLE TO ENGAGE DEMONSTRATORS UP TO THIS POINT. THE MOB ARRIVED INTO DELARAM DC AND APPEARED TO REGROUP ALONG RTE 1. 2/3 COC CONTINUED TO MAINTAIN VISUAL ON THE MOB VIA SCAN EAGLE AND ECHO 3 MAINTAINED VISUAL ON THE MOB FROM THE ANP STATION. THE MOB APPROACHED THE DELARAM ANP STATION AND BEGAN TO THROW ROCKS WITHIN THE ANP STATION AT THE ANP AND THE MARINES. THEY ALSO ATTEMPTED TO CLIMB THE HESCO WALLS ON THE WESTERN SIDE OF THE COMPOUND. THE MOB BEGAN TO DESTROY THE CONCERTINA WIRE ON THE HESCO WALL IOT TO BREACH THE ANP STATION. KANE JUMP (2/3 BN PSD) LAUNCHED FROM FOB DELARAM AS A QUICK REACTION FORCE FOR ECHO CO. UPON ARRIVAL, KANE JUMP ESTABLISHED A ROAD BLOCK ON RTE 1 IVO THE ANP STATION WITH THE LEAD AND SECOND VIC IOT DENY THE MOB ACCESS INTO THE ANP STATION, AND TO ALLOW MARINES IN POSITION ACROSS THE STREET TO EGRESS. THE MOB BEGAN TO THROW ROCKS AT KANE JUMP'S VEHICLES WHICH STRUCK THE TURRET GUNNER OF THE LEAD VEHICLE SEVERAL TIMES. KANE JUMP EMPLOYED SMOKE GRENADES IOT TO DETER THE MOB FROM APPROACHING THE VEHICLES. KANE JUMP IN TURN, EGRESSED BACK TO THE ANP STATION. ONCE KANE JUMP AND ECHO ELEMENTS RE-ENTERED THE ANP STATION, THE MOB SURROUNDED THE ANP STATION AND CONTINUED TO THROW ROCKS AND ATTEMPT TO PULL DOWN OR

CLIMB THE HESCO WALL ON THE WESTERN SIDE OF THE COMPOUND. KANE JUMP REPORTED THE ANP STATION RECEIVING SAF AND DECLARED TIC. KANE JUMP AND ECHO 3 CONTINUED TO EMPLOY PEN FLARES AND SMOKE GRENADES IOT DISPURSE THE MOB. THE ANP FIRED OVER HEADS OF THE MOB AS THEY CLOSED ON ANP TRUCKS IN THE STREET. THE ANP THEN WITHDREW THEIR TRUCKS BACK WITHIN THE ANP STATION. MARINES FIRED WARNING SHOTS INTO HESCO AT RANGE OF APPROX 15-20 METERS AS THE MOB TORE AT CONCERTINA ON NORTH SIDE AND STARTED CLIMBING OVER THE WALL. ECHO 1-3 LAUNCHED FROM FOB DELARAM WITH (70) ANA SOLDIERS AND PROCEEDED TO RESPOND TO THE MOB SURROUNDING THE ANP STATION. UPON ARRIVAL, THE ANA APPROACHED THE MOB IN THEIR VEHICLES CAUSING THE MOB TO PUSH WEST INTO DELARAM DC. THE MOB DISPURSED AND SCATTERED THROUGHOUT DELARAM DC. WHILE THE ANA MAINTAINED A CORDON AROUND THE ANP STATION, ECHO 3 AND KANE JUMP CONDUCTED A DAMAGE ASSESSMENT. ECHO 3 REPORTED DAMAGED MIRRORS AND GLASS TO THE VEHICLES WITHIN THE COMPOUND.
(2) US MARINES WERE SUFFERED BROKEN TEETH AS A RESULT OF THE MOB THROWING ROCKS. (2) LN MALES WERE TRANSPORTED TO FOB DELARAM AFTER BEING SHOT WHILE IVO THE BAZAAR. (1) LN CASUALTY CLAIMED TO BE INSIDE HIS SHOP WHEN STRUCK WITH A ROUND.
ECHO 3 REPORTED EMPLOYING (181) RD OF 5.56MM, (15) RDS OF 7.62MM, (12) SMOKE GRENADES, (4) PEN FLARES, (2) FLASHBANGS.

Reference ID: AFG20091208n2505
Latitude: 33.64477539
Date: 2009-12-08 06:06
Category: Demonstration
Detained: 0
Region: RC WEST
Longitude: 62.2662468
Type: Non-Combat Event
Affiliation: Neutral

	Enemy	Friend	Civilian	Host Nation
Killed in Action	0	0	0	0
Wounded in Action	0	0	0	0

Alcatraz (ABP TEAM) REPORTS:
S: 150 200 PAX W/ MULTIPLE BUSSES, JINGLE TRUCKS, SEPTIC TANK TRUCK
A: PEACEFUL DEMONSTRATION
L: 41SMT3195823012 (Adraskan)
T: 081020DEC09
R: PROTESTING THE FACT THAT THE REPRESENTATIVE THEY VOTED FOR TO REPRESENT THEM IN KABUL WAS NOT ALLOWED TO GO, BUT SOMEONE ELSE WAS PICKED TO REPRESENT THEM THAT THEY DID NOT VOTE FOR. PEACEFUL DEMONSTRATION, BLOCKED THE ROAD AND HAD TO TAKE DIFFERENT ROUTE AROUND LOCATION.

Enemy Actions

The difference between an ordinary policeman and a counter-insurgent in an occupied country, of course, is that in ordinary police work, the armed gangs don't ambush the police with AK-47's or blow them up with roadside bombs. In Afghanistan, they do. Afghanistan is a *war*.

The Afghan insurgents are not strong enough to stand toe-to-toe with American forces. For the most part, therefore, their tactics consist of surprise ambushes, in which they suddenly open fire on a convoy or a detachment of US troops, then quickly run away before the Americans can gather for a counterattack or call in heavy weapons or air support. The insurgents also have a small number of anti-aircraft weapons, which they have used in attempts to shoot down helicopters and fixed-wing aircraft. In general, large-scale firefights only occur when American forces surround an insurgent stronghold and force the guerrillas to fight. Given the choice, the Afghan insurgents prefer to take a hit-and-run approach, and prefer not to expose themselves to superior American firepower.

Individual ambush actions normally result in few American casualties (indeed, most enemy attacks don't result in anyone getting hurt at all), but collectively they are deadly. Although the Iraq War has produced a higher number of total American casualties, the size of the US force in Afghanistan is much smaller, making Afghanistan proportionately more deadly to troops than Iraq—a soldier in Afghanistan has a significantly higher chance of being wounded or killed than a soldier in Iraq.

The casualty rates among insurgents, however, particularly when they are forced by American operations into a large-scale firefight, can be tremendously high. A key US tactic, therefore, has been to surround insurgent pockets and force them to fight, where they are often wiped out by air strikes and artillery. However, since the scale of Taliban attacks has increased over the past few years, in both frequency and geographic area, it is apparent that the insurgents are able to recruit enough new members to make up for their losses. Guerrilla fighters, to be successful, do not actually have to win the war—they only have to avoid *losing* it, to keep the insurgency going at a level which will allow the opponent to grind himself down so much that he finally makes the political decision to give up and leave.

Reference ID: AFG20040115n6
Latitude: 33.57249069
Date: 2004-01-15 00:12
Category: Direct Fire
Detained: 0

Region: RC EAST
Longitude: 69.25
Type: Enemy Action
Affiliation: Enemy

	Enemy	Friend	Civilian	Host Nation
Killed in Action	0	0	0	0
Wounded in Action	0	0	0	0

CJSOTF -AFGCUROPS REPORTS: TIC GARDEZ S= UNK 1 VEHICLE, A= I VEHICLE DROVE BY AND FIRED APPROX 4 MAG OF SMALL ARMS ROUNDS AT FIREBASE, L= 42SWC232148 SOUTH GATE, U=UNK, T= 151550ZJAN04, E= UNK, NO INJURIES AT THIS TIME.

Reference ID: AFG20040401n16
Latitude: 33.21250153
Date: 2004-04-01 10:10

Region: RC EAST
Longitude: 69.77805328
Type: Enemy Action

Category: Direct Fire   Affiliation: Enemy
Detained: 0

	Enemy	Friend	Civilian	Host Nation
Killed in Action	1	0	0	0
Wounded in Action	0	0	0	0

TF 1-501 KILLS ONE, AND DETAINS TWO ACMS SOUTHWEST OF KHOWST. AT 011057APR04, TF 1-501 REPORTED ACMS THREW GRENADES AT A US CONVOY SOUTH OF KHOWST (42S WB 7251 7510); THERE WERE NO US CASUALTIES OR DAMAGE TO EQUIPMENT. TF 1-501 REPORTED ONE GRENADE DETONATED BETWEEN TWO VEHICLES IN THE CONVOY, THE OTHER TWO GRENADES FAILED TO DETONATE. TF 1-501 KILLED ONE OF THE ACM'S WITH DIRECT FIRE, CAPTURED A SECOND, AND PURSUED THE REMAINING THREE ACM'S TO A COMPOUND. TF 1-501 IS CURRENTLY CONDUCTING A CORDON AND SEARCH OF THE COMPOUND. AT 1346Z, THE SEARCH WAS COMPLETED, NO ACM'S PRESENT.
NFI

Reference ID: AFG20040415n17   Region: RC WEST
Latitude: 33.42625046   Longitude: 64.01112366
Date: 2004-04-15 00:12   Type: Enemy Action
Category: Direct Fire   Affiliation: Enemy
Detained: 0

	Enemy	Friend	Civilian	Host Nation
Killed in Action	0	0	0	11
Wounded in Action	0	0	0	0

(S//REL TO USA AND ISAF) ON 15 APRIL 2004 AKHUNZADA THE POLICE CHIEF OF MIZAN DISTRICT, ZABUL PROVINCE, AFGHANISTAN TRAVELED ALONG WITH 10 OF HIS SOLDIERS TO SHAWALI KOT DISTRICT IN KANDAHAR PROVINCE IN SEARCH OF TALIBAN FIGHTERS. THE TALIBAN KILLED AKHUNZADA AND ALL OF HIS SOLDIERS.
TEXT: (S//REL TO USA AND ISAF) ON 15 APRIL 2004 ((AKHUNZADA)) THE POLICE CHIEF OF MIZAN DISTRICT, ZABUL PROVINCE, AFGHANISTAN TRAVELED ALONG WITH 10 OF HIS SOLDIERS TO SHAWALI KOT DISTRICT IN KANDAHAR PROVINCE IN SEARCH OF TALIBAN FIGHTERS. THE TALIBAN KILLED AKHUNZADA AND ALL OF HIS SOLDIERS. THE LEADER OF THE TALIBAN GROUP THAT KILLED AKHUNZADA IS MULLAH MOHAMMED ((UNIS)) AKHUNZADA. UNIS IS THE FORMER KABUL PROVINCE POLICE CHIEF DURING THE TALIBAN RULE OF AFGHANISTAN, NFI.
COMMENTS: (S//REL TO USA AND ISAF) (FIELD COMMENTS)-- 1. THIS REPORT ADDS TO THE FACT THAT THE TALIBAN AND OTHER ANTI-COALITION FORCES ARE IN THE AREA JUST NORTH OF HIGHWAY 1. THIS ALSO INDICATES A POSSIBLE INCREASE IN ATTACKS IN THE DISTRICTS NEAR MIZAN.

Reference ID: AFG20040426n17   Region: RC SOUTH
Latitude: 31.56500053   Longitude: 65.42111206
Date: 2004-04-26 00:12   Type: Enemy Action

Category: Direct Fire   Affiliation: Enemy
Detained: 18

	Enemy	Friend	Civilian	Host Nation
Killed in Action	0	0	0	2
Wounded in Action	0	0	6	0

(S//REL GCTF) PANJWAYI CITY. THE LOCAL GOVERNMENT DISTRICT OFFICES AND THE NEIGHBOURING COMPOUND OF A LOCAL NGO WERE ATTACKED BY BETWEEN TEN AND FIFTEEN ARMED MEN. WITNESSES REPORT THAT FIRING BEGAN AT THE GOVERNMENT OFFICES AROUND 10:45 HRS AND THAT WITHIN THE NEXT HALF HOUR SOME OF THE ATTACKERS MOVED TO THE AID AGENCYS AREA, WHERE THEY KILLED TWO NATIONAL STAFF MEMBERS, WOUNDED ONE GUARD AND SET FIRE TO SOME VEHICLES. IT IS ALSO REPORTED THAT ABOUT FIVE OTHER PERSONS WERE WOUNDED INCLUDING MEMBERS OF THE LOCAL SHURA, WHO SHARE THE COMPOUND WITH THE NGO, AND SOME GOVERNMENT OFFICIALS AND SOLDIERS. AN UNCONFIRMED NUMBER OF ATTACKERS MAY HAVE BEEN KILLED OR INJURED. AFGHAN AUTHORITIES HAVE ARRESTED 18 MEMBERS OF THE OUSTED TALIBAN REGIME SUSPECTED OF KILLING TWO LOCAL AID WORKERS IN THE RESTIVE SOUTHERN PROVINCE OF KANDAHAR, A SENIOR OFFICIAL SAID ON THURSDAY. (AS REPORTED BY ANSO, ASSOCIATED PRESS AND OTHER PRESS SOURCES).

Reference ID: AFG20040503n10   Region: RC SOUTH
Latitude: 32.51665878   Longitude: 67.41665649
Date: 2004-05-03 04:04   Type: Enemy Action
Category: Direct Fire   Affiliation: Enemy
Detained: 0

	Enemy	Friend	Civilian	Host Nation
Killed in Action	0	0	0	15
Wounded in Action	0	0	0	0

BODYGUARDS ASSIGNED TO PROTECT ZABOL PROVINCE GOVERNOR KILLED BY TALIBAN MILITIA DURING AMBUSH: AS MANY AS 15 BODYGUARDS ASSIGNED TO PROTECT ZABOL PROVINCE GOVERNOR MOHAMMAD HOSAYNI KHIAL WERE KILLED ON 3 MAY 2004 IN AN AMBUSH IN SHAJOY (3231N 06725E). GOVERNOR KHIAL, WHO WAS TRAVELING IN A SEPARATE VEHICLE AHEAD OF HIS BODYGUARDS, WAS NOT INVOLVED IN THE ATTACK. IN ADDITION TO KILLING THE BODYGUARDS, THE ATTACKERS MANAGED TO STEAL A VEHICLE.
CTF BRONCO DISE ANALYST COMMENT: BY ATTACKING AND ATTEMPTING TO KIDNAP MEMBERS OF THE ATA, THE TALIBAN, PARTICULARLY ROZI KHAN, WHO IS THE TALIBAN SUB-COMMANDER FOR THE ZABOL DISTRICT, WOULD BE ABLE TO INFLUENCE PEOPLE TO NOT SUPPORT THE ATA. HE HAS AND WILL CONTINUE TO BE EXTREMELY VIGOROUS IN HIS ATTEMPTS TO KIDNAP ATA MEMBERS OR ANYBODY WHO SUPPORTS IT. BY INSTILLING FEAR IN THE PEOPLE AROUND THE TOWNS IN WHICH HE OPERATES HE CREATES A SAFE HAVEN FOR HIMSELF AND HIS ASSOCIATES. THIS WILL ALLOW FOR FREEDOM OF MOVEMENT IN ORDER TO CONDUCT ATTACKS IN THE COMING MONTHS.

Reference ID: AFG20040510n29
Latitude: 36.84500122
Date: 2004-05-10 00:12
Category: Other (Hostile Action)
Detained: 0

Region: RC NORTH
Longitude: 68.91278076
Type: Enemy Action
Affiliation: Enemy

	Enemy	Friend	Civilian	Host Nation
Killed in Action	0	0	12	0
Wounded in Action	0	0	16	0

(S//REL GCTF) KABUL, JUNE 10 (AFP) - ELEVEN CHINESE CONSTRUCTION WORKERS WERE GUNNED DOWN THURSDAY IN A USUALLY PEACEFUL AREA OF NORTHEASTERN AFGHANISTAN IN THE WORST ATTACK ON FOREIGNERS SINCE THE FALL OF THE TALIBAN NEARLY THREE YEARS AGO. AROUND 20 ARMED MEN STORMED A COMPOUND HOUSING CHINESE WORKERS BUILDING A ROAD IN KUNDUZ PROVINCE, 250 KILOMETRES (150 MILES) NORTH OF KABUL, AND OPENED FIRE ON SLEEPING WORKERS WITH AUTOMATIC WEAPONS, THE CHINESE EMBASSY SAID.

THE NIGHT-TIME KILLING WAS THE SECOND MURDER OF FOREIGNERS IN A WEEK IN NORTHERN AFGHANISTAN, UP UNTIL NOW CONSIDERED FREE OF THE BLOODY INSURGENCY WRACKING THE SOUTH AND SOUTHEAST. ON JUNE 2 THREE EUROPEANS WORKING FOR MEDECINS SANS FRONTIERES AND THEIR TWO LOCAL ASSISTANTS WERE SHOT DEAD ON A ROAD IN THE NORTHWEST PROVINCE OF BADGHIS. ONE AFGHAN ALSO DIED IN THURSDAY'S RAID AND FOUR CHINESE NATIONALS WERE INJURED, REGIONAL MILITARY COMMANDER GENERAL MOHAMMED DAUD SAID. A SPOKESMAN FOR NATO-LED GERMAN PEACEKEEPERS BASED IN KUNDUZ CITY SAID A TOTAL OF 16 PEOPLE WERE HURT. THE CHINESE EMBASSY IN KABUL DESCRIBED THE RAID AS A "TERRORIST ATTACK" WHILE GENERAL DAUD BLAMED "THE ENEMIES OF AFGHANISTAN, TALIBAN AND AL-QAEDA"

THE ATTACKERS WERE ARMED WITH MACHINE GUNS AND AK-47S AND TRAVELLED IN TWO SMALL VEHICLES, A COROLLA AND A STATIONWAGON, INTERIOR MINISTRY SPOKESMAN LUTFULLAH MARSHAL TOLD AFP. THE INTERNATIONAL SECURITY ASSISTANCE FORCE SOLDIERS PROVIDED BLOOD FOR TRANSFUSIONS FOR THE INJURED, WHO WERE TAKEN TO A HOSPITAL IN KUNDUZ, A SPOKESMAN FOR THE PEACEKEEPERS TOLD AFP. THE COMPOUND, SOME 36 KILOMETERS (22 MILES) SOUTH OF KUNDUZ CITY IN JALAWGEER DISTRICT, WAS HOME TO AROUND 90 CHINESE WORKERS WHO ARE BUILDING A ROAD FOR THE CHINA RAILWAY CONSTRUCTION SHISIJU GROUP CORPORATION.

MANY OF THE WORKERS HAD ONLY ARRIVED IN AFGHANISTAN IN THE PAST WEEK AND WERE BEING HOUSED IN TEMPORARY TENT ACCOMMODATION AT THE SITE, ACCORDING TO A SECURITY OFFICIAL. CHINE

Reference ID: AFG20040517n21
Latitude: 32.17694092
Date: 2004-05-17 00:12

Region: RC SOUTH
Longitude: 66.51027679
Type: Enemy Action

Category: Direct Fire Affiliation: Enemy
Detained: 0

	Enemy	Friend	Civilian	Host Nation
Killed in Action	1	0	0	2
Wounded in Action	0	0	0	2

(S//REL GCTF) TB TAKEOVER MIZAN DISTRICT, ZABOL THE EVENING OF 18 MAY TALIBAN FORCES TOOK CONTROL OF MIZAN DISTRICT, ZABUL PROVINCE TO INCLUDE THE PROVINCIAL CAPITAL MIZAN, AND THE VILLAGES OF BUSTAN, MURIANY AND ABDUL AHAD, THE LATTER TWO IN SOUTHERN MIZAN DISTRICT. THEY REMAIN THERE AS OF 1000Z 19 MAY. TALIBAN FORCES ATTACKED THE DISTRICT HEADQUARTERS FOR THE SECOND NIGHT IN A ROW THE EVENING OF 18 MAY, AND DUE TO LACK OF PERSONNEL AND AMMUNITION THE DISTRICT CHIEF ((RAHMATULLAH)) FLED TO QALAT, THE CAPITAL OF ZABUL PROVINCE, WITH HIS REMAINING FORCES. THE ZABUL PROVINCIAL GOVERNMENT ATTEMPTED TO SEND 50 MEN FROM THE POLICE AND MILITARY FORCES BASED IN QALAT, BUT HEAVY FIGHTING WITH TALIBAN ELEMENTS ENROUTE FORCED THEM TO TURN BACK. TWO 27TH BRIGADE FORCES WERE KILLED AND TWO WOUNDED AND ONE TALIBAN FIGHTER WAS KILLED. THE MORNING OF 19 MAY THE ZABUL PROVINCIAL GOVERNMENT MET AND APPEALED TO THE CENTRAL GOVERNMENT FOR ASSISTANCE WITH EXTRA TROOPS, VEHICLES, MONEY AND AMMUNITION. THERE IS NO SPECIFIC AFGHAN PLAN DRAWN UP TO RETAKE THE PROVINCE AS OF 1000Z 19 MAY. (SOURCE COMMENT: THE FORMER POLICE CHIEF OF MIZAN DISTRICT, ((YAR MOHAMMAD)), WAS KILLED BY TALIBAN ELEMENTS THREE WEEKS AGO IN SHAH WALI KOT DISTRICT, QANDAHAR PROVINCE. HE HAD NOT BEEN REPLACED.)

Reference ID: AFG20040518n26 Region: RC EAST
Latitude: 33.30443954 Longitude: 68.24582672
Date: 2004-05-18 02:02 Type: Enemy Action
Category: Direct Fire Affiliation: Enemy
Detained: 0

	Enemy	Friend	Civilian	Host Nation
Killed in Action	0	2	0	0
Wounded in Action	1	1	0	0

AT 0200Z, THE WAZA KHWA POLICE CHIEF AND 20 POLICEMEN WERE AMBUSHED IVO 42S VB 298 853 (GAZNI) ENROUTE BACK FROM OBJ STARS (VIC. 42S VB 306 117) WITH 6 JINGLE TRUCKS LOADED WITH CERP THAT THE GOVERNOR HAD GIVEN THEM. THE ENGAGEMENT LASTED 30 MINUTES. THE POLICE CHIEF FEELS THAT THE ENEMY FORCE WAS ABOUT 20 PERSONNEL ON MOTORCYCLES. THERE WERE 2 FRIENDLY KIAS AND 1 WIA. THERE WAS ONE POSSIBLE ENEMY WIA AND A MOTORCYCLE WAS CAPTURED. US FORCES HEARD SOME OF THIS CONTACT ON SCANNERS, BUT WERE TOO FAR AWAY TO REACT BY GROUND.

Reference ID: AFG20040602n14 Region: RC NORTH
Latitude: 35.89999008 Longitude: 64.48332977

Date: 2004-06-02 00:12
Category: Ambush
Detained: 0
Type: Enemy Action
Affiliation: Enemy

	Enemy	Friend	Civilian	Host Nation
Killed in Action	0	0	5	0
Wounded in Action	0	0	0	0

AMBUSHED THE CAR OF AN AID WORKER ORGANIZATION IN BADGHIS PROVINCE, KILLING ALL FIVE OCCUPANTS. MEMBERS OF THE TALIBAN HAVE CLAIMED RESPONSIBILITY FOR THE ATTACK ASSESSMENT OF THE CRIME SCENE DETERMINED THAT TWO ATTACKERS COMMITTED THE AMBUSH WHILE TRAVELING ON A MOTORCYCLE. THEY USED AN AK-47 AND A PISTOL. THEY DID NOT ROB THE VEHICLE. TALIBAN COMMANDER HAJI LATIF HAKIMI, LOCATED IN HERAT STATED THAT TALIBAN IS CLAIMING RESPONSIBILITY FOR THE INCIDENT. HE SAID THE ATTACK WAS MADE ON MSF BECAUSE THE GROUP WORKS FOR AMERICANS UNDER THE COVER OF AID WORK. HE FURTHER THREATENED UNSPECIFIED AID GROUPS. (SOURCE COMMENT: SOURCE STATES THAT THE STATEMENT MAY NOT BE ACCURATE BECAUSE IT IS HARVEST SEASON IN BADGHIS PROVINCE AND SO IT IS MORE LIKELY TO BE POPPY RELATED. ANOTHER SOURCE STATES THAT ALTHOUGH THERE WAS NO ROBBERY, THERE HAVE BEEN NO RECENT REPORTS OF TALIBAN ACTIVITY IN QADIS DISTRICT AND SO TALIBAN IS UNLIKELY.

THERE IS HEIGHTENED TENSION IN THE PROVINCE AS A CONSEQUENCE OF THE ATTACK. THE UNITED NATIONS AND AFGHAN NON-GOVERNMENT ORGANIZATION SECURITY ORGANIZATION (ANSO) HAVE RECOMMENDED THAT ALL ROUTES IN QADIS DISTRICT BE CONSIDERED HIGH RISK AT THIS TIME, AND ALL BADGHIS ROUTES ARE AT ELEVATED RISK DUE TO THE POPPY HARVEST

Reference ID: AFG20040624n16
Latitude: 32.34999847
Date: 2004-06-24 00:12
Category: Other (Hostile Action)
Detained: 0
Region: RC SOUTH
Longitude: 67.43332672
Type: Enemy Action
Affiliation: Enemy

	Enemy	Friend	Civilian	Host Nation
Killed in Action	0	0	14	0
Wounded in Action	0	0	0	0

(S//REL GCTF) CONFLICTING REPORTS HAVE BEEN RECEIVED INDICATING THAT 14 PEOPLE HAVE BEEN MURDERED. IT APPEARS FROM REPORTS THAT TALIBAN INSURGENTS DID SET UP A VCP ALONG THE ROAD INTO THE VILLAGE ON 24 JUN 04. THE INSURGENTS WERE STOPPING VEHICLES RANDOMLY, WHEN THEY STOPPED A MINI-BUS TRANSPORTING 17 PERSONS. THE TALIBAN INSURGENTS FORCED THE PASSENGERS TO EXIT THE BUS AND EMPTY THEIR POCKETS (THE INSURGENTS ARE REPORTED TO HAVE BEEN LOOKING FOR PEOPLE WITH VR CARDS). THE MAJORITY OF THE PASSENGER DID INDEED HAVE VR CARDS. IT APPEARS THE TALIBAN WERE SO UPSET WITH THE NUMBER OF PASSENGERS CARRYING VR CARDS, AS THIS WENT AGAINST THE TALIBAN IDEALS. THE TALIBAN LINED THE

PASSENGERS UP TO SHOOT THEM. THE PASSENGERS REQUESTED TO PRAYER BEFORE THEY WERE TO BE EXECUTED. QUICK THINKING ON THE PART OF A FEW OF THE PASSENGERS, 3 MANAGED TO ESCAPE WHILE PRAYING. 14 INDIVIDUALS WERE KILLED. AMONG THEM A TEAM LEADER WITH THE VOTER REGISTRATION (MR RHIMI). THE TEAM LEADER DID NOT HAVE ANY SPECIAL RECOGNITION CARD OF HIS POSITION OTHER THAN HIS PERSONAL VOTER REGISTRATION CARD. THE THREE PERSONS MANAGE TO ESCAPE TO TIRINKOT AND INFORMED OFFICIALS OF THE INCIDENT.

Reference ID: AFG20040707n19
Latitude: 32.47415161
Date: 2004-07-07 00:12
Category: Other (Hostile Action)
Detained: 0
Region: RC WEST
Longitude: 62.46527863
Type: Enemy Action
Affiliation: Enemy

	Enemy	Friend	Civilian	Host Nation
Killed in Action	0	0	6	0
Wounded in Action	0	0	2	0

(S//REL GCTF) AT APPROXIMATELY 1600 07 JUL TWO USPI HERAT BASED ESCORT UNITS WERE AMBUSHED IN THE AREA OF CHAKAB ON THE KANDAHAR/HERAT ROAD. 6 KILLED AND 2 WOUNDED AND TAKEN TO THE FARAH HOSPITAL. NO INTERNATIONAL PERSONNEL WERE INVOLVED. REPORTEDLY THE TWO ESCORT UNITS WERE RETURNING TO HERAT FROM DELARAM WHEN THE AMBUSH OCCURRED. IT HAS BEEN REPORTED THAT 3 TAXI CABS WERE PARKED ON THE SIDE OF THE ROAD AND WHEN THE TWO ESCORTS UNITS APPROACHED THE PEOPLE IN THE TAXI CABS OPEN FIRE. THE FIRST UNIT, A SURF, WAS HIT WITH AN RPG. THE SECOND UNIT, A PICKUP, WAS HIT WITH AK 47 FIRE A 60 MAN SECURITY FORCE WAS DISPATCH FROM HERAT TO RECOVER THE VICTIMS AND TAKE ANY APPROPRIATE ACTION.

Reference ID: AFG20040922n38
Latitude: 34.95442963
Date: 2004-09-22 15:03
Category: Inirect Fire
Detained: 0
Region: RC EAST
Longitude: 69.33055878
Type: Enemy Action
Affiliation: Enemy

	Enemy	Friend	Civilian	Host Nation
Killed in Action	0	0	0	0
Wounded in Action	0	1	0	0

TF EAGLE REPORTS ROCKET ATTACK AT BAF. 1 X US MILITARY SUFFERED SHRAPNEL WOUNDS AND IS BEING TREATED AT TF WINGS AID STATION, PATIENT IS STABLE. SALT FOLLOWS: S- UNK, A- RECEIVED 3X ROCKETS, L- POO WD 3019 6805, POI IVO 42S WD 231 668, T- 1523Z. REMARKS: ROCKET IMPACTED IVO CAMP ALBERT. FIRE WAS REPORTED AT STEEL BEACH AT 1529Z. AIR QRF WAS LAUNCHED AT 1532Z. FIRE WAS PUT OUT AT 1537Z. 1 X HESCO AND 1 X CONEX WERE DAMAGED. 1636Z UPDATE, GROUND QRF IS LAUNCHED TO INVESTIGATE POO SITE. 1749Z UPDATE: THERE HAVE BEEN TWO CONFIRMED POI AT WD 2340 6660 AND WD 20406 65530. BASED OFF

INFORMATION FROM TOWERS 10 AND 12, THE ESTIMATED POO IS 2520 7020. QRF IS W/D AND M/C BACK AT BAF AT 1801Z. 1833Z UPDATE: TWO PERSONNEL THAT LEFT THE SUSPECTED POO HAVE RETURNED TO A BUILDING AT THE SUSPECTED POO WD 2520 7020. BASEOPS IS ALERTING THE 2X SQUADS FROM THE RRF TO INVESTIGATE THE BUILDING. OSI WILL BE WITH THE RRF. 1941Z UPDATE: THE THIRD POI IS IVO 42SWD 2190 6480. 2108Z UPDATE: QRF MISSION IS POSTPONED BECAUSE THE LOCATION IS IN A SUSPECTED MINEFIELD. MISSION WILL GO IN THE MORNING.

Reference ID: AFG20050224n62
Latitude: 31.56526947
Date: 2005-02-24 08:08
Category: Direct Fire
Detained: 0

Region: RC SOUTH
Longitude: 65.36110687
Type: Enemy Action
Affiliation: Enemy

	Enemy	Friend	Civilian	Host Nation
Killed in Action	0	0	0	0
Wounded in Action	0	0	0	0

TF BRONCO 3-7 REPORTS RECEIVING FIRE FROM A VEHICLE 32K W OF KANDAHAR. S: 2X ACM, A: OPENED FIRE FROM A VEHICLE WHILE DRIVING BY, L: 41R QQ 241 947, T: 0830Z. REMARKS: 3-7 WAS INVESTIGATING AN IED SITE AT THE TIME OF INCIDENT. 1X US MILITARY SHOT IN THE FOOT, 1X ACM SHOT IN THE NECK, NO MEDEVAC IS NEEDED, BOTH ARE STABLE AND ENROUTE TO KAF. MTF

Reference ID: AFG20050321n66
Latitude: 33.71694946
Date: 2005-03-21 16:04
Category: Direct Fire
Detained: 0

Region: RC EAST
Longitude: 68.91361237
Type: Enemy Action
Affiliation: Enemy

	Enemy	Friend	Civilian	Host Nation
Killed in Action	0	0	0	0
Wounded in Action	0	0	0	0

TWO GROUPS OF TB WITH APPROXIMATELY 21 MEMBERS IN ONE GROUP AND APPROXIMATELY 10 IN THE SECOND GROUP CONDUCTED ATTACKS LAST NIGHT AT APPROXIMATELY 1630Z AGAINST A POLICE CHECKPOINT AND A POLICE STATION IN THE KHARWAR AREA (42S VC 920 308). THE INSURGENT ELEMENTS INITIATED WITH SMALL ARMS FIRE, AND BROKE CONTACT WHEN THE LOCAL POLICE RETURNED FIRE. TB MEMBERS ALSO FIRED TWO ROCKETS AT THE POLICE STATION. THE TWO TB GROUPS WERE LED BY MULLAH SAMULLAH AND DAOUD SURKH.

Reference ID: AFG20050326n80
Latitude: 32.91500092
Date: 2005-03-26 12:12
Category: Indirect Fire
Detained: 0

Region: RC EAST
Longitude: 69.50470734
Type: Enemy Action
Affiliation: Enemy

	Enemy	Friend	Civilian	Host Nation
Killed in Action	0	0	0	0
Wounded in Action	0	0	0	0

TODAY AT APPROXIMATELY 1200Z, ELEMENTS FROM FB TILLMAN CAME UNDER 82MM MORTAR FIRE FROM A Q-36 ACQUIRED POO FROM THE SOUTHEAST, 42SWB 472 420. THE IMPACT OF THE FIRST TWO ROUNDS WERE VISUALLY OBSERVED BY VCP1 AT 42S WB 445 448, APPROXIMATELY 500M FROM THEIR POSITION. SUBSEQUENT IMPACTS WERE ACQUIRED BY Q-36 VICINITY 42S WB 445 437, A TOTAL OF 5 RDS WERE RECEIVED, ALL FROM THE SAME POO. WE RETURNED 16 RDS 105 HE AT TGT SARA IN THE VICINITY OF THE ACQUISITION. THE LAST RDS WAS RECEIVED AT 1211Z, RDS WERE COMPLETE AT 1215Z. WE RECEIVED A SECOND VOLLEY OF 7 82MM RDS FROM THE SAME POINT OF ORIGIN AND IMPACT AT 1224Z, WE RETURNED 8 MORE 105MM HE RDS IN COUNTER-BATTERY AT TGT SARA AGAIN. COUNTER-BATTERY RDS WERE COMPLETE AT 1230Z. INITIALLY WE BELIEVED THAT THEY WERE SHOOTING AT VCP1 ON THE DASTA, BUT BASED ON THEIR SUBSEQUENT CORRECTIONS THAT WERE MORE IN LINE WITH THE CAMP, IT IS LIKELY THAT THE FIRST TWO LONG ROUNDS AND OUR VCP1 POSITION WAS COINCIDENCE.

Reference ID: AFG20050624n100
Latitude: 32.59693909
Date: 2005-06-24 15:03
Category: Direct Fire
Detained: 0

Region: RC EAST
Longitude: 68.04582977
Type: Enemy Action
Affiliation: Enemy

	Enemy	Friend	Civilian	Host Nation
Killed in Action	0	0	0	0
Wounded in Action	0	0	0	0

UNOPS reported that an unknown number of Taliban attacked Dila District Commissioners Compounds/Voter Registration Centers late on 24JUN05. TB attacked the Dila District Commisioners Coumpound/VRC, using AK47s, RPGs and UNK type MGs. The TB overran the compound once the ANP onsite ran out of ammunition. The TB took one ANP hostage, the DCs Thuraya and the voter registration kits. During the same period the Kushamond District Commisioners Compound was attacked by TB, however this attack was unsuccessful because the ANP onsite had sufficient ammunition.

Reference ID: AFG20050811n153
Latitude: 34.34030914
Date: 2005-08-11 19:07
Category: Direct Fire
Detained: 0

Region: RC EAST
Longitude: 68.84996033
Type: Enemy Action
Affiliation: Enemy

	Enemy	Friend	Civilian	Host Nation
Killed in Action	0	0	0	0
Wounded in Action	0	0	0	0

TF Devil reports an ambush 39km SW of Kabul. A TF Devil convoy was ambushed by 7-10 ACM with an IED, RPGs and small arms fire. The convoy returned fire repelling the attack. There were no injuries reported and 1x 5-Ton received a flat tire. TF Devil requests CAS at this time. Boar 13 (2x A-10s) is on station. The convoy continued on route after changing the tire. A QRF team has secured the site and will investigate the scene. Upon further investigation the IED was classified as a command detonated IED due to wires found at site. Unit returned to base without incident, NFI.

Reference ID: AFG20051116n195
Latitude: 34.71072006
Date: 2005-11-16 13:01
Category: Direct Fire
Detained: 0

Region: RC EAST
Longitude: 70.8956604
Type: Enemy Action
Affiliation: Enemy

	Enemy	Friend	Civilian	Host Nation
Killed in Action	0	0	0	0
Wounded in Action	0	0	0	0

Task Force Devil reported troops in contact (TIC) 27 kilometers southwest of Asadabad (ABAD). At 1323Z, a 2d Battalion, 3d Marines patrol participating in Operation Sorkh Khar was engaged with heavy small arms fire from two locations from an unknown size ACM element. Two attack airplanes (A10s) were sent to support the patrol. At 1921Z, the unit reported that they cleared the area and were unable to reestablish contact with the enemy. There were no casualties or damages reported.

Reference ID: AFG20060411n221
Latitude: 34.85527039
Date: 2006-04-11 05:05
Category: Indirect Fire
Detained: 0

Region: RC EAST
Longitude: 71.13925934
Type: Enemy Action
Affiliation: Enemy

	Enemy	Friend	Civilian	Host Nation
Killed in Action	0	0	6	0
Wounded in Action	0	0	29	0

TF Spartan reported rocket attack 1 KM from ABAD. TF Spartan reported rockets impacted near Asadabad PRT and at local school (42SXD 95570 59080) , RESULTING IN 6x LN children KIA, 28x LN children wounded, and 1x adult wounded. All casualties are coming to the A-bad FST. US elements will exploit this in conjunction with JTF Effects. A-bad PRT Cdr will work to get Gov. Wafa to make an announcement on the radio. 2x A-10 sent ISO attack on ABAD PRT and school attack. Update: 13 personnel currently at ABAD FST. 11X were released to their families, and 6X PAX were evaced to BAF.

Reference ID: AFG20060610n299
Latitude: 32.57833862
Date: 2006-06-10 09:09
Category: Direct Fire
Detained: 0

Region: RC EAST
Longitude: 69.35691833
Type: Enemy Action
Affiliation: Enemy

	Enemy	Friend	Civilian	Host Nation
Killed in Action	0	0	0	0
Wounded in Action	0	3	0	0

TF Catamount reports US Troops in Contact. At 0932Z, TF Catamount reported that a patrol received heavy RPG, machine gun, and small arms fire. Patrol reports 3 US Soldiers casualty and 3 HMMWV disabled. Patrol conducting a recon of the cave complex came under heavy RPG, Machine Gun, and small arms fire. 3 vehicles were damaged and 3 casualties were sustained (GSW to Ankle, GSW to Arm, GSW to lower spine). Catamount launched a US PLT and a ANA PLT as QRF to support TIC, meanwhile patrol at TIC site was getting outflanked by enemy forces. QRF enroute encountered enemy forces while manuevering to the TIC site and Enemy moved elements to reinforce. AH-64s came on station at approximately 1030Z. GCAS came on station at approximately 1048Z. Enemy broke contact and audio reported they moved into caves and are awaiting for helicopters to move out before they re-attack. Audio indicated 15 enemy moved into cave. At 1230Z, Aircraft dropped ordinance and eliminated cave complex. Third aircraft pass was complete on cave complex. Cave Complex destroyed. At 1018Z, MEDEVAC was requested and at 1020Z CJTF76 approved MEDEVAC 06-10C w/ SAL assets. MEDEVAC was prepositioned at FOB Orgun-E at 1010Z. At 1030Z, MEDEVAC w/u OE to Bermel. At 1101Z, MEDEVAC w/d. At 1102Z, MEDEVAC w/u at Bermel for Salerno. At 1131Z, MEDEVAC w/d at Salerno. MC. At 1352Z, TF Catamount declared TIC complete, all personnel and vehicles have been recovered to FOB. 1x Soldier is in stable but guarded condition at BAF from GSW to spine. 2x Soldiers are in stable condition at Salerno with GSWs to arm/ankle. PMR is being worked to move 1x Soldier with GSW to spine to LRMC. NFTR. [UPDATED ON 06/10/2006 2127]:

Reference ID: AFG20060621n279
Latitude: 35.41062164
Date: 2006-06-21 14:02
Category: Direct Fire
Detained: 0

Region: RC EAST
Longitude: 71.56376648
Type: Enemy Action
Affiliation: Enemy

	Enemy	Friend	Civilian	Host Nation
Killed in Action	0	4	0	0
Wounded in Action	0	1	0	0

At 1415z TF Titan reported that their K-TM, was in small arms fire contact with 10-20 enemy fighters approximately 14 KM NW of Camp Bari Khowt. The K-TM returned fire and the enemy continued to try and maneuver on the US position. 2xUS KIA and 2xUS WIA were reported. The K-TM consisted of 15 PAX. A BIB A/C came on station at approximately 1500 and dropped ordinance 5 times in support of the TIC. 2xAH-64s came on station at 1611z in support of the MEDEVAC mission of the WIA and KIA soldiers. Ground CAS, arrived on station to continue support of the TIC at 1700z and an AC-130, came on station in support of the TIC at 1740z. The MEDEVAC A/C successfully loaded one casualty onto the a/c the flight medic was in the basket with the second PT when the cable broke and both pt and medic fell 30 feet to the ground. Both the medic and the PT were killed. MEDEVAC A/C from ABAD dropping off a WIA from TF Chosin diverted to support the MM 06-21G mission. Patient is in stable condition. At 0235Z, Hero Recovery Mission w/u from BAF. At 0736Z, TF Titan report that all casualties have been extracted.

Reference ID: AFG20060624n250
Latitude: 31.55422974
Date: 2006-06-24 12:12
Category: Direct Fire
Detained: 0

Region: RC SOUTH
Longitude: 65.42503357
Type: Enemy Action
Affiliation: Enemy

	Enemy	Friend	Civilian	Host Nation
Killed in Action	0	2	0	0
Wounded in Action	0	1	0	0

At 1223Z, CJSOTF reported a TIC 19KM W of FOB Ghecko. Unit reported receiving SAF from 8X Taliban. Enemy fled area to a near by compound and unit was maneuvering to clear compound ATT. Unit reported Taliban were reinforcing from the south and CAS was requested. Unit reported 2X US MIL WIA and a MEDEVAC was requested. PT 1 had GSW to leg and PT 2 has GSW to shoulder and graze to head. Update 1352Z, 2X US casualties and 4X ANA received heavy SAF 75m from their position. CAS could not engage ATT due to close proximity of friendly forces. Unit requested AH-64 support. Unit reported a 3rd PT has GSW to the head with perfuse bleeding. PT 3 has DOW. A second WIA has DOW ATT. MEDEVAC 06-24D is W/U at 1541Z. W/D at grid 1621Z. W/U from grid 1630Z. W/D KAF 1646Z M/C. 1 x WIA is stable awaiting evac to BAF and LRMC.

Reference ID: AFG20060708n334
Latitude: 34.91453171
Date: 2006-07-08 10:10
Category: Direct Fire
Detained: 0

Region: RC EAST
Longitude: 70.10088348
Type: Enemy Action
Affiliation: Enemy

	Enemy	Friend	Civilian	Host Nation
Killed in Action	0	0	0	0
Wounded in Action	0	1	0	1

At 1017Z, Mehterlam PRT reported Taliban ambushed a patrol 26 km N of FOB Mehterlam. Unit reported receiving SAF and RPG fire and a Jingle truck was blocking the road. Unit was returning fire. At 1021Z Mehterlam PRT reported 1X ANA WIA. MEDEVAC was requested for ANA soldier and one US MIL with a broken ankle. At 1110Z, MEDEVAC 07-08F was W/U from JAF. MEDEVAC W/D at JAF at 1348Z. M/C

Reference ID: AFG20060709n352
Latitude: 32.7016983
Date: 2006-07-09 20:08
Category: Direct Fire
Detained: 0

Region: RC SOUTH
Longitude: 65.89360046
Type: Enemy Action
Affiliation: Enemy

	Enemy	Friend	Civilian	Host Nation
Killed in Action	0	0	0	1
Wounded in Action	0	1	0	1

At 2040Z, CJSOTF reported an element received PKM, SAF, and RPG fire 8KM N of TK. At 2222Z, CJSOTF reported 1x US WIA with GSW to the left leg, 1x ANSF with GSW to left arm and 1x ANSF KIA. Both WIAs will remain with the unit and will be ground exfilled. At 0121Z, CJSOTF requested a MEDEVAC for 1x QSF soldier.

MEDEVAC W/U at 0207Z. MEDEVAC W/D at grid at 0214Z. MEDEVAC W/D KAF 0229. MC. AC-130 engaged targets and estimated 40X EKIA. A weapons cache was destroyed. Unit recieved fire from flanks for seceral km on way out of target area. NFTR

Reference ID: AFG20060718n372
Latitude: 31.5033493
Date: 2006-07-18 08:08
Category: Indirect Fire
Detained: 0

Region: RC SOUTH
Longitude: 65.84674072
Type: Enemy Action
Affiliation: Enemy

	Enemy	Friend	Civilian	Host Nation
Killed in Action	0	0	0	0
Wounded in Action	0	3	0	0

At 0851Z TF Aegis reported a rocket attack at Camp Faraway near KAF. 2X rocket impacts were reported and 3X US MIL were WIA Pts were taken to Role 3. Extent of injuries were 1X US MIL with shrapnel injury to shoulder and 1X US MIL with minor injuries to the face. The 3rd PT was not admitted as he had no injuries and was just shaken up. Unit was assessing BDA and exploiting the POI ATT. Unit reported discovering a fuse at grid 41R QQ 70898 90400. Incident closed at 0945Z. Patients are all in stable condition. NFTR.[UPDATED ON 07/19/2006 0050]

Reference ID: AFG20060803n312
Latitude: 31.56428909
Date: 2006-08-03 02:02
Category: Direct Fire
Detained: 0

Region: RC SOUTH
Longitude: 65.42855835
Type: Enemy Action
Affiliation: Enemy

	Enemy	Friend	Civilian	Host Nation
Killed in Action	0	1	0	0
Wounded in Action	0	3	0	1

At 0327z on 03 August, TF Aegis reported RPG fire IVO PBW, Kandahar Province. Aegis element began taking mortar fire at 0545z. 3x CF WIA, 1x CF KIA, 1x ANP WIA. Aegis element moved to site where a bridge had been blown and remained in contact.

Reference ID: AFG20060811n313
Latitude: 35.13077927
Date: 2006-08-11 08:08
Category: Direct Fire
Detained: 0

Region: RC EAST
Longitude: 70.84279633
Type: Enemy Action
Affiliation: Enemy

	Enemy	Friend	Civilian	Host Nation
Killed in Action	0	3	0	0
Wounded in Action	0	3	1	0

At 0814z TF Chosin reports element receiving SAF approx 16km N of Camp Blessing. TF Chosin reports that they are firing indirect ATT. Element reports 6x enemy PAX and element has been pinned down for 30 minutes. Elemant was engaged wit SAF, RPG, and RKG fire from approx 50m. At 0902z TF Chosin initially reports 2x US KIA,

2x US WIA and MEDEVAC is being requested. [update]0944z TF Chosin reports total of 3x US KIA, 3x US WIA, and 1x LN who was with element. MEDEVAC MM 08-11B approved and in route to grid ATT. At 1302Z Medical Mission 08-11B/HERO w/d at JAF, MC.

Reference ID: AFG20060812n344
Latitude: 32.50918961
Date: 2006-08-12 20:08
Category: Direct Fire
Detained: 0
Region: RC EAST
Longitude: 69.22676086
Type: Enemy Action
Affiliation: Enemy

	Enemy	Friend	Civilian	Host Nation
Killed in Action	0	0	0	5
Wounded in Action	0	0	0	6

At 2152Z, CJSOTF reported BCP 213 received SAF/RPG fire IVO Shkin. CJSOTF returned fire with SAF and indirect fires from FOB Bermel. ASF manning OP 8km from FB SHKIN came under SAF/RPG fire by approx. 40-150 ACM. Indirect fire from FB SHKIN and FB Bermel are ISO TIC. ANA Company with USMC ETTs maneuvered from FB Bermel to BCP. ANA Company regained contact with TB who were collecting casualties. Subsequent contact resulted in 5x ANA KIA and 6x ANA WIA (KIA/WIA in MEDEVAC 08-13A/B). 87x 105mm HE rounds fired ISO TIC. BDA: 12x EKIA, unknown of additional EKIA due to destruction of bodies caused by indirect fire. 15x seperate blood trails leaving the area. At 2208Z, MEDEVAC was requested for 1x ANA. 2221Z, MM08-12A was approved. W/U SAL 2235Z. W/D AT SKN 2311. W/U AT SKN 2314. W/D AT OE 2333. CJSOTF reports an additional 3x ANA WIA and 1x ANA KIA. W/U FOB SKN 0025z. W/D O-E 0045z. M/C. CJSOTF reports an additional 2x ANA WIA and 4x ANA KIA. Total 6x ANA WIA and 5x ANA KIA. MEDEVAC 08-13B approved for launch from BAF-OE-BAF. MEDEVAC 08-13B W/U BAF 0112z. W/D O-E 0215z. W/U O-E 0220z. W/D BAF 0322z. M/C. Patient status: 3x ANA WIA with lacerations, all RTD; 1x ANA WIA with broken arm; 1x ANA WIA GSW to abdomen, currently enroute to BAF for further treatment; 1x ANA WIA with shrapnel to shoulder and back of head, currently enroute to BAF for further treatment. Patients are in stable condition.

Reference ID: AFG20060828n366
Latitude: 31.58369064
Date: 65.43373871
Category: Indirect Fire
Detained: 0
Region: RC SOUTH
Longitude: 31.58369064
Type: Enemy Action
Affiliation: Enemy

	Enemy	Friend	Civilian	Host Nation
Killed in Action	0	0	0	0
Wounded in Action	0	1	0	1

At 281317Z Aug 06, Patrol Base WILSON, Panjwayi district, Kandahar province came under mortar attack. 2x mortars impacted north of base, and 1x impacted inside. A fourth impact was also reported. A TIC was declared. 1x (CAN) WIA, PRI 1. 1x (ANA) WIA, also PRI 1.

Reference ID: AFG20060901n397
Latitude: 31.11675835
Date: 2006-09-01 16:04
Category: Direct Fire
Detained: 0

Region: RC SOUTH
Longitude: 64.04110718
Type: Enemy Action
Affiliation: Enemy

	Enemy	Friend	Civilian	Host Nation
Killed in Action	0	0	0	4
Wounded in Action	0	0	0	1

At 011638Z Sept 06 it was reported that TFH elements have spoken to Gereshk Chief of Police. TB have taken 1 x ANP checkpoint and a contact is ongoing. ANP still have control of the power station. 2x ANP reported KIA. Chief of Police says situation is in hand. At 011716Z a report from PSCC (Provincial Security Coordination Centre) suggested that 3 x ANP kidnapped, 2 x killed and 1 x wounded in Gereshk by TB at a check point north of the power station. At 011915Z The Chief of Police reported that 100-200 TB are massing in the area of the bazaar. 1x ANP check point overrun and communications lost with power station. At 011934Z ANA stated that the hospital in Gereshk has been overrun. And TB are now marching to the town centre. ANA stood to and prepared to respond. General Naim said TB intent is to close Route 1 (between Gereshk and FOB Price).

Reference ID: AFG20060904n335
Latitude: 32.51636124
Date: 2006-09-04 02:02
Category: Direct Fire
Detained: 0

Region: RC EAST
Longitude: 67.8065033
Type: Enemy Action
Affiliation: Enemy

	Enemy	Friend	Civilian	Host Nation
Killed in Action	0	0	0	0
Wounded in Action	0	0	0	0

At 0240, TF Warrior reported that a patrol was engaged by small arms fire from an unkown number of insurgents, 30k south east of FOB Warrior. Unit returned fire and pursued the insurgents to the east and lost contact. The element could not reestablish contact with the insurgents and continued on with the mission. No damage to US forces or equipment. NFTR

Reference ID: AFG20060904n373
Latitude: 31.11675835
Date: 2006-09-04 17:05
Category: Indirect Fire
Detained: 0

Region: RC SOUTH
Longitude: 64.04110718
Type: Enemy Action
Affiliation: Enemy

	Enemy	Friend	Civilian	Host Nation
Killed in Action	0	0	0	5
Wounded in Action	0	0	0	6

At 041759Z Sept 06 Governor Daud reported that TB were attacking Garmser police posts with mortars (Grid unknown). At 042042Z it was reported that the Garmser ANP station was under attack and needed ammunition resupply. In recent fightings, ANP lost: 5x ANP KIA, 6x ANP WIA, 4x ANP MIA, 13x ANP MIA believed joined TB. ANP further lost the following due to capture: 2x vehicles, 1x mortar, 2x rockets,

40x grenades, 2,2000 rounds AK ammunition, 8x PK ammunition, 30x AK magazines and additional material. Afterwards there was reported that support will move at first light and conduct a show of force ivo Garmser. NFI ATT.

Reference ID: AFG20060912n388
Latitude: 34.76454163
Date: 2006-09-12 16:04
Category: Direct Fire
Detained: 0
Region: RC EAST
Longitude: 71.13067627
Type: Enemy Action
Affiliation: Enemy

	Enemy	Friend	Civilian	Host Nation
Killed in Action	0	0	0	0
Wounded in Action	0	0	0	0

(DELAYED REPORT)At 13:00z TF Chosin reports an ANA element at Camp Joyce in Sarkani received SAF, RPGs, and mortars on their camp from their SE Ridgeline. They returned SAF, and the enemy broke contact. No injuries or damage to equipment, and no BDA determined. NFTR.

Reference ID: AFG20060913n390
Latitude: 32.83543015
Date: 2006-09-13 13:01
Category: Direct Fire
Detained: 0
Region: RC SOUTH
Longitude: 66.01569366
Type: Enemy Action
Affiliation: Enemy

	Enemy	Friend	Civilian	Host Nation
Killed in Action	0	0	0	0
Wounded in Action	0	0	0	0

At 131355Z Sept 06 TFU reported that a ANP/Militia checkpoint was attacked by approximatly 60x insurgents (3.9 km S/W of Chora DC, Chora district, Oruzgan province). SF moved towards scene to get overwatch. At 1505Z SF reported of a possible second attack ongoing to the N of original attack. After a show of force from an A-10 the firing stopped. SF moved into ANP post to investigate further. No friendly casualties, post was still in our hands. TIC closed at 131642Z.

Reference ID: AFG20060914n427
Latitude: 31.1045208
Date: 2006-09-14 09:09
Category: Direct Fire
Detained: 0
Region: RC SOUTH
Longitude: 64.19539642
Type: Enemy Action
Affiliation: Enemy

	Enemy	Friend	Civilian	Host Nation
Killed in Action	0	0	0	0
Wounded in Action	0	0	0	1

Delayed reporting: At 140947Z Sept 06 elements of the ANA came under sporadic RPG and SAF at their consolidated positions E of the DC at the 43 northing. CAS was tasked and engaged 2 x targets(2.8km N/W of Garmser DC, Helmand province). FF eng with .50 cal and SAF. 1x ANP WIA cat A. TIC closed at 1317Z.

Reference ID: AFG20060915n418
Latitude: 32.07460022
Date: 2006-09-15 08:08
Category: Direct Fire
Detained: 0

Region: RC SOUTH
Longitude: 64.83483887
Type: Enemy Action
Affiliation: Enemy

	Enemy	Friend	Civilian	Host Nation
Killed in Action	0	0	0	0
Wounded in Action	0	0	0	0

At 150847Z SANGIN District, HELMAND Province was engaged with 1x RPG . FF returned fire with SAF, mortars and 105 mm, insurgents were seen to the N of the compound, CAS was utilized to engage with rockets. TIC closed at 150905Z.

Reference ID: AFG20060918n424
Latitude: 32.83543015
Date: 2006-09-18 14:02
Category: Direct Fire
Detained: 0

Region: RC SOUTH
Longitude: 66.01569366
Type: Enemy Action
Affiliation: Enemy

	Enemy	Friend	Civilian	Host Nation
Killed in Action	0	0	0	0
Wounded in Action	0	0	0	0

At 181458 Sept 06 ANP reported they were engaged by 120x TB with HMG and SAF (3.8km S/W of Chora DC, Oruzgan province). ANP also received SAF from houses north of post. ANP returned fire. CAS was sent for support. TIC closed at 181656Z.

Reference ID: AFG20060920n358
Latitude: 32.1747818
Date: 2006-09-20 11:11
Category: Direct Fire
Detained: 0

Region: RC SOUTH
Longitude: 66.47691345
Type: Enemy Action
Affiliation: Enemy

	Enemy	Friend	Civilian	Host Nation
Killed in Action	0	0	0	0
Wounded in Action	0	0	0	0

At 201135Z Sept 06 a patrol was engaged with SAF by 4-5 insurgents 3.5km S/W of Mizan base (Zabol province). FF returned fire and were trying to flank the enemy. Afterwards FF tried to recover a humvee and returned to base. BDA: no casualties, 1x humvee damaged. TIC closed at 1626Z.

Reference ID: AFG20060921n354
Latitude: 32.74406052
Date: 2006-09-21
Category: Direct Fire
Detained: 0

Region: RC EAST
Longitude: 69.35640717
Type: Enemy Action
Affiliation: Enemy

	Enemy	Friend	Civilian	Host Nation
Killed in Action	0	0	0	0
Wounded in Action	0	0	0	0

At 1055Z, CJSOTF reported while conducting a patrol 15km NE of FB Bermel received 26x rockets on their location. CAS was utilized and BDA is pending. POO was identified as 42S WB 3339 2290. POO was located 2.5km southeast of CJSOTF patrol and 5km west of the Afghan/Pak border. GFC declares TIC complete at 1420Z. No injuries to personnel or damage to equipment. NFTR.

Reference ID: AFG20061002n401
Latitude: 32.64173889
Date: 2006-10-02 11:11
Category: Direct Fire
Detained: 0

Region: RC EAST
Longitude: 67.71527863
Type: Enemy Action
Affiliation: Enemy

	Enemy	Friend	Civilian	Host Nation
Killed in Action	0	0	1	0
Wounded in Action	0	0	2	1

(DELAYED REPORT)At 1146Z, TF Warrior reports an ANA element guarding a construction site (approximately 13km southeast of FOB Warrior) received SAF from approximately 20x Taliban. TF Warrior requested a MEDEVAC for the following injured during the attack: 1x ANP with GSW to hand and Stomach, 1x LN Female with GSW to chest and groin/hip, 1x LN female child (est. age 9) shrapnel to jaw, and 1x LN KIA (child, age UNK). Medical Mission 10-02D was approved, w/u from OE at 1215z, w/d 1341z at OE, m/c. An MP squad was sent to the location (village of Spedar) to confirm or deny the contact and search the area for suspected Taliban, and at 1500z began searching with ANP. While conducting the search of Spedar, TF Warrior received intel that TB went to the town of Ahmaday (42S UB 821 168) IOT to find medical treatment. After the search of Spedar TF Warrior moved to Ahmady IOT confirm or deny TB presence. Updates will follow once the TF Warrior element arrives at Ahmady. ISAF Tracking # 10-030.

Reference ID: AFG20061002n414
Latitude: 32.50569916
Date: 2006-10-02 19:07
Category: Direct Fire
Detained: 0

Region: RC EAST
Longitude: 68.86052704
Type: Enemy Action
Affiliation: Enemy

	Enemy	Friend	Civilian	Host Nation
Killed in Action	0	0	0	2
Wounded in Action	0	0	0	12

At 1932Z, TF Catamount reports an ABP Compound receiving RPG/MG/SAF from 100x enemy pax approximately 41km southwest of FB Bermel. The ANP Chief is requesting CF assisstance. The nearest TF Catamount element is 5x hr ground movement from the DC. At 2200z the Paktika PCC reports the attack is ceased. No casualties, but a few buildings in the compound are on fire, and are being extinguished by the ANP ATT. PCC reports 2 ANP KIA, 12 ANP WIA. NFTR. ISAF

Reference ID: AFG20061003n409
Latitude: 31.56678963

Region: RC SOUTH
Longitude: 65.43377686

Date: 2006-10-03 11:11
Category: Direct Fire
Detained: 0

Type: Enemy Action
Affiliation: Enemy

	Enemy	Friend	Civilian	Host Nation
Killed in Action	0	2	0	0
Wounded in Action	0	8	0	0

At 1208Z, TF Aegis reported receiving heavy SAF and mortar fire SW of Patrol Base Wilson. They were withdrawing toward the Patrol Base under cover of LAV MG fire with 2x AH-64 in support. 1x M1114 and 1x Husky damaged. At 1332Z Aegis requested Medevac for 2x CND KIA, 4x US WIA and 4x CND WIA. US Mil WIAs were part of Engineer Route Clearance Package 6 (RCP6). MM(S)10-03C was approved for Kandahar. W/U KAF 1356z, W/D Grid 1419z, W/U Grid 1424z, W/D KAF 1514z, M/C. Patient status: 1x CDN WIA shrapnel to both legs; 1x CDN WIA shrapnel to arm, fracture to arm; 2x CDN WIA with minor shrapnel wounds; 1x US WIA foot/head laceration and shrapnel to both legs; 1x US WIA minor shrapnel injuries; 1x US WIA shrapnel wound to ankle; 1x US WIA right leg amputation. CDN patients are in stable condition, 2x US Mil in stable condition, 1x US Mil in guarded condition. Patients are being prepared for transfer to LRMC. Recovery assets have recovered the damaged vehicles (both mobility kills)have been recovered to Patrol Base Wilson in Kandahar for assessment and repair.

Reference ID: AFG20061006n512
Latitude: 34.9454689
Date: 2006-10-06 19:07
Category: Direct Fire
Detained: 0

Region: RC EAST
Longitude: 71.04229736
Type: Enemy Action
Affiliation: Enemy

	Enemy	Friend	Civilian	Host Nation
Killed in Action	0	0	0	0
Wounded in Action	0	4	0	0

At 1905Z, TF Chosin reports receiving RPG, PKM, RPK, and SAF at a vehicle patrol base approximately 14km west of ABAD along the Pech river. The fire came from both the north and south of the vehicle patrol base (and the Pech river), and impacted inside the patrol base. TF Chosin fired indirect at enemy positions, and CAS and CCA were diverted. CAS engaged an enemy position with 2x WP rockets and 30mm. There are 4x US WIA (1x shrapnel to head, 1x shrapnel to back, 1x shrapnel to throat, 1x GSW to leg and fractured leg). Medical Mission 10-06G approved, w/u from JAF at 1953z, w/d at grid at 2035z, at 2037z w/u from grid, at 2043z w/d at ABAD, m/c. At 2153z TF Chosin updates that 5x enemy pax engaged ANA forces at an OP to the north of the vehicle patrol base (believed to be enemy exfilling from earlier attack) with SAF. TF Chosin fired indirect, and CAS was diverted. CAS did not identify any targets. At 2330, no further contact. Total indirect fired: 155mm: 4xHE, 2xWP; 81mm: 52xHE, 14xWP, 18xRP, 1xIllum; 60mm: 68xHE, 24xWP. No BDA identified. Event closed at 2220Z. ISAF Tracking # 10-151.

Reference ID: AFG20061008n459
Latitude: 31.72310066
Date: 2006-10-08 11:11

Region: RC SOUTH
Longitude: 66.82581329
Type: Enemy Action

Category: Direct Fire   Affiliation: Enemy
Detained: 0

	Enemy	Friend	Civilian	Host Nation
Killed in Action	0	0	0	1
Wounded in Action	0	0	0	8

(Delayed Report) At 081130Z Oct 06 it was reported that the ANP were in heavy contact with 200x TB ivo Gari Kalay village (Arghistan district, Kandahar province). 40x ANP were pinned down and had no freedom of movement. ANP asked for support. TB were centered at two grids that are features held by TB; ANP all located in town. ANP moved forward to East and will not venture outside. UPDATE: 1x ANP KIA, 8x ANP WIA (unconfirmed). ANP were low on ammo. CAS conducted effective show of force. TIC was closed at 1730Z.

Reference ID: AFG20061014n481   Region: RC SOUTH
Latitude: 31.5615406   Longitude: 65.43060303
Date: 2006-10-14 10:10   Type: Enemy Action
Category: Direct Fire   Affiliation: Enemy
Detained: 0

	Enemy	Friend	Civilian	Host Nation
Killed in Action	1	2	0	0
Wounded in Action	0	2	0	0

At 141035Z Oct 06, FF were engaged by incoming SAF and RPG 3km NW of PANJWAYI DC (PANJWAYI District, KANDAHAR Province). FF returned with 25mm and artillery. Cas came in for support. 2x CDN VSA and 3x CDN WIA moved to PBW, and to be Medevacd from there. Consolidating in Strong Point Center, 2x VSA confirmed, 2x Injuries confirmed, still engaging enemy. A reliable source states enemy withdrawing to conduct Ambush or IED. UPDATE:At 1130Z Oct 06, FF engaged from rooftop in objective Rubgy. At 1204Z, FF consolidated in strong point center, 2x KIA confirmed, 2x WIA confirmed, still engaging enemy, reliable source states enemy withdrawing to conduct ambush or IED. At 1253Z, 2x WIA extracted from Patrol Base Wilson along with KIA. Patrol was moving ammo to FOB Zettlemayer, FF consolidated. At 141259Z, FF engaged flashes in treeline, large bangs in tree line. At 1345Z FF going firm, ammo, and vehicle priority. At 1500Z, 1x pers approached FF position with apparent hostile intent. FF engaged with 6x 25mm and destroyed the target. Consolidation of forces now complete, all required recovery has been effected.TIC closed at 1753Z.

Reference ID: AFG20061017n430   Region: RC EAST
Latitude: 32.66704941   Longitude: 69.22609711
Date: 2006-10-17 03:03   Type: Enemy Action
Category: Direct Fire   Affiliation: Enemy
Detained: 3

	Enemy	Friend	Civilian	Host Nation
Killed in Action	16	0	0	1
Wounded in Action	1	3	0	0

At 170319ZOCT06 TF Catamount reported RCP receiving heavy SAF 5km Northwest of FOB Bermel from 10-20 TB. Ground QRF was dispatched. AH QRF, CAS and ISR was diverted. 3x US WIA (1-GSW to left arm below the elbow, possible fracture; 1-shrapnel to lip, 1 minor shrapnel RTD in a couple days). MEDEVAC was requested. MM 10-17A, w/u OE 0423Z, w/u BER 0437Z, w/d OE 0447Z, MC.

At 0415Z ANA/QRF regained contact with 10-15 TB on the high ground. AH QRF engaged enemy element and TB engaged helos with SAF. AH QRF reported 5 EKIA, 1x EWIA (missing legs and will die soon). 1 AH received a hole in the fuel tank from MG Fire with no leaking. 0517Z reporting indicated an additional 1 EKIA and 1 EWIA. 0602Z Unit reports ANA captured 2 enemy, 1 with superficial wounds. 0649Z 13 enemy with sporadic fire on patrol attempting to egress to Margah. AT Platoon is moving to interdict, ANA/QRF is clearing the high ground. 0802Z Unit reported have not had contact in 60 mins. The unit collected BDA and returned to FB Bermel, and will scrutinize LN clinics for enemy wounded. 0851Z Unit reported recovered body parts of 15-20 EKIA. 1 ANA was KIA and was loaded onto a ANA helo for disposition. 1006Z One Enemy surrendered to ANA. 1020Z ANA regained contact with enemy to the Northeast of original TIC site and 1 EWIA, 1 EKIA. Totals: 3 US WIA, 1 ANA KIA, 16-21 EKIA, 1 EWIA, 3 EPWs. Catamount conducted leader engagement. TIC declared closed at 1210Z. ISAF Tracking# 10-392.

Reference ID: AFG20061030n367
Latitude: 32.53572083
Date: 66.74022675
Category: Direct Fire
Detained: 0

Region: RC SOUTH
Longitude: 66.74022675
Type: Enemy Action
Affiliation: Enemy

	Enemy	Friend	Civilian	Host Nation
Killed in Action	55	1	0	0
Wounded in Action	20	0	0	0

At 300643ZOCT06 CJSOTF reported TIC 10km S of Daichopan. Unit reported they were receiving RPG and machine gun fire from an unknown size enemy element. CAS was requested and arrived on station. The unit returned fire and the enemy retreated. 1X US MIL (C/1-4 IN) was KIA. CJSOTF reported using CAS and unit estimates 55x EKIA and 20x EWIA. The US MIL KIA arrived at KAF. Event closed at 1224Z. ISAF Tracking #10-641

Reference ID: AFG20061102n444
Latitude: 33.74399948
Date: 2006-11-02 13:01
Category: Direct Fire
Detained: 0

Region: RC EAST
Longitude: 69.95723724
Type: Enemy Action
Affiliation: Enemy

	Enemy	Friend	Civilian	Host Nation
Killed in Action	0	0	0	0
Wounded in Action	0	3	0	2

At 021335ZNOV06 TF Vanguard reported a patrol had received RPG and SAF 15km SE of FB Chamkani. The unit had 2x vehicles destroyed. At 1421Z, CJSOTF requested a MEDEVAC for 3x US MIL and 2x ABP. MM11-02E was approved at 1436Z. W/U Sal 1444z, W/D CMK 1503z, W/U CMK 1509z, W/D Sal 1518z. M/C. Patient status: 1x US Mil in stable condition with shrapnel wounds to hand, 1x US Mil in stable condition with shrapnel wounds to legs, 1x US Mil in stable condition with shrapnel wounds to face and ruptured TM. 1x ABP in stable condition with multiple shrapnel wounds and 1x ABP in stable condition with GSW to shoulder and shrapnel wounds. NFTR. ISAF Tracking# 11-030. Event closed at 1518z

Reference ID: AFG20061103n437
Latitude: 34.90620041
Date: 2006-11-03 06:06
Category: Direct Fire
Detained: 0

Region: RC EAST
Longitude: 70.10608673
Type: Enemy Action
Affiliation: Enemy

	Enemy	Friend	Civilian	Host Nation
Killed in Action	0	0	0	0
Wounded in Action	0	3	4	2

At 030627ZNOV03 METHAR LAM reported a patrol received SAF from an unknown sized enemy element 27km North of Methar Lam PRT. CAS requested. 0638Z Spartan approved SAL AH QRF to support TIC. 0640Z Unit requested MEDEVAC for 9 WIA (3 US MIL, 2 US Contractors, 1 US Terp, 1 LN TERP, 2 ANA). 0730Z CAS on station. Unit reported taking indirect fire. Unit reports that security elements to flank of patrol could not locate enemy positions but believed they were being maneuvered on. 0745Z AH/UH CCA from BAF on station and MED staged at Methar Lam. 0821Z MED A/C w/u and ground element began movement South out of TIC site. 0801Z SAL AH QRF on station. 0839Z ANA reported that enemy was setting in mines and establishing an ambush position to interdict unit movement South back to FOB Methar Lam (vic XD 009 559). Reporting indicated numerous individuals along route. Unit continued movement South with AH escort conducting route clearance and convoy security. 0937Z Ground element linked up with additional forces coming from the South. 0950Z First element closed on FOB Methar Lam. 1139Z remainder of convoy closed on FOB Methar Lam. 9 WIA(3 US MIL, 2 US Contractors, 1 US Terp, 1 LN TERP, 2 ANA) MM 11-03A w/d Grid 0820Z, w/u Grid 0826Z, w/d BAF 0840Z.Closed 1140Z. ISAF Tracking# 11-040.

Reference ID: AFG20061103n439
Latitude: 32.63809967
Date: 2006-11-03 07:07
Category: Indirect Fire
Detained: 0

Region: RC EAST
Longitude: 69.2665329
Type: Enemy Action
Affiliation: Enemy

	Enemy	Friend	Civilian	Host Nation
Killed in Action	0	0	0	0
Wounded in Action	0	3	0	0

At 030756ZNOV06 TF Catamount reported a rocket impacted vic FOB Bermel. Unit returned counter-battery at the POO site. 0856Z unit reported 9 rockets impacted. 2nd was a 122mm, last 3 impacts were 3km, 2km then 800m away from FOB. The 9th rocket impacted Gun 2. 0858Z Unit reported 2 US WIA. 0918Z Unit conducted dropped 2 GBU 38 (500lbs) and 1 GBU 31 (2000lbs) on POO site and observed multiple secondary explosions. 0931Z Unit dropped 1 GBU 31 (2000lbs) on enemy position. Reporting indicated injured Uzbeks in second location. 1200Z Unit reported 3rd WIA. ((both minor, 1 scratch to forehead, 1 to face, 1 with minor Shrapnel wound to calf, all will be RTD), Hesco Barrier damaged and Shower container pipe broke.

POO 1- WB 32556 07743 2-WB 3221 0827. 2 GBU 31, 2 GBU 38. Event closed at 1220Z. ISAF Tracking#11-044.

Reference ID: AFG20061212n506
Latitude: 32.41672897
Date: 2006-12-12 07:07
Category: Direct Fire
Detained: 0

Region: RC SOUTH
Longitude: 64.4553833
Type: Enemy Action
Affiliation: Enemy

	Enemy	Friend	Civilian	Host Nation
Killed in Action	0	1	0	0
Wounded in Action	0	0	0	0

At 120735ZDEC06, TFH reported SAF and RPG from a TB FP 1.9 km NW of NOW ZAD DC, NOW ZAD District, HELMAND Province. FF used SAF to suppress TB. ANP engaged with DF wpns. CAS was on station and released 25x rockets, 5x 540lbs, 3x 500lbs and 2x1000lbs bombs. TB remained around areas of known FPs and engaged by air as targets were presented. TB FP destroyed. 1x UK KIA. TIC closed at 1008Z.

Reference ID: AFG20070117n564
Latitude: 31.82665062
Date: 2007-01-17 07:07
Category: Direct Fire
Detained: 0

Region: RC SOUTH
Longitude: 64.59159851
Type: Enemy Action
Affiliation: Enemy

	Enemy	Friend	Civilian	Host Nation
Killed in Action	2	0	0	4
Wounded in Action	0	0	0	4

At 170756Z Jan 07, TFH reported ANP were in contact with 50x TB IVO GERESHK Hydro Electric Dam (GERESHK, NAHRI SARRAIJ District, HELMAND Province). No coalition forces involved. Chief of Police liaised with FF and he did not request any assistance. CAS released from ROBINSON TIC to support. TB pulled out once air came on station. TIC closed at 0835Z. TIC reopened at 0931Z. 50-75x TB re-attacked Dam CP. ANA were re-enforcing and CAS was on station. TB moved off expecting to get bombed. The area had calmed down. ANA and ANP were in control of the situation. 4x ANP KIA, 4x ANP WIA and 2x TB captured. TIC closed at 1112Z.

Reference ID: AFG20070215n621
Latitude: 31.11792946
Date: 2007-02-15 06:06
Category: Direct Fire
Detained: 0

Region: RC SOUTH
Longitude: 64.20710754
Type: Enemy Action
Affiliation: Enemy

	Enemy	Friend	Civilian	Host Nation
Killed in Action	8	0	0	0
Wounded in Action	0	4	0	0

At 0530Z 15 February, CF were engaged by multiple groups of 1-3 x TB. CF engaged TB with HMG. TIC closed. Following SHOTREP at 0732Z TIC reopened. CF received SAF at JTAC Hill. FP PID and 7 x TB engaged with HMG. At 1506Z 15 February,

JTAC Hill received SAF and heavy RPG fire. FF received 4 casualties(UK Mil) which were CASEVACED to Bastion. FF engaged TB FP 400m south of JTAC Hill with Javelin and 105mm light gun resulting in 8 x TB KIA. TIC closed.

Reference ID: AFG20070216n570
Latitude: 33.31155014
Date: 2007-02-16 07:07
Category: Indirect Fire
Detained: 0

Region: RC EAST
Longitude: 70.03019714
Type: Enemy Action
Affiliation: Enemy

	Enemy	Friend	Civilian	Host Nation
Killed in Action	0	0	0	0
Wounded in Action	0	0	0	0

The first POO site we came across was seen from the trucks and we got out and took a look. The locals there were harvesting rocks and said that the men in the compound to the south of it had some information about everything. So we moved to the only compound there and questioned them. They took us up the ridge and showed us the other two rockets. He said he didnt hear anything until the fire started coming in and out last night. My guess is that the Kuchi Camp to the south of the second POO site are responsible for the attack. They could have easily moved up the ridge undetected and put in the rockets and ran when we started firing artillery. The elder of the village was not present for questioning. There was another elder that was supposedly on his way to Salerno or to the police with information. I assume that he went to the NDS, because right as we were preparing to destroy the rockets, the NDS came to our location to conduct an investigation on a tip they received about rockets. I told the commander what I knew and he said he was going to check things out. We left with RCP and returned to the FOB around 0745z.

Reference ID: AFG20070219n576
Latitude: 34.89030075
Date: 2007-02-19 05:05
Category: Direct Fire
Detained: 0

Region: RC EAST
Longitude: 70.90273285
Type: Enemy Action
Affiliation: Enemy

	Enemy	Friend	Civilian	Host Nation
Killed in Action	0	0	0	0
Wounded in Action	0	0	0	0

At 190516ZFEB07 TF Chosin reported 3 individuals observing the KOP and has received reports that these individuals may be coordinating an attack from multiple directions on the KOP and OP3. KOP fired 155mm and 120mm on the observed enemy and historic POO sites. Event closed at 0900Z.

Reference ID: AFG20070220n570
Latitude: 31.12214088
Date: 2007-02-20 03:03
Category: Direct Fire
Detained: 0

Region: RC SOUTH
Longitude: 64.19299316
Type: Enemy Action
Affiliation: Enemy

	Enemy	Friend	Civilian	Host Nation
Killed in Action	0	0	0	0
Wounded in Action	0	0	0	0

At 0252Z 20 February, CF observed heat sources in a known TB FP. CF engaged with GPMG. TIC closed.

Reference ID: AFG20070221n585
Latitude: 33.98035812
Date: 2007-02-21 19:07
Category: Direct Fire
Detained: 0

Region: RC EAST
Longitude: 68.78347778
Type: Enemy Action
Affiliation: Enemy

	Enemy	Friend	Civilian	Host Nation
Killed in Action	0	0	0	0
Wounded in Action	0	0	0	0

*** NEED TO ENTER CORRECT GRID LOCATION ***
At 211930FEB07 TF 2Fury reports ANP at Wardak checkpoint on HWY1 in contact with 15 dismounted personnel behind covered positions with small arms. The enemy broke contact after relizing their fire was ineffective. The checkpoint returned fire and defended its position. A patrol was sent to investigate but did not report anything and returned. NSTR

Reference ID: AFG20070223n545
Latitude: 34.95185089
Date: 2007-02-23 17:05
Category: Direct Fire
Detained: 0

Region: RC EAST
Longitude: 70.95529175
Type: Enemy Action
Affiliation: Enemy

	Enemy	Friend	Civilian	Host Nation
Killed in Action	0	0	0	0
Wounded in Action	0	0	0	0

231702Z TF CHOSIN ELEMENTS IN FOB BLESSING AND AT PECH RIVER BRIDGE CROSSING REPORT A COORDINATED ATTACK FROM 7-9 ENEMY PERSONNEL WITH MACHINE GUN, RPG, AND MORTAR FIRE. REQUESTING CAS TO INTERDICT ENEMY EXFIL ROUTES TO THE NORTH
231713Z ELEMENTS NO LONGER TAKING FIRE. FOB BLESSING RECEIVED 5 MORTAR ROUNDS. PATROL BASE RECEIVED HEAVY FIRE AND 1 RPG, ROUNDS WENT HIGH OVER PATROL BASE.
231940Z TIC COMPLETE. JAF QRF W/D AT JAF. 31 HE 155MM FIRED AT ENEMY POSITIONS. NO BDA.

Reference ID: AFG20070303n625
Latitude: 32.08531952
Date: 2007-03-03 07:07
Category: Indirect Fire
Detained: 0

Region: RC SOUTH
Longitude: 64.84327698
Type: Enemy Action
Affiliation: Enemy

	Enemy	Friend	Civilian	Host Nation
Killed in Action	0	0	0	0
Wounded in Action	0	0	0	0

At 0710Z TF Helmand reported receiving 107mm rockets of both HE and White Phos. FF returned 105mm on enemy positions 1.5km NE of the Sangian DC. ISAF Tracking# 03-059

Reference ID: AFG20070303n633
Latitude: 32.08224106
Date: 2007-03-03 09:09
Category: Attack
Detained: 0

Region: RC SOUTH
Longitude: 66.73864746
Type: Enemy Action
Affiliation: Enemy

	Enemy	Friend	Civilian	Host Nation
Killed in Action	0	0	0	0
Wounded in Action	0	0	0	0

ON 03 MARCH 2007, TWENTY FIVE INSURGENTS, WITH TWELVE MOTORCYCLES, WERE HIDING ALONG HIGHWAY ONE WAITING TO ATTACK ANY COALITION FORCES THAT TRAVEL ALONG THAT ROUTE. THESE MEN ARE LEAD BY TALIBAN COMMANDERS MULLAM MORAD KHAN AND MOHAMMED NOUR. THESE TWO MEN ARE TALIBAN COMMANDERS OF THE RAMAZI KALAY VILLAGE//MGRS: 42STA86575179//, TARNAK WA JALDAK DISTRICT, ZABUL PROVINCE, AF. THE 25 MEN ARE HIDING IN THE TARNAK WA JALDAK DISTRICT.

Reference ID: AFG20070321n611
Latitude: 34.88785172
Date: 2007-03-21 10:10
Category: Sniper Ops
Detained: 0

Region: RC EAST
Longitude: 70.90956879
Type: Enemy Action
Affiliation: Enemy

	Enemy	Friend	Civilian	Host Nation
Killed in Action	0	0	0	0
Wounded in Action	0	1	0	0

211045Z TF Chosin received 1x single small arms round approximately 700m south of the KOP. The single round struck a US soldier in the thigh (going through and through with entry and exit wound approximately 1 inch apart). The soldier was treated on site, and will not require a MEDEVAC (soldier will move back with the patrol under his own control tonight). NFTR. ISAF 03-431

Reference ID: AFG20070402n602
Latitude: 33.39112091
Date: 2007-04-02 03:03
Category: Attack
Detained: 0

Region: RC EAST
Longitude: 69.75105286
Type: Enemy Action
Affiliation: Enemy

	Enemy	Friend	Civilian	Host Nation
Killed in Action	0	0	0	0
Wounded in Action	0	0	0	0

S: UNK

A: INSURGENTS ATTACKED SCHOOL IN NSK DISTRICT. TIED UP GUARDS, STOLE WEAPONS AND DETONATED MINES IN THE SCHOOL.
L: 42S WB 6985 9490
T: 020300ZAPR07
A: ANP HAVE INVESTIGATED THE SITE. REPORTED NO INJURIES. THEY BELIEVE THIS WAS AN INSIDE JOB WITH TB SUPPORT. NO INJURIES WERE REPORTED.
THE SCHOOL IS CURRENTLY CLOSED BECAUSE OF DAMAGED CLASSROOMS.

Reference ID: AFG20070403n666
Latitude: 33.65702057
Date: 2007-04-03 08:08
Category: Attack
Detained: 0

Region: RC EAST
Longitude: 69.77763367
Type: Enemy Action
Affiliation: Enemy

	Enemy	Friend	Civilian	Host Nation
Killed in Action	1	0	0	0
Wounded in Action	0	0	0	2

S: 2 X ANP Kidnapped
A: Sabari Police chief reports: Last night 2x ANP officers were kidnapped by an unknown # of ACM in the Janat Kheyl district of Paktia province. He believes it is possible they are being held somewhere along the northern border of Sabari District. Janat Kheyl police chief reports to PCC: There was an attack on the D.C. last night that resulted in 2xANP Kidnapped and 1xACM KIA. He has received a tip from a LN who conducted the attack last night
L: 42S WC 721 244
T: 0824Z
R: Gardez PRT reports,ANP police chief from Gardez told them that the Jani Kehl ANP (in the Chamkani area) got hit by 100to 200 ACM. They burned the station and our codan radio. 5 ANP are missing. The Police Chief in JK is new. The ACM had AK47, RPG, and other small arms. Equipment losses include vehicles, uniforms, and the prior mentioned CODAN Radio. Contacted SF BTL CPT and they are passing information to ODA in Chamkani.
UPDATE - 031757ZMAR07
Diablo 6 called GOV Rahmat and confirmed the following:
1) 3 rooms burned
2) 3 vehicles destroyed
3) 5 ANP missing
The GOV doesnt think it was insurgents, but a Tribal dispute. GOV Rahmat is not asking assistance from the CF ATT. Additionally, Diablo gave HA to 80 ANP which went out to the ANP HQ today. CODAN radio and power source accessories were also destroyed.
UPDATE - 041450ZMAR07
From ODA 755 CDR:
Our reports have indicated that there were approx. 70 ACM armed with PKMs, AKs and RPGs that attacked the district HQ. ACM incurred two WIA and one KIA, all of whom were evaced to Zanbar using improvised litters. There was ANP injured who was treated for minor schrapnal wounds and five are missing. The codan radio tower and solar panels are intact however the radio itself is missing and the batteries are

destroyed. Additionally, three police vehicles were destroyed and the facilities recieved significant damage to the roof and the walls.

It is believed that their are 5 ANP missing and possible 2 KIA. The Senior Captain of Jani Kheyl (Avzal-T) was relieved of his station, because it is beleived he was involved. A new guy named LTC Alizai will take his place. The NDS and ANP are reporting 20-30 insurgents involved. It is unknown who is responsible, but we are working on that. This information was provided to the ODA, by way of General Dasiagir Rostomyar a representative of the Provincial Police Chief. Also reporting this information is Ali Ahmad Morzar the Provincial NDS Chief.

BDA Photos in "Attachments"; Tab

UPDATE - 041652ZAPR07

From ODA TM 753. CDR'S COMMENTS: SFODA 753 CONTINUED WITH COORDINATION WITH TF DIABLO AND ETT FORCES. THE DETACHMENT CONDUCTED CONOP 753-005 LEADER ENGAGEMENTS IN GARDEZ. THE DETACHMENT MEET WITH RTC PERSONNEL TO DISCUSS ACQUIRE ADDITIONAL RESOURCES FOR OUR PARTNERED ANP FORCE. THE DETACHMENT ATTEMPTED TO MEET WITH GEN SARJAN WHO IS THE PROVINCIAL POLICE CHIEF FOR PAKTYA. GEN SARJAN HAD TRAVELED TO THE JANAKEYL DISTRICT, APPROXIMATELY 12KM SOUTH OF CHAMKANI, IN RESPONSE TO A ACM ATTACK THIS MORNING ON THE TOWN DISTRICT CENTER. THE DETACHMENT LEADERSHIP WAS ABLE TO TALK TO SECOND MAN IN CHARGE GEN DASIAGIR ROSTOMYAR WHO IS THE PROVENCIAL SECURITY OFFICER. ACCORDING TO GEN ROSTOMYAR, THE ATTACK HAPPENED AT APPROXIMATELY 0200L WITH THE ACM FIGHTERS NUMBERING AROUND 10-20. THE INITIAL REPORTS ARE OF FOUR ANP OFFICERS MISSING AND ONE OFFICER IS PRESUMED TO BE KIA. AT THE BEGINNING OF THE MEETING THE DETACHMENT WAS INTRODUCED TO AN ANP LTC NAMED ALIZAI THAT WAS DEPARTING IMMEDIATELY TO THE JANAKEYL DISTRICT TO BE APPOINTED AS THE NEW POLICE CHIEF IN THE DISTRICT. ACCORDING TO GEN ROSTOMYAR THE CURRENT POLICE CHIEF OF JANAKEYL, SR. CPT DASHTEE HAS BEEN RELIEVED OF DUTY AFTER THE ATTACK LAST NIGHT. IT WAS INFERRED THAT SR. CPT DASHTEE HAS TIES WITH HIG AND WAS INDIRECTLY RESPONSIBLE FOR THE ATTACK ON HIS OWN DISTRICT CENTER. THE DETACHMENT ALSO MEET WITH THE PROVINCIAL NDS CHIEF IN GARDEZ ALI AHAMD MORZAR. MORZAR WAS VERY SURPRISED TO SEE THE DETACHMENT AND LOOKED TO BE SOMEWHAT NERVOUS. MORZAR IS KNOWN TO BE CORRUPT AND HAS ON NUMEROUS OCCASIONS RELEASED DETAINEES THAT HAVE BEEN SENT TO NDS. THE DETACHMENT DISCUSSED THE INFORMATION THAT WAS OBTAINED FROM THE ANP SECURITY OFFICER ON THE ATTACK IN JANAKEYL. THE SAME INFORMATION WAS OBTAINED FROM THE ANP AND NDS WITH THE NDS WANTING TO QUESTION SR. CPT DASHTEE ON HIS INVOLVEMENT OF THE JANAKEYL ATTACK. THE DETACHMENT ALSO DISCUSSED THE NDS DETAINEE PROCEDURE, WHICH ACCORDING TO MORZAR THE RELEASE AUTHORITY OF DETAINEES LIES ON THE LOCAL PROSECUTOR.

ISAF Tracking # 04-038
HEADQUARTERS
INTERNATIONAL SECURITY ASSISTANCE FORCE

AFGHANISTAN
NEWS RELEASE [2007 - : RELEASE]
Insurgents attack Afghan police station
KHOST, Afghanistan (3 APRIL)   Five Afghan National Police officers are reported missing after insurgents attacked the Jani Khail District Coordination Center in Paktya Province, Afghanistan. (For the rest of the release, see attachment)

Reference ID: AFG20070429n595
Latitude: 34.75244904
Date: 2007-04-29 12:12
Category: Attack
Detained: 0

Region: RC CAPITAL
Longitude: 69.13437653
Type: Enemy Action
Affiliation: Enemy

	Enemy	Friend	Civilian	Host Nation
Killed in Action	0	0	0	0
Wounded in Action	0	0	0	0

(C//NF) AFGHAN ERADICATION FORCE COMES UNDER HOSTILE FIRE: (Source: AMEMBASSY KABUL 01455, 29 Apr 07)
The US-funded Afghan Eradication Force (AEF) came under hostile fire twice on April 29 during its deployment in Uruzgan province. The first time came at the beginning of the day when the AEF was initiating its operations. On the way back to base, the AEF encountered an ambush necessitating QRF response from the Dutch-led Task Force Uruzgan. INL Air Wing grounded two Huey helicopters due to damage from small arms fire. The AEF captured one combatant who is at the FOB and will be turned over to Task Force Uruzgan. Several Afghan members of the AEF were wounded, but there were no fatalities. The AEF will not conduct eradication on April 30 as we assess their capabilities to continue their mission.

Reference ID: AFG20070515n782
Latitude: 33.33778
Date: 2007-05-15 15:03
Category: Ambush
Detained: 0

Region: RC EAST
Longitude: 69.95832062
Type: Enemy Action
Affiliation: Enemy

	Enemy	Friend	Civilian	Host Nation
Killed in Action	0	1	0	0
Wounded in Action	0	0	0	1

At 1550z TF Bushmaster reported ambush, RPG and PKM fire, engaged from enemy on both sides of the road (42R TA 6958 3256) while moving west. At 1556, CAS came on station in supporo of the TIC.
ISAF Tracking # 05-333
At 1615Z TF Bushmaster Requested a medevac for 1 non US and 1 US Mil.
[1-42R TA 6519 3059
2-SC 22
3-Ax1, Cx1
4-A
5-Lx2
6-P
7-E IR STROBE

8-Ax1, Cx1
9-SECURE
US WIA NON RESPONSIVE
MM(S) 05-15D
UPDATE: 1 x US KIA
COMBINED JOINT TASK FORCE- 82
COMBINED PRESS INFORMATION CENTER
BAGRAM AIRFIELD, AFGHANISTAN
APO AE 09354
Press Center: 0799-063-013
bagrammediacenter@afghan.swa.army.mil
FOR IMMEDIATE RELEASE
May 16, 2007
RELEASE # 098
One Coalition servicemember killed in action during engagement with enemy fighters
BAGRAM AIRFIELD, Afghanistan Afghan Border Police and Coalition forces were attacked by an unknown number of enemy forces while operating near the village of Chinah, 43 kilometers southwest of Qalat in Zabul Province May 15. (For the rest of the release, please see attachment)

Reference ID: AFG20070517n769
Latitude: 32.96757126
Date: 2007-05-17 15:03
Category: Patrol
Detained: 0

Region: RC EAST
Longitude: 69.49320221
Type: Enemy Action
Affiliation: Enemy

	Enemy	Friend	Civilian	Host Nation
Killed in Action	0	0	0	0
Wounded in Action	0	2	0	0

Event Summary: ON 17 MAY 2007, OP4 IDENTIFIED 12 PAX CROSSING THE PAKISTAN BORDER VIC WB 4609 4780 WITH AKS AND RPGS AND BEGAN MOVING WEST. 30 X ROUNDS OF 105MM HE WERE FIRED AT (1) WB 4488 4863. 10 PAX BEGAN TO MOVE EAST TOWARD THE PAKISTAN BORDER. 20 X ROUNDS 105MM HE WERE FIRED ALONG DIRETION OF TRAVEL (2), CHANGING THEIR DIRECTION OF MOVEMENT TO THE NORTH. 2 X AH64S ENGAGED STATIONARY PAX IN WOODLINE AT (3) WB 4615 4762. 4 PAX FLED ACROSS THE BORDER TO PAKISTAN. 105MM ILLUM WAS FIRED ISO PAKMIL WHO SET UP A BLOCKING POSITION EAST OF THE RUINS. AT 1834 A26 WERE ENGAGED BY PAX ON EGRESS ROUTES. A/26 ENGAGED ONE PAX AT WB 457 473 AND TOOK 2 FRIENDLY WIAS. THE 2 FWIA WERE MEDEVAC'D TO OE. MM(E) 05-17H IS ASSOCIATED WITH THIS REPORT.

Analyst Comments: These 12 insurgent pax were observed in close proximity to the site where approximately 40 insurgent pax were observed crossing the border and subsequently engaged beginning on the evening of 12 MAY 07. These recent attempts (and almost stubborn infiltration) and the ensuing losses sustained in personnel indicate a growing desperation on the part of insurgent leadership who are seeking some kind of IO victory along the AF-PK border during what has been a disappointing start to 2007 for higher level HQN leadership. With these continued

setbacks we can feasibly anticipate insurgent leadership to eventually resort to suicide attacks against CF and IRoA targets along the AF-PK border which are virtually guaranteed to gain widespread attention and can be spun as an IO victory as attempts at infiltration and direct fire engagement will ultimately result in heavy insurgent defeat.
-BDA patrol will be conducted at first light-
More to Follow
EVENT NUMBER 05-383
HEADQUARTERS
INTERNATIONAL SECURITY ASSISTANCE FORCE
AFGHANISTAN
NEWS RELEASE [2007 - : DRAFT]
ANSF prevails over Taliban in Paktika
FORWARD OPERATING BASE SALERNO, Khowst, Afghanistan (17 May) The Afghan National Security Forces showed their capability and determination after an exchange of gunfire with the Taliban, followed by an indirect fire artillery strike in Bermel District, Paktika Province today. (For the rest of the release, please see the attachment)

Reference ID: AFG20070520n711
Latitude: 31.10124969
Date: 2007-05-20 14:02
Category: SAFIRE
Detained: 0

Region: RC SOUTH
Longitude: 64.18733215
Type: Enemy Action
Affiliation: Enemy

	Enemy	Friend	Civilian	Host Nation
Killed in Action	0	0	0	0
Wounded in Action	0	0	0	0

At 1445Z TF Helmand reported 4 enemy with a vehicle and an AA gun engaged an F-18 4km south of the Garm Seer DC. FF engaged the enemy with CAS. ISAF Tracking# 05-455.

Reference ID: AFG20070522n748
Latitude: 34.75244904
Date: 2007-05-22 12:12
Category: Indirect Fire
Detained: 0

Region: RC CAPITAL
Longitude: 69.13437653
Type: Enemy Action
Affiliation: Enemy

	Enemy	Friend	Civilian	Host Nation
Killed in Action	0	0	0	0
Wounded in Action	0	0	0	0

(C) TRUCKS DESTROYED IN ROCKET ATTACK AT TORKHAM BORDER: (Source: AMEMBASSY ISLAMABAD 02292, 22 May 07)
According to Mission contacts, at approximately 0400 local time Monday, May 21, unknown persons fired two Russian-made MRB-12 rockets at a group of fuel trucks bound for Coalition forces in Afghanistan. The trucks were parked in a lot near the Torkham border crossing, about 35 miles west of Peshawar. At least four of the trucks were destroyed, and the media reported another six trucks severely damaged. Local Frontier Corps soldiers confiscated three additional rockets of the same type

from a nearby hilltop and detained eight Afghan refugees for questioning. (Note: At this time, authorities cannot verify that the eight detained refugees were associated with the rocket attack. End Note.)

Reference ID: AFG20070524n580
Latitude: 33.33750916
Date: 2007-05-24 00:12
Category: Attack
Detained: 0

Region: RC EAST
Longitude: 68.59351349
Type: Enemy Action
Affiliation: Enemy

	Enemy	Friend	Civilian	Host Nation
Killed in Action	0	0	1	0
Wounded in Action	0	0	3	0

Sharana PRT received a report from the contractors awarded the SHARAN-ORGUN Road contract that their 12 truck convoy was attacked on Thursday while traveling from Ghazni to Sharan. The initial report stated that the convoy was hauling asphalt-making equipment for the road construction and that one driver was killed, three were injured and taken to Sharan Hospital, and three were kidnapped. Additionally, it was reported yesterday that the contractors paid $75K (to an unknown group) for the return of 7 vehicles and 3 drivers. Today our engineers met with the contractors and were told that 10 trucks arrived in Sharana, and one other was towed in from Ghazni while they were there. There is still one truck at the attack site; it will be towed in as soon as a wrecker can get there to recover it. Today they said that $33K was paid to the attackers for the returned vehicles. Another update to this story is that there are still four (4) people in the insurgents custody: an engineer, a plant foreman, an equipment operator, and a truck driver. They are negotiating their release, but the insurgents are asking too much money. The owner of the contracting company has already paid a ransom for the engineer and he is due to be returned within days. Most of the damage to the trucks is repairable, but two of the trucks are totally destroyed. The truck owner has refused to accept the trucks until all damages are repaired. The contractor is in the process of assessing the damage.

PRT Engineering conducted the SHARAN to ORGUN Road project QA/QC today. In conjunction with their inspection, they collected more information regarding the attack last Thursday on the 12-truck convoy.

Reference ID: AFG20070530n650
Latitude: 32.2677803
Date: 2007-05-30 16:04
Category: SAFIRE
Detained: 0

Region: RC SOUTH
Longitude: 65.04860687
Type: Enemy Action
Affiliation: Enemy

	Enemy	Friend	Civilian	Host Nation
Killed in Action	0	7	0	0
Wounded in Action	0	1	0	0

At 302104LMAY07, on egress of TF Fury insertion of Lift 1 , Flipper 75 (CH-47D) was engaged and struck with a Missile at 41S PR 919 727 shortly after crossing over the Helmand River. Suspected POO site is 41S PR 92801 71833. A/C was traveling at approx. 70-80 Knots, 200-250ft AGL on an easterly heading when it was hit from the rear. The missile struck the aircraft in the left engine. The impact of the missile projected the aft end of the aircraft up as it burst into flames followed immediately by a nose dive into the crash site with no survivors. A/C was Lift 1, Serial 1, Chalk 2, but due a delay on HLZ to offload a gator, Flipper 75 along with Chalk 3 took off significantly after Chalk 1 and in effect became a second serial on the same route. Chalk 3 witnessed a burst come from their SE approx. 300-500m away. Chalk 3 did not witness a flare launch from Flipper 75 which is consistent with later missile launch at Arrow 25 (AH-64D) in same location that did not bring about CMWS flare launch. Based on description of launch, size of round, and impact force of the projectile, it is assessed to be bigger then an RPG and possibly a Surface-to-Air Missile. Witness statements from Chalk 3 suggest Flipper was struck by MANPAD and is consistent with MANPAD event described by Arrow 25. ODA responded to crash site and eventually secured the site and recovered crew and passengers.

Reference ID: AFG20070531n419
Latitude: 33.48630142
Date: 2007-05-31 11:11
Category: Other (Hostile Action)
Detained: 0

Region: RC EAST
Longitude: 69.05259705
Type: Enemy Action
Affiliation: Enemy

	Enemy	Friend	Civilian	Host Nation
Killed in Action	0	0	0	0
Wounded in Action	0	0	0	0

311135zMAY07 TF DIABLO reports massing of vehicles; a red datsun, a white datsun, white corolla, a red corolla, and six motorcycles total of 50 insurgents in the vicinity, Tatanak 42S WC 04886 05202. 311250zMAY07 CF reports that they are surrounded by the insurgents and are under attack by the 50 insurgents. 311257zMAY07 TF Diablo pushes their ANA element out of Zormat as a QRF element to assist in TIC.
SALTR Follows
S- 1x Red Datsun
1x Whtie Datsun
1x white corolla HB
1x red corolla HB
6x motorcycles
~50x PAX
A- Massing
L-Tatanak 42S WC 04886 05202, MTF
T- 311135ZMAY07
Report was received from CF.
CF says They are surrounded by the 50 pax and being attacked at or around above grid
CF being attacked reported at 1250Z
311257zMAY07 Zormat push ANA out
UPDATE
ISAF Tracking# 05-722

Reference ID: AFG20070605n811
Latitude: 34.91160965

Region: RC EAST
Longitude: 70.90638733

Date: 2007-06-05 13:01 Type: Enemy Action
Category: Attack Affiliation: Enemy
Detained: 0

	Enemy	Friend	Civilian	Host Nation
Killed in Action	0	1	0	0
Wounded in Action	0	1	0	0

At 1355z, Battle 26 reported a contact near Korengal Outpost (XD 7416 6490). They took RPG and small arms fire. At 1405z, they reported 1 X US MIL WIA, urgent - gunshot wound to the shoulder, 1 X US MIL KIA. The platoon returned fire and TF ROCK supported them with 155mm until CCA and CAS could be divereted to their location.

At 1405Z, TF Talon is working MOD risk approval for CCA att due to high winds warning. At 1406Z, TF Bayonet approved CCA. At 1407, TF BAYONET approved CCA ISO TF Rock TIC. At 1434, 2xA10s were enroute to TF ROCK TIC.

At 1411Z, the urgent MEDEVAC posted for the US MIL with GSW to the shoulder. MEDEVAC approved, MM(E) 06-05F with the KOP as a PZ. At 1526z, while enroute to the KOP, TF Rock called in CCA, and continued to move. At 1535, TF ROCK reported that casualty had been moved to the KOP.

Flight Plan: JAF-KOP-ABAD.
Mission Authority @ 1418Z
Launch Authority @ 1424Z
W/U JAF @ 1430Z
W/D KOP @ 1504Z
W/U KOP @ 1535Z
W/D ABAD @ 1545Z

At 1829Z A-10s dropped 1xGBU 12 (500lb Laser Guided Bomb) IVO 42S XD 750 630. TF Rock RTB FOB Phoenix at 1611Z.
Event closed at 1700Z.
ISAF EVENT NUMBER 06-123

Headquarters
International Security Assistance Force Afghanistan

NEWS RELEASE [2007-XXX: Draft]
One ISAF servicemember dead, one wounded in Kunar province ambush
BAGRAM AIRFIELD, Afghanistan (05 June) An International Security Assistance Force servicemember was killed and another was wounded June 5 when their patrol was ambushed at approximately 6:30 p.m. in Kunar province.
SEE ATTACHMENTS FOR COMPLETE RELEASE

Reference ID: AFG20070605n825 Region: RC SOUTH
Latitude: 32.28310013 Longitude: 64.98763275
Date: 2007-06-05 23:11 Type: Enemy Action
Category: Direct Fire Affiliation: Enemy
Detained: 0

	Enemy	Friend	Civilian	Host Nation
Killed in Action	9	1	0	0
Wounded in Action	0	0	0	0

At 2330z TF 1FURY (3/C) reported 1 X INS fired upon a FF platoon, FF RTN fire with HMG. At 2345Z, TF 1 Fury reported 4 insurgents engaging friendly forces with SAF and RPG. At 0015Z Fury elements were clearing different locations while enemy forces engaged with mortars.
UPDATE 8-10 INS KIA, 1X FF KIA NATIONALITY IS US
At 0038Z CCA was requested and granted. At 0152Z the TIC was reported as intense and AH was due to leave station in 30 mins. RIP was requested for AH.
ISAF Tracking # 06-130
Headquarters
International Security Assistance Force Afghanistan

NEWS RELEASE [2007-XXX: Draft]

Servicemember dies during combat operations
BAGRAM AIRFIELD, Afghanistan (06 June) An ISAF servicemember was killed during combat operations early morning June 6 in Helmand province.
SEE ATTACHED FOR COMPLETE RELEASE

Reference ID: AFG20070621n783
Latitude: 32.89640045
Date: 2007-06-21 15:03
Category: Ambush
Detained: 0

Region: UNKNOWN
Longitude: 69.86029053
Type: Enemy Action
Affiliation: Enemy

	Enemy	Friend	Civilian	Host Nation
Killed in Action	0	0	0	2
Wounded in Action	0	0	0	2

At 15:20Z on 21 June, the Polish Battle Group (PPG), reported ANP Patrol was ambushed by 50 ACM in the Omna District IVO 42S VB 8870 4030 along RTE Dodge. PBG reported 7 ANP WIA 8 ANP KIA one truck destroted. Medevac 06-21H was launched to grid vb 8046 4014. Inital report: 3 GSW to the stomack and 1GWS to the leg, all seperate. Medevac was coordinated through Sharona PRT (SHR Xray). Later confirmed through Desert Hawk 2 KIA and 2 WIA. KIA were left at location, 2 x WIA evaced OE, one head shot DOA, and the other is currently being treated at OE for broke femur. Can not confirm ACM activity ATT. Reports systemic from SHR PRT, PBG, TF Eagle TOC and NDS.
Solider will be evaced to Sal approximately 220600ZJune07 for further treatment.
ISAF Tracking # 06-577.
NFTR

HEADQUARTERS
INTERNATIONAL SECURITY ASSISTANCE FORCE
AFGHANISTAN
NEWS RELEASE [2007 - : DRAFT]
Police killed defending town
FORWARD OPERATING BASE SALERNO, Khowst, Afghanistan (21 June) Two Afghan policemen were killed and two were wounded today as they defended the Omna District Center during a firefight with insurgents in the Paktika Province.
FOR THE COMPLETE PRESS RELEASE, SEE ATTACHMENT

Reference ID: AFG20070625n723
Latitude: 33.34167099
Date: 2007-06-25 11:11
Category: Attack
Detained: 0
Region: RC EAST
Longitude: 68.60212708
Type: Enemy Action
Affiliation: Enemy

	Enemy	Friend	Civilian	Host Nation
Killed in Action	0	0	0	0
Wounded in Action	0	0	0	0

HEB TRUCKING COMPANY REPORTS 8 JINGLE TRUCKS ATTACKED BY TALIBAN BETWEEN SHARANA AND GHAZNI, NEAR THE TOWN OR CHARDEWAL. EF ENGAGED USING AK47S AND RPGS. 2 TRUCKS WERE LEFT BURNING AND 1 DRIVER WOUNDED. NO FURTHER INFO ATT. ISAF tracking # 06-672.

Reference ID: AFG20070720n800
Latitude: 35.40761185
Date: 2007-07-20 02:02
Category: SAFIRE
Detained: 0
Region: RC EAST
Longitude: 71.41251373
Type: Enemy Action
Affiliation: Enemy

	Enemy	Friend	Civilian	Host Nation
Killed in Action	2	0	0	0
Wounded in Action	0	0	0	0

At 0220Z TF Bushmaster reported a UH-60 was shot down by an RPG 8km east of Kamdesh PRT. No casualties reported. TF Saber's JTAC had eyes on the crash site and comms with aircraft supporting. At 0259Z close air support (2xF-15Es) was on station and QRF was enroute. At 0306Z, 2xA-10s were enroute to take over after the F-15s. At 0313Z, TF Bushmaster reported all personnel (4 cew members, 1 LN interpreter, and 4 passengers) had been recovered from the crash site and taken to Naray by the trail aircraft in the section. There were no injuries reported.
There were 2 US squads and 2 ANA squads in overwatch and support, while QRF rendered safe the aircraft. At 0315Z, TF Saber and Bushmaster reported the coalition forces were taking small arms fire in the vicinity of the aircraft. Friendly forces returned fire with rotary wing and ground units. At 0334Z, TF Saber reported an update to the personnel at the crash site as 31xUS, 3xETT, 15xANA. At 0347Z, TF Saber reported the enemy atempting to exfil northeast, and TF Saber attempting to block them with attack helicopters.
At 0423Z, TF Bushmaster declared TIC Complete at 0416Z. Event remains open as TF Saber units are still at a/c site and are in contact. TF Bushmaster no longer has forces at this location.
ISAF Tracking# 07-467.
Headquarters
International Security Assistance Force Afghanistan
NEWS RELEASE [2007-XXX: Draft]
ISAF helicopter makes precautionary landing in Nuristan; all on-board safe
BAGRAM AIRFIELD, Afghanistan   An ISAF helicopter made a precautionary landing near Kamdesh in the Nuristan province early this morning. (See attachment)

Reference ID: AFG20070720n824
Latitude: 32.54259872
Date: 2007-07-20 12:12
Category: Ambush
Detained: 0

Region: RC WEST
Longitude: 63.20555115
Type: Enemy Action
Affiliation: Enemy

	Enemy	Friend	Civilian	Host Nation
Killed in Action	0	0	0	0
Wounded in Action	0	0	0	0

At 1245Z, RC(W) reported an American security company (Kompas) was ambushed by an unknown number of insurgents as they were escorting a fuel convoy to RC(S). They broke contact and began their return to Herat. There was an unconfirmed casualty report, which RC(W) will confirm. ISAF Tracking # 07-490.

Reference ID: AFG20070722n833
Latitude: 34.87342834
Date: 2007-07-22 05:05
Category: Direct Fire
Detained: 0

Region: RC EAST
Longitude: 70.89785767
Type: Enemy Action
Affiliation: Enemy

	Enemy	Friend	Civilian	Host Nation
Killed in Action	0	1	0	0
Wounded in Action	0	0	0	0

At 0550z, Battle 26 reported taking small arms and recoilless rifle fire from 4-5 ACM located at vic. XD 7346 6065 and XD 7478 6149. Battle element returned fire with crew-served and below, and called for 120mm and 155mm support. At 0558z, Battle sent an update in which they reported 1x WIA - soldier shot through the neck. CCA/CAS requested at 0608z. CCA approved at 0611z. At 0618z, Battle updated the enemy situation to four locations - two new grids were XD73096187 and XD73246227. The casualty was ground evac'ed by guntruck to the KOP for pickup. CCA with the MEDEVAC aircraft arrived on station at 0646z. CAS (2x Mirages) came on station at 0658z. Contact ceased, nothing follows. Event closed at 1100z.
MEDEVAC
At 0606z TF Rock called in a 9-Line MEDEVAC request for on US Soldier who had been shot in the neck during the Battle TIC (see associated report). Battle ground evac''ed the casualty to the KOP for pickup. MM(E)07-22B went wheels up from JAF at 0628z. Wheels down at the KOP at 0650z. Wheels up to ABAD at 0700z. Wheels down ABAD at 0710z.
SM presented to FST w penetrating wound
Entry point: L cheek traveling down L side of neck causing damage to L sub clavian / main arteries but not limited to said anatomy
Penetration consistent c frag/bullet wound
SM went into cardio pulmonary arrest secondary to exsanguinating hemorrhaging on the a/c
SM did not respond to aggressive surgical intervention
As a result pronounced TOD at ABAD FST 0751z.
Medevac flew follow on HERO Mission to BAF.
Ramp Ceremony conducted at 1415z.

Reference ID: AFG20070728n850
Latitude: 32.01177979
Date: 2007-07-28 01:01
Category: Attack
Detained: 0

Region: RC SOUTH
Longitude: 66.80435181
Type: Enemy Action
Affiliation: Enemy

	Enemy	Friend	Civilian	Host Nation
Killed in Action	1	0	0	1
Wounded in Action	5	0	0	3

Ghazni (Jul 27). The Taliban this morning attacked a convoy of the Afghan National Army [ANA] on the Kabul-Kandahar highway in Hazartak, an area near Qalat, the provincial capital of Zabul. One ANA soldier was killed, and three others wounded. In retaliatory fire, the Afghan soldiers killed one Taliban and wounded five others. A Taliban spokesman claimed to have destroyed three ANA convoys and killed all the soldiers onboard.

Reference ID: AFG20070728n856
Latitude: 33.87593079
Date: 2007-07-28 03:03
Category: Ambush
Detained: 17

Region: RC EAST
Longitude: 68.99134827
Type: Enemy Action
Affiliation: Enemy

	Enemy	Friend	Civilian	Host Nation
Killed in Action	0	0	0	4
Wounded in Action	0	0	0	1

At 0330Z, an ANP patrol was ambushed in the Dasht-e-Altamur area northeast of the Dabar Bridge by an unknown number of ACM with small arms. One ANP WAS WIA. ACM broke contact and withdrew to a village (still waiting on the name). The ANP surrounded the village and requested support from more ANP and ANA. ANP from Puli-ALam and two ANA trucks reinforced at 0510Z.

The Dasht-e-Altamur encompasses a large area northeast of the Dabar Bridge. Center mass grid for the area is, 42S VC 99200 48400. This is the same area TF Roughneck was hit earlier in the month. This is the same area the National Solidarity Project NGO personnel were murdered as well.
CHARKH AMBUSH UPDATE- Charkh confirmed 4 ANP KIA 1 ANP WIA, 17 detainees at Puli Alam ANP Station, confiscated one British rifle with approximately 25 rounds. NFTR

Reference ID: AFG20070729n726
Latitude: 31.71903992
Date: 2007-07-29 02:02
Category: Attack
Detained: 0

Region: RC SOUTH
Longitude: 63.11294174
Type: Enemy Action
Affiliation: Enemy

	Enemy	Friend	Civilian	Host Nation
Killed in Action	0	0	0	0
Wounded in Action	0	0	0	0

Kabul (Jul 28). Taliban militants have used a heat-seeking surface-to-air missile to attack a Western aircraft over Afghanistan for the first time. The Taliban attempted to bring down an American C-130 Hercules aircraft flying over the south-western province of Nimroz on July 22. The crew reported that a missile system locked on to their aircraft and that a missile was fired. It closed in on the large C-130 aircraft, pursuing it as the pilots launched a series of violent evasive maneuvers and jettisoned flares to confuse the heat sensors in the nose of the missile. Crew members said that they saw what they believed was a missile passing very close to the aircraft. The C-130 was not damaged in the attack. NATO officials yesterday refused to confirm or deny that such an attack had taken place.

Reference ID: AFG20070802n813
Latitude: 34.99929047
Date: 2007-08-02 07:07
Category: Ambush
Detained: 0

Region: RC EAST
Longitude: 70.41108704
Type: Enemy Action
Affiliation: Enemy

	Enemy	Friend	Civilian	Host Nation
Killed in Action	0	1	0	0
Wounded in Action	0	2	1	0

On 02 Aug 07, Assassin 1 conducted a joint VCP just south of Gandalaluk Village at grid (42S XD 28230 76110). On the return trip the convoy was ambushed by approx 3-5 enemy forces. The ambush was initiated by a two round RPG volley and followed SAF. The first RPG round stuck the third vehicle in the convoy entering through the cradle of the turret and traveling through the other side. The second RPG round hit the ground before it reached the convoy spraying shrapnel on the fourth vehicle causing minor damage.
REACTION: CF responded with .50 caliber machine gun fire, 5.56mm rifle fire, and immediately suppressed with 155mm artillery fire. The enemy broke contact after US forces gained fire superiority.
COUNTERACTION: QRF (Hydra) was activated to recover the destroyed vehicle while the Assassin element medevaced the WIA. Once the QRF was on site, the Assassin element returned to FOB Kalagush. A-10s, Red Ridge, F-15s, and Senior Scout were on station. There were multiple ICOM chatter reports on 144.00 and 145.00 from Red Ridge and Senior Scout. EC 130 arrived on stationed as ICOM chatter indicated ACM planning another attack. The Hydra element returned the next morning and used an Amerifa crane to hoist the vehicle onto a flat bed. The flat bed moved the vehicle to FOB Kalagush. CF used their own crane to place the vehicle on a five-ton. Casualties: 1x US KIA, 3x US WIA. ISAF Tracking # 08-040
*****EVENT CLOSED ATT*****

Reference ID: AFG20070803n863
Latitude: 34.95423889
Date: 2007-08-03 07:07
Category: Other (Hostile Action)
Detained: 1

Region: RC EAST
Longitude: 69.26286316
Type: Enemy Action
Affiliation: Enemy

	Enemy	Friend	Civilian	Host Nation
Killed in Action	0	0	0	0
Wounded in Action	0	0	0	0

03 0739Z AUG 07: A.F. Security Forces reported that 2 LNs were spotted by a A-10 EAMXS Soldier attempting to breech the perimeter vic TOWER 13. The soldier used

EOF measures and the LNs fled to the nearby village of Bakhsheikyel when the Airman showed his weapon. Another A.F. Airman spotted the same two individuals attempting to breech the perimeter fence. The A.F. Security Force LNO was notified and the C Co. Commander and SOG were dispatched to TOWER 13 where they questioned a known LN named Bobby and awaited the ANPs arrival to the village of Bakhsheikyel to collect up all individuals that fit the description of those who attempted the breech. At ~0833Z C Co. Commander reports that the ANP have placed Bobby into custody and are contacting the village elders to inform them Bobby was in custody and being questioned.

Reference ID: AFG20070811n875
Latitude: 35.37670898
Date: 2007-08-11 08:08
Category: Other (Hostile Action)
Detained: 0

Region: RC EAST
Longitude: 71.54728699
Type: Enemy Action
Affiliation: Enemy

	Enemy	Friend	Civilian	Host Nation
Killed in Action	0	0	0	0
Wounded in Action	0	0	0	0

At 08:12Z, TF SABER received a report that an unknown number of enemy fighters overran the GOWARDESH BRIDGE ABP checkpoint. TF SABER reports the bridge location to be YE 314 178 and unit is Afghanistan Border Police. At 08:16Z, It was reported to TF Saber that seventeen ABP personnel have been taken hostage by ACM. TF SABER reports the source is an ABP member that escaped from the bridge.

At 08:17Z, TF SABER states enemy weapon capabilities are1x82mm Mortar, 2xRPG launchers with approximately 12 rounds and 2x RPK. At 08:18Z, TF SABER report those are the weapon system ABP possessed before being overrun and currently in ACM control. At 08:19Z, TF SABER request ISR assets in order to observe GOWARDESH BRIDGE area, to confirm or deny ACM in area control GOWARDESH BRIDGE. TF SABER JTAC reports F15s on station at 09:05Z in AO SABER. At 11:11Z, VINO OPS informs BAYONET and SABER TOC DUDE off station at this time.

At 11:22Z, TF SABER informs BAYONET TOC 1-91 has not communicated with provincial leadership at this time. The reason being 1-91 has no proof that the GOWARDESH BRIDGE ABP checkpoint has been overrun or compromised by ACM. TF SABER is currently passing information to PRT in order to update provincial leadership and possibly obtain additional information. At 12:08Z, TF SABER has not reported damage to U.S. personnel and equipment at this time.

Reference ID: AFG20070811n878
Latitude: 32.09732819
Date: 2007-08-11 08:08
Category: Direct Fire
Detained: 0

Region: RC SOUTH
Longitude: 64.8973465
Type: Enemy Action
Affiliation: Enemy

	Enemy	Friend	Civilian	Host Nation
Killed in Action	0	0	0	0
Wounded in Action	0	7	0	1

At 0850Z TF Helmand reported an unknown number of insurgents engaged FOB Ink with small arms fire and RPG fire. Friendly forces returned fire with direct fire weapons. Friendly foreces requested close air support with POD capability. At 0919Z TF Helmand requested a medevac for 2 Urgent, 1 Priority, and 1 Routine UK, injuries unknown att. MM(S) 08-11A. At 1002Z TF Helmand reported coalition forces not in contact at this time. IRT complete at BSN. B1B is on station, friendly forces engaged with 15 HE 105MM rounds. At 1016Z TF Helmand requested a 2nd medevac for 1 urgent surgery UK with injuries unknown at this time. Patient has loss of memory and hearing, fast pulse and increased amount of pain. MM(S) 08-11B. NFTR. TIC Closed at 1040Z. UPDATE: 7x UK WIA, 1x ANA WIA. ISAF tracking number 08-280.

Reference ID: AFG20070822n877
Latitude: 35.12807083
Date: 2007-08-22 00:12
Category: Direct Fire
Detained: 0

Region: RC EAST
Longitude: 70.95794678
Type: Enemy Action
Affiliation: Enemy

	Enemy	Friend	Civilian	Host Nation
Killed in Action	5	0	0	2
Wounded in Action	0	11	0	0

At 0036Z 2 ACM wearing BDUs walked into an ASG OP 3 at Ranchouse (XD 78399 89000) and wounded the two ASG in the OP. 20xACM then breached the perimeter of the ASG section of Ranchhouse with two inside the perimeter firing small arms and RPGs. Chosen 1-6 and ASG returned fire with small arms, M-240s, mk19 and 120mm mortars. 7xUS WIA and 1xANA WIA and 1xASG KIA 9-line Medevac request sent 0150Z.
CCA and A-10s were on station at 0110Z. At least two danger close gun runs into the compound. Predator on station at 0357. Force protection box in place. After CAS performed gun runs (at 0157z and 0202z) ACM broke contact 0213Z.
Follow on reporting received from rc(e) indicates two ACM dressed in ANA uniforms approached an Afghan Security Group (ASG) entry point, fired multiped RPGs to over powered it and allowed 18-20 more ACM into the wire. Simultaneously, the ACM launched a 15-rpg volley onto the CP at the Ranchhouse knocking out comms. Reports indicated that 18-20 ACM were in the Ranchhouse compound and close fighting was underway.
Reports indicated planned RPG fire on MEDEVAC A/C. Medevac options being worked. However, terrain is extremely difficult and options are limited. This will be a high risk medevac. 0305 1xRPG was fired at Medevac. Both Medevac birds MC in JAF 0455 (see associated report).
QRF is being spun up at Asadabad. 0434: QRF U/U JAF. 0541 w/d Bella to pick-up 1xsquad. 0525 w/d NGM to pick-up resupply and ANA replacements, 0529 w/u NGM enroute to Ranchhouse. 0545 QRF inserted 2x squad at Ranchhouse with ANA replacements. 0600 Additional 4x US WIA walking wounded identified. 0644 QRF A/C Extracted walking wounded to ABAD and subsequently to JAF. 1xANA WIA dies of wounds while being treated at ABAD. QRF MC JAF 0711.
Update: Unit reports 5xenemy KIA, 2xenemy WIA.
Event closed at 0918z. Event number 08-577.
Headquarters
International Security Assistance Force Afghanistan
NEWS RELEASE [2007-XXX: Draft]

Insurgents attack ISAF base
JALALABAD, Afghanistan An Aug. 22 attack on an International Security Assistance Force forward operating base in Afghanistan resulted in two Afghan National Army soldiers killed and 11 ISAF soldiers wounded.

Reference ID: AFG20070822n897
Latitude: 34.89608002
Date: 2007-08-22 06:06
Category: Direct Fire
Detained: 0

Region: RC EAST
Longitude: 69.78473663
Type: Enemy Action
Affiliation: Enemy

	Enemy	Friend	Civilian	Host Nation
Killed in Action	0	0	0	0
Wounded in Action	0	0	0	0

Pathfinder 3 reports while coducting clear operations in Ala Say valley:
S: UNK
A: engaging with RPGs
L: 42S WD 717 618
T: 0632Z
R: Request CCA from BAF
ISAF Tracking # 08-584.
Update (0708Z): Contact was 1x RPG round.
Update (0911Z): 10 ENY A: Engaging with SAF L: 42S WD 710 612 T: 0911Z
Update (1000Z): CCA on station for approx. 3 hours. Unit has exfilled from the valley to Ala Say DC at 1215Z.
Total AAR/BDA from 21-22 AUG ops in Askin Valley:
Detainees: ANA capture two personnel during their TIC from today (22 AUG), they were turned over to the ANP check point at Nijrab. I do not have their names at this point due to the fact that ANA was forward when they captured them.
Total rounds shot: 2000 .50cal, 384 MK-19 rounds, 1200 7.62mm, 1 x AT4
Total enemy kills: We were unable to visually verified enemy kills, however one of the detainees stated that 6 enemy were killed yesterday with 5 enemy wounded, while 3 enemy were wounded today
Anything blown up: Gunmetal 11 spotted a cave opening in the side of the southern ridgeline. They closed it with a Hellfire missile and did multiple passes using 30mm and 2.75 rockets.
Caches found : No caches were located
Gunmetal (CAS) target hits/ kills: Kills are unknown due terrain
Enemy BDA : 6 killed 5 wounded yesterday and another three today as we were told by the detainee, however he was not certain and it could have been more
Friendly BDA: N/A
Villages searched (name and # count): 2 villages searched, the first named Lowndi WD 686 617, the second was not named but was located IVO WD 720 624

Reference ID: AFG20070822n940
Latitude: 34.66804886
Date: 2007-08-22 18:06

Region: RC EAST
Longitude: 70.2115097
Type: Enemy Action

Category: Direct Fire	Affiliation: Enemy
Detained: 0

	Enemy	Friend	Civilian	Host Nation
Killed in Action	0	0	0	0
Wounded in Action	0	2	1	0

TF DIAMOND BACK SALTUR 030200ZAUG07
S: UNknown
A: Possible GRENADE TOSSED AT tcp BEING CONDUCTED BY NIGHT PATROL
L: XD 1085 3685
T: 1900Z
U: 3/66 MP CO
R: MP'S RETURNED TO FOB MHL. QRF DEPLOYING WITH ANP IOT TO ASSESS AREA.
MEDIVAC TO FOLLOW
UPDATE:
QRF RESPONDED WITH ANP TO THE ATTACK SITE. A SEARCH FOR POTENTIAL INSURGENTS CONTINUING TO OPERATE IN THE AREA WAS CONDUCTED. QRF/ANP REPORTED NO SIGACT.
EOD/QRF WILL RESPOND TO THE SCENE ON 23AUG07 IOT EXPLOIT THE SITE AND CONDUCT A BLAST ANALYSIS. 2x US WIA, 1x LN (TERP) WIA. ISAF Tracking # 08-613.

Reference ID: AFG20070825n815	Region: RC EAST
Latitude: 34.46168137	Longitude: 68.6202774
Date: 2007-08-25 05:05	Type: Enemy Action
Category: Attack	Affiliation: Enemy
Detained: 0

	Enemy	Friend	Civilian	Host Nation
Killed in Action	0	0	0	0
Wounded in Action	0	0	0	0

TWO JINGLE TRUCKS CONTRACTED FROM BAF ENROUTE TO FOB GHAZNI AND FOB ORGUNE WERE ATTACKED IVO SALAR (42SVC6938851627). THE TRUCKS WERE ATTACKED BY UNIDENTIFIED NUMBER OF PERSONNELL WITH RPGs. THE 2 TRUCKS AND THE CONTENTS THEY WERE CARRYING ARE COMPLETLEY DESTROYED . ONE DRIVER IS EXPECTED TO BE CAPTURED BY THE OPPOSING FORCE , AND THE WHEREABOUTS OF THE OTHER DRIVER ARE NOT KNOWN .
*TMR 1772 BA CARRYING GEN CARGO KBR CJOA
*TMR 1776 BA CARRYING CLS IX

Reference ID: AFG20070827n867	Region: RC EAST
Latitude: 33.13241196	Longitude: 69.27445221
Date: 2007-08-27 04:04	Type: Enemy Action
Category: Ambush	Affiliation: Enemy
Detained: 0

	Enemy	Friend	Civilian	Host Nation
Killed in Action	4	1	0	0
Wounded in Action	0	2	0	0

At 0445Z the commander of B/864Engineers, reported that 2 PAX IVO of Zerok COP were flashing mirrors for about 5 minutes. Immediately after, radio intercepts were reported that indicated that an enemy ambush was emplaced.

At 0455Z, ACM fighters ambushed a platoon from Workhorse (HHC/1-503) that was en route to Zerok COP. The platoon was engaged at 42S WB 256 660. This is a historic area of the route known to TF Eagle as ambush alley. The attack resulted in one US KIA and two US WIA. A BDA patrol confirmed four enemy KIA. The fighters wore BDUs, with foliage for additional camouflage, and white turbans.

Two Mirages (C/S Comet 37) came on station and dropped the following bombs:
1 x GBU12 at 42S WB 25793 66590
1 x GBU12 at 42S WB 23993 67515
Two F-15s also dropped bombs at the following locations:
1 x GBU38 at 42S WB 24697 68214
1 X GBU31 at 42S WB 24198 67713
1 X GBU31 at 42S WB 23713 66725
1 X GBU38 at 42S WB 23066 66384
2 X GBU38 at 42S WB 25203 66188
2 X GBU38 at 42S WB 25391 66182
2 x Fighting positions were found along the ridge line
BDA:
   Friendly 2 x WIA, 1 x KIA
   Enemy 4 x KIA
0915z TM Havoc SPs to conduct QRF ISO Workhorse
1230z TM Attack SPs to conduct QRF ISO Workhorse
More to follow.
ISAF Tracking # 08-752.
Headquarters
International Security Assistance Force Afghanistan
NEWS RELEASE [2007-XXX: Draft]
ISAF soldier killed, one wounded in ambush
FORWARD OPERATING BASE SALERNO, Afghanistan (27 August) One International Security Assistance Force soldier was killed and one wounded in Paktika Province in eastern Afghanistan today.
FOR THE COMPLETE PRESS RELEASE, PLEASE SEE ATTACHMENT.

Reference ID: AFG20070906n1041
Latitude: 32.34603119
Date: 2007-09-06 01:01
Category: Direct Fire
Detained: 0

Region: RC SOUTH
Longitude: 66.13905334
Type: Enemy Action
Affiliation: Enemy

	Enemy	Friend	Civilian	Host Nation
Killed in Action	22	0	0	0
Wounded in Action	0	0	0	0

At 0125Z TF BUSHMASTER reported audible SAF at 42S TA 3074 8239 IVO FOB PACEMAKER. Special Intel suggests OMF maneuvering on position. TF

BUSHMASTER requested close air support. At 0352Z TF Bushmaster reported they have seized high ground vic 42S TA 314 807, insurgents fled. At 0554Z TF Bushmaster reported currently positioned tactically on the high ground awaiting emergency resupply. BDA is 20 EKIA and insurgnet forces are reinforcing. Reports indicate enemy reinforcing with heavy weapons and are prepared to engage. At 0847Z, TF Bushmaster reportes receiving recoilless and SAF from a village IVO 42S TA 319 806. Continuing to assess the situation ATT. At 1042Z, TF Bushmaster reported PID of 3X OMF maneuvering on them so they are engaging with mortars. Emergency resupply is w/u ATT. CAS: 2x A-10 dropped 1x GBU-12, 1x GBU-38 and fired 1200 rds 30mm.

At 1101Z, Event closed. NFTR. ISAF tracking# 09-194.

COMBINED JOINT TASK FORCE- 82
COMBINED PRESS INFORMATION CENTER
BAGRAM AIRFIELD, AFGHANISTAN
APO AE 09354
Press Center: 0799-063-013
bagrammoc@afghan.swa.army.mil
FOR IMMEDIATE RELEASE
September 6, 2007
RELEASE # 037

More insurgents killed as government forces continue operations in Kandahar Province

BAGRAM AIRFIELD, Afghanistan An eight-hour-long battle this morning in the Kandahar Province ended with another defeat of the Taliban by Islamic Republic of Afghanistan forces. (See attachment)

Reference ID: AFG20070907n1071
Latitude: 31.11812973
Date: 2007-09-07 20:08
Category: Direct Fire
Detained: 0

Region: RC SOUTH
Longitude: 64.18718719
Type: Enemy Action
Affiliation: Enemy

	Enemy	Friend	Civilian	Host Nation
Killed in Action	0	2	0	0
Wounded in Action	0	7	0	0

At 2016Z, TF Helmand reported an unknown number of insurgents at 41R PQ 132 433, 2.2km of GARMSER DC in Helmand province. Friendly forces engaged with small arms fire. 2X friendly forces KIA. Update posted at 2018Z Friendly forces in heavy contact with multiple casualties. Friendly forces are currently engaging with small arms fire and 81mm and 105mm mortar. MTF. 9 line to follow. Update 2031Z, request AH support. Update posted at 2034Z Friendly forces report 5X casualties, 3X T1, 2X T2 no 9 line at this time. At 2056Z MEDEVAC requested by TF Helmand MM(S) 09-08A, for 6x UK WIA. Update posted at 2118Z Friendly forces still in contact and attempting to extract. All casualty wounds are gunshot wounds with possibly more than 6X casualties. Over watch units established. Update posted at 2122Z, additional forces in readiness for support. At 2234Z, TF Helmand reports 1x FF (UK) KIA and 1xFF (UK) MIA. Update posted at 2308Z Request for further AH RIP IVO GARMSER DC. Update posted at 2321Z Friendly forces are now extracting 1X T1 and 1X CF KIA, request launch IRT. Update posted at 2338Z Friendly forces are extracting north. AH is currently in the north carrying out over watch and there is still 1X missing PAX. Update posted at 2347Z TF Helmand requests aviation assets to re-supply 81mm HE and 105mmHE to DELHI as soon as possible. Update posted at 0023Z Last known GRID for missing PAX is 41R PQ 129 432. Update posted at 0102Z Friendly forces are establishing overhead GMR and are searching for missing PAX. Update posted at 0155Z Friendly forces confirm MIA found. MIA status is unknown at this time. TF HELMAND is sending recovery assets and AH is remaining in over watch. MTF. Update posted at 0206Z Friendly forces are in position and about to extract the MIA from the vicinity of GRID 41R PQ 12974 43228. There are no friendly forces IVO of GRID currently. Friendly forces close air support is being engaged and is reengaging. Update posted at 0301Z 2X F15 dropped 2X GBU-31 at 2311Z at N31:07.057, E064:11.11, 6X GBU-38 9 with no impact GRIDS given. AH in overwatch spotted 1X insurgent moving tactically IVO 41R PQ 1289 4303. At 0323Z TF Helmand reported that in support of TIC 300 30MM 41R PQ 136 435 at 0230Z. Event closed at 0612Z, final BDA 2 UK KIA, 7 UK WIA. ISAF tracking # 09-263.

Reference ID: AFG20070912n902
Latitude: 34.96747971
Date: 2007-09-12 05:05
Category: Indirect Fire
Detained: 0

Region: RC EAST
Longitude: 70.37473297
Type: Enemy Action
Affiliation: Enemy

	Enemy	Friend	Civilian	Host Nation
Killed in Action	0	0	0	0
Wounded in Action	0	0	0	0

12SEP07 Rocket Attack:
4 x 107mm Rockets were fired at FOB Kalagush from a suspected POO location in the Wadawu Valley (42S XD 227 700). Two rockets landed west of the FOB at grids 42S XD 240 701 and 42S XD 251 702. The other two rockets were unobserved but impacts were heard west of the FOB. TF King sent out a crater analysis element to confirm impact areas and type of munitions fired. They returned with the remains of 2 X 107mm rocket shells, shrapnel, and their POIs.
Crater Analysis Debrief
The dismounted Patrol SPed from FOB KLG with 4 ASG at 0520Z to investigate the craters from the indirect attack earlier that morning. There seemed to be little reaction from the locals in the area around the FOB. The patrol pushed up the ridge to the West of the FOB and investigated the initial suspected impact location. The patrol found a 107mm casing at grid 42S XD 25619 70009. Upon further investigation, the patrol found an impact crater at 42S XD 25794 68659. The patrol sent 2 of the ASG to the village just to our North West vic 42S XD 255 703. They returned and told the patrol that there was another impact location just to our West. The patrol moved to investigate and found the fragments of another 107mm Rocket with what was left of the casing. The patrol took pictures of all sites and recovered all of the fragments that we found. Both craters were poor due to the initial impact on rock. From the first crater, we think that the casing that the patrol found to its East is from that impact. That puts the rounds coming from the West of the impact location. The second crater the patrol found was long and it appeared that the rocket had hit and exploded out to the North East and the rocket traveled in that direction for about 15 feet before

stopping. The patrol found what was left of the canister on the West side of the crater and found most of the shrapnel on the East end of the crater.

Upon recovering all of the fragments found, the patrol returned to FOB KLG along a different route to the South and entered the gate around 0910Z. NFI

Reference ID: AFG20070919n960 Region: RC EAST
Latitude: 32.51057053 Longitude: 68.86180878
Date: 2007-09-19 10:10 Type: Enemy Action
Category: Attack Affiliation: Enemy
Detained: 0

	Enemy	Friend	Civilian	Host Nation
Killed in Action	0	0	0	0
Wounded in Action	0	0	1	0

FROM: 2PL , D Co, 1/503 INF
TO: CHOPS, Battle Captain, Eagle 2
SUBJECT:
Size and Composition of Patrol: 13x US, 1x Cat 2 TERP, 1x PUC
Traveling with RCP
A. Type of patrol: Mounted
B. Task and Purpose of Patrol: 2/D/1-503 IN conducts mounted patrol to FOB Orgun-E NLT190330SEP07 IOT transport detainee and resupply the Bandar checkpoint.
C. Time of Return: 1030z
D. Routes used and Approximate times from point A to B:
From Grid/FOB To Grid/FOB Route Travel
Bandar Checkpoint FOB Orgun-E RTE Charger to RTE Honda to F-150 back to RTE Honda 10-15 km/h
E. Disposition of routes used: RT Charger IVO Aman Kheyl continues to get more and more washed out as we travel it. RTE F-150 is getting better, but still has a few spots where the rocky and canalizing terrain are restricting. RTE Honda is highly trafficable with numerous jungle truck convoys going both north and south. Coming out of the wadi IVO Mangrah Towry (VB 009 241) (RTE F-150) onto RTE Honda is becoming an known enemy area for ambushes and possible IEDs (a jingle truck convoy was ambushed today)
F. Enemy encountered: U.S. Forces did not encounter any enemy, but roughly thirty minutes to an hour before we arrived IVO Mangrah Towry (VB 009 241), a jungle truck convoy was ambushed coming out of the wadi onto the high ground. The ACM forces had started to burn one of the jingle trucks and shot the windows and tires out of two of the five trucks. Upon arrival of the jingle trucks, we secured the site, cleared the surrounding area, and extinguished the fires.
G. Equipment status: One RCP vehicle had to change a tire. All Havoc vehicles have minor maintenance issues to be looked at within the next 24 hours.
H. Intelligence: H6 and H1-6 detained an individual who was using a signaling mirror on the high ground IVO Mangrah Towry (VB 009 241) on 18 SEP. Today there was an ambush on a jingle truck convoy that had been at the Bandar checkpoint. These two encounters are most likely related and the detainee possibly has information on whereabouts of these ACM forces.

I.   Local Nationals encountered:
Name: unknown
Position: jingle truck driver
Location: Mangrah Towry (headed to Orgun)
General Information: I briefly spoke with one of the jingle truck drivers who was in the ambush this afternoon. They were all very nervous and scared, and one was cut from the windshield shattering after being fired upon. The drivers were coming out of the wadi (RTE F-150) up the hill when a small number of ACM forces were dismounted along the road; they signaled for the drivers to halt and then engaged the two lead vehicles. The jingle truck drivers all fled once the hasty ambush was initiated and flagged down our convoy in the village of Mangrah Towry. The men were distraught, and we tried to help calm him down while we put out the fires.
J.   Disposition of local security: There was a three truck private security convoy that was suppose to be with these jingle trucks; however, they somehow got stuck behind the U.S. convoy and were not present during the ambush. Each security guard carried an AK-47 and wore a chest rack.
K.   HCA Products Distributed: N/A
L.   Atmospherics: (reception of HCA, reactions to ANSF and Coalition forces, etc): N/A
M.   Reconstruction Projects QA/QC: N/A
N.   Conclusion and Recommendation (Patrol Leader): (Include to what extent the mission was accomplished and recommendations as to patrol equipment and tactics.)
The endstate was that we arrived at FOB Orgun-E following our timeline, thus the mission was accomplished. However, the more we travel RTE Honda and RTE F-150, the more likely it is that we will see attacks and IEDs along the route. The enemy observes our route on every movement, and this is the third time in one month that an element has been attacked between FOB Orgun-E and Bandar. The ACM forces still have not engaged a U.S. convoy along this route, but target our jingle truck convoys and local ANA and ABP convoys. I believe it is only a matter of time before a U.S. convoy is decisively engaged along this route. It is wise to travel before daylight on this route to deter any opportunities for IED emplacement and direct fire engagement, but we also need to conduct actual patrols IVO of Mangrah Towry (VB 009 241). We simply bypass this village every time because it is not part of the mission, and we are neglecting to collect information on the threat in the immediate area.

Reference ID: AFG20070922n1001 Region: RC EAST
Latitude: 34.18046951 Longitude: 70.65261078
Date: 2007-09-22 21:09 Type: Enemy Action
Category: Attack Affiliation: Enemy
Detained: 0

	Enemy	Friend	Civilian	Host Nation
Killed in Action	0	0	0	0
Wounded in Action	0	0	0	0

The NDS chief Agha Jan reports that the Kot District Center (DC) was attacked by 6-8 groups that had about 5-6 individuals each. Agha Jan stated enemy forces were firing on the DC from approx. 200m away, with PKMs and rockets. The NDS chief reports they are still around the village, although he's not exactly sure. He states some are wounded, and he would like help to go after them. There are currently no known casualties. NFI

Reference ID: AFG20070923n939
Latitude: 31.83529091
Date: 2007-09-23 17:05
Category: Direct Fire
Detained: 0

Region: RC SOUTH
Longitude: 64.67282104
Type: Enemy Action
Affiliation: Enemy

	Enemy	Friend	Civilian	Host Nation
Killed in Action	15	0	0	0
Wounded in Action	20	0	0	0

At 1705Z TF Helmand reported receiving small arms fire and RPG from insurgents at 41R PR 583 234, 4.1 KM south southeast of PB SANDFORD in Nahri Sarraj, Helmand province. Friendly forces returned fire with small arms fire. At 1824Z TF Helmand reported an unknown number of insurgents engaged friendly forces with small arms fire and RPG from 2X fighting positions. Friendly forces have returned fire with small arms, JAV and 105MM LT GUN. CAS and AH have been requested ISO TIC. AH now on station at 1839Z. BDA 15X EKIA 20X EWIA. Event closed at 1942Z ISAF tracking # 09-769.

Reference ID: AFG20070925n918
Latitude: 32.14392853
Date: 2007-09-25 09:09
Category: Direct Fire
Detained: 0

Region: RC SOUTH
Longitude: 64.80240631
Type: Enemy Action
Affiliation: Enemy

	Enemy	Friend	Civilian	Host Nation
Killed in Action	61	1	0	0
Wounded in Action	0	3	0	0

At 0910Z, TF Bushmaster reported receiving ineffective Russian AGS 40mm from an unknown size enemy at 41S PR 69993 57814. Friendly forces attempting to locate point of origin site by maneuvering. At 0920Z friendly forces reported enemy locations at 41S PR 70100 57711 and 41S PR 70809 57712. At 0941Z TF Bushmaster reported that they are receiving effective RPG fire and small arms fire from Grid 41S PR 70444 57866. At 0949Z TF Bushmaster reported that 10X EKIA and insurgents are attempting to re-enforce from Musa Qala. There are 15 insurgents at Grid 41S PR 70444 57866 from Falah with AK 47's. At 1035Z TF Bushmaster reported they moved into the green zone, and received multiple RPG and returned suppresive fire. At 1057Z Reported 1X US WIA with shrapnel to shoulders and back. No medevac required and WIA is continuing to fight. At 1112Z TF Bushmaster reported receiving heavy effective fire. Friendly forces location is at 41S PR 70170 58479 and friendly forces requested emercency close air support. At 1220Z, TF Bushmaster requested a medevac MM(S)09-25E for 3 US Mil, 1 urgent and 2 priority. At 1230Z, friendly forces reported 1xUS MIL KIA, 4xUS MIL WIA. Injuries are unknown. The initial MEDEVAC landed and collected 1 x US KIA and 2 x US WIA. They couldnt wait any longer for the third patient to get to the MEDEVAC site, due to imminent danger, so they took off and returned to Camp Bastion. While returning to Bastion, they

received ineffective RPG fire and requested MED HLZ be changed when they return for last patient. They are enroute to secure final patient att. CAS is off station and CCA is supporting TIC. Close air support will be on station to support at 1520Z with a playtime until 1700Z. TF Bushmaster has requested an emergency re-supply and will likely use the MEDEVAC HLZ grid for PI, but not certain as of yet. The drop should take place at approximately 1545Z. At 1411Z TF Bushmaster reported still being engaged with AH support as overwatch. At 1514Z TF Bushmaster reported 61X EKIA. Event reopened at 0700Z on the 26th of September. Friendly forces, identified an insurgent carring AK-47, that was reporting on coalition forces activities. TF Bushmaster engaged with GMLRS from FOB Robinson. At 0817Z TF Bushmaster reported that insurgent outpost on hilltop at 41S PR 66351 68284. Attempted to engage but insurgents fled back into the greenzone, TF Bushmaster occupied the outpost and have a good observation of the AO. At 0851Z TF Bushmaster reported TIC complete, No BDA and NFTR.Requested resupply of :8000x rds .50CAL, 120x 60mm HE, 30X CARL GUSTAF HE, 2GAL. CLP, 70 CAS of water, 220 gallons of fuel, 30x cases of 40mm(MK19), 4x cases of 60mm WP,8x cases of 7.62mm link. TF Bushmaster reported they have supplies at KAF and requests aviation assets to move from KAF to HLZ. At 1008Z TF Bushmaster reported that insurgents are back on the hilltop reported at 41S PR 66351 68284. Close air support was requested and attempted to engaged.Update to current location 41S PR 6604 6556. At 1022Z TF Bushmaster reported that insurgents were identified and engaged friendly forces at 41S PR 67149 67934, 41S PR 66343 68284, 41S PR 65446 69178. At 1212Z TF Bushmaster reported maneuver elements have come under small arms contact from 5-10 insurgents in a north to south running trenchline, VIC 41S PR 68363 64611. Friendly forces continued to manuever on the enemy. At 1435Z, TF Bushmaster reported pushing east into the green zone. The enemy is reinforcing the 7 vehicles already gathered in the trench where TF Bushmaster is heading. At 1513Z TF Bushmaster reported an additional 38 EKIA. Event closed at 1856Z, 26Sep07. ISAF Tracking # 09-826.
COMBINED JOINT TASK FORCE- 82
COMBINED PRESS INFORMATION CENTER
BAGRAM AIRFIELD, AFGHANISTAN
APO AE 09354
Press Center: 0799-063-013
bagrammoc@afghan.swa.army.mil
FOR IMMEDIATE RELEASE
September 25, 2007
RELEASE # 110
ANSF, Coalition inflict heavy insurgent losses in Helmand province
BAGRAM AIRFIELD, Afghanistan   Members of the 205th Afghan National Army Corps, advised by Coalition forces, killed more than 60 insurgents during combat operations near the Musa Qalah Wadi in Helmand Province today.
SEE ATTACHED FOR COMPLETE RELEASE

Reference ID: AFG20070930n887
Latitude: 31.56385994
Date: 2007-09-30 06:06

Region: RC SOUTH
Longitude: 65.35479736
Type: Enemy Action

Category: Direct Fire Affiliation: Enemy
Detained: 0

	Enemy	Friend	Civilian	Host Nation
Killed in Action	0	0	0	0
Wounded in Action	0	0	0	0

At 0655Z TF Kandahar reported a USPI convoy that consisted of 16x security vehicles and 8x fuel tankers were ambushed by an unknown number of insurgents with small arms and RPG fire at grid 41R QQ 235 945, in the Zharmi district, Kandahar province. A Coalition OMLT that was with the ANA engaged the insurgents position with small arms fire and mortars. The insurgents disengaged and retreated into a wadi. The convoy continued on to Helmand covered by a smoke screen. At 0740Z, 3x US vehicles arrived on the scene and engaged the insurgents from the North. Incident closed at 0902Z. ISAF tracking # 09-993.

Reference ID: AFG20071019n1002 Region: RC SOUTH
Latitude: 32.17367935 Longitude: 64.79564667
Date: 2007-10-19 05:05 Type: Enemy Action
Category: Direct Fire Affiliation: Enemy
Detained: 0

	Enemy	Friend	Civilian	Host Nation
Killed in Action	15	0	0	0
Wounded in Action	0	1	0	0

At 0527Z TF Bushmaster reported a squad sized element of insurgents engaged friendly forces with small arms and RPG fire at 41S PR 693 611, in the Mosa Qala district, Helmand province. Friendly forces returned fire and worked pre-planned close air support on the enemy fighting positions. At 0535Z TF Bushmaster was still in heavy contact. At 0637Z friendly forces requested a MM(S)10-19A for 1 urgent surgical US MIL (USMC) with crushed abdomen and thorax from a collapsed wall during a breach. At 0702Z, TF Bushmaster reported that the OMF were heavily re-enforcing their positions along the east side of a wadi. TF Bushmaster engaged the maneuvering OMF with fire from the close air support and confirmed OMF commander Mohammad Hak was killed during the engagement. At 0727Z, TF Bushmaster reported that 7X OMF had been engaged in a compound with 2X JDAMS. BDA of the engagement was 15 x OMF KIA. At 0801Z TF Bushmaster reported approximately 50 OMF in the green zone and 25 reinforcements enroute. Close air support is to draw insurgents in the open. TF Bushmaster reported receiving 1X round of indirect fire and engaged the point of origin. Event was closed at1042Z. ISAF tracking # 10-479.
COMBINED JOINT TASK FORCE- 82
COMBINED PRESS INFORMATION CENTER
BAGRAM AIRFIELD, AFGHANISTAN
APO AE 09354
Press Center: 0799-063-013
bagrammoc@afghan.swa.army.mil
FOR IMMEDIATE RELEASE
October 19, 2007
RELEASE # 062
ANSF, Coalition forces disrupt terrorist actions

BAGRAM AIRFIELD, Afghanistan   Afghan National Security and Coalition forces engaged and killed more than a dozen Taliban fighters to include a suspected Taliban commander in the Musa Qaleh Wadi region of Helmand Province today.
SEE ATTACHED FOR COMPLETE RELEASE

Reference ID: AFG20071023n966
Latitude: 34.86886978
Date: 2007-10-23 06:06
Category: Direct Fire
Detained: 0

Region: RC EAST
Longitude: 70.94621277
Type: Enemy Action
Affiliation: Enemy

	Enemy	Friend	Civilian	Host Nation
Killed in Action	0	1	0	0
Wounded in Action	0	2	0	0

At 0655z, Battle 6 on OBJ Taylor (vic. XD 7789 6023) reported that 5-10 ACM had engaged their positions with small arms fire from the south, vic. XD 768 588. Battle elements, spread along the top of the Abas Ghar, returned fire with small arms and called for 120mm indirect support out of the KOP. Battle continued to receive heavy ICOM chatter from the south and west.
At 0713z, Rock reported 1x WIA (gunshot wound to the arm) from the ongoing contact. Battle also began to engage the enemy with 155mm indirect fire.
Contact continued, with ICOM intercepts indicating that the ACM were attempting to maneuver on Battle's positions.
0732z: CAS on station (DE01/05) moved to drop 1x GBU-38 on enemy positions at XD 76811 58775. At this time, Battle 6 reported a second casualty - gunshot wound to the abdomen - and one Fallen Soldier.
0738z: DE01 released 1x GBU-38 which was a dud, DE01came around for a re-attack on the same target with another GBU-38 which was observed safe and on target
0744z: CAS dropped 1x GBU-31 on a known enemy fighting position at XD 78482 61162.
0750z: CAS came around to re-attack the same position. Impact observed, and ICOM intercepts stated that it had come close to the enemy's position.
0840z: CAS Dropped another GBU-3 on enemy located at XD 77742 59241. Battle observed the rounds safe, and reported them on-target. Shortly thereafter, CCA, also on-station, conducted a 30mm gun run on enemy locations in the same vicinity.
1048z: CAS prepared to drop 1x GBU-31 on enemy located at XD 76302 61643. Impact at 1051z, round observed safe and on-target.
Battle 6 called up at aprox. 1110z and reported that Battle was preparing to maneuver in the vicinity of the Village of Landigal (vic. XD 603 751) in order to conduct SSE.
1205z: CAS engaged yet another enemy position at XD 78165 60456 with 1x GBU-38. Battle observed the rounds safe and on target.
1430z: After extensive target analysis and consultation with BDE, TF Rock prepared to engage aprox. 10 ACM that they had PID'ed in a house (vic. XD7536 6017) near the village of Landigal. Predator maintained eyes one, and Battle Company had reported observing 2-7 ACM rotating postions on the deck of the house, with 1x PKM, AK47s. The next closest structure was a small house aprox. 55m way, with the next closest 80 to 100m away.

Collateral damage was assessed to be a risk, but the on-scene commander judged the military value of the target high enough to risk engaging.
1435z: CAS engaged the above target with 1x GBU-31. Impact was observed safe, but off-target.
1510z: ISR observed aprox. 12 ACM exfilling from target house cleared to go hot with a GBU-38 and engage them at vic. XD 7495 6055. Impact observed safe, but ACM continued to exfil.
TF Rock has ripped from TF Bayonet and stated NFTR

Reference ID: AFG20071023n981
Latitude: 33.01998901
Date: 2007-10-23 10:10
Category: Patrol
Detained: 0

Region: RC EAST
Longitude: 69.49610901
Type: Enemy Action
Affiliation: Enemy

	Enemy	Friend	Civilian	Host Nation
Killed in Action	0	0	0	0
Wounded in Action	0	0	0	0

EXSUM: TF Eagle Joint IDF/DF Border Interdiction of ACM with PAKMIL (23 OCT) At 1008z, PAKMIL reported via field phone to TF Eagle forces (A Company) PID on four armed ACM to the north of OP5 and opposite the PAKMIL Checkpoint #5 in the Lawara Dashdah. A Company briefly had eyes on the enemy personnel before the ACM moved behind OP5. PAKMIL requested fires on OP5 in order to drive the enemy into small arms range of their OPs. A Company cleared the ground of friendly forces (OGA is in the vicinity) through OP4 and BCP-10 before firing 4rds of 105mm HEVT on OP5. At 1040z, PAKMIL reported the egress of enemy personnel towards their position where the ACM were engaged by PAKMIL with small arms fire. PAKMIL then reported to A Company that ACM had broken contact with their OP and moved north and east out of visual contact. No further information was reported by PAKMIL, we will continue to press for a joint BDA evaluation.

Reference ID: AFG20071030n935
Latitude: 31.49662971
Date: 2007-10-30 04:04
Category: Direct Fire
Detained: 0

Region: RC SOUTH
Longitude: 65.38155365
Type: Enemy Action
Affiliation: Enemy

	Enemy	Friend	Civilian	Host Nation
Killed in Action	0	1	0	0
Wounded in Action	0	1	0	1

At 0425Z, TF Kandahar reported an unknown number of insurgents ambushed friendly forces with small arms fire at 41R QQ 262 871 IVO Panjwayi District center in Kandahar province. Friendly forces returned fire. BDA is 1x ANP WIA with gunshot wound, 1x US PMT WIA with gunshot wound and 1x US MIL vital signs absent. At 0539Z TF Kandahar requested a medevac for 2x urgent US Mil and 1 routine ANP. At 0700Z all patients were brought to PBSG and evacuated to KAF. 1x US MIL with shrapnel to the right side of the head will remain overnight for observation. At 0701Z No further BDA reported. Event closed at 0658Z. ISAF tracking # 10-789.

Reference ID: AFG20071104n1063
Latitude: 32.62899017
Date: 2007-11-04 15:03
Category: Surveillance
Detained: 0

Region: RC EAST
Longitude: 68.2591095
Type: Enemy Action
Affiliation: Enemy

	Enemy	Friend	Civilian	Host Nation
Killed in Action	1	0	0	0
Wounded in Action	0	0	0	0

At 041500ZNOV07, the QRF from FOB Kusahmond was sent to check on a suspicious man approaching to FOB. The suspicious man was seen earlier by the guard towers. After warning signals and warning shots, the suspicious man opened fire at PBG QRF. The QRF returned fire and killed the individual. PBG QRF investigated body of suspicious and found:
1 x AK-47, Chinese manufacture
3 x AK magazines with approx. 90 rounds
1 x F-1 fragmentation grenade
1 x Scissors
1 x Watch
1 x Calculator
300 USD in Pakistan Rupees
Misc. documents
Analysts comment: Considering he was alone and lightly armed, the insurgent was probably observing the base, checking our security and did not want to engage CF. He probably underestimated the quick reaction of the PBG security team. This quick and violent reaction by the PBG will likely discourage future dismounted actions against the base
UPDATE
NDS reporting indicates that the insurgent may have been a man named Yaqoob. Other sources indicate that a man named Yaqoob belonged to an ACM cell from Mest, Yousef Khel District, Paktika (42S VB 587 475). Further investigation is ongoing.

Reference ID: AFG20071109n1071
Latitude: 35.13190079
Date: 2007-11-09 11:11
Category: Direct Fire
Detained: 0

Region: RC EAST
Longitude: 70.943573
Type: Enemy Action
Affiliation: Enemy

	Enemy	Friend	Civilian	Host Nation
Killed in Action	0	0	0	0
Wounded in Action	0	5	0	0

A combined element of US/ANA conducted a shura at Aranas and were moving back to COP Bella. At 1124z, Chosen Company reported that ACM had engaged Chosen 16's patrol at XD 7708 8940z with small arms fire and RPGs. Chosen 16 returned fire with small arms and called for 120mm and 155mm indirect support. They reported taking heavy effective direct fire from enemy at multiple locations.
1150z: CAS (2xF-18C/Sword 31/32) came on station in support of ongoing contact. (From A/C MISREP: Sword 31/32 performed XCAS. Checked in at 1200Z. Received fuel at 1240Z. Checked back on station at 1308Z. Attempted strafing run but unable

due to HUD malfunction. Conducted armed overwatch from 1330Z-1423Z and checked off at 1423Z).

1200z: TF Rock posted a 9-Line MEDEVAC Report, in which they reported 5 US casualties.

1217z: TF Rock reported that ACM had also engaged Bella's OP1 with more small arms and RPG fire.

1237z: TF Rock updated the event, reporting a total of 9 casualties (6 Urgent, 3 Priority). During this time, contact with the enemy continued - Chosen 16 reported that the enemy had approached points of his position to within 100 meters

1240z: CAS executed a simultaneous drop of 3x GBU-31s on enemy positions at the following targets: XD 75300 89800,

XD 74800 88700, and XD 74600 89350. Rounds observed safe and on-target. (From A/C MISREP: Bone 22 released 3xGBU-31v1 on 3 targeted insurgent fighting positions at 1244Z IOT neutralize. JTAC reported JDAMs successfully neutralized enemy. Unable to strike 4th target due to its close proximity to friendlies (200 meters). Ground commander disapproved any bomb drops that close without better SA. Bone 22 off station at 1251Z).

TF Rock requested the use of UH-60L's in order to effect a combat resupply and re-inforcement for the troops in contact. 2x Sling loads of 120mm mortar rounds were put together at Blessing for transport to Bella - reinforcements, composed of platoons from Able and Battle Companies, and a detachment of ANA staged at Blessing as well. Rock also requested that the AH-64s accompanying the MEDEVAC mission stay on-station after pickup, in order to act as CCA. (From A/C MISREP: Dude 21 received the order to scramble at 1320Z. Dude 21 checked in at 1348Z and conducted overwatch IVO of MEDEVAC operation with NSTR. Dude checked off station at 1517Z.)

1323z: AH-64s escorting the MEDEVAC mission arrived and came on station to provide CCA. They engaged multiple enemy positions with gun runs. (From TF Talon Air Mission AAR: Gunmetal 71/75 arrived on station at 1310Z. At 1330Z Gunmetal 75 conducted 3x strafing passes on SAF POO (1st 20x30mm, 2nd 1xWP, 3rd 1xWP and 40x30mm) while Gunmetal 71 conducted overwatch. After engagement, both conducted reconnaissance for ACM on the run with NSTR.)

1358z: ASG OP Speedbump, outside COP Bella, reported taking small arms fire from another group of ACM.

1404z: TF Rock prepared to send 1x PLT and HQ Element (including C6 and C7) from Blessing to Bella (2x non-standard HLZs: XD 767 898; XD 774 891 - Alternate: XD 760 897). However, initial recon of the LZs proved that they were not suitable for low-illum. The re-inforcements instead were to move to Bella, and link up with the platoon in contact by foot.

1450: OP Speed Bumb no longer receiving SAF

(From A/C MISREP: Sword 33/34 (2xF-18C) conduted armed overwatch from 1500-1545Z ISO Chosen 12 ISO TIC IE. NSTR. Anvil 13/14 (2xF-18F) conducted XCAS ISO TIC IE from 1515-1540Z and 1615-1645Z with NSTR.)

1554z: Reinforcemnt Mission Aircraft w/d Blessing

1601z: w/u to Bella

1611z: w/d Bella

1642z: w/d Blessing to pick up Lilft 2

1703z: w/d Blessing to pick up Lift 3

1753z: C6 SP'ed from Bella with 37 PAX, enroute to C16's position.
1854z: w/u 3rd Lift to Bella
1900z: w/d Bella, return flight to Blessing. At this time as well, TF Rock reported a further 9x ANA WIA at
C16's last location, that would require yet another MEDEVAC. 6 Fallen Heros enroute to JAF
1910z: w/u 4th lift from Blessing
1921: Rock reports locating 3X ANA MIA and 1X US MIA. All MIA accounted for
1950z: w/d Blessing
1954z: w/u lift 5 from Blessing
2002z: w/d lift 5 Bella
2100z: Flight crew reports fallen Hero slipped from hoist during initial extraction, was unobserved by ground forces due to visibility, and is still IVO PZ.
2139z: HH60 flight(with hoist capabilities) to recover fallen Hero IVO Bella w/u JAF
(From A/C MISREPs: Claw 01 (Warrior-A) arrived on station at 2000z and conducted ISR during casualty evacuation. Ripped with Ramit 03 (2xF-16) at 0122z and RTBed at 0125z.)
~~10 NOVEMBER~~
0030z: US and ANA Fallen Heroes extracted by hoist IVO Bella by HH60s.
0038z: HH60 enroute to ABAD with Heroes.
0200z: Final US Hero located and secured. US and ANA Heroes being moved to more accessible area for hoist operations.
0522: Recovery A/C on site; all Fallen Heros enroute to JAF, then BAF
0530: TF Rock reports all equipment recovered and all Chosen elements have initiated movment back to Bella COP
0642: TF Rock reports all elements are RTB
(From A/C MISREPs: Beginning at 012z, Ramit 03 conducted ISR to look for suspicious movements in the area with NSTR. Ramit 03 ripped with Bone 11 (B-1B) at 0344z. At 0558z, Vino 23 reported casualties extracted and platoon exfilling on foot. At 0611z, Bone 11 did a SOP over this position to deter further enemy activity during exfil and JTAC reported good effects. Bone 11 off station at 0639z.)
BDA
6 x US KIA
8 x US WIA (6 Urgent, 2 Priority)
3 X ANA KIA
11 X ANA WIA
WAY AHEAD
Coordination for Ramp Side Ceremony
Memorial Ceremony scheduled for 17 NOV
2/C/2-503 will RIP into Bella, sending 1/C back to Blessing for refit and recovery. They will occupy the FOB and execute counter-insurgency patrols and follow them up with regular KLEs throughout the region in order to deny sanctuary to the ACM and to separate them from the local population.
ISAF Tracking #11-232

Reference ID: AFG20071110n1070
Latitude: 34.89178085
Date: 2007-11-10 04:04
Region: RC EAST
Longitude: 69.63668823
Type: Enemy Action

Category: Direct Fire   Affiliation: Enemy
Detained: 0

	Enemy	Friend	Civilian	Host Nation
Killed in Action	0	0	0	0
Wounded in Action	0	6	0	0

At 0417Z TF Bushmaster reported that 40x ACM surrounded friendly forces at Grid 42S WD 58176 61227, in the Tag Ab District,Kapisa province. Friendly forces assessed the situation while an AH-64 and 2x GR-7's came on station.

At 0558Z, TF Bushmaster reported that CAS dropped 2x EPW (540lbs Bombs) at grid 42S WD 61831 61188.The first bomb exploded prematurely and JTAC request another run on the same target and reported a successful strike.

At 0659Z, TF Bushmaster reported taking 1x 107mm rocket at FB Pathfinder. The point of origin was located at grid 42S WD 580 535. TF Bushmaster responded with counter battery on that location.

At 1210Z, TF Bushmaster reported observing 7-10 OMF still engaging friendly forces with small arms fire and RPG's. The enemy were located at 42S WD 599 602.

At 1323Z, Jumpmaster 06 reported linking up with TF Bushmaster at grid 42S WD 598 520. They also reported that they were still receiving sporadic SAF and that they had casualties and a 9 line would follow.

At 1356Z, TF Bushmaster requested a medevac for 3x Urgent US MIL and 1x French soldier. MM(E)11-10D.

At 1420Z TF Bushmaster reported another 3x US soldiers were wounded and required a medevac.

At 1454Z TF Bushmaster reported a total of 7X WIA 6X US MIL 1X French ETT. All WIA are being medevaced.

At 1513Z TF Bushmaster reported returning to FB Anaconda and awaiting emergency resupply.

At 1557Z TF Bushmaster reported receiving small arms fire and theres a suspected IED in vicinity of 42S WD 5954 6091.At 1558Z TF Bushmaster 4X WIA were evacuated from FB Pathfinder, (3X USSF and 1 X Terp) 1 X French WIA was treated at FB and RTD (Laceration to face and broken tooth)Final correction to BDA is 1x US MIL KIA, 2x US MIL WIA, 1x FRA WIA, and 1x civilian interpreter WIA.

At 0450Z on NOV 11th , TF Bushmaster reported that Gremlin 25 and Jumpmaster 06 were receiving small arms fire VIC. 42S WD 5942 5425. It was also reported that 2x F-16's were on station in support of the units on the ground. There were 2x EKIA from this engagement.

At 0631Z, TF Bushmaster reported that elements were preparing a move south down the MSR in order to investigate reports of 100x OMF possibly gathering.

At 0808Z, Gremlin 25 received small arms fire from 2-3 OMF in the vicinity of 42S WD 6004 5005. A recovery team also made link up with the Pathfinder 06 vehicle that was NMC at 42S WD 584 537. Once the vehicle was recovered Jumpmaster 06 was going to move south to link up with Gremlin 25. At 111548Z Gremlin 36 reported houses along the Wadi IVO 42S WD 596 550 flickered their lights to signal the presence of coalition forces. All houses turned off their lights. Gremlin 25 awaited link up with Gremlin 14 and Gremlin 36 to plan future operations.At 0818Z on November 12th Gremlin 25 reported that they were receiving small arms fire and RPG fire from 2-3 OMF vicinity of 42S WD 5953 5240.

Tic closed at 1500Z on the 12 of November, no further BDA was reported. NFTR. ISAF tracking # 11-243.

Reference ID: AFG20071119n1054
Latitude: 32.99819946
Date: 2007-11-19 05:05
Category: Indirect Fire
Detained: 0

Region: RC SOUTH
Longitude: 65.51631927
Type: Enemy Action
Affiliation: Enemy

	Enemy	Friend	Civilian	Host Nation
Killed in Action	80	0	0	0
Wounded in Action	0	0	0	0

At 0547z, TF Bushmaster reported an unknown number of insurgents engaged friendly forces with indirect fire at 41S QS 351 539 in the Shaheed Hasas district of Uruzgan province. Friendly forces are developing the situation.
At 0600Z, TF Bushmaster reported that the attack is located in the vicinity of 41S QS 365 606, the FOB is still receiving indirect fire.
At 0624Z, TF Bushmaster reported close air support engaged the enemy in the tree line in the location of where the mortar fire came from. (From A/C MISREP: At 0638z, Bone 21 dropped 3xGBU-31 on ACM in tree line. JTAC reported good hits with estimated 30x EKIA)
At 0640Z, TF Bushmaster reported a friendly forces element at 41S QS 3628 5815 engaged enemy with close air support. Sporadic mortar fire is still incoming.
(A/C MISREP) At 0656z, Bone 21 engaged ACM leader in tree line with 3xGBU-31; JTAC reported good hits with estimated 15 EKIA.
(A/C MISREP) At 0713z, Bone 21 engaged C2 ACM with 2xGBU-38; JTAC reported good hit with estimated 10 EKIA.
(A/C MISREP) At 0737z, Bone 21 engaged ACM in tree line with 2xGBU-31 and 1xGBU-38; JTAC reported good hit with estimated 10 EKIA.
(A/C MISREP) At 0750z, Bone 21 engaged ACM compound with 3xGBU-38; JTAC reported good hits with estimated 5 EKIA and possible weapons cache.
At 0757Z, TF Bushmaster reported an estimated 80x insurgents KIA in the vicinity of 41S QS 374 663. Close air support is continuing to be worked.
(A/C MISREP) At 0813, Bone 21 released 5xGBU-38 on ACM in treeline; JTAC reported weapons released within parameters.
At 0900Z, TF Bushmaster reported close air support was still being worked on insurgent targets around Sarsina.
Additional close air support will arrive on station at 0910Z. 3x insurgents fighting positions have been destroyed.
At 1004Z, TF Bushmaster reported they identified insurgents inside Sarsina, an additional close air support mission is being worked.
(A/C MISREP) Recoil 43 spotted 2xPAX moving in an easterly direction along the alley. Recoil 43 tracked them and observed them entering a building. Jaguar 01 was also able to ID the PAX by using Rover downlink and declared them as hostile based on pattern of previous attacks from this location. ICOM chatter confirmed this. At 1014z, Recoil launched 20x CRV-7 rockets at ACM in building. JTAC confirmed successful strike and confirmed zero expectation of civilian casualties.
At 1028Z, TF Bushmaster reported their location is at 41S QS 3596 5440. Close air support engaged additional OMF IVO 41S QS 3635 5851 and killed an estimated 5x OMF. Additional close air support is enroute, ETA 1045Z.
(A/C MISREP) Recoil 43 observed 1xPAX moving from an orchard to the cover of woodlandd. Again Jaguar 01 was able to see the location using Rover downlink and declared the PAX as EF based again on pattern of life, ICOM chatter, and known

location of POO of previous attacks. At 1045z, Recoil 44 launched 8x CRV-7 rockets at ACM in wood land. JTAC confirmed successful strike with ICOM chatter indicating 1xEKIA and again confirmed zero expectation of civilian casualties.
At 1304Z no further BDA reported. An estimated 85x EKIA were reported. Event closed at 1304Z.
ISAF tracking # 11-487.

Reference ID: AFG20071128n1076
Latitude: 35.35166931
Date: 2007-11-28 04:04
Category: Attack
Detained: 0

Region: RC EAST
Longitude: 71.54640198
Type: Enemy Action
Affiliation: Enemy

	Enemy	Friend	Civilian	Host Nation
Killed in Action	0	0	0	0
Wounded in Action	0	0	0	4

OVERALL SITUATION: This is part of SPITAMENES OPERATION; an ANSF led operation and support by 1-91 (See attached Spitamenes CONOP). The TF is conducting EXFIL after 3 days of KLE/HA distribution in upper and lower Gowerdesh, they are conducting GAC from Lower Gowerdesh back to JSS CP D and the to FOB Naray when ACM initiated the attack.
TF OBJECTIVE: conducting KLE/HA distributions in Kamdesh area IOT separate the insurgents from the local populace.
IMMEDIATE OBJECTIVE:
1. Dropped bombs to destroy enemy to allow GAC to exfil to the FOB
2. Dude 01 SOF to deter ACM from engaging CF.
EFFECT:
1. Bombs neutralize the ACM
2. SOF deterred ACM from engaging CF
SEQUENCE OF EVENTS:
At 0400z, Workhorse 6 element located YE 3139 1502 was engaged w/ 8x RPGs and SAF by estimated 2x squad-size elements from vic YE 3071 1494. WarriorA pushed to observe the ridgeline for enemy exfil.
At approximately 0410z CAS (Hawg01 A-10) performed a 30mm gun run and dropped 2x MK82 AB on YE 307 147 IOT destroy the UECs. Enemy fire ceased after HG01 conducted the runs.
Around the same time the LLVI team at OP Mace (YE 3269 1790) reported a 245 LOB, "Turn around you have more rounds to shoot. Shoot it. Did you see the bird? Were you successful? Yes we were! Do your job we have more to shoot."
At approximately 0422z FOB Naray fired 155mm to YE 3049 1458 (KE 4470).
At approximately 0445z WH reported 1x WIA (ANA CDR). The ANA CDR received a small piece of shrapnel to his right pectoral muscle. The medic onsite treated the wound and the ANA CDR was RTD. Three additional ANA Soldiers sustained superficial wounds as well--all were RTD.
At 0522z DUDE01 (F-15) dropped 1x GBU-31 on YE 3032 1488 IOT destroy UECs engaging Workhorse 6.
At 0649z, en route back to CP D, WH6/Hatchet 15 elements were engaged with SAF from the high ground above the LOC, vic YE 315 145.

At approx 0648z CP D reported icom chatter indicating insurgents had eyes on the Workhorse convoy. A few minutes later, at approximately 0656z, Darkhorse elements at CP D reported RPG fire from a suspected C2 house at YE 311 141. At 0703z, Workhorse received SAF from east of the river POO vic YE 321 143, and approximately 0705z WorkhorseBlue4 reported enemy movement IVO YE 319 135. DUDE01 executed a show of force at 0711z as he came on station.

All Workhorse elements made it to CP D at 0738z and all friendly ground elements were at CP D as of 0857z. BDA was unable to be assessed, and there was no collateral damage observed.

Reference ID: AFG20071201n1082
Latitude: 34.93872833
Date: 2007-12-01 08:08
Category: Direct Fire
Detained: 0

Region: RC EAST
Longitude: 70.98639679
Type: Enemy Action
Affiliation: Enemy

	Enemy	Friend	Civilian	Host Nation
Killed in Action	0	0	0	0
Wounded in Action	0	0	0	0

At 0852z, Sapper 27 (RCP) while on patrol on the Pech Road, reported taking small arms and indirect fire from 5-10 enemy located south of the river, at vic. XD 8087 6699. They returned fire with small arms and called for indirect fire support. 120's out of Combat Main and 155's out of Blessing fired in support in order to suppress the enemy. Rounds observed by Sapper 27, who reported the enemy attack disrupted. Contact ceased, and the enemy exfilled to the high ground to the south. Terrain prevented Sapper from conducting on-site SSE, and they continued movement. All contact was directed away from populated areas, and there was no collateral damage.

Enemy regrouped and moved back into the same location, from which they re-engaged Sapper 27 at 1013z with small arms and RPG fire. Sapper 27 returned fire with small arms and heavy weapons, and again called for indirect support. 155's out of Blessing fired to suppress the enemy and to restrict their freedom of movement. A6 sent a QRF element out from Combat Main to link up with the Sapper element, which did so at 1036z, at vic. XD 814 680. There, they identified 2x ACM moving south along the ridgeline across the river, and continued to engage with heavy weapons and indirect fire.

Enemy exfilled to the south under fire. They managed to break contact with no confirmed casualties. The river and restrictive terrain prevented the element from conducting on-site BDA. All contact directed away from populated areas, and there was no collateral damage. Able element returned to Combat Main, and Sapper returned to ABAD.

After contact had ceased, Sapper reported that two soldiers had received minor wounds in the course of the event. One soldier had been shot in the back - the plate in the back of his IOTV stopped the round, but he still sustained an acute chest wall injury. The other soldier was struck in the face with shrapnel from an enemy RPG. Both soldiers were treated at the ABAD FST and were returned to duty; they did not require any MEDEVAC.

ISAF Tracking # 11-011

Reference ID: AFG20071211n1120
Latitude: 31.62402916
Date: 2007-12-11 07:07
Category: Indirect Fire
Detained: 0

Region: RC SOUTH
Longitude: 65.05592346
Type: Enemy Action
Affiliation: Enemy

	Enemy	Friend	Civilian	Host Nation
Killed in Action	0	0	0	0
Wounded in Action	0	0	0	0

At 0730Z, TF Kandahar reported insurgents engaged an ANSF convoy with mortar fire at 41R PR 950 006, 39.5km southeast of FOB Arnhem IVO Hutal in the Maywand district, Kandahar province. TF Kandahar requested close air support for a show of force.

At 0824Z, after the initial attack on the convoy the insurgents attacked the Maywand DC headquarters and deputy commanders house. 16x insurgents were using PKM, mortars and RPG. Friendly forces casualties were reported. The ANP from Zharey COP sent 3x Ford Rangers to assist.

At 0945Z, the convoy consisted of 22x vehicles and the ambush commenced at 0600Z. TF Kandahar intended to monitor the situation, since the ANP was already enroute.

At 1011Z, F-16 conducted a show of presence with 2x passes at 200 ft.

At 1326Z, BDA is 4x ANP KIA, 3x ANP WIA and 2xANP vehicles damaged. The enemy BDA is 2x EKIA, 2x EWIA, 2X AK captured and 2x MOTORCYCLES captured. 4x CIVILIANS were held for questioning.

At 1333Z, no further BDA was reported. Event closed at 1333.

ISAF tracking # 12-301.

Reference ID: AFG20080104n1153
Latitude: 32.6547699
Date: 2008-01-04 16:04
Category: Attack
Detained: 0

Region: RC WEST
Longitude: 62.10514069
Type: Enemy Action
Affiliation: Enemy

	Enemy	Friend	Civilian	Host Nation
Killed in Action	0	0	0	0
Wounded in Action	0	0	0	0

NDS REPORTED THAT LAST NIGHT 14 VEHICLES OF TALIBAN SURROUNDED THE KHAKE SAFED DISTRICT CENTER (41S MS 16080 13370), KHAKE SAFED DISTRICT, FARAH PROVINCE, AF AND SUBSEQUENTLY SET IT ON FIRE THIS MORNING. NDS COMMENTED THAT BY THE TIME THE TALIBAN ARRIVED THE DISTRICT CENTER WAS ALREADY ABANDONED BECAUSE THE DISTRICT MANAGER WAS AWARE OF THE IMPENDING ATTACK. THERE WERE NO SHOTS FIRED. NDS BELIEVES THE ACTING POLICE CHIEF, JUMA GULL, WAS NOT HAPPY WITH THE RECENT APPOINTMENT OF HAJI LABHEJ JAN AS THE DISTRICT MANAGER. JUMA GULL WANTED TO BE BOTH THE DISTRICT MANAGER AND DISTRICT POLICE CHIEF. NDS BELIEVES JUMA GULL WAS WORKING WITH THE TALIBAN COMMANDER MULLAH SALAAM TO ORGANIZE LAST NIGHTS ATTACK. POLICE CHIEF JUMA GULL LEFT THE DISTRICT CENTER AND TOOK HIS ANP WITH HIM LEAVING JUST THE DISTRICT MANAGER AND HIS 5 ANP OFFICERS. NDS BELIEVES THE TALIBAN HAVE LEFT THE DISTRICT CENTER AND IT IS NOW VACANT. ANP

REPORTED THAT THEY WOULD SEND 40 ANP OFFICER TODAY TO SECURE THE AREA. (PRT FARAH S2; DOI: 05 JAN 08)

Reference ID: AFG20080113n1106
Latitude: 31.59428024
Date: 2008-01-13 01:01
Category: Direct Fire
Detained: 0

Region: RC SOUTH
Longitude: 65.16486359
Type: Enemy Action
Affiliation: Enemy

	Enemy	Friend	Civilian	Host Nation
Killed in Action	0	0	0	10
Wounded in Action	0	0	0	0

At 0130Z, TF Kandahar reported an unknown number of insurgents attacked checkpoint Kala Shmeer at 41R QQ 054 975, 6.4km north of Ata Mohammad Kariz, 15.8km west of PB H-E-M in the Maywand district, Kandahar province. 10x ANP KIA, 1x ford ranger, 1x motorcycle and 9x AK's were stolen. Friendly forces investigated the situation.
At 0822Z, TF Kandahar reported the ANP removed the bodies and reassumed the checkpoint. Event closed at 0821Z.
At 1157Z, TF Helmand reported friendly forces left the checkpoint. All the bodies, their weapons and the Ford Ranger were gone. The incident occurred at 0100Z. The crime scene indicated all but one of the victims were shot while asleep. The ANP did not return fire. A minimum of 4 shooters was suspected an they escaped to the north in the stolen Ford Ranger. A RCMP officer assisted in the investigation.
At 1431Z, the Kandahar COP reported the insurgents infiltrated the checkpoint by dressing as ANP personnel in an ANP vehicle. The license plate number of the stolen vehicle was PO30MAYWAND.
ISAF tracking # 01-235.

Reference ID: AFG20080123n1097
Latitude: 35.35720825
Date: 2008-01-23 04:04
Category: Patrol
Detained: 0

Region: RC EAST
Longitude: 71.55317688
Type: Enemy Action
Affiliation: Enemy

	Enemy	Friend	Civilian	Host Nation
Killed in Action	0	0	0	0
Wounded in Action	0	0	0	0

BACKGROUND INFORMATION: The situation began on 21Jan 2008 when ABC contractors were engaged north of CP D on 21 JAN. At approx. 210440zJan08, ABC contractors reported to CP D that they were surrounded by approx. 50-60 ACM IVO 42S YE 318 128. The ABC supervisor at CP D initially reported four to five ABC personnel (42S YE 313 159) were wounded by small arms fire. Enemy element composition and disposition were reported to be 20-30 PAX IVO 42S YE 314 167, 15-20 PAX 42S YE 313 163, 3-4 groups of 3-4 PAX each IVO 42S YE 3227 1402, and 3-4 groups of 3-4 PAX each IVO 42S YE 3162 1408. The ABC personnel reported to be fired upon by PKM machineguns from the east side of the river. At approx. 0545z, US elements at CP D request 155mm support from FOB Naray IOT facilitate the CASEVAC of the three wounded and one KIA ABC Construction personnel. 0725z,

CP D reports 45 ABC workers were still north of CP D, and that they were no longer in contact, stated that the ACM had moved off the 16 gridline, likely due to the IDF, in which the ABC claimed killed two to three ACM. The ABC Construction personnel also claim to have killed two to three ACM with small arms fire. At approx. 0810z, all ABC Construction personnel were south of CP D. ABC personnel sustained 3x WIA and 1x KIA

iCOM intercepts on 22Jan indicated that enemy forces can monitor coalition movement from various observatory positions. Other indications include that the enemy knows the terrain well and can communicate effectively as needed.

23JAN:

iCOM intercepts basically mirror those of yesterday. They indicate that the enemy has observation of CF, from multiple vantage points, and are continuing to move forces into position based off of our movements

- At 0425z, Workhorse received a report of 2 possible spotters IVO 42S YE 309 158
- 0940z, CF north of CP D observes 3 PAX with weapons enter a cave IVO 42S YE 3199 1565

Size: 3pax w/ weapons
Activity: running into cave
Location: enemy: YE 3199 1565
Time: 1003z
Unit: Workhorse 6
Remarks: Hatchet observed 3pax with AK's running into cave, firing 120, Working BE 11 att

- 1041z, BONE 11 engaged Cave with 2x GBU38s
- 1131z, HAWG 05 engaged cave with 1x GBU 12
- 1140z, HAWG 05 engaged cave with 1x GBU 12
- 1418z, DUDE 05 engaged cave with 1x GBU 31

At 1515z, Saber closed the TIC
UPDATE:
Saber re-opens TIC

At approximately 1530z Dude 05 observed 6 pax carrying packs walking in a file approximately 15m apart. At 1615z 4 of the pax entered a house at YE 3086 1630. Dude oberserved two pax leave the house and move onto the highground IVO YE 3116 1637, which is the origin of hostile icom chatter over the past two days. The pax stopped under a tree giving them direct line of sight to CF OPs approx 1 KM to the south. Workhorse fired 120mm illum IOT observe the pax. They dug in deeper to avoid being seen. At 1752z hostile intent was determined and Dude06 dropped 1x GBU-38 on the enemy Op. Dude continued to observe the house which now guarded by one pax at each corner.

NFTR

(from JTAC report)

TF Saber declared a TIC when they observed 3 ACM with AK-47s run into a cave. VO32 had eyes on the cave, He used type 2 controls and dropped 2xGBU-38 on the coordinates that he generated for the cave using his map, and GPS, VO32 crosschecked his grids with VO30 who had falconview. They dropped 2xGBU-38s because they could not drop the 1xGBU-31 Inst, and 1xGBU-31 Delay that was weaponeered for this target using all players inputs. BE11 reported that he had issues programming the 31s. HG05 dropped 1xGBU-12, and HG 06 dropped 1xGBU-12 on the cave. HG05 perfect hit observed from VO32, HG06 bomb landed 50m short of cave. DE05 checked in and dropped 1xGBU-31 on the cave using his sniper pod to derive good coordinates, his bomb was on target and left the cave mostly closed. Later DE05 observed six pax walking on the road to the south towards the US Ops. The pax then went to a house; two pax broke off and set up an OP to observe the US Ops. Saber6 declared hostile intent, and VO30 dropped a single GBU-38 on top of their position using type 2 control with DE05, and the coordinates derived off of DE05 sniper POD. DE05 continued to observe the OP after impact. He confirmed that no squiters left the area, and when the smoke cleared he confirmed that there was nobody in that position anymore.

Reference ID: AFG20080311n1228
Latitude: 31.92676353
Date: 2008-03-11 05:05
Category: Direct Fire
Detained: 0
Region: RC SOUTH
Longitude: 64.76858521
Type: Enemy Action
Affiliation: Enemy

	Enemy	Friend	Civilian	Host Nation
Killed in Action	0	0	0	0
Wounded in Action	0	1	2	0

At 0545Z, TF Bushmaster received small arms fire, RPG and indirect fire from an unknown number of insurgents at 41R PR 67197 33683, Nahr Surkh District, Helmand. Friendly forces developed the situation. At 0621Z, 2x F15Es engaged target 41R PR 67197 33683 with 1x GBU31 and 1x GBU38. TF Bushmaster requested a priority MEDEVAC for 1x US MIL WIA and 2x Civilian Terps WIA at 41R PR 70411 34109. The US MIL has a GSW to the right arm with a fracture. Patient 2 has a GSW to the right elbow. Patient 3 has a GSW to the buttocks.

At 0721Z, TF Bushmaster continued to receiving heavy SAF and IDF. CAS engaged multiple enemy positions at 41R PR 6719 3368, 41R PR 674 340, 41R PR 679 341. MEDEVAC mission complete at 0742Z. At 0823Z, TF Bushmaster discovered 1,600lbs of Amonium Nitrate and will destroy with CAS.

At 0837Z, TF Bushmaster PID what appeared to be a wheeled multi rocket launcher and 8x insurgents moving into a structure at 41R PR 6627 3318. CAS engaged the target. At 0932Z, TF Bushmaster reported firing 3x Hellfires on 41R PR 6627 3318. Remains of the ruins show numerous entrances, living quarters, guard towers, underground tunnels, and brass casings which indicate it was used as a firing position.

At 1007Z, TF Bushmaster reported destroying the cache of ammonium nitrate with a 2,000lbs bomb. At 1019Z, TF Bushmaster reported that 2x 500lbs bombs were dropped on the ammonium nitrate cache but both were duds. Event closed at 1330Z. No confirmed enemy BDA.

ISAF Tracking # 03-258

Reference ID: AFG20080325n1174
Latitude: 32.85628891
Date: 2008-03-25 06:06
Category: Attack
Detained: 0
Region: RC EAST
Longitude: 68.45012665
Type: Enemy Action
Affiliation: Enemy

	Enemy	Friend	Civilian	Host Nation
Killed in Action	0	0	0	0
Wounded in Action	0	0	0	0

S- 1 ANP, 17 ACM
A- Hijacked 3 Jingle Trucks, kidnapped drivers, shot ANP trying to escape
L- VB 48551 35489
T- 0500L (0030Z) 25 Mar 08
R- At approximately 0500L, 25 Mar, an ANP Officer (NOORO) stationed at Yahaya Khel, was shot by Taliban Forces when he escaped from Capture. At approximately 22 March, while on leave, he was helping drive 3 jingle trucks with his father at the Andar Province when his 3 trucks were ambushed. His father, another driver and himself were taken into captivity and kept in a well without food or water for 2 days. On 25 Mar, Talibans forced them to drive the 3 trucks to Yayah Khel where they said they would burn the trucks and then release them. 1 ACM rode with each truck and another 14 ACM on 7 motorcycles rode with them. All ACM armed with AK47. After entering Mest along Route Audi at VB 588 477, the trucks began heading east towards Yayah Khel. Approximately 10 - 15 KM along the road, trucks stopped and drivers were removed. At this point, ACM recognized NOORO as ANP and told him that they were going to kill him. NOORO began to run and was hit on his left rear hip. ACM burned one of the trucks and kept the other 2. Both father and other driver were released unharmed. All 3 were found by Yayah Khel ANP Soldiers when they came to investigate the truck on fire. ANP brought NOORO to FOB KKC for MEDEVAC at 0640 local. NOORO was MEDEVAC from FOB KKC at 0802 Local. At this time, ANA is investigating 2 jingle trucks being downloaded at Mest / Samali Zanki.

Reference ID: AFG20080326n1158
Latitude: 32.53768921
Date: 2008-03-26 16:04
Category: Patrol
Detained: 0
Region: RC EAST
Longitude: 69.20059967
Type: Enemy Action
Affiliation: Enemy

	Enemy	Friend	Civilian	Host Nation
Killed in Action	0	0	0	0
Wounded in Action	0	0	0	0

On 26 1626z March 2008, TF Eagle declared Imminent Threat due to 18-20 pax spotted in groups of three bounding about 1k from the Pakistan border inside Afghanistan. These pax were spotted and reported by FB Lilley at 1610z in the vicinity of grid WB 265 005. In response, FB Lilley fired 4 x 105mm HEPD on Target 1 grid WA 267 994, 4 x 105mm HEPD on Target 2 grid WB 265 005, and 4 x 105mm HEPD on Target 3 grid WB 265 998. Icom chatter was intercepted in the vicinity of Targets 2 and 3 stating that a guy named Kalam was wounded. At 1749z, two 9 x 105mm Sweep In Zones were conducted on Targets 2 and 3 in response to the intercepted Icom chatter. Bone 22, 1 x B1, came on station at 1653z in response to the Imminent Threat. At 1834z, Bone 22 dropped 3 x GBU-38s with an observed and confirmed splash on target. Imminent Threat was closed with no CF casualties, collateral damage, or damage to equipment.

Reference ID: AFG20080412n1218
Latitude: 31.54449654
Date: 2008-04-12 07:07
Category: Direct Fire
Detained: 0

Region: RC SOUTH
Longitude: 64.8919754
Type: Enemy Action
Affiliation: Enemy

	Enemy	Friend	Civilian	Host Nation
Killed in Action	0	0	0	4
Wounded in Action	0	0	0	0

GLE conducting eradication patrols. INS engaged with SAF (significant explosions heard). FSG RBG Recce are deploying to the site with caution. FSG RBG requesting CAS
UPDATE:
GLE was engaged with SAF and 82mm.
The GLE returned fire and a fire fight ensued. FSG Reece had eyes on from the North. The Predator on station IOT defined the INS disposition. FSG Recce will keep a 2KM distance and assist in any medical evacuation. It has been reported that there are 15-20 killed and several wounded.
UPDATE:
FSG RBG(S) will push forward approximately 1 km 93N, IOT Observe/Support ANP extraction.
ANP has been informed to withdraw E60, and fire flares for recognition. FF intend to CASEVAC seriously wounded.
JPCC reported that the District CoP is confirming that he has 150x uniformed ANP, 17x Blue Rangers and 2x white Tunis.
UPDATE:
RBG(S) FSG intend to move back to link up with their Echelon. FF did not receive any casualties. The final report from MAYWAND DL states : 4x ANP KIA, No mention of wounded, 1x tractor burned, 1x tractor stolen and 1x ANP white Ranger stolen.
The final BDA will not be confirmed until RC(S) CJ9 has made calls through the hospital chain with reference to this event. Event closed at 1705D*. ISAF tracking # 04-306.

Reference ID: AFG20080413n1226
Latitude: 34.89029312
Date: 2008-04-13 09:09
Category: Indirect Fire
Detained: 0

Region: RC EAST
Longitude: 70.90338898
Type: Enemy Action
Affiliation: Enemy

	Enemy	Friend	Civilian	Host Nation
Killed in Action	0	0	0	0
Wounded in Action	0	3	0	0

At 0907z Battle company reported a complex attack in the southern Korengal Valley. COP Korengal Outpost, COP Restrepo, and OP Dallas all reported receiving effective SAF and IDF from multiple groups of AAF located to their southeast and west. Battle company responded with SAF, heavy weapons (M2 and MK19), 120mm mortar IDF out of COP Korengal Outpost, and 155mm artillery IDF out of FOB Blessing.
0913z: COP Restrepo and OP Dallas reported direct hits from IDF and RPGs.
0922z: COP Restrepo and OP Dallas reported they were still receiving sustained effective SAF from multiple groups of AAF.

0931z: CAS (2 x A10) arrived on station controlled by Vino 20, prepared to engage AAF fighting positions with GBU strkes.
0941z-1010z: CAS received clearance and engaged 3 AAF fighting positions with bomb strikes:
DELTA: 42S XD 72623 63147 @ 0941z w/ 1 x MK-82
BRAVO: 42S XD 74834 61462 @ 0951z w/ 1 x GBU-12
ALPHA: 42S XD 72766 61839 @ 1010z w/ 1 x MK-82
Battle 9N reported all three strikes to be safe and on target.
1014z: CAS conducted a SOF through southern Korengal Valley, south to north.
1017z: Battle company reported they were no longer receiving DF ATT.
1055z: Battle company continued to observe the area for further AAF movement but was unable to regain contact with the enemy. Battle reported 3 x US WIA from the attack, all with minor shrapnel wounds and are all RTD ATT. No other damage to MWE reported. TIC Closed.ISAF #04-333

Reference ID: AFG20080414n1322
Latitude: 31.7466526
Date: 2008-04-14 03:03
Category: Direct Fire
Detained: 0

Region: RC SOUTH
Longitude: 65.73091125
Type: Enemy Action
Affiliation: Enemy

	Enemy	Friend	Civilian	Host Nation
Killed in Action	0	0	0	11
Wounded in Action	0	0	0	1

At 0300Z TF Kandahar reported unknown number of AAF engaged ANP CP IVO 41R QR 587 156 in Arghandab district of Kandahar province. ANP CP was over run all vehicles destroyed and burned and weapons stolen. BDA 11 ANP KIA, 1 ANP WIA. ANP WIA was treated at another ANP checkpoint. ISAF # 04-349.

Reference ID: AFG20080422n1282
Latitude: 34.74126816
Date: 2008-04-22 23:11
Category: Direct Fire
Detained: 0

Region: RC EAST
Longitude: 71.18229675
Type: Enemy Action
Affiliation: Enemy

	Enemy	Friend	Civilian	Host Nation
Killed in Action	0	0	0	5
Wounded in Action	0	1	0	10

At 2315z TF Rock reported that an ABP OP IVO Nawa Pass was receiving heavy effective SAF, RPG, and heavy weapons fire (suspected to be recoilless rifle) from AAF just to their east. This contact resulted in the ABP OP building being completely destroyed. ABP responded with SAF and RPGs, and Ghost 6 (ABP ETT from COP Sarkani) launched as a QRF from COP Sarkani to assist the ABP on the border.
2258z: CCA (2 x AH-64) arrived on station controlledy by Destined 6.
2313z: CCA reported observing SAF IVO 42S XD 9985 4659.
2326z: CCA PID and engaged armed AAF IVO 42S YD 0005 4724.
2338z: Ghost 6 reported receiving effective SAF, resulting in 1 x US WIA with a GSW to the arm.
2346z: CCA PID and engaged armed AAF IVO 42S XD 9958 4594.

2358z: CCA PID and engaged armed AAF IVO 42S XD 9960 4600.

0049z: TF Rock reported 16 casualties had been taken during the TIC: 1 x US WIA, 5 x ABP KIA, and 10 x ABP WIA. The 1 x US WIA was MEDEVAC'd by air, and all 10 x ABP WIA were ground CASEVAC'd to FOB ABAD FST.

0309z: Ghost 6 and ABP elements continued to observe the area for further AAF movement and improved their position IOT repel any further AAF attacks. Rock 6 will be airlifted to the attack location later today to have a meeting with the Pakistan Military leadership to discuss the way ahead for the incident. Rock 6 also ordered that CF will maintain a presence at the Nawa Pass ABP location while the ABP rebuilt the defensive positions there. No further damage to MWE reported. TIC Closed.

Reference ID: AFG20080618n1367
Latitude: 33.1576004
Date: 2008-06-18 07:07
Category: Indirect Fire
Detained: 0

Region: RC EAST
Longitude: 69.3045578
Type: Enemy Action
Affiliation: Enemy

	Enemy	Friend	Civilian	Host Nation
Killed in Action	0	2	0	0
Wounded in Action	0	10	0	0

UNIT: TF EAGLE
TYPE: AAF IDF
TIMELINE:
AT 0713Z, ZEROK COP REPORTS AAF IDF IMPACTING 300METERS OUTSIDE COP. NO DAMAGE OR INJURIES REPORTED.
ZEROK COP HAS RECEIVED 2 X AAF IDF. VISUAL ACQUIRED POO WB 2908 7212.
SIGINT: AAF ARE ADJUSTING FIRES.
TF EAGLE SITREP:
The second round reported as impacting however there was no direction or distance passed up
TF Eagle fired 5 rounds of 81mm HE on WB WB 305 671
10 rounds of 120mm HE on WB 273 710 (TGT Mets)
5rounds of 81mm HE on WB 3052 6658
Update: Dude 03 is on station in support of Zerok COP and will drop on the following grids:
TGT# 1 305 671 x GBU31s
TGT# 2 2685 7084 2x GBU38s
UPDATE: 0825z Zerok received 2x107 rockets-effective fire visually acquired POO at WB 281 729.
UPDATE: 0830z Zerok received 2x107 rocket impacting within 10m of COP. 1 hit District Center resulting in wounded ATT.
UPDATE: Zerok has received 6x107 rockets ATT all effective hitting on the COP and District Center.
UPDATE: 0846z seventh round impact within 10m of COP, suspected WP round.
In response TF Eagle fired 30x81 HE on visually acquired POO at WB 281 729. And 2xGBU31 and 5xGBU38 on vicinity same grid.
Correction second grid was canceled due to CDE issues.

UPDATE 1100Z: Due to SIGINT stating "we will use the reccoilless rifle on them." Havoc prepped 3 HIF targets at WB 232 667, WB 209 671, and WB 207 652.
SIGINT pickedup from COP WILDERNESS (North of COP Zurok): 4 my friends be patient i will talk to him adel go to your own number/ we dont have that other guy know it khitab all your friends ok congratulations to all of you Aubi you hear me one of the rockets hit the compound Wahib that is right what you do with wahib the chip is broken. hear me one of the hit the target get off the line, you hear me go to your own number on friday you take guys over there it is very far. i dont have any news take those 2 people they are very good. Commander says god bless you his best aubi cant do anything not later i will talk with them tell them we will do it in the evening. Rockatee are you on the phone?
SUMMARY:
AAF IDF: 7
MM(E) 06-18C OE-ZER-OE-SAL-OE
MM(E) 06-18E SAL-OE-SAL
BDA:
US KIA: 2
US WIA: 10
EVENT CLOSED AT 1621Z

Reference ID: AFG20080620n1263
Latitude: 33.1000824
Date: 2008-06-20 05:05
Category: Direct Fire
Detained: 0

Region: RC EAST
Longitude: 69.25045776
Type: Enemy Action
Affiliation: Enemy

	Enemy	Friend	Civilian	Host Nation
Killed in Action	22	0	0	0
Wounded in Action	12	6	0	0

Unit: C/1-503
Type: SAF
Timeline: Charlie company called via FM and said that they were in contact small arms and RPGs on RTE Honda. RCP reported they lost one vehicle (it is damaged and cant move) so far at grid WB 2337 6241 C co reported that the fire is coming from the East. FLT for C co is WB 2324 6230.
Update: C co (MOD) reported that the contact has shifted to the west MOD asked for a Jdam strike on hill top at grid WB 2360 6180
Update: MOD reported that an MRAP is on fire and destroyed all pax are out of the vehicle at grid WB 230 621
Update: 2 urgent surgical causalities shrapnel wounds to the neck and face.
JDAM Grids WB 2250 6300, WB 2190 6190, WB 2360 6180 1x GBU 31s on all as of right now first drop went coming around for the next target
We received 2 SIGINT gists "We have two more locations set up. Saying final Salams!"
"We have just hit one, moving to another location!"
Update: MOD is pushing out of the kill zone current FLT WB 223 614 hill top 2581is where MOD believes that that is where the contact is coming from.
pdate:
MOD is in contact again at grid WB216 604 from the East AWT will be on station

Update: Bearcat 6 is on station MOD is reporting 5 down vehicles to include a HEMMIT wrecker HAWG is on station ATT
MOD HLZ for medevac WB 2121 5957
Enemy Gist was received stating A number of Vehicles are destroyed a C2 node at WB 2272 5600 HAWG is coming in on a gun run on that grid
Update: 60mm mortars are engaging pax exfiling to the north west form the ambush site at grid WB 237 638
Update: Medevac WD OE 4x paxs
Update: MOD FLT WB 211 578 going to consolidate at that location and send an update
Update:TF Eagle dropped 3x JDAMs on enemy location at WB 225 630
UPDATE: NEW 9 LINE CALLED UP. 2 MORE PAX WITH SHRAPNEL WOUNDS FROM INITIAL CONTACT
SUMMARY:
RPG/SAF
MM(E) 06-20A OE-GRID-OE
MM(E) 06-20E SAL-GRID-SAL
MM(E) 06-20G OE-GDE(T2T)-OE
FRIENDLY BDA: 1 MRAP DESTROYED
ENEMY BDA: BASED UPON SIGINT 22 AAF WERE KIA, 12 WOUNDED
US WIA: 6

Reference ID: AFG20080713n1298
Region: RC EAST
Latitude: 35.05212021
Longitude: 70.90773773
Date: 2008-07-13 00:12
Type: Enemy Action
Category: None Selected
Affiliation: Enemy
Detained: 0

	Enemy	Friend	Civilian	Host Nation
Killed in Action	15	9	0	0
Wounded in Action	40	16	0	4

S: UKN A: SAF L: FRIENDLY: 42S XD 73985 80487 23:54 ROCKL: ENEMY: 42S XD 74488 80992 T: 12 2353 JULY 08 U: TF ROCK: C.CO R: SAF, 155MM TF ROCK REQUESTS CAS AND CCA ISO TIC 2358z: COP HAS RECEIVED EFFECTIVE SAF AND RPG ATT. ONE VEHICLE IS ON FIRE ATT. ALL PERSONNEL HAVE BEEN MOVE FROM THE VEHICLE. 0000z: COP KHALER HAS SUSTAINED 2XCASUALTIES ATT. 0004z UPDATE TO CASULATIES NOW HAVE 3XURGENT SURGICAL CASUALTIES. 0006z: AAF ARE LOCATED 100M WEST OF COP KAHLER. CURRENTLY ENGAGING WITH 155MM AND 120MM, CONTINUING TO RECEIVE EFFECTIVE SAF AND RPG 0014Z BONE-23 ON STATION 0016z: COP KAHLER IS CONTINUING TO RECIEVE EFFECTIVE SAF AND RPG. OP KAHLER IS UNDER EFFECTIVE SAF AND RPG. 0022Z DUDE-27 ON STATION 0024z: COP KHALER HAS A TOTAL OF 9 CASUALTIES ATT. STILL RECEIVING EFFECTIVE SAF. 0028Z SIJAM DEVIRTED 0029z: AAF ARE MANUVERING IVO OP KHALER. AAF ARE VERY CLOSE TO THE WIRE OF COP KHALER. AAF CONTINUING TO ENGAGE WITH EFFECTIVE SAF AND RPG. 0035z: CAS IS PREPAIRING TO REATTACK CAS TGT A. 0048Z DUDE-15 ENROUTE 0053z: COP KHALER IS RECEIVING SPORADIC SAF ATT. CCA CURRERNTLY MOVING INTO THE VALLEY ATT. 0056Z BONE-23 DROPPED 3xGBU-38s 0100z: CAS (DUDE-27) IS

PREPAIRING TO CONDUCT A SHOW OF FORCE IN THE VALLEY. 0102Z CASEVAC AND SWT (2x OH-58 WEAPONS TEAM) PERPARING TO LAUNCH 0103z; CAS (DUDE-27) HAS COMPLETED SOF ATT. 0104z: MEDEVAC IS CURERNTLY INBOUND ATT TO COP KAHER FOR 1ST LIFT. 0108Z W/U JBAD ENROUTE TO COP KAHLER 0113Z BONE-23 DROPPED 1xGBU-38s 0122z: WILL UTILIZE THE OH'S TO ESCORT MEDEVAC A/C AND WILL CONTINUE TO USE AH'S TO SUPPORT COP KHALER. 0123z: AAF ARE CURRENTLY LOCATE WITHIN 400M TO THE WEST OF THE OP. CONTINUING TO UTILIZE AH'S ISO COP KAHLER. 0125z: MEDEVAC IS CURERNTLY W/D AT COP KAHLER ATT FOR FIRST LIFT. 0128z: ABLE COMPANY IS CURENTLY ENROUTE TO RE-ENFORCE COP KHALER ATT. 0138z: CHOSEN QRF HAS ARRIVED AT COP KHALER ATT. ABLE CO QRF WILL MOVE DIRECTLY TO COP KAHLER IOT RE-ENFORCE COP KHALER. 0152z: INTEL REPORTS HAVE INDICATED AN IED THREAT IN THE WANAT VALLEY IVO 42S XD 744 795 AND 42S XD 746 776. 0157z CASEVAC A/C ARE CURRENTLY W/D COP KHALER ATT. ABLE CO QRF IN MOVING INTO WANAT VALLEY ATT. 0203z: COP KHALER IS STILL RECEIVING SAF AND RPG'S ATT. 0215Z DUDE-27 ENGAGED ENEMY TARGETS WITH 1xGBU-31 0234z: CAS IS CURERNTLY ENGAGING CAS TGT. CAS CONTROLLED BY VINO-20. 0235Z DUDE-27 HAD DROPPED 4xGBU-38's 0302Z HARDLUCK (2xAH-64'S) W/U BAF ENROUTE TO COP KHALER 0312Z DUDE-27 HAD DROPPED 1xGBU-31 0324z: UPDATE FOR COP KHALER: AAF IN WANAT ENGAGED COP KAHLER AND THE HEDGEROW ELEMENT FROM THE NORTH SIDE OF THE WANAT BAZAAR, THE MOSQUE, AND FROM DWELLINGS IN PROXIMITY OF THE COP. THE AAF MOVED THROUGH THE POPULATION. GOV WAHIDI (KONAR GOV) HAS ALREADY BEEN NOTIFIED AND DOING HIS OWN PRESS RELEASE. 0324z: COP KHALER OP IS RECEIVING EFFFECTIVE PKM ATT/CURERNTLY HAVE AN ADDITIONAL 3XWIA AT THE OP. 0327Z: D/O ELEMENT IS CURRENTLY ENROUTE ITO P/U ADDITIONAL CASULTIES. ~ 0355z: (AWT:HL76/74) LINKED UP WITH MEDEVAC (DO36/34) EN ROUTE TO FOB BLESSING. 0356z: CAS (B-1:BE11) CONTROLLED BY VINO 20 PREPARING TO ENGAGE CAS TGT M. 0410z: ABLE 6 LINKED UP WITH CHOSEN 6, CONDUCTING RECONSOLIDATION, REORGANIZATION, AND EMPLACING SECURITY. 0413z: CCA (AWT:HL76/74) ON STATION CONTROLLED BY CHOSEN 6. 0415z: CAS CONTROLLED BY VINO 20 PREPARING TO ENGAGE CAS TGT L, CAS TGT O, AND CAS TGT P. 0434z: CAS CONTROLLED BY VINO 20 PREPARING TO ENGAGE CAS TGT J AND CAS TGT K. 0452z: CAS CONTROLLED BY VINO 20 PREPARING TO ENGAGE CAS TGT R AND CAS TGT S. 0530z: CAS CONTROLLED BY VINO 20 ENGAGING CAS TGT Q AND CAS TGT Q.1 0549z: CAS CONTROLLED BY VINO 20 PREPARING TO ENGAGE CAS TGT T AND CAS TGT V. 0600z: C6 REPORTS LRAS AND ITAS DESTROYED IN THE ATTACK, NO GBISR AVAILABLE AT COP KAHLER. 0607z: CAS RIP- CAS (A-10:HG53) ON STATION CONTROLLED BY VINO 20. 0642z: CAS CONTROLLED BY VINO 20 ENGAGING HG TGT A. 0645z: CCA (AWT:HR50/53) ON STATION CONTROLLED BY C6. 0658z: CAS CONTROLLED BY VINO 20 ENGAGING HG TGT B 0758z: PREDATOR OBSERVES THREE AAF MOVING EAST IVO XD 779 837. 0815z: PREDATOR PREPARING TO ENGAGE THREE AAF IVO XD 779 837 WITH HELLFIRE. 0821z: PREDATOR ENGAGED WITH HELLFIRE. CAS CONTROLLED BY VINO 24 PREPARING FOR RE-ATTACK. 0855z: REINFORCEMENT ACFT W/D COP KAHLER. 0903z: (AWT:HL74/76) ON STATION ISO COP KAHLER. 0940z:

CURRENT FORCE AT COP KAHLER: 43 CHOSEN PAX 30 ABLE PAX 4 LLVI PAX 17 BATTLE PAX 5 ENGINEERS 1 THT 2 MEDICS 3 ETT 3 TERP 19 ANA 1130z: ROCK TAC(-) W/D COP KAHLER 1226z: PREDATOR, WARRIOR-A, AND CAS OBSERVING TWO PERSONNEL MANEUVERING IVO XD 742 792. 1442z: PREDATOR IDENTIFIED THREE PERSONNEL CARRYING EQUIPMENT IVO XD 7924 8248. 1448Z PT67(299) PT72(595) (WANAT RE-SUPPLY) W/U BLE ENROUTE COP KAHLER ~ 1555z: B-36 PID 2 AAF PAX MANUVERING INTO A FIGHTING POSITION LOCATED NORTH-WEST OF B-36 POSITION. CURRENTLY ENGAGING PID AAF PAX WITH SAF AND CCA IS MOVING TO B-36 POSITION ATT. 1559z: CCA IS CURRENTLY ENGAGING PID AAF PAX ATT. 1612z: LOCATION FOR PID AAF 42S XD 7424 8054. 1651z: TWO NEW INTEL EFFORTS HAVE BEEN MADE.ONE REFERENCES ICOM TRAFFIC AND THE OTHER IS A THREAT REPORT FOR COP KHALER. 1757z: AFGHAN COMMANDOS ARE CURERNTLY BEGINING CLEARENCE OPERATIONS OF DRAWS AROUND COP KHALER. 1846zCAS(SLASHER) HAS CHECKED ON STATION ATT. 1921:z BAJA (F-18) HAS REPORTED THEY HAVE RECEIVED SOME TYPE OF S/A FIRE THAT ORIGINATED 6 KILOMETERS TO WEST COP KHALER IN THE HIGH GROUND. 2121z: SLASHER HAS SPOTTED 4XPAX MOVING IVO 42S XD 778 807. CONTINUING TO OBS PAX ATT. 2147z:SLASHER IS STILL OBSERVING PAX. PAX ARE MOVING IN A MILITARY TYPE(STYLE) OF FORMATION. 2152z: SLASHER IS PREPAIRING TO ENGAGE PID AAF PAX. PID HAS BE EN DETERMINED BY PATTERNS OF LIFE IN THE AREA, PAX ARE MOVING IN ENGAGEMENT AREA AND PAX ARE TRYING TO AVOID CF A/C. 2156z: SLASHER IS ENGAGING PID AAF PAX ATT. 2201z: CCA IS MOVING INTO SLASHER ENGAGMENT AREA ATT. 2315Z: COP KHALER IS CURENTLY CONDUCTING STAND-2 ATT. 0110z:COP KHALER HAS BEEN REC EIVING INCREASED ICOM CHATTER. MAJORITY OF ICOM CHATTER IS IN NURISTANI AND UNABLE TO BE TRANSLATED. 0214z: AFGHAN COMMANDOS ARE CURRENTLY CLEARING HOUSES AND STRUCTURES TO THE NORTH AND SOUTH. MULTIPLE AK-47'S AND BLASTING CAPS HAVE BEEN FOUND FROM THE SEARCHES. IT APPEARS THE AAF USED A LARGE HOUSE TO STAGE FROM FOR THE ATTACK. 0226z:PRED CURENTLY HAS EYES ON 8XPAX MOVING IVO 42S XD 80070 82425. ~ 0350z: SUB-EFFORTS WILL BE USED FROM THIS POINT FORWARD.
Pilot Debrief Report:
WHO: HEDGEROW 53/50, DUSTOFF 35/36, PROPHET 67/71 (2 x AH-64, 2 x UH-60, 2 x UH-60 MEDEVAC; ISO TF ROCK)
WHEN: 130023ZJUL08
WHERE: 42S XD 73985 80487 (400FT AGL, HDG 360, SPD 80KTS)
WHAT: At 2353Z, COP Kahler was engaged with heavy and effective SAF/RPG fire from an unspecified number of Anti-Afghanistan Forces (AAF), estimated at approximately 100-120. AAF elements used civilian structures as cover as well as 12 x fighting positions in the draws to the NE. HEDGEROW (HR) elements (AH-64s) were called in to support the engagement. AAF were reportedly attempting to breach the wire into the COP; CHOSEN elements requested that HR elements engage 30 meters east of their location IVO 42S XD 74100 80500 with 30mm runs. HR conducted multiple strafing runs 100-200 meters east, IVO COP Kahler. DUSTOFF elements arrived at the COP to pick-up the casualties from the engagement area, when HEDGEROW elements observed multiple muzzle flashes toward the DUSTOFF aircraft originating from 42S XD 7397 8143; HEDGEROW elements

engaged the AAF location with organic weapons. HEDGEROW elements conducted FARP operations at Camp Blessing and returned to the engagement area and then were briefed that AAF elements had moved closer to CHOSEN elements. CHOSEN 6 requested that HR elements engage 10 meters from friendly units in the area IVO 42S XD 7400 8040. HR elements conducted a northbound engagement on AAF positions; multiple targets were called in 200 meters of the OP IVO 42S XD 742 805. At 0430Z, a battle handover was conducted with TF SHADOW HARDLUCK (HL) elements (AH-64s). HEDGEROW elements departed for ABAD then RTB to JAF. Total rounds expended: 945 x rounds .30mm, 82 x HE rockets, 4 x Flechettes, 11 x WP rockets, 3 x Hellfire missiles. TF OUT FRONT ASSESSMENT: During the engagement there was an estimated 15 x EKIA, at least 40 x EWIA. Current Coalition losses include: 14 x US WIA, 4 x ANA WIA, and 9 x US KIA from the engagement at COP Kahler. Current reporting indicates that AAF from villages in Dara Noor District are moving to reinforce AAF elements in Wanat Village. AAF are re-supplying and restructuring for additional attacks reportedly scheduled for this evening. Reporting has indicated reinforcements of 100 x AAF from surrounding areas are prepared to conduct future attacks. SIGINT intercepts have placed 2 x AAF Aid Stations north of Wanat, and that both have reached capacity to treat wounded. AAF will continue to conduct surveillance on COP Kahler in attempts to discern Coalition vulnerabilities prior to a follow on attack.

TF DESTINY ASSESSMENT: Over the last 30 x days there have been 6 x SAFIREs within 10NM (all of which were categorized as Minor, with the exception of 1 x Major Hit approximately 8.5NM SE). This SAFIRE is assessed as a Minor, target of opportunity engagement, as the area was taking heavy enemy fire at the time of the casualty extraction. The large scale attack has indicated the increasing enemy presence in this region, which may increase the air threat. Recent HUMINT reporting has also indicated the presence of DShKs throughout the Waygal Valley in the surrounding area. Insurgent forces will continue to coordinate attacks in this region in an attempt to obtain control of the area.

Reference ID: AFG20080802n1358
Latitude: 34.97849655
Date: 2008-08-02 16:04
Category: Surveillance
Detained: 0

Region: RC EAST
Longitude: 70.38537598
Type: Enemy Action
Affiliation: Enemy

	Enemy	Friend	Civilian	Host Nation
Killed in Action	0	0	0	0
Wounded in Action	0	0	0	0

AT 1627Z OP LOYALTY OBSERVED 4 AAF ARMED WITH AK-47'S TRYING TO CRAWL UNDERNEATH THE PERIMETER WIRE. OP LOYALTY RESPONDED WITH SAF, AND THE AAF FLED DOWN THE MOUNTAIN.

Reference ID: AFG20080806n1506
Latitude: 33.045681
Date: 2008-08-06 03:03

Region: RC EAST
Longitude: 69.51698303
Type: Enemy Action

Category: Indirect Fire   Affiliation: Enemy
Detained: 0

	Enemy	Friend	Civilian	Host Nation
Killed in Action	0	0	0	0
Wounded in Action	0	0	0	0

Unit: White Currahee
Type: Direct Fire and IDF
UPDATE: OP ESAST TOOK IDF AND DIRECT FIRE @ 0356Z by 18 AAF
ENEMY EXFILLED BACK INTO PAKISTAN
COUNTERFIRE:
5 X 60MM HE @ WB 4827 5647
SHOT 0404Z R/C 0404Z
SUMMARY:
OP EAST TOOK IDF AND DIRECT FIRE RETURNED WITH 5 X60MM NO KIA/WIA
EVENT: closed 0453Z

Reference ID: AFG20080818n1449   Region: RC CAPITAL
Latitude: 34.64517593   Longitude: 69.81837463
Date: 2008-08-18 11:11   Type: Enemy Action
Category: Direct Fire   Affiliation: Enemy
Detained: 0

	Enemy	Friend	Civilian	Host Nation
Killed in Action	1	10	0	0
Wounded in Action	0	21	0	2

An unknown number of insurgents engaged a dismounted French BG with SAF in the Uzbin Valley as the French BG awaited medical support, the insurgents called in reinforcements resulting in 12x FF WIA. UPDATE: As of 181700LAUG08 the FBG was still in contact with insurgent fighters. CAS (A-10) was on site and engaging insurgents. At 1830 FBG engaged ACF with 81mm mortars and air MEDIVAC was on site to evacuate casualties. At 1845L, A-10 CAS support replaced by F-15 air support and at, 1915L one APC was damaged. As of 182000AUG08 FBG had cleared FOB Tora. At 190853AUG08 FBG Carmin 4 (Grid: 42S WD 752 346) received mortar fire from INS and FBG Carmin 1 engaged ACF at (Grid: 42S WD 78300 36980).
BDA as of 190900AUG08: 10x ISAF KIA, 21x ISAF WIA, 2x ANA WIA, 1x EKIA, 1x APC Damaged.

Reference ID: AFG20080825n1313   Region: RC SOUTH
Latitude: 32.07290649   Longitude: 64.84133911
Date: 2008-08-25 08:08   Type: Enemy Action
Category: Direct Fire   Affiliation: Enemy
Detained: 0

	Enemy	Friend	Civilian	Host Nation
Killed in Action	0	0	0	0
Wounded in Action	1	1	1	0

ISAF # 08-1336

At 0648Z, 2/7 USMC reported while passing under a bridge an Antif Afghan Force dropped a grenade into turret of the vehicle at 41S PR 73800 50000, 200m East of FOB Sangin, Helmand. Friendly Forces report 1x US MIL WIA, and 1x AAF WIA. MEDEVAC was requested for both. US MIL was priority, and AAF was urgent surigical.
AT 0908Z, FF ENGAGED THE AAF AND RETURNED TO SANGIN DC WITH THE CASUALTY. A LN WITH A GSW TO THE FOOT LATER SHOWED UP AT SANGIN DC. HE IS BELIEVED TO BE LINKED WITH THE ATTACK.
EVENT CLOSED AT 0908Z

Reference ID: AFG20081224n1467
Latitude: 32.76454926
Date: 2008-12-24 04:04
Category: Indirect Fire
Detained: 0
Region: RC EAST
Longitude: 69.33551025
Type: Enemy Action
Affiliation: Enemy

	Enemy	Friend	Civilian	Host Nation
Killed in Action	0	1	0	0
Wounded in Action	0	3	0	0

S UKN
A IDFX1EFF
L MARGAH
T 0825L
R ONE EFFICTIVE ROUND   MARGAH 4xCAS.
UNIT: TF CURRAHEE(1/D/2-506)
TYPE: IDF
TIMELINE: 0353Z MARGAH COP REPORTS TAKING 1x RND AAF IDF EFFECTIVE FIRE. NO POO ATT. POI: INSIDE COP.STRUCK HMMWV
-BDA 3x US CASUALTIES. 1x KIA 2x WIA
UPDATE: 1 MORE US CASUALTIE IS REPORTED MAKING 3x WIA AND 1x KIA
-JUST AQUIRED A RADAR POO
GRID WB 3524 2522.
FIRES:
9x 155mm HEVT FROM BORRIS AT GRID WB 3524 2522.
SHOT: 0406Z   R/C: 0410Z
-NO BDA ATT
FIRES:
4x 120mm HE/PROX FOLLOWED BY 4x 120mm WPPD AT GRID WB 3524 2522.
SHOT: 0413Z   R/C: 0416Z
-NO BDA ATT
-CAS IS ON STATION ATT.
UPDATE:
FIRES:
10x 120mm HE/PROX AT GRID: WB 3524 2522.
SHOT: 0443Z   R/C: 0458Z
SUMMARY:
GRIDS: WB 3524 2522
RNDS:
9x 155mm HEVT

14x 120mm HE/PROX
4x 120mm WPPD
UPDATE 0816Z
FRIENDLY BDA 1XHMMWV DAMAGE LEFT REAR
MWR SATALITE DISH DAMAGED
EVENT: CLOSED 1105Z

Reference ID: AFG20090214n1757
Latitude: 32.03742599
Date: 2009-02-14 11:11
Category: Direct Fire
Detained: 0

Region: RC SOUTH
Longitude: 64.8620224
Type: Enemy Action
Affiliation: Enemy

	Enemy	Friend	Civilian	Host Nation
Killed in Action	0	1	0	0
Wounded in Action	0	0	0	0

X COY 45 CDO conducting a framework patrol report that INS engaged FF with SAF from GR 41S PR 7635 4686, resulting in 1 x GBR WIA CAT B who later on DOW. FF returned fire with mortar and QRF is deployed. CAS has been requested. FF extracted back to FOB NOLAY.
UPDATE 2151D*
No further INS activity has been observed.
BDA: 1 x GBR KIA.
***Event closed at 2151D*1 Died of Wounds british (citizen)(GBR) NATO/ISAF

Reference ID: AFG20090314n1780
Latitude: 32.29915237
Date: 2009-03-14 03:03
Category: Direct Fire
Detained: 0

Region: RC SOUTH
Longitude: 64.78855896
Type: Enemy Action
Affiliation: Enemy

	Enemy	Friend	Civilian	Host Nation
Killed in Action	0	1	0	0
Wounded in Action	0	0	0	0

C COY 2 RW reported that while conducting a probing patrol, FF were engaged by INS with SAF and RPG. FF returned fire with SAF and declared an Air TiC. 2x AH (UG 50/51) and 1x A10 (HAWK 51/52) supported ground troops and engaged INS FPs with 30mm and CRV7 rockets. FF returned fire with 81mm mortar and 105mm artillery IOT cover FF extraction N. Warrior IFV despatched to assist the foot patrol's extraction. FF had 1 x casualty who was extracted to USPB but declared KIA at the HLS.
UPDATE 0903D*
FF are still in contact. FF are using AH and A10 against INS FP. FF using 81mm smoke grenades into a wadi to screen suspected INS on the W flank. FF intent is to break contact and move north to extract.
UPDATE 1336D*
At 0958D*, FF suggests that INS are planning a coordinated attack from E and W. FF fired 90 x 30 mm warning shots and suppressive fire into clear area S of FF IOT allow FF to extract to USPB. FF lost a sniper rifle at GR 41SPR68437497. FF fired 60x 30mm

IOT destroy the rifle. At 1009D*, The intention is for Warrior to deploy to the area of the AH engagement to search for BDA on the sniper rifle because FF cannot confirm if it is destroyed ATT. FF have requested that CAS remains on station to provide over watch as they move to the location. At 1052D* On station CAS (HG 51) has PID'd 3x INS IVO of the earlier engagements (41SPR 68557490) and engaged with 30mm. At 1118D*, FF patrol in Warrior IFV on route to investigate the area of previous engagement. INS fired 3 x RPG rounds from IVO 41SPR686749. FF from Warrior fired back with platoon weapons and 30mm from grid 41SPR684750 to the INS FP. HG 51 engaged INS FP with 30mm before being RIP by a F18 (MT). CAS remains overhead and intends to engage with 500lb. At 1128D* CAS has engaged the INS RPG FP with 2 x GBU38. The 1st dropped short (No CD) and the second a DH onto the INS position at GR 41SP6861274913. At 1158D*, Ref update 1128D* 2x GBU 38 were fired resulting in 1x GBU 38 dropped in the wadi (No collateral damage), 1 x GBU 38 dropped on INS FP. INS FP neutralized, compound destroyed, ICOM has gone quite. The neutralisation of the INS RPG team enabling the FF patrol to extract from the area.
***Event closed at 1336D*1 Killed in Action british (citizen)(GBR) NATO/ISAF

Reference ID: AFG20090316n1704 Region: RC SOUTH
Latitude: 32.71136475 Longitude: 65.89644623
Date: 2009-03-16 06:06 Type: Enemy Action
Category: Direct Fire Affiliation: Enemy
Detained: 0

	Enemy	Friend	Civilian	Host Nation
Killed in Action	0	1	0	0
Wounded in Action	0	0	0	0

ISAF # 03-0857
MRTF CONDUCTING A FRAMWORK PATROL
S-UNK
A-SAF
L-F-41S QS 71500 23200
   E-41S QS 71500 23000
T-0459Z/0929D
A-URUZGAN
INS ENGAGED WITH SAF RESULTING IN 1 x CASUALTY AUS CAT B NO FURTHER INFO ATT
0540Z MM(S)03-16B
1X AUS WIA
GSW LEFT SIDE OF HEAD RECOMEND TAKE PATIENT TO TF NLD R2E
CONFIREMED 1 xAUS DOW
1400Z EVENT CLOSED

Reference ID: AFG20090406n1871 Region: RC SOUTH
Latitude: 32.60563278 Longitude: 65.87567139
Date: 2009-04-06 13:01 Type: Enemy Action
Category: Indrect Fire Affiliation: Enemy
Detained: 0

	Enemy	Friend	Civilian	Host Nation
Killed in Action	0	1	0	0
Wounded in Action	0	5	0	1

AUS MRTF reported that INS fired 1 x 107mm rocket at FOB RIPLEY, POO 41S QS 695 202. Several casualties, BDA to follow.
UPDATE 1931D*
INS fired 2 x further 107mm rockets at FOB RIPLEY. FF searching the area ATT.
UPDATE ON CASUALTIES 2114D*
see personnel details.
UPDATE 2129D*
No further INS activity observed.
***Event closed at 2133D*5 Wounded in Action, Category B dutch(NLD) NATO/ISAF
1 Wounded in Action, Category C None(None) National Military/Security Force
1 Killed in Action dutch(NLD) NATO/ISAF

Reference ID: AFG20090408n1792
Latitude: 32.41867447
Date: 2009-04-08 02:02
Category: Direct Fire
Detained: 0
Region: RC SOUTH
Longitude: 64.47402954
Type: Enemy Action
Affiliation: Enemy

	Enemy	Friend	Civilian	Host Nation
Killed in Action	0	1	0	0
Wounded in Action	0	1	0	0

S- LIMA COMPANY 2ND PLT 3RD SQUAD- SAF
A-LIMA 2-3 AND RECON TEAM 3 WERE ESTABLISHING AN OP IN VICINITY OF PURPLE 10 AND 12 WHEN THEY TOOK SAF FROM 100 METERS SOUTH OF PURPLE 17.
L-41S PR 386 878
T-080647DAPR09
A-UNIT RETURNED FIRE AND DECLARED TIC. SUSTAINED ONE FRIENDLY KIA.
L CO 3/8 USMC CONDUCTING A FRAMEWORK PATROL.
INS ENGAGED WITH SAF. FF REQUESTED HIMARS STRIKE.
UPD1-0801D
FF WERE ESTABLISHING AN OP IVO PURPLE 10 NAD 12 WHEN INS ENGAGED 100M S OF PURPLE 17. FF RETURNED FIRE WITH SAF. AS A RESULT OF THE ENGAGEMENT FF SUFFERED 1 x USA KIA CASUALTY.
9 LINER RECIEVED FOR GSW.
1 WIA CAT E (USA) CONFIRMED.
MISSION CANCELLED 0758D.
1 VSA ISAF (USA) CONFIRMED.
THIS INCEDENT CLOSED AT 758D

Reference ID: AFG20090529n1711
Latitude: 35.58096313
Date: 2009-05-29 03:03
Region: RC WEST
Longitude: 63.32074356
Type: Enemy Action

Category: Indirect Fire   Affiliation: Enemy
Detained: 0

	Enemy	Friend	Civilian	Host Nation
Killed in Action	20	0	1	11
Wounded in Action	10	3	1	5

TF NORTH and ANA Forces reported while conducting a clearing ops IAW OP MURGHAB, they were engaged by INS with SAF and FOB COLUMBUS and ANA BALA MURGHAB DC were attacked by INS with mortars. A CAS mission is going on to provide ground troops safety. First BDA report 1 ANA WIA (CAT UNK). At 0738D*, TFN is providing self defence using mortars against taliban positions.
UPDATE 1026D*
The clearing up operation is still ongoing. Casualties to be evacuated to QIN. See BDA.

UPDATE 1726D*
All WIA evacuated to CAMP ARENA Role 2 in HERAT. TF North is in FOB COLUMBUS. We are waiting the last BDA Updated.
Change of Title from INSURGENT ATTACK ---> OFFENSIVE ENGAGEMENT
UPDATE 302115D*
BDE update. See personnel details.
UPDATE 310945D*
RC(W) re-witten the story of whole event as follow:
During the execution of Op. Mourghab phase II, on 290730D*MAY09, ANA forces moving toward blocking positions in BM area has been engaged by INS with SAF, RPG and mortars fire. TFN personnel, while securing flanks and rear of ANA formation, has been attacked by INS from different fire sources south of BM area. As a target acquisition detachment, deployed in OP SOUTH, spotted two different INS fire sources, FF mortar fire has been led and INS were neutralized. CAS performed show the force from 290740D*MAY09 to 291006D*MAY09. On 291100D*MAY09 the engagement was over and FF reached predetermined reinforce position in BM. On 310945D*MAY09 TF North in Bala Murghab reported that local people leaved in front of the main gate of FOB COLUMBUS 1 body of a died ANA member. new current ANA KIA number confirmed is 11.
UPDATE 011435D*JUN09
BDE updated with 3 x ANA MIA.
UPDATE 051240D*JUN09
NFI AVAILABLE ATT.
***Event closed at 051240D*JUN20095 Killed None(None) Insurgent
9 Missing in Action None(None) National Military/Security Force
1 Wounded, Category B None(None) Local Civilian
1 Killed None(None) Local Civilian
3 Wounded in Action, Category B afghan(AFG) National Military/Security Force
11 Killed in Action afghan(AFG) National Military/Security Force
2 Wounded in Action, Category C italian(ITA) NATO/ISAF
2 Wounded in Action, Category C afghan(AFG) National Military/Security Force
1 Wounded in Action, Category D italian(ITA) NATO/ISAF
20 Killed None(None) Insurgent
10 Wounded None(None) Insurgent
3 Missing in Action afghan(AFG) National Military/Security Force

Reference ID: AFG20090603n1808
Longitude: 64.63587952
Type: Enemy Action
Affiliation: Enemy
Detained: 0
Latitude: 31.836689
Date: 2009-06-03 03:03
Category: Direct Fire

	Enemy	Friend	Civilian	Host Nation
Killed in Action	0	0	0	6
Wounded in Action	0	0	0	0

At 1808Z, RC South reported an IED strike:
FF reported ANP allowed an UNK individual to stay overnight at the CP. When ANP deployed to GSK Bazaar, the UNK individual shot and killed 4x ANP with an AK-47 and escaped with the weapon. There was no ISAF assistance required. At 0630Z, the Commander of AAB Pashak ANP CP was driving to Power Dam CP to investigate the incident and struck an IED killing him and his driver. Total BDA: 6x ANP KIA. NFTR. Event closed at 1845Z.
ISAF # 06-0221

Reference ID: AFG20090623n1839
Latitude: 36.63774872
Date: 2009-06-23 09:09
Category: Attack
Detained: 0
Region: RC NORTH
Longitude: 68.84004211
Type: Enemy Action
Affiliation: Enemy

	Enemy	Friend	Civilian	Host Nation
Killed in Action	0	3	0	0
Wounded in Action	0	0	0	0

RC North reported a IED Strike with SAF. FF reported German troops came under attack by unknown number of INS. 1x FOX vehicle flipped into river as a result of IED Strike. FF reported that the attack was an IED followed by SAF. TIC resulted in casualties. BDA: 3 X ISAF/NATO (DEU) KIA (1 X DROWNED), 3 X INS KIA (UNCONFIRMED). At 1245Z, vehicle recovery is ongoing.
ISAF # 06-1777
Final Summary
PRT KDZ reported that INF PLT E reported about an attack with RPG and SAF at 42SVF859546 IVO LOC LITTLE PLUTO. PROTECTION COY PRT KDZ was executing an IED sweep and observation with INF PLT A, INF PLT C, INF PLT D and INF PLT E, RECCE SQD, EOD, EW and MEDICAL FORCES. INF PLT E returned fire immediately without noticing effect on target. No own casualties and damages. At 1204D* MINIMIZE was activated. At 1219D* CAS showed of force. At 1224D* INF PLT C and INF PLT D withdrew under observation of INF PLT A and INF PLT E into NW direction via WESTPLATEAU. At 1238D* INF PLT E reported about an accident of tactical FOX vehicle at 42SVF 857 547 during withdrawing. Probably own casualties. At 1240D* Medical troops initiated first aid. At 1304D* IRF with recovery forces left PRT to the place of accident. At 1308D* COM PROT COY reported SAF IVO place of accident from eastern direction. At 1320D* Two wounded soldiers from crew of accident FOX were still treated by medic. One soldier was still encircled in vehicle. At 1348D* Two soldiers from FOX crew died, one soldier was still encircled in vehicle. At 1420D* IRF with recovery forces were on scene. At 1547D* Encircled soldier from FOX crew died. At 1500D* INF PLT D and INF PLT E were back at PRT.

Three soldiers got shock status. Immediate treatment by MTF. Recovery was ongoing. No enemy contact was at that moment. At 1510D* Report from COM PROT COY: Approximately one additional hour necessary for recovery. At 1555D* COM PROT COY reported one additional hour necessary for recovery. At 1606D* ANA QRF PLT was having for reinforcement along LOC KAMINS between points J93 and X04 in contact with COM INF PLT at PHQ CHAHAR DARA.
UPDATE 1645D*
ANA QRF PLT established observation position along LOC KAMINS between J93 and X04 for further movement of own forces back to PRT KDZ. At 1702D* Damaged FOX vehicle was recovered out of little river at place of accident by crane. At 1731D* Recovery was still ongoing. Positions of own forces were unchanged.
UPDATE 1802D*
Report from COM PROT COY: Recovery finished and they were ready for movement. At 1825D* Due to initial reports of PLT leaders who already returned at PRT: 3x INS probably killed. UAV LUNA was still on scene for observation of movements from own forces.
UPDATE 1830D*
UAV LUNA still on scene for observation of own forces movements. At 1920D* Position PLT PROT COY at OP LEBACH (42S VF 825 569). At 1925D* ANA QRF PLT withdrew because of because of increasing darkness. At 1959D* RECCE SQD A2 received SAF from eastern direction. INS (number UNK) withdrew into eastern direction. UNK effect on target. NFI.
UPDATE 2128D*
ASOC reported CAS IG KINETIC//IG 1777//HG61// 1xWP (warning shot)// 42S VF 80064 61510
UPDATE 2226D*
At 2001D* RECCE SQD A2 reported place of mentioned fire struggle: OP LEBACH (VF825 569), RECCE SQD A2 returned fire immediately. Effect on target UNK. At 2052D* PROTECTION COY and IRF started to march back to PRT KDZ. At 2140D* PROTECTION COY and IRF arrived in PRT KDZ. INF COY (INF PLT H, INF PLT G, RECCE SQD A3) was in PHQ CHAHAR DARA to stay over night and to march back to PRT KDZ on 24th. NFI.3 Killed in Action german(DEU) NATO/ISAF
3 Killed None(None) Insurgent
End Duplicate report Summary

Reference ID: AFG20090702n1898
Latitude: 30.91064072
Date: 2009-07-02 08:08
Category: Direct Fire
Detained: 0

Region: RC SOUTH
Longitude: 64.13737488
Type: Enemy Action
Affiliation: Enemy

	Enemy	Friend	Civilian	Host Nation
Killed in Action	0	1	0	0
Wounded in Action	0	0	0	0

E COY 2/8 USMC reported while conducting a NFO, INS engaged with SAF. FF responded with SAF. FF have requested air support.
UPDATE 1844D*
INS still engaging with sporadic fire.
UPDATE 1915D*

As a result of the first engagement FF suffered 1 x USA WIA (CAT A) who was MEDEVACED IAW MM(S)07-02S to DWYER STP, but later DOW.
UPDATE 2101D*
Contact ceased. NFTR. BDA: 1 x USA DOW.
***Event closed at 2103D*1 Died of Wounds american(USA) NATO/ISAF

Reference ID: AFG20090728n2156
Latitude: 34.78262711
Date: 2009-07-28 20:08
Category: Direct Fire
Detained: 0
Region: RC CAPITAL
Longitude: 69.89164734
Type: Enemy Action
Affiliation: Enemy

	Enemy	Friend	Civilian	Host Nation
Killed in Action	0	1	0	0
Wounded in Action	0	0	0	0

DELAYED REPORT
TF 10 reported while conducting a joint NFO, TF 10 with ANA (2/3/201) was engaged by 10-15x INS with DF resulting in 1x ISAF (USA) WIA (CAT A). Casualty was MEDEVACd to BAF where he later DOW. NFTR.
***Event closed at 1800D*1 Killed in Action american(USA) NATO/ISAF

Reference ID: AFG20090730n1934
Latitude: 30.98882866
Date: 2009-07-30 13:01
Category: Direct Fire
Detained: 0
Region: RC SOUTH
Longitude: 64.16976929
Type: Enemy Action
Affiliation: Enemy

	Enemy	Friend	Civilian	Host Nation
Killed in Action	0	2	0	0
Wounded in Action	0	0	0	0

WHEN: 30 1735D JULY 09
WHO: 4TH SQD, 2ND PLT
WHERE: 41R PQ 11690 28951
1.2KM FROM COP KOSTAY
WHAT: SAF/ URGENT MEDEVAC
EVENT: WHILE CONDUCTING A PATROL, GOLF 2/8 RECEIVED APPROXIMATELY (30) ROUNDS OF SAF FROM 2-4 ENEMY FIGHTERS RESULTING IN (2) CASUALTIES. GOLF 2/8 EGRESSED TO THE NORTH AND REQUESTED AN URGENT MEDEVAC FOR THE (2) CASUALTIES. (1) CASUALTY SUSTAINED A GSW TO THE FACE AND THE OTHER A GSW TO THE CHEST. THE CASUALTIES WERE TAKEN TO DWYER STP FOR TREATMENT. AT 1815D, GOLF 2/8 REPORTED NOT TAKING ANY ENEMY FIRE SINCE INITIAL CONTACT AND THAT ICOM CHATTER SUGGESTS POSSIBLE ENEMY FOLLOW ON ATTACK. AT 1832D, GOLF 2/8 REPORTED THE ENEMY FORCE IS MOVING WEST TOWARDS THE HELMAND RIVER FROM THEIR ORIGINAL FIRING POINT.
AT 1840D ONE OF THE WOUNDED MARINES DOW AT DWYER STP.
AT 2333D SECOND MARINE DOW AT BSN ROLE III.

BDA: (2) DOW
ISAF REF # 07-2699(CLOSED)
MEDEVAC# 07-30M (COMPLETE)

Reference ID: AFG20090814n2168   Region: RC SOUTH
Latitude: 31.60458565   Longitude: 65.70304871
Date: 2009-08-14 10:10   Type: Enemy Action
Category: Direct Fire   Affiliation: Enemy
Detained: 0

	Enemy	Friend	Civilian	Host Nation
Killed in Action	0	0	0	2
Wounded in Action	0	0	0	2

While an UN-MENTORED ANP unit were manning CP RORABAT, 2 x INS dressed in burqa's walked into CP RORABAT and started shooting ANP resulting in 2 x ANP KIA and 2 x ANP WIA.
UPDATE 0046D*
INS withdrew. Nothing further to report.
BDA: 2 x ANP KIA and 2 x ANP WIA.
***Event closed 0047D*2 Killed in Action afghan(AFG) ANP
2 Wounded in Action afghan(AFG) ANP

Reference ID: AFG20091120n2620   Region: RC SOUTH
Latitude: 31.49095345   Longitude: 65.84068298
Date: 2009-11-20 13:01   Type: Enemy Action
Category: Indirect Fire   Affiliation: Enemy
Detained: 0

	Enemy	Friend	Civilian	Host Nation
Killed in Action	0	0	0	0
Wounded in Action	0	4	0	0

JDOC reported a rocket attack. INS fired 1 x ROCKET at KAF. POO GR QQ 6848 9378, POI GR 41R QQ 6984 8751.
JDOC reported 2 x casualties
UDPATE 201408Z
4 x WIA (1 x CAT A, 3 x CAT UNK)
BDA: 4 x ISAF WIA (1 x CAT A, 3 x CAT UNK)

IEDs

By far, the favorite weapon of the Afghan insurgents is the improvised explosive device (IED). These take many forms; the CWIED ("Command Wired Improvised Explosive Device") consists of a bomb that is hard-wired to a switch by an electrical line that runs some distance away from the buried bomb to an operator, who manually pushes the switch to detonate the bomb when the convoy or troop unit is passing. The PBIED ("Pedestrian-Borne Improvised Explosive Device") is a suicide bomber who wears a vest that is fitted with explosives and a switch. The bomber runs into a crowded area and sets off the device, blowing himself up as well as everyone around him. The RCIED ("Radio-Controlled Improvised Explosive Device"), consists of a buried bomb that is fitted with a wireless signal receiver, often made from a cellphone but also sometimes a doorbell receiver or garage-door opener, that is attached to the bomb's blasting cap. An operator standing nearby presses a switch to send a signal to the bomb's receiver and set it off. The SVBIED ("Suicide Vehicle-Borne Improvised Explosive Device") is a car bomb that is driven into its target by a driver, who is then killed in the explosion. There are indications in some reports that at least some suicide-bomb drivers were recruited by the insurgents simply to drive a car along a certain route, without knowing that they carried a bomb. The VOIED ("Vehicle-Operated Improvised Explosive Device") is a buried bomb that is set off by a pressure plate when a vehicle drives over it.

A variety of tactics can utilize IEDs. Pressure-detonated devices are simply buried in a likely spot, where they hit the first random vehicle that runs over them. Command-detonated devices, whether radio-controlled or command-wire, can be specifically aimed at a particular target, exploding only when it comes into range. Some reports indicate the use of booby traps—in one case, a hidden bomb was deliberately left behind in an abandoned insurgent position, to be detonated when American forces entered. In other instances, bombs are set off to disable the lead vehicle of a convoy to block the road and thereby allow insurgents to ambush the other vehicles with gunfire and RPGs. The insurgents are also reported to set off an IED and then later trigger a second nearby bomb to attack any US units that respond to the first explosion. Bombs can also be used to attack buildings such as police stations or schools. Suicide IEDs in effect function as a "poor man's smart bomb"—they can be aimed at specific targets with pinpoint accuracy. Such targets have even been attacked inside major American bases, like Bagram Airfield. Many of the reported roadside bomb attacks seem to be targeted at specific individuals, indicating that the insurgents have an efficient intelligence network that allows them to reliably track the movements of people they consider as targets.

IED attacks allow the insurgents to inflict casualties on American forces without exposing their own forces to attack. With the use of only a handful of insurgents, the guerrillas can inflict heavy damage on US convoys or troops. According to the reports, children as young as 11 or 14 have been used as partners in IED attacks.

IED attacks have probably been the single largest cause of American casualties in Afghanistan.

Reference ID: AFG20040104n4
Latitude: 31
Date: 2004-01-04 00:12
Category: IED EXPLOSION
Detained: 0

Region: RC SOUTH
Longitude: 65.74999237
Type: Explosive Hazard
Affiliation: ENEMY

	Enemy	Friend	Civilian	Host Nation
Killed in Action	0	0	0	0
Wounded in Action	0	0	0	0

04 JAN: AT LEAST 15 DEAD IN TRUCK BOMB ATTACK IN KANDAHAR, AF. REPORT OVER VIDEO.

Reference ID: AFG20040217n7
Latitude: 33.32471085
Date: 2004-02-17 00:12
Category: IED EXPLOSION
Detained: 0

Region: RC EAST
Longitude: 69.98805237
Type: Explosive Hazard
Affiliation: ENEMY

	Enemy	Friend	Civilian	Host Nation
Killed in Action	0	0	0	0
Wounded in Action	0	0	0	0

(S//REL GCTF) RCIED ATTACK ON US FORCES IN KHOWST: ON 16 FEB 04 AT 0428Z, A RCIED EXPLODED AS US CONVOY PASSED IVO 331929N 0695917E. SEARCH OF THE AREA REVEALED THAT THE RCIED WAS PLACED IN A ONE AND A HALF FOOT DEEP DITCH. THE DITCH TOOK MOST OF THE BLAST. APACHE ELEMENT OBSERVED ONE PERSON RUNNING INTO A VILLAGE AFTER THE EXPLOSION, INDIVIDUAL EVADED THE APACHE ELEMENT. THERE WAS NO DAMAGE OR INJURIES TO US EQUIPMENT OR PERSONNEL.

Reference ID: AFG20040422n12
Latitude: 30.98055077
Date: 2004-04-22 00:12
Category: IED EXPLOSION
Detained: 0

Region: RC SOUTH
Longitude: 66.18055725
Type: Explosive Hazard
Affiliation: ENEMY

	Enemy	Friend	Civilian	Host Nation
Killed in Action	0	0	1	0
Wounded in Action	0	0	1	0

THREE IEDS EXPLODED WITHIN 20 HOURS DURING 21-22 APRIL. ON 21 APRIL, A TIME-DELAY IED ATTACHED TO A MOTORBIKE EXPLODED IN THE COMPOUND OF THE DISTRICT COMMISSIONERS OFFICE IN SPIN BOLDAK DURING A MEETING AT WHICH GOVERNOR PASHTUN OF KANDAHAR, THE DIRECTOR GENERAL OF CUSTOMS, THE DEPUTY MINISTER OF FINANCE, AND THE DISTRICT COMMISSIONER WERE PRESENT. ONE CIVILIAN WAS KILLED AND ONE INJURED.

Reference ID: AFG20040425n19
Latitude: 32.25777817
Date: 2004-04-25 11:11
Category: IED EXPLOSION
Detained: 0

Region: RC SOUTH
Longitude: 65.73750305
Type: Explosive Hazard
Affiliation: ENEMY

	Enemy	Friend	Civilian	Host Nation
Killed in Action	0	0	0	0
Wounded in Action	0	3	0	0

(S) SUMMARY OF 24 APRIL ATTACK ON TF LINEBACKER CONVOY: AT APPROX 241130Z 3-5 ACM ENGAGED A LINEBACKER CONVOY VIC OF THE PASS SOUTH OF DAYLANOR (41SQR579723) RESULTING IN 3 X MARINE WIA WHO WERE SUBSEQUENTLY CASEVAC'D TO KANDAHAR AIRFIELD (KAF). THE AMBUSH WAS INITIATED USING AN IED, WHICH DESTROYED 1X MTVR (7 TON TRUCK). AN EOD MARINE ASSESSED THE IED WAS REMOTELY DETONATED WITH A "SPIDER" INITIATING DEVICE. SMALL ARMS FIRE AND

POSSIBLY AN RPG WERE ALSO USED IN THE AMBUSH. THE ACMS THEN WITHDREW INTO THE SURROUNDING TERRAIN (NFI). LINEBACKER FORCES HAVE FREQUENTED THIS ROUTE DURING THE LAST SEVERAL DAYS. THE CONVOY ENGAGED TODAY WAS SMALLER (4 X IFAVS, 1X HMMWV, 1X MTVR) THAN MOST LINEBACKER CONVOYS THAT HAVE TRAVELED THE PASS, AND WAS LIKELY TARGETED AS A RESULT. OF NOTE, THE AMBUSH DID NOT OCCUR IN THE HEART OF THE PASS, BUT AT THE SOUTHERN ENTRANCE WHERE ACM ELEMENTS WOULD BE AFFORDED A GREATER OPPORTUNITIES TO WITHDRAW. ACM ELEMENTS WILL CONTINUE ATTEMPTS TO INTERDICT LINEBACKER LOCS.

Reference ID: AFG20040529n15
Latitude: 32.0886116
Date: 2004-05-29 11:11
Category: IED EXPLOSION
Detained: 0
Region: RC SOUTH
Longitude: 67.24276733
Type: Explosive Hazard
Affiliation: ENEMY

	Enemy	Friend	Civilian	Host Nation
Killed in Action	0	4	0	0
Wounded in Action	0	0	0	0

CJSOTF REPORTS MINE ATTACK 32K EAST OF QALAT, 4X US SOLDIERS INJURED. MEDEVAC 32K EAST OF QALAT, FOR 4X US MILITARY WHOSE VEHICLE STRUCK AN IED. LINE 1: 42S UA 34176 51624, LINE 2: 345540 FOX 11, LINE 3: 1A, LINE 4:A, LINE 5: 3 AMBULATORY, LINE 6: P, LINE 7: AC, LINE 8: A, LINE 9: N/A. 1147Z CJTF76 APPROVES THE MEDEVAC. MEDEVAC WU AT 1205Z. 1210Z UPDATE, LINE 5: 4L. MEDEVAC WU AT 1205Z. W/D AT 1341Z. UPDATE: ALL 4X US SOLDIERS NOW REPORTED KIA.

Reference ID: AFG20040614n26
Latitude: 33.59917068
Date: 2004-06-14 07:07
Category: IED Explosion
Detained: 0
Region: RC EAST
Longitude: 69.22055817
Type: Explosive Hazard
Affiliation: ENEMY

	Enemy	Friend	Civilian	Host nation
Killed in action	0	0	0	0
Wounded in action	0	0	0	0

14 JUNE- GARDEZ , CITY HIGH SCHOOL WHICH HAS BEEN OPERATING AS A MALE REGISTRATION SITE HAD AN IED PLACED AT THE DOOR OF THE SCHOOL WHICH EXPLODED AT 0715. REGISTRATION WAS DUE TO RECOMMENCE AT 0800HRS. NO INJURIES DAMAGE TO WINDOWS AND DOORS. (VOTER REGISTRATION, ELECTION, NGO) 333557N 691314E VOTER

Reference ID: AFG20040616n34
Latitude: 36.71665955
Date: 2004-06-16 05:05
Region: RC NORTH
Longitude: 68.8666687
Type: Explosive hazard

Category: IED Explosion Affiliation: ENEMY
Detained: 0

	Enemy	Friend	Civilian	Host nation
Killed in action	0	0	4	0
Wounded in action	0	0	1	0

ALONG THE A-ROUTE FROM THE PRT CAMP TO THE AIRPORT NEAR THE MEAT MARKET (BESIDE THE SPINZA FACTORY) AN IED (PROBABLY REMOTE CONTROL) EXPLODED AT 0935L (0505Z). A TOTAL OF 4X LNS (2X SCHOOL CHILDREN, 1X OLD MAN AND THE DRIVER) DIED AND ONE OTHER SCHOOL KID WAS INJURED.

Reference ID: AFG20040711n36 Region: RC WEST
Latitude: 34.30028152 Longitude: 62.42028046
Date: 2004-07-11 05:05 Type: Explosive Hazard
Category: IED Explosion Affiliation: ENEMY
Detained: 0

	Enemy	Friend	Civilian	Host nation
Killed in action	0	0	5	0
Wounded in action	0	0	32	0

TF PHOENIX REPORTS VEHICLE BORNE IED IN DOWNTOWN HERAT. AT 0633Z THE FOLLOWING SALUTE REPORT WAS SENT: SALUTE (WOLVERINE TOC IN HERAT), S - 1 VBIED (MOTORCYCLE), A - DETONATED KILLING 2 X LN AND INJURING SEVERAL OTHERS, L - DOWNTOWN HERAT, U UNKNOWN, T - 0500Z, E - 1 X MOTORCYCLE AND UNKNOWN EXPLOSIVES. UPDATE 1505Z: 5X LN KILLED, 32X LN WOUNDED. VEHICLE WAS ACTUALLY BICYCLE, NOT MOTORCYCLE AS PREVIOUSLY REPORTED. NFI.

Reference ID: AFG20040718n37 Region: RC EAST
Latitude: 34.340271 Longitude: 68.31777191
Date: 2004-07-18 08:08 Type: Explosive Hazard
Category: IED Explosion Affiliation: ENEMY
Detained: 0

	Enemy	Friend	Civilian	Host nation
Killed in action	0	0	0	0
Wounded in action	0	0	0	0

(S//REL TO USA/GCTF/ISAF) AT APPROXIMATELY 0828 HOURS LOCAL, 18 JULY 2004, A REMOTE CONTROLLED IMPROVISED EXPLOSIVE DEVICE (RCIED) EXPLODED ON THE RING ROAD AT KILOMETER MARKER 98 IN WARDAK PROVINCE. THE RCIED WAS DETONATED BY CELLULAR TELEPHONE. UNITED STATES PROTECTION AND INVESTIGATION (USPI) FORCES WERE WORKING IN THE AREA AND RECOVERED THE CELLULAR TELEPHONE THAT WAS USED TO DETONATE THE DEVICE. THE TARGET OF THE ATTACK WAS AFGHAN NATIONAL ARMY (ANA) SOLDIERS THAT WERE PASSING BY THE AREA. THE ANA SOLDIERS STOPPED AND SEARCHED FOR THE RESPONSIBLE PARTY BUT WERE UNSUCCESSFUL. THE EXPLOSION LEFT A THREE-METER IN DIAMETER HOLE, BUT THE FORCE OF THE BLAST WAS

CENTERED OFF THE ROAD AND THERE WERE NO INJURIES. UPON INSPECTION OF THE AREA, THE USPI FORCES SAW THAT A HOLE WAS DUG UNDER THE ROAD IN WHICH THE RCIED WAS PLACED.

Reference ID: AFG20040720n28
Latitude: 32.37694168
Date: 2004-07-20 12:12
Category: IED Explosion
Detained: 0

Region: RC WEST
Longitude: 62.11944962
Type: Explosive Hazard
Affiliation: ENEMY

	Enemy	Friend	Civilian	Host nation
Killed in action	0	0	0	0
Wounded in action	0	0	0	0

(S//REL TO USA/ISAF) AT APPROXIMATELY 0500 HOURS LOCAL, 20 JULY 2004, AN EXPLOSION OCCURRED AT THE FARAH TELEVISION AND RADIO STATION, FARAH CITY, //GEOCOORD:322237N/620710E//, FARAH PROVINCE, AF. THE SINGLE-STORY BUILDING IS APPROXIMATELY ONE KILOMETER WEST OF THE UNITED NATIONS (UN) COMPOUND. DAMAGE OCCURRED TO FIVE GENERATORS AND A LARGE ROOM ON THE BUILDING'S NORTH FACE. A FIVE-METER DIAMETER HOLE WAS BLOWN IN THE ROOF ABOVE THE GENERATORS. INTERIOR AND EXTERIOR DOORS WERE BLOWN OFF THEIR FRAMES AND SPLINTERED. THE BUILDING HAD A GUARD FORCE OF SIX PERSONNEL WHO REPORTED INJURIES BUT DID NOT NOTICE ANYTHING SUSPICIOUS BEFORE THE EXPLOSION. THE DAMAGE SUGGESTED THAT A DEVICE WITH A TIMER HAD BEEN PLACED AT THE LOCATION. THE DAMAGE WAS DETERMINED TO NOT BE THE RESULT OF A ROCKET PROPELLED GRENADE OR MORTAR ATTACK.
(S//REL TO USA/ISAF) THE NEW CHIEF OF POLICE HAS MADE EFFECTIVE USE OF THE TELEVISION STATION SINCE HIS ARRIVAL TO COMMUNICATE HIS ACTIVITIES AND INTENTIONS TO THE PEOPLE IN FARAH CITY, AF.
(S//REL TO USA/ISAF) THERE HAVE BEEN RUMORS, ORIGINATING FROM THE BAZAAR, OF A DESIRE TO PERSUADE SOMEONE WITH ACCESS TO THE UN COMPOUND TO DELIVER AN EXPLOSIVE DEVICE THERE.

Reference ID: AFG20040818n44
Latitude: 32.93611145
Date: 2004-08-18 22:10
Category: IED Explosion
Detained: 0

Region: RC SOUTH
Longitude: 66.6847229
Type: Explosive Hazard
Affiliation: ENEMY

	Enemy	Friend	Civilian	Host nation
Killed in action	0	0	0	0
Wounded in action	0	0	0	0

PART 1 OF 2 REPORTS (SECRET//REL GCTF) A CO REPORTS THAT LAST NIGHT (18 AUG) AT 2215 AND 2220 2 IEDS EXPLODED AT GRIDS 42STB 8354 4659 AND 42STB 7953 4916. ALPHA COMPANY SENT A PATROL OUT TO INVESTIGATE THE SITE AND FOUND A MOTORCYCLE BATTERY AND BOOSTER BUT NO REMNANTS FROM THE BLAST. THE BLAST HOLE WAS 4 FEET IN DIAMETER AND 1 FOOT DEEP. THE SECOND BLAST REPORT CAME IN

AT 0700 THIS MORNING AND THEY ARE ASSESSING RIGHT NOW. PATROL SEARCHED THREE COMPOUNDS THAT MOHAMMED SHAW LED THEM TO. MOHAMMAD SHAW WAS A VICTIM OF THE 16TH AUGUST KIDNAPPING. HE LED THE PATROL TO 3 COMPOUNDS IN KOCAK. THEY FOUND A DISASSEMBLED WALKMAN/TAPE RECORDER. 3 LIGHT BALLASTS AND WIRE. LIGHT BALLASTS ARE NOT THE SAME THAT WERE USED IN THE IEDS BUT STILL VERY SUSPICIOUS.

Reference ID: AFG20041015n57
Latitude: 34.90304947
Date: 2004-10-15 00:12
Category: IED Explosion
Detained: 0
Region: RC EAST
Longitude: 71.23557281
Type: Explosive Hazard
Affiliation: ENEMY

	Enemy	Friend	Civilian	Host nation
Killed in action	0	0	5	0
Wounded in action	0	0	0	0

A REMOTE-CONTROLLED BOMB EXPLODED NEAR A TRUCK SUPPLYING FOOD TO US BASES IN AN AREA ABOUT 125 KILOMETERS (80 MILES) EAST OF THE CAPITAL KABUL. THE ATTACK CAME DAYS AFTER AFGHANISTAN'S LANDMARK PRESIDENTIAL POLL WENT AHEAD PEACEFULLY DESPITE VOWS BY LOYALISTS OF THE OUSTED HARDLINE ISLAMIC TALIBAN TO DISRUPT THE VOTE.

Reference ID: AFG20041030n45
Latitude: 31.5574894
Date: 2004-10-30 04:04
Category: IED Explosion
Detained: 0
Region: RC SOUTH
Longitude: 66.94917297
Type: Explosive Hazard
Affiliation: ENEMY

	Enemy	Friend	Civilian	Host nation
Killed in action	0	0	0	0
Wounded in action	0	0	0	0

(S) JSOTF-AFGCUROPS-1 (2) (05:58:18): SALT REPORT FROM TG ARES FOLLOWS: SIZE -1 CONSTRUCTION AND INITIATION UKNOWN. ACTIVITY -PARTIAL OR LOW ORDER DETONATION. LOCATION - 42R UV 05366 93218. TIME - 30446ZOCT04. ADDITIONAL INFO:NO COALITION VEHICLES OR PAX DAMAGED. CURRENTLY SECURING THE AREA FOR ASSESSMENT. HAVE PHOTOGRAPHED THE SCENE. AFTER IT IS DETERMINED NO MORE IED IN THE VICINITY. THIS IED STRIKE WAS FOCUSED AGAINST FRENCH SOF FORCES OF TG ARES.

Reference ID: AFG20041116n57
Latitude: 34.63360977
Date: 2004-11-16 00:12
Category: IED Explosion
Detained: 0
Region: RC CAPITAL
Longitude: 69.71749878
Type: Explosive Hazard
Affiliation: ENEMY

	Enemy	Friend	Civilian	Host nation
Killed in action	0	0	0	0
Wounded in action	0	0	0	0

(S//REL GCTF) SOURCE: UNSECOORD SIZE: A MINE (TYPE UNKNOWN) ACTIVITY: WAS DETONATED LOCATION: INSIDE A NEWLY CONSTRUCTED GIRLS SCHOOL IN NAGHALO VILLAGE, KABUL PROVINCE (IVO 42S WD 6577 3266)TIME: 15 0001L NOVEMBER 04 REMARKS: THE EXTENT OF THE DAMAGES IS NOT KNOWN AT THIS TIME.
THE SCHOOL WAS TO BE INAUGURATED THIS WEEK.
ASSESSMENT: POSSIBLY PARTIALLY RESPONSIVE TO CJTF76 ENVIRONMENT CCIR 1 ON DISRUPTIONS OF RECONSTRUCTION AND DEVELOPMENT OPERATIONS.

Reference ID: AFG20041116n64
Latitude: 32.67139053
Date: 2004-11-16 10:10
Category: IED Explosion
Detained: 0
Region: RC SOUTH
Longitude: 65.48249817
Type: Explosive Hazard
Affiliation: ENEMY

	Enemy	Friend	Civilian	Host nation
Killed in action	0	0	0	4
Wounded in action	0	0	0	5

(S//REL GCTF) SOURCE: SAFETY ADVISOR FOR SOUTHERN REGION AFGHANISTAN NGO SECURITY OFFICE (ANSO)
SIZE: RCIED
ACTIVITY: EXPLODED, TARGETING PROVINCIAL CHIEF OF POLICE WHO WAS TRAVELING WITH 9 POLICEMEN
LOCATION: DEHRAWOOD DISTRICT, URUZGAN PROVINCE
TIME: 16 1300L NOV 04
REMARKS: 4 POLICE OFFICERS WERE KILLED AND ANOTHER 5 WOUNDED. THE ATTACK CLEARLY TARGETED THE CHIEF OF POLICE; MOTIVATIONS BEHIND THE INCIDENT ARE NOT KNOWN FOR THE MOMENT.

Reference ID: AFG20050107n89
Latitude: 33.34582901
Date: 2005-01-07 00:12
Category: IED Explosion
Detained: 0
Region: RC EAST
Longitude: 70.09028625
Type: Explosive Hazard
Affiliation: ENEMY

	Enemy	Friend	Civilian	Host nation
Killed in action	0	0	0	0
Wounded in action	0	0	0	0

(S//REL GCTF) EARLY TODAY AN IED BLEW UP A JINGA TRUCK IVO KARNUM ON THE EXACT ROUTE THAT A PRT VEHICLE TOOK EARLIER IN THE DAY. THE EXPLOSION HAPPENED DURING THE SAME TIME THE PRT VEHICLE WAS HEADING BACK TO CHAPMAN. IF THE VEHICLE HAD TAKEN THE SAME ROUTE THAT THEY HAD EARLIER IN THE DAY, THEY WOULD

HAVE BEEN INVOLVED IN THE EXPLOSION. INTELLIGENCE REPORT STIPULATES THAT THE TARGET HAD AN EXACT DESCRIPTION OF THE PRT VEHICLES IN THE CONVOY. NEED TO EMPHASIZE TO NOT ESTABLISH A PATTERN OF TRAVEL AND BE COGNOSCENTE OF ACTIONS EVEN WHEN TRAVELING ON REGULAR ROUTES BETWEEN DESTINATIONS. KEY TO THIS, IS TO DRIVE DETERRENCE AT BCPS WHERE WE CHOSE THE BATTLE SPACE, NOT IN THE INTERIOR OF THE KHWOST BOWL AND WE BECOME CASUALTIES AS A RESULT OF IEDS.

Reference ID: AFG20050203n57
Latitude: 31.7002697
Date: 2005-02-03 07:07
Category: IED Explosion
Detained: 0

Region: RC SOUTH
Longitude: 65.70639038
Type: Explosive Hazard
Affiliation: ENEMY

	Enemy	Friend	Civilian	Host nation
Killed in action	0	0	0	0
Wounded in action	0	0	0	0

(S//REL GCTF) EXPLOSION IVO 300TH ROMANIAN PATROL A: ROMANIANS HAVE LEFT SCENE, HHS PATROL IS BEING DIVERTED TO INVESTIGATE L: 41R QR 565 104 T: 03 0755Z FEB 05(S//REL GCTF) TF BRONCO 3-7 FA REPORTS RCIED EXPLOSION 9K N KANDAHAR. AT 0830Z THE FOLLOWING SALT REPORT WAS SENT: S- 1X RCIED, A- DETONATED, L- 41R QR 565 104, T- 0755Z. REMARKS: MINE DETONATED IVO COALITION PATROL. COALITION UNIT HAS DEPARTED SCENE AND 3-7 PATROL IS BEING DIVERTED TO INVESTIGATE ATT. UPDATE 1205Z: EOD RECOVERED SPIDER DEVICE FROM SITE AND DETERMINED IT WAS AN RCIED ANTI-TANK MINE. NO INJURIES OR DAMAGE TO EQUIPMENT. SPIDER DEVICE IS ENROUTE TO BAF ATT. NFI

Reference ID: AFG20050303n62
Latitude: 33.19361115
Date: 2005-03-03 00:12
Category: IED Explosion
Detained: 0

Region: RC EAST
Longitude: 69.26389313
Type: Explosive Hazard
Affiliation: ENEMY

	Enemy	Friend	Civilian	Host nation
Killed in action	0	0	0	0
Wounded in action	0	0	0	0

05 MAR 05: C/2-5 IN FORCES MET WITH ABDUL ALIME, THE INTERIM DISTRICT CHIEF IN CEHAR CINEH. ALIME REPORTED THAT THERE WAS AN IED THAT EXPLODED ON 03 MAR 05 NEAR YAKHDAN. HE SAID THAT THE IED EXPLODED BEFORE ANY VEHICLES CAME CLOSE TO IT. ALIME STATED THAT THE IED WAS ON THE ROAD JUST NORTH OF THE BRIDGE IN REGAK (41S QS 3449). THE EXACT LOCATION OF THE IED WAS UNCLEAR, BUT IT APPEARED THAT IT WAS ALONG THE ROAD ON THE WESTERN SIDE OF THE RIVER BETWEEN REGAK AND THE TOP OF THE WISHBONE. ALIME SAID THAT HE WAS PLANNING ON GATHERING ALL THE ELDERS TOGETHER FROM YAKHDAN AND TELLING THEM THAT THEY NEED TO REPORT ON THE INDIVIDUALS THAT ARE RESPONSIBLE FOR THE RECENT IEDS. ALIME

AND COBRA 6 TALKED ABOUT THE LACK OF ELDERS COMING FORWARD WITH INFORMATION IN CEHAR CINEH AND HOW C/2-5 IN FORCES CAN IMPROVE ON THE INFORMATION FLOW AND SECURITY SITUATION IF ELDERS COME FORWARD (COBRA REPORTING).

Reference ID: AFG20050322n72
Latitude: 31.69750023
Date: 2005-03-22 10:10
Category: IED Explosion
Detained: 0

Region: RC SOUTH
Longitude: 65.70388794
Type: Explosive Hazard
Affiliation: ENEMY

	Enemy	Friend	Civilian	Host nation
Killed in action	0	0	0	0
Wounded in action	0	1	0	0

POSSIBLE AT BLAST LANDMINE CONFIGURED WITH A MOD 1 SPIDER DEVICE AND 6 D-CELL BATTERIES
TF BRONCO REPORTS IED STRIKE 9K N OF KANDAHAR. THE FOLLOWING SALT REPORT WAS SENT: S: 1X IED, A: IED STRIKE, L: 41R QR 563 101, T: 1040Z. REMARKS: 1X HMMWV DAMAGED (UNDRIVEABLE) NO CASUALTIES OR INJURIES. TF STEEL IS STANDING UP IRF WITH EOD SENDING THEM TO THAT LOCATION SITE IS SECURE. AT 1358Z EOD ARRIVES AT IED SITE TO CONDUCT SSE.
ONE OF THE VEHICLES IN THE CONVOY HAD AN ECM DEVICE.
RECOVERED FROM SITE:
(1) MOD 1 SPIDER DEVICE WITH THE FOLLOWING NUMBER WRITTEN ON THE TOP. (159.160 2 8 0).
(1) BLACK CASE BATTERY PACK CONTAINING SIX (6) D-CELL 1.5 VOLT BATTERIES.
(2) RED LEAD WIRES APPROXIMATELY THREE (3) FEET IN LENGTH EACH.
APPROXIMATELY TWENTY-FIVE (25) FEET OF WHITE DOUBLE STRAND ELECTRICAL WIRE.
ON 22 MAR 05, AT APPROXIMATELY 1046Z, TF BRONCO REPORTED AN IED STRIKE ON U.S. CONVOY APPROXIMATELY 9 KM NORTH OF KANDAHAR. THE LEAD VEHICLE, AN UP-ARMORED HUMMWV, WAS STRUCK BY THE BLAST AND SUSTAINED MODERATE DAMAGED. THE EXPLOSIVE CHARGE, LIKELY AN AT MINE, HAD BEEN BURIED IN THE MIDDLE OF THE ROAD AND DETONATED JUST IN FRONT OF THE VEHICLE. LOCATED OFF THE ROAD WAS THE POWER SOURCE AND DTMF MOD-1 RECEIVER, SPIDER DEVICE. NO CASUALTIES OR INJURIES WERE REPORTED. EOD EXPLOITED THE SITE AND TOOK PHOTOGRAPHS OF THE SCENE. EOD ALSO REPORTED ANOTHER IED STRIKE AT THIS SAME LOCATION ON 03 FEB 05, ALTHOUGH THE TM-62P2 AT MINE LOW ORDERED AS THE ROMANIAN CONVOY PASSED.

Reference ID: AFG20050328n75
Latitude: 31.59444046
Date: 2005-03-28 09:09
Category: IED Explosion
Detained: 0

Region: RC SOUTH
Longitude: 64.37499237
Type: Explosive Hazard
Affiliation: ENEMY

	Enemy	Friend	Civilian	Host nation
Killed in action	0	0	0	0
Wounded in action	0	0	3	0

AT 1310 HOURS LOCAL AFGHAN TIME, ON 28 FEBRUARY 2005, AN IMPROVISED EXPLOSIVE DEVICE (IED) EXPLODED OUTSIDE THE MAIN GATE OF THE INFORMATION AND CULTURAL CENTER IN LASHKAR GAH //GEOCOORD:313540N/0642230E//, LASHKAR GAH DISTRICT, AFGHANISTAN. A ONE BY ONE METER BOX OF ORANGES, CONTAINING THE IED, WAS PLACED UNDER A TRUCK PARKED IN FRONT OF THE MAIN GATE. WHEN THE IED EXPLODED, IT SERIOUSLY INJURIED ((MAZULLAH)), THE SON OF ABDUL ((RAHMAN)), AND SLIGHTLY INJURIED MAKMAD ((AWAIZ)) AND ((ASADULLAH)). MULLAH ((MAHMOOD)), THE GUARD FORCE COMMANDER, PARKED THE TRUCK EARLIER IN THE DAY AND THEN LEFT IN A DIFFERENT VEHICLE. THE HELMAND NATIONAL DIRECTORATE OF SECURITY DETAINED TWO SUSPECTS ASSOCIATED WITH THIS IED. THE POSSIBLE PURPOSE BEHIND THE ATTACK MAY HAVE BEEN TO KILL JAN ((GUL)), THE CHIEF OF THE INFORMATION AND CULTURE AND CENTER.

Reference ID: AFG20050329n60
Latitude: 32.96083832
Date: 2005-03-29 06:06
Category: IED Explosion
Detained: 0

Region: RC SOUTH
Longitude: 65.5147171
Type: Explosive Hazard
Affiliation: ENEMY

	Enemy	Friend	Civilian	Host nation
Killed in action	0	0	0	0
Wounded in action	0	2	0	0

S: 1X IED, A: IED STRIKE, AND SMALL ARMS AMBUSH, L: 41S QS 348 498, T: 0650Z. REMARKS: C/2-5 PATROL RETURNING FROM BCF 3H HAD UP-ARMORED HMMWV STRUCK BY IED. 2X US MILITARY PERSONNEL INJURED. AT 0926Z UP-ARMORED HMMWV STRUCK BY IED CAN NOT BE TOWED OR SLUNG. MECHANIC ON SITE ASSESS VEHICLE AS DETROYED. ALL COMMUNICATIONS, ECM, AND EQUIPMENT HAVE BEEN STRIPPED FROM VEHICLE. AT 0933Z C/2-5 CONTINUES TO SEARCH THE VILLAGE OF SAKHAR. 1X PERSON HAS BEEN DETAINED. HE WAS FOUND ATTEMPTING TO HIDE FROM SEARCH ELEMENTS. INDIVIDUAL IS NOT KNOWN TO BE CONNECTED TO IED IN ANY WAY AT THIS TIME.

THE UPDATED GRID LOCATION FOR YESTERDAYS IED ATTACK AGAINST C/2-5 IN FORCES IN VICINITY OF REGAK BRIDGE WAS AT 41S QS 35075 49769. PART OF THE C/2-5 IN CONVOY HAD CROSSED THE REGAK BRIDGE, AND THE VEHICLE THAT WAS STRUCK WAS THE FIRST ONE IN THE CONVOY AND WAS APPROXIMATELY 250 METERS PAST THE BRIDGE. INITIAL FEEDBACK FROM THE FBI IS THAT THE IED WAS DEFINITELY A REMOTE-CONTROLLED IED (RCIED) AND HAD A MOD-1 SPIDER DEVICE. THE IED WAS NOT ASSESSED TO HAVE BEEN A PROJECTILE ROUND DUE TO THE LACK OF SHRAPNEL ON THE SITE AND IT IS BEING ASSESSED TO HAVE BEEN AT LEAST 2X AT MINES DUE TO THE SIZE OF THE CRATER. THE CRATER WAS THREE FEET DEEP BY EIGHT FEET WIDE.

THE TARGETED VEHICLE, AN UP-ARMORED HMMWV WAS THE FIRST VEHICLE IN AN 11 VEHICLE CONVOY. THE CONVOY WAS TRAVELLING EAST ALONG THE HELMAND RIVER AND STOPPED BEFORE APPROACHING THE BRIDGE WHERE THE IED WAS BURIED. THERE HAD BEEN AN EARLIER IED AT THIS LOCATION, SO CONVOY PERSONNEL DISMOUNTED AND SEARCHED THE AREA. THE SEARCH FAILED TO LOCATE AN IED AND AS THE FIRST VEHICLE APPROACHED THE BRIDGE CROSSING THE IRRIGATION CANAL THE IED DETONATED CAUSING THE VEHICLE TO FLIP BACKWARDS.

Reference ID: AFG20050329n63
Latitude: 34.36832047
Date: 2005-03-29 09:09
Category: IED Explosion
Detained: 0
Region: RC EAST
Longitude: 70.31916809
Type: Explosive Hazard
Affiliation: ENEMY

	Enemy	Friend	Civilian	Host nation
Killed in action	0	0	0	0
Wounded in action	0	0	0	0

ON 29 MARCH AN IED STRUCK A HALO TRUST NGO VEHICLE IN THE SURK ROD DISTRICT, SHEKH MESRI (42S XD 213 038), LOCATED IN THE DESERT AREA SOUTHWEST OF JALALABAD. THE IED WAS REMOTE DETONATED ON THE MAIN ROAD.

Reference ID: AFG20050329n64
Latitude 34.36832047
Date: 2005-03-29 10:10
Category: IED Explosion
Detained: 0
Region: RC EAST
Longitude: 70.31916809
Type: Explosive Hazard
Affiliation: ENEMY

	Enemy	Friend	Civilian	Host nation
Killed in action	0	0	0	0
Wounded in action	0	0	0	0

ON 29 MARCH AN IED STRUCK A MOD VEHICLE IN THE SURK ROD DISTRICT, SHEKH MESRI (42S XD 213 038), LOCATED IN THE DESERT AREA SOUTHWEST OF JALALABAD. THE IED WAS REMOTE DETONATED ON THE MAIN ROAD. THE MOD VEHICLE WAS RESPONDING TO THE EARLIER IED STRIKE AGAINST HALO TRUST.

Reference ID: AFG20050403n73
Latitude: 31.57943916
Date: 2005-04-03 09:09
Category: IED Explosion
Detained: 0
Region: RC SOUTH
Longitude: 65.82389069
Type: Explosive Hazard
Affiliation: ENEMY

	Enemy	Friend	Civilian	Host nation
Killed in action	0	0	0	0
Wounded in action	0	0	0	0

TF BRONCO REPORTS EXPLOSION 10K SE OF KANDAHAR. THE FOLLOWING SALT WAS SENT: S: 1X, A: UNKNOWN EXPLOSION, L: 41R QQ 680 973, T: 0930L.

REMARKS: WE ARE CURRENTLY NOT SURE IF THIS IS AN IED OR MINE, RCAG PTRL REPORTED THIS, CURRENTLY ASSESSING SITE. AT 1300Z TF STEEL REPORTS, EXPLOSION WAS RC IED. EXPLOSION ONLY MADE A SMALL HOLE IN THE GROUND. THE IED EXPLODED AFTER THE ANA PATROL PASSED THE IED. DETONATION TIMING WAS POOR. LOCALS SAW A LN GRAB SOMETHING NEAR THE SITE OF THE EXPLOSION AFTER DETONATION AND FLEE THE SCENE PRIOR TO IRF/EOD ARRIVAL ON SITE. LOCALS WERE UNABLE TO IDENTIFY THE LN.

THE FIRING POINT FOR THIS DEVICE WAS DETERMINED TO BE APPROXIMATELY 200 M EAST OF THE BLAST SITE

BEHIND A SIX FOOT WALL. A DETAILED SEARCH OF THE FIRING POSITION FURTHER YIELDED A BURIED SOVIET 100 MM PROJECTILE WHICH COULD HAVE BEEN USED IN FUTURE IED ATTACKS AS WELL AS A PIECE OF DETONATING CORD,PIECES OF BLACK ELECTRICAL TAPE, CLEAR PLASTIC CONSISTENT WITH PACKAGING MATERIAL FOR D CELL BATTERIES,AND EMPTY SONY AUTOMATIC HEATER TIMER 12 VDC BOX. A ROCK WAS PLACED TO ALLOW THE TRIGGERMAN TO STAND ON IT AND HAVE AN UNOBSTRUCTED VIEW OF THE IED SITE FROM OVER THE WALL. ADDITIONALLY, A TERRAIN MODEL (SAND-TABLE) WAS FOUND THAT COULD HAVE AIDED THE PERPETRATORS IN EXECUTING THIS OR OTHER OPERATIONS.

Reference ID: AFG20050416n86
Latitude: 32.01860809
Date: 2005-04-16 11:11
Category: IED Explosion
Detained: 0

Region: RC SOUTH
Longitude: 67.02832794
Type: Explosive Hazard
Affiliation: ENEMY

	Enemy	Friend	Civilian	Host nation
Killed in action	0	0	0	0
Wounded in action	0	0	0	0

TF BRONCO REPORTS MINE STRIKE 15K SW OF QALAT. THE FOLLOWING SALT REPORT WAS SENT: S: 1X UN VEHICLE, A: MINE STRIKE, L: 42S UA 138 442, T: 1125Z. REMARKS: 6X LNS INJURED IN THE BLAST, 4X LNS NOT SERIOUSLY INJURED. 1X INJURED LN IS A UN WORKER
FIBERGLASS ENCASED LANDMINE WITH IMPROVISED PRESSURE PLATE. NO EVIDENCE OF SPIDER OR OTHER RC DEVICE WAS RECOVERED.

Reference ID: AFG20050423n86
Latitude: 35.16278076
Date: 2005-04-23 07:07
Category: IED Explosion
Detained: 0

Region: RC EAST
Longitude: 71.41750336
Type: Explosive Hazard
Affiliation: ENEMY

	Enemy	Friend	Civilian	Host nation
Killed in action	0	0	0	0
Wounded in action	0	0	0	0

CJSOTF REPORTS A CONVOY WAS ATTACKED WITH A RCIED 11K SW OF FOB NARAY. THE FOLLOWING SALT WAS SENT BY B43: S- RCIED; ITALIAN, AT,

TC/2.4, A- COALITION CONVOY OF ASF, WAS ATTACKED WITH AN IED (MISFIRE), L- 42SYD202938 (POINT OF MISFIRE OF IED), T- 230730ZAPR05. REMARKS-ASF BROUGHT THE IED MATERIALS BACK TO THE FIREBASE. MTF

Reference ID: AFG20050505n101
Latitude: 33.33181
Date: 2005-05-05 12:12
Category: IED Explosion
Detained: 0
Region: RC EAST
Longitude: 69.85637665
Type: Explosive Hazard
Affiliation: ENEMY

	Enemy	Friend	Civilian	Host nation
Killed in action	0	0	0	0
Wounded in action	0	0	0	0

IT WAS REPORTED THAT AN RCIED STRIKE 9K WEST OF FB CHAPMAN TOOK PLACE ON COALITION FORCES. A COALITION CONVOY WAS TRAVELLING EAST TOWARDS KHOWST WHEN THEY CAME ACROSS A BICYCLE (POSTIONED IN THE MIDDLE OF THE ROAD). MOMENTS LATER THE BICYCLE EXPLODED AND THE CONVOY CLEARED THE KILL ZONE (42SWB 79700 88400). UNIT REPORTED SMALL ARMS FIRE WHILE SPEEDING THROUGH THE AMBUSH AREA. NO INJURIES OR DAMAGE REPORTED. THE IED WAS REMOTELY CONTROLLED. UPDATE:

Reference ID: AFG20050512n93
Latitude: 34.23694992
Date: 2005-05-12 02:02
Category: IED Explosion
Detained: 0
Region: RC EAST
Longitude: 70.18054962
Type: Explosive Hazard
Affiliation: ENEMY

	Enemy	Friend	Civilian	Host nation
Killed in action	0	0	0	0
Wounded in action	0	0	0	0

(DELAYED REPORT) CJSOTF reports two ANA Police vehicles were attacked by a RCIED 31km SW of Jalalabad on 12 MAY 2005. The two-vehicle convoy was struck in the late evening while on the way from the old bazaar heading towards Kaga (small village). The second vehicle sustained broken windows, and no reported injuries or casualties.

Reference ID: AFG20050514n83
Latitude: 32.03250122
Date: 2005-05-14 07:07
Category: IED Explosion
Detained: 0
Region: RC SOUTH
Longitude: 66.95881653
Type: Explosive Hazard
Affiliation: ENEMY

	Enemy	Friend	Civilian	Host nation
Killed in action	0	0	0	2
Wounded in action	0	0	0	5

TF Bayonet reports IED detonation and requests MEDEVAC 10K S of QALAT to KAF. TF Bayonet reported that 5 ASF soldiers were WIA and 2 ASF were KIA by an IED IVO 42S UA 0725 4586 at 0740Z. All PTs are reported as URGENT with multiple shrapnel wounds. The LZ has been secured by US Forces and will be marked by white smoke. KAF QRF will be used to transport TF IED to perform site expoitation. CJTF76 approves MEDEVAC 05-14A at 0754Z. W/U at 0804Z. W/D at 0934Z. The convoy took a creek bed to by pass an overpass. The second vehicle in the convoy a NTV struck the device. TF IED believes is was a TC-6 pressure plate mine judging by the crater 7 feet in diameter and 3 feet deep, they estimate 13 lbs of explosives were used.

Reference ID: AFG20050517n100
Latitude: 31.08856964
Date: 2005-05-17 09:09
Category: IED Explosion
Detained: 0

Region: RC SOUTH
Longitude: 64.16375732
Type: Explosive Hazard
Affiliation: ENEMY

	Enemy	Friend	Civilian	Host nation
Killed in action	0	0	0	0
Wounded in action	0	0	0	0

(Delayed Report) TF Bayonet reports an IED attack on a convoy (AIP) 27K S of the Garmser bazaar (41RPQ 1100 4000)in South Helmand. No injuries reported. The detonation occurred 2m in front of the 1st vehicle causing moderate damage. Armed police, who were acting in the role of escort, debussed and arrested 17 personnel on site. All detained personnel were taken to the Garmser authorities and held for questioning. The device was powered by a six-volt sealed lead battery of Japanese manufacture. A quantity of fine copper wire and the remains of the aluminum housing for the explosive were found in the close vicinity of the crater. The crater measured 3m x 3m x 70cm. NFI.

Reference ID: AFG20050520n90
Latitude: 32.16794968
Date: 2005-05-20 14:02
Category: IED Explosion
Detained: 0

Region: RC SOUTH
Longitude: 66.0951767
Type: Explosive Hazard
Affiliation: ENEMY

	Enemy	Friend	Civilian	Host nation
Killed in action	0	0	0	0
Wounded in action	0	1	0	0

TF Sword reports IED strike on recovery team from earlier IED attack on TK. A LTMV was hit by the IED. 1x US Military injured. TF Sword requests Medevac 15km NE of FOB Tiger (42S TA 26075 62751) at 1417Z. CJTF76 approves Medevac 05-20F at 1419Z. MEDEVAC 05-20F cancelled. PT will be ground EVACd.

Reference ID: AFG20050521n77
Latitude: 31.9769001
Date: 2005-05-21 09:09
Category: IED Explosion
Detained: 0

Region: RC SOUTH
Longitude: 67.494133
Type: Explosive Hazard
Affiliation: ENEMY

	Enemy	Friend	Civilian	Host nation
Killed in action	0	1	0	0
Wounded in action	0	2	0	0

TF Bayonet requested a MEDEVAC due to an IED strike 11K E of Sweeney (42R UA 5765 3895). PTs are 3X US-MIL one is listed as urgent, and one is listed urgent surgical, and the third not seriously injured. Patient one suffered a head injury and possible internal bleeding and was being given CPR on site and on board the medevac aircraft. The second patient had both lower extremities amputated by the explosion. Both patients were medevaced to KAF. No enemy in the area and PZ is marked with panels. CJTF76 approves medevac mission 05-21D at 0911Z. The visibility at KAF is less than 1 mile due to blowing dust preventing medevac aircraft from taking off. The medevac aircraft originated from Tarin Kowt due to the dust at KAF. Both JSRC at KAF and a medevac from Tarin Kowt were launched in response to TF Bayonets request. The medevac from Tarin Kowt arrived first at the scene and JSRC support was called off. Medevac was W/U at 0949Z and W/D at 1110Z. The patient suffering head injuries died of his wounds. The second patient has been evaced to Germany for further treatment.

Reference ID: AFG20050530n76　　Region: RC CAPITAL
Latitude: 34.54401016　　Longitude: 69.26351929
Date: 2005-05-30 05:05　　Type: Explosive Hazard
Category: IED Explosion　　Affiliation: ENEMY
Detained: 0

	Enemy	Friend	Civilian	Host nation
Killed in action	0	0	0	0
Wounded in action	0	0	0	0

TF Phoenix reported an explosion 1K SW of Phoenix (42S WD 24179 22509) at 0500Z. There was a large explosion south of Jalalabad Road and east of Kabul. TF Phoenix and ISAF patrols are investigating. There were no US or coalition injuries, and one Swedish was vehicle damaged. The explosion appears to have been caused by a land mine attached to a bicycle (VBIED).

Reference ID: AFG20050603n94　　Region: RC SOUTH
Latitude: 31.57575035　　Longitude: 64.34784698
Date: 2005-06-03 09:09　　Type: Explosive Hazard
Category: IED Explosion　　Affiliation: ENEMY
Detained: 0

	Enemy	Friend	Civilian	Host nation
Killed in action	0	0	0	1
Wounded in action	0	0	0	0

TF Bayonet reports an IED exploded 4km SW of the Lashkar Gah PRT (41R PQ 27900 94200). ANP reported that an IED exploded near the Bullan bridge and killed the former Dishu District ANP Chief. The PRT is sending a squad and EOD team to gather more information. IED was a 60mm mortar that was remotely detonated. NFI.

Reference ID: AFG20050604n84
Latitude: 34.40121841
Date: 2005-06-04 04:04
Category: IED Explosion
Detained: 0
Region: RC EAST
Longitude: 70.29141998
Type: Explosive Hazard
Affiliation: ENEMY

	Enemy	Friend	Civilian	Host nation
Killed in action	0	0	0	0
Wounded in action	0	0	0	0

TF Devil reports an IED exploded, followed by small arms fire 13km West of Jalalabad (42SXD 18700 07400) at 0345Z. Lima, 3-3 Marines reported an IED exploded (center of a road) near one of the ANA vehicles while on convoy; Small arms fire then followed. No injuries or damage reported. The convoy consisted of 9 vehicles with ECM devices. The IED detonated in front of the 5th vehicle a spider device and 2X projectile devices were found at the IED site. Fragments of the IED will be analyzed by EOD.

Reference ID: AFG20050623n116
Latitude: 33.8158493
Date: 2005-06-23 14:02
Category: IED Explosion
Detained: 0
Region: RC EAST
Longitude: 69.89684296
Type: Explosive Hazard
Affiliation: ENEMY

	Enemy	Friend	Civilian	Host nation
Killed in action	0	0	0	0
Wounded in action	0	0	0	0

CJSOTF reports an IED exploded at an ASF Checkpoint 7km E Chamkani at 1420Z. A second IED is still intact. Unit is requesting EOD team to exploit. No injuries reported. ASF recovered the IED and returned to Firebase. They reported that it was of a type they had not seen before and components will be forwarded by CJSOTF for exploitation.

Reference ID: AFG20050624n101
Latitude: 31.5978508
Date: 2005-06-24 19:07
Category: IED Explosion
Detained: 0
Region: RC SOUTH
Longitude: 64.36300659
Type: Explosive Hazard
Affiliation: ENEMY

	Enemy	Friend	Civilian	Host nation
Killed in action	0	0	0	0
Wounded in action	0	0	0	0

ON 20050624, AT APPROXIMATLEY 2330L, A RCIED WAS DETONATED ON THE SIDE OF A ROAD IN LASHKAR GAH CITY, BETWEEN THE FOLLOWING GRIDS //MGRS:41RPQ2930896668// AND //MGRS:41RPQ2932396458//. A BROWN GRAIN BAG WAS PLACED ON THE SIDE OF THE ROAD IN FRONT OF HAJI ((AMINULLAH))S HOUSE, A LOCAL GOVERNMENT OFFICIAL. LOCAL NATIONALS (LN) REPORTED SEEING THE BAG PRIOR TO THE DETONATION. THE RCIED WAS DETONATED WHILE A POLICE VEHICLE WAS PASSING, NO INJURIES WERE SUSTAINED AND NO DAMAGE WAS DONE TO THE VEHICLE.

THE RCIED APPEARS TO BE CONSTRUCTED USING A LARGER MUNITION. SOURCE STATED THAT LN WERE ACTUALLY KICKING THE BAG PRIOR TO DETONATION TO SEE WHAT WAS INSIDE. THE VEHICLE WAS NOT DAMAGED BECAUSE THE SHRAPNEL TRAVELED AWAY FROM THE VEHICLE.

Reference ID: AFG20050629n105
Latitude: 33.45014954
Date: 2005-06-29 14:02
Category: IED Explosion
Detained: 0

Region: RC EAST
Longitude: 69.04595947
Type: Explosive Hazard
Affiliation: ENEMY

	Enemy	Friend	Civilian	Host nation
Killed in action	0	0	0	0
Wounded in action	0	0	0	0

TF PhoenixreportsIEDexploded22km SW of Gardez while conducting convoy operations. After the initial explosion the site was secured andTF Phoenixfound a second unexploded IED. There wereno reported coalition casualties; EOD enroute to location.It has been determined that the convoy rolled over pressure plates that were linked to two anti-tank mines but the mines did not explode; only the blasting caps detonated. EOD secured the 2 mines and the convoy continued mission to Gardez. There were no reported casualties and no damage to equipment.

Reference ID: AFG20050714n123
Latitude: 33.33924103
Date: 2005-07-14 19:07
Category: IED Explosion
Detained: 0

Region: RC EAST
Longitude: 69.91755676
Type: Explosive Hazard
Affiliation: ENEMY

	Enemy	Friend	Civilian	Host nation
Killed in action	0	0	0	0
Wounded in action	0	0	1	2

TF Devil reports 2X IED strikes at Khowst. ANP reports 1X IED detonated at Khowst Central Mosque resulting in 1X LN child being injured. The LN was taken to FOB Salerno. An ANP detachment responded to the blast and as they entered the Mosque the other IED exploded injuring Col Hairulla and another ANP. EOD and a 2/504 element will go to the Mosque in the morning to conduct BDA.

Reference ID: AFG20050719n118
Latitude:
Date: 2005-07-19 00:12
Category: IED Explosion
Detained: 0

Region: RC EAST
Longitude:
Type: Explosive Hazard
Affiliation: ENEMY

	Enemy	Friend	Civilian	Host nation
Killed in action	0	0	0	0
Wounded in action	0	0	0	0

An IED exploded outside the house of Mufti Habibur Rahman who opted for reconcillation program last month. There was no casualties but structural damage to the house occured.

Reference ID: AFG20050801n138
Latitude:
Date: 2005-08-01 00:12
Category: IED Explosion
Detained: 0
Region: RC EAST
Longitude:
Type: Explosive Hazard
Affiliation: ENEMY

	Enemy	Friend	Civilian	Host nation
Killed in action	1	0	0	0
Wounded in action	0	0	0	7

On 01 Aug 05, Afghan Border Police contacted AGE in Kamdesh approx 20 klms east of Kamu village, Nuristan/Kunar Province, which resulted in 1 AGE being killed, 1 ANA killed and 3 police injured. Additional police and soldiers from Kunar Province were dispatched to the location, which resulted in one vehicle in which they were traveling in being hit with an IED, which injured 3 police and 4 soldiers.

Reference ID: AFG20050804n109
Latitude:
Date: 2005-08-04 00:12
Category: IED Explosion
Detained: 0
Region: RC NORTH
Longitude:
Type: Explosive Hazard
Affiliation: ENEMY

	Enemy	Friend	Civilian	Host nation
Killed in action	0	0	0	0
Wounded in action	0	0	0	0

It was reported that last Night around 0100hrs an IED Explosion took place in Kunduz city in the direction of Bandary Imamsahib about 200m in the West of Police training center. Reportedly the timer device probably detonated the IED prior to the defined time. It was likely planed IED attack against police trainers usually use this routs. But police believe that it was a destructive action, which was conducted by AGEs. The further investigation is underway.

Reference ID: AFG20050804n115
Latitude: 32.94974899
Date: 2005-08-04 10:10
Category: IED Explosion
Detained: 0
Region: RC EAST
Longitude: 69.22841644
Type: Explosive Hazard
Affiliation: ENEMY

	Enemy	Friend	Civilian	Host nation
Killed in action	0	1	0	0
Wounded in action	0	1	0	1

CJSOTF reported an IED strike 7km E of FOB Orgun-E at 1018Z. A M1114 UAH struck an IED. 1X US/MIL was KIA. 1X US/MIL was WIA, he sustained a bruised left thigh, lacerations, and 2 left ribs fractured (did not penetrate chest cavity). one ANA soldier was also wounded. All PAX were taken to Orgun-E, and the WIA was conscious and responsive and is being treated in the Forward Surgical team clinic. The ANA soldier was operated on at the clinic. The site has been secured by the ANA. At 1110Z 2X PLTs from TF Devil and CJSOTF elements moved from Orgun-E to recover the vehicle from the IED site. 4 suspected ACM were immediately detained at the IED site by the ANA soldiers. One possible initiator was found at the site. IED TF was taken to the site for further exploitation. Initiation system was a long range cordless telephone, two charges were used one exploded behind the vehicle and one directly underneath. The wounded US/MIL was transfered to BAF and evaced to LRMC.

Reference ID: AFG20050806n179
Latitude:
Date: 2005-08-06 00:12
Category: IED Explosion
Detained: 0
Region: RC EAST
Longitude:
Type: Explosive Hazard
Affiliation: ENEMY

	Enemy	Friend	Civilian	Host nation
Killed in action	0	0	1	0
Wounded in action	0	0	3	0

In the early morning a private car hit an IED/ mine approx 2 km from Governors office on the road between Sharan and Yusuf Khel resulted two occupants of the veh killed on the spot. At 1500 hrs a veh carrying supporters of the Gen Daud Shar (candidate), whilst campaigning was attacked by an IED resulted 1X KIA and 3X WIA in Kotani village of Sar Hawza district.

Reference ID: AFG20050809n152
Latitude: 34.27793121
Date: 2005-08-09 09:09
Category: IED Explosion
Detained: 0
Region: RC EAST
Longitude: 70.46929169
Type: Explosive Hazard
Affiliation: ENEMY

	Enemy	Friend	Civilian	Host nation
Killed in action	0	0	0	0
Wounded in action	0	0	0	0

On 09 August 2005, ANP and coalition forces escorted press representatives to a local school for a ceremony. Enroute to the ceremony, the convoy passed the IED attack site without incident. After leaving the ceremony, three and half hours later and travelling the same route, the fourth vehicle in the convoy a U.S. M1114, was hit by an IED.

Reference ID: AFG20050810n137
Latitude: 33.99642944
Date: 2005-08-10 03:03
Category: IED Explosion
Detained: 0
Region: RC EAST
Longitude: 69.021698
Type: Explosive Hazard
Affiliation: ENEMY

	Enemy	Friend	Civilian	Host nation
Killed in action	0	0	0	0
Wounded in action	0	0	0	0

JEMB reports an explosion 53km S of Kabul, in Puli Alam, at 0305Z. The device was placed under the hood of a vehicle that was parked at the JEMB compound. The device detonated destroying the vehicle and damaging two nearby vehicles. No injuries were reported. ANP PAX on scene swept the compound and found nothing of significance. JEMB LNO did not ask for any further assistance.

Reference ID: AFG20050810n142
Latitude: 32.19725037
Date: 2005-08-10 08:08
Category: IED Explosion
Detained: 0

Region: RC EAST
Longitude: 68.35978699
Type: Explosive Hazard
Affiliation: ENEMY

	Enemy	Friend	Civilian	Host nation
Killed in action	0	0	0	0
Wounded in action	0	0	0	0

TF Devil reported an IED strike 54km northwest of FOB Funk at 0810Z. IED consisted of double stacked Anti-Tank Mines and a pressure plate. The vehicle was the 15th of the 20 vehicle convoy. The vehicles rear end was destroyed. No injuries to personnel were reported. While conducting a search of the surrounding area an 82mm mortar round was found in a tent of a near by village. 1/325 is coordinating for a wrecker and for EOD to destroy the mortar round.

Reference ID: AFG20050817n139
Latitude: 31.61417007
Date: 2005-08-17 11:11
Category: IED Explosion
Detained: 0

Region: RC SOUTH
Longitude: 65.72702789
Type: Explosive Hazard
Affiliation: ENEMY

	Enemy	Friend	Civilian	Host nation
Killed in action	0	0	1	0
Wounded in action	0	0	20	0

TF Bayonet reports IED strike 3km SW of Kandahar PRT. The IED struck a bus that was transporting trainees from the local police academy. The Provincial Coordination Center reports 20-25 LN wounded and 1x LN killed. Canadian soldiers were the first in arrive and secure the site. EOD arrived and conducted a preliminary investigation and determined that the IED consisted of 3x artillery shells and it was detonated by remote control.

Reference ID: AFG20050826n124
Latitude: 32.9406395
Date: 2005-08-26 15:03
Category: IED Explosion
Detained: 0

Region: RC EAST
Longitude: 68.54000092
Type: Explosive Hazard
Affiliation: ENEMY

	Enemy	Friend	Civilian	Host nation
Killed in action	0	1	0	0
Wounded in action	0	4	0	0

TF Devil reports IED strike 36k SW of Sharona PRT. A TF Fury convoy consisting of 4x HMMWVs and 3x jingle trucks struck an IED. The 1st vehicle of seven, an M114 up-armor HMMWV, in convoy was struck in the rear right after it crested a hill. At 1546Z TF Devil requests MEDEVAC to Orgun-E. PT1 suffers from possible lumbar spine injury, right anterior knee superficial thru and thru wound, left posterior rib fracture, and simple facial laceration. PT2 has an open right leg fracture, probable pulse, and is unable to move toe and ankle. PT3 has a right leg soft tissue injury and is stable. PT 4 appears to have no injuries at this time. PT5 is reported as critical and is receiving CPR. At 1552Z CJTF76 formally requests JSRC for MEDEVAC 08-26A. At

1614Z JSRC accepts MEDEVAC 08-26A. W/U at 1630Z. At 1705Z PT5 is reported as KIA. W/D at Orgun-E at 1839Z. 2044Z Update: PT1 is stable and is pending transfer from Orgun-E to BAF. PT2 is currently at KAF. PT3 is stable and RTD (light duty). PT 4 is stable and RTD. W/D at KAF at 2122Z. IED TF arrived on scene and determined the IED was an anti-tank mine that was detonated by a remote control device. TF Fury is massing combat power in the area to gain intelligence on the perpetrators who executed this attack. M/C.

Reference ID: AFG20050828n132
Latitude: 32.96915817
Date: 2005-08-28 04:04
Category: IED Explosion
Detained: 1

Region: RC SOUTH
Longitude: 65.49388885
Type: Explosive Hazard
Affiliation: ENEMY

	Enemy	Friend	Civilian	Host nation
Killed in action	2	0	0	0
Wounded in action	0	0	0	3

CJSOTF reports an IED strike 8km NW of FB Cobra at 0410Z. An ANP HILUX was struck by an IED that consisted of a 107mm rocket. 2x ANP were reported to have minor injures and have been EVACED of the scene. A search of the area revealed a pressure plate IED and a motorcycle with 4x AK-47 mags w/ 120x rounds, 1x grenade, and a pistol. No enemy contact reported. At 0722Z CJSOTF reports TIC 16km SW of IED site. A third IED struck an ANA NTV, followed by small arms fire, 300m S of the original IED. As a result of the TIC CJSOTF requests a MEDEVAC 15km W of FB Cobra at 0729Z. PT1 is ANA and is listed as urgent suffers from multiple injuries. PT 2 and 3 are ANA, listed as routine, and suffer from leg wounds. There is enemy in the area. PZ will be marked with smoke. CJTF76 approves MEDEVAC 08-28A at 0729Z. PT will be taken to TK FST. At 0918Z CJSOTF reports 2x EKIA and 1x detainee. CJSOTF will finish the destruction of first IED. At 0929Z CJSOTF reported troops are no longer in contact. CJSOTF reports TIC with an unknown ACM element at 1003Z. CJSOTF reported troops are no longer in contact and the area is secure at 1010Z.

Reference ID: AFG20050904n120
Latitude:
Date: 2005-09-04 00:12
Category: IED Explosion
Detained: 0

Region: RC SOUTH
Longitude:
Type: Explosive Hazard
Affiliation: ENEMY

	Enemy	Friend	Civilian	Host nation
Killed in action	0	0	1	0
Wounded in action	0	0	0	0

On 04 September at 0800 hours it was reported that a vehicle in which a Provincial Council candidate, Habibullah was traveling in suffered an IED strike. Habibullah had just departed his residence and was seriously injured in the incident. He was later transferred to Lashkargah Hospital where he died from his wounds. Police are continuing their investigations into the incident.

Reference ID: AFG20050913n144
Latitude:
Date: 2005-09-13 00:12
Category: IED Explosion
Detained: 0

Region: RC EAST
Longitude:
Type: Explosive Hazard
Affiliation: ENEMY

	Enemy	Friend	Civilian	Host nation
Killed in action	0	0	0	0
Wounded in action	0	1	0	0

Approx 08:20 hrs, Border of Baraki Barak and Sayed Abad District (Lachi Khail village) report that an IED attack had taken place in Lachi Khail area. The IED was detonated towards a CF vehicle patrol as it drove past, 1 x soldier slightly injured.

Reference ID: AFG20050915n162
Latitude: 33.49053955
Date: 2005-09-15 08:08
Category: IED Explosion
Detained: 0

Region: RC EAST
Longitude: 69.14694214
Type: Explosive Hazard
Affiliation: ENEMY

	Enemy	Friend	Civilian	Host nation
Killed in action	0	0	0	0
Wounded in action	0	0	0	0

TF Devil reports an IED strike 13km SW of Gardez at 0826Z. The IED detonated in front of the lead vehicle in a 5x vehicle convoy. The lead vehicle was a M1114 that was equipped with ECM, It is unknown if it was active. No injuries to personnel or significant damage to equipment was reported. IED was believed to have consisted of 2-3 stacked AT-mines with a spider device and the detonation left a 6x6 crater.

Reference ID: AFG20050917n152
Latitude: 35.18822861
Date: 2005-09-17 07:07
Category: IED Explosion
Detained: 0

Region: RC EAST
Longitude: 71.50845337
Type: Explosive Hazard
Affiliation: ENEMY

	Enemy	Friend	Civilian	Host nation
Killed in action	0	0	0	0
Wounded in action	0	0	0	3

CJSOTF reports an IED strike on ANP IVO Naray at 0641Z. believed to be 3x ANP casualties, all being taken to FOB Naray. An ANP element is enroute to IED site to investigate. At 0748Z CJSOTF requests a MEDEVAC IVO FB Naray to BAF at 0748Z. 1x ANP has an amputated right hand and blast injuries to the upper extremities, hands, and face. The PT is listed a urget precedence. Green smoke marks the PZ. CJTF76 approves MEDEVAC 09-17B at 0758Z. W/U at 0824Z. W/D at 1029Z. No significant findings reported by ANP.

Reference ID: AFG20050917n173
Latitude: 31.12291908
Date: 2005-09-17 18:06

Region: RC SOUTH
Longitude: 66.4150238
Type: Explosive Hazard

Category: IED Explosion   Affiliation: ENEMY
Detained: 0

	Enemy	Friend	Civilian	Host nation
Killed in action	0	1	0	0
Wounded in action	0	1	0	0

CJSOTF reports IED strike 13k N of Spin Buldak to KAF. A COLSOF convoy was hit by a T5Z pressure plate mine in the middle of the road. A P4 non up-armored Mercedes was struck by the mine while heading north to a polling site. At 1858Z CJSOTF requests MEDEVAC for 2x CJSOTF PAX. PT1 reported as critical with carotid artery severed and cervical spine injury and reported as urgent surgical. PT2 is reported as routine with lower left leg fracture. At 1903 CJTF76 accepts MEDEVAC mission 09-17G. W/U at 1947Z. W/D AT 2049. PT1 was declared DOA.

Reference ID: AFG20050926n127
Latitude:
Date: 2005-09-26 00:12
Category: IED Explosion
Detained: 0

Region: RC SOUTH
Longitude:
Type: Explosive Hazard
Affiliation: ENEMY

	Enemy	Friend	Civilian	Host nation
Killed in action	0	0	2	2
Wounded in action	0	0	0	0

On 26 September it was reported that two civilians and two police officers were killed when their vehicle was hit by a RCIED in Nawzad District. No arrest has been made in relation to the incident.

Reference ID: AFG20050928n142
Latitude: 34.56093979
Date: 2005-09-28 12:12
Category: IED Explosion
Detained: 0

Region: RC CAPITAL
Longitude: 69.31394196
Type: Explosive Hazard
Affiliation: ENEMY

	Enemy	Friend	Civilian	Host nation
Killed in action	0	0	0	6
Wounded in action	0	0	0	25

TF Phoenix reports an IED detonation IVO Kabul. KMNB reported a LN dressed in an ANA uniform drove in between 2x buses detonated a VBIED or an IED. 2x buses exploded and a total of 4x buses are on fire. ISAF and CF are on scene and are conducting a mass casualties MEDEVAC. No assistance is requested as of 1238Z. 1255Z Update: KCP reported 25x WIA taken to the Kabul Medical Center and 6x KIA. . The incident has been confirmed as a suicide bomb attack. No CF or US forces were involved in the attack. The occupants of the buses were ANA officers in training.

Reference ID: AFG20050930n127
Latitude:
Date: 2005-09-30 00:12

Region: RC EAST
Longitude:
Type: Explosive Hazard

Category: IED Explosion   Affiliation: ENEMY
Detained: 0

	Enemy	Friend	Civilian	Host nation
Killed in action	0	0	0	0
Wounded in action	0	4	0	0

On 30 Sep 2005 about 1530hr, a CF convoy was hit with an IED approx 3kls west of the village if Daag, Pech district, Kunar. As a result of the incident, 4 CF members were injured, 3 of them are classed as serious. It should be noted that the CF were hit by an IED in this same spot on 24 Jul 2005.

Reference ID: AFG20051002n166   Region: RC EAST
Latitude: 33.91846848   Longitude: 69.70458984
Date: 2005-10-02 15:03   Type: Explosive Hazard
Category: IED Explosion   Affiliation: ENEMY
Detained: 0

	Enemy	Friend	Civilian	Host nation
Killed in action	0	0	0	0
Wounded in action	0	0	0	0

CJSOTF reports an IED strike on the lead vehicle of a convoy 16km NW FOb Chamkani. Personnel were moving from north to south on the south side of Ali Kheyl, to the NE of GARDEZ when the lead vehicle was subject to an IED attack. There were no injuries or damage to the vehicle and two LN were detained for questioning. The device was found to be a Radio Controlled IED (RCIED) with a Mod 2 Dual Tone Multi Frequency (DTMF) Receiver linked explosively to a main charge buried in the center of the road.

Reference ID: AFG20051007n212   Region: RC SOUTH
Latitude: 32.00170898   Longitude: 64.81800842
Date: 2005-10-07 04:04   Type: Explosive Hazard
Category: IED Explosion   Affiliation: ENEMY
Detained: 0

	Enemy	Friend	Civilian	Host nation
Killed in action	0	1	0	0
Wounded in action	0	0	0	0

TF Bayonet reported a mine strike 31km NE of Geresk. At 0435Z, TF Bayonet reported that a US-MIL soldier stepped on a AP mine. As a result of this mine strike, TF Bayonet requested a MEDEVAC for one US-MIL listed as urgent. There is no enemy in the area. The PZ is secure and will be marked with panels. CJTF76 approves MEDEVAC 10-07B at 0437Z. PT will be taken to KAF. W/U at 0452Z. MEDEVAC 10-07B declared PT KIA after arriving onsite and will take the remains back to KAF. W/D at 0548Z in KAF. M/C. A pressure plate was discovered on the site and an investigation is ongoing to determine if the mine was an IED. 081738ZOCT05 Update: TF IED investigation revealed the improvised pressure device triggered the IED as the soldier ran over it moving from one vehicle to another. No components were recovered from the site. Fragmentation pieces at the site are consistent with an artillery projectile (unknown type). NFTR.

Reference ID: AFG20051009n177
Latitude: 31.61586952
Date: 2005-10-09 05:05
Category: IED Explosion
Detained: 0

Region: RC SOUTH
Longitude: 65.73235321
Type: Explosive Hazard
Affiliation: ENEMY

	Enemy	Friend	Civilian	Host nation
Killed in action	0	0	0	0
Wounded in action	0	2	0	0

TF Bayonet reported an VIED strike IVO Kandahar. At 0500Z, Kandahar PRT reported a VBIED strike on a UK convoy. Convoy consisted of two up-armored SUVs both with active ECMs on board. Convoy was driving along the roadway when a vehicle pulled alongside of the rear vehicle and self detonated 1m from the right front of the vehicle. As a result of the detonation two UK personnel were injured, both sustained shrapnel wounds to the arms and face. PTs were EVACED to Kandahar PRT. TF Bayonet IRF and TF IED responded to the site.

Reference ID: AFG20051014n185
Latitude: 33.24723053
Date: 2005-10-14 09:09
Category: IED Explosion
Detained: 0

Region: RC EAST
Longitude: 69.8265686
Type: Explosive Hazard
Affiliation: ENEMY

	Enemy	Friend	Civilian	Host nation
Killed in action	0	0	1	0
Wounded in action	0	0	20	0

TF Devil reported a direct fire attack IVO Khowst. At 0944Z, Provincial Coordination Center reported an unknown size bomb detonated and destroyed a local mosque. The mullah was killed and more then 20x PAX was injured. ANA and ANP are enroute to the site to investigate. The LN injured were taken to the Khowst Hospital. ANP did not request any CF assistance. No CF damages or injuries were reported. Attack appears to be directed at civilian populace. 1620Z Update: TF IED, 2/504th QRF went to the site and EOD swept the area for secondary explosives and found none. Damage to mosque was determined to be minor damage located at the main entryway. Explosive was determined to be placed in front of or underneath the mullah and a MOD-1 DTMF receive was recovered. Approximately 350x PAX were inside when the explosion happened. Approximately 16x to 20x PAX were sent to the hospital with injuries. TF IED and QRF RTB. NFTR.

Reference ID: AFG20051015n182
Latitude:
Date: 2005-10-15 00:12
Category: IED Explosion
Detained: 0

Region: RC NORTH
Longitude:
Type: Explosive Hazard
Affiliation: ENEMY

	Enemy	Friend	Civilian	Host nation
Killed in action	0	0	0	0
Wounded in action	0	0	0	0

It was reported that a roadside IED targeted a Dutch Military convoy on Saturday at 0830hrs while driving towards Baghlan Jaded district 35km East of PIK. It believes that the IED was home made and detonated by remote controlled device. Reportedly the DPRT vehicle sustained serious damages but no human casualties reported in this incident.The road from Kunduz to Polikhumri classified the most risky areas in the NER.

Reference ID: AFG20051018n214
Latitude: 31.59782982
Date: 2005-10-18 05:05
Category: IED Explosion
Detained: 0
Region: RC SOUTH
Longitude: 65.49230957
Type: Explosive Hazard
Affiliation: ENEMY

	Enemy	Friend	Civilian	Host nation
Killed in action	0	0	2	0
Wounded in action	0	0	2	0

At 0549z a four vehicle USPI convoy was eastbound on Highway 1, about 22.5 km west of Kandahar City, when the lead vehicle, a Toyota Hilux, was struck in the left rear by an IED. The force of the explosion flipped the vehicle forward end over end on to its roof, killing two LN and seriously injuring three others. Five PAX were detained, questioned and then released. The injured LNs were taken to a local hospital. No CF were involved in the IED strike. NFTR.

Reference ID: AFG20051019n160
Latitude:
Date: 2005-10-19 00:12
Category: IED Explosion
Detained: 0
Region: RC SOUTH
Longitude:
Type: Explosive Hazard
Affiliation: ENEMY

	Enemy	Friend	Civilian	Host nation
Killed in action	0	0	0	2
Wounded in action	0	0	0	2

On 20 October at 2000 hrs it was reported that the Chief of Security of Nimroz province was killed by a VBIED in Zaranj City. Nafas Khan was moving on foot to the mosque at 1925 hrs west of the city between the Iranian/Afghanborder crossing point and Zaranj City. A white Toyota Corolla Taxi exploded as it passed him, killing Nafas Khan and his bodyguard Sheramat, and injuring 2 other guards. At 1930 hrs gunfire was heard to the southeast of the city. More information to follow.

Reference ID: AFG20051024n141
Latitude: 34.12078857
Date: 2005-10-24 13:01
Category: IED Explosion
Detained: 0
Region: RC EAST
Longitude: 69.06109619
Type: Explosive Hazard
Affiliation: ENEMY

	Enemy	Friend	Civilian	Host nation
Killed in action	0	0	0	0
Wounded in action	0	0	0	0

TF Devil reported TIC 41km S of Kabul. At 1342Z, Gardez PRT reported while on a patrol they were engaged by an IED strike and small arms fire by an unknown size ACM element.

1354Z: Gardez PRT reported ACM broke contact and fled the area. Contact was not reestablished. No damages or injuries were reported. Unit RTB.
NFTR.

Reference ID: AFG20051107n224
Latitude: 31.58555984
Date: 2005-11-07 04:04
Category: IED Explosion
Detained: 0

Region: RC SOUTH
Longitude: 64.3585434
Type: Explosive Hazard
Affiliation: ENEMY

	Enemy	Friend	Civilian	Host nation
Killed in action	1	0	0	0
Wounded in action	0	0	0	1

CJSOTF reported a VBIED explosion 2km SW of Lashkar Gah. At 0433Z, a CJSOTF element reported a VBIED explosion at the Governors Palace at Lashkar Gah. A foreign national male stopped near the wall of the governors compound in a new black car and detonated the VBIED, however the ordnance inside only partially exploded. The auto caught on fire, as did the bomber, who ran from the vehicle. The bomber failed to follow the commands of nearby Afghan Special Forces (ASF) personnel and was then shot by ASF and was transported to a local hospital, where he died of his wounds. One ANA was slightly wounded with a cut to his forehead. CJSOTF requests TF IED at 0509Z. CJTF76 approves request at 0517Z. Awaiting final report from TF IED. NFTR

Reference ID: AFG20051114n191
Latitude:
Date: 2005-11-14 00:12
Category: IED Explosion
Detained: 0

Region: RC EAST
Longitude:
Type: Explosive Hazard
Affiliation: ENEMY

	Enemy	Friend	Civilian	Host nation
Killed in action	0	0	2	0
Wounded in action	0	0	0	0

On 141105, 0400hrs, two tribal militia members (force stood up by Kunar governor) were targeted by an IED near Gul Baba village (MGRS 42 XD 75 73)in the Mano Gai area of Pech district. Both individuals were killed by the blast. NFD at this stage, police are investigating.

Reference ID: AFG20051114n197
Latitude: 34.54399109
Date: 2005-11-14 10:10
Category: IED Explosion
Detained: 0

Region: RC CAPITAL
Longitude: 69.23432159
Type: Explosive Hazard
Affiliation: ENEMY

	Enemy	Friend	Civilian	Host nation
Killed in action	1	0	0	0
Wounded in action	0	0	0	0

TF Phoenix reported four VBIED strikes IVO Kabul. At 1029Z, ISAF reported a vehicle drove alongside a German ISAF vehicle (non-armored) and detonated adjacent to checkpoint V3 on route Violet. As a result of the explosion ISAF reported one ISAF KIA, two ISAF WIA, two ANP WIA and two LN WIA. ISAF KIA and WIA were German. All injured were ground EVACD. At 1159Z, ISAF reported a second VBIED detonated IVO checkpoint V4 on route Violet. After the explosion the checkpoint was engaged with small arms fire from an unknown size ACM element, who quickly broke contact and fled the area. As a result of the explosion and small arms fire ISAF reported three ISAF WIA, one KCP WIA, and four LN WIA. ISAF WIA were Greek. Injured were ground EVACD. At 1210, ISAF reported a third VBIED detonation adjacent to checkpoint V1, no damages or injuries reported. At 1229Z, ISAF reported sniper fire occurring IVO Dyne Corp compound. As a result of the fire ISAF reported two ISAF WIA (unknown country). ANP responding to the sniper fire mistakenly shot at ANA. As a result of the fire two ANA were WIA. All injured were ground EVACD. All ISAF personnel were treated at the ISAF warehouse. All ANA and LN were treated at local hospitals. At 1345Z, ISAF reported a fourth attempted VBIED adjacent to checkpoint V3. ISAF reported a taxi attempted to drive through a cordon adjacent to the checkpoint and was engaged by British troops. As a result the driver of the vehicle was killed. The vehicle was destroyed by a controlled detonation at 1900Z. No further injuries or damages were reported.

Reference ID: AFG20051116n190
Latitude:
Date: 2005-11-16 00:12
Category: IED Explosion
Detained: 0

Region: RC EAST
Longitude:
Type: Explosive Hazard
Affiliation: ENEMY

	Enemy	Friend	Civilian	Host nation
Killed in action	0	0	0	0
Wounded in action	0	0	0	0

On 161105, approx 2200 hrs, it was reported that AGE destroyed a new three room building which was built by the PRT for tribal militiamen, by using an IED. The building is situated within the Sirkanay District Center and was not occupied at the time of the incident. No causalities have been reported.

Reference ID: AFG20051116n191
Latitude: 31.61750984
Date: 2005-11-16 04:04
Category: IED Explosion
Detained: 0

Region: RC SOUTH
Longitude: 65.73977661
Type: Explosive Hazard
Affiliation: ENEMY

	Enemy	Friend	Civilian	Host nation
Killed in action	0	0	1	0
Wounded in action	0	4	0	0

TF Bayonet reported a suicide VBIED strike 1.5km SE of Kandahar PRT. At 0441Z, a convoy which consisted of two up-armored vehicles, two gun trucks with Afghan escorts, one locally contracted Mercedes-Benz flat-bed truck and one Toyota Hilux.was struck by a taxi SVBIED. The flatbed was destroyed and its LN driver was killed. A LN riding a motorcycle near the blast and the SVBIED driver was also killed. Three American contractors sustained minor injuries. They were ground evacuated to KAF, and later released. One contractor SUV was also destroyed in the detonation.

Reference ID: AFG20051121n153
Latitude: 32.42290115
Date: 2005-11-21 20:08
Category: IED Explosion
Detained: 0
Region: RC EAST
Longitude: 68.35054016
Type: Explosive Hazard
Affiliation: ENEMY

	Enemy	Friend	Civilian	Host nation
Killed in action	0	0	2	0
Wounded in action	0	0	1	0

TF Devil reported an IED strike on a LN Vehicle 25km N of FOB Wazi Khwa. At 0348Z (MIRc), TF Fury reported two LNs killed, one adult and one child. One adult was injured. The last occupant, a child, was uninjured in the detonation. The jingle truck was transporting bricks to FOB Wazi Khwa when it was struck. As a result of the IED strike, TF Devil requested a MEDEVAC at FOB Waza Khwa at 0033Z. PT was a LN, listed as urgent surgical and requires a litter. PT had an open fracture of the right leg. CJTF76 approved MEDEVAC 11-22A at 0043Z. PT was be taken to SAL. W/U at 0102Z. W/D at 0255Z. M/C. After an investigation of the site, it was determined that the IED was a double stacked AT mine with saw blades, inter tubes and a pressure plate. The vehicle struck the IED at approximately 212000ZNOV05.

Reference ID: AFG20051204n173
Latitude: 31.6185894
Date: 2005-12-04 11:11
Category: IED Explosion
Detained: 0
Region: RC SOUTH
Longitude: 65.73137665
Type: Explosive Hazard
Affiliation: ENEMY

	Enemy	Friend	Civilian	Host nation
Killed in action	1	0	1	0
Wounded in action	0	1	2	0

TF Bayonet reported a suicide bomber attack IVO Kandahar. At 1142Z, Kandahar PRT reported while enroute back to the PRT compound from a meeting, a unknown person ran towards the convoy and detonated an unknown explosive on his person. As a result of the explosion KPRT reported one CAN/MIL injured with minor cut to the eye. Two LNs were reported injured, and one LN was killed. KPRT QRF and IED were sent to the site. Convoy continued to the PRT compound. CAN/MIL WIA was treated at the PRT and RTD. LN injured were taken to a local hospital. No further injuries or damages were reported.

Reference ID: AFG20051228n172
Latitude: 34.66635895
Date: 2005-12-28 10:10
Category: IED Explosion
Detained: 0
Region: RC EAST
Longitude: 70.87345123
Type: Explosive Hazard
Affiliation: ENEMY

	Enemy	Friend	Civilian	Host nation
Killed in action	0	1	1	0
Wounded in action	0	2	0	0

TF Devil reported an IED strike 32km SW of ABAD. At 1029Z, TF Devil reported that the first vehicle in a four vehicle patrol was struck by an IED. The blast caused significant damage to an up-armor HMMWV (M1114). An explosive ordnance disposal (EOD) team moved to the site and began sensitive site exploitation. The unit will recover the damaged vehicle upon completion of the site exploitation. As a result of the IED strike, two US/MIL (one US Marine and one US Airman) were wounded in action, one US soldier was killed, and one LN was killed. TF Devil requested a MEDEVAC to ABAD at 1035Z. The two patients were PRIORITY and LITTER. The wounded Marine sustained shrapnel wounds to his leg, and the airman suffered from a bruised left arm and a possible left ankle injury. Oxygen was required for the MEDEVAC. Green and red smoke marked the PZ. CJTF76 approved MEDEVAC 12-28C at 1036Z. W/U at 1058Z. W/D at 1138Z. 2209Z Update: EOD exploited the site and discovered a MOD 4 device, and believes the mine was a AT TC-6. Vehicle was recovered back to base.

Reference ID: AFG20051229n179
Latitude: 30.98454094
Date: 2005-12-29 13:01
Category: IED Explosion
Detained: 0

Region: RC SOUTH
Longitude: 64.19390869
Type: Explosive Hazard
Affiliation: ENEMY

	Enemy	Friend	Civilian	Host nation
Killed in action	0	0	0	5
Wounded in action	0	0	0	4

(Delayed Report) ANP reported an effective IED strike on an ANP checkpoint 68km S of Lashkar Gah. At 1216Z, TF Bayonet reported that an unknown sized ACM element in a Toyota Landcruiser detonated an RCIED on a mud hut shortly after prayer time, killing four ANP and wounding five ANP. The ANP speculate that the RCIED was emplaced on the roof of the hut. The LKG ANP QRF responded to the incident, and no CF were involved.

Reference ID: AFG20060114n224
Latitude: 33.29351044
Date: 2006-01-14 10:10
Category: IED Explosion
Detained: 0

Region: RC EAST
Longitude: 69.91507721
Type: Explosive Hazard
Affiliation: ENEMY

	Enemy	Friend	Civilian	Host nation
Killed in action	0	0	2	0
Wounded in action	0	0	40	0

TF Devil reported two explosions in the vicinity of Khowst. At 1000Z, a local Afghan Security chief reported an explosion in front of the Khowst radio station. At 1130Z, TF Devil reported that a second explosion occurred approximately 500m from the first site. There were no coalition forces involved at the time of the first blast. However, Task Force Devil immediately responded to the site after the first blast. Task Force IED cleared and exploited the site. As a result of the two blasts, 40 local national Afghan citizens were injured. Twelve of the injured were treated at the US facility at FOB Salerno. The remainder were treated at local national facilities. Two of the injured individuals subsequently died of wounds. The initial report from the unit is that the first blast was possibly caused by the detonation of a C4 explosive and the second was possibly caused by a propane based device. TF IED will submit a final report when complete. There were no friendly injuries or damages reported.

Reference ID: AFG20060116n218
Latitude: 31.00431061
Date: 2006-01-16 12:12
Category: IED Explosion
Detained: 0
Region: RC SOUTH
Longitude: 66.3920517
Type: Explosive Hazard
Affiliation: ENEMY

	Enemy	Friend	Civilian	Host nation
Killed in action	0	0	25	0
Wounded in action	0	0	17	1

CJSOTF reported a possible suicide IED strike in Spin Buldak. At 1230Z, a CJSOTF element reported an explosion at a wrestling match resulting in 17 x LN killed and 25 x LN wounded. Initial report is a suicide motorcycle-borne IED. There were no coalition involved at the time of the attack; however, a unit moved to the location of the explosion. The Takhteh Pol COP and the local ABP commander were among the injured. ABP commander was evacuated from Spin Buldak to KAF under MEDEVAC 01-16B. He was listed as URGENT SURGICAL with severe abdominal wounds. IR strobe marked the PZ, which was a HLZ. Possible enemy in the area. CJTF76 approved MEDEVAC 01-16B at 1452Z, which will be accomplished in conjunction with AMR 01-16I. The unit will provide updates as available. W/U at 1527Z. W/D at 1617Z. M/C.

Reference ID: AFG20060120n200
Latitude:
Date: 2006-01-20 00:12
Category: IED Explosion
Detained: 0
Region: RC EAST
Longitude:
Type: Explosive Hazard
Affiliation: ENEMY

	Enemy	Friend	Civilian	Host nation
Killed in action	0	0	0	0
Wounded in action	0	0	0	0

Wazian Village, South of Khost City. One IED was detonated in front of the house of Mullah by the name of Rahmatullah Mansoor, ex-taliban commander who turned to the AG. Structural damages reported to the house.

Reference ID: AFG20060207n263
Latitude: 31.61828995
Date: 2006-02-07 06:06
Category: IED Explosion
Detained: 0
Region: RC SOUTH
Longitude: 65.70291138
Type: Explosive Hazard
Affiliation: ENEMY

	Enemy	Friend	Civilian	Host nation
Killed in action	0	0	7	16
Wounded in action	0	0	8	10

TF Bayonet reported a Suicide bomber detonation in Kandahar. At 0619Z TF Bayonet reported an explosion at the ANP HQ. There were no CF involved at the time of the explosion. KPRT responded immediately, and TF IED moved to the site. After exploiting the site, TF IED reported that a man with Asian features detonated explosives strapped to his chest and back while being searched prior to entering the ANP HQ. The unit reported that eight ANP were killed, five ANP were wounded, six LN were killed, one person unknown killed, and eight LN were injured. The wounded were evacuated by ground to LN hospital in Kandahar City.

Reference ID: AFG20060208n226
Latitude: 32.62580109
Date: 2006-02-08 03:03
Category: IED Explosion
Detained: 0
Region: RC WEST
Longitude: 62.54190063
Type: Explosive Hazard
Affiliation: ENEMY

	Enemy	Friend	Civilian	Host nation
Killed in action	0	4	0	0
Wounded in action	0	0	0	0

(CEXC 065_06) At approx 071230ZFeb06 a US Protection and Investigations (USPI) convoy of three vehicles was traveling, at approx 60 Kph, on highway 517 approx 4Km from Shawan. As the convoy passed a distinctive mound of earth on the side of the road, a series of explosions occurred under and around the center vehicle. A total of two explosions occurred simultaneously destroying the center vehicle and killing all four occupants.USPI secured the scene and US EOD assets were tasked to make the area safe.
INVESTIGATORS COMMENTS
11. The Mod 2 DTMF was buried on the side of the road, and was connected to the mine and artillery shells, at a distance of 4.5m and 4.1m respectively. It is likely Ethat this convoy was targeted specifically due to its regular use of the route and lack of ECM. USPI regularly travel the route, at least three times daily, and never travel with ECM. On a previous occasion the same USPI group was involved in an ambush consisting of a hand grenade and small arms fire. It is not known how often Coalition Forces patrol this route. Unfortunately the receiver was damaged during the explosion or render safe procedure which precluded bench testing.
12. As is commonly seen within this theater the receiver was initiated a short distance from the main charge. This close distance is probably to allow the bomber to recover the receiver for use at a later date.
13. The damage to the vehicle, dimensions of the crater, and lack of fragmentation are consistent with the functioning of a non-metallic anti-tank mine under the vehicle. Fragmentation found at the second seat of the explosion was consistent with the functioning of three HE 122mm projectiles. The use of two or more charges could indicate a desire to attack more than one vehicle or simply to increase the chances of a successful attack on a single target.
14. Of significance in this incident is the effective targeting of vehicles not carrying ECM and the inclusion of a daisy chained main charge.
Updated 3 Nov 07, Maj Harmon -- 065_06

Reference ID: AFG20060209n231
Latitude: 32.91814041
Date: 2006-02-09 04:04
Region: RC SOUTH
Longitude: 65.41526794
Type: Explosive Hazard

Category: IED Explosion Affiliation: ENEMY
Detained: 0

	Enemy	Friend	Civilian	Host nation
Killed in action	0	0	0	0
Wounded in action	0	0	2	0

CJSOTF reported TIC 14KM W of FOB Cobra. At 0442Z CJSOTF reported TIC with approximately 4 - 5 ACM fighters. The enemy initiated the contact with a command detonated IED followed by small arms fire. The unit immediately returned fire and maneuvered on the enemy positions. ANA elements with the patrol flanked the enemy positions. The enemy attempted to break contact. The unit later reported several command detonated IED were nearby. The unit requested and received CAS. A set of GR7 attack airplanes and one B52 bomber supported the unit. At 0843Z, CJSOTF reported that the patrol regained contact with the four ACM fighters. The unit again returned fire and maneuvered on the enemy. However, the enemy broke contact and fled. Two LN were injured in the incident, and both were MEDEVACED as detailed in SIGACT 6040-14406. 0843Z CJSOTF regained contact with 24 ACM with AK47s were firing on a friendly convoy. Enemy broke contact. No injuries or damage reported.

Reference ID: AFG20060210n214 Region: RC EAST
Latitude: 34.94562149 Longitude: 71.03825378
Date: 2006-02-10 00:12 Type: Explosive Hazard
Category: IED Explosion Affiliation: ENEMY
Detained: 0

	Enemy	Friend	Civilian	Host nation
Killed in action	0	0	0	7
Wounded in action	0	0	0	12

TF Devil reported troops in contact and three improvised explosive device (IED) strikes 13 kilometers southeast of Camp Blessing. Beginning at 0048Z and lasting until 1109Z, TF Lava reported three separate attacks against one of its patrols and two ANA patrols. All the attacks occurred between Camp Blessing and Asadabad along the Pech River Road. At 0048, TF Lava reported the first IED attack on the Pech River Road. The blast damaged one ANA vehicle. It also wounded two ANA soldiers and killed three ANA soldiers. A Marine patrol moved to the site to assist the ANA element. Enroute to the site, the patrol was struck by a second IED and received small arms fire from an unknown size ACM on the high ground at 0302Z. The Marines returned fire but were unable to maneuver on the enemy due to terrain. The ACM later broke contact. Two ANA soldiers were wounded in the contact, and were evacuated to BAF via helicopter on MEDEVAC 02-10A. One of the ANA soldiers was listed as URGENT, with internal injuries and a fractured left leg and tourniquet, and the other ANA soldier was ROUTINE. The unit reported possible enemy in the area. Yellow smoke marked the PZ, which was secured with two squads. CJTF76 approved MEDEVAC 02-10A at 0347Z. MEDEVAC 02-10A W/U at 0353Z. MEDEVAC 02-10A W/D and M/C at 0612Z. A third IED strike occurred at 0515Z at 42S XD 960 650 which was also along the Pech River Road. The third IED targeted an ANA patrol moving east along the Pech River. The blast killed five ANA soldiers and wounded seven ANA soldiers. At 1109Z, TF Devil declared that troops were no longer in contact. As a result of all three contacts, seven ANA soldiers were killed in action and twelve ANA were wounded. There were also three ANA vehicles damaged in the contacts.

Reference ID: AFG20060213n212
Latitude: 32.65343857
Date: 2006-02-13 04:04
Category: IED Explosion
Detained: 0

Region: RC SOUTH
Longitude: 65.39362335
Type: Explosive Hazard
Affiliation: ENEMY

	Enemy	Friend	Civilian	Host nation
Killed in action	0	4	0	0
Wounded in action	0	0	0	0

CJSOTF reported IED strike 37KM N of Deh Rawod . At 0433Z CJSOTF reported a M1114 vehicle struck an IED and was destroyed with 4X US KIA. 9 Line MEDEVAC requested for 4 X US KIA. MEDEVAC approved as 02-13A.
Update: TIC.
At 0553Z CJSOTF reported that ACM were attacking from western side of riverbed at 41SQS 309 502 with heavy direct fire. 1x B-52 dropped 8X GBU 31s on ACM positions. MEDEVAC 02-13A was cancelled and the remains were GROUNDEVACED to FOB Cobra, where they were CASEVACED by a resupply helicopter to Kandahar.
Update:
1st set of AH-64s on scene fired 200 X 30MM rounds, 42 X rockets. SIGINT determined ACM were in buildings, BDA was 3 X buildings destroyed, 2 X vehicles destroyed including the M1114 involved in the initial IED strike. No assessment received on insurgent losses. A-10s fired an additional 150 X 30MM HE rounds. All aircraft returned to base.

Reference ID: AFG20060401n247
Latitude: 34.94001007
Date: 2006-04-01 06:06
Category: IED Explosion
Detained: 1

Region: RC EAST
Longitude: 71.01785278
Type: Explosive Hazard
Affiliation: ENEMY

	Enemy	Friend	Civilian	Host nation
Killed in action	0	0	0	0
Wounded in action	0	5	0	0

TF Spartan reported an IED detonation 11KM SE of Camp Blessing. At 0649Z TF Spartan reported a Route Clearing Package enroute to Camp Blessing struck an IED. IED attack was followed by SAF from an unknown size enemy element. 5 x US MIL sustained injuries and a 9 Line MEDEVAC was requested at grid 42S XD 84330 68330. MEDEVAC was approved as 04-01A, W/U from JAF 0720Z.
At 0744Z TF Spartan reported friendly IND FR at enemy position 42SXD 8448069220.
At 0827Z TF Spartan reported no enemy contact at this time. Size of enemy at initial contact was unknown, initiator was IED detonation, followed up by SAF and RPG fire. Site is secured by RCP, and exploitation by CEXC is ongoing.
Recovery assets launched out of ABAD with EOD.
1x TB has been detained for questioned and turned over to FDS at ABAD.

AT 1050Z CEXC exploited the site, and will have report will be submitted.
1325Z PT Update: all 5x personnel were RTD.

Reference ID: AFG20060401n257
Latitude: 34.55408859
Date: 2006-04-01 15:03
Category: IED Explosion
Detained: 0

Region: RC CAPITAL
Longitude: 69.32198334
Type: Explosive Hazard
Affiliation: ENEMY

	Enemy	Friend	Civilian	Host nation
Killed in action	0	0	0	0
Wounded in action	0	0	0	0

(Delayed Report) IED detonation occurred at a market in Kabul. French EOD responded and recovered a Mosque Clock modified to act as an IED trigger a long with an attached power source. IED components were taken to CEXC BAF for exploitation.

Reference ID: AFG20060408n261
Latitude: 34.34592056
Date: 2006-04-08 06:06
Category: IED Explosion
Detained: 0

Region: RC WEST
Longitude: 62.22180939
Type: Explosive Hazard
Affiliation: ENEMY

	Enemy	Friend	Civilian	Host nation
Killed in action	1	0	2	0
Wounded in action	0	0	7	0

PRT Farah reported a SVBIED detonated 50M from Heart PRT main gate. At 0956Z, PRT Farah reported a SVBIED detonated near the main gate of the Heart PRT resulting in 3x Civilian deaths, 7x civilians wounded, and severe damages to the buildings surrounding the area. The explosion took place in the street by the South wall from PRT/RAC West compound leaving a crater of 5 cm deep on the pavement. The VBIED was a white Mitsubishi car with afghan plates, which was possibly circulating from West to East, in the direction of the main gate compound. The 3x civilian KIAs are: 1x suicide bomber (TBC), 1x of the afghan personnel guarding PRT main gate, and 1x civilian who was probably a passer-by. 7x were wounded, 1x badly and 1x Italian Civilian slightly this one who belonged to MAE staff (Civil IT). In an area of approximately 20x50 M, the level of destruction was clearly seen: 3x Cars destroyed in the street, metal rests from the VBIED and 3x Buildings with their facade glasses completely broken, one of them belonging to the PRT compound. No casualties in ISAF forces are reported. [UPDATED ON 09/04/2006 0450]: [UPDATED ON 09/04/2006 0452]:

Reference ID: AFG20060412n244
Latitude: 32.92731857
Date: 2006-04-12 00:12
Category: IED Explosion
Detained: 0

Region: RC EAST
Longitude: 69.39682007
Type: Explosive Hazard
Affiliation: ENEMY

	Enemy	Friend	Civilian	Host nation
Killed in action	0	0	0	0
Wounded in action	0	0	0	1

(Delayed Report) On 12 APR 06, Apache 6 reported that ANA/ASG elements were engaged in a direct fire ambush while on patrol to recover an overturned jingle fuel truck IVO Mane Kandow Pass. The ambush was initiated with an IED which was detonated under the fuel truck and was followed by RPG and small arms fire.

Reference ID: AFG20060419n234
Latitude: 34.25582886
Date: 2006-04-19 07:07
Category: IED Explosion
Detained: 0
Region: RC EAST
Longitude: 70.79318237
Type: Explosive Hazard
Affiliation: ENEMY

	Enemy	Friend	Civilian	Host nation
Killed in action	1	0	0	0
Wounded in action	0	0	0	0

TF VIGILANT REPORTS VBIED. AT 0700Z, TF VIGILANT REPORTED A VBIED ATTACK VIC 42S XC 65108 91977, ON THEIR CONVOY VIC TORKHAM. THE CONVOY WAS TRAVELING FROM TORKHAM TO JAF WHEN A VEHICLE TRIED TO PULL ALONGSIDE THEIR CONVOY. AS THE DEUCE1-3 CONVOY TRAVELED WEST, A LOCAL NATIONAL VEHICLE TRAVELING EAST CROSSED-OVER THE CENTERLINE NEAR THE SECOND VEHICLE OF THE THREE VEHICLE CONVOY. THE GUNNER IN THE VEHICLE REPORTED HEARING AN AUDIBLE EXPLOSION AS THE DRIVERS WINDOWS BLEW OUT. THE LN VEHICLE THEN IMMEDIATELY HALTED BEHIND THE CONVOY.
AS DISMOUNTS APPROACHED, THE DRIVER EXITED THE VEHICLE, SAT DOWN WITH A GRENADE AND PULLED THE PIN, DETONATING HIMSELF. AS EOD/CEX-C INSPECTED THE REAR OF THE VEHICLE THEY DISCOVERED (17) 82MM MORTAR ROUNDS, (4) AP MINES, (28) TNT-BOOSTERS, AND 10-LBS OF PROPELLANT. EOD REMOVED THE MUNITIONS TO A FIELD AND DETONATED THEM. CEX-C AND EOD WILL SUBMIT FURTHER REPORTING.

Reference ID: AFG20060422n233
Latitude:
Date: 2006-04-22 00:12
Category: IED Explosion
Detained: 0
Region: RC NORTH
Longitude:
Type: Explosive Hazard
Affiliation: ENEMY

	Enemy	Friend	Civilian	Host nation
Killed in action	0	0	0	0
Wounded in action	0	0	0	0

On 21 Apr 06 at 0300hrs, Two IEDs detonated in front of residential houses of Akhtar Mohammad Ebrahim Khil in charge of Mahaaz Milli party and his son Wali Mohammad Ebrahim Khil in Elabad village of Charbolak district. No casualties or injures were reported.

Reference ID: AFG20060422n246
Latitude: 32.23139954
Date: 2006-04-22 10:10
Category: IED Explosion
Detained: 0

Region: RC SOUTH
Longitude: 65.91356659
Type: Explosive Hazard
Affiliation: ENEMY

	Enemy	Friend	Civilian	Host nation
Killed in action	0	4	0	0
Wounded in action	0	0	0	0

TF Ageis reported IED Strike 5KM N of FOB Gumbad PRT. At 0309Z, TF reported IED detonation on convoy composed of 1 LAV, 1 LUVW, 1 GSK, 1 BISON. The detonation flipped the LUVW on its side, and injured 4X Pax. TF Aegis requested a MEDEVAC, for 1X Urgent and 3X KIA coalition soldiers. MEDEVAC was approved as 04-22B, and W/U from KAF 0356Z. MEDEVAC W/D at 0458Z. M/C AT 0456Z, TF Aegis reported that vehicle is too damaged for sling load recovery. The wreckage will be towed, TF IED will exploit the site. Unit on the ground believed the IED to be an RCIED, as a spider box was found. At 0738Z TF Aegis reported WIA DOW. At 1036Z, TF IED reported that the IED was comprised of 4X AT mines staked in two stacks, also was a RCIED. The IED detoanted under the 3rd vehicle of the convoy, the vehicle being a gun truck G-wagon. The 4X Coalition KIA arrived at KAF at 1003Z. Coalition element still maintaining security on site for vehicle extraction.

Reference ID: AFG20060425n232
Latitude:
Date: 2006-04-25 00:12
Category: IED Explosion
Detained: 0

Region: RC CAPITAL
Longitude:
Type: Explosive Hazard
Affiliation: ENEMY

	Enemy	Friend	Civilian	Host nation
Killed in action	0	0	0	0
Wounded in action	0	0	2	0

On 25 Apr 06 at approx 21:45 hrsTwo IEDs, believed to be remote controlled mines, exploded minutes apart on Kabul airport road close to the ANA Quick Reaction Force compound. The mines were placed inside a garbage container near a mosque. The details of the explosions remain unknown. It is not clear who the intended target was. A press release claimed people dead, but the official report only indicate two civilians injured.

Reference ID: AFG20060505n249
Latitude: 32.37033081
Date: 2006-05-05 04:04
Category: IED Explosion
Detained: 0

Region: RC SOUTH
Longitude: 65.08004761
Type: Explosive Hazard
Affiliation: ENEMY

	Enemy	Friend	Civilian	Host nation
Killed in action	0	0	3	0
Wounded in action	0	0	0	0

TF Aegis reported an IED strike. At 0435Z TF Aegis reported an IED strike against the police chiefs family near Kajaki Dam. ANA and ANP were dispatched to investigate.

It was later reported that 3x of the police chief's family were KIA. All ANP in the area responded to the strike, causing Operation Shepherd's reach to be delayed by 24 hours.

Reference ID: AFG20060505n259
Latitude: 33.42625427
Date: 2006-05-05 16:04
Category: IED Explosion
Detained: 0

Region: RC WEST
Longitude: 64.01112366
Type: Explosive Hazard
Affiliation: ENEMY

	Enemy	Friend	Civilian	Host nation
Killed in action	0	2	0	0
Wounded in action	0	4	0	0

(Delayed Report) ISAF reported an Italian patrol struck a mine 18 KM SE of Kabul. 2 Coalition troops KIA, 4 Coalition WIA. Patrol was responding to a Ghazni report of police chief striking a mine (SIGACT 15728). French patrol responded to the Italian mine strike. A third device was identified by the French (SIGACT 15729). ISAF requested MEDEVAC support for Italian WIAs. CJTF-76 provided MEDEVAC support from Camp Warehouse (German Role III facility) to Kabul IA where patients were transferred to Coalition aircraft for evacuation of WIAs out of country. NFTR. [UPDATED ON 05/06/2006 1749]:

Reference ID: AFG20060509n287
Latitude: 34.43661118
Date: 2006-05-09 06:06
Category: IED Explosion
Detained: 0

Region: RC EAST
Longitude: 68.8117981
Type: Explosive Hazard
Affiliation: ENEMY

	Enemy	Friend	Civilian	Host nation
Killed in action	0	0	0	0
Wounded in action	0	0	0	0

(Delayed Report) TF Paladin (Salerno)received a MOD 5 device from an IED detonation approximately 33 km SW of Kabul on 09 MAY that was turned in by ANP. RCP recovered the device from ANP at the scene. Crater was 4" wide by 2"; deep and contained no metal fragments. Team believes that plastic AT mines were used. The firing device had been located approximately 8" from center of crater and hidden behind a rock.

Reference ID: AFG20060518n320
Latitude: 34.34999084
Date: 2006-05-18 05:05
Category: IED Explosion
Detained: 0

Region: RC WEST
Longitude: 62.20000076
Type: Explosive Hazard
Affiliation: ENEMY

	Enemy	Friend	Civilian	Host nation
Killed in action	0	0	1	0
Wounded in action	0	3	2	0

ISAF CJOC reported 1x SVBIED strike occurred 1 KM N of Herat PRT. At 0507Z, ISAF CJOC reported a SVBIED strike occurred 1 KM N of PRT compound. The target seemed to be 2x US vehicles from training team with ANP. 1x vehicle was destroyed, 5x WIA. At 0529Z, ISAF CJOC reported 1x US Civilian KIA. 2x US Civilians WIA (Minor Injuries). 2x LN interpreter WIA (Minor Injuries), 1x Romanian security pax WIA (Minor Injuries). MEDEVAC is in progress. At 0645Z, BAF QRF approved to move TF Paladin to Kandahar to make movement to Herat.

Reference ID: AFG20060522n263
Latitude: 36.14364624
Date: 2006-05-22 00:12
Category: IED Explosion
Detained: 0

Region: RC NORTH
Longitude: 68.74119568
Type: Explosive Hazard
Affiliation: ENEMY

	Enemy	Friend	Civilian	Host nation
Killed in action	0	0	0	0
Wounded in action	0	0	0	0

It was reported that a RIED went off on the main road in Baghlan Jaded district while a big convoy of ANA was driving from Kunduz towards Mazar destination. According to ANA Battalion Commander the IED was remote control and had been placed in the farm field 12m away from the main road. The RIED said to be a 107mm rocket that was propelled by remote and went over the convoy and exploded in the other side of the road in an open area. The IED explosion left no casualties or damages to the ANA convoy. Police is investigating the incident.

Reference ID: AFG20060606n333
Latitude:
Date: 2006-06-06 00:12
Category: IED Explosion
Detained: 0

Region: RC SOUTH
Longitude:
Type: Explosive Hazard
Affiliation: ENEMY

	Enemy	Friend	Civilian	Host nation
Killed in action	1	0	6	0
Wounded in action	0	0	12	0

On 04 June, District 1, Kandahar City, Kandahar Province; at approximately 0930 hrs, a suicide VBIED detonated prematurely as the Governors convoy was approaching the Eidga Jada area of District 1, Kandahar City. The VBIED was parked outside a teahouse when the detonation occurred. Casualties to date are six civilians killed and twelve injured. The suicide bomber was killed in the explosion. The Governor was not injured in the blast.

Reference ID: AFG20060606n357
Latitude: 34.94512939
Date: 2006-06-06 14:02
Category: IED Explosion
Detained: 0

Region: RC EAST
Longitude: 71.06199646
Type: Explosive Hazard
Affiliation: ENEMY

	Enemy	Friend	Civilian	Host nation
Killed in action	0	0	0	2
Wounded in action	0	0	0	3

At 1415Z TF Chosin reported an ANA vehicle was destroyed by an IED. Unit moved to the site and found 2xANA KIA and 2xANA WIA. All ANA were ground evacuated to ABAD. Unit secured the site until TF Paladin exploitation. No additional IEDs or mines were found in the area. Update to SALTUR posted 1432Z: Engineers secured the site, and assessed 4x ANA casualties, PTs were ground EVACED to ABAD. TF Chosin reported two of the ANA are KIA and two WIA are being ground EVACED to ABAD. Update to SALTUR posted 1432Z, Engineers checked the site and found no further IEDS and unit secured the site until TF Paladin conducted post blast analysis, the IED appeared to have been an AT mine based on the size of the crater. At 0712Z, ABAD FST requested patient transfer for 2 ANA soldiers that were injured in the IED strike. At 0715Z, CJTF 76 approves MEDEVAC 06-06J. At 0748Z, MEDEVAC w/u from BAF to JAF. At 0759Z, MEDEVAC w/u from JAF to ABAD. At 0833Z, MEDEVAC W/U from ABAD to JAF. At 0939Z, MEDEVAC W/D at BAF. M/C.

Reference ID: AFG20060608n310
Latitude: 33.56039047
Date: 2006-06-08 09:09
Category: IED Explosion
Detained: 0

Region: RC EAST
Longitude: 68.34078217
Type: Explosive Hazard
Affiliation: ENEMY

	Enemy	Friend	Civilian	Host nation
Killed in action	0	0	0	0
Wounded in action	0	0	0	0

TF Iron Gray reported an IED strike on a US convoy. At 0908Z, TF Iron Gray reports that the 554th MPs struck an IED approximately 7 km W Ghazni City. One vehicle was overturned. Minor injuries were treated at site and no MEDEVAC was requested. At 1028Z, TF Iron Gray reported that are able to return the vehilcle to base. TF Paladin was with the patrol when it was hit and conducted site exploitation. TF Paladin recovered a pressure plate.

Reference ID: AFG20060610n286
Latitude:
Date: 2006-06-10 00:12
Category: IED Explosion
Detained: 0

Region: RC EAST
Longitude:
Type: Explosive Hazard
Affiliation: ENEMY

	Enemy	Friend	Civilian	Host nation
Killed in action	0	0	0	0
Wounded in action	0	0	0	0

An IED primed with time fuse was laid in front of the residence of the Head Master, Dargah High School. The IED exploded causing damage to the house but no cas occurred.

Reference ID: AFG20060613n28
Latitude: 36.82223892
Date: 2006-06-13 09:09

Region: RC NORTH
Longitude: 68.7387619
Type: Explosive Hazard

Category: IED Explosion   Affiliation: ENEMY
Detained: 0

	Enemy	Friend	Civilian	Host nation
Killed in action	0	0	0	0
Wounded in action	0	0	0	0

(Delayed Report) ISAF reports an IED detonation on a PSYOPs patrol in Kunduz City, Kunduz province. Device was an RCIED; exploitation team recovered a battery pack and Mod-5 DTMF. Suspected explosives were a 100mm Soviet projectile and bulk HE. No injury to personnel or damage to equipment was reported.

Reference ID: AFG20060615n304   Region: RC SOUTH
Latitude: Longitude:
Date: 2006-06-15 00:12   Type: Explosive Hazard
Category: IED Explosion   Affiliation: ENEMY
Detained: 0

	Enemy	Friend	Civilian	Host nation
Killed in action	0	0	0	0
Wounded in action	0	0	0	0

: On 15 June, Delaram District, Nimroz Province: at approximately 0930 hrs a demining team vehicle with four men on board, struck an RCIED ten kilometers east of Delaram. The vehicle was part of an UNMACA contracted de-mining team convoy. One deminer died at the scene and another whilst waiting for an air medivac. Two other occupants of the vehicle were injured. No additional information is available.

Reference ID: AFG20060628n299   Region: RC SOUTH
Latitude: 32.38294601   Longitude: 64.78833771
Date: 2006-06-28 01:01   Type: Explosive Hazard
Category: IED Explosion   Affiliation: ENEMY
Detained: 0

	Enemy	Friend	Civilian	Host nation
Killed in action	0	1	0	0
Wounded in action	0	2	0	0

At 0151Z, CJSOTF requested a MEDEVAC for 3x US soldiers injured in an IED strike 40KM N of FOB Robinson. MEDEVAC 06-28A W/U at 0258Z from BSN. W/D at PU site at 0329Z, W.D at BSN 0352Z. PT 1 died on arrival at Bastion, PT 2 had head injuries, and PT 3 had minor injuries to head and hands. Both patients were released from the hospital.

Reference ID: AFG20060629n266   Region: RC NORTH
Latitude: 36.76753998   Longitude: 67.59445953
Date: 2006-06-29 05:05   Type: Explosive Hazard
Category: IED Explosion   Affiliation: ENEMY
Detained: 0

	Enemy	Friend	Civilian	Host nation
Killed in action	0	0	0	0
Wounded in action	0	0	0	0

(DELAYED REPORT)On 29 June, a report was received that a rocket had been fired at a coalition convoy in route from Konduz to Pul e Khumri (PeK). The rocket was remotely fired and passed between the first and second vehicle, both vehicles were PATRIA armoured vehicles. The rocket seemed to be aimed to high according to witness reports and exploded well past the convoy. The rocket was launched approximately 15 to 20m from the convoy. One (1) DTMF Mod 2 and (5) D cell batteries were recovered by ISAF/PRT Pul e Khumri (PeK) elements. WIS arrived in PeK on 30 JUN 06 to recover components and brought all items to CEXC Kabul on 1 JUL 06. Items retrieved (1) heavily damaged DTMF Mod 2. Written on top of broken casing in white pen was the frequency 158 and firing code #8-. Two (2) holes had been bored in the casing piece that was still attached to the circuit board; one (1) had a green LED in it, the other had nothing. Five (5) separate wires had at one time extended from the DTMF casing: one (1) white, multi strand antenna wire measuring approximately 293cm that was broken into two (2) pieces ones measuring 67cm and the other measuring 226cm. Two (2), one (1) white and one (1) red, single-conductor multi-strand power input wires measuring approximately 14.3cm and 13.6cm respectively. Two (2) white, single-conductor multi-strand power output wire measuring 13.5cm that were then taped to two (2) red single-conductor multi-strand wires that measured 234.5cm giving the power output wires an overall length of 234.5cm. The receiver and decoder board measured 8.2cm (l) x 7.1cm (w). Written in black ballpoint pen on damaged tape adhered to a damaged integrated circuit was the frequency 58.345 and the firing code -2. The decoder board also contained one (1) red and one (1) yellow LED and a green LED attached to 8.2cm of white, dual conductor, multi-strand wire ran to the Mod 2 casing denoting the safe to arm feature. The Mod 2 was heavily damaged during firing preventing a bench test of the device.

One (1) white, multi-strand antenna wire measuring approximately 293cm that was broken into two (2) pieces ones measuring 67cm and the other measuring 226cm. Two (2) white, single-conductor multi-strand power output wire measuring 13.5cm that were then taped to two (2) red single-conductor multi-strand wires that measured 234.5cm giving the power output wires an overall length of 248cm Five (5) D Cell 1.5v Durata Heavy Duty batteries that were wrapped in paper and taped together. Multiple pieces of what appears to be a tire inner tube.

Reference ID: AFG20060707n353 Region: RC NORTH
Latitude: 36.12741852 Longitude: 68.70674133
Date: 2006-07-07 00:12 Type: Explosive Hazard
Category: IED Explosion Affiliation: ENEMY
Detained: 0

                        Enemy   Friend   Civilian Host nation
Killed in action
Wounded in action
A BBIED was detonated next to the car of KAMIN, the BAGHLAN City CoP. 2 local civilians were wounded. This may have been as a result of the criminal activities of the CoP and an alleged shoot out between his men and locals in NARIM District, just to the e

Reference ID: AFG20060709n328
Latitude: 34.51523972
Date: 2006-07-09 03:03
Category: IED Explosion
Detained: 0

Region: RC CAPITAL
Longitude: 69.17105103
Type: Explosive Hazard
Affiliation: ENEMY

	Enemy	Friend	Civilian	Host nation
Killed in action	0	0	1	0
Wounded in action	0	0	4	0

(Delayed Report) MOL Command Center reports, at 0730L IVO police district 15, a bus struck an IED while transporting the Ministry of Commerce employees. 4 local nationals WIA, 1 local national KIA.

Reference ID: AFG20060716n316
Latitude: 35.1464386
Date: 2006-07-16 14:02
Category: IED Explosion
Detained: 0

Region: RC EAST
Longitude: 71.39083099
Type: Explosive Hazard
Affiliation: ENEMY

	Enemy	Friend	Civilian	Host nation
Killed in action	0	0	0	0
Wounded in action	0	0	0	0

(DELAYED) At 0500Z, TF Titan received a report from ANP, of an IED, located 14 kilometers SW of FOB Narray, detonated on a Jingle Truck followed by SAF targeting the ANP element responding to the site. Unknown enemy size element. ANP secured the site, no injuries reported. ANP is not requesting CF support.

Reference ID: AFG20060726n277
Latitude: 32.6634407
Date: 2006-07-26 04:04
Category: IED Explosion
Detained: 1

Region: RC EAST
Longitude: 69.22640991
Type: Explosive Hazard
Affiliation: ENEMY

	Enemy	Friend	Civilian	Host nation
Killed in action	0	0	0	0
Wounded in action	0	0	0	0

At 0445, TF Chamberlain reported elemnts of the 27th EN BN was traveling from FOB Bermel to a construction site on OE-Bermel Rd when an IED detonated approx 5 meters in front of lead vehicle. Slight damage to Husky, no damage to personnel. Immediately after detonation, 2 x enemy personnel were witnessed fleeing the scene, leading ground personnel to believe IED was command detonated. ANA pursued and detained 1 x individual. Detainee was being taken to FOB Bermel for questioning by TF Catamount. 27th EN BN secured the IED remnants and took post blast photos for EOD at Orgun-E. IED materials have been returned to FOB O-E for further inspection. NFTR.

Reference ID: AFG20060729n279
Latitude: 36.94200134

Region: RC NORTH
Longitude: 66.78528595

Date: 2006-07-29 00:12 Type: Explosive Hazard
Category: IED Explosion Affiliation: ENEMY
Detained:
                         Enemy   Friend   Civilian   Host nation
Killed in action
Wounded in action
During our trip back to Mazar-e Sharif from Sheberghan we got a phone call from the Swedish PO Sheb at 1900hrs. They had got the information from ANP Sheb that a IED attack had been set off against one of their vehicles. No injuries reported. From our loc

Reference ID: AFG20060731n164   Region: RC EAST
Latitude: 34.35948944   Longitude: 70.47345734
Date: 2006-07-31 06:06   Type: Explosive Hazard
Category: IED Explosion   Affiliation: ENEMY
Detained: 0
Enemy	Friend	Civilian	Host nation
Killed in action	0	0	3	5
Wounded in action	0	0	27	0

At 0727 TF Chosin reports a VBIED detonated into a crowd of LNs. TF Chosin Received a report from JBAD PCC that during the conclusion of a funeral for a former Mujahedin CDR, a VBIED drove into the crowd around Governor Sherazis vehicle convoy IVO of the mosque and detonated. Governor is uninjured and was moved directly to the Gov compound in JBAD. The casualty reports is 8 x KIA and 16x WIA. OGA reports that a vehicle from the canal ministry was either the VBIED or was parked on top of the bomb. Governor has not asked for CF assistance ATT. At 0800Z, TF Paladin JAF team on site.

Reference ID: AFG20060803n324   Region: RC SOUTH
Latitude: 31.54844093   Longitude: 65.45552826
Date: 2006-08-03 09:09   Type: Explosive Hazard
Category: IED Explosion   Affiliation: ENEMY
Detained: 0
	Enemy	Friend	Civilian	Host nation
Killed in action	0	0	15	0
Wounded in action	0	0	15	0

(DELAYED REPORT) TF Orion reports and IED STRIKE IVO Panjwayi. ANP reports 10-15 civilian KIA and 10-15 civilian WIA. A civilian car advanced rapidly to the Orion 79 convoy, who where inroute to support a TIC in Panjwayi. Troops stopped the car and after a few minutes the vehicle advanced again and detonated. 5x CA WIA but no MEDEVAC requested. No major damage to the vehicles. WIA was treated in Role 3 at KAF.

Reference ID: AFG20060814n396   Region: RC EAST
Latitude: 34.01301956   Longitude: 69.0104599
Date: 2006-08-14 10:10   Type: Explosive Hazard

Category: IED Explosion
Detained: 0
Affiliation: ENEMY

	Enemy	Friend	Civilian	Host nation
Killed in action	0	0	0	0
Wounded in action	0	0	1	0

At 1024Z TF Vanguard reports they received a report from Dyna Corps. that an unidentified male rode his bicycle, which carried an unknown type of explosive device, into the path of a moving ANP truck approximately 4 KM NW of Pul-i Alam. The bicycle detonated, injuring the U/I male and blowing out the windows of the ANP truck. The man is currently in the Puli-Alam clinic under guard. ANSF investigation continues.

Reference ID: AFG20060819n346
Latitude: 34.93063354
Date: 2006-08-19 13:01
Category: IED Explosion
Detained: 0

Region: RC EAST
Longitude: 70.95763397
Type: Explosive Hazard
Affiliation: ENEMY

	Enemy	Friend	Civilian	Host nation
Killed in action	0	3	0	0
Wounded in action	0	3	0	0

At 0858z TF Chosin reports troops in contact approx. 8km SE of Camp Blessing. A convoy was moving north to south escorting jingle trucks to the KOP and IED detonated. Shortly after SAF was received from the east. Unit is currently returning fire and shooting 120mm Mortars at enemy positions. A separate patrol is in overwatch at Comcer Bandeh, approximately 3 km to the north, observing movement. TF Chosin reports 5x USA WIA casualties (unknown injuries att), 1x M1114 vehicle destroyed , and still recieving sporadic small arms fire. At 0940Z, 3x USA WIA are urgent and 2x USA WIA are unknown and still stuck in destroyed vehicle. One is going into shock, one is burned fairly bad, one received facial wounds and burns, and other 2 are unknown. At 1027Z, casuaties is now 3x USA KIA, 3x USA WIA (1 Urgent, 1 Expectant, 1 Priority). MEDEVAC 08-19B approved. W/U JAF 0959z. W/D ABAD 1023z. W/U ABAD 1029z. W/D grid 1035z. W/U grid 1045z. W/D ABAD 1109z. W/U BAF 1043z. W/D JAF 1110z. Transfer of burn patients from ABAD to BAF. W/U ABAD 1207z. W/D BAF 1314. M/C. Patient status: 1x USA WIA amputation of finger, stable condition; 1x USA WIA 40% burns to torso and arms, post surgery in guarded condition; 1x USA WIA 55% burns to torso and arms, post surgery in guarded condition.

Reference ID: AFG20060825n338
Latitude: 34.23165894
Date: 2006-08-25 10:10
Category: IED Explosion
Detained: 0

Region: RC EAST
Longitude: 70.18171692
Type: Explosive Hazard
Affiliation: ENEMY

	Enemy	Friend	Civilian	Host nation
Killed in action	0	2	0	0
Wounded in action	0	2	0	0

At 1030Z, TF Chosin reports IED strike approx. 38km SE of FOB Methar Lam. TF Chosin reports IED detonated on the last vehicle of a US/French patrol. The patrol was receiving SAF and MG fire on their position. CAS was requested. At 1041Z TF Chosin requested a MEDEVAC for 4 Litter Urgent. Medevac MM(E) 08-25C. 2x A-10s were on station in support of patrol. w/u BAF at 1141Z, w/d at BAF at 1249Z. All 4x pax were French soldier and 2x pax DOW.

Reference ID: AFG20060827n343
Latitude: 34.58327103
Date: 2006-08-27 08:08
Category: IED Explosion
Detained: 0

Region: RC CAPITAL
Longitude: 69.16866302
Type: Explosive Hazard
Affiliation: ENEMY

	Enemy	Friend	Civilian	Host nation
Killed in action	0	0	0	0
Wounded in action	0	0	0	0

(Delayed Report) An explosion occurred in Kabul City in District 15, Qasaba area, north of Kabul Airport. Conflicting reports state that an RCIED constructed of an anti tank mine was remotely detonated when a convoy belonging to a private company (Dynacorp) was passing a road on the north side of the Kabul Airport. The RCIED was planted on the roadside. Only the last car of the convoy was involved. No injuries reported and the only damage was broken glass.

Reference ID: AFG20060829n313
Latitude: 31.82028961
Date: 2006-08-29 08:08
Category: IED Explosion
Detained: 0

Region: RC SOUTH
Longitude: 64.56944275
Type: Explosive Hazard
Affiliation: ENEMY

	Enemy	Friend	Civilian	Host nation
Killed in action	0	0	1	1
Wounded in action	0	0	0	0

at 290819 Aug 06 the ANP passed to PSCC that the ANP Commander and his son were killed in an attack on the Gereshk Bridge, Nahri Sarraj district, Helmand province. It is believed that a landmine was used in the attack as either a RCIED or CWIED. PSCC was trying to gather more information and TFH PRT would post when collated.

Reference ID: AFG20060831n187
Latitude: 32.18318939
Date: 2006-08-31 06:06
Category: IED Explosion
Detained: 0

Region: RC SOUTH
Longitude: 67.01963043
Type: Explosive Hazard
Affiliation: ENEMY

	Enemy	Friend	Civilian	Host nation
Killed in action	1	0	1	0
Wounded in action	0	0	2	1

At 0640Z, TF Aegis reported the last vehicle of an MoI convoy, traveling from Kabul to Zabul, was hit by a SVBIED 11 KM NE of Qalat. 4 passengers from the convoy were wounded, including the Adj of the Chief of Highway Police. One civilian car traveling behind the convoy was also affected by the blast with 1 civilian killed and 2 wounded. The area was secured by Romanian MP platoon and 2x ANA platoons. The MoI convoy continued movement. Possible 2x RPG rounds and 2x 100 mm rounds. The EOD team will be sent to investigate.

Reference ID: AFG20060901n371
Latitude: 32.64808655
Date: 2006-09-01 05:05
Category: IED Explosion
Detained: 0

Region: RC EAST
Longitude: 69.23831177
Type: Explosive Hazard
Affiliation: ENEMY

	Enemy	Friend	Civilian	Host nation
Killed in action	0	0	0	0
Wounded in action	0	0	0	0

At 0505Z, TF Catamount reports the Malekshay school (just built with opening ceremony next week) was destroyed by an artillery round wired up inside the school. 3 rounds were in the hallway, the middle detonated, the other 2 failed to detonate. Detonation caused damage to the roof and most of the inside of the school. EOD TM was sent to exploit the site. At 0917Z Catamount reports the school in Malekeshay was destroyed and they recovered to 2 artillery rds. NFTR.

Reference ID: AFG20060907n398
Latitude: 31.70420647
Date: 2006-09-07 03:03
Category: IED Explosion
Detained: 0

Region: RC SOUTH
Longitude: 67.52156067
Type: Explosive Hazard
Affiliation: ENEMY

	Enemy	Friend	Civilian	Host nation
Killed in action	0	0	0	0
Wounded in action	0	0	0	0

At 070315Z Sept 06 a convoy reported (13 km northeast of FOB VARNER, along HWY 1, Shahjoy district, Zabol province), an ambush with SAF, RPGs and multiple IEDs. At first they returned fire and after that they broke contact. QRF has left FOB VARNER to support. TIC was closed at 0400Z.

Reference ID: AFG20060909n388
Latitude: 36.31159973
Date: 2006-09-09 05:05
Category: IED Explosion
Affiliation: ENEMY
Detained: 0

Region: RC NORTH
Longitude: 68.82681274
Type: Explosive Hazard

	Enemy	Friend	Civilian	Host nation
Killed in action	0	0	0	0
Wounded in action	0	0	0	0

(Delayed report) At 0340Z, RC(N) reported a patrol was attacked by a rocket. A timing device, remote control, battery pack and detonator have been found at the firing position. EOD and QRF arrived at police station in order to investigate found BM-1 rocket. The police have arrested an unknown number of suspects (TBC). MTF.

Reference ID: AFG20060913n383
Latitude: 35.31015015
Date: 2006-09-13 11:11
Category: IED Explosion
Detained: 0
Region: RC EAST
Longitude: 71.540802
Type: Explosive Hazard
Affiliation: ENEMY

	Enemy	Friend	Civilian	Host nation
Killed in action	0	0	0	4
Wounded in action	0	0	0	0

At 1237Z, TF Titan reports IED ambush approximately 11km north of FOB Naray. The ABP District Chief Ahmed Shah, his mess officer, and 2x of his bodyguards were killed when their vehicle was struck by the IED while on patrol (inspecting checkpoints). The KIA are currently located with TF Titan at the Naray ANBP station. The TF Titan element at the scene is going to move the remains of the ANBP Chief to ABAD in the morning. NFTR.

Reference ID: AFG20060908n388
Latitude: 33.42625427
Date: 2006-09-08 06:06
Category: IED Explosion
Detained: 0
Region: RC WEST
Longitude: 64.01112366
Type: Explosive Hazard
Affiliation: ENEMY

	Enemy	Friend	Civilian	Host nation
Killed in action	1	2	14	0
Wounded in action	0	0	0	0

At 0550z, CFC-A reports an SVBIED at US Embassy, Mossoud Circle, Camp Eggers, Kabul City. An SVBIED attacked a Methar Lam PRT convoy on the way to the embassy in Massoud circle, Kabul at 0600Z. Convoy was in route to the embassy in Kabul to pick up PRT members as said in the CONOP and the OOA. Securing the site ATT. Two US KIA were US PRT CA members. Vehicle bumper number CA31. MTF

Reference ID: AFG20060929n341
Latitude: 31.56027985
Date: 2006-09-29 08:08
Category: IED Explosion
Detained: 0
Region: RC SOUTH
Longitude: 65.43077087
Type: Explosive Hazard
Affiliation: ENEMY

	Enemy	Friend	Civilian	Host nation
Killed in action	0	1	0	0
Wounded in action	0	0	0	0

At 290820Z Sep 06, a dismounted platoon 2.5km S of ZHARI DC (ZHARI District, KANDAHAR Province) struck an IED. 1x CDN KIA. TF PALADIN/CEXC/NIS transported to PBW to exploit the site. Initial investigation stated explosion caused by suspected 1x AT, 1x 107mm, pressure plate (UNCONFIRMED). At 291750L Sept 06: TF PALADIN exploited the site. The explosion was very powerful, it left a crater of 3 meters in diameter and 1 meter deep. The explosion threw the victim 15 meters away. Few remains of the device could be recovered, this made it difficult to determine the construction of the explosive device, possibly an anti-personnel mine initiated an anti-tank mine. Further investigation on recovered items is being conducted to bring more clarification. Detailed report to follow through EOD channels. Incident closed at 1409Z.

Reference ID: AFG20061006n483
Latitude: 31.11675835
Date: 2006-10-06 02:02
Category: IED Explosion
Detained: 0

Region: RC SOUTH
Longitude: 64.04110718
Type: Explosive Hazard
Affiliation: ENEMY

	Enemy	Friend	Civilian	Host nation
Killed in action	0	0	0	0
Wounded in action	0	0	0	1

(Delayed Reporting) 050230L Oct 06:. After fighting between ANSF and TB forces ivo Gereshk, 1x ANP pax was injured by an explosion whilst re-occupying a former TB position. Assessment by ANSF was that TB had emplaced VOIED or landmine. EOD did not deploy due to FP issues and unknown loc of incident. Possible new TTP in Helmand province. NFTR.

Reference ID: AFG20061012n442
Latitude: 32.9242897
Date: 2006-10-12 14:02
Category: IED Explosion
Detained: 0

Region: RC EAST
Longitude: 68.0427475
Type: Explosive Hazard
Affiliation: ENEMY

	Enemy	Friend	Civilian	Host nation
Killed in action	0	0	0	0
Wounded in action	0	2	0	0

While conducting a planned movement, CJSOTF received 1x IED which resulted in 2x US WIA (1x fractured leg/compartment syndrome, 1x ambulatory). 1x GMV destoyed. QRF was launched with recovery assets from Organ-E. CAS was on station, no BDA, USSF WIA were taken to Organ-E. MEDEVAC was approved as MM(E)10-12C. W/U OE 1545z, W/D Grid 1621z, W/U Grid 1625z. MM10-12C W/D OE MC 1652Z. Patients are in stable condition. NFTR.ISAF Tracking # 10-273.

Reference ID: AFG20061015n430
Latitude: 37.11100769
Date: 2006-10-15 00:12
Category: IED Explosion
Detained:

Region: RC NORTH
Longitude: 70.56298065
Type: Explosive Hazard
Affiliation: ENEMY

	Enemy	Friend	Civilian	Host nation
Killed in action				
Wounded in action				

Vehicle of COM PRT FEYZABAD was attacked with an IED (donkey-born IED). COM PRT and his CPT were able to leave the area and return to PRT Feyzabad. No ISAF casualties, the vehicle is lightly damaged. 4xLN wounded. All forces of PRT FEYZABAD are back in ca

Reference ID: AFG20061019n388
Latitude: 31.59233093
Date: 2006-10-19 06:06
Category: IED Explosion
Detained: 0

Region: RC SOUTH
Longitude: 64.35748291
Type: Explosive Hazard
Affiliation: ENEMY

	Enemy	Friend	Civilian	Host nation
Killed in action	0	1	2	0
Wounded in action	0	1	7	0

At 191248ZOCT06, TF Helmand reports that a UK patrol struck an SIED that resulted in 1x UK MIL KIA, 1x UK MIL WIA, 2x LN Children KIA and 7x LNs WIA. TF Helmand believes the attack was not just against British forces but also innocent LNs. The soldiers were MEDEVAC to Cp Bastion.

Reference ID: AFG20061031n239
Latitude: 35.10147858
Date: 2006-10-31 04:04
Category: IED Explosion
Detained: 0

Region: RC EAST
Longitude: 70.91771698
Type: Explosive Hazard
Affiliation: ENEMY

	Enemy	Friend	Civilian	Host nation
Killed in action	0	3	0	0
Wounded in action	0	1	0	0

At 310417ZOCT06 TF CHOSIN reported a patrol struck an IED 13km north of FB Blessing. Unit requested AH QRF support and MEDEVAC. 0449Z Unit reported 1 US WIA, 3 US KIA. Patrol moving patients to LZ. 0455Z Unit reported 3 US KIA, 1 US WIA (PT 1- Fx Arm, shrapnel and concussion). TF Paladin was requested to exploit IED site. MM 10-31A W/U Jaf 0441Z, W/D LZ Bella 0537Z, W/D Abad 0610z. 0700Z unit reported 1x US WIA at ABAD DOW. HERO Mission W/U Baf 0601z, W/D Jaf 0631z, W/U Jaf 0814z, W/D Grid 0820z, W/U Grid 0824z, W/D Abad 0833z, W/U Abad 0920z, W/D Baf 1004z. M/C. 3x US KIA, 1x US WIA. Event closed at 1007Z. ISAF Tracking#10-655

Reference ID: AFG20061031n246
Latitude: 33.32081985
Date: 2006-10-31 06:06
Category: IED Explosion
Detained: 0

Region: RC EAST
Longitude: 68.42842865
Type: Explosive Hazard
Affiliation: ENEMY

	Enemy	Friend	Civilian	Host nation
Killed in action	1	0	0	1
Wounded in action	0	3	0	0

At 310703ZOCT06 TF IRONGRAY reported a Suicide Bomber detonated himself while trying to enter the Miri DC. Unit reported ANP Soldier stopped a suspicious elderly male attempting to enter the Miri DC at the check point. When the ANP approached the man, he detonated himself. 1 ANP KIA, 3 US WIA (minor shrapnel wounds). Three US were ground evacd to FOB Sharana for treatment of minor injuries. QRF/Paladin responded. Paladin will forward the completed report. Closed 0945Z. ISAF Tracking# 10-661.

Reference ID: AFG20061114n529
Latitude: 32.1457901
Date: 2006-11-14 10:10
Category: IED Explosion
Detained: 0

Region: RC SOUTH
Longitude: 66.50406647
Type: Explosive Hazard
Affiliation: ENEMY

	Enemy	Friend	Civilian	Host nation
Killed in action	0	0	0	0
Wounded in action	0	3	0	0

At 141132ZNOV06 TF Taurus reported a Charlie 1-4 convoy was taking SAF and RPG fire when they struck an IED 5km S of Mizan Base. The convoy engaged the enemy with SAF and requested to blow in place 1x M1151 HMMWV struck by the IED because it was unrecoverable. Contact with the enemy was lost. At this point CAS was approved to destroy the HMMWV. The convoy confirmed the HMMWV was destroyed by a CAS gun run. 3x US Mil WIA were ground evacuated to FOM Mizan. 1x US Mil was wounded with 2 puntures through the upper thigh, 2x US Mll with blast injuries and will be medevaced at first light to Qalat FST for further evaluation and treatment. Wounded US mil arrived in Qalat at 150339ZNOV06.
M/C.
ISAF Tracking# 11-230.

Reference ID: AFG20061203n477
Latitude: 31.62048912
Date: 2006-12-03 06:06
Category: IED Explosion
Detained: 0

Region: RC SOUTH
Longitude: 65.71856689
Type: Explosive Hazard
Affiliation: ENEMY

	Enemy	Friend	Civilian	Host nation
Killed in action	0	0	0	0
Wounded in action	0	3	0	0

At 030630ZDEC06, TF TAURUS reported A VBIED attack against ISAF Convoy 2km SW of CAMP Nathan Smith. 3xUK WIA, 3xLN KIA, and 22xLN WIA. British WIA were transported to KAF. ISAF vehicle was recovered by the ANA and the VBIED was put on the low bed and moved back to PRI for exploitation. Event closed at 0933Z. ISAF Tracking# 12-028.

Reference ID: AFG20061215n532
Latitude:
Date: 2006-12-15 11:11

Region: RC EAST
Longitude:
Type: Explosive Hazard

Category: IED Explosion Affiliation: ENEMY
Detained: 0

	Enemy	Friend	Civilian	Host nation
Killed in action	0	1	0	0
Wounded in action	0	2	0	0

At 151150ZDEC06 Mehtar Lam PRT reported a patrol struck an IED approximately 3km northwest of FB Mehtar Lam. There are 2x US WIA, 1x US KIA(DOW: severe amputation). Mehtar Lam PRT reported there are multiple IEDs still at the location. MEDEVAC was requested, and at 1203z MM(E)12-15B was approved. At 1208Z Mehtar Lam PRT reported that additional IEDs at the location detonated. ANA/QRF/EOD/TF Paladin moved to the site. The element ground evacuated the casualties to FB Methar Lam, due to the remaining IED threat. QRF secured site, EOD determined IED's were daisy chained, 5xIED total. MM(E)12-15B W/U BAF 1235Z, W/D at ML PRT at 1302z, W/U from ML PRT at 1417z, W/D at BAF at 1449z, M/C. At 1655z TF Iron Grays updates that the element securing the site for TF Paladin received SAF. TF Iron Grays returned fire with 81mm (illum), and IR Illum from CAS on station. There is no further contact ATT. TF Paladin exploited site and RTB to JAF. The QRF element recovered the disabled vehicle, and all elements are RTB at 2030z. NFTR. ISAF tracking #12-185

Reference ID: AFG20061222n518 Region: RC CAPITAL
Latitude: 34.503479 Longitude: 69.19608307
Date: 2006-12-22 05:05 Type: Explosive Hazard
Category: IED Explosion Affiliation: ENEMY
Detained: 0

	Enemy	Friend	Civilian	Host nation
Killed in action	1	0	0	0
Wounded in action	0	0	8	0

At 220535ZDEC06, RC Central reported a SVBIED attack directed against the vehicle of a representative of PAKTIA Province near Sah Sehid area-PD8 in Kabul. The Parliament member was not in the vehicle. 1 EKIA, 3 bodyguards and 5 LNs injured. TU BG QRF and IRT are alerted. MoI officials collected evidence at the scene. The scene has been cleared. NFTR. ISAF Tracking#12-265.

Reference ID: AFG20070105n533 Region: RC EAST
Latitude: 32.76966476 Longitude: 69.32778931
Date: 2007-01-05 11:11 Type: Explosive Hazard
Category: IED Explosion Affiliation: ENEMY
Detained: 0

	Enemy	Friend	Civilian	Host nation
Killed in action	1	0	0	0
Wounded in action	0	4	0	0

At 051200ZJAN07 TF CATAMOUNT/27th EN reported a SVBIED (Black Hilux) with 3 PAX attacked the Margah COP construction site. Unit reported as the Hilux approached the CF outer cordon, it failed to halt. CF then engaged the vehicle and at that time it detonated. Catamount reported 4 US WIA, 3 EKIA. 1205Z Medevac requested and approved. MM 01-05C w/u 1227Z, w/d Grid 1252Z, w/u Grid 1305Z, w/d OE 1311Z, MC. Paladin exploited site and found only 1xPAX in the VBIED from previously reported 3xPAX. ISAF Tracking # 01-061.

Reference ID: AFG20070109n561   Region: RC SOUTH
Latitude: 31.54845047   Longitude: 65.42346191
Date 2007-01-09 03:03   Type: Explosive Hazard
Category: IED Explosion   Affiliation: ENEMY
Detained: 0

	Enemy	Friend	Civilian	Host nation
Killed in action	0	0	0	0
Wounded in action	0	0	0	0

(DELAYED REPORT) At 090355ZJAN07 a CF Canadian clearance convoy hit a suspected IED IVO of Route Cornerbrooke. EOD and Paladin deployed and recovered a s mall amount of fragmentation from an unknown AT mine and a small piece of black rubber. CEXC Report: CEXC_AFG_017_07. NFTR.

Reference ID: AFG20070113n557   Region: RC EAST
Latitude: 33.39704514   Longitude: 70.24733734
Date: 2007-01-13 07:07   Type: Explosive Hazard
Category: IED Explosion   Affiliation: ENEMY
Detained: 0

	Enemy	Friend	Civilian	Host nation
Killed in action	0	0	0	0
Wounded in action	0	0	0	0

At 130943ZJAN07 TF WOLFPACK reported PCC reported they received a report at 0745Z that 5 different GOA employees had a mine or IED placed in front of their house last night. All 5 explosions were mines set on timers and happened at separate times during the night. No components recovered as of yet. ANP believes this was used as a scare tactic and no suspects have been identified. The first was Salekhan s/o Besmilik of Belawud Village (no casualties). Second was Namat s/o Bakul of same village (2 children slightly injured). Third was Mohammad Nabi s/o Mohammad Rasul of the same village who works for the Khowst municipality (no casualties). Fourth was Malem Khan of the Jarobi Village who works for the Khowst Criminal Office (no casualites). The fifth was Alem Khan s/o Fazal of Jarobi Village a driver for Khowst Attorney (no casualties). The only damage caused was the gates to the compounds were destroyed. NFTR. [No grid with report. Grid is a ballpark grid in the Tirzaye district] ISAF Tracking #01-213

Reference ID: AFG20070114n616   Region: RC SOUTH
Latitude: 31.62638092   Longitude: 65.54369354
Date: 2007-01-14 23:11   Type: Explosive Hazard
Category: IED Explosion   Affiliation: ENEMY
Detained: 0

	Enemy	Friend	Civilian	Host nation
Killed in action	0	0	0	0
Wounded in action	0	2	0	0

At 142346ZJAN07, TF Grizzly reported a US NSE 5-ton wrecker, traveling in a convoy consisting of 8 x vehicle and 27 x pax, struck a PPIED while enroute to PB Wilson. The element was operating as part of a LEVEL I CONOP GUNDAY. Following the blast the element secured the location, identifying a secondary device (possibly an RCIED) IVO the initial blast site. 2 x US MIL were wounded in the blast and were MEDEVAC'd to KAF where they are currently being treated (1x Urgent Surgical, 1x priority).
At 0636Z TF Paladin reported that they had exploited the scene, the IED was command wired activated pressure plate and all elements had been returned to base. 1 x suspect in custody. Incident closed.
ISAF TRACKING# 01-241.

Reference ID: AFG20070116n549
Latitude: 34.54743958
Date: 2007-01-16 04:04
Category: IED Explosion
Detained: 0

Region: RC CAPITAL
Longitude: 69.25887299
Type: Explosive Hazard
Affiliation: ENEMY

	Enemy	Friend	Civilian	Host nation
Killed in action	0	0	0	0
Wounded in action	0	0	8	0

At 160503ZJAN07 TF Phoenix reported one silver Toyota Corolla rammed the Camp Phoenix front gate at 0430Z. The gate personnel noted wires hanging from the vehicle. The Pakistan driver was removed from the car by guards and detained. EOD was notified and a 200 meter safe zone was established. A cordon was set on route violet, and route violet and the main gate were declared BLACK. Gate 8 remained open and was RED. The detained driver said there was a bomb in the vehicle and the interpreter at the gate verified the presence of a bomb. EOD inspected the vehicle with a robot. ANP were at the scene to assist with the cordon. Based on the amount of explosives in the vehicle, the inside perimeter was increased to 300 meters, EOD continued to work on clearing the vehicle and reported they would not intentionally detonate the vehicle in place to allow exploitation by TF Paladin. The vehicle was being exploited by the robot when it detonated resulting in minor injury to several Local Nationals who were treated by TF Phoenix Medics and 1x robot destroyed. The main gate was damaged in the explosions and is not accessible. Event was closed at 1130Z. ISAF Tracking #01-256
==
Summary from duplicate report CEXC
(CEXC) On 16 JAN 07, at approximately 0915L, a silver Toyota Corolla, license number KBL15768SL, attempted to breach the front gate at Camp Phoenix. The driver of the vehicle was observed handling some wires before he was removed from the vehicle by guards.
Updated 18 Dec 07, Maj Harmon - 8 LN were injured when device high-ordered during RSP. However, these injuries will not be counted becasuse they were not the result of the suicide bomber detonating as planned.
1x SILVER/GOLD TOYOTA COROLLA WAS DRIVEN INTO THE MAIN GATE OF CAMP PHEONIX. THE DRIVER (PAKISTANI) WAS PULLED FROM THE VEHICLE AND CLAIMS THAT THE VEHICLE IS A VBIED. THE DRIVER HAS BEEN

DETAINED AND A PERIMETER ERECTED. ROUTE VIOLET IS OOB BETWEEN V3 AND V5. 42SWD236226 CAMP PHEONIX / KABUL / RC
UPDATE AS AT 161300D*:
EOD CONDUCTED A CONTROLLED EXPLOSION OF THE VEHICLE. AN UNKNOWN NUMBER OF LNs SUSTAINED MINOR INJURIES AS A RESULT. THE TQ OF THE DRIVER IS ONGOING. A US GUARD REPORTED THAT A LN WAS PHOTOGRAPHING THE INCIDENT AS IT TOOK PLACE. THE LN WAS NOT APPREHENDED.
End duplicate report summary

Reference ID: AFG20070119n546
Latitude: 32.89636612
Date: 2007-01-19 04:04
Category: IED Explosion
Detained: 0
Region: RC SOUTH
Longitude: 66.227005
Type: Explosive Hazard
Affiliation: ENEMY

	Enemy	Friend	Civilian	Host nation
Killed in action	0	0	0	0
Wounded in action	0	0	6	0

A convoy with the District Commissioner was subjected to an IED blast on the Trin Kot - Chora Road. 6 CIV wounded, including the DC.

Reference ID: AFG20070121n537
Latitude: 34.40288925
Date: 2007-01-21 10:10
Category: IED Explosion
Detained: 0
Region: RC CAPITAL
Longitude: 69.16533661
Type: Explosive Hazard
Affiliation: ENEMY

	Enemy	Friend	Civilian	Host nation
Killed in action	0	0	0	0
Wounded in action	0	0	0	0

At 21 1030Z Jan 07, Lightning Main reported to TF Phoenix that a TF PHX convoy was struck by an VBIED 19KM S of Camp Phoenix at approximately 1010Z. When the VBIED detonated the lead UAH sustained damage to the front of the vehicle, flattening the front two tires. A KBR vehicle was also damaged during the strike by debris from the explosion. The convoy pushed through the strike and continued on to Pul-e-Alam. No casualties are reported, however, the driver and the gunner are being examined as a precaution in Pul-e-Alam. VBIED was a yellow/white corolla (taxi). NFTR. Event closed at 1300Z. ISAF TRACKING # 01-327.

Reference ID: AFG20070123n494
Latitude: 33.36355209
Date: 2007-01-23 02:02
Category: IED Explosion
Detained: 0
Region: RC EAST
Longitude: 69.95665741
Type: Explosive Hazard
Affiliation: ENEMY

	Enemy	Friend	Civilian	Host nation
Killed in action	1	0	6	2
Wounded in action	0	0	4	1

At 230256ZJAN07 TF SPARTAN reported an PBIED detonated at FB Salerno KPF gate. 0309 Spartan reported ALL CLEAR. QRF and TF Paladin responded to PBIED Site. 0542Z Paladin reported a suicide bomber with a vest was attempting to enter the FOB through the pedestrian gate. When the PBIED arrived at the search point, he then detonated his vest resulting in 2 KPF KIA, 6 LN KIA, 4 LN WIA, 1 KPF WIA, 1 suicide EKIA. Event closed at 0550Z. ISAF Tracking# 01-353. JDIGS: 774TH EOD / 774-28-07 \2007 JAN 23\07:30\42SWB9071693013\EXPLOSIVE

Reference ID: AFG20070126n475
Latitude: 32.48624039
Date: 2007-01-26 07:07
Category: IED Explosion
Detained: 0
Region: RC SOUTH
Longitude: 64.37525177
Type: Explosive Hazard
Affiliation: ENEMY

	Enemy	Friend	Civilian	Host nation
Killed in action	1	0	0	0
Wounded in action	0	0	0	1

At 260754ZJAN07 TF Helmand reported a 1xPAX approached the guard of a Global Security Compound. 1xPax had a letter which he claimed allowed him access to the compound. The guard refused entry and shot the individual suspecting him as a SBIED. While the 1xPAX was lying on the ground he detonated himself. The blast killed the bomber and seriously injured the guard which was taken to a local hospital. Primary and Secondary QRF are on standby. The FF C/S at the NDS compound recovered to LKG MOB, QRF's stood down, threat warning decreased and event is closed at 1600Z. NFTR. ISAF Tracking # 01-394.

Reference ID: AFG20070209n600
Latitude: 34.80599976
Date: 2007-02-09 06:06
Category: IED Explosion
Detained: 0
Region: RC EAST
Longitude: 71.11643219
Type: Explosive Hazard
Affiliation: ENEMY

	Enemy	Friend	Civilian	Host nation
Killed in action	0	0	0	0
Wounded in action	0	0	0	0

At 0641Z ABAD PRT reported having two IEDs detonate in front of and behind their convoy that was heading to Camp Joyce in Sarkony. No damage to men or equipment. No further enemy activity.
NFTR.

Reference ID: AFG20070226n499
Latitude: 33.34033966
Date: 2007-02-26 04:04
Category: IED Explosion
Detained:
Region: RC EAST
Longitude: 69.92523956
Type: Explosive Hazard
Affiliation: ENEMY

	Enemy	Friend	Civilian	Host nation
Killed in action	1	0	0	1
Wounded in action	0	0	0	1

At 260445ZFEB07, TF FURY reported 1 X Suicide bomber dressed in ANP uniform walked up to ANP police substation and attempted to enter.
ANP did not recognize the bomber and stopped him.
He continued to try to enter ANP shot at him and he detonated himself kill 1 X SIED, 1 X ANP KIA, 1 X ANP WIA.
TF PALADIN C-IED team from Salerno responding to post blast.
Update 1150Z: Salerno team returned to base, full report to follow.
Event Closed at 1151Z.
ISAF Tracking# 02-384.

Reference ID: AFG20070227n583
Latitude: 34.93420029
Date: 2007-02-27 11:11
Category: IED Explosion
Detained: 0

Region: RC EAST
Longitude: 69.24318695
Type: Explosive Hazard
Affiliation: ENEMY

	Enemy	Friend	Civilian	Host nation
Killed in action	1	3	15	1
Wounded in action	0	2	15	0

At approximately 0517Z a suicide bomber detonated himself at the Movement Control Team (MCT) shack near ECP 1 on Bagram Airfield (BAF). It is undetermined at this time, but the bomb may have been a vest packed with explosives and ball bearings. Initial reporting stated that the suicide bomber may have been a truck driver coming from Tagab by way of FOB 33. This information is unsubstantiated at this time. The drivers papers stating that there was a driver coming from Tagab was taken from the scene by local ANP and retrieved by BAF CI. It is undetermined at this time if the information actually belonged to the bomber. Reporting from the scene stated that there was 1 US KIA, 1 KBR KIA, one Korean KIA, 21 LNs WIA, 1 US WIA (who has returned to duty) and 1 GOV or KBR WIA. Further reporting from CJTF-76 stated that the Taliban announced on BBC and Al Jazeera that they were responsible for the attack and that the intended target was Vice President Cheney. The report of a possible second bomber or trigger man wasunfounded when BAF CI questioned the individuals captured at Tower 24. There was a LN that was injured during the blast and attempted to get help from the US Hospital. He was redirected to the Egyptian Hospital and apprehended when he was thought to have discarded a possible trigger mechanism for the bombing. This was found to be a tourniquet that was applied after the explosion to wounds sustained by the suicide bombing.
===
Summary from duplicate report
CEXC Report
(CEXC) Post blast investigation revealed that the explosion...was the result of a suicide device delivered on foot. The suicide device was initiated IVO of the shelters. In the local area were 1 x US MCT soldier, 1 x Korean escorting soldier, numerous LNs and several contractors. A 1012 man US PRT had moments prior, passed the point of initiation as they left BAF in armored HMMWVs. The explosion resulted in significant casualties. CEXC BAF conducted scene exploitation.
CASUALTIES AND DAMAGED EQUIPMENT
4. (S//REL) a. Casualties: 20 KIA, (1xUS, 1xRoK, 1xUS Contactor, 1xANA, 15xLNs), 1xEKIA

17 WIA (1xUS, 1xUS Contactor, 15 x LNs) fig approx due to walking wounded leaving scene.
(S//REL) b. Equipment: 2x HMMWV Light fragmentation damage
1x LN vehicles with heavy fragmentation damage
Multiple LN vehicles with light fragmentation damage
At 0517ZFEB07 TF Gladius reported a SIED at ECP1 of Bagram AB. TF PALADIN exploited the scene while TF GLADIUS secured the scene. ECP1 was closed and BAF was locked down. ECP3 was then opened to Coalition Traffic. Buildings around the ECP were secured. F-15's conducted a show of force in the vicinity of BAF. Initial Casualty figures include 9 KIA (1 US Mil, 1 ROK Mil, 1 AMC Contractor, 3 Local Nationals, 2 Pakistani Nationals, 1 Suiced Bomber). 24 WIA (1US Mil-RTD, 1 KBR contractor, 22 Local Nationals). Further reporting from CJTF-76 stated that the Taliban announced on BBC and Al Jazeera that they were responsible for the attack and that the intended targetwa Vice President Chaney. The report of a possible second bomber or trigger man was unfounded when BAF CI questioned the individuals captured at Tower 23. There was an LN that was injured during the blast and attempted to get help from the US Hospital. He was directed to the Egyptian Hospital and apprehended when he thought to have discarded a possible trigger mechanism fo the bombing. This was found to be a tourniquet that was applied after the explosion to wounds. ISAF Trackting #02-405

Reference ID: AFG20070305n622
Latitude: 33.32484818
Date: 2007-03-05 18:06
Category: IED Explosion
Detained:

Region: RC EAST
Longitude: 68.48255157
Type: Explosive Hazard
Affiliation: ENEMY

	Enemy	Friend	Civilian	Host nation
Killed in action	0	0	0	0
Wounded in action	0	0	0	0

At 051848mar07, TF 2Furys element was in a convoy of 6 vehicles, 18 personnel, and 1 interpreter traveling from FB Miri to FOB Ghazni along route Rebel when the lead vehicle struck an IED at VB 5184 8742. The lead vehicle was disabled. The element immediately cleared and secured the immediate area. They moved to the Abdul Val ANP station (VB 5478 8825) after the area was cleared and 100% accountability was achieved. No injuries were reported. NFTR
Assessment: Initial assessment is that the IED was a pressure plate IED since the convoy was using Duke ECM and when they cleared the area immediately following the incident they found no evidence of either command detonation or enemy in the area. Also, looking at IED history in the area, several pressure plate IEDs have been used in the past in very close proximity to tonights location.
Future Actions: Convoy will split, with one element remaining with the vehicle disabled by the IED (UAH) as security, and the other element linking up with the local ANP to move to the Abdul Val ANP station at four corners. One of the convoy vehicles was a wrecker already carrying a disabled UAH, so this wrecker will transport the UAH it is carrying to Abdul Val. It will then return to the IED site to pick up the UAH disabled tonight and carry it back to the ANP station along with the security element originally left at the IED site. 3/A will stay at the Abdul Val ANP station for the night and return to FOB Ghazni at first light 6 mar. The BN will

arrange for local assistance in transporting the UAH disabled by the IED back to FOB Ghazni with the convoy. FOB Ghazni QRF will escort TF Paladin to the IED site in the morning of 6 MAR to enable a complete evaluation of the incident.

Reference ID: AFG20070312n632
Latitude: 32.20064926
Date: 2007-03-12 10:10
Category: IED Explosion
Detained:

Region: RC WEST
Longitude: 62.75154877
Type: Explosive Hazard
Affiliation: ENEMY

	Enemy	Friend	Civilian	Host nation
Killed in action	0	0	0	9
Wounded in action	0	0	0	1

On 121030ZMAR07 PST element reports that an ANP vehicle in their convoy, traveling from PRT Farah to Bakwa District Center, struck an IED. The route of travel was along RTE 515, and the location of incident was reported to be 41S MR 76584 62704. They are reporting the District Chief of Police along with 8 other ANP are KIA along with 1 ANP WIA. PRT QRF and EOD Team are prepparring to move to the site. RC West has been notified in an effort to alert requirement for MEDEVAC.
ISAF 03-254

Reference ID: AFG20070319n622
Latitude: 34.16627502
Date: 2007-03-19 14:02
Category: IED Explosion
Detained: 1

Region: RC EAST
Longitude: 71.07019043
Type: Explosive Hazard
Affiliation: ENEMY

	Enemy	Friend	Civilian	Host nation
Killed in action	0	0	0	0
Wounded in action	0	0	0	0

A bomb was planted on a fuel truck in Pakistan. The vehicle went thru Torkham gate and proceeded to Torkham Toll Gate. The IED fell off the truck at the gate and detonated. There was some damage to the fuel truck, no other damage. Kerosene drained from a 4-6 inch gash but failed to ignite; the Torkham QRF with TF Paladin element was sent out to assess the situation; the driver of the fuel truck is currently being detained at 1st BN ABP. ISAF 03-398

Reference ID: AFG20070325n575
Latitude: 32.46531296
Date: 2007-03-25 10:10
Category: IED Explosion
Detained: 0

Region: RC WEST
Longitude: 63.55599213
Type: Explosive Hazard
Affiliation: ENEMY

	Enemy	Friend	Civilian	Host nation
Killed in action	0	0	2	0
Wounded in action	0	0	0	0

(Delayed Entry) At 251030ZMAR07 a Local National Motorcycle driven by two LNs were struck by a PPIED IVO grid 41S NR 52250 92150. 2 LNs KIA.

Reference ID: AFG20070326n555
Latitude: 32.00045013
Date: 2007-03-26 15:03
Category: IED Explosion
Detained: 0
Region: RC SOUTH
Longitude: 65.14684296
Type: Explosive Hazard
Affiliation: ENEMY

	Enemy	Friend	Civilian	Host nation
Killed in action	0	0	1	0
Wounded in action	0	2	0	0

At 261553z MAR 07, 1 Fury Scout vehicle struck a AT mine that was emplaced in a waddi along a trail. The blast wounded two paratroopers and killed one of our Interpreters (Billy, 18 years of age). Post blast recovery was conducted by 1FURY EOD element, and subsequently the vehicle and all equipment were recovered. Paratroopers were evacuated to TK, and are in good condition at this time (1x possible ACL tear; 1x Concussion). TF 1Fury assessment is that the AT mine was laid in an IV line in a WADII.
ISAF Tracking # 03-548
N2

Reference ID: AFG20070401n638
Latitude: 34.68261719
Date: 2007-04-01 10:10
Category: IED Explosion
Detained: 0
Region: RC EAST
Longitude: 70.19753265
Type: Explosive Hazard
Affiliation: ENEMY

	Enemy	Friend	Civilian	Host nation
Killed in action	0	0	5	0
Wounded in action	0	0	5	8

011023Z TF Iron Grays reports a VBIED detonated at the ANA gate to FB Mehtarl Lam. There were 6x ANA casualties, 4x LN casualties (3x LN children, 1x LN adult male - amputated leg and was taken to ML Hospital), and 5x LNs killed (3x LN female children, 1x LN adult male, and 1x adult male suicide bomber). 1x ANA (eye injury) and 2x LN (1x burn victim and shrapnel wound, 1x arm in sling) were evacuated by US aircraft with an adult LN escort to BAF for further treatment. It is believed the intended target was an ANA patrol returning to the FB approximately 120m from the gate. The site is being secured by ANP/ANA/US, and TF Paladin is enroute to exploit the blast. MTF. ISAF 04-011
Headquarters
International Security Assistance Force Afghanistan
NEWS RELEASE [2007-XXX: Draft]
5 Afghans killed, 10 wounded during
Mehtar Lam attack
JALALABAD AIRFIELD, Afghanistan Five Afghans were killed and 10 wounded April 1 during a suicide vehicle borne improvised explosive device terror attack near Forward Operating Base Mehtar Lam. (For the rest of the release, please see sttachment)

Reference ID: AFG20070412n658
Latitude: 31.88705063
Date: 2007-04-12 07:07
Category: IED Explosion
Detained: 0

Region: RC SOUTH
Longitude: 64.79573822
Type: Explosive Hazard
Affiliation: ENEMY

	Enemy	Friend	Civilian	Host nation
Killed in action	0	0	0	0
Wounded in action	0	0	0	0

AT 0725Z on 12 APR 07, while conducting a CLP from Kandahar Airfield to FOB Robinson in support of the TTF (1-508th PIR), TF Denali reported RCP 2 struck a pressure plate IED at 41R PR 69837 29323, traveling north parallel to Route 611, between Highway 1 and FOB Robinson. No casualties reported. RCP 2 and TF Denali are currently installing a new redpack to bring the Husky to FMC before continuing mission.

7. (S//REL) On 12 April 07, C/S Hardcore 6 was traveling north on route 611 towards FOB Robinson when the left front tire of the Husky struck an explosive device. This occurred at the crest of a hill where the one lane road split into two lanes. Investigation of the scene revealed the vehicle was traveling north in the left lane when the left front tire riding on the outside track initiated the PPIED. It appears that the PP was located on top of the explosive charge with the power source offset the device. After the scene was exploited, and recovery of the vehicle was complete, the convoy was preparing to regroup and depart when a HMMWV set off another PPIED in the same vicinity as the first incident. The second device was placed on the opposite side of the road, again placed under the outside track. No injuries and minor equipment damage in each instance. CEXC KAF was embedded with the convoy traveling to FOB Robinson and exploited both sites

10. (S//REL) The placement of all the components in the same hole is an older ETTP in relationship to PP devices. Fortunately this tactic generally results in mobility damage and not personnel injuries. It is also noted that two devices were placed in close proximity of each other, probably not intended to be secondary devices, but to cover both lanes of the road, which had the secondary effect. These pressure plates are similar inn construction to those profiled in CEXC_AFG_Profile_005 (Twin Spring PPIED).

Reference ID: AFG20070416n636
Latitude: 36.72341919
Date: 2007-04-16 04:04
Category: IED Explosion
Detained: 0

Region: RC NORTH
Longitude: 68.86673737
Type: Explosive Hazard
Affiliation: ENEMY

	Enemy	Friend	Civilian	Host nation
Killed in action	1	0	0	9
Wounded in action	0	0	4	24

At 0445Z TF Phoenix reported a suicide bomber detonated his vest inside an ANP HQ building in Kunduz. Approx casualties were 10 ANP KIA, 13 ANP WIA and 4 LN WIA with 1 suicide bomber dead. ISAF Tracking# 04-318.
Update 1: Total Casualties of the event: 9 x ANP KIA, 24 x ANP WIA, and 1x INS KIA.

Reference ID: AFG20070424n555
Latitude: 34.85327148
Date: 2007-04-24 12:12
Category: IED Explosion
Detained: 0
Region: RC CAPITAL
Longitude: 69.13498688
Type: Explosive Hazard
Affiliation: ENEMY

	Enemy	Friend	Civilian	Host nation
Killed in action	0	0	0	6
Wounded in action	0	0	0	0

(SBU) PRT NURISTAN: ROAD EXPLOSION KILLS SIX, INJURES FOUR NATIONAL DIRECTORATE OF SECURITY PERSONNEL: (Source: AMEMBASSY KABUL 01393, 24 Apr 07)
At about 0930, April 23, on the main Alingar Road connecting Laghman and Nuristan provinces, an explosive device destroyed a small pick-up truck, killing six National Directorate of Security (NDS) personnel and injuring four. No one has claimed responsibility. PRT Nuristan is collaborating with PRT Laghman to mobilize the police in Laghman province to conduct an investigation.

Reference ID: AFG20070426n608
Latitude: 32.41143036
Date: 2007-04-26 22:10
Category: IED Explosion
Detained: 0
Region: RC SOUTH
Longitude: 66.81053162
Type: Explosive Hazard
Affiliation: ENEMY

	Enemy	Friend	Civilian	Host nation
Killed in action	0	0	0	0
Wounded in action	0	0	0	0

We left FOB Lane approximately 0205 to conduct a combat patrol to the valley area of Marah. We left with 16 vehicles total. The 5 ANA rangers were in the front of the convoy followed by 3 2nd plt trucks, 3 gmv SF trucks, and my 5 trucks in the rear. The lead humvee from 2nd platoon hit an IED approximately 0255-0300 vic 42STA 985 912. I was 7 vehicles behind the blast, so I didn't actually see the blast. However, I saw the flash from my location. There were no injuries, just a few bruises. The element stopped and set up security around the blast site. We sent 2nd sqd with two ANA rangers back to Lane approximately 0345 to get the bucket loader in order to recover the damaged vehicle. 2nd sqd returned to the IED site approximately 0435 with the bucket loader. The vehicle was hooked up and we began our movement back to FOB Lane approximately 0815 and returned to the FOB around 0900 with all personnel and equipment.
It is my assessment after surveying the blast site and talking to the individuals involved is that the ANA rangers may have detected a disturbance in the road and avoided the IED location. The IED was placed on the right side of the road in a pass that was very restrictive and afforded no alternative to bypass. However, it was placed just outside of the most restrictive portion of the pass to allow at least civilian size vehicles the opportunity to pass along the road. The IED seems to be a US or British model AT mine with a tilt rod as the detination device. The blast was 1/4 of the power of the 8APR IED strike. It is possible that the IED/mine would have been detected if we were traveling in daytime. As stated by CPT Aviles, it is very likely the insurgents implaced the mine after 2nd plt drove through the area, assuming they

would have to return on the same route. Also, due to this being the only available road to travel and with the absence of a strong ANP presence in the district center, RTE Mule between FOB Lane and the district center will become a greater threat for mounted travel.

I believe that the likelyhood of IED strikes will greatly decrease once we are able to cross the river and alter our travel with multiple avenues of approach to choose from. And I would argue that others need to alter their TTP for travel at night to travel at day if they wish to increase the chances of detecting IEDs. Much of the terrain in the Arghendab area is extremely restrictive, and the only way to travel is by using the roads. We cannot assume that we will be able to travel off the roads much of the time. And even if we are able to travel off the roads, in most cases we have to converge on the road again where the IEDs are most probable. Therefore, the most effective way to avoid IEDs is to detect them before running over them and by altering our routes as much as possible.

At 2233z TF Bushmaster reported IED strike 100M east of FB Lane. 1 vehicle destroyed, no injuries reported. Units from TF Bushmaster hit an IED. 1 X Vehicle destroyed. No injuries reported. Destroyed Vehicle will be ground evacuated back to FOB Lane. FF remained on site until daylight to SSE area. TF Bushmaster returned to base at 0440Z with the damaged vehicle. TIC Closed at 0600Z. ISAF # 04-0494

Reference ID: AFG20070501n698
Latitude: 33.65835953
Date: 2007-05-01 11:11
Category: IED Explosion
Detained: 0

Region: RC EAST
Longitude: 69.22887421
Type: Explosive Hazard
Affiliation: ENEMY

	Enemy	Friend	Civilian	Host nation
Killed in action	1	0	1	0
Wounded in action	0	0	0	0

At 011140zMAY07 Suicide bomber who was wearing traditional clothing approached an ANP Graduation Ceremony IVO 42S WC 2122 2430 (Gardez). When he was discovered, he blew himself up and damaged only a nearby jingle truck. He was wearing pineapple grenades. TF Diablo receives report that a child died in the explosion. At 011400Z Gardez PRT RTB at FOB Gardez. ANP exploiting site. NFTR. ISAF Tracking# 05-023.

Reference ID: AFG20070510n722
Latitude: 33.1336174
Date: 2007-05-10 16:04
Category: IED Explosion
Detained: 0

Region: RC EAST
Longitude: 68.83655548
Type: Explosive Hazard
Affiliation: ENEMY

	Enemy	Friend	Civilian	Host nation
Killed in action	1	0	3	0
Wounded in action	0	0	7	0

Last 24: Unit: PRT SHARANA   DTG: 2007-05-10
Commanders Summary:
(S//REL) Today we hosted and briefed JFC-Brunnsum NATO General Ramms (German GO) at the PRT. Also, briefing were the Governor of Paktika, the 4-73rd

CAV, The Polish Battle Group and an RCP (Route Clearing Package) display put on by TF Rugged. After the briefing and tour of the display we traveled to the SHARAN CEE so that our distinguished visitors could get a first hand view of the types of projects we do with the IROA.

(S//REL) Our weapons slant for the M2 .50 Cal is one out of four operational. We will test fire an M2 tomorrow morning which should bring us to two of four operational. We continue to borrow one M2 .50 Cal and one MK19 from the Engineer battalion here at FOB Sharana. However, AECON is working with us to expedite repair of the M2s as well as we received help today from the BSB. Ten of seventeen HMMWVs are FMC. Six vehicles have critical parts on order, one less than yesterday, since a transfer case arrived today which is being installed.

Political: (S//REL) NSTR
Military: (S//REL) NSTR
Economic: (S//REL) NTSR
Security: (S//REL) NTSR
Infrastructure: (S//REL) LT Cooke participated in VIP site tour of the SHARAN Center for Educational Excellence. The construction is progressing as scheduled. Workmanship on the project is improving. The PRT Commander, the Governor of Paktika, and our USAID rep discussed the SHARAN 100 bed hospital, it was agreed that the project needs to move forward. Conducted weekly project progress meeting with BACC for the MATA KHAN and SAR HAWZA District Centers. Scheduled contract meetings for bids related to the purchase of 500 chairs for the government of Paktika. Scheduled meeting with contractor to bid on proposed 3 story Justice Center to be located in SHARAN. Prepared for project closeout of MUSHKHEL Retention Dam Project and Solar Waterworks System located at Governors compound in SHARAN

Information:
- (S//REL) We received a request from Catamounts IO officer to have the Governor approve an IO response in regards to the MARGAH suicide bombing. Once the response is approved it will be aired on Voice of Paktika and SWBS OE.
- Voice of Paktika report:
(S//REL) A suicide attack took placed in BERMEL district. This attack killed three people and seven other injured. The district sub governor said that the attack was close to the CF base in Margha.
(S//REL) This morning Governor Akhpal Wak held a staff meeting with his directors. In this meeting, the director of public works and social affairs talked about the vocational centers to be built in the different districts.
(S//REL) The director of education told Voice of Paktika that a school will be built in SAR HOWZA district. He added that the sub governor had a ground breaking ceremony for a elementary school in this district. He also said there are plans to build more Madrass in other districts.

Reference ID: AFG20070517n787
Latitude: 35.03000259
Date: 2007-05-17 18:06
Category: IED Explosion
Detained: 0

Region: RC EAST
Longitude: 71.35237122
Type: Explosive Hazard
Affiliation: ENEMY

	Enemy	Friend	Civilian	Host nation
Killed in action	0	0	0	0
Wounded in action	0	0	0	1

A LN brought an ANP chief to CAMP MONTI. The ANP chief was in the LNs home drinking tea when a bomb that was planted in the home exploded. Urgent medevac was requested for the ANP chief.

Reference ID: AFG20070519n697
Latitude: 36.72974014
Date: 2007-05-19 05:05
Category: IED Explosion
Detained: 0
Region: RC NORTH
Longitude: 68.86852264
Type: Explosive Hazard
Affiliation: ENEMY

	Enemy	Friend	Civilian	Host nation
Killed in action	1	3	5	0
Wounded in action	0	5	22	0

At 190532Z TF Phoenix reported an PBIED detonation IVO of Kunduz Bazaar. SALTA posted:
S-UNK
A- Initial report is that a Suicide Bomber detonated in downtown Kunduz this morning, ANA reporting possible 3xGerman KIA, 7xGerman WIA, UNK LN casualties, ETTs still trying to develope situation. MTF
L- IVO Downtown Kunduz
T- Morning of 19 MAY 07
Update: In earlier suicide attack report it was stated that 3 Germans were KIA and seven wounded. That information was incorrect. 3 Germans on foot patrol near a bazaar (42S VF 8826 6490) were severely wounded 1 was slightly wounded. Amounts of civilian casualties are unknown at this time. Suicide bomber detonated himself at approximately 1002L this morning (19MAY).
Update 2: The final BDA : 3 X CF KIA, 5 X CF WIA, (2 serious, 3 light), 5 X LN KIA, 22 X LN WIA (1 X interpretor)
ISAF Tracking # 05-421.

Reference ID: AFG20070522n737
Latitude: 33.34642029
Date: 2007-05-22 06:06
Category: IED Explosion
Detained: 0
Region: RC EAST
Longitude: 69.49112701
Type: Explosive Hazard
Affiliation: ENEMY

	Enemy	Friend	Civilian	Host nation
Killed in action	0	0	0	3
Wounded in action	0	0	0	2

At 0626Z ETT reported an IED detonation on ANA Convoy at GRID 42S WB 4570 8980. IED Strike killed 3 ANA Soldiers. 2xANA WIA.
ETT REPORTS: ANA Convoy was returning from FOB Wilderness when it was struck by an IED. ANA QRF responded and moved wounded to Camp Clark. TF Deserthawk MEDEVAC'd injured to SAL CSH. ETT added that this is the fourth IED in this area in two weeks.

UPDATE: The vehicle was struck by an AT mine. 3 X ANA riding in the rear of the vehicle were killed. Two passengers in the front of the vehicle were injured when the LTV rolled.
One remains at Camp Clark with a head laceration. The other WIA is at the SAL CSH in a coma. He is expected to be transported to BAF for further treatment.
Exploitation found it to be 2xRCIED detonating at the same time.
Associated MEDEVAC Report for ANA Trooper.
ISAF Tracking # 05-489.

Reference ID: AFG20070528n748
Latitude: 36.72496033
Date: 2007-05-28 03:03
Category: IED Explosion
Detained: 0
Region: RC NORTH
Longitude: 68.86083221
Type: Explosive Hazard
Affiliation: ENEMY

	Enemy	Friend	Civilian	Host nation
Killed in action	1	0	0	0
Wounded in action	0	0	5	0

At 0330Z RC North reported a PBIED Strike against Dyno Corp IVO Kunduz City resulting in 4xUS CIV WIA, 1xLN WIA, and 1xEN KIA. All casualties brought to field hospital. The Dyno Corp vehicle is destroyed lying next to the road. The area is currently cordoned off by the police and initial investigations have been initiated. ISAF Tracking # 05-622.

Reference ID: AFG20070606n920
Latitude: 32.43540955
Date: 2007-06-06 16:04
Category: IED Explosion
Detained: 0
Region: RC WEST
Longitude: 62.17346954
Type: Explosive Hazard
Affiliation: ENEMY

	Enemy	Friend	Civilian	Host nation
Killed in action	0	0	0	0
Wounded in action	0	0	0	0

At 1630Z RC West reported that a VBIED, blue Toyota Corolla, was placed along the road and exploded. The intended target was the NDS Chief of Farah, Col. Baraktullah Hamidi, but he was not involved in the blast. Reportedly no insurgant in the car which exploded. ISAF Tracking # 06-181.

Reference ID: AFG20070616n745
Latitude: 34.52436066
Date: 2007-06-16 04:04
Category: IED Explosion
Detained: 0
Region: RC CAPITAL
Longitude: 69.05883789
Type: Explosive Hazard
Affiliation: ENEMY

	Enemy	Friend	Civilian	Host nation
Killed in action	1	0	4	0
Wounded in action	0	1	4	0

On 16 June, at 0430, a 2x HMMWV US convoy, which was being trailed by a 2x vehicle DynCorp convoy, was struck by an SVBIED on Route Red, 11km W of Camp

Eggers (MGRS 42S WD 05597 20162). The SVBIED, which was a Yellow station wagon Taxi, struck the HMMWVs in the lead of the convoy. Both HMMWVs were disabled. 1x US MIL suffered relatively minor injuries and 4x LNs were killed along with 4x LNs wounded due to the initial IED blast. A Camp Eggers BDOC QRF, a JIOC-A THT team and a TF Phoenix Response Team responded to the blast site. While at the scene of the detonation, a perimeter security force was set-up around the damaged vehicles while the site was being exploited and the damaged vehicles were being prepared for extraction. A security gunner mounting a M-240B had an accidental discharge of 2x rounds. The rounds struck 2x separate LNs in a crowd that had gathered around the incident site. One LN may have been fatally wounded but that is unconfirmed at this time. THT reported that a strong negative reaction among the LNs and the local police ensued after the accidental discharge. ISAF Tracking # 06-412.

Reference ID: AFG20070617n810
Latitude: 34.52334976
Date: 2007-06-17 03:03
Category: IED Explosion
Detained: 0

Region: RC CAPITAL
Longitude: 69.17215729
Type: Explosive Hazard
Affiliation: ENEMY

	Enemy	Friend	Civilian	Host nation
Killed in action	1	4	7	24
Wounded in action	0	0	15	47

At 0345Z RC Capital reported an SVBIED detonation 1.9km SW of ISAF HQ. The SVBIED detonated close to a bus nearby the KCP Station. Reported BDA is 13xKIA and 16xWIA (Nationality Unknown). Afghan authorities are not requesting any assistance at this time. All injuries are being taken to the Afghan Military Hospital. Update 0531Z: Updated BDA is 20xLN KIA, 2xJAP KIA, 1xKOR KIA, and 1xPAK KIA. Update 0614Z: The attack might have been from a suicide bomber who was inside a bus. 2xBuses have been destroyed. Last BDA 24xKIA and between 15 and 50 WIA. According to RC(C) LNO, KCP confirmed the information about the 2xJAP,1xKor, and 1xPAK KIA. MTF.
Update 0704Z: KJSCC reported the bus an ANP bus, and most of the casualties are ANP, accurate number of WIA is unsure ATT. MTF.
***UPDATE: This was a suicide bomber (PBIED) who jumped onto the bus near the bus station, not a SVBIED.
***UPDATE from MOI ISAF LNO on 25 Jun 07: Final BDA: 24xANP KIA 47xANP WIA 7xLN KIA 15xLN WIA 4xFN KIA
ISAF Tracking # 06-442

Reference ID: AFG20070701n807
Latitude: 34.39595413
Date: 2007-07-01 08:08
Category: IED Explosion
Detained: 0

Region: RC EAST
Longitude: 68.86890411
Type: Explosive Hazard
Affiliation: ENEMY

	Enemy	Friend	Civilian	Host nation
Killed in action	1	0	0	1
Wounded in action	0	0	0	6

At 0840Z, a VBIED detonated IVO the gate to Camp Airborne. ANP/ANA and French OMLT had secured the site and found that there were 2 x unexploded AT-6 mines in the road (Highway 1) to the rear of the VBIED. Chief of Police reported 6x ANP WIA, 1x ANP KIA. The WIA ground MEDEVAC to a local hospital. ANP have detained 1 x individual with a possible detonator. 1406D, ISAF EOD (French) were responding from Camp Warehouse. At 1145Z, 2 M1114s, 1 JERV, 1 ASV, 16 personnel, 1 interpreter, 2 ANP Rangers and about 14 ANP moved to the SVBIED site from FOB Ghazni. They arrived on scene at 1339z and report a grid of VD 8795 0607 for the strike site. The blast was not on HWY 1, but on a side road between the ANP and NDS compound. The element reports that no elements were securing the site when they arrived. The vehicle was reported to be a white Toyota Corolla, but had already been moved by the ANP and NDS prior to the QRF and Paladin arriving. TF Paladin and the 2 Fury LEP conducted an investigation of the site, but were not able to examine the vehicle. All ANSF on site confirm that there were two pax in the car prior to detonation. Prior to detonation, the passenger ran away from the car. This individual was detained by NDS. When questioned by the 2 Fury LEP, he stated that he was a hitch hiker picked up prior to the blast. He over heard the driver speaking in code on a cell phone and then noticed UXOs in the car and the driver wearing an oversized vest. At that time he ran out of the car and away from the vehicle. Shortly after that, the driver detonated himself. NDS detained the passenger believing that it was an RC VBIED and the passenger used his cell phone to detonate the vehicle. Paladin and the LEP were not able to confirm this. The ANP produced the remains of the driver. The 2 Fury LEP examined them and they are consistent with that of a suicide vest, and not necessarily a VBIED. It is believed, but not confirmed, that additional UXOs in the vehicle acted as a secondary explosion. At 1443z the 2 Fury element reports that the ANP on site had also produced the two AT mines that they report were ejected from the vehicle during the blast. The ANP had secured the UXOs and moved them to their ANP station. EOD took control of the UXOs and reduced them at 1523z. At 1640z the QRF and Paladin returned to FOB Ghazni. At 1702z TF Fury reported the event closed.
ISAF Tracking # 07-013

Reference ID: AFG20070708n947
Latitude: 32.6346283
Date: 2007-07-08 15:03
Category: IED Explosion
Detained: 0

Region: RC EAST
Longitude: 68.20648193
Type: Explosive Hazard
Affiliation: ENEMY

	Enemy	Friend	Civilian	Host nation
Killed in action	0	0	0	0
Wounded in action	0	4	0	0

At 1535Z TF White Eagle reported a 3rd vehicle in a convoy struck an IED in the vicinity of FOB Bruin. 4 polish WIA, 3 have minor injuries and 1 has burns to the lower extremities. TF white eagle requested medevac. At 1555Z TF white eagle was informed about Medevac they are preparing reinforcement. At 1625Z the Landing zone is at 42S VB 25501 11221 and is secured at this time. At 1648Z Medevac approved, W/D in 5 minute, 35 minute estimated time of arrival. At 1655Z a platoon from Kushamond is 5km away from the site. At 1733Z medevac wheels down, at

1740Z medevac wheels up to Qualat. ISAF Tracking number 07-189. Medevac number: MM(S) 07-08D,E
1. 42S VB 25568 11061
2. 40800 FM/ B 06A
3. A4
4. A
5. A3, L1
6. N
7. E T Stick
8. C4 (Polish)
9. Flat terrain
Remarks:
PT: 1,2,3 with minor injuries
PT: 4 burns to lower extremities
Headquarters
International Security Assistance Force Afghanistan
NEWS RELEASE [2007-XXX: Draft]
ISAF servicemembers injured while returning from peacekeeping mission
BAGRAM AIRFIELD, Afghanistan (09 July) Four ISAF servicemembers were medically evacuated for wounds sustained when their armored High Mobility Multipurpose Wheeled Vehicle struck an improvised explosive device in southern Paktika Province during the evening of July 8.

Reference ID: AFG20070709n836
Latitude: 33.45497894
Date: 2007-07-09 05:05
Category: IED Explosion
Detained: 0

Region: RC EAST
Longitude: 70.20141602
Type: Explosive Hazard
Affiliation: ENEMY

	Enemy	Friend	Civilian	Host nation
Killed in action	0	0	0	0
Wounded in action	0	0	0	0

At 0506Z ASG REPORTED A SECOND RCIED WAS LOCATED APPROXIMATELY 20 METERS WEST OF THE FIRST IED AND WAS DETONATED WHEN ANSF FORCES INITIATED MOVEMENT FROM THE SITE. NO INJURIES OR SIGNIFICANT DAMAGE WAS SUSTAINED AND FURTHER COMPONENTS WERE RECOVERED FROM THE SECOND SITE FOR EXPLOITATION. COMPOUNDS IN THE VICINITY OF THE IEDS WERE SEARCHED AND NO MALES WERE FOUND AT THESE LOCATIONS.Tracking # 07- 199.
Duplicate report summary
ASG RECEIVED TWO REPORTS OF IED EMPLACEMENTS IN THE VIC OF BCP 7 ALONG THE PRIMARY MSR LEADING INTO KHOWST CITY. THE FIRST IED WAS DISCOVERED AT 42S XC 11656 02373 AND WAS CONCEALED BY A FRESHLY CUT PILE OF GRASS APPROXIMATELY 1 METER FROM THE ROADSIDE. THIS RCIED CONSISTED OF A 122MM MORTAR ROUND AND BATTERY PACK. ANSF DEFUSED THE IED AND RECOVERED THE COMPONENTS FOR EXPLOITATION BY TF PALADIN
NFTR, Event closed.
End duplicate report summary

Reference ID: AFG20070712n808
Latitude: 33.45872116
Date: 2007-07-12 03:03
Category: IED Explosion
Detained: 0

Region: RC EAST
Longitude: 69.95932007
Type: Explosive Hazard
Affiliation: ENEMY

	Enemy	Friend	Civilian	Host nation
Killed in action	0	0	0	6
Wounded in action	0	0	0	0

At 120300ZJUL07 in the Sabari district Punisher 2 reported that an ANP vehicle that was part of their convoy at grid WC 89253 02558 hit and IED. 4 ANP KIA, 1 ANP WIA. Air medevac was sent to the IED site and evacuated the 1 x WIA. The patient was pronounced dead at the SAL CSH. He died of internal injuries suffered from the blast.
TF Paladin, TF Kodiak RCP and EOD from Bak DC was sent to exploit site.
ISAF Tracking# 07-273.
LINE 1 WC 89253 02558
LI NE 2 -38.900 PUNISHER 3A
LINE 3 1B
LINE 4- None
LINE 5-1 L
LINE 6 N
LIN E 7 C
LINE 8 C
LINE 9 OPEN FIELD
IED STRIKE, NO NOI ATT, VEHICLE DESTROYED, 4 KIAs FROM BLAST
SAL-GRID-SAL
CJTF82 MED OPS (2) (12 Jul 07 03:33:03): MM(E) 07-12B
110300ZJUL07
SALT REPORT
S UNKNOWN
A IED
L WC 89253 02558
T 0304
R - PUNSHER 2 REPORTS ANP TRUCK   WAS HIT BY AN IED. 4 ANP KIA, 1 WIA
TF Paladin exploited site and discovered IED was 2 AT mines double stacked with a trip wire initiator. All components will be brought back to Salerno by Rock 16 and given to TF Paladin.
Total KIA revised to 6 X ANP.
Three similar VOIED reports associated.
Headquarters
International Security Assistance Force Afghanistan

NEWS RELEASE [2007-XXX: Draft]

Five ANP Killed in IED Attack
FORWARD OPERATING BASE SALERNO, Afghanistan (12 July) Five Afghan National Police were killed as a result of an improvised explosive device attack in Sabari District, Khowst Province today. (See attachment)

Reference ID: AFG20070723n796
Latitude: 32.85396576
Date: 2007-07-23 12:12
Category: IED Explosion
Detained: 0

Region: RC EAST
Longitude: 69.01389313
Type: Explosive Hazard
Affiliation: ENEMY

	Enemy	Friend	Civilian	Host nation
Killed in action	0	4	0	0
Wounded in action	0	1	0	0

0915Z: Havoc 16 SPs for a patrol to Charbaran and Gomal. The patrol consisted of 9 US vehicles, 1 Jingle Truck, and 38 US soldiers.
1155Z: Havoc 16 (D/1-503) hits an IED at   WB 013 351. 4x US KIA and 1x WIA. 1x UAH destroyed. One element (Havoc 16) stays to secure the site and detains 16 personnel IVO the blast.
1320Z: 4 vehicles move back to FOB OE IOT ground CASEVAC wounded paratrooper.
1335Z: CAS on station 2x A-10s (Hawg 11).
1410Z: 2x AH-64s (Conquest 13) over the TIC site and have comms with Havoc 16
1458Z: 1x WIA transferred out of OE to BAF
1535Z: QRF (Havoc 36), RCP (Grizzly 26), THT and Paladin elements depart OE to clear south along routes and exploit the site.
MTF pending TF Paladin exploitation and recovery operations.

Reference ID: AFG20070730n792
Latitude: 31.81591034
Date: 2007-07-30 14:02
Category: IED Explosion
Detained: 0

Region: RC SOUTH
Longitude: 64.5668335
Type: Explosive Hazard
Affiliation: ENEMY

	Enemy	Friend	Civilian	Host nation
Killed in action	0	0	0	0
Wounded in action	0	0	0	3

At 1435Z an explosion has injured 3 afghan national police (2 X Stretcher cases, and 1 walking wounded). A bicycle has been retrieved from the center of the explosion. JDCC DO JEOD are going to exploit the bike for forensics.The Pt's are being assessed by the medical officer at FOB Price and still awaiting details. update as of 1812Z Police have been questioned referencing the explosion target was believed to be a police Ranger vehicle that was traveling to the JDCC from bridge "DICK". Device was concealed behind some awaiting wis to inspect mortorcycle which is being held in JDCC GSK for possible forensic evidence possibly sometime tomorrow.
Incident closed at 2247L/1817Z
ISAF Tracking # 07-794

Reference ID: AFG20070731n458
Latitude: 34.5439415
Date: 2007-07-31 04:04
Category: IED Explosion
Detained: 0

Region: RC CAPITAL
Longitude: 69.25829315
Type: Explosive Hazard
Affiliation: ENEMY

	Enemy	Friend	Civilian	Host nation
Killed in action	1	0	2	0
Wounded in action	0	4	1	0

At 0420Z TF Phoenix reported a VBIED Detonation at the front of Camp Phoenix on 1xHMMVW. HMMVW was damaged and reported BDA is 3xUS MIL WIA and 3xUNK Nationality WIA. MEDEVAC has been requested and approved MM(E) 07-31A. Updated BDA: 6xUS MIL WIA (2 were MEDEVACd to BAF), 1xEKIA. Kabul CEXC Team on site for exploitation, issue report from CSTC-A is that a Jingle Truck drove into the HMMVW and detonated.MTF. ISAF Tracking # 07-800.
COMBINED JOINT TASK FORCE- 82
COMBINED PRESS INFORMATION CENTER
BAGRAM AIRFIELD, AFGHANISTAN
APO AE 09354
Press Center: 0799-063-013
bagrammediacenter@afghan.swa.army.mil
FOR IMMEDIATE RELEASE
July 31, 2007
RELEASE # 150
Coalition forces attacked in suicide bombing
BAGRAM AIRFIELD, Afghanistan (July 31) A Coalition force convoy was attacked by a vehicular-borne suicide bomber in Kabul today.
SEE ATTACHED FOR COMPLETE RELEASE

===
Summary from duplicate report
On the road VIOLET in front of the CAMP PHOENIX 1xUS Humvee was damaged by VBIED attack. During the VBIED attack 2XLN are wounded and 1XUS WIA(broken leg) One of the LN is killed and brought to CAMP WAREHOUSE and the other LN wounded is in FR ROLE-2. 1xLN DOW and in Camp Warehouse. 1xN WIA and in Camp Warehouse FR Role-2 now. 1xUS soldier WIA (broken leg) and in Camp Phoenix now. There were some friendly fires between Afghan security units because of the tension on the spot. One boduguard of KCP was injured during the friendly fire.
Due o the VBIED at PHOENIX, there is a trafficjam on road DESPERADO and this between D1 and D2. UK Coy QRF was on the spot as of 920D* FR IRT is on the spot now. Camp Phoenix requested additional patrols in the south of Camp Phoenix to clear the area. 1044D*FR BG IRT will come back to Camp Warehouse. RC C will send FR BG QRF on the spot IOT conduct patrols in the south of CAMP PHOENIX to clear the area. 1131D* FR BG QRF arrived at the spot and the platoon leader is in Camp Phoenix now IOT coordinate the patrols that will be conducted in the south of Camp Phoenix. CFC has VIN for Small Jingle Truck. Mid-scale explosion. BDA unchanged but one of the four US WIA was not injured during the SVBIED ATK but after, when KCP and NDS exchanged SAF due to the following reasons: ??When chief of counter criminal directorate of KCP BG PAKTIWAL has reached the spot he had a dispute with deputy of Kabul NDS HQ. Both of their personnel started shooting over at each other injuring four people including two bodyguards of BG PAKTIWAL. The security forces have launched an inquiry into the case and it is ongoing at present?. Information given by RC C LNO TO KCP. Event closed at 311917D*JUL.
End duplicate report summary

Reference ID: AFG20070804n820
Latitude: 32.43635559
Date: 2007-08-04 00:12
Category: IED Explosion
Detained:

Region: RC SOUTH
Longitude: 66.85459137
Type: Explosive Hazard
Affiliation: ENEMY

Enemy   Friend   Civilian   Host nation
Killed in action
Wounded in action
(Storyboard from ODA team) 4 X VEHICLES DROVE OVER DEVICE BEFORE DISCOVERY ETT AND ANA PAX SAW A SMALL FLAME AND PUFF OF SMOKE COME FROM DEVICE
ETT PERSONNEL EXPOSED SWITCH BY REMOVING TOP LAYER OF DIRT ODA DISCOVERED EXPLOSIVE DEVICE WITH FURTHER SITE

Reference ID: AFG20070806n992
Latitude: 34.23505783
Date: 2007-08-06 03:03
Category: IED Explosion
Detained: 0

Region: RC EAST
Longitude: 70.3138504
Type: Explosive Hazard
Affiliation: ENEMY

	Enemy	Friend	Civilian	Host nation
Killed in action	0	0	0	0
Wounded in action	0	0	0	0

On 6 AUG at approx 0330 the PCC reported that ANP had informed them of an explosion in Chapahar District near the village of Srah Kala vic XC 2189 to PCC, PCC dispatched ANP to the site, ANP discovered a motorcycle battery, 2 yellow wires and a remote were the explosion detonated. The PCC has secured the items and has coordinated to transfer them to TF Paladin for futher exploitation.
ISAF Tracking # 08-126

Reference ID: AFG20070812n867
Latitude: 34.27350616
Date: 2007-08-12 05:05
Category: IED Explosion
Detained: 0

Region: RC EAST
Longitude: 70.20467377
Type: Explosive Hazard
Affiliation: ENEMY

	Enemy	Friend	Civilian	Host nation
Killed in action	0	3	1	0
Wounded in action	0	1	0	0

At 0532Z TF Bushmaster reported that SE41 struck an IED IVO OSB Khogyani, reported BDA is 3xUS MIL Non-responsive, 3xUS MIL WIA, 1xTERP KIA, 1 US MIL WIA and 1xVehicle damaged and flipped. Recovery assets have SP'ed along with Paladin to conduct Post Blast. MEDEVAC was requested and approved MM(E) 08-12B. Updated BDA: 3xUS KIA, 1xLN TERP KIA, 1xUS MIL WIA with minor wounds, twisted ankle and minor cuts to face. All have been brought to FOB Fenty (JAF). At 1040Z TF Bushmaster reported TIC complete. Friendly forces RTB at OSB Khogi at this time. Final BDA 3 US KIA, 1 Terp KIA, 1 US WIA, 1 government vehicle destroyed.
ISAF Tracking # 08-301

COMBINED JOINT TASK FORCE- 82
COMBINED PRESS INFORMATION CENTER
BAGRAM AIRFIELD, AFGHANISTAN
APO AE 09354
Press Center: 0799-063-013
bagrammoc@afghan.swa.army.mil
FOR IMMEDIATE RELEASE
August 12, 2007
RELEASE # 051
Three Coalition service members killed in IED strike
BAGRAM AIRFIELD, Afghanistan Three Coalition forces service members and one civilian interpreter died of wounds sustained from an IED blast during a combat operation in Nangarhar Province this morning.
SEE ATTACHED FOR COMPLETE RELEASE

Reference ID: AFG20070816n881
Latitude: 31.56031036
Date: 2007-08-16 06:06
Category: IED Explosion
Detained: 0

Region: RC SOUTH
Longitude: 65.34896851
Type: Explosive Hazard
Affiliation: ENEMY

	Enemy	Friend	Civilian	Host nation
Killed in action	0	0	0	0
Wounded in action	0	0	0	0

The team responded to a detonation on Ring South involving a Canadian TLAV. The team recovered components consistent with a CIED (two Motorcycle batteries wired in a series circuit and 300 yards of wire). All evidence was turned over to CEXC personnel for exploitation.

Reference ID: AFG20070817n928
Latitude: 31.61433029
Date: 2007-08-17 00:12
Category: IED Explosion
Detained: 0

Region: RC SOUTH
Longitude: 65.7618103
Type: Explosive Hazard
Affiliation: ENEMY

	Enemy	Friend	Civilian	Host nation
Killed in action	1	0	4	0
Wounded in action	0	0	3	0

(SECRET//REL TO GCTF) At 0615Z TF Kandahar reported that a suicide bomber detonated himself in the Kandahar City District 6, Kandahar Province. Killing the Zharey District leader along with his 2 sons and daughter. At 1233Z TF Kandahar reported that the KIA will be buried at GRID 41R QQ 250 953, in a joint op with ANP who are providing security for the ceremony. There were also 3 LN WIA. Incident closed at 1241Z. ISAF Tracking # 08-424

Reference ID: AFG20070822n924
Latitude: 31.52636147
Date: 2007-08-22 13:01

Region: RC SOUTH
Longitude: 65.28437805
Type: Explosive Hazard

Category: IED Explosion   Affiliation: ENEMY
Detained: 0

	Enemy	Friend	Civilian	Host nation
Killed in action	0	2	1	0
Wounded in action	0	2	0	0

At 1349Z TF Kandahar reported that 12.9KM west of Sperwan Ghar in Panjwayi district, Kandahar province a company while on patrol hit a IED, site is secured. Medevac was requested for 4 urgent canadian, injuries unknown at this time. Medevac mission was complete at 1505Z. TIC closed at 1816Z. Medevac number MM(S) 08-22C, Final Casualties: 2x NATO(CAN) KIA, 1x LN (Terp) KIA, 2x NATO(CAN) WIA, 2x CIV(CAN reporters) WIA. ISAF tracking # 08-606.

Reference ID: AFG20070823n835   Region: RC SOUTH
Latitude: 31.80838013   Longitude: 64.51813507
Date: 2007-08-23 07:07   Type: Explosive Hazard
Category: IED Explosion   Affiliation: ENEMY
Detained: 0

	Enemy	Friend	Civilian	Host nation
Killed in action	0	0	3	0
Wounded in action	0	0	14	0

Khaleej Times
At least three killed, 14 hurt in Afghan blast
KANDAHAR (Aug 23) At least three civilians were killed and 14 others injured when a bomb aimed at a police commander exploded Thursday in southern Afghanistan, officials and a medic said. Helmand provincial police chief Mohammad Hussin Andiwal was the target of the bombing in the town of Greshk, but he emerged unscathed.
I was in the same convoy. As our first vehicle passed ... the bomb was detonated. Me and my entire team are unharmed, were fine, Andiwal told AFP. The police chief said a total of 10 people had been killed or wounded, but said he had no further details. A doctor in the towns hospital said at least three people were killed and 14 others all passers-by were injured. Weve received 14 people with injuries. Five of them are in critical condition. Three dead have also been brought to our hospital, doctor Mohammad Tahire Rasouli told AFP. The police chief said he was traveling from the provincial capital of Lashkar Gah to visit local authorities in Greshk when the attack took place. The bomb was planted in a hand-cart parked at the side of the road near a bridge, and operated by remote control, local official Abdul Manaf told AFP, blaming the attack on the Taliban.

Reference ID: AFG20070824n756   Region: RC EAST
Latitude: 33.29237366   Longitude: 70.13318634
Date: 2007-08-24 04:04   Type: Explosive Hazard
Category: IED Explosion   Affiliation: ENEMY
Detained: 0

	Enemy	Friend	Civilian	Host nation
Killed in action	0	0	0	6
Wounded in action	0	0	0	2

At 0400Z TF Professional reported that an ANSF convoy with 3 vehicles and 30 personnel were moving NE enroute to an ABP checkpoint when they hit an IED, at grid XB 05449 84272. The explosion resulted in 6 KIA and 2 WIA. A 9 line was submitted to BDE and approved. Medevac was w/d at grid XB 05510 84273 at 0434z and w/u at 0436z. The MEDEVAC arrived (w/d) at FOB Salerno at 0444z. OGA/KPF elements arrived on site to police and collect evidence of IED. EVENT Closed at 1209Z. ISAF Tracking # 08-658.
. 04:06 9 Line MEDEVAC:
MM(E) 08-24B
Line 1: XB 05510 84272
Line 2: Cardinal 30, 36.050
Line 3: 3A
Line 4: None
Line 5 3L
Line 6: No Enemy
Line 7: Vs-17, Green Smoke
Line 8: C
Line 9: None
TF Fury approves MEDEVAC mission SAL-GRID-SAL
Headquarters
International Security Assistance Force Afghanistan

NEWS RELEASE [2007-XXX: Draft]

Six killed by IED blast in Khowst
FORWARD OPERATING BASE SALERNO, Afghanistan (24 Aug.) A convoy led by a Khowst Provincial Force east of Khowst City was hit by an improvised explosive device early today.
FOR THE COMPLETE PRESS RELEASE, PLEASE SEE ATTACHMENT.

Reference ID: AFG20070825n810
Latitude: 31.62694931
Date: 2007-08-25 05:05
Category: IED Explosion
Detained: 0

Region: RC SOUTH
Longitude: 65.54506683
Type: Explosive Hazard
Affiliation: ENEMY

	Enemy	Friend	Civilian	Host nation
Killed in action	0	0	3	0
Wounded in action	0	0	2	0

At 0505Z TF Kandahar reported that 11.5KM northeast of Patrol Base Wilson in Panjwayi District, Kandahar province a report from Warrior 6, that a US PMT team that a private contractor convoy has been hit with an IED at GRID 41R QR 414 019. They reported 3 KIA and 2 WIA. TIC closed at 0641Z. ISAF tracking number: 08-698.

Reference ID: AFG20070828n931
Latitude: 33.93743896
Date: 2007-08-28 06:06

Region: RC EAST
Longitude: 69.69550323
Type: Explosive Hazard

Category: IED Explosion   Affiliation: ENEMY
Detained: 0

	Enemy	Friend	Civilian	Host nation
Killed in action	0	3	0	0
Wounded in action	0	6	2	0

585th ENGs (Roughneck 3/6) reports attack by a suicide bomber while conducting construction of the Jaji Bridge.
Roughneck reported 3x CF KIAs, 6x CF WIAs and 2 LN WIA. 1 Local construction vehicle dmaged in the attack.
Roughneck 3/6 maintained security positions on the site of attack until arrival of CEXC. 1/C 4-73 acted as QRF providing security to reduce the possibility of secondary attacks. CEXC exploited the site and RTB to FB Jaji with Roughneck and 1/C elements, TF 3 Fury is awaiting debrief information from CEXC exploitation att.
ISAF Tracking # 08-798
S- 1 PAX
A- Suicide bombing
L- WC 64276 55437
T- 0630Z
R- Roughneck 3/6 (585th ENG) reports suicide bombing VIC Jaji bridge construction site.
0633z MEDEVAC called
0639z MEDEVAC W/U SAL
0704z MEDEVAC W/D
0717z MEDEVAC W/U
0726z 2nd MEDEVAC W/D
0731z 2nd MEDEVAC W/U

Reference ID: AFG20070829n794   Region: RC EAST
Latitude: 32.97871017   Longitude: 69.4825592
Date: 2007-08-29 03:03   Type: Explosive Hazard
Category: IED Explosion   Affiliation: ENEMY
Detained: 0

	Enemy	Friend	Civilian	Host nation
Killed in action	0	0	0	1
Wounded in action	0	0	0	4

At approx 282228AUG2007, as 2xUH47s flew over the Dashta. Possibly spooked by the helicopter, OP4 reported 5 pax emerging from dead space and running from Afghanistan into Pakistan vic. WB 46201 49335 with backpacks and 3 possible weapons. PAKMIL was immediately notified, but unable to quickly confirm that no patrols were in the area.
After monitoring for about 1 minute, pax crossed the border.A/3-6 departed OP4 at 290058AUG2007 with 3 vehicles IOT conduct hasty clearance vic. previous nights sighting and conduct resupply. They conducted hasty clearance of area where 5 pax were seen. 3-6 conducted clearance of the path without actually driving on the path b/c of the IED threat.
At approximately 0325, ASG HILUX traveling alone to resupply OP4 hit an IED (reported by OP4) at WB 45090 49030. 3 minutes later 2 x ASG HILUXES dispatched as QRF. At 0412, ASG arrived at FOB Tillman with 1 x KIA and 4 x WIA (1 urgent). 9

Line submitted at 0420 and MEDEVAC wheels down at FOB Tillman at 0450. ISAF Event # 08-826.

Reference ID: AFG20070829n816　　Region: RC EAST
Latitude: 32.64398956　　　　　　　Longitude: 69.25802612
Date: 2007-08-29 07:07　　　　　　　Type: Explosive Hazard
Category: IED Explosion　　　　　　 Affiliation: ENEMY
Detained: 0

	Enemy	Friend	Civilian	Host nation
Killed in action	0	0	4	2
Wounded in action	0	0	10	1

At 0705z a suicide bomber detonated in the Bermel bazaar at WB 2420 1185. The bomber was a 16-18 yr old male in an all white turban with new clothes on.
Two ANA soldiers identified the bomber and told him to approach. At this point the Bomber detonated himself, causing 10 civilian injuries, 1 ANP WIA, 4 Civilian KIA, and 2 ANA KIA. The bomb was strapped around the bomber and underneath his clothing. MTF. ISAF Event # 08-834.
2 ANA KIA (42s WB 251 112)
4 CIV KIA
13 CIV WIA MEDEVAC Mission is in support of the civilians wounded during suicide bombing. The range of injuries is not known at this time. OE-BERMEL-OE/Rushmore
From 203rd RCAG:
A 16-18 year old young man was identified by 1/2/203rd ANA soldiers as a possible suicide bomber. They told him to stop and put his hands up, at which point he detonated himself inside the Bermel Bazar, located just outside the Mosque. Injured were treated at the Bermel TMC with US and ANA doctors. Presently 9 LNs are being helod to FOB Rushmore, to be ground transported to local Sharana hospital. No ETT or American soldiers were injured.

Reference ID: AFG20070830n829　　Region: RC SOUTH
Latitude: 32.04810715　　　　　　　Longitude: 64.84083557
Date: 2007-08-30 06:06　　　　　　　Type: Explosive Hazard
Category: IED Explosion　　　　　　 Affiliation: ENEMY
Detained: 0

	Enemy	Friend	Civilian	Host nation
Killed in action	0	0	0	0
Wounded in action	0	0	0	0

This incident is reported in WIS/RC(S)/07/101. The report refers to an Improvised Explosive Device (IED) that detonated ahead of an ANA route clearance patrol on 300520ZAUG07. The ANA were able to recover components believed to be associated with IEDs.
ITEMS RECOVERED:
a. Remains of one (1x) battery pack, black plastic, commercial construction, with DURATA batteries.
b. One (1x) large aluminum US First Aid tin.

c. One (1x) piece of circular iron, the investigators are calling an attempt at making an Explosive Formed Penetrator (EFP).
d. One (1x) length of orange detonation cord.
e. An unknown quantity (estimated at 1 kg) of Composition C-4 explosive. This C-4 is suspected of being counterfeit, further analysis is required in order to verify the origin of this explosive.
f. Various electronic components.
g. A length of white plastic coated, single core wire.
f. A length of green/black plastic coated single core wire.
CEXC_AFG_849_07

Reference ID: AFG20070831n503
Latitude: 34.55755997
Date: 2007-08-31 03:03
Category: IED Explosion
Detained: 0

Region: RC CAPITAL
Longitude: 69.20928955
Type: Explosive Hazard
Affiliation: ENEMY

	Enemy	Friend	Civilian	Host nation
Killed in action	1	0	0	2
Wounded in action	0	4	3	5

At 0310Z RC Capital reported one explosion just occurred at KAIA Main Gate. The IED was placed just against the exterior wall. The blast pushed the wall inside. Initial reported BDA is 1xWIA, confirming at this time what the actual BDA of KIA and WIA totals are. Due to the explosion at KAIA, RTE Abbey is closed between A1 and PU1 for ISAF Vehicles. According to KJSCC it was a SVBIED that was targeting an ANA Vehicle and they reported 5xANA WIA. MTF on the event as details come in.
Update as of 0451Z: Video proof shows the explosion was a SVBIED, a dark sedan type coming from center Kabul on Road Abby. Referring to a report from GE MP, the target was a GE MP Patrol. The SVBIED crashed into a MP car and detonated the vehicle. The GE MP Patrol took the 1xGE WIA, in the second MP Car and withdrew to HQ ISAF.
Updated BDA: 1xINS KIA, 1xLN KIA (DOW), 3xLN WIA, 1xGER WIA, 4xBEL WIA, 2xCIV (Philippines) in shock, and 2xVehicles damaged (1xISAF 1xLN). KAIA main gate is closed to vehicles but open for pedestrians.
Final BDA:
2 ANA KIA
5 ANA WIA
1LN injured
2 x Phillipine injured
3 x BE WIA (v minor)
1 x GE WIA (v minor)
ISAF Tracking # 08-892

Reference ID: AFG20070905n958
Latitude: 31.73901749
Date: 2007-09-05 05:05

Region: RC SOUTH
Longitude: 64.34915924
Type: Explosive Hazard

Category: IED Explosion   Affiliation: ENEMY
Detained: 0

	Enemy	Friend	Civilian	Host nation
Killed in action	0	2	0	0
Wounded in action	0	2	1	0

At 0505Z TF Helmand reported that an RCIED exploded and flipped a vehicle and trapped 3x UK and 1x Interpreter under the vehicle at grid 41R PR 278 123, in the Nad Ali district, Helmand province. The second vehicle in the convoy hit an RCIED consiting of 2 x Anti Tank mines and a mod 5 spider device. It is believed that the RCIED was originally suspected to target ANA however, it is believed that the insurgents hit the ISAF convoy as a target of oppurtunity. A medevac was requested and 2x AH's sent in support of the incident. At 0601Z TF Helmand reported that fire rescue team and EOD team were on site in order to support. Event closed at 1019Z. FINAL BDA: 2x UK KIA, 2x UK WIA, 1x LN (Terp) WIA. ISAF Tracking # 09-163.
LINE 1: HLS GR 41R 278 123
LINE 2: TOPAZ 10, CAG
LINE 3: 4X A
LINE 4: A
LINE 5: 4X L
LINE 6: P
LINE 7: C (BLUE)
LINE 8: 3XA (UK) 1X D (TERP)
LINE 9: SECURE HLS
MM(S)09-05B BSN R2E

Reference ID: AFG20070923n932   Region: RC NORTH
Latitude: 37.52127075   Longitude: 70.38285828
Date: 2007-09-23 14:02   Type: Explosive Hazard
Category: IED Explosion   Affiliation: ENEMY
Detained: 0

	Enemy	Friend	Civilian	Host nation
Killed in action	0	0	0	10
Wounded in action	0	0	0	2

At 1430Z, PRT Fayzabab received a report of an IED strike against a bus of ANP. An ANP convoy was traveling from RAGH via Yavan to Fayzabab 10X ANP KIA, 2X ANP WIA. ISAF Tracking #09-762.

Reference ID: AFG20070929n868   Region: RC CAPITAL
Latitude: 34.53239822   Longitude: 69.1427536
Date: 2007-09-29 02:02   Type: Explosive Hazard
Category: IED Explosion   Affiliation: ENEMY
Detained: 0

	Enemy	Friend	Civilian	Host nation
Killed in action	1	0	0	27
Wounded in action	0	0	6	20

At 0215Z RC Capital reported an explosion in downtown Kabul. Ambulances and firefighters are en route to site. According to the first reported BDA is many were dead and wounded are not known at this time. Update 0347Z: RC C LNO to KJSCC reported that 1xINS with a uniform entered the bus and detonated himself. KCP or ANA did not request any help from RC C. Update 0436Z: Updated BDA from ARTEC is 27xANA KIA, and 20xANA WIA, 6xNC Injured. Update 0650Z: All of the wounded have been brought to the MOI Hospital for treatment ATT. The 1xEKIA detonated himself once he got onto the bus from the middle door. Event closed at 1355Z. ISAF Tracking # 09-961.

Update as of 1830Z: GEN BK has been actively involved in the follow up to this mornings attack on the ANA bus. He was at the scene within 20 minutes of the attack and spoke to an ANP eye witness. The attacker was wearing an ANA uniform and waited at the normal bus stop along with several ANA officers for the bus to come. When the bus arrived, the attacker rushed the rear door of the blue bird bus and detonated the explosives either just inside or outside the bus. The explosion knocked out windows of buildings as far as 50 meters away. The bus was completely destroyed. CSTC-A representatives visited the ANA hospital later in the morning. They have a list of everyone that normally rides that particular bus. The ANA Surgeon General said that the casualties/injuries include 27 ANA KIA, 3 LN KIA, 2 ANP KIA, 23 ANA WIA, and 2 ANP WIA. Of the 23 ANA WIA, 11 are in a coma and 6 were being operated on when we visited. GEN BK arranged ground and air transportation for the ANA KIAs to their hometowns across Afghanistan while we were there. 15 of the KIAs had already been identified and linked up with family members by the time we got to the hospital around 1000 hrs. The major effort on-going now is to link up identified KIAs with family members and identify some of the remaining KIAs based on the few body parts recovered. Neither GEN BK nor the Surgeon General said that they needed any coalition assistance at this time.

CSTC-A Commander engaged GEN BK on TTPs that might be used to prevent such an incident happening in the future and will continue to press this point with him in the coming days. Although the incident is tragic, the response to the incident was done well.

Reference ID: AFG20071002n924
Latitude: 34.53335953
Date: 2007-10-02 03:03
Category: IED Explosion
Detained: 0

Region: RC CAPITAL
Longitude: 69.0817337
Type: Explosive Hazard
Affiliation: ENEMY

	Enemy	Friend	Civilian	Host nation
Killed in action	1	0	4	6
Wounded in action	0	0	0	12

At 0334Z TF Phoenix reported that in the vicinity of Kabul, Kabul province; 1 PBIED suicide bomber detonated himself in police district 5 Kabul. Kabul police district 5 is on the west side of Kabul, no coalition involved at this time. PBIED detonated on a ANP bus. BDA 12 ANP KIA, 5 ANP WIA.

Update: Afghan male wearing an Afghan uniform boarded a Kabul City Police Bus and detonated himself. According to Kabul City Police there are 12 KIA and 5 WIA so far. The bomber was checked by security guards before he could enter the bus. He proceeded to run toward the front door of the bus while the security guards were shooting at him, he exploded upon reaching the door. UPDATED BDA: 12ANP WIA, 6xANP KIA, 4xNon-Combatants killed. Event is closed. ISAF Tracking # 10-036.

Reference ID: AFG20071002n958
Latitude: 34.01272202
Date: 2007-10-02 10:10
Category: IED Explosion
Detained: 0

Region: RC EAST
Longitude: 68.7270813
Type: Explosive Hazard
Affiliation: ENEMY

	Enemy	Friend	Civilian	Host nation
Killed in action	0	0	0	0
Wounded in action	0	0	0	8

At 1000Z TF 2Fury reported the Ghazni ANP reported through the Ghazni PCC that there was an assassination attempt on LTG Ali Shah, the Ghazni Province Chief of Police with an IED consisting of a bicycle with an RCIED attached. The CoP was moving in a convoy from Kabul to Ghazni when an IED attached to a bike was detonated in Sayed Abad District, Wardak Province. They report the attack took place between the villages of Shater (VC 748 636) and Sayd Serazr Baba (VC 750 649). The ANP convoy reported that they recovered the remains of the bike and continued to Ghazni. They also reported that there were 8 x ANP WIA and were brought to the Ghazni City Hospital. Additionally they reported that LTG Ali Shah was not injured in the attack. NFTR. Event Closed at 0344Z.
ISAF Tracking # 10-058.

Reference ID: AFG20071110n1080
Latitude: 33.55682755
Date: 2007-11-10 06:06
Category: IED Explosion
Detained: 0

Region: RC EAST
Longitude: 69.05409241
Type: Explosive Hazard
Affiliation: ENEMY

	Enemy	Friend	Civilian	Host nation
Killed in action	0	0	0	0
Wounded in action	0	0	0	0

On 100619z NOV07, RCP-7 while conducting deliberate clearance of RTE Virginia ISO 3 Fury recovery operation of 1x damaged UAH in IED attack on 2/B elements in vicinity of Gurjay Village 09 NOV 07, RCP-7 struck 1x PPIED equipped with 1x TC-6 AT mine at grid WC 0502 1302. The detonations of the device cause minor damage to the lead vehicle and no injuries to personnel. CEXC team that was currently traveling with RCP-7 assessed the munition that was used was too old and was ineffective in this attack; given that reason meant why the vehicle took as little damage as it did.
At 0806z, Exploitation of the post blast site was completed RCP-7 continued mission and event was closed at that time. ISAF Tracking # 11-248
Analysis: This IED was located along RTE Virginia in the same vicinity as another IED attack on 17 AUG 07. This attack occurred less than 2km S of where RCP 7 discovered an IED on 09 NOV 07. ACM IED cells in this region are assessed to emplace PPIEDs along routes that lead to support areas. ACM were likely observing RCP 7s movements and activated the PPIED accordingly. The age of the AT mine was likely the reason for such minor damage to the Buffalo.
Event Closed

Reference ID: AFG20071112n1005
Latitude: 32.59381104

Region: RC EAST
Longitude: 69.3068924

Date: 2007-11-12 04:04
Category: IED Explosion
Detained: 0

Type: Explosive Hazard
Affiliation: ENEMY

	Enemy	Friend	Civilian	Host nation
Killed in action	0	2	0	0
Wounded in action	0	1	0	0

At 0449z, an Anvil convoy moving from Bermel to Malekshay COP hit an IED at 42S WB 2987 0613 in the vicinity of historic attack locations. The vehicle was destroyed and 2 x US soldiers were KIA. 1 soldier was MEDEVACd from the site to OE for stabilization then to GHZ for further treatment. At 0532Z (CAS) BE21 priovide overwatch of FF MEDEVAC and 0550Z conduct a SOF dispensing 7 flares and at 0600 conducted another SOF dispensing 5 flares, at 0632Z DE21 was directed to search for ACM with NSTR, at 0910 DE21 was directed to conduct another SOF due to fuel restrictions DE21 suggested a SOP which was authorized; all missions where successful. Anvil is securing the site att and MOD/RCP/Paladin were pushed down IOT conduct route clearance and neutralize a suspected second IED at site.

EOD Report

On 12 Nov 2007 Anvil Co. 1/503D - TF Eagle struck a Pressure Plate IED on the Malkeshay COP access road IVO FOB Bermel. FOB Orgun-E CIED / CEXC, 720 EOD TM 1, RCP-3, and 720 EOD TM3 were notified of the IED strike on US forces, and prepared to move. Initial report stated that the IED strike had resulted in US casualties (2) KIA (1) WIA, and that a second IED had been encountered at the same location. Based on the late arrival time of the element from FOB Orgun-E to FOB Bermel, it was decided to RON on FOB Bermel, and conduct the Post Blast Analysis (PBA) in the AM. Site was secured by US Forces. The Orgun-E element arrived on site the morning of 13 Nov 07.

After resetting the security perimeter, EOD TM 1 conducted an initial recon with the robot. TM interrogated the suspect second IED, and determined that it was the pressure plate from the original IED. A secondary search of the area was conducted remotely - via robot. TM Leader cleared the area of possible secondary IEDs, and UXO remaining from the destroyed UAH. OE CIED CEXC element and EOD Teams conducted PBA, resulting in the recovery of: 1 ea - pressure plate (3.14 in width x 23.46 in length) and 1 ea - power source (8 ea D-Cell batteries). TM believes main charge was bulk HE (type and quantity unknown). PBA did not reveal any fragmentation or otherwise within the blast seat or surrounding area. Blast Seat measured: 10 x 10 5 x 3.15 in depth. The UAH that struck the PPIED was the third vehicle in a convoy of six. All components were retained by OE CIED CEXC element for further exploitation.

Historical Comparisons:
(F) This is the third IED with in this general area in recent history.
(F) PP IEDs are common in the Bermel Malkeshay COP AOR.
Lessons Learned:
(F) INS place IEDs in areas that convoys must stay on the roads.
New TTPs: N/A
ISAF Tracking #11-294.

Reference ID: AFG20071114n1110
Latitude: 32.06674576

Region: RC SOUTH
Longitude: 64.83624268

Date: 2007-11-14 06:06
Category: IED Explosion
Detained: 0

Type: Explosive Hazard
Affiliation: ENEMY

	Enemy	Friend	Civilian	Host nation
Killed in action	0	1	1	0
Wounded in action	0	0	0	0

(S//REL) At 0626Z on 14 Nov 07, seven ANA and one CF officer were conducting a foot patrol in a small town when an IED detonated, killing the CF officer and injuring the LN interpreter. Investigation revealed a Command Wire was used. An EOD search revealed a second undetonated charge approx 15m away (Grid Ref: 7334 4933) from the detonation along the direction of travel, consisting of 2 x 81mm mortars and detonation cord. This charge was wired to the first charge with copper wire, but it did not function. Several lengths of wire were also recovered from the second charge. A motorcycle battery, lengths of wire and fragments from an artillery shell were recovered from the first explosion. The Patrol consisted of six (6x) ANA Pax followed by a gap, a CF Officer, another gap, then another individual to the rear. Exact spacings are not known.
ITEMS RECOVERED:
a. (C//REL) One (1x) 12v motorcycle battery.
b. (C//REL) Four (4x) lengths of single core wire tied together in a rough square with one piece of green cord. The report is not clear where this was found and its use.
c. (C//REL) Five (5x) lengths of twin flex wire. The wire may have originally been all one piece. It was cut into five pieces. The report did not state which cuts came from the detonation and which from recovery efforts. The bags list the five pieces as: three pieces of wire that ran from the firing point to way to the crater, from this point the next wire ran to the crater of the first charge and then way to the second charge, the last wire ran from this point to the second charge. The last piece still had the remains of the electric detonator taped to the wire.
d. (S//REL) Four (4x) pieces of an artillery shell from the first explosion.
CEXC_AFG_1133_07

Reference ID: AFG20071124n951
Latitude: 34.58211899
Date: 2007-11-24 05:05
Category: IED Explosion
Detained:

Region: RC CAPITAL
Longitude: 68.93000031
Type: Explosive Hazard
Affiliation: ENEMY

	Enemy	Friend	Civilian	Host nation
Killed in action	1	1	9	0
Wounded in action	0	3	9	0

At 0525Z RC Central reported that 1x insurgent armed with a suicide vest detonated himself on an Italian convoy at Grid 42S VD 963 255 in the Paghman district of the Kabul province. As a result of the blast, 3x Italian soldiers were wounded, 6x civilian children were killed and 9x civilians were in injured, along with the death of the bomber. The 3x Italians were medevac'ed to Bagram Airfield.
Update: French MEDEVAC diverted to Camp Warehouse while enroute to BAF to stabilize a patient. As of 1115Z, 3 x Italian WIA are still at Camp Warehouse.
At 0829Z, updated BDA: 4 x ITA WIA, 9x Civilians KIA, 9 x Civilians WIA, 1xINS KIA

At 1402Z, 1x Italian DOW. Updated BDA: 1x ITA KIA, 3xITA WIA, 9x Civilians KIA, 9 X Civilians WIA, 1xINS KIA.
At 1111Z, an updated grid for the attack was reported as 42S VD 93580 26705, 21.9 km NW of Camp Dubs.
ISAF Tracking # 11-624

Reference ID: AFG20071204n1073
Latitude: 34.55531311
Date: 2007-12-04 03:03
Category: IED Explosion
Detained: 0

Region: RC CAPITAL
Longitude: 69.20580292
Type: Explosive Hazard
Affiliation: ENEMY

	Enemy	Friend	Civilian	Host nation
Killed in action	1	0	0	0
Wounded in action	0	0	22	0

At 0340Z, RC Capital reported that a VBIED detonated on 2xUS Vehicles convoy on RTE White at 42S WD 1888 2375, Kabul district of Kabul province. The VBIED was a Toyota Corolla license plate number 44453 and the vehicle was on the suspicious vehicle list. A QRF from ISAF HQ was dispatched to secure the area. All wounded civilians were transferred to Kabul Hospital for treatment.
BDA: 22xCIV WIA and no military casualties reported.
Event closed at 0804Z, NFTR.
ISAF Tracking #12-067.

Reference ID: AFG20071216n1069
Latitude: 32.56548691
Date: 2007-12-16 00:12
Category: IED Explosion
Detained:

Region: RC SOUTH
Longitude: 65.98107147
Type: Explosive Hazard
Affiliation: ENEMY

	Enemy	Friend	Civilian	Host nation
Killed in action			5	
Wounded in action				

Local Nationals (2 adults, 3 children) killed when their vehicle struck a probably pressure plate IED 15 km SE of FOB Ripley. NFI

Reference ID: AFG20071212n1079
Latitude: 32.79460144
Date: 2007-12-12 12:12
Category: IED Explosion
Detained: 0

Region: RC EAST
Longitude: 68.91625977
Type: Explosive Hazard
Affiliation: ENEMY

	Enemy	Friend	Civilian	Host nation
Killed in action	0	2	0	0
Wounded in action	0	3	0	0

At 1200z, Havoc 16 convoy (1st vehicle) traveling from FOB Curry to Charbaran DC struck an IED at VB 9216 2852. Direct HIF fires were conducted on the ridges along the road as soldiers moved and recovered 3 x wounded soldiers from the vehicles. 2

soldiers were killed in the strike and were initially unable to be retrieved from the vehicle due to fire and ammunition cooking off.

At 1215z, TF Eagle posted a 9 line for 3 x urgent US Soldiers (2 Litter, 1 Ambulatory) who were wounded in the IED strike. MM(E) 12-12B was approved for launch and went w/u OE at 1236z. The MEDEVAC went w/d at the grid at 1240z and returned to OE, dropped off all 3 PTs, MC at 1249z.

At 1323z, TF Eagle posted a 9-Line Patient transfer for the 3 x wounded soldiers IOT move them up to BAF for further treatment. Remarks follow: PT1: US male, with 3rd degree burns to arm, legs and hands, has had escharotomy, PT2: US male with broken left leg and ankle, fx right leg, and lac above left eye, possible spinal injury has been placed on spine board, and PT3: US male with head concussion, swollen below and above ear. MM(E) 12-21B (Dingo 55) was launched from BAF at 1251z, w/d OE at 1400z. NFTR. Event closed.

ISAF Tracking # 12-336
Event Closed
FM TF PALADIN

A patrol was traveling north from FOB Curry to the Charbaran DC and struck a PPIED. The detonation resulted in: 2 ea US KIA and 3 ea US WIA; the team responded to the site by aviation assets to conduct a post blast investigation of the site. The 1st vehicle (UAH) in a convoy of five had struck the PPIED with the left rear tire, the detonation occurred in the rear centerline of the vehicle. The vehicle was flipped on to the roof and caught on fire. The device was determined to have consisted of 1ea AT landmine (likely plastic as no fragmentation or remains were located), 1 ea 6 volt battery contained in a clear plastic container inside of a blue plastic bag; 1 ea pressure plate contained in an inner tube, sewn together with red yarn containing 2 ea hack saw style blades. The blast seat measured 78 inches in diameter and 20 inches deep. The team disposed of 40ea 40mm HEDP and 1ea AT-4 that had been damaged in the attack by detonation. The recovered components were turned into CEXC for exploitation.

Team Leaders Assessment
-This was the second PPIED in this area. The first was 18 July 2007 (prior to 720th EOD arrival in theater).

Lessons Learned
-It is extremely important to obtain all EOD mission related data when responding to Post Blast investigations via rotary wing. Based on limited space and resources, every attempt must be made by the EOD team, and the supported unit to obtain a clear picture of the scene.

Mission Complete. For further details please see associated reports. NFTR
****

ISAF convoy hits IED in southern Afghanistan
KHOWST PROVINCE, Afghanistan (12 Dec.) Two International Security Assistance Force servicemembers were killed and three others wounded today when their vehicle struck an IED during a convoy in Paktika Province, Afghanistan.
SEE ATTACHED FOR COMPLETE RELEASE
EXSUM:
On the evening of 12 DEC, a Task Force Eagle (D Company) patrol traveling north on Route Charger from FOB Curry to the Charbaran District Center struck an IED and began to burn, killing two Task Force Eagle paratroopers and wounding three others. The lead vehicle in the convoy hit the IED. The D company patrol secured the blast

site and pulled the three wounded from the vehicle. The vehicle TC and the passenger in the right rear seat were killed instantly and could not be extracted from the burning vehicle, as ammunition began to cook off. The three wounded were MEDEVACd to FOB Orgun FST and onto BAF. One paratrooper remains sedated in stable condition with third degree burns over 50% of his body. Another suffered two ankle fractures, a torn knee ligament, and a fractured rib. The third suffered head trauma and a severely bruised jaw. TF Paladin and Mortuary Affairs will arrive at the strike site the morning of 13 DEC to conduct site exploitation and recover the remains of our fallen paratroopers. D Company is securing the blast site and will link up with the RCP 3 tomorrow to clear the Route Charger south to FOB Curry.

Reference ID: AFG20071221n1080
Latitude: 31.55198097
Date: 2007-12-21 05:05
Category: IED Explosion
Detained: 0

Region: RC SOUTH
Longitude: 65.68309784
Type: Explosive Hazard
Affiliation: ENEMY

	Enemy	Friend	Civilian	Host nation
Killed in action	0	0	1	1
Wounded in action	0	0	2	0

At 0515Z, TF Kandahar reported friendly forces rolled a cadaver over triggering an IED at 41R QQ 547 939, 0.8km northeast of Monar, 10.2km southwest of Camp Nathan Smith in the Kandahar district of Kandahar province. ISAF assistance was requested. BDA is 1x ANP KIA, 1x LN KIA, 2x LN WIA.
At 0727Z, A second IED was discovered IVO the same location. TF Kandahar sent a QRF from KPRT. The QRF picked up an IED team from KAF and then proceeded to the site. At 0756Z, the ANP found another IED at Munara Ghundi at 41R QQ 547 939. The ANP was on site.
At 0815Z, TF Kandahar reported the CEXC was scheduled to link up with EOD on KAF at 0825Z. Those 2x elements were planned to then link up with the TF Kandahar QRF at the main gate at 0900Z. They then were tasked to continue to site and possibly continue to Arghendab.
At 1117Z, EOD confirmed 1x explosion and 1x ANP KIA. Nothing was found at the site. Event closed at 1116Z.
ISAF tracking # 12-540.

Reference ID: AFG20080107n1248
Latitude: 34.10984802
Date: 2008-01-07 06:06
Category: IED Explosion
Detained: 0

Region: RC EAST
Longitude: 70.53524017
Type: Explosive Hazard
Affiliation: ENEMY

	Enemy	Friend	Civilian	Host nation
Killed in action	0	2	0	0
Wounded in action	0	1	0	0

AT 070620ZJAN08 173D STB Report a UXO IVO of KOT Grid follows .42S XC 416 745   ANP in the Kot district reported an IED in the village of Laghar Juy. Description of 1 mine on the side of the road with wires.   ANP have secured the site and we are going to link up with EOD and escort them to the IED location

173D STB REPORTS AN IED STRIKE AT 1150Z LOCATION XC 448 774. NANGAHAR PRT SECFOR COMPLETED AN ESCOURTE OF TF PALADIN TO RECOVER A UXO AND HIT AN IED. OF THE 6 VEHICLE CONVOY THE FIFTH VEHICLE STRUCK THE ACTUALL IED. THE IED WAS DESCIRBED AS A COMMAND WIRED IED, WITH THE WIRE BEING BURIED IN THE MUD ALONG A DRAINAGE DITCH, DETONATED WITH A BATTERY. THE LOCATION OF THE IED IS APPROXIMANATLY 2 KM FROM THE UXO THAT THE UNIT REPSONED TO. IN THE AREA OF THE IED THERE ARE TWO LOCAL SHOPS WHICH IS COMMONLY VERY POPULATED WITH LOCAL NATIONALS WAS VACANT PRIOR TO THE INCIDENT. THE PERSONELL INSIDE THE VEHICLE SUSTAINED INJURY, CAUSING ONE KIA, AND TWO ADDITIONAL WIAS. THE WIA"S INJURIES DESCIRBED WERE, ONE SUSTAINING INJURY TO BOTH LEGS, THE OTHER SUSTAINIED INTERNAL INJURIES. THE PRTSEC FOR CONVOY HAD ONE MEDIC THAT WAS HAS CIVILAIN EMT EXPERIENCE. MEDIVAC WAS REQUESTED AT 1155Z, AT 1218 A REPORT OF 3 MINUTES OUT WAS GIVEN. AT 1247 THE MEDIVAC WAS CANCELLED DUE TO WEATHER. UNIT HAD TO CONDUCT A CASEVAC AT 1308 OF THE WIA"S TO FOB FENTY AND LEFT THE KIA ON SITE WITH A SQUAD FROM THE 66TH MP SECURING THE LOCATION. PATEINTS ARRIVE AT FST 1435, ONE OF THE WIA"S REPORTED WITH NO CHANGE TO CONDITION, THE OTHER THAT WAS REPORTED AS HAVING A WEAK PULSE. THE CASULTY WITH INTERNAL INJURIES LATER DIED AT FENTY HOSPITAL. 66TH MPS ARE ON SITE AND WILL SECURE THE AREA OVERNIGHT. TF RAPTOR WILL CONDUCT SSE IN THE MORNING.
INCIDENT: IED ATTACK
RESULTS: 1 x CF KIA, 2 X CF WIA
SIGACT/EVENT ID:
DTG: 07 1151Z, JAN 08
UNIT: TF RAPTOR (STB) / 173D ABCT
LOCATION: Kot District, NANGARHAR PROVINCE
TIMELINE OF EVENTS:
07 JAN 08
07 JAN 08
At 0604 PCC reported ANP have secured an IED site (XC 416 745) in the Kot district and requested EOD
At 0824 PRT SECFOR (Phoenix 6) and EOD SP FAF to the IED site
At 1027 EOD and Phoenix 6 arrived at IED site. EOD conducted a controlled detonation and began to return to FAF
At 1151 one of the EOD trucks (4th in order of movement) was struck by an IED at XC 44894 77484. Resulting in 1 KIA and 2 WIA.
At 1155 a 9 line was sent
At 1218 Report that MEDEVAC is 3 MIN out
At 1227 Apocalypse 2 (66th MP QRF) arrived on site. ANP also responded and sent 3 vehicles and 15 PAX.
At 1247 the MEDEVAC was recalled to FAF due poor visibility cause by weather
At 1308 Phoenix 6 SP to FAF for ground MEDEVAC, carrying 2x WIA, leaving 1 x KIA on site with Apocalypse 2
At 1403 Apocalypse 2 reports all SI have been removed and all personal affects secured with KIA still at IED site. AP 3 in over watch position
1435 Phoenix 6 RP at FAF

1556 Phoenix 6 SP FAF to PRT
1604 Phoenix 6 arrive at PRT
08 JAN 08
At 0443 the recovery assets under Grizzly 16 SP FAF to recover the vehicle and KIA
At 0730 Grizzly 16 discover a mine at grid XC 4963 8639 and detonate the mine
At 0843z Recovery element arrives at IED and begin recovery & exploitation
At 1401 all elements at IED site SP for FAF/TKM
At 1706 recovery assets RP FAF
At 1722 AP2 & AP3 RP TKM
At 1758 PHX 2 RP JBAD Mission Complete
****

Team responded to a call for a mine with wires in the road at grid 42S XC 416 754. EOD arrived on scene to find wire, det cord, a DTMF receiver (possible MOD5), something buried wrapped in tape, and a little plastic jug. EOD recovered mod device with wire and little plastic jug. The taped wrapped object was disposed of by detonation and some explosive contribution was witnessed. Remains of detonation appeared to be some type of projo fuse and thin metal fragment. Evidence that was collected was given to CEXC on site. While returning from the IED call, convoy was struck by a CWIED at 42S XC 44894 77484 . The Paladin vehicle was destroyed, resulted in 2 US KIA (1 DOW at JAF), 1 US WIA. WIA were ground evacd to JAF. A hasty post blast analysis was conducted by the EOD element within the convoy. EOD teams 1 and 3 responded on 8 Jan for SSE. Evidence from original mission was in the Paladin vehicle and team will attempt recovery with post blast investigation.

Paladin update

While returning from an IED call, 071151ZJan08 at 42S XC 41880 75504, convoy was struck by a CWIED at 42S XC 44894 77484. Detonation resulted in 2X US KIA (1 DOW at JAF), 1 US WIA. WIA were ground evacuated to JAF with remaining first responders. A hasty post blast analysis was conducted by the EOD team leader within the convoy. 703rd EOD Teams 1 and 3 returned to IED site on 8 Jan for SSE. Evidence collected was Umbrella (with possible biometrics), Battery, Wire, and red cloth aiming flag. Enroute to Post blast location, a landmine was discovered by the Husky. EOD team disposed of landmine by detonation and continued mission. While returning to base, multiple rocks/boulders were placed in the road as to make a vehicle go around them. Convoy also encountered a 30 gallon cloth bag with a box leaning against it in the middle of the road. Husky received no metallic signature of item and convoy continued.

TF Paladin Observations

-The convoy took the same route back and CWIED was used in the attack.
-Initial response could have been a come-along.
-IED was emplaced prior to response and insurgents waited for convoys return due to anticipated short response on initial response.
****

.COMBINED JOINT TASK FORCE- 82
COMBINED PRESS INFORMATION CENTER
BAGRAM AIRFIELD, AFGHANISTAN
APO AE 09354
Press Center: 0799-063-013
bagrammoc@afghan.swa.army.mil
FOR IMMEDIATE RELEASE

January 07, 2008
RELEASE # 029
One servicemember killed, two wounded by IED
BAGRAM AIRFIELD, Afghanistan One Coalition servicemember was killed and two were wounded by an improvised explosive device in the Kot District of Nangarhar Province, Afghanistan, today.
SEE ATTACHED FOR COMPLETE RELEASE
Nothing further to report Event Closed

Reference ID: AFG20080114n1232
Latitude: 34.51882553
Date: 2008-01-14 13:01
Category: IED Explosion
Detained: 1

Region: RC CAPITAL
Longitude: 69.17649078
Type: Explosive Hazard
Affiliation: ENEMY

	Enemy	Friend	Civilian	Host nation
Killed in action	1	0	5	0
Wounded in action	0	0	8	0

At 1345Z, the Kabul City Police reported that four men ran into the main entrance of the Serena Hotel in Kabul and opened fire with small arms. The men were armed with small arms and wore suicide vests. One of the insurgents detonated his suicide vest, killing himself. Five civilians were killed in the attack. These include three Afghans, one Norwegian, and one unknown. Eight individuals, one Norwegian and one from the United Arab Emirates, as well as six Afghans were wounded and evacuated by ground to the Czech Role 2 Hospital at Kabul International Airport.
Approximately 26 Americans staying at the hotel were evacuated to the US Embassy by Embassy security personnel. The TF Gladius QRF deployed from Camp Eggers to provide additional security. Three of the attackers were killed in the attack. The disposition of the final gunman is unknown at this time.ISAF tracking # 01-268.
ASSESSMENT: Historical reporting indicates that the Serena Hotel remains a primary target for the insurgency because it is known to be the hotel of choice for visiting western dignitaries. AQ along with HQN elements increased their focus on Kabul in 2007, and this complex SIED event coupled with the HQN claim of responsibility and indirect linkages back to Abu Layth make these two groups the most likely culprits.

Reference ID: AFG20080217n1231
Latitude: 31.61611938
Date: 2008-02-17 06:06
Category: IED Explosion
Detained: 0

Region: RC SOUTH
Longitude: 65.63436127
Type: Explosive Hazard
Affiliation: ENEMY

	Enemy	Friend	Civilian	Host nation
Killed in action	1	0	55	0
Wounded in action	0	0	48	0

At 0600Z, TF Kandahar reported a suspected Suicide Bomber detonated killing himself, Abdul Hakin Jan, and approximately 50x Local Nationals at 41R QR 499 009, Kandahar district of Kandahar province. Friendly forces investigated the situation.
AT 0733Z, TF Kandahar reported Al Jazeera reported the incident took place in Kandahar City, at a dog fight related picnic.

At 0737Z, TF Kandahar reported a local hospital, Miriwais hospital, is full of patients. Patients have been taken to the ANA hospital at Camp Hero. ANA has declared a mass casualty.15x ISAF ambulances from KAF and FP are on standby for patient transfer when necessary. 4x ambulances, 10x patients are enroute from local hospital to Camp Hero.
At 0806Z, TF Kandahar reported multiple sources indicated the event took place at 41R QR 43 01.
At 0832Z, TF Kandahar reported Al Jazeera is reported multiple explosions. TF Kandahar QRF is responding with EOD and has requested air support.
At 0946Z, TF Kandahar reported all ISAF ambulances returned to Kandahar Air Field and all Afghan National Army ambulances returned to Camp Hero.
At 10255Z, TF Kandahar reported the location of the SIED was 41R QR 445 024 in an open area around some farms. This description was based on verbal descriptions.
At 1327Z, friendly forces exploited the IED site and returned to base.
BDA 1x EKIA, 48x WIA, and 55 LN killed
Event closed at 1632Z.
ISAF Tracking # 02-291

Reference ID: AFG20080226n1092   Region: RC EAST
Latitude: 33.47724152   Longitude: 70.03356171
Date: 2008-02-26 04:04   Type: Explosive Hazard
Category: IED Explosion   Affiliation: ENEMY
Detained: 0

	Enemy	Friend	Civilian	Host nation
Killed in action	0	0	1	5
Wounded in action	0	0	0	0

At 26 0424Z Feb 08, Sabari DC reported that the Sabari ANP Company Commander (Raziq Noor) struck an RCIED near 42S WC 96030 04674 while traveling to work in a civilian vehicle. ANP arrived at the site and found that all 6 passengers of the vehicle were KIA; Names follow:
 1) Raziq Noor s/o Ajab Noor (ANP CO)
 2) Kamal Noor s/o Raziq Noor (ANP)
 3) Jamal Noor s/o Raziq Noor (ANP)
 4) Gul Noor s/o Raziq Noor (12 yrs old s/o Raziq Noor)
 5) Halim Jan s/o Majan (ANP)
 6) Zaman Khan s/o Gul Hanan (ANP)
Sabari ANP reported that Latfullah, the Sabari Sub Governor, was in the vehicle behind Raziq Noor.
FM TF PALADIN PBA concluded 5 ANP KIA, and 1 noncombatant KIA. Two separate means of initiation were found, one of which had been at the location for an extended period of time. The first system consisted of: A battery pack w/ six D-cell batteries wrapped in black electrical tape. Two lengths of white lamp cord extended in opposite directions parallel to the route terminating with clothes pins on each end. Each clothes pin had an insulator consisting of black electrical tape wrapped upon itself multiple times. The second system was discovered IVO the blast seat, and had been emplaced recently. This system consisted of: A battery pack w/ 3 ea D-cell batteries wrapped in black electrical tape, a Uniden PMR model GMR 635. The PMR was wrapped in plastic and black electrical tape concealing the PMR and DTMF

board. The blast seat measured 130 in Long x 100 in Wide x 28 in deep. Based on the size of the blast seat and fragmentation recovered, main charge is consistent with two Mk 7/1landmines, placed side by side. All evidence from the scene was turned over to CEXC for exploitation.

Reference ID: AFG20080226n1103
Latitude: 31.81693077
Date: 2008-02-26 06:06
Category: IED Explosion
Detained: 0

Region: RC SOUTH
Longitude: 65.78356171
Type: Explosive Hazard
Affiliation: ENEMY

	Enemy	Friend	Civilian	Host nation
Killed in action	1	2	0	0
Wounded in action	0	1	0	0

At 0612Z, TF Eagle reported that an SVBIED hit a vehicle in a US convoy at 41R QR 6349 2352 in the Shah Wali Kot district, Kandahar. Friendly forces reported no BDA.
At 0704Z, TF Bushmaster responded to the scene of the incident as QRF. TF Bushmaster reported having 3x ambulatory casualties, none that were reported as being life-threatening at this time. They were ground evac''d to FOB Maholic and based on a further assessment of the patients a MEDEVAC may be requested.
Event closed at 1031Z.
ISAF Tracking # 02-515
Press Release # 087
BAGRAM AIRFIELD, Afghanistan (26 Feb.) Two ISAF Servicemembers were killed and one was wounded Feb. 26 when their vehicle was struck by an improvised explosive device in the Shah Wali Kot District in Kandahar Province.
For full release see attachments

Reference ID: AFG20080404n1234
Latitude: 32.3001976
Date: 2008-04-04 04:04
Category: IED Explosion
Detained: 0

Region: RC SOUTH
Longitude: 65.09685516
Type: Explosive Hazard
Affiliation: ENEMY

	Enemy	Friend	Civilian	Host nation
Killed in action	0	2	0	0
Wounded in action	0	2	0	0

(S//REL) C Coy, 40 Cdo Regt was conducting a mounted patrol and reconnaissance to clear a route to the southern FLET for the use of Close Combat Troops. The FSG was tasked to provide over-watch and fire support to the combat troops. The FSG, comprised of Whiskey 1-4, evaluated the use of two over-watch positions, Electric Hill and Thortons Rise. These two locations had been used previously but not frequently. The tracks leading to both locations channel the FSG vehicles through choke points. As such, the commander mandated the use of Op BARMA to clear a safe route to the over-watch positions. Ultimately, the FSG commander chose to use Electric Hill as the over-watch and fire-support position. As the FSG cleared a route up Electric Hill, one of the vehicles struck a PPIED. IEDD was called and responded to the scene. After conducting a search for secondary devices, IEDD cleared the scene via the use of a Render Safe Procedure (RSP).

Reference ID: AFG20080407n1351
Latitude: 32.01094437
Date: 2008-04-07 11:11
Category: IED Explosion
Detained: 0

Region: RC SOUTH
Longitude: 64.81716156
Type: Explosive Hazard
Affiliation: ENEMY

	Enemy	Friend	Civilian	Host nation
Killed in action	0	0	0	0
Wounded in action	0	0	0	0

SUMMARY OF EVENTS

(S//REL). At approx 071100ZAPR08 C/S Spatacus 20 (C/S S20) was conducting a dominance, reassurance and influence patrol in the local area following up on previous patrols. C/S S20 was patrolling along a large bundline to the only crossing point on the river for approx 2kms to move back to FOB Robin. Two members of C/S S20 and the interpreter had already crossed the river. The third member of the patrol was at the bottom of the bundline and was about to cross, the fourth member of the patrol was on top of the bundline. The explosion occurred approx 1m in front of the fourth member of the patrol.

ITEMS RECOVERED

(C//REL) One (1x) RC Pack consisting of a MOD 5 DTMF Spider attached to a 12v motorcycle battery. The Spider device measures approx 150mm (L) x 55mm (W) x 30mm (H). The 12v motorcycle battery measures 110mm (L) x 95mm (W) x 50mm (H). Three (3x) wires exit the IED, two (2x) SSMC wires with a blue outer sheath measure 100mm (L) which are attached and secured to DSMC wire with a clear outer sheath and measures approx 4170mm (L). This wire is predominately used with audio speakers. The third wire is a SSMC wire with a black outer sheath which measures 4141mm (L).

(C//REL) Quantity of metal fragments consistent with a 105mm illumination artillery shell.

Reference ID: AFG20080416n1284
Latitude: 33.53086472
Date: 2008-04-16 15:03
Category: IED Explosion
Detained: 0

Region: RC EAST
Longitude: 69.89517212
Type: Explosive Hazard
Affiliation: ENEMY

	Enemy	Friend	Civilian	Host nation
Killed in action	0	0	0	0
Wounded in action	0	0	0	0

While conducting route clearance, RCP9's lead Husky triggered a VOIED (Trip Wire) in the Kholbesat Wadi Southwest of Maktab Bazaar. The trip wire was emplaced across the route, and was detonated by the vehicle's front tires. The Husky received damage to its rear mod and the driver was shaken up by the detonation. However, no casualties. RCP9 immediately secured the surrounding area while the EOD TL expeditiously cleared the SOE and surrounding area of hazards. TM conducted Post Blast Analysis (PBA). VOIED consisted of: white electrical wire (lamp cord); x1 Clothes Pin (plastic tan), and a Power Source consisting of a battery pack with x14 D-cell batteries. The SOE measured 14 across by 46 deep. TM estimates the main charge to have been 65-75 lbs of an unknown HME. RCP requested CCA from TF

Glory, self recovered and CM 161700ZAPR08. Components were turned over to C-IED SAL CEXC for further exploitation.

C Co 70th EN OPS: (20:24) RCP 9 IED REPORT
1. 16 1540z APR 08
2. WC 8312 1050
3. RCP 9 Rock 36 44650
4. IED exploded on Husky
5. none
6. RTE Ford; Zambar Route
7. Halt Patrol
8. 360 Security, conducting 5/25/100m checks
9. PRIORITY EOD is with them
Event Closed

Reference ID: AFG20080506n1413
Latitude: 31.61888313
Date: 2008-05-06 02:02
Category: IED Explosion
Detained: 0
Region: RC SOUTH
Longitude: 65.71768951
Type: Explosive Hazard
Affiliation: ENEMY

	Enemy	Friend	Civilian	Host nation
Killed in action	1	0	3	0
Wounded in action	0	0	4	3

FF reported a SBIED (explosive built into a bicycle) strike targeted an ANP Academy Ranger. Initial exploitation indicates the attack was a bicycle borne IED detonated by a remote or command wire. Reports by QRF on ground state that three of the casualties were regional training center personnel. All casualties were transported to LN hospital. PRT QRF with EOD /TET responded.
BDA: 3 x ANP WIA, 3 x LN Killed, 4 x LN Wounded, 1 x ACF Killed, 1 x Ford Ranger Vehicle Damaged
ISAF# 05-180

Reference ID: AFG20080528n1329
Latitude: 33.13933945
Date: 2008-05-28 04:04
Category: IED Explosion
Detained: 0
Region: RC EAST
Longitude: 68.07613373
Type: Explosive Hazard
Affiliation: ENEMY

	Enemy	Friend	Civilian	Host nation
Killed in action	0	0	0	0
Wounded in action	0	0	0	0

SUMMARY OF EVENTS
(S//REL) Guam 16 was traveling South bound on MSR OHIO when a detonation occurred from within a culvert as the lead vehicle passed over it. No casualties or vehicle damage was reported. A Post Blast Analysis (PBA) was conducted and determined the culvert was not severely damaged and there was no damage to the roadway. One (1x) British Landmine, Anti Tank, Model Mk 7/1 (burned out) and remnants from three (3x) 82 MM Mortars (model and country unknown) were found at the scene. A command pull string was also located approximately 300m to the East

side of road. The main charge did not fully detonate but instead burned violently in a low order event. The pull string and casing of the burned out Mk 7/1 Landmine were recovered. The mortars were destroyed by EOD.
ITEMS RECOVERED
(C//REL) One (1x) ball of burnt orange colored pull string. Total length of the pull string is approximately 378 meters.
(C//REL) Two (2x) red cardboard tubes measuring approximately 100mm (L) x 34mm (H).
(C//REL) One (1x) casing of burned out British, Anti tank, Mk 7/1 Landmine (to be destroyed by EOD).

Reference ID: AFG20080531n759
Latitude: 34.42733765
Date: 2008-05-31 07:07
Category: IED Explosion
Detained: 0

Region: RC EAST
Longitude: 70.45505524
Type: Explosive Hazard
Affiliation: ENEMY

	Enemy	Friend	Civilian	Host nation
Killed in action	1	2	0	0
Wounded in action	0	4	0	0

FF were on routine patrol when they were struck by an IED strike. The BDA is 4x US MIL WIA and 1x UAHMMWV damaged. All of the wounded have been MEDEVAC. QRF is on site with wrecker to secure and recover the UAHMMWV. FF are reporting that it is a possible secondary device in a white sedan (VBIED). The area is cordoned off and FF are maintaining a 200m standoff from the vehicle. NFI att.
At 0954Z, TF Raptor reported update:
EOD arrived on site and confirmed the initial IED was a SVBIED strike and the secondary device is a VBIED. EOD conducted a controlled detonation of the VBIED. At 0944Z, EOD identified a possible third device and they are exploiting the site att. NFI att.
At 1103Z, TF Raptor reported update:
FF report that the third device was an UXO that ejected from the VBIED following the controlled detonation. NFI att.
At 1359Z, TF Raptor reported update:
Update to casualties is 2x US MIL KIA and 4x US MIL WIA. NFI att.
At 1928Z, TF Raptor reported: Site has been cleared and everything has been recovered. NFTR. Event closed at 1906Z.
ISAF #05-1280

Reference ID: AFG20080607n1390
Latitude: 33.31153107
Date: 2008-06-07 01:01
Category: IED Explosion
Detained: 0

Region: RC EAST
Longitude: 70.03491211
Type: Explosive Hazard
Affiliation: ENEMY

	Enemy	Friend	Civilian	Host nation
Killed in action	0	0	0	0
Wounded in action	0	0	0	0

SUMMARY OF EVENTS

(S//REL) On 7 June 2008 at approximately 0100 local time, FOB Salerno received InDirect Fire (IDF) and 720th EOD was tasked to investigate a POO site at first light on 7 June 2008. EOD team was escorted by A/3-321 FA from the Terezai DC. EOD discovered one (1x) Chinese Rocket, Ground-to-Ground, 107mm, HE, Model Type 63-2 with a Chinese Rocket Fuze, PD, Model MJ-1 Fuze. Team leader noticed that the rocket had a MUV-2 firing device in the venturi and after clearing the site the unfired rocket was disposed of in place by detonation. TM also found one (1x) Mosque Shape Clock connected to a power source (6x D-Cell batteries) with wires leading to a launch site. A flashlight with POLICE written on the side was found next to the unfired rocket. While continuing to clear the site after disposing of the rocket, team leader noticed trash at the bottom of the hill and moved down to investigate. Team leader found three (3x) empty boxes for Mosque Clocks along with stripped wire and other pieces of trash. TM leader also noticed fresh and old mule tracks leading in and out of the rocket preparation area, below the POO site.

Reference ID: AFG20080609n1283
Latitude: 33.43384171
Date: 2008-06-09 05:05
Category: IED Explosion
Detained: 2

Region: RC EAST
Longitude: 69.99873352
Type: Explosive Hazard
Affiliation: ENEMY

	Enemy	Friend	Civilian	Host nation
Killed in action	0	0	0	0
Wounded in action	0	0	0	0

While conducting routine patrol FF observed an IED explosion. FF detained 2x INS. NFI, att.
At 0909Z, TM Khowst reported:
The 2x INS were released because they were both under 10 years old. FF conducted site exploitation and determined the device to have been a CPIED with 20-25lbs of explosives. NFI, att.
ISAF # 06-411

Reference ID: AFG20080620n1261
Latitude: 31.81858826
Date: 2008-06-20 05:05
Category: IED Explosion
Detained: 0

Region: RC SOUTH
Longitude: 64.56900024
Type: Explosive Hazard
ffiliation: ENEMY

	Enemy	Friend	Civilian	Host nation
Killed in action	1	1	9	0
Wounded in action	0	3	8	0

While on a routine patrol, FF struck an IED. BDA: 1x NATO/ISAF KIA, 2x NATO/ISAF (US) WIA (CAT B), 2x LNs wounded (CAT B) one of the LNs is a 7 year old. NFI att.
At 0628Z, RC South reported:
BDA: 1x NATO/ISAF (US) KIA, 1x LN (interpreter) Killed, 2x NATO/ISAF (US) WIA (CAT B), 2x LN Wounded (CAT B), no damages were reported. Device was a possible PBIED. NFI, att.

At 0900Z, RC South reported:
Update to casualties: 1x NATO/ISAF (US) KIA, 2x LN (1x interpreter and 1x child) Killed, 2x NATO/ISAF (US) WIA (CAT B), 1x CIV (US) wounded (CAT C), 2x LN wounded (1x CAT B and 1x CAT C). NFI, att.
At 1942Z, RC South reported:
Due to the casualties, FF returned to base and was not able to maintain a cordon. FF have no further intentions to exploit the site. NFTR. Event closed at 1152Z.
At 2030Z, RC South reported:
Update to casualties is 1x NATO/ISAF (US) KIA, 2x NATO/ISAF (US) WIA, 1x CIV (US) wounded, 9x LN killed (1x interpreter,1x child) and 8x LN wounded and 1 x INS KIA. NFTR. Event remains closed at 1152Z.
ISAF # 06-0903

Reference ID: AFG20080707n1425
Latitude: 34.52786636
Date: 2008-07-07 03:03
Category: IED Explosion
Detained: 0

Region: RC CAPITAL
Longitude: 69.16671753
Type: Explosive Hazard
Affiliation: ENEMY

	Enemy	Friend	Civilian	Host nation
Killed in action	1	0	42	0
Wounded in action	0	0	147	0

A SVBIED detonated while trying to enter the Indian Embassy front gate. BDA 1x INS Killed, 12x LN Killed, 4x LN Wounded. NFI att
At 0710Z, RC Capital reported:
BDA: 29x LN Killed, 1x INS Killed, 112x LN Wounded, several buildings damaged. NFI, att.
At 1230Z, RC Capital reported:
BDA: 42x LN Killed, 1x INS Killed, 147x LN Wounded, several buildings damaged. NFI, att.
ISAF# 07-308

Reference ID: AFG20080711n1337
Latitude: 32.68467331
Date: 2008-07-11 14:02
Category: IED Explosion
Detained: 0

Region: RC EAST
Longitude: 68.2828598
Type: Explosive Hazard
Affiliation: ENEMY

	Enemy	Friend	Civilian	Host nation
Killed in action	0	2	0	0
Wounded in action	0	1	0	0

T: TF HAMMER(GUAM 3-2)
TYPE: IED DETONATION
TIMELINE: AT 1400Z, GUAM 3-2 REPORTED TO TF HAMMER THAT THEY STRUCK AN IED ON RTE AUDI, 6 KILOMETERS NORTH OF FOB KUSHAMOND, GUAM ELEMENTS RESPONDED IN KUSHOMOND AND ARRIVED ON THE SCENE AND SECURED THE IED SITE THAT CAUSED 2 X US KIA, AND 1 X US WIA. GUAM 3-2 SECURING THE SITE ATT

TF WHITE EAGLE WILL BE SENDING A 4 VEHICLE PATROL FROM FOB KUSHAMOND TO THE IED SITE TO ASSIST IN SITE SECURITY.
CAS IN RTE ISO OF IED STRIKE
VEHICLE TYPE: M1151
IED DEFEAT SYSTEM: DUKE
FRAG 5 KIT
UPDATE 1543Z PBG QRF ON SITE ATT
UPDATE: 1659z GUAM REPORT POSSIBLE SECONDARY IED DEVICE, CURRENTLY SECURING AND CORDON THE AO TILL EOD GETS ON SITE ATT.
UPDATE: AT 1730Z GUAM 3-6 REPORTED THAT THEY SPOTTED A LIVE GRENADE AND STILL SECURING AND CORDON AO TILL EOD GETS ON SITE
UPDATE: AT 0110 EOD IS ON SITE
SUMMARY:
IED DETONATION
MM(E) 07-10C OE-GRID-OE
BDA:
US KIA: 2
US WIA: 1
EVENT OPEN PENDING RECOVERY OPERATIONS
UPDATE: 0740Z EOD CONDUCTED SITE EXPLOITATION. THE VEHICLE WAS SELF RECOVERED BACK TO FOB KUSHMOND. ALL ELEMENTS HAVE RETURNED TO THE FOB
EVENT CLOSED. @ 0755Z
Summary from duplicate event
At 1400Z, TF Currahee reported an IED strike. FF were on patrol when they struck an IED along route AUDI. BDA: 2x NATO/ISAF (US) KIA, 1x NATO/ISAF (US) WIA (CAT A). A 4 vehicle patrol from FOB Kushamond deployed to assist in site security. The Polish Battle Group QRF is on site att. NFI att.
ISAF # 07-475 End of summary from duplicate event

Reference ID: AFG20080814n1454
Latitude: 32.05557251
Date: 2008-08-14 09:09
Category: IED Explosion
Detained: 0

Region: RC SOUTH
Longitude: 64.85476685
Type: Explosive Hazard
Affiliation: ENEMY

	Enemy	Friend	Civilian	Host nation
Killed in action	0	3	0	0
Wounded in action	0	1	0	0

While conducting dismounted patrol FF struck an IED. BDA: 3x NATO/ISAF (US) KIA, 1x NATO/ISAF (US) WIA (CAT C), no damages were reported. NFI, att.
At 1808Z, RC South reported:
FF reported that there were 2x IED strikes. BDA remains the same. MEDEVAC was completed. NFI, att.
ISAF # 08-709

Reference ID: AFG20080816n1398
Latitude: 32.09568024

Region: RC SOUTH
Longitude: 66.10131073

Date: 2008-08-16 08:08
Category: IED Explosion
Detained: 0
Type: Explosive Hazard
Affiliation: ENEMY

	Enemy	Friend	Civilian	Host nation
Killed in action	0	0	0	11
Wounded in action	0	0	0	0

At 0830Z, TF Bushmaster reported an IED strike. FF reported that ANP with Scorpion 30 struck an IED. BDA: 10x ANP KIA, 1x ANP WIA and 1x ANP vehicle (Ford Ranger) destroyed. MEDEVAC was requested. FF established cordon. NFI att.
At 1207Z, TF Bushmaster reported:
BDA: 11 ANP KIA (1x DOW), 1x ANP vehicle (Ford Ranger) destroyed. FF positively identified the INS who emplace the IED and are moving to his position. CAS was requested. NFI, att.
At 1622Z, TF Bushmaster reported:
FF did not report site exploitation. NFTR. Event closed at 1416Z.
ISAF # 08-801

Reference ID: AFG20080820n1330
Latitude: 31.57152939
Date: 2008-08-20 06:06
Category: IED Explosion
Detained: 0
Region: RC SOUTH
Longitude: 65.37923431
Type: Explosive Hazard
Affiliation: ENEMY

	Enemy	Friend	Civilian	Host nation
Killed in action	0	3	0	0
Wounded in action	0	1	0	0

At 0600Z, TF Kandahar reported an IED strike. FF were conducting mounted NFO patrol along HWY 1 when they struck an IED. BDA: 4x NATO/ISAF (CAN) WIA (3x VSA, 1x CAT A) and 1x vehicle (unknown type) destroyed. FF established cordon. NFI att.
At 0749Z, TF Kandahar reported update:
The destroyed vehicle was a LAV III. 1x WIA has been extracted and MEDEVAC. 3x WIA are still inside the vehicle. The vehicle is burning and rounds are cooking off. Final extraction of casualties and exploitation of the site will not be conducted until rounds have stopped cooking off. NFI att.
At 1503Z, TF Kandahar reported:
BDA: 3x NATO/ISAF (CAN) KIA, 1x NATO/ISAF (CAN) WIA (CAT A), 1x LAV III destroyed. MEDEVAC was completed. EOD arrived on scene and conducted exploitation. While clearing the scene EOD BIP several UXOs. FF did not report the type of IED. NFTR. Event closed at 1430Z.
ISAF # 08-1047
Updated IAW CEXC level 2 report
see associated CEXC level 2 report for details
TF Paladin QAQC

Reference ID: AFG20080822n1383
Latitude: 33.41119385
Date: 2008-08-22 05:05
Region: RC EAST
Longitude: 68.51140594
Type: Explosive Hazard

Category: IED Explosion Affiliation: ENEMY
Detained: 0

	Enemy	Friend	Civilian	Host nation
Killed in action	0	1	0	0
Wounded in action	0	0	0	0

FF were on patrol when they found a CWIED. FF traced the command wire to the trigger man hiding location, but there were no INS found. RCP 7 deployed to the site. NFI att.
At 0723Z, TM Ghazni reported update:
FF secured the IED, command wire was cut and while removing the IED it detonated. BDA: 1x US MIL KIA. NFI att.
ISAF # 08-1166

Reference ID: AFG20080825n1321 Region: RC SOUTH
Latitude: 32.06839371 Longitude: 64.83453369
Date: 2008-08-25 11:11 Type: Explosive Hazard
Category: IED Explosion Affiliation: ENEMY
Detained: 0

	Enemy	Friend	Civilian	Host nation
Killed in action	0	0	0	0
Wounded in action	1	0	0	1

While conducting dismounted security patrol FF struck an IED. BDA: 1x ANP WIA, 1x LN wounded, no damages were reported. FF established cordon and EOD was requested. NFI, att.
At 260638Z, RC South reported:
EOD arrived on scene and conducted exploitation. TM determined the device to have been a CWIED daisy chain. FF returned to base. BDA: 1x INS wounded (CAT B), 1x ANP WIA (CAT B), no damages were reported. NFTR. Event closed at 260440Z.
ISAF # 08-1366

Reference ID: AFG20080901n1384 Region: RC SOUTH
Latitude: 31.4866066 Longitude: 65.3381424
Date: 2008-09-01 08:08 Type: Explosive Hazard
Category: IED Explosion Affiliation: ENEMY
Detained: 0

	Enemy	Friend	Civilian	Host nation
Killed in action	0	0	0	0
Wounded in action	0	0	0	0

FF were conducting a clearance patrol in support of OP Mutafiq Tandar when the mine roller of the lead tank in the patrol struck an IED. No casualties were reported and the mine roller was destroyed. FF conducted exploitation with organic assets and will submit a full report through the C-IED chain. FF installed a new mine roller on another tank and continued on mission. NFTR. Event closed at 0919Z.
ISAF # 09-019

Reference ID: AFG20080917n1492
Latitude: 33.37672043
Date: 2008-09-17 04:04
Category: IED Explosion
Detained: 0

Region: RC EAST
Longitude: 69.39196777
Type: Explosive Hazard
Affiliation: ENEMY

	Enemy	Friend	Civilian	Host nation
Killed in action	0	4	0	0
Wounded in action	0	1	0	0

FF were on patrol when they struck an IED. BDA: 4x US MIL KIA, 1x LN (Interpreter) KIA and 1x M1151 possibly destroyed. The M1151 flipped over and is on fire with rounds cooking off inside. The casualties have not been removed from the vehicle. QRF and CIED team Gardez deployed to conduct exploitation of the site. NFI att.
At 1111Z, TM Paktia reported:
CIED team completed exploitation and confirmed the device used in the strike to be a CWIED consisting of 40-60lbs of HME. The firing point was located 800-1200 meters away from the explosion site.
FF have returned to base.
NFTR.
Event closed at 1107Z.
ISAF # 09-0803

Reference ID: AFG20080924n1345
Latitude: 33.15427017
Date: 2008-09-24 12:12
Category: IED Explosion
Detained: 0

Region: RC WEST
Longitude: 62.18401718
Type: Explosive Hazard
Affiliation: ENEMY

	Enemy	Friend	Civilian	Host nation
Killed in action	0	0	0	0
Wounded in action	0	3	0	0

IED STRIKE
At 0810Localhrs on 24 Sep, an vehicle was struck by an IED, 3 pax were injured during the incident, 2 have lost their legs and remain in a critical condition in Herat hospital and 1 is in stable condition.
ARMOR GROUP MINE ACTION TEAM CONDUCTED EXPLOITATION AND DETERMINED IED TO BE VOIED CONSISTING OF- POSSIBLE 156MM MORTAR
3 Civilian Contracters

Reference ID: AFG20081022n1494
Latitude: 32.64674759
Date: 2008-10-22 15:03
Category: IED Explosion
Detained: 0

Region: RC WEST
Longitude: 62.59162521
Type: Explosive Hazard
Affiliation: ENEMY

	Enemy	Friend	Civilian	Host nation
Killed in action	0	3	0	0
Wounded in action	0	1	0	0

At 1609Z, 2/7 USMC COY reported an IED Strike:
FF were conducting a mounted security patrol when the struck an IED. FF have assessed the BDA: 3x KIA (USA, OEF), 1x WIA (USA, OEF, CAT A). NFI att.
ISAF # 10-1121

Reference ID: AFG20081227n1598 Region: RC EAST
Latitude: 33.84874725 Longitude: 69.62787628
Date: 2008-12-27 09:09 Type: Explosive Hazard
Category: IED Explosion Affiliation: ENEMY
Detained: 0

	Enemy	Friend	Civilian	Host nation
Killed in action	0	0	0	0
Wounded in action	0	0	0	0

ISAF # 12-1136
UNIT: TF PANTHER (COP HERRERA)
TYPE: IED STRIKE
TIMELINE: 0704Z A 201 ENGINEERS REPORTED THAT THE REAR VEHICLE IN THE CONVOY STRUCK AN IED ON RTE KEYSTONE AT GRID 42SWC 58086 45563
UPDATE: 0920Z ALL PAX THAT WERE IN THE REAR VEHICLE ARE BEING CHECKED BY A MEDIC AS A PRECAUTION
SUMMARY:
THIS REPORT IS A LATE POST DUE TO A / 201 ENGINEERS WAITING UNTIL THEY ARRIVED TO COP HERRERA BEFORE NOTIFING THAT THEY HAD HIT AN IED
BDA: NO CAS
NO DAM
ASSESSMENT OF EVENTS:
PLAN OF ACTION:
AIR ASSETS:
EXPENDITURE REPORT:
EVENT: CLOSED 0930Z

Reference ID: AFG20090106n1730 Region: RC SOUTH
Latitude: 31.69642258 Longitude: 64.72134399
Date: 2009-01-06 08:08 Type: Explosive Hazard
Category: IED Explosion Affiliation: ENEMY
Detained: 0

	Enemy	Friend	Civilian	Host nation
Killed in action	0	0	4	0
Wounded in action	0	0	0	0

At 0853Z, RC South reported an unknown explosion. While conducting a convoy from LKG to CSC, FF observed a LN vehicle suffer an unknown explosion. The explosion occurred behind the convoy. BDA: 4x LN KIA. 1x LN vehicle destroyed. Convoy continued on task. NFI att.
At 1002Z, RC South reported. At 0957Z, Due to lack of available EOD assets, TFH has no intention of exploiting the scene. NFTR. Event closed at 0957Z.
ISAF # 01-208

Reference ID: AFG20090202n1596
Latitude: 32.61549377
Date: 2009-02-02 05:05
Category: IED Explosion
Detained: 0

Region: RC SOUTH
Longitude: 65.89388275
Type: Explosive Hazard
Affiliation: ENEMY

	Enemy	Friend	Civilian	Host nation
Killed in action	1	0	1	21
Wounded in action	0	0	6	8

At 0715Z, RC South reported a PBIED Strike. FF reported they were struck by a PBIED. BDA: 15x ANP KIA, 1x LN killed, 2x ANP (no CAT reported) WIA, and 6x LN wounded. NFI att.
At 0827Z, RC South reported:
UPDATE BDA: 19x ANP KIA (2x Officers, 17x Soldiers unconfirmed), 9x ANP WIA (including Deputy Commander of Provincial CID, No CATs reported-unconfirmed). No reports of damages. NFI att.
At 1703Z, RC South reported:
Updated BDA: 21x ANP KIA, 8x ANP WIA.
At 1038Z on 03FEB09, RC South reported:
NFTR. Event closed at 1038Z on 03FEB09.
ISAF # 02-054

Reference ID: AFG20090208n1707
Latitude: 31.62860489
Date: 2009-02-08 08:08
Category: IED Explosion
Detained: 0

Region: RC SOUTH
Longitude: 64.26943207
Type: Explosive Hazard
Affiliation: ENEMY

	Enemy	Friend	Civilian	Host nation
Killed in action	0	2	1	1
Wounded in action	0	0	1	1

At 0818Z, RC South reported an IED Strike. While conducting a framework patrol with support from US PMT, FF reported they struck an IED. BDA: 2X US MIL KIA, 1x ANP KIA, 1x ISAF TERP WIA (CAT UNK), 1x ANP WIA (CAT UNK). FF exploited the site and suspected the IED to be a VOIED (pressure plate). FF removed the pressure plate and power source but the device functioned detonated. Initial reports suggested that the device was a remote controlled. No reports of damage. NFI att.
At 1009Z, RC South reported:
UPDATED GRID: 41R PQ 17873 01239. NFI att.
At 1103Z, RC South reported:
UPDATE BDA: 2x US PMT KIA, 1x ANCOP KIA, 1x TERP killed, and 1x ANCOP (CAT B) WIA, MEDEVACd to BSN R2E. No reports of any damages. IEDD TM have no intentions to exploit the site. The cordon has been collapsed and FF RTB. NFI att.
At 1307Z, RC South reported:
NFTR. Event closed at 1255Z.
ISAF # 02-0285

Reference ID: AFG20090211n1613　　　Region: RC CAPITAL
Latitude: 34.56396484　　　　　　　　Longitude: 69.14607239
Date: 2009-02-11 02:02　　　　　　　　Type: Explosive Hazard
Category: IED Explosion　　　　　　　Affiliation: ENEMY
Detained: 0

	Enemy	Friend	Civilian	Host nation
Killed in action	2	0	10	0
Wounded in action	0	0	10	0

At 0906Z, RC Capital reported a PBIED Strike. FF reported a PBIED strike on a US Convoy between PD4 and PD11. BDA: 2x INS killed, 10x LN killed (unconfirmed), and 3x vehicles (Type not reported-lightly) damaged. FF reported the detonation was located near the General Director of Personnel and that the convoy continued on with their mission. NFI att.
At 0644Z on 12FEB09, RC Capital reported:
NFTR. Event closed at 0632Z on 12FEB09.
ISAF # 02-0420

Reference ID: AFG20090211n1624　　　Region: RC CAPITAL
Latitude: 34.52244568　　　　　　　　Longitude: 69.17324066
Date: 2009-02-11 05:05　　　　　　　　Type: Explosive Hazard
Category: IED Explosion　　　　　　　Affiliation: ENEMY
Detained: 0

	Enemy	Friend	Civilian	Host nation
Killed in action	10	0	10	14
Wounded in action	0	0	55	0

At 0721Z, RC Capital reported a PBIED Strike. FF reported a PBIED Strike. FF reported 3-4x PBIED near a crossroad. FF engaged and killed 1x INS. The other PBIEDS went to the MINISTRY OF JUSTICE and only 1x PBIED detonated. HQ CJ2 reported a second explosion by the KHORASAN HOTEL in KHAIR KHANA area of KABUL. At 0630Z, ARTEC reported an attack by a minimum of 2x PBIEDs in the direction of the Penitentiary Affairs at grid 42S WD 13588 24588. No reports of amount of casualties or damage. NFI att.
At 1554Z, RC Capital reported:
At 0720Z, near the penitentiary ministry 2x Suicide Bombers entered the building.1x INS detonated himself just around the corner while the other detonated near the ministry of foreign affairs. At 0530Z, near crossroad Patshoun in the Serena Hotal there was an attack consisting of SAF. Police shot INS Vehicle by on rocket. From CJ2X, the minister was attacked by 6x INS with 5x INS being killed. Unknown volume of INS have hostage in. The hostage include The Minister on Interior, Minister of Justice, Deputy Minister of Interior and UNK members of the Ministery of Defense. Hostage situation ended when CF headed in and assaulted the building. BDA: 20x UNK, And 57x wounded. NFI att.
At 1847Z, RC Capital reported:
Updated BDA: 10x Afghan Gov. Employees killed, 10x LN killed, 3x NDS KIA, 1x ANP KIA, 55x LN wounded and 10x INS killed.
At 1145Z on 13FEB09, RC Capital reported:

At 1145Z on 13FEB09, Ff reported that due to the great amount of contradictory information it has been difficult to have a clear view and timeline of the events. The chronology is assumed to be the following: Approx. 8x INS (Suicide Bombers) were operating in Kabul. At 0510Z, 2x INS detonated themselves in Jails General Office injuring 31 personnel and killing 9 others. At 0630Z, 1x INS attempted to enter into the Education Ministry but was killed by a guard. At the same time 5x INS travelled by Land Cruiser VHL near the Ministry of Justice and killed 2x Policemen at the main gate. 1x INS detonated himself within the ministry. Another INS, equipped with small arms, entered the MOJ building and took several hostages to include the Minister of Justice and the Deputy Minister of Interior. At 0755Z, an assault infiltrated the MOJ building and resolved the hostage situation.
At 0020Z on 19FEB09, RC Capital reported:
NFTR. Event closed at 0636Z on 17FEB09.
ISAF # 02-0413

Reference ID: AFG20090218n1679
Latitude: 34.52125168
Date: 2009-02-18 07:07
Category: IED Explosion
Detained: 0

Region: RC CAPITAL
Longitude: 69.04748535
Type: Explosive Hazard
Affiliation: ENEMY

	Enemy	Friend	Civilian	Host nation
Killed in action	0	0	0	0
Wounded in action	0	0	0	0

At 1603Z, RC Capital reported an SVBIED Strike:
FF reported that an US ISAF Convoy from RCE was struck by a SVBIED at 0750Z. According to US Troops at the scene the explosion was weak. It could mean that only the fuse exploded and the secondary charge is still intact. At 1600Z, CIED Team reported that upon exploitation that the detonator in the SVBIED exploded but the Det Cord and device did not. The device contained 2x Propane Cylinders, a Container of Fuel, 50kg of HME and a Safe Arm Switch.
NFI att.
At 1343Z on 20FEB09, RC Capital reported:
NFTR. Event closed at 1302Z on 20FEB09.
ISAF # 02-0747

Reference ID: AFG20090224n1580
Latitude: 31.77201271
Date: 2009-02-24 07:07
Category: IED Explosion
Detained: 0

Region: RC SOUTH
Longitude: 65.78404236
Type: Explosive Hazard
Affiliation: ENEMY

	Enemy	Friend	Civilian	Host nation
Killed in action	0	4	1	0
Wounded in action	0	0	0	0

ISAF # 02-1010
US PMT STRUCK AN IED 4 x US PMT VSA 1 x TERP VSA
0730Z US PMT IED STRIKE

GRID-41R QR 63663 18540
UPDATE:9-LINE
0803Z
4X VSA, 1 CAT UNKNOWN
UPDATE 1
US PMT CONDUCTING NORMAL FRAMEWORK PATROL IED STRIKE ON FF
UPDATE 2
3RCR BG ELEMENT ON SCENE
BDA:4 x US VSA 1 x UNK VSA
UPDATE 2 1820D
VEHICLE INVOLVED WAS A HUMVEE AND IT IS BEING RECOVERED ALL FF RTB

Reference ID: AFG20090228n1713 Region: RC SOUTH
Latitude: 32.82078171 Longitude: 65.40910339
Date: 2009-02-28 07:07 Type: Explosive Hazard
Category: IED Explosion Affiliation: ENEMY
Detained: 0

	Enemy	Friend	Civilian	Host nation
Killed in action	0	1	0	0
Wounded in action	0	3	0	0

ISAF # 02-1208
CJSOTFA Unit reported they suffered an IED strike. CAS was requested. There were no casualties or damage reported ATT.
UPDATE 2020D*
CJSOTFA were conducting a CRP IVO DIHRAWUD. The IED strike destroyed 1 x vehicle and caused casualties.
UPDATE 2100D*
Following the IED-S, INS were on the high ground, but out of SAF range. CAS dropped 5 x GBU to destroy the confirmed INS positions. Another 2 were used to destroy unsalvageable FF VEH.
FOX 25
S: UNK
A: IED STRIKE
L: 41SQS25533399
T: 0738
0738Z: FOX25 reports IED stike at GRID 41sqs25533399. Nine Line Follows
0827Z: Medevac W/U en Route TO FB Ripley ATT.
0835Z: Medevac is W/D ATT.
0952Z: FOX 25 is going to move a safe distance from down vehicle so A/C can destroy it.
1030Z: FOX 25 confirms Positive hit on vehicle will conduct SSE.
1209Z: FOX 25 reports 1st ordance did not destroy vehicle. Second ordance was successful in destroying vehicle.
1714Z: TIC CLOSED
28 FEB 2009, JOCWATCH EVENT 1208, NSI INSURGENT ATTACK (update 04) as of 282340D*FEB2009 CJSOTFA Unit reported they suffered an IED strike. CAS was requested. There were no casualties or damage reported ATT. UPDATE 2020D*

CJSOTFA were conducting a CRP IVO DIHRAWUD. The IED strike destroyed 1 x vehicle and caused casualties. UPDATE 2100D* Following the IED-S, INS were on the high ground, but out of SAF range. CAS dropped 5 x GBU to destroy the confirmed INS positions. Another 2 were used to destroy unsalvageable FF VEH. NFI ATT. ***Event closed at 2143D* This Incident closed at: 010546D*MAR2009 41SQS2553033990 Afghanistan/Oruzgan [Uruzgan]/Dihrawud 10km NW of PB JAHAN GUL Personnel: 1 KIA OEF (USA) 1 WIA Cat C OEF (USA) 2 WIA Cat D OEF (USA) Personnel Details: MM(S)02-28G to TK MM(S)02-28I to KAF R3 Equipment
Details: 1 x up armoured HUMVEE destroyed Actions: CAS IC 7 x GBU

Reference ID: AFG20090307n1748 Region: UNKNOWN
Latitude: 33.98295212 Longitude: 71.54129791
Date: 2009-03-07 07:07 Type: Explosive Hazard
Category: IED Explosion Affiliation: ENEMY
Detained: 0

	Enemy	Friend	Civilian	Host nation
Killed in action	0	0	0	0
Wounded in action	0	0	0	0

Some time in the morning of 7 MAR 09 an RCIED detonated on the south side of Peshawar, Pakistan Police were responding to an abandoned vehicle when the vehicle detonated via remote control The blast resulted in 6 x Police KIA and 2 x Civilians KIA All RC-E LNOs are accounted for. Summary: 6 x Police KIA 2 x Civilians KIA 0900Z EVENT CLOSED

Reference ID: AFG20090316n1691 Region: RC SOUTH
Latitude: 31.59802818 Longitude: 64.37346649
Date: 2009-03-16 05:05 Type: Explosive Hazard
Category: IED Explosion Affiliation: ENEMY
Detained: 0

	Enemy	Friend	Civilian	Host nation
Killed in action	1	0	3	8
Wounded in action	0	0	27	0

At 0929Z, RC South reported a PBIED Strike. FF reported that while conducting a NFO there was a large Suicide IED explosion. Multiple ANP casualties. ANP on scene. FF are deploying to ANP PHA. OCCP attempting to coordinate. OPS Co QRF stood to. LKG PRT Med Center prepared for MASCAS. BDA: 9X KIA ANP, 2X Killed LN, 27X Wounded LN. NFI att.
UPDATED BDA: 9X KIA ANP, 2X Killed LN, 28X Wounded LN, 1X Killed INS.
At 0930Z, FF reported an Updated BDA: 8X KIA ANP, 2X Killed LN, 27X Wounded LN, 1X Killed INS.
At 0522Z, FF reported an PBIED detonated outside of ANP HQ in LASHKAR GAH. The PBIED INS, was dropped off by a second INS in a vehicle 200m from ANP front gate. The vehicle then departed from scene. The PBIED INS (dressed in ANP uniform) approached outer cordon and was challenged by ANP sentry approximately 50m from gate.

The PIED then detonated. BDA: 8x ANP officers killed, 3x LN killed, 27x ANP and LN wounded. QRF deployed to scene to provide support. ANP investigation is in progress.
ISAF # 03-0860

Reference ID: AFG20090322n1711
Latitude: 34.01398087
Date: 2009-03-22 12:12
Category: IED Explosion
Detained: 0

Region: RC EAST
Longitude: 68.79627228
Type: Explosive Hazard
Affiliation: ENEMY

	Enemy	Friend	Civilian	Host nation
Killed in action	1	0	0	0
Wounded in action	0	4	0	0

ISAF #03-1248
1138Z RCP 13 lead vehicle just hit a CWIED
UPDATE: 1145Z RECIEVING SMALL ARMS FIRE 30M SOUTHWEST
update: 1151Z GUNNER OF 1-2 INJURED   AWAITING STATUS OF WHETHER MEDEVAC IS NEEDED OR NOT
UPDATE: 1203Z REQUEST QRF TO 42S VC 81200 63706 ONE MRAP ON SIDE   FM 52.200   PL BFT ROLE ID
TM1-5321-DOD
UPDATE: 1206Z RCP13 TAKING RPG FIRE from the east ATT at 1600 MLS and 600M away
UPDATE: 1323Z QRF on sites no longer receiving fire at this time
UPDATE: 1357Z CLEARING SUSPECTED ENEMY POSITIONS ATT
UPDATE: 1400Z 4x US MIL WIA, 1x INS KIA.
UPDATE: 1426Z RCP truck on its side still, 3C will begin clearance of qalat VC 80845 63347 where RCP took fire from
UPDATE: 1455Z wrecker is onsite in addition to RCP lowboy and crane (local national). vehicle is out of the hole and onto the road but still on its side
UPDATE: 1541Z RCP reports road crater is 15'x10'x4' deep.
UPDATE: 1609Z QRF IS TRACKING DISMOUNTS SOUTH OF THEIR POSITION. THE COLT IS TRACKING ENY DISMOUNTS WITH WEAPONS VIA AVN.
OPEN 1139Z / CLOSED 1722Z

Reference ID: AFG20090330n1626
Latitude: 31.10529709
Date: 2009-03-30 12:12
Category: IED Explosion
Detained: 0

Region: RC SOUTH
Longitude: 64.18943787
Type: Explosive Hazard
Affiliation: ENEMY

	Enemy	Friend	Civilian	Host nation
Killed in action	0	0	0	0
Wounded in action	0	0	0	0

At 1338Z, RC South reported an IED strike:
FF reported while conducting an offensive patrol, a donkey lashed to a tree was remotely detonated as the last FF passed it. FF are trying to interdict motorcyclists

seen in the area. FF intend on gathering as much evidence as possible from the scene and return to FOB Delhi. There were no casualties or damage reported. NFI att.
At 1604Z, FF reported device type unknown. There was no IEDD team that deployed due to the tactical situation. Scene not exploited. NFTR. Event closed at 1649Z.
ISAF #03-1652

Reference ID: AFG20090408n1800   Region: RC SOUTH
Latitude: 31.542202   Longitude: 65.85353088
Date: 2009-04-08 05:05   Type: Explosive Hazard
Category: IED Explosion   Affiliation: ENEMY
Detained: 0

	Enemy	Friend	Civilian	Host nation
Killed in action	0	0	3	0
Wounded in action	0	0	5	0

At 0604Z, RC South reported an IED Strike
FF reported that a Compass convoy was enroute from Camp Bastion to the Convoy Supply Center when they suffered an IED Strike. FF assessed damage to be 1x fuel tanker damaged. No casualties reported. NFI att.
At 0850Z, FF report that HWY 4 is damaged and the road will not support through traffic, cross country passage is possible around the IED strike site. KPRT took pictures and PRT SET will deal with the road. FF assess the IED was placed in a culvert and the culvert collapsed when the IED detonated.
At 0849Z, FF reported the strike was observed from JDOC units. UAV was launched to observe situation. At 1222Z, the convoy returned to CSC Kandahar. At 1305Z, FF reported the Compass vehicle was traveling behind 2x civilian Toyota Corollas when one of the Corollas struck the IED. The driver of the Compass vehicle had an accident trying to avoid the Corollas, 3x LNs in civilian Corollas died, 5x LNs wounded (including driver of Compass vehicle who also suffered wounds). All LNs were evacuated to KAF. NFTR. Event closed at 1225Z.
BDA: 3x LNs killed, 5x LNs wounded 1x fuel tanker damaged, HWY 4 damaged (bypass available).
ISAF # 04-0319
Exploitation of site was conducted negligible evidence remaining, unable to detemine type

Reference ID: AFG20090417n1825   Region: RC NORTH
Latitude: 36.74110031   Longitude: 66.95813751
Date: 2009-04-17 05:05   Type: Explosive Hazard
Category: IED Explosion   Affiliation: ENEMY
Detained: 0

	Enemy	Friend	Civilian	Host nation
Killed in action	1	1	0	0
Wounded in action	0	1	0	0

FF reported that a Norwegian convoy (2x NOR vehicles) traveling from Camp Marmal towards Balkh region struck an IED. A MEDEVAC was launched and returned with 2x NOR WIA (1x CAT A, 1x CAT D). QRF arrived on scene and cordoned area. The vehicles in the incident were 2x Toyota Land Cruisers. FF at the

scene reported the IED to be a SVBIED. Area was searched for possible secondary IED with no finds. PBA ongoing att. 1x NOR WIA casualty later DOW. Updated BDA: 1x NOR (DOW), 1x NOR WIA (CAT D), 1x INS killed. At 1020Z, recovery unit left Camp Marmal, linked up with QRF and recovered damaged vehicle. At 1225Z, all units RTB. NFI att.
Event closed at 1638Z.
ISAF #04-0743

Reference ID: AFG20090425n1677
Latitude: 31.61904144
Date: 2009-04-25 07:07
Category: IED Explosion
Detained: 0

Region: RC SOUTH
Longitude: 65.71031189
Type: Explosive Hazard
Affiliation: ENEMY

	Enemy	Friend	Civilian	Host nation
Killed in action	0	0	0	3
Wounded in action	0	0	5	6

At 0821, RC South reported an Unknown Explosion. FF reported 3x loud explosions followed by SAF at South and West entrances to the Governor Palace in Kandahar City. OCCP attempting to define. ANA QRF moved to site. Governor and his wife are secured in the OCCP building. Significant casualties reported in central courtyard.
At 0950Z FF reported that 3 x suicide bombers exploded around Governor Palace in Kandahar City. The Governor of Kandahar and his family are secured in the OCC-P building. NFI ATT.
At 1757Z, EOD conducted an investigation of the site. It is unknown if the attacks were all PBIEDs or 2x PBIEDs and 1x SVBIED. Further details will follow from EOD report. NFTR. Event closed at 2038Z.
Event reopened for updated BDA: 2X KIA ANSF, 1X KIA ANP, 3X WIA ANP, 3X WIA ANSF, AND 5X WOUNDED LNs (ALL AFGHAN, ALL CONFIRMED). NFTR. Event closed 260730ZAPR09.
ISAF # 04-1110

Reference ID: AFG20090510n1828
Latitude: 31.8293705
Date: 2009-05-10 11:11
Category: IED Explosion
Detained: 0

Region: RC SOUTH
Longitude: 64.57235718
Type: Explosive Hazard
Affiliation: ENEMY

	Enemy	Friend	Civilian	Host nation
Killed in action	2	0	6	6
Wounded in action	0	0	13	14

At 1340Z, RC South reported an PBIED strike:
FF reported that INS engaged with SAF on an ANP CP followed by a PBIED strike. ANP QRF responded to attack and were struck by a second PBIED. BDA: 16x ANP WIA (15x CAT B, 1x CAT C) and 1x ANP DOW. At the second PBIED strike, IEDD team did not deploy due to J2 reports of possible PBIED INS in AO. Scene not exploited. NFI att.

At 1737Z, FF reported total of 40 casualties. BDA: 1x ANP DOW, 5x ANP KIA, 1x ANA KIA, 6x LN killed, 13x ANP WIA (CAT B), 1x ANA WIA (CAT C), 13x LN wounded.
At 1800Z, OCCP GSK reported the event as follows: 1x INS in vehicle drove towards ANP CP 3 opening fire. ANP returned fire with SAF. 1x PBIED INS moved in and detonated himself close to CP 3 resulting in massive LN casualties. ANP SWAT unit deployed to secure area and treat LN wounded. During the move towards the hospital, another PBIED INS detonated himself between two vehicles in the column.
BDA: 1 X ANP DOW, 10 X ANP WIA (CAT B)
BDA (UPDATE 1): 1 X ANP DOW, 16 X ANP WIA (CAT B), 1 WIA (CAT C)
BDA (UPDATE 2): 1 X ANP DOW, 16 X ANP WIA (CAT B), 1 WIA (CAT C)
BDA (UPDATE 3): 6 X ANP KIA, 13 X ANP WIA (CAT B), 1 X ANA WIA (CAT C), 6 X LN KILLED, 13 X LN WOUNDED, 2 X INS KILLED
Event closed at 1804Z.
ISAF #05-0551

Reference ID: AFG20090512n1794
Latitude: 33.33999252
Date: 2009-05-12 07:07
Category: IED Explosion
Detained: 3
Region: RC EAST
Longitude: 69.91730499
Type: Explosive Hazard
Affiliation: ENEMY

	Enemy	Friend	Civilian	Host nation
Killed in action	8	0	6	0
Wounded in action	0	3	15	3

At 0830Z, RC East reported an IED Explosion:
CJSOTF reported that an attack at a girls by 4x suicide bombers at a girls school IVO PRT Khowst.
UPDATE: At 0650Z, TF Steel reported that the Governors compound in Khowst city is receiving SAF from an UNK number of INS. TF also reported an explosion with 2x vehicles on fire at 42SWB 85420 88810. No casualties reported att.
At 1124Z NPCC reported seven additional suicide bombers entered the city. 3x were killed by ANP, 1x removed his vest and ran off, 3x others entered the municipal building and are holding an unknown number of hostages. At 1345L, FF started their attack on the municipal building . CORRECTED BDA: 1x SVBIED wearing an ANSF uniform (DETONATED), 2x suicide bombers (DETONATED), 3x suicide bombers killed by ANP, 1x POSS suicide bomber removed his vest and ran away, 3x suicide bombers held up in the municipal building
At 1220Z, QRF arrived on site. Attacks appear to be over with the exception of unspecified number of INS in the municipal building. No additional reports confirming the initial attack on girls school. Girls school does not appear to have been attacked. Governor is unharmed in his compound.
At 1235Z, ANP cleared the municipal building. There appears to be no more INS in the municipal building. EOD is on scene to check for and clear the area of booby traps. Updated BDA: 4x LNs hostages rescued, 3x ANA WIA (CAT UNK), 3x ANP WIA (CAT UNK), 3x USA WIA (CAT UNK), 15x LNs wounded (CAT UNK) and 6x INS killed.

At 1720Z, RC East reported BDA update as follow: 3x US MIL WIA, 3x ANA WIA, 8x INS KIA, 3x INS Detained, 15x LNs wounded, 6x LNs killed. All WIA and wounded CAT UNK att.
ISAF # 05-0656

Reference ID: AFG20090520n1738   Region: RC CAPITAL
Latitude: 34.67224503   Longitude: 69.28100586
Date: 2009-05-20 03:03   Type: Explosive Hazard
Category: IED Explosion   Affiliation: ENEMY
Detained: 0

	Enemy	Friend	Civilian	Host nation
Killed in action	0	2	0	0
Wounded in action	0	0	0	0

At 0529Z, RC Capital reported an IED Explosion. Camp Phoenix reported that a US convoy struck an IED resulting in 1x US MIL KIA and 1x US CIV KIA. ITA IRT has been deployed to the site. NFI att. BDA: 1x US MIL KIA, 1x US CIV KIA
ISAF # 05-1162
CEXC # 09/1169
CPoF Summary of events
Event Title:D1 0339Z
Zone:null
Placename:ISAF # 05-1162
Outcome:null
MEDEVAC REFERANCE # 05-20B
LINE 1: 42SWD 25744 36733
LINE 2: CALL SIGN VICE 37 Task 30.100
LINE 3: 2B
LINE 4 NONE
LINE 5 2 L
LINE 6 N
LINE 7 C
LINE 8; 1A;1B
LINE:9 NONE
WEATHER FOR MEDEVAC * LOCATION: BAF - GRID - BAF * WINDS: VRB06KT * ENRTE MIN VIS/WX: 8000 HZ * CLOUDS: SKC * ENRTE MIN CIG: NONE * MAX TEMP: +25 (BAF) * MIN ALSTG: 3002INS (BAF) * HAZARDS: LGT TURB SFC-100 * ILLUMINATION: N/A * RMK: N/A * BRIEF TIME/INITIALS: 20/0413Z
04:22Z) CHOPS APPROVES MM(E) 05-20B BAF-GRID-BAF
04:25Z)MM(E) 05-20B DO45(020) HN57(832) REDCON1
04:29Z)EL APPROVES MM(E) 05-20B ROF BAF-GRID-BAF
0427Z) MM(E) 05-20B W/U BAF
0439Z) MM(E) 05-20B W/D GRID
0441Z) MM(E) 05-20B W/U GRID
0501Z) MM(E) 05-20B W/D BAF
INITIAL REPORT
ONE PATIENT IS REPORTED KIA THE OTHER DOUBLE AMPUTEE
MISSION COMPLETE

EVENT CLOSED 0501Z
20 MAY 09 RC-EAST SIGACTS
D1.0339Z TF Phoenix IED Strike Northern Kabul
RC-C 2x Urgent Surgical MM(E)05-20B BAF-GRID-BAF
1x US MIL KIA
1x US CIV KIA
At 0339Z, TF Phoenix reported that a CSTC-A convoy struck an improvised explosive device while on a convoy on Route Bottle at 42S WD 25744 36733, 0415Z, 13km northwest of Camp Blackhorse, Kabul. At 0415Z, TF Phoenix requested 2x Urgent MEDEVACs for 1x US MIL WIA and 1x US CIV WIA at the above grid. Both patients suffered from blast injuries associated with an IED blast. At 0446Z, TF Phoenix reported 1x US CIV DOW. The 1x US MIL sustained bi-lateral amputations of his legs. The MEDEVAC mission was completed at 0501Z. At 0520Z, TF MED (BAF) reported the 1x US MIL DOW. TF Phoenix reported the vehicle the casualties were riding in was an up-armored Land Rover SUV. This event will continue to be investigated and reported through RC Central channels.
This event closed at 0630Z.
ISAF Tracking #05-1162
End of CPoF summary

Reference ID: AFG20090603n1848
Latitude: 31.01193047
Date: 2009-06-03 11:11
Category: IED Explosion
Detained: 0
Region: RC SOUTH
Longitude: 66.39196777
Type: Explosive Hazard
Affiliation: ENEMY

	Enemy	Friend	Civilian	Host nation
Killed in action	1	0	4	0
Wounded in action	0	0	1	0

At 1136Z, RC South reported a PBIED strike:
FF reported Convoy Y from Chaman to CSC Kandahar suffered an IED strike resulting in 4x CIV (Int) killed, 1x CIV (Int) wounded and 1x escort vehicle damaged. The wounded was brought to a local hospital by Compass security guards. At 1445Z, FF reported the IED was a PBIED INS, who jumped in front of the fourth vehicle and detonated himself. Event closed at 1526Z.
ISAF #06-0194

Reference ID: AFG20090606n1983
Latitude: 32.40360641
Date: 2009-06-06 06:06
Category: IED Explosion
Detained: 0
Region: RC SOUTH
Longitude: 64.47737885
Type: Explosive Hazard
Affiliation: ENEMY

	Enemy	Friend	Civilian	Host nation
Killed in action	0	1	0	0
Wounded in action	0	2	0	0

At 0630Z, RC South reported an IED Explosion. 2/3 USMC reported that while conducting a NFO patrol, FF suffered an IED (VOIED (PP)) strike followed by SAF and IDF resulting in 1x US MIL KIA and 2x US MIL WIA. FF engaged INS with

organic weapons IOT break contact. Casualties were MEDEVAC to R3 (UK) BSN. NFTR. Event closed.
BDA: 1x US MIL KIA, 1x US MIL WIA (CAT A), 1x US MIL (CAT B)
ISAF # 06-0388

Reference ID: AFG20090611n1856
Latitude: 31.50559807
Date: 2009-06-11 04:04
Category: IED Explosion
Detained: 0

Region: RC SOUTH
Longitude: 65.32292938
Type: Explosive Hazard
Affiliation: ENEMY

	Enemy	Friend	Civilian	Host nation
Killed in action	1	1	0	0
Wounded in action	0	1	0	0

A Coy 3 Scots BG reported that while conducting an offensive patrol ISO Op TORA ARWA 1, 2 x INS engaged with 1 x burst of SAF. FF are observing.
UPDATE 1007D*
INS engaged with sporadic fire from FP at GR 41R QQ 2094 8850. FF retuned fire and snipers killed 1 x INS.
UPDATE 1041D*
At 1005D* FF suffered an IED strike, resulting in 1 x GBR KIA and 1 x GBR WIA (CAT C) MEDEVACED IAW MM(S) 06-11C to KAF R3 MMU.
UPDATE 1620D*
Nothing further to report. BDA: 1 x INS killed, 1 x GBR KIA, 1 x GBR WIA (CAT C).
***Event closed at 1626D*1 Killed not otherwise specified(NOS) Insurgent
1 Killed in Action british (citizen)(GBR) NATO/ISAF
1 Wounded in Action, Category C british (citizen)(GBR) NATO/ISAF

Reference ID: AFG20090618n1879
Latitude: 31.61743927
Date: 2009-06-18 06:06
Category: IED Explosion
Detained: 0

Region: RC SOUTH
Longitude: 65.70078278
Type: Explosive Hazard
Affiliation: ENEMY

	Enemy	Friend	Civilian	Host nation
Killed in action	0	0	2	0
Wounded in action	0	0	2	0

At 0800, RC South reported an IED Explosion. TFK reported that while providing FP to ANP HQ, ANP suffered an IED explosion resulting in 2x LN killed and 2x LN wounded. The IED possibly consisted of a cooking pot mounted on the back of a bicycle. ANP is on site. NFI att. BDA: 2x LN killed, 2x LN wounded
ANP investigated the explosion. IED was confirmed to be a VBIED (cooking pot tied to a bicycle). Event closed at 1540Z.
ISAF # 06-1334

Reference ID: AFG20090620n1866
Latitude: 31.59568405
Date: 2009-06-20 10:10

Region: RC SOUTH
Longitude: 65.48011017
Type: Explosive Hazard

Category: IED Explosion   Affiliation: ENEMY
Detained: 0

	Enemy	Friend	Civilian	Host nation
Killed in action	0	1	0	0
Wounded in action	0	3	0	0

2R22R BG reported that an UNK convoy suffered an IED strike resulting in 1x LN killed and 2x LN wounded. NFI att. At 1118Z, FF reported casualties taken to Mirwais hospital. FF believe they are PSC (private security convoy). At 1146Z, QRF deployed to site to assess damage and to temporarily repair the road. EOD exploited IED remnants. NFTR. Event closed at 1328Z.
(See attached IED Exploitation Report) states that personnel involved in incident were USPS (American private security)
ISAF # 06-1533

Reference ID: AFG20090706n2076   Region: RC NORTH
Latitude: 36.64458084   Longitude: 69.09545135
Date: 2009-07-06 06:06   Type: Explosive Hazard
Category: IED Explosion   Affiliation: ENEMY
Detained: 0

	Enemy	Friend	Civilian	Host nation
Killed in action	0	4	0	0
Wounded in action	0	0	0	0

PRT KDZ TOC reported that US police mentoring team CENTRAL in a M1151 HMMWV suffered an IED strike resulting in 4x US MIL KIA. At 0939Z, IRF started with a VP-Check IVO, it took 30 minutes after they started recovery of destroyed HMMWV, it took 60 more minutes, road was still not passable so that US Convoy was separated, IRF integrated two of them for marching back to PRT KDZ. US Forces tried to fix road with a backhoe to reintegrate all separated HMMWVs. At 1401Z, all forces at PRT KDZ. Investigation started. NFI att.
ISAF # 07-0522

Reference ID: AFG20090708n2032   Region: RC SOUTH
Latitude: 31.30099487   Longitude: 64.22779083
Date: 2009-07-08 14:02   Type: Explosive Hazard
Category: IED Explosion   Affiliation: ENEMY
Detained: 0

	Enemy	Friend	Civilian	Host nation
Killed in action	0	2	0	0
Wounded in action	0	3	0	0

RC South reported an IED strike:
: FF reported that while conducting a NFO patrol they struck an IED resulting in 2x US KIA and 2x US WIA (CAT A). Casualties were MEDEVACd to FOB Dwyer. FF cordoned area. NFI att.
At 2015Z, vehicle and remaining convoy vehicles and unit RTB. UPDATED BDA: 2x US MIL KIA, 2x US MIL WIA (CAT A), 1x US MIL WIA(CAT B). NFTR. Event closed.
Update: EOD assessed as VOIED. See attached EOD report. ISAF # 06-0738

Reference ID: AFG20090713n1884
Latitude: 31.74694252
Date: 2009-07-13 03:03
Category: IED Explosion
Detained: 0

Region: RC SOUTH
Longitude: 64.76642609
Type: Explosive Hazard
Affiliation: ENEMY

	Enemy	Friend	Civilian	Host nation
Killed in action	0	0	4	0
Wounded in action	0	0	0	0

FF reported that while convoy enroute from BSN to CSC with 52x Vehicles they suffered an IED Strike. BDA: 4x Killed LN (CIVSEC), and 1x Vehicle destroyed. COMPASS security guards secured site and are assessing. At 0453Z, COMPASS security guards report finding 1x possible IED in culvert. 1 lane of HWY-1 destroyed by the IED Strike.
NFTR. Event closed.
ISAF# 07-1138
CIDNE#20090713033641RPR6731713744

Reference ID: AFG20090714n2099
Latitude: 31.62893105
Date: 2009-07-14 22:10
Category: IED Explosion
Detained: 0

Region: RC SOUTH
Longitude: 65.71165466
Type: Explosive Hazard
Affiliation: ENEMY

	Enemy	Friend	Civilian	Host nation
Killed in action	0	0	0	1
Wounded in action	0	0	0	0

FF reported that a Bicycle-IED exploded South of PSS 13 in Kandahar City. BDA: 1x KIA ANP. ANP cordoned area, and conducting search for possible suspects. No damage reported. NFTR. Event closed at 0042Z.

Reference ID: AFG20090720n1972
Latitude: 34.47209549
Date: 2009-07-20 10:10
Category: IED Explosion
Detained: 0

Region: RC EAST
Longitude: 68.78050232
Type: Explosive Hazard
Affiliation: ENEMY

	Enemy	Friend	Civilian	Host nation
Killed in action	0	4	0	0
Wounded in action	0	0	0	0

At 1013Z, TM Wardak reported that 3rd HHB struck an IED while on a mounted patrol at 42S VD 79843 14525, 3km northeast of COP Garda, Maydan Shahr District, Wardak. CF reported after striking the IED, they received SAF and RPG fire from 5-7 INS. CF reported the vehicle that struck the IED, an M1151, was completely destroyed. CF reported the vehicle had 4x US MIL occupants. At 1028Z, CF requested 4x Urgent MEDEVAC for the 4x US MIL in the destroyed vehicle. CF reported due to the condition of the vehicle, they were having difficulty reaching the occupants to determine their status. At 1058Z, CF confirmed 3x US MIL KIA. They were still searching for the 4th US MIL who was in the vehicle. At 1117Z, HAWG-61 (2x A-10s) arrived on station. At 1134Z, CF reported the 3x HEROs were transported on the (M) mission MEDEVAC. At 1143Z, CF reported they located the 4th US MIL who was KIA. At 1400Z, Blackjack was on site securing the area until OED arrives. Gladiator 16 attempted to recover the vehicle. At 1437Z, Archangel 23 departed COP Garda with EOD to the site. At 2244Z, the vehicle was recovered and all elements RTB. The (M) MEDEVAC mission was completed at 1212Z. This event closed at 2300Z.

Reference ID: AFG20090722n1965
Latitude: 32.1678009
Date: 2009-07-22 04:04
Category: IED Explosion
Detained: 0
Region: RC SOUTH
Longitude: 67.00176239
Type: Explosive Hazard
Affiliation: ENEMY

	Enemy	Friend	Civilian	Host nation
Killed in action	0	2	0	0
Wounded in action	0	2	0	0

4th ENG BN reported that while conducting a patrol, FF suffered an IED strike resulting in 2x US MIL KIA and 2x US MIL WIA (CAT A). Casualties were MEDEVAC to Qalat FST. EOD are en route to site. NFI att.
At 0947Z, EOD reported that it was a CWIED attached to a camera flash for extra power and a 500lbs HME. FP was 150 meters NW of strike. NFTR. Event closed.

Reference ID: AFG20090722n1965
Latitude: 32.1678009
Date: 2009-07-22 04:04
Category: IED Explosion
Detained: 0
Region: RC SOUTH
Longitude: 67.00176239
Type: Explosive Hazard
Affiliation: ENEMY

	Enemy	Friend	Civilian	Host nation
Killed in action	0	2	0	0
Wounded in action	0	2	0	0

4th ENG BN reported that while conducting a patrol, FF suffered an IED strike resulting in 2x US MIL KIA and 2x US MIL WIA (CAT A). Casualties were MEDEVAC to Qalat FST. EOD are en route to site. NFI att.
At 0947Z, EOD reported that it was a CWIED attached to a camera flash for extra power and a 500lbs HME. FP was 150 meters NW of strike. NFTR. Event closed.

Reference ID: AFG20090726n1817
Latitude: 31.79203606
Date: 2009-07-26 01:01
Category: IED Explosion
Detained: 0
Region: RC SOUTH
Longitude: 64.58255005
Type: Explosive Hazard
Affiliation: ENEMY

	Enemy	Friend	Civilian	Host nation
Killed in action	0	0	0	0
Wounded in action	0	0	4	2

COMPASS Convoy #8 was travelling from BSN to GSK with 26 vehicles. FF reported that the convoy suffered an IED strike that resulted in 2 x ANP WIA. Convoy halted. GSK OCC-D is investigating the site.

UPDATE:
0516Z - Contact ceased at 0210Z. Confirmed 4 x WIA CIV (CAT UNK).
BDA: 2 x ANP WIA (1 x CAT A, 1 x CAT C), 4 x WIA CIV (CAT UNK). No damage reported.
Event Closed At 0526Z

Reference ID: AFG20090727n1969
Latitude: 32.29277039
Date: 2009-07-27 04:04
Category: IED Explosion
Detained: 0

Region: RC SOUTH
Longitude: 65.08680725
Type: Explosive Hazard
Affiliation: ENEMY

	Enemy	Friend	Civilian	Host nation
Killed in action	0	1	0	0
Wounded in action	0	0	0	0

FF reported that while conducting NFO patrol, they struck an IED that resulted in 1 x KIA. Following the explosion, INS engaged with RPG fire (FP: 41SPR 963 771). CAS (A-10) is on station trying to locate INS. Angel Flight has been released to evacuate the casualty.
UPDATE:
0546Z - UNK x INS engaged NPVCP(?) with 3-4 bursts of automatic fire. FP in UNK. FF are returning to FOB.
BDA: 1 x ISAF KIA (GBR), no damage reported.
EVENT CLOSED AT 0851Z

Reference ID: AFG20090728n2078
Latitude: 31.82108498
Date: 2009-07-28 04:04
Category: IED Explosion
Detained: 0

Region: RC SOUTH
Longitude: 64.56909943
Type: Explosive Hazard
Affiliation: ENEMY

	Enemy	Friend	Civilian	Host nation
Killed in action	0	0	8	0
Wounded in action	0	0	4	0

ISAF HQ Reported that while on an operation, a CIV Security Group vehicle struck an IED in the Yahchal area of the Gerishk district in Helmand province.
ATT there is no information available on the mission, affiliation, or nationality of the Security Company or it's employees.
BDA: 8 x CIV KIA (NAT UNK), 4 x CIV WIA (NAT UNK, CAT UNK), 2 x Toyota Surf vehicles destroyed.
***Event closed at 0730Z*

Reference ID: AFG20090731n1157
Latitude: 32.62004852
Date: 2009-07-31 05:05
Category: IED Explosion
Detained: 0

Region: RC WEST
Longitude: 62.52355957
Type: Explosive Hazard
Affiliation: ENEMY

	Enemy	Friend	Civilian	Host nation
Killed in action	0	0	0	4
Wounded in action	0	0	0	5

FF reported that an ANA convoy suffered an IED strike resulting in 5 x KIA, 5 x WIA. Casualties MEDEVAC to Farah IAW MM(S) 07-31E
BDA: 5 x ANA KIA, 5 x ANA WIA (2 x CAT A, 1 x CAT B, 2 x CAT C), no damage reported.
Updated BDA: 4x ANA KIA, 6x ANA WIA (2x CAT A, 2x CAT B, 2x CAT C). Event closed at 1313Z.

Reference ID: AFG20090801n1997
Latitude: 31.47167778
Date: 2009-08-01 07:07
Category: IED Explosion
Detained: 0

Region: RC SOUTH
Longitude: 65.26042938
Type: Explosive Hazard
Affiliation: ENEMY

	Enemy	Friend	Civilian	Host nation
Killed in action	0	3	0	0
Wounded in action	0	9	0	0

FF reported that while conducting NFO patrol, they suffered 2 x IED strikes resulting in 3 x WIA, and 1 x KIA. The 1st IED strike was at 0610Z 41RQQ 1475 8409, the 2nd IED strike was at 0703Z 41RQQ 145 840. Casualties MEDEVAC IAW MM(S) 08-01J to KAF R3 MMU.
UPDATE:
0915Z - CAS on station ISO ground troops observed 2 x INS at a suspected mortar site. SH-60 engaged INS. INS returned fire with RPG.
BDA: 3 x US MIL WIA (CAT A), and 1 x US MIL KIA, no damage reported.
At 1018Z, FF reported an updated BDA of 3x US KIA, 9x US WIA (CAT A). Casualties were MEDEVAC'D to KAF.
NFI att.
***Event closed at 2030Z*

Reference ID: AFG20090805n2133
Latitude: 32.20066833
Date: 2009-08-05 16:04
Category: IED Explosion
Detained: 0

Region: RC SOUTH
Longitude: 63.10893631
Type: Explosive Hazard
Affiliation: ENEMY

	Enemy	Friend	Civilian	Host nation
Killed in action	0	1	0	0
Wounded in action	0	2	0	0

WHEN: 05 2112D AUGUST 09
WHO: FOX 2/3
WHERE: 41S NR 10267 62684 (STRIKE)
    41S NR 10226 62084 (PIED)
1.5 MI WEST OF COP BARROWS
200 METERS SOUTH OF RTE 515
WHAT: IED STRIKE

EVENT: WHILE RETURING TO COP BARROWS AFTER RECOVERING JAEGER 4, THE 4TH VEH (M1114) OF THE MOVEMENT STRUCK AN IED RESULTING IN A INITIAL REPORT OF (3) URGENT CASUALTIES. A MEDEVAC WAS REQUESTED. UNIT REPORTED THAT THE HUMVEE THAT STRUCK THE IED WAS FLIPPED UPSIDE DOWN AND (1) MARINE WAS TRAPPED WHILE THE VEH WAS ON FIRE AND LEAKING FUEL. NO MINE ROLLER WAS ON THE VEH. ECM WERE OPERATIONAL ON SOME VEH AND DEGRATED ON OTHERS.
THE MARINE WHO WAS TRAPPED WAS LATER REPORTED AS (1) ROUTINE ANGEL. PEDRO 35 WAS LAUNCHED IN RESPONSE TO MEDEVAC THE CASUALTIES TO BSN ROLE III, AND PEDRO 36 WENT WHEELS DOWN AT THE SITE AND RECOVERED THE FALLEN ANGEL AT 2224D.
A WRECKER WITH CBT DFL FROM GOLESTAN AT 0100, AND IS CURRENLTY EN RTE TO DELARAM TO LNK UP WITH A QRF.
AT 2238D FOX REPORTED A POSSIBLE SECONDARY IED NEAR THE STRIKE SITE.
UPDATE: AT 0125D THE FALLEN ANGEL ARRIVED IN KAF. BOTH WIA ARE AT BSN IN STABLE CONDITION.
BDA:
2x US WIA (CAT A), 1 x USA DOW,
{1 x INS KIA, 1 x INS WIA(fled area) contained in associated report}
ISAF REF # 08-0419 (CLOSED)
MEDEVAC # 08-05Y (COMPLETE)

Reference ID: AFG20090806n2193 Region: RC WEST
Latitude: 32.25416565 Longitude: 62.94042206
Date: 2009-08-06 10:10 Type: Explosive Hazard
Category: IED Explosion Affiliation: ENEMY
Detained: 0

	Enemy	Friend	Civilian	Host nation
Killed in action	0	4	0	0
Wounded in action	0	1	0	0

WHEN: 06 1433D AUG 09
WHO: 2ND SQD, 1ST PLT
WHERE: 41S MR 94388 68610 2KM N OF FOB BAKWA
WHAT: IED STRIKE / URGENT MEDEVAC
EVENT: WHILE CONDUCTING A MOUNTED SECURITY PATROL BACK TO BAKWA. THE LEAD VEHICLE (M1114) IN A FOUR VEHICLE PATROL, STRUCK AN IED THAT WAS LOCATED ON THE SOUTH SIDE OF AN UNNAMED ROAD. ECMS WERE OPERATIONAL AND NO MINE ROLLER WAS USED. THE VEHICLE CAUGHT FIRE IMMEDIATELY AND MARINES WERE TRAPPED INSIDE. URGENT MEDEVAC FOR (4) CASUALTIES WAS REQUESTED. AS THE SITUATION DEVELOPED, IT WAS REPORTED THAT THERE WAS ACTUALLY (1) URGENT MEDEVAC AND (4) MARINES REMAINED TRAPPED IN THE VEHICLE . THE ANGELS REMAINS WILL BE TAKEN TO FOB BAKWA AND WRECKER IS EN ROUTE. THE (1) URGENT WAS TAKEN TO FARAH FOR FURTHER TREATMENT.
UPDATE: THE ANGELS REMAINS WERE TRANSPORTED TO KAF. THE WIA WAS TRANSFERRED TO FRH FOR FUTHER TREATMENT AT 1540D.

THE VEH WAS RECOVERED AND TRANSPORTED TO BAKWA.
BDA: (1) USMC WIA, (4) USMC KIA (1) M1114 DESTROYED
ISAF REF # 08-0536 (CLOSED)

Reference ID: AFG20090815n2018   Region: RC CAPITAL
Latitude: 34.53126144   Longitude: 69.18836212
Date: 2009-08-15 04:04   Type: Explosive Hazard
Category: IED Explosion   Affiliation: ENEMY
Detained: 0

	Enemy	Friend	Civilian	Host nation
Killed in action	0	0	5	0
Wounded in action	0	10	2	7

ISAF HQ CJOC reported that a SVBIED exploded 20 meters sounth of ISAF HQ maingate. FRA BG QRF and ITA BG IIERT deployed to the site. According to US Emabassy the vehicle was an up-armored Toyota Land Cruiser. License plate number: 44787.
BDA: 5x LN killed, 2x LN wounded, 9x ISAF WIA, 7x ANA WIA, 1x FRA CIV wounded.
10x vehicles including 2 x ISAF vehicles damaged in explosion
EVENT OPEN
CEXC # 09/CEXC-A/2713
WISREP FLR # WIS/RC(C)09/049

Reference ID: AFG20090815n2108   Region: RC WEST
Latitude: 34.24258804   Longitude: 62.26292419
Date: 2009-08-15 21:09   Type: Explosive Hazard
Category: IED Explosion   Affiliation: ENEMY
Detained: 0

	Enemy	Friend	Civilian	Host nation
Killed in action	0	1	0	1
Wounded in action	0	4	0	0

At 2328Z, FF reported that on completion of a cordon and search while on OP Mountain Rush, one of the FF vehicles struck an IED which was followed by heavy SAF and RPG from INS resulting in 1x US KIA, 4x US WIA (3x CAT A, 1x CAT UNK) and 1x LN TERP killed. FF returned suppressive fire and rendered first aid to the casualties who were then ground evacuated to the Spanish hosptial on Camp Arena. The body of the LN TERP was unrecoverable due to the vehicle fire and the heavy contact. All sensitive materials were removed from the vehicle or destroyed. FF will attempt to recover the vehicle at a later date. The vehicle was too close in proximity of compounds to destroy via CAS. CAS on station fired 14 x 40mm as containment fire. No collateral damage or CIVCAS due to CAS fire. All of the casualties currently at the Spanish hospital at Camp Arena in Herat Airfield. Event closed at 0042Z, 16 Aug 09.
Summary from duplicate report
MSOT 8211 AND MSOC 8210 DEPARTED CAMP MILAM AT 2000Z FROM THE FRONT GATE OF CAMP ZAFAR AND PROCEEDED NORTH ALONG HWY 1. AFTER THE PATROL ARRIVED AT NAI 5 AROUND 2100Z, VEHICLE 2 PUSHED

NORTH TO 41S MT 32923 89420 WHILE THE REST OF THE MAIN EFFORT MOVED TO 41S MT 33484 88727 AND DISMOUNTED THEIR VEHICLES TO BEGIN ACTIONS ON. MSOC 8210 SET IN A BLOCKING POSITION AT 41S MT 32895 89163. AS THE DISMOUNTED ASSAULT FORCE MOVED NORTH TO CLEAR TAI 3, THE AC-130 OVERHEAD SPOTTED A GROUP OF 5 INDIVIDUALS MOVING TOWARDS THEIR POSITION ON FOOT. AROUND THIS TIME, THE DISMOUNTED ASSAULT FORCE TOOK SMALL ARMS FIRE FROM THE 5 INDIVIDUALS AND A TIC WAS DECLARED BY MSOC 8210. THE DISMOUNTED ASSAULT FORCE CONTINUED MISSION AND PROCEEDED TO TAI 5 WHERE IT CONTINUED THE CORDON AND SEARCH.

DURING THIS TIME, THE AC-130 CONTINUED TO OBSERVE SMALL GROUPS PROBING THE AREA. THE DISMOUNTED ASSAULT FORCE CONTINUED TO CLEAR TAI 5 AND CONDUCT SSE/KLE. THEY FOUND A SMALL AMOUNT OF EXPLOSIVES. AFTER SSE AND KLE WERE COMPLETE, THE ASSAULT FORCE MOVED TO MSOC 8210'S POSITION AT THE FOUR WAY INTERSECTION TO MOUNT BACK UP INTO THEIR VEHICLES. DURING THIS TIME, THE AC-130 CONTINUED TO OBSERVE SMALL GROUPS OF INDIVIDUALS PROBE THE AREA. VEHICLE 1 POSITIVELY IDENTIFIED AN ARMED INSURGENT AND ENGAGED WITH A BURST OF .50 CALIBER FROM ITS REMOTE WEAPON SYSTEM. ONCE THE PATROL HAD ACCOUNTABILITY OF ALL PERSONNEL AND WEAPONS, IT MOUNTED BACK UP INTO ITS VEHICLES AND BEGAN TO EXFIL ALONG ROUTE JADE. AT APPROXIMATELY 2315Z, THE SIXTH VEHICLE IN THE PATROL, A GMV, SUSTAINED A CATASTROPHIC IED STRIKE THAT IMMEDIATELY KILLED THE DRIVER AND A TERP AND SERIOUSLY WOUNDED THE REMAINING 4 PASSENGERS. AT THIS TIME, THE PATROL BEGAN TAKING HEAVY SMALL ARMS AND RPG FIRE FROM BOTH SIDES OF THE ROAD. AS THE FIREFIGHT ENSUED, MEMBERS OF THE PATROL BEGAN TO RECOVER THE CASUALTIES FROM THE DESTROYED VEHICLE.

ONCE THE CASUALTIES WERE LOADED UP, TWO VEHICLES DEPARTED THE SCENE WITH THE MEDEVAC TO CAMP ARENA. THE REMAINDER OF THE PATROL CONTINUED THE FIGHT WHILE TRYING TO RECOVER ANYTHING THEY COULD FROM THE BURNING VEHICLE. THE ENTIRE TIME THE FIREFIGHT WAS RAGING, THE AC-130 CONTINUED TO IDENTIFY ENEMY REINFORCEMENTS WHO WERE MASSING ON THE AREA.

THE AC-130 ENGAGED ENEMY IN OPEN AREAS WITH 40MM FIRE. ONCE THE PATROL RECOVERED THE FEW ITEMS THAT WERE NOT COMPLETELY DESTROYED, IT CONTINUED TO EXFIL THE OBJECTIVE AREA.

DURING THE EXFIL, THE PATROL CONTINUED TO TAKE SMALL ARMS AND RPG FIRE FOR APPROXIMATELY 3KM AS IT FOUGHT ITS WAY BACK TO HWY 1. AT HWY 1, THE PATROL TURNED SOUTH AND RTB BACK TO CAMP MILAM AND WENT GAME OVER.

MSOT 8212

WHEN THE MSOT LEFT CAMP MILAM AT 1730Z, A COMMANDO VEHICLE SWERVED TO AVOID A CIVILIAN TRUCK AND CUT OFF AN RG-33. THE RG AND THE COMMANDO VEHICLE WENT OFF THE ROAD AND THE RG-33 TIPPED OVER DUE TO THE STEEP EMBANKMENT ON THE SIDE OF THE ROAD. THE SOTF-73 QRF BROUGHT OUT A WRECKER TO RECOVER THE RG AND PROVIDED ANOTHER RG. AFTER CROSSLOADING EQUIPMENT INTO THE NEW RG, MSOT 8212 DEPARTED AGAIN AT 2115Z. MSOT 8212 MOVED NORTH

FROM CAMP MILAM AND MOVED THROUGH THE DESERT, SOUTH OF ARENA FSB, TOWARD THE TEAM'S NAIS. WHEN 8212 REACHED THE DISMOUNT POINT FOR THE TEAM'S FIRST OBJECTIVE, 8210 NOTIFIED THE TEAM LEADER THAT A VEHICLE FROM THE 8211/8210/ANP CONVOY HAD BEEN STRUCK BY AN IED.
8212 IMMEDIATELY RELOADED VEHICLES AND MOVED WEST THROUGH THE DESERT TO HIGHWAY 1. AFTER STAGING AT CAMP ARENA TO SUPPORT THE WITHDRAWAL OF 8211 AND 8210 8212 LINKED UP 8211 AND 8210 ENROUTE BACK TO CAMP MILAM.
Summary from duplicate report

Reference ID: AFG20090818n2120
Latitude: 34.54396057
Date: 2009-08-18 08:08
Category: IED Explosion
Detained: 0

Region: RC CAPITAL
Longitude: 69.24958038
Type: Explosive Hazard
Affiliation: ENEMY

	Enemy	Friend	Civilian	Host nation
Killed in action	1	1	11	0
Wounded in action	0	2	52	0

TF PHOENIX reported that a possible SVBIED exploded between a UN vehicle and a GBR convoy on Route Bottle. ITA BG, RC C MP and FRA QRF deployed to the site to investigate. RC-C Provost Marshal reports the BDA: 1x GBR ISAF KIA, 4x LN killed and multiple LN wounded. NFI att.
UPDATE: BDA: 1x US KIA, 2x UNAMA KIA (AFG),9x LN killed, 2x GBR WIA, 1x UNAMA wounded, 51x LN wounded

Reference ID: AFG20090821n1998
Latitude: 34.95846939
Date: 2009-08-21 01:01
Category: IED Explosion
Detained: 0

Region: RC EAST
Longitude: 70.81329346
Type: Explosive Hazard
Affiliation: ENEMY

	Enemy	Friend	Civilian	Host nation
Killed in action	0	1	0	0
Wounded in action	0	3	0	0

TF LETHAL WARRIOR reported that while conducting a patrol, RCP 8 struck an IED resulting in 4x US MIL WIA and causing a vehicle (MRAP) to roll over on its side. A second vehicle (EOD) rolled into a river. Casualty # 1 has lower body extremities wounds. Casualty # 2 has lower body injuries. Casualty # 3 has broken left arm, right index finger missing, lower back pain, broken right ankle, and Casualty # 4 head injury, possible broken arm. CF also reported receiving SAF and RPG. NFI att.
UPDATE: 0518Z: 1x US WIA has DOW. BDA: 1x US MIL KIA, 3x US MIL WIA, 1x MRAP destroyed, 1x MRAP damaged.
EOD ANALYSIS: RCP8 was conducting a route clearance in the Konar District when an IED detonated on the second vehicle. RCP personnel began treating casualties immediately. EOD conducted a post blast analysis and found a battery pack consisting of 6x D cell batteries and 1x 9 volt battery buried near the hole. A sewing machine pedal was also found. The main charge was estimated at 75-100lbs of UBE

and it was placed between a deep wash out on the South side of the road and the mountain on the North side of the road. The IED breached the RG-31 hull and flipped the vehicle resulting in 1x US KIA and 3x US WIA.

Reference ID: AFG20090831n1320
Latitude: 30.99594498
Date: 2009-08-31 12:12
Category: IED Explosion
Detained: 0

Region: RC SOUTH
Longitude: 64.17017365
Type: Explosive Hazard
Affiliation: ENEMY

	Enemy	Friend	Civilian	Host nation
Killed in action	0	1	0	0
Wounded in action	0	2	0	0

WHEN: 31 1641D AUG 09
WHO: 3RD SQD, 1ST PLT
WHERE: 41R PQ 1172 2974, 630M NE OF PB BURROWS
WHAT: IED STRIKE
EVENT: WHILE CONDUCTING A DISMOUNTED LOCAL SECURITY PATROL, G/2/8 RECEIVED SAF AND DECLARED TIC. AS THE UNIT WAS RETROGRATING (1) SQD STRUCK AN PPIED, RESULTING IN (2) WIA AND (1) ANGEL. G/2/8 REQUESTED AN URGENT MEDEVAC. WHILE THE MEDEVAC WAS DEPARTING THE LZ, G/2/8 RECEIVED SAF FROM 4 INDIVIDUALS POSITIONED TO THE NORTH. THE EN BROKE CONTACT AND EGRESSED NORTH. THE CASUALTIES WERE TAKEN TO BSN. (1) URGENT CAS SUFFERED A MAXILLA FRACTURE, AND SHRAPNEL TO HIS LEFT EYE. HE WILL BE AEROVAC'D TO BAF WITHIN 24 HRS. (1) PRIORITY SUFFERED A GRADE 3 CONCUSSION. HE IS STABLE AND UNDER OBSERVATION AT BSN ROLE 3.
BDA: (2) USMC WIA (1) US ANGEL
ISAF # 08-3492 (CLOSED)
MEDEVAC # 08- 31R (COMPLETE)
JOCWatch summary
G Co 2-8 USMC reported that while conducting a NFO dismounted patrol, FF struck an IED followed by INS engaging with SAF. PPIED struck the dismounted patrol which resulted in 2x US WIA and 1 x US KIA who were MEDEVACd IAW MM(S)08-31R to BASTION R3. FF are securing area, MEDEVAC complete, FF received additional SAF from the north of the LZ after HELO departed. FF return fire and working Arty mission.
BDA 1 x US KIA 2x US WIA

Reference ID: AFG20090902n2112
Latitude: 31.63408089
Date: 2009-09-02 08:08
Category: IED Explosion
Detained: 0

Region: RC SOUTH
Longitude: 65.03697968
Type: Explosive Hazard
Affiliation: ENEMY

	Enemy	Friend	Civilian	Host nation
Killed in action	0	0	1	0
Wounded in action	0	0	3	0

COMPASS CONVOY #6 reported that while supporting Logistic Convoy with 25 vehicles from KAF to JUNO, they struck an IED resulting in 1 x KIA, 3 x WIA, and moderate damage to 1 x vehicle.
UPDATE:
Info sourced from TF 1-12, MAYWARD indicated that an INS on a motorcycle threw a bomb under the JMCC vehicle. NFTR.
BDA: 1 x LN KIA, 3 x LN WIA (CAT UNK), 1 x Vehicle damaged (Type and status UNK).

Reference ID: AFG20090903n2177
Latitude: 30.5787468
Date: 2009-09-03 11:11
Category: IED Explosion
Detained: 0
Region: RC SOUTH
Longitude: 63.67315674
Type: Explosive Hazard
Affiliation: ENEMY

	Enemy	Friend	Civilian	Host nation
Killed in action	0	3	0	0
Wounded in action	0	2	0	0

WHEN: 03 1555D SEP 09
WHO: 2D LAR
WHERE: 41R PR 64548 83110 5.2KM W OF QUAL YE ANP STATION
WHAT: IED STRIKE EVENT: WHILE CONDUCTING A DISMOUNTED SWEEP OF A COMPOUND, A MEMBER OF THE PATROL STEPPED ON A PRESSURE PLATE IED RESULTING IN (2) KIA, AND (3) WIA. AN URGENT MEDEVAC WAS REQUESTED.
EOD ON SITE CONDUCTED A PBA AND DETERMINED THE IED WAS PRESSURE PLATE ACTIVATED WITH 20-30LBS HME LOCATED NEAR A METAL DOOR FRAME. THE PATROL'S METAL DETECTOR PICKED UP A SIGNATURE FOR THE DOOR FRAME, BUT NOT THE PRESSURE PLATE LOCATED AT THE BASE OF THE DOOR.
BOTH ANGELS ARE AT KAF. (2) WIA ARE CURRENLTY IN STABLE CONDITION AND WILL BE TRANSPORTED TO LUNDSTUHL. THE OTHER WIA IS CURRENTLY IN THE ICU AT KAF R3.
UDPATE 10 1530D SEPT 09:
(1) MARINE WIA DOW AT LUNDSTUHL.
BDA: (1) USN ANGEL, (2) USMC ANGEL, (1) USMC WIA (1) USN WIA
ISAF # 09- 0268 (CLOSED)
MEDEVAC # 09-03Q (COMPLETE)
WAITING ON EOD REPORT

Reference ID: AFG20090904n2002
Latitude: 34.94760513
Date: 2009-09-04 03:03
Category: IED Explosion
Detained: 0
Region: RC EAST
Longitude: 69.42719269
Type: Explosive Hazard
Affiliation: ENEMY

	Enemy	Friend	Civilian	Host nation
Killed in action	0	1	0	0
Wounded in action	0	9	0	0

IED STRIKE---
0309Z: TF KORRIGAN--- KAPISA, MAHMOOD RAQI DIST, 13.5KM W FOB MORALES-FRAZIER. BDA: 1X FRENCH MIL KIA, 9X FRENCH MIL WIA (5X URGENT, 4X PRIORITY), 1X VAB DESTROYED. CASUALTIES MEDEVAC (MM(E)09-04B) TO BAF.
FRENCH EOD CONDUCTED A POST BLAST ANALYSIS AND ASSESSED A CWIED CONSISTING OF 50-100 LBS. EXPLOSIVES EMPLACED IN SOFT MOIST DIRT. THE REAR END OF THE APC (LAST VEHICLE IN CONVOY) WAS HIT AND ROLLED OVER, COMING TO REST ON ITS SIDE. THE CRATER AT THE BLAST SITE MEASURED 8 FT. ACROSS AND HAD FILLED WITH WATER BY THE TIME THE EOD TEAM HAD ARRIVED ON SITE. NFI ATT.

Reference ID: AFG20090904n2026
Latitude: 32.15177155
Date: 2009-09-04 06:06
Category: IED Explosion
Detained: 0

Region: RC SOUTH
Longitude: 63.43897247
Type: Explosive Hazard
Affiliation: ENEMY

	Enemy	Friend	Civilian	Host nation
Killed in action	1	0	4	0
Wounded in action	0	0	10	0

WHEN: 04 1046D SEP 09
WHO: ECHO 2/3
WHERE: 41S NR 41500 57600, COP DELARAM ECP
WHAT: VBIED
EVENT: WHILE CONDUCTING STATIC SECURITY OPERATIONS ON COP DELARAM, A VBIED EXPLODED APPROX 50M FROM THE VCP AT THE COP ENTRANCE IN FRONT OF POST 6. THE SVBIED DETONATED NEAR A LN FOOD TRUCK HEADED WEST ON HWY 1. (4) LN'S WERE KILLED. (7) LN PRIVATE SECURITY CONTRACTORS AND (3) LN BYSTANDERS SUSTAINED INJURIES. (4) OF THE CAS WILL BE TRANSPORTED TO LASHKAR GAH FOR FURTHER TREATMENT. ANA TOOK CONTROL OF PROPER BODY RETURN AND DISPOSAL. 2/3 EOD CONDUCTED A PBA AND CONFIRMED THE SVBIED WAS A GREEN TRUCK WITH 82MM, 120MM MORTARS, A 107MM ROCKET AND AN UNK AMOUNT OF HME IN PLASTIC YELLOW JUGS WRAPPED WITH DETCORD. THE IED WAS POORLY CONSTRUCTED AND ALL THE ORDNANCE / HME WAS NOT DETONATED. EOD CONDUCTED A CONTROLLED DETONATION OF THE REMAINDER. 2/3 CLEARED THE ROAD AND TRAFFIC IS BACK TO NORMAL. THE SECURITY COMPANY HAS BEEN CONTACTED.
BDA: (4) LN KIA, (10) LN WIA, (1) EKIA (SUICIDE BOMBER)
ISAF # 09-0342 (CLOSED)

Reference ID: AFG20090912n2105
Latitude: 32.6203537
Date: 2009-09-12 02:02
Category: IED Explosion
Detained: 0

Region: RC WEST
Longitude: 62.50199509
Type: Explosive Hazard
Affiliation: ENEMY

	Enemy	Friend	Civilian	Host nation
Killed in action	0	2	0	2
Wounded in action	0	0	0	2

FF REPORTED THAT WHILE MENTORING A 1/1 KANDAK, FF WERE AMBUSHED BY INS SAF, RPG'S AND IED'S. RESULTING IN 1 X US WIA AND 1 X ANA KIA. THESE PERSONNEL WERE MEDEVAC'D TO FARAH. THE ETT PULLED BACK FROM THEIR POSITION AND HIT A SECOND IED, WHICH LED TO ANOTHER COMPLEX ATTACK RESULTING IN 1 X US WIA AND 3 X ANA WIA. THESE PERSONNEL WERE MEDEVAC'D ON A SECOND FLIGHT. THE 2 X US MIL AND 2 X ANA SUBSEQUENTLY DOW. THEIR REMAINS ARE PENDING MOVEMENT TO KAF.
BDA: 2 X US MIL KIA, 2 X ANA KIA AND 2 X ANA WIA

Reference ID: AFG20090914n2231
Latitude: 31.63754845
Date: 2009-09-14 03:03
Category: IED Explosion
Detained: 0

Region: RC SOUTH
Longitude: 65.02933502
Type: Explosive Hazard
Affiliation: ENEMY

	Enemy	Friend	Civilian	Host nation
Killed in action	0	2	0	0
Wounded in action	0	5	1	0

At 140355SEP09 (Z) TF Stryker reports TF Legion (B/2-1 IN) struck an IED VIC 41RPR92450205, Maiwand district, Kandahar province. EF engaged Stryker element with an IED during joint patrol with 1-12 IN. Stryker was hit with the IED and landed on its side. Initial BDA assessment was 1x US KIA, 4 x US WIA but crew are currently still in the vehicle. TOTAL BDA 5x US WIA (2 x CAT A, 3 x CAT B) 1x LN WIA(CAT B) and 2x US KIA, 1 Stryker Damaged.

Reference ID: AFG20090915n2134
Latitude: 31.72166252
Date: 2009-09-15 04:04
Category: IED Explosion
Detained: 0

Region: RC SOUTH
Longitude: 64.40251923
Type: Explosive Hazard
Affiliation: ENEMY

	Enemy	Friend	Civilian	Host nation
Killed in action	1	0	0	0
Wounded in action	0	2	0	0

FF reported while conducting framework patrol:
1 x PBIED ATTACK. The suicide bomber had 2 devices. 1 x British grenade which was id by the fly off lever (batch # SM02-3) and 1 x suicide vest. The ATF at that location said that INS shouted "Salam mother F'ers" while he detonated himself. FF at the location stated it was a Pakistani phrase not a local one..
Casualties: 1 x UK WIA (CAT A), 1 x UK WIA (CAT B) MEDEVACED IAW MM-S 15E TO BSN R3
INS approached via the western enterance and threw a grenade at the sentry point. He entered into the compound between one veh. and a wall and detonated the suicide vest. It was not possible to id the exact point detonation due to body parts being spread over a wide area.

UPDATE AT 0754Z, POSSIBLE PARTS NOT FULLY DETONATED YET. IEDD HAS BEEN REQUESTED.
AT 0856Z, EOD WAS UNAVAILABLE. FF MARKED THE AREA FOR FUTURE EXPLOTATION. NFTR.
BDA: 1 x UK WIA (CAT A), 1 x UK WIA (CAT B), 1 X INS KIA (SUICIDE BOMBER)
EVENT CLOSED AT 151101ZSEP2009

Reference ID: AFG20090917n2375 Region: RC SOUTH
Latitude: 32.3331604 Longitude: 64.41225433
Date: 2009-09-17 13:01 Type: Explosive Hazard
Category: IED Explosion Affiliation: ENEMY
Detained: 0

	Enemy	Friend	Civilian	Host nation
Killed in action	0	0	0	0
Wounded in action	0	3	0	0

WHEN: 17 1801D SEP 09
WHO: 8TH ESB (AMUCK 12)
WHERE: 41S PR 29160 78241, 9KM SW OF COP CAFFERETTA
WHAT: IED STRIKE EVENT: WHILE CONDUCTING A MOUNTED CONVOY TO COP CAFFERETTA, THE 5TH VEH (AMK-23, MTVR) STRUCK AN IED RESULTING IN (3) CASUALTIES AND A MOBILITY KILL (ECM'S ON, MINEROLLER USED). A CORDON WAS SET AND A ROUTINE MEDEVAC WAS REQUESTED. CAS WERE TRANSPORTED TO BASTION ROLE 3 FOR FURTHER TREATMENT. THE VEH HAS BEEN SELF RECOVERED TO NOW ZAD. WHILE EN RTE TO COP CAFFERETTA, UNIT HALTED DUE TO A STUCK VEH (870 TRAILER). THE CONVOY CONTINUED ON MISSION; (5) VEH'S HAVE REMAINED ON SITE AS SEC UNTIL RECOVERY TEAM ARRIVES.
UPDATE: THE DOWNED VEHICLE HAS BEEN RECOVERED TO FOB CAFFERETTA.
BDA: (3) WIA, (1) M-KILL MTVR
ISAF # 09-1790 (CLOSED)
MEDEVAC # 09-17T (COMPLETE)

Reference ID: AFG20090918n2309 Region: RC WEST
Latitude: 32.51967239 Longitude: 63.59688568
Date: 2009-09-18 15:03 Type: Explosive Hazard
Category: IED Explosion Affiliation: ENEMY
Detained: 0

	Enemy	Friend	Civilian	Host nation
Killed in action	0	0	0	0
Wounded in action	0	0	0	0

WHEN: 18 1930D SEP 09
WHO: HAVOC 2A
WHERE: 41S NR 56059 98197 7MI S OF PB GOLESTAN
WHAT: IED STRIKE
EVENT: WHILE ON A MOUNTED PATROL, THE 3RD VEH'S MINEROLLER (PANAMA CITY GEN II) STRUCK AN IED (40LBS UBE) RESULTING IN A

DESTROYED MINEROLLER AND MINOR DAMAGE TO THE VEH (MINEROLLERS USED, ECM'S ON). A CORDON WAS SET AND SWEEP FOR SECONDARIES CONDUCTED.
UPDATE: UNIT SELF RECOVERED AND CONTINUED ON MISSION TO PB GOLESTAN.
BDA: NO CASUALTIES REPORTED. (1) RG-31 MRAP MINOR DAMAGE, (1) DESTROYED MINEROLLER
(PANAMA CITY GEN II).
ISAF # 09-1892 (CLOSED)
UPDATE: EOD ASSESSED AS UNKNOWN INITATION - SEE ASSOCIATED EXPLOITATION REPORT.

Reference ID: AFG20091020n2497
Latitude: 31.30515289
Date: 2009-10-20 08:08
Category: IED Explosion
Detained: 0

Region: RC SOUTH
Longitude: 64.19933319
Type: Explosive Hazard
Affiliation: ENEMY

	Enemy	Friend	Civilian	Host nation
Killed in action	0	1	0	0
Wounded in action	0	2	0	0

WHEN: 20 1315D OCT 09
WHO: 1/5 / ANA
WHERE: 41R PQ 14133 64042, 2.2 KM SW OF OP HUSEY
WHAT: IED STRIKE/MEDEVAC
EVENT: WHILE CONDUCTING A PARTNERED DISMOUNTED PATROL, 1/5 STRUCK AN IED RESULTING IN (1) USMC ANGEL, AND (2) USMC CAT A CASUALTIES. AN URGENT MEDEVAC WAS REQUESTED AND THE CASUALTIES WERE TRANSPORTED TO BASTION ROLE 3 FOR TREATMENT. THE ANGEL WAS TRANSPORTED TO BASTION WHERE A RAMP CEREMONY WAS HELD, AND WAS THEN FLOWN TO KAF. EOD CONDUCTED A PBA AND DETERMINED THE IED CONSISTED OF A YELLOW JUG OF APPROX 50LBS HME, A WOODEN PRESSURE PLATE WITH A ROLLED OUT OIL CAN FOR CONTACTS THAT WAS WRAPPED IN RUBBER AND YELLOW AND CLEAR TAPE. THE WIRING WAS WHITE LAMP CORD AND THERE WERE (6) POWER FLASH BATTERIES AS A BATTERY SOURCE.
BDA: (1) USMC ANGEL, (2) URGENT USMC WIA
ISAF # 10-1866 (CLOSED)
MEDEVAC # 10-20I

Reference ID: AFG20091027n2301
Latitude: 31.64707947
Date: 2009-10-27 06:06
Category: IED Explosion
Detained: 0

Region: RC SOUTH
Longitude: 65.63578033
Type: Explosive Hazard
Affiliation: ENEMY

	Enemy	Friend	Civilian	Host nation
Killed in action	1	7	1	0
Wounded in action	0	1	0	0

At 270615OCT09 (Z) TF Stryker reports TF Buffalo (2/C/1-17 IN) was engaged in a complex attack IVO 41RQR4995204336 (Arghandab District, Kandahar Province). EF engaged a mounted Stryker element with an IED while Stryker element was establishing blocking positions for future operations in the area. Initial BDA of the engagement was 8 x KIA (7 x US KIA, 1 x LN interpreter KIA) and 1 X US WIA (CAT A). Air Tic was declared within the AO; CAS and UAS assets were redirected to the area. EF engaged the Stryker element with SAF 400m NE of the IED Strike location. CAS engaged possible trigger man and 2 x EF, BDA could not be confirmed. MEDEVAC arrived on location and received SAF during the recovery of the 1 x US WIA; wounded soldier was taken back to KAF for further treatment. EF broke contact from the Stryker element at 0642 (Z). CAS reported receiving SAFIRE 400-500m SE from IED Strike location, CAS attempted to engage with Hellfire but misfired, switched over to rockets IVO 41RQR50200431. CAS confirmed with Stryker element at least 1 x EKIA from SAFIRE engagement. Intel reports indicated a possible compound of interest IVO 41RQR5069504839. UAS asset was utilized to observe the compound but no activity was noticed at the location. Stryker element is reporting SAF IVO dismounted Stryker element. Shamus is engaging the source of the SAF. EF broke contact and exfiled north; CAS maneuvered to IOT attempt re-engagement with enemy. Final BDA: 7 x US KIA, 1 x US WIA, 1 x LN Interpreter KIA. 1 x Stryker (ICV) catastrophic loss. NFTR ATT. MTF

Reference ID: AFG20091030n2227
Latitude: 31.58716202
Date: 2009-10-30 11:11
Category: IED Explosion
Detained: 0

Region: RC SOUTH
Longitude: 65.80841827
Type: Explosive Hazard
Affiliation: ENEMY

	Enemy	Friend	Civilian	Host nation
Killed in action	0	0	0	3
Wounded in action	0	0	0	0

National Directorate Security (NDS) agents were chasing a suspected VBIED which failed to stop and subsequently rammed into an NDS vehicle resulting in 3 X NDS KIA and an unknown number of NDS WIA which were transported to MIRWAIS hospital. DAMAN Chief of Police en route to investigate.
UPDATE 2331Z NDS WILL BE INVESTIGATING, NFTR.
BDA: 3 X NDS KIA, unknown number of NDS WIA.

CPSIA information can be obtained
at www.ICGtesting.com
Printed in the USA
LVHW052157210523
747647LV00012B/517